SUMMARY KU-466-974

Nicholas Moussis

Guide to
European policies

14th revised edition
2008 - 2009

European Study Service

ISBN 978-2-930119-51-9

© European Study Service
Avenue Paola 43 - B-1330 RIXENSART
TEL.: (+32 2) 652 02 84 - FAX: (+32 2) 653 01 80
RCN: 51147 - TVA: BE-659 309 394

CONTENTS

FOREWORD

The Flemish master Pieter Bruegel the elder has well illustrated the lack of interest of people for a historic event that takes place under their very eyes. In a painting of 1564, entitled "The Procession to Calvary", he has depicted the Messiah as a small figure sinking down under the cross on his way up the Golgotha. No one of the crowd of Roman soldiers and ordinary people around Him pays any attention to His Martyrdom. They are all looking at a couple of peasants struggling with three soldiers in the forefront of the picture. This everyday brawl is the centre of attention of the crowd and not the event that has changed the course of history. One can hardly blame these people who, at the time of the Crucifixion, were going about their business and were attracted by a boisterous albeit banal happening. As demonstrated by Brueguel, they had not the hindsight that we now have about the importance of the event that they were witnessing.

Likewise, the majority of contemporary Europeans have no notion that they are witnessing an experience that will most probably change again the history of mankind. This history is marked by wars and all kinds, of bloody fights between ethnic, religious and other groups, fights for power, for land, for ideals (real or supposed) or just for the survival of a nation or a group attacked by other nations or groups. The extraordinary event that takes place under our eyes is the fifty-year old experience of peaceful and voluntary unification of different and formerly conflicting nations. The European experience is unique by virtue of its objective of establishing the basis for an increasingly closer union between formerly hostile nations. It is also unique because of its institutions, which have no equal in other international organisations. Lastly, it is unique on account of its achievements: never in human history have different nations cooperated so closely with one another, implemented so many common policies or, in such a short space of time, harmonised ways of life and economic situations which differed so greatly at the outset.

Yet this unique experiment is hardly exciting. It is hidden behind tedious negotiations by complicated institutions using a peculiar jargon incomprehensible to ordinary citizens. Curiously enough it is not the lack but the abundance of information that clouds the European horizon. Information about the work of European institutions is abundant and freely available to citizens for the asking, particularly in electronic form. The problem is that the great majority of citizens do not and never will go asking for information about an experiment that they consider as extremely complex and distant from their everyday problems and interests. On their part, many European mass media report on a daily basis new European policies, laws, programmes and internal and external disputes. Yet, these media accounts are for most citizens like the leaves of a tree, which hide the forest that is stretching out behind. Leaves, like the daily news are ephemeral and unexciting, not worthy of particular attention. On the other hand, the dense forest of European institutions, policies and laws, which produces the political and economic oxygen necessary for the blossoming of small and medium European nations, is obscure and terrifying, if there is no roadmap showing the way through it.

The *Guide to European policies* attempts to provide the reader with an overall view and the perspective necessary for understanding the complex organisation, which is the European Community/Union (EC/EU). The emphasis of the book is placed on the common policies developed by the EC/EU. Indeed, **an approach to multinational integration** is advanced, based on the setting up and development of common policies by the participating states. This approach is based on the empirical evidence of the European Union, but may also be applied *mutatis mutandis* to other multinational integration schemes elsewhere in the world.

This book aspires to being a textbook for **any student of European integration**, whether academic student of the European integration process, lawyer interested in Community law, which is ceaselessly growing and modified, economist wishing to acquire the latest information on European economic policies, historian wanting to understand the recent history of the continent or businessman seeking to understand the mechanisms of the large market in which he operates. In fact, European integration cannot be properly approached with the particular methods and tools of political science, international relations, economics or law. The *Guide to European policies* follows, therefore, an interdisciplinary, pragmatic approach, which is somewhat distinct from the precise precepts of the disciplines that compose it. European policies, as all public policies, have both positive and negative aspects and can therefore be approached either in a positive or a negative way according to the viewpoint of the writer. The empirical or pragmatic approach followed here endeavours to present European policies as they are, with a minimum of value judgments as to their performance.

To help the reader find easily the details of any policy or measure he or she is interested in and/or deduce in an unprejudiced way whether a certain policy is good or bad or whether it has achieved the objectives assigned to it, facts and references are presented in a precise, almost scholastic, manner. All statements about past, present and future developments of common policies as well as all references to European law are based on the official texts of Community acts, published in the **Official Journal of the European Union (OJ)** or in Commission publications, such as the monthly **Bulletin of the European Union** and the annual **General Report** on the Activities of the European Union. In addition to their documentary purpose, the references to the OJ are also meant to help researchers find the official texts of their particular interest, as published in the collections of the OJ or in the electronic database EUR-Lex in the Europa server of the Commission.

PART I: Treaties, law and institutions

Chapter 1.   *Introduction to European integration*
Chapter 2.   *The European Treaties*
Chapter 3.   *European law and finances*
Chapter 4.   *The European institutions*

In this part of the book we review, in an introductory chapter, the various theories that have endeavoured to **explain the phenomenon of European integration**. We ascertain that all these theories have shed some light on various aspects of the integration process, but they have all missed the fundamental aspect of this process: the building and management of common policies. We, therefore, propose a theoretical synthesis based on the common policies of the European Union, which are, indeed, the main subject of this book. The theoretical propositions advanced in section 1.1.2 are empirically verified in the rest of the book. In the second section of the introductory chapter we briefly recall how, after the Second World War, an ever-increasing number of European States have decided to set aside their differences and engage themselves in **the process of European integration**.

The main objective of the second chapter is to emphasise the **role of the treaties and their reforms in setting new common policies** and ever-higher objectives for pre-existing ones. It shows how the success of the common policies based on the Treaty on the European Coal and Steel Community (ECSC), signed in Paris in April 1951, led to the signing in March 1957, in Rome, of the Treaties on the European Atomic Energy Community (EAEC or Euratom) and of the most important European Economic Community (EEC), extending integration in all economic sectors. We will note that in order to attain their expanding goals, the Member States decided, in Maastricht in 1992, to supplement the amended Treaty establishing the European Community (TEC) as well as the Treaties on the ECSC and EAEC with the new Treaty on the European Union (TEU), which set the objective of political integration. We will see that five years later, the Treaty of Maastricht was replaced by the Treaty of Amsterdam, in order to accommodate the objectives of the new policies on home and judicial affairs and on foreign affairs. We will finally note that the **Treaty of Nice, now in force**, allowed the accession of twelve more Member States, but that the **Treaty of Lisbon**, actually in the process of ratification by the twenty-seven Member States, whose leaders signed it on 13 December 2007, is needed to help Europe advance in the path of its integration.

In chapter three a metaphorical image is used to explain how **the European Union covers under its roof** the main edifice of the European construction, which is the European Community, and the new wings of the common foreign and security policy and of justice and home affairs. The original **decision-making process** of the Community is clarified, a process that leads to the formation of an equally **original legal system**, based on the treaties and taking the form of regulations, directives and decisions. A particular attention is paid to the **unique financing system** of the European Community based on its own resources inscribed in the Community budget, managed by the Commission.

The final chapter of this part examines the structure and the functions of the **main European institutions**, in the order that they appear in the decision-making process: the European Council, the European Commission, the European Parliament, the Council of Ministers and the Court of Justice. This chapter deals also with other important institutions, the European Central Bank and the Court of Auditors, and with the consultative bodies of the EC/EU, the Economic and Social Committee and the Committee of the Regions. The interaction of these institutions and organs, examined in the section on the European decision-making process, is essential for the development of **the common policies that are analysed in this book**.

Chapter 1

INTRODUCTION TO
EUROPEAN INTEGRATION

In 1945, just after the Second World War, Winston Churchill described Europe as "a rubble heap, a charnel house, a breeding ground for pestilence and hate". A year later, on 19 September 1946, in his famous Zurich speech, he proposed as a remedy "to recreate the European Family ... and to provide it with a structure under which it can dwell in peace, in safety and in freedom ... a kind of United States of Europe". Half a century later, realising and exceeding Churchill's vision, the western part of the "European Family" had become an island of peace and prosperity in a world ravaged by hatreds, conflicts, civil wars and misery. The successful formula that European nations had invented to overcome their depression was the integration of the formerly antagonistic nation-states into a union of peacefully interacting and competing nations. The multinational integration formula involves the gradual creation of imperceptible albeit innumerable links between the nations taking part in the process. Those links consist of common laws and common policies, which govern the Member States' economic activities and influence the day-to-day lives and occupations of their citizens.

1.1. The theoretical framework

Many theories, stemming mainly from the theoretical frameworks of political science or international relations, have been developed during the second half of the twentieth century about international and, more especially, European integration. Each has focused on a particular aspect of the phenomenon, while neglecting most of the other aspects. Each, therefore, has had its own merits in shedding scientific light on some parts of a very complicated phenomenon, but none has succeeded in explaining the whole, in structuring scientific observations on all its parts and in predicting its future development. After pointing out the main points of prevalent theories, we attempt in section 1.1.2. to present an explanation of the phenomenon of multinational integration based on the evolutionary development of common policies.

1.1.1. A synopsis of prominent integration theories

As early as the 1920s, **federalists** like Coudenhove-Kalergi perceived that European nations, which had just devastated each other in a nonsensical civil war, were a natural entity that could become a significant global force, if only they could succeed in having a federal constitution[1]. After the second catastrophic war for supremacy of one European nation over the others, Altiero Spinelli expressed the view that the national states had lost their *raison d'être*, since they could no longer guarantee the political and economic safety of their citizens and should give way to a federation, called by him "the European Union"[2]. Federalists, thus, put the cart (the ultimate state of European integration) before the horse (the creation of solidarity among former bitter enemies). They had a bright vision, but had not found the means to reach it.

Functionalists like Mitrany[3] rightly pointed out that international organisations are not an end in themselves, but rather the means of addressing the priorities dictated by human needs and have, therefore, to be flexible and modify their tasks (functions) according to the needs of the moment. In their over-optimism, however, for the creation of a cobweb of really international (worldwide), task-oriented organisations, they overlooked and even mistrusted the peacekeeping and welfare functions of a regional organisation like the European Economic Community.

Closer to the European reality, the **transactionalist** theory of Karl Deutsch defines international integration as the attainment, within a territory, of a "sense of community" and of institutions and practices strong enough to assure dependable expectations of "peaceful change" among its population[4]. The assertion that the sense of community among states would depend on establishment of a network of mutual transactions[5] is borne out by the experience of the European Communities. However, this experience proves that first comes the formal institutional framework and on it are built the informal transactions and hence the community spirit, necessary for an effective multinational integration.

Relatively close to the Jean Monnet method of "common action which is the core of the European Community"[6], is the **neofunctionalist** theory, developed mainly by Ernst Haas[7]. Both Monnet and neofunctionalist theo-

---

[1] COUDENHOVE-KALERGI Richard N., *Pan-Europe*, Knopf, New York, 1926.

[2] SPINELLI Altiero, "The Growth of the European Movement since the Second World War", in M. Hodges (ed.), *European Integration*, Penguin, Harmondsworth, 1972.

[3] MITRANY David, *A Working Peace System*, Quadrangle Books, Chicago, 1966.

[4] DEUTSCH Karl W., *Nationalism and Social Communication*, 2nd edition, MIT Press, Cambridge, MA, 1966.

[5] DEUTSCH Karl W., *The Analysis of International Relations*, Prentice Hall, Englewood Cliffs NJ, 1968.

[6] Monnet Jean. "A Ferment of Change", *Journal of Common Market Studies*, n. 1, 1962, p. 203-211.

[7] HAAS Ernst B. The Uniting of Europe: Political, Social and Economic Forces 1950-1957, 2nd edn. Stanford: Stanford University Press, 1968.

rists rejected federalist idealism and brought down Mitrany's functionalism from its international high spheres to the concrete level of several neighbouring states. The Monnet inspired famous declaration of Robert Schuman of 9 May 1950 was quite explicit on the road to be followed by European integration: "Europe ... will be built through concrete achievements which first create a *de facto* **solidarity**". Integration was viewed as a process where the constructive functions of the main actors, the common institutions, would induce positive reactions of the political and economic elites, influence the behaviour of other societal groups and bring together the citizens of the different nations. Neofunctionalist logic was built on the "spillover" effect. This meant that economic integration would gradually build solidarity among the participating nations and would in turn create the need for further supranational institutionalisation. Leon Lindberg (1963)[1] defined the "spillover effect" as: "a situation in which a given action, related to a specific goal, creates a situation in which the original goal can be assured only by taking further actions, which in turn create a further condition and a need for more action and so forth".

Many other neofunctionalist assumptions have been proved correct by European experience, notably that: action by interest groups would not be motivated by idealistic pursuit of the common good, but would be self-regarding and goal driven; perceptions by these groups of shifts in the loci of authority and power would increasingly direct their activity towards the developing supranational arena; the supranational scheme of government at the regional level would be the appropriate regional counterpart to the national state, which would no longer feel capable of achieving welfare aims within its own narrow borders. In economic terms, the creation of a customs union would generate pressures for the establishment of a common market and monetary union. The close economic integration brought about would require supranational regulatory capacity. Thus, political integration would follow economic integration[2].

Some neofunctionalist assertions, namely the withering away of the power-based states system, prompted a strong **intergovernmentalist** alternative to neofunctionalism, despite the strong European evidence in its favour. The Treaties of Maastricht and Amsterdam have, indeed, disproved Stanley Hoffmann's prediction that states would not compromise their sovereignty by moving their integration from the areas of "low politics" (read economics) to the sphere of "high politics", i.e. foreign and security policy[3]. **Liberal intergovernmentalist** analysis provided by Andrew Moravcsik (1993)[4] has failed to explain how national interests, voiced by national

---

[1] LINDBERG Leon, The political Dynamics of European Economic Integration, Stanford CA, Stanford University Press.

[2] BALASSA Bela, *The Theory of Economic Integration*, Allen and Unwin, London, 1962.

[3] HOFFMANN Stanley, "The European Process at Atlantic Crosspurposes", *Journal of Common Market Studies*, No 3, 1964.

[4] MORAVCSIK Andrew, "Preferences and Power in the European Community: A Liberal Intergovernmentalist Approach, Journal of Common Market Studies, No 31 (4).

governments in international negotiations, can merge and allow European integration to prosper.

Although the neofunctionalist theory has come closer to the European integration process, particularly thanks to its emphasis on the spillover effect, some critics rightly point out certain deficiencies in neofunctionalist reasoning. By highlighting the **multi-level governance** (European, national, regional, etc) of the EC/EU and the interaction of political actors across those levels, Gary Marks *et al.* (1996)[1] have shown the theoretical trap of imagining either the withering away of the state or its stubborn resilience. **Neoinstitutionalists**, like March and Olsen (1984)[2], have demonstrated the importance of institutions (not just formally established supranational organs, but also informal interactions) in providing contexts where actors can conduct a great number of positive sum bargains.

Although the neofunctionalist theory has come closer to the European integration process, particularly thanks to its emphasis on the spillover effect, it, like the other integration theories has overlooked the main element of this process, which is the gradual formulation, development and multiplication of common policies. In the next section an empirical approach is advanced taking into consideration this important element.

1.1.2.   An empirical approach based on the development of common policies

The multinational integration process may de defined as the voluntary establishment by treaty, concluded between independent states, of common institutions and the gradual development by them of common policies pursuing common goals and serving common interests. Being "voluntary", a multinational integration process is clearly distinguished from any form of coercive governance or coalition of nations or states. A "multinational" integration process between several nations should be distinguished from a Mitranian "international integration", involving all or most nations of the world. It should also be distinguished from "regional integration", a concept frequently used to denote the integration of various states of a region of the world, but which should, in fact, be reserved to the integration of various regions of a state, a process that is going on in most countries of the world. Multinational integration may go on inside one state containing different nationalities, but, in this case, its institutions are based on a federal constitution rather than on a treaty between independent states.

The "gradual development" of common policies implies that multinational integration is a constantly evolving process without a clearly defined end. Since the process is voluntary, it ensues that independent states may

[1]   MARKS G., SCHARPF F., SCHMITTER P.C. and STREECK W., Governance in the European Union, London, Sage.
[2]   MARCH J.G. and OLSEN J.P., "The New Institutionalism: Organizational Factors in Political Life", American Political Science Review, No 78.

join it at any point, following the procedures and criteria laid down by the group, or leave it, if they consider that the common policies developed or envisaged by the group, according to the majority definition of the common interest, do not coincide any more with their national interests.

The primary goal of multinational integration is the **achievement of peace and security** among the member states as well as between them and the rest of the world. But, unlike a military alliance where this goal is pursued by various pledges of a political and military nature, a multinational integration scheme is built gradually **by means of a large number of common policies**, cementing common interests and creating a real solidarity among the member states. In the words of Jean Monnet, the intellectual father of European integration, "union between individuals or communities is not natural; it can only be the result of an intellectual process... having as a starting point the observation of the need for change. Its driving force must be **common interests** between individuals or communities".

In EC/EU usage, "common policies" are the ones that take the place of the essential elements of national policies (notably, agriculture, fisheries and foreign trade). The policies that support and supplement national policies are called "**Community policies**". But, in fact, the distinction, between the two categories is not at all clear-cut. Indeed, all common policies, whether called thus by the Treaties or by Community practice, are in a process of development. They start as mere objectives set in general terms by the Treaties or the institutions and are gradually built up by common or "Community" legal acts. The Treaty establishing the European Community (TEC) clearly declares in its Article 2 that "the Community shall have as its task, by establishing a common market and an economic and monetary union and by implementing **common policies or activities** referred to in Articles 3 and 4, to promote throughout the Community a harmonious, balanced and sustainable development of economic activities...". Articles 3 and 4 of the TEC serve, in fact, as legal bases for common policies in a great number of sectors or for common measures in some other fields (the distinction between common policies and common measures being quantitative rather than qualitative). In this book, the terms "common policy" and "Community policy" are used alternatively, as the latter is taken to mean "the common policy of the Member States of the Community" in a certain field.

Common policies, developed gradually by the actors of the process, foster both **political and economic integration** of the participating states. Although multinational integration depends on political decisions, it greatly affects the economies of the member states. Increasingly, through the stages of customs union, common market and economic and monetary union [see part II], it opens up the participating economies to multinational trade and competition. Obviously, the economies of the member states are greatly influenced by common economic and other policies. As these economies are gradually opened up to multinational trade and competition, **all economic parameters change**: trade increases enormously within the large internal market, both supply and demand conditions are modified drastically, state intervention is seriously curbed and new dynamics are set in motion, notably concerning trade and investment opportunities. The creation and/or extension of multinational companies and the cross invest-ments between them and national companies tend to bind the economies more closely together. The common policies build, in fact, a new concept and context of political economy, which affects the actions of political leaders and the activities of businessmen of the member states.

Indeed, by bringing about tougher conditions of competition than the ones existing inside the previously protected economies, multinational in-tegration brings about **radical changes in business habits** and creates new business opportunities. Not surprisingly, business associations, constituting powerful interest groups, try to influence the integration process in their favour. They intervene by way of demands, suggestions or criticisms ad-dressed to the principal actors - the common institutions and the govern-ments of the Member States - at various stages of the decision-making process concerning particular policies or the advancement of the integra-tion process itself.

In the case of the EC/EU it is clear that the political elite were and still are influenced by **open-minded and dynamic economic elite**. In fact, more than by considerations of security or balance of power at world level, over-emphasised by political scientists, the historic decisions of the Mem-ber States were motivated by economic factors: revitalising the two most important economic sectors in the post-war period, coal and steel; creating a large market in order to give a new dynamism to their economies stifled by protectionism; completing the single market to further facilitate trade and investment within a large market; strengthening the single market with a single currency to further facilitate internal transactions and allow Euro-pean businesses to better face global competition. These decisions and the ensuing common policies were supported, if not provoked, by influential economic groups in the Member States.

Although they are of paramount importance, economic pressures alone cannot start the integration process. The necessary condition for setting the multinational integration process in motion is that the political, economic and other elite of neighbouring countries are earnestly seeking to **serve the interests of their nations**, rather than their own interests or those of a par-ticular class or societal category. Under this condition - which implies de-mocratic regimes - economic and political leaders would sooner or later concur that trade liberalisation better serves the supreme national goals of peace and prosperity than existing protectionist economic policies [see sec-tions 5.1. and 6.1.]. They would then have an option: either to pursue mu-tual trade liberalisation through intergovernmental cooperation or through multinational integration.

Intergovernmental cooperation is a conventional shelter of national interests, entrenched in the solid and familiar bulwark of national sover-eignties defended by national governments. It does not need strong central institutions or a great deal of common legislation. Although it is usually based on a treaty, which prescribes governmental action and behaviour for the reduction of trade barriers and sanctions in case of infringement by a participating state, the respect of the agreement depends more on the goodwill of the participating governments than on common legislation enacted and enforced by supranational bodies. In contrast, **multinational integration** is a dynamic venture of promoting national interests, depending on many unpredictable internal and external parameters and moved forward perpetually by the ever-changing requirements of the partners and by the extra energy provided by the combination of their forces. While safeguarding the interests of big and small countries alike, it requires common institutions and leads progressively to the establishment of a great number of common policies, to the harmonisation of legislations and to the common management of significant parts of national sovereignties. Small and big countries participating in the process have the same rights and obligations. They pledge themselves to pursue common objectives, which go much beyond trade liberalisation. In addition to this goal, the nations participating in an integration process also want to liberalise the movements of persons and capital and to facilitate the establishment and provision of services by companies from the partner countries.

Hence, the **fundamental decision** of a number of states to establish a multinational integration process, outlined in a treaty, signed and ratified by willing governments, is the catalyst, which precipitates a sequence of secondary decisions formulating various common policies. If the implementation of these initial common policies gave satisfactory but not optimal economic results, it would reveal the necessity for more common policies and would thus have a multiplicative effect on the process. There is no predictable end to this process, as it depends on all sorts of internal and external factors. Depending on the stimuli exerted on the actors by those factors, the process may temporarily be slowed down or speeded up, but its general trend is progressive. An abrupt end to the multinational integration process is theoretically possible, but becomes increasingly improbable as the process itself continuously strengthens and multiplies the economic, political and cultural links between the participating nations.

Multinational integration is based on common policies, which develop and multiply thanks to the Community decision-making method that characterizes it. Hence, common policies are the basic elements of a multinational integration process. **A common policy**, as far as multinational integration is concerned, is defined as a set of decisions, measures, rules and codes of conduct adopted by the common institutions set up by a group of states [see section 4.1.] and implemented by the common institutions and the member states. A "real" common policy (to be distinguished from a so-called one) has to be implemented by all the participants and, therefore, needs to be monitored by supranational executive and judiciary authorities. Hence, by adopting a common policy, the participants agree to transfer some of their sovereign powers to common supranational institutions. This transfer of sovereign rights in the framework of common policies is the main drawback but also the fundamental characteristic of multinational integration. It explains why common policies are difficult to adopt, but also why, once adopted, they are the binding (or integrating) elements of the whole multinational structure. Common policies, thus, distinguish multinational integration from intergovernmental cooperation and explain nationalistic scepticism towards the former.

There are four main types of common policies: fundamental and secondary, horizontal and sectoral. **Fundamental** are the common policies, whose basic objectives and scope are inscribed in the Treaty itself and are, therefore, agreed by both the governments and the parliaments of all the Member States. **Secondary** common policies are the ones that are defined by the common legislative bodies within the framework of the fundamental common policies and in accordance with the Community decision-making process. Both fundamental and secondary common policies can be divided into **horizontal** (such as social, competition or environment protection), which affect the overall conditions of the economies and societies of the Member States and **sectoral**, which concern certain sectors of the economies of the Member States (namely industry, energy, transports, agriculture and fisheries). All common policies can be classified in a decreasing order of importance, depending on the scope of the area covered by each one.

Common policies materialise when, where and to the extent that the governments, representing the parties to an integration treaty, believe that the individual interests of their states are better served by them than by national policies. To create a sentiment of mutual confidence, the formulation of a common policy by the common institutions must clearly indicate the **common need** that it addresses, the **common goal** that it pursues and the **common interest** that it serves [see section 3.2.]. The essential element in a common policy is the definition of the common interest in the objectives and measures framed by it. This definition has to satisfy all Member States as far as fundamental common policies are concerned and most Member States concerning secondary common policies. It is possible that some common policies better satisfy the national interests of some participants than those of others. It is inadmissible and hence impracticable that all common policies better satisfy the interests of some members of the group to the detriment of the rest. Indeed, no party to a multinational integration scheme should feel that its national interests are being permanently and systematically damaged by the common policies pursued by the majority of its partners; but, on the other hand, no party to such a scheme may systematically obstruct the common policies proposed by claiming that they do not fully satisfy its national interests. Hence, all parties to a multinational integration scheme must be prepared to accept compromise solutions formulated in the various common policies and, sometimes, to give ground in one field, expecting to gain ground in another field. The hundreds of decisions taken every year by the EC/EU institutions demonstrate the fact that its Member States play the game according to this rule. The few exceptions confirm the rule.

A common policy may develop in two senses: in the sense of its legal evolution, which is required in order to keep up with economic and technical progress in the subject matter that it covers; and in the sense of the expansion of its field, which may happen in order to cover peripheral needs not formerly attended to in the formulation of the policy or new needs, either encountered during the implementation of the measures originally adopted or created by the geopolitical environment of the moment. Moreover, a common policy tends to spill over into the areas of other common policies, produce needs, cause reactions and nourish their development. Thus, common policies are closely knit together, support each other, foster their joint evolution and multiplication and, in so doing, promote the progress of the multinational integration process.

This book brings enough empirical evidence to test the hypotheses advanced above. Chapter 4 examines the structure, the functions and the role of the main actors of European integration, which are the common institutions. The second part of the book examines the most fundamental common policies, which concern the **stages of the European integration process**. Part III focuses on policies that are of particular interest to the citizens of the Union. Part IV examines the **common horizontal policies** - such as social, competition or environment protection - which affect the overall conditions of the economies and societies of the Member States. Part V analyses the **common sectoral policies**, which concern certain sectors of the economies of the Member States. Part VI, presents the **common external policies**, which steer the relations of the Member States with third countries. In the final chapter, conclusions are drawn on the effectiveness of the European integration process and on its possible future development.

1.2. Birth and growth of the Community

In his declaration of 9 May 1950, Robert Schuman proposed the creation of a **common market in two important economic sectors** which had until then been used for military purposes, namely the coal and steel sectors: it would be a matter of integrating Germany economically and politically into a European Coal and Steel Community with France and other willing countries. He advocated some transfer of sovereignty to an independent High Authority, which would exercise the powers previously held by the States in those sectors and the decisions of which would bind those States. That was to say that the cooperation of the Member States in those sectors should be much closer than that obtained with a traditional inter-governmental cooperation. The choice of coal and steel was not fortuitous. In the early 1950s those sectors were the basis of a country's industrial and military power. In addition to the economic benefits to be gained, the pooling of French and German resources in coal and steel was to mark Franco-German reconciliation.

Beyond the Coal and Steel Community, Robert Schuman envisaged the creation of a common market for all products, on a scale comparable to that of the United States, in which the conditions would be fulfilled for rapid and regular economic expansion through economies of scale, better division of labour and the improved use of new production techniques. It is true that, beyond economic integration through the merging of the essential economic interests of the European countries, Schuman looked forward to political integration through the creation in stages of a **"European Federation"**. But this was to be achieved in an advanced stage of European integration, after the creation of conditions of mutual trust through concrete achievements based on common policies.

Although the appeal from the French Minister for Foreign Affairs was addressed to all European countries, only five - Germany, Italy, Belgium, the Netherlands and Luxembourg - gave a favourable reply. Therefore, only six States signed the Treaty establishing the **European Coal and Steel Community (ECSC)** in Paris on 18 April 1951 [see section 2.1.]. The "little Europe of Six" began its construction on 23 July 1952, the date of entry into force of the ECSC Treaty. The United Kingdom, on the other hand, favoured the intergovernmental method of liberalising trade through a European free trade area, which would not involve any transfer of national sovereignty. According to the British standpoint, customs duties should be abolished between member countries, but the latter should remain autonomous with regard to commercial policy vis-à-vis third countries. Denmark, Norway, Iceland, Austria, Portugal and Switzerland supported that argument and, therefore, did not sign the ECSC Treaty.

In parallel with the integration of their economies, the six founding States of the ECSC wanted to integrate their armies. They, therefore, signed in Paris, on 27 May 1952, the Treaty instituting the **European Defense Community (EDC)**, which aimed at the creation of a supranational integrated army, placed, however, under the supreme command of NATO, barring unanimous opposition of the Six. The EDC project was rejected, on 30 August 1954, by the French parliament. This project may develop in the framework of amended European treaties, after the creation of the conditions, which were lacking fifty years ago [see European perspectives in the conclusions].

The very first years of the functioning of the common market in coal and steel showed, however, that economic integration was possible and worthwhile and that it could be extended to all economic sectors. Already in June 1955, the Ministers for Foreign Affairs of the Six discussed the possibility of creating a common market embracing all products and a separate Community for nuclear energy. Speedy negotiations conducted by the Belgian Minister for Foreign Affairs, Paul-Henri Spaak, were concluded in April 1956 and on 25 March 1957, the Six were able to sign, on Capitol Hill in Rome, the Treaties establishing the two new Communities [see section 2.1.].

The United Kingdom proposed then to the Six the creation of a vast European free trade area between the European Economic Community and the other Member States of the OECD, but the discussion were interrupted during the autumn of 1958 owing to intractable differences of opinion between France and the United Kingdom. The separation between states, which wanted to try the Community method and those, which preferred the intergovernmental cooperation for trade liberalisation took shape in 1959 with the creation of the **European Free Trade Association (EFTA)**, to which the United Kingdom, Norway, Sweden, Denmark, Austria, Portugal, Iceland and Switzerland acceded, with Finland joining at a later date.

Having been impressed, however, by the early successes of the European Community, it was not long before the British Government was rethinking its refusal to play an active role in the work of European unification. It was aware that the United Kingdom could not maintain its political influence in Europe and the world through the intergovernmental association of the EFTA. So in August 1961, the United Kingdom submitted an initial official application to become a full member of the European Community. UK candidature of the EEC was followed by two other EFTA member countries, namely Denmark and Norway, and also by Ireland.

Accession of those countries initially met with the opposition of the President of the French Republic, General de Gaulle, who, being very distrustful of the United Kingdom's intentions, declared, right in the middle of the negotiations in 1963, that he wished to discontinue them. The second British application for accession, in 1967, with which Ireland, Denmark and Norway were yet again associated, was not examined for much time owing to France's misgivings. The issue of the accession of those countries could not be resolved until, following General de Gaulle's resignation in April 1969. After laborious negotiations, the Treaties of Accession were finally signed on 22 January 1972. The **accession of the United Kingdom, Ireland and Denmark** took effect on 1 January 1973, following favourable referenda (Ireland and Denmark) and ratification by the national parliaments. Norway's accession was prevented, however, after 53.49% of the Norwegian population opposed accession to the European Community in a referendum.

Once democracy was restored in Greece, Portugal and Spain, those countries submitted applications for accession to the European Community, in 1975 in Greece's case and in 1977 in the other two cases. **Greece** acceded to the Community on 1 January 1981, and **Spain and Portugal** on 1 January 1986. Those countries thus chose to step in the novel and hence risky experiment of the EEC rather than in the secure but limited refuge of the EFTA.

With the signature of the Single European Act, in June 1987, the Twelve Member States of the EEC decided to complete their internal market on 31 December 1992. One year before that date, in December 1991, they decided in Maastricht to develop within the single market an economic and monetary union, a judicial and home affairs policy and a common foreign and security policy, thus transforming the European Economic Community into a **European Union (EU)**, including a refurbished European Community (EC).

Since the 1st January 1995, the Europe of Twelve became the Europe of Fifteen, with the **accession of Austria, Finland and Sweden**, the people of Norway having again voted against membership of the Union by a majority of 52.8%. The remaining countries of the European Free Trade Area (minus Switzerland), i.e., Norway, Iceland and the Liechtenstein signed with the European Community a Treaty on the **European Economic Area (EEA)**, which came into force on 1 January 1994, creating a large free trade area involving several common policies of the EC/EU [see section 25.1.].After the fall of the iron curtain in 1989, one after the other the countries of Central and Eastern Europe applied for membership to the EU, thus clearly opting for multinational integration rather than for intergovernmental cooperation inside EFTA. Their preference was guided both by expectations of faster economic development and by hopes of increased political stability inside a Union of democratic countries. The EU encouraged their application by political and financial means [see section 25.2.] and started accession negotiations with **Poland, Hungary, the Czech Republic, Slovakia, Slovenia, Estonia, Latvia, Lithuania** plus **Cyprus** and **Malta**. After conclusion of the negotiations, these ten countries signed the Treaty of Accession in Athens on 16 April 2003[1] and have been full members of the EC/EU since 1 May 2004. **Bulgaria** and **Romania** acceded to the EU on 1 January 2007. We, therefore, now speak of the Union of Twenty seven.

The enlargement of the EC/EU is still in progress. In December 2004, the EU accepted to start accession negotiations with Croatia and Turkey. As soon as their economic and political situation allows, all Balkan countries are expected to seek a safe haven inside the Union, which, in the next decade, could thus number more than thirty members [see sections 15.2 and 25.3].

1.3. The attractiveness of the Community method

The growing membership of the Community/Union demonstrates the **extraordinary attractiveness of the multinational integration process**, the Community method, compared to its rival, the intergovernmental cooperation method. The countries, which had originally advocated the latter method, have come, one after the other, to solicit their participation in the integration process. The countries of Western Europe, which still shy away from this process, are nevertheless following many of the policies decided by the countries participating in the process, thanks to the European Economic Area agreement (EEA) [see section 25.1.]. The countries of Central and Eastern Europe, which, after their liberation from the iron curtain, had the option of joining the outer circle of the free trade EFTA/EEA or the inner circle of the EC/EU, have unhesitatingly opted for the latter. The facts speak for themselves. There could be no better demonstration of the valid-

---

[1] OJ L 236 and OJ C 227E, 23.09.2003.

ity of the multinational integration (Community) method than the attraction that it exerts on outsider neighbouring countries.

What is even more extraordinary is that the membership has kept growing together with the tasks assumed by the team, which means that the newcomers accede to an ever closer union and undertake to adopt all the "acquis communautaire", i.e. all the ever-growing legislation enacted by the institutions set up by the elder members. Earlier accessions happened at the time that the Community had just realised its customs union and was struggling to complete its common market in order to make it a single market. The newcomers could well believe that the integration process would stop at this stage and, in fact, some still wish that it had and feel betrayed that it marches on and on. But, later day accessions happened at times that the Community/Union had declared, in revised Treaties, its intention to proceed to the stages of economic and monetary union and even to political union. Hence, when they signed and ratified these Treaties, they were fully aware that European integration is a process without a specified end, but with the declared objective of bringing the European peoples ever closer together. This means that recent newcomers and applicants are attracted by the economic and political advantages of integration, which, for them, outweigh the disadvantage of ceding parts of their national sovereignties to supranational institutions.

The 2004 and 2007 enlargements were successes of the European Union. They have helped to overcome the division of Europe and contributed to peace and stability throughout the continent. They have inspired reforms and have consolidated common principles of liberty, democracy, respect for human rights and fundamental freedoms and the rule of law as well as the market economy. The wider internal market and economic cooperation have increased prosperity and competitiveness, enabling the enlarged Union to respond better to the challenges of globalisation. Enlargements have also enhanced the EU's weight in the world and made it a stronger international partner.

The attraction continues and it seems likely that all the countries in the periphery of the Union will someday ask for accession to it. In fact, the problem is not so much the continuous enlargement of the Union as that **its actual structures and institutions cannot support its expansion** without their reinforcement. The signing of the Lisbon Treaty, on 13 December 2007, was an initial endeavour to strengthen the structures and institutions of the Union. But, it seems likely that the reforms brought about by this Treaty will not be enough to allow the Union to satisfy the aspirations of its citizens both on the internal and particularly on the external front [see the European perspectives in the conclusions].

General bibliography on the EU

- AHRENS Joachim (et al.). "Enhanced cooperation in an enlarged EU", in: *Jahrbuch für Wirtschaftswissenschaften*, v. 58, n. 2, 2007, p. 130-150.

- DIMITROVA Antoaneta, TOSHKOV Dimiter. "The dynamics of domestic coordination of EU policy in the new Member States: impossible to lock" in *West European Politics*, v. 30, n. 5, November, 2007, p. 961-986

- KAISER Wolfram. *Christian democracy and the origins of European Union.* Cambridge: Cambridge University press, 2007.

- KIRSCHBAUM Stanislav (ed.). *Central European history and the European Union: the meaning of Europe.* Basingstoke: Palgrave MacMillan, 2007.

- MOUSSIS Nicholas. *Access to European Union: Law, Economics, Policies,* 17th revised edition. Brussels: European Study Service, 2008.

- SAJDIK Martin, SCHWARZINGER Michael. *European Union enlargement: background, developments, facts.* London: Transaction Publishers, 2008.

- SCHÄFER Wolf (et al.). "The EU on the 50th anniversary of the Treaty of Rome", in Intereconomics, v. 42, n. 1, January-February, 2007, p. 4-31.

- SCHIEMAN Konrad. "Europe and the loss of sovereignty" in *International and Comparative Law Quarterly*, v. 56, n. 3, July, 2007, p. 475-489.

- STIVACHTIS Yannis (ed.). *The state of European integration.* Aldershot: Ashgate, in association with Athens Institute for Education & Research - ATINER, 2007.

- TAYLOR Paul. *The end of European integration: anti-europeanism examined.* London: Routledge, 2008.

DISCUSSION TOPICS

1. On the basis of the contents of this book, can you assess the importance of common policies for multinational integration?
2. Why did R. Schuman call for a treaty on coal and steel and not for the constitution of a federal state?
3. Does multinational integration imply the disappearance of nation-states?
4. Discuss the evolution of the membership of the European Community/Union.
5. Which in your view are the primary objectives of the nations that take part or are seeking participation in European integration and how do they pursue them?

Chapter 2

EUROPEAN TREATIES

Paris 1951	Rome 1957		Brussels
ECSC Treaty p. 20	EAEC Treaty p. 20	**EEC Treaty p. 21**	Single Act p. 21

Maastricht 1991, p. 22			
ECSC Treaty	EAEC Treaty	EU Treaty	EC Treaty

Amsterdam 1997, p. 23			
ECSC Treaty	EAEC Treaty	EU Treaty	EC Treaty

Nice 2000, p. 22		
EAEC Treaty	EU Treaty	EC Treat

Lisbon 2007, p. 23		
EAEC Treaty	EU Treaty	Treaty on the functioning of the EU

The Treaties are the primary source of European law and hence the legal basis of common policies. The emphasis in this chapter is put on the Treaties as instruments of progress of the European integration. We, therefore, review the main objectives of the original Treaties and those of the Treaties which have replaced them in order to revise some of their provisions and to lay the foundations for more advanced stages of European integration.

2.1. The original Treaties

As we saw above, the first European Treaty, the one establishing the **European Coal and Steel Community (ECSC)**, was signed in Paris on 18 April 1951 by France, Germany, Italy and the Benelux countries and entered into force on 23 July 1952. Its main objective was to eliminate the various barriers to trade and to create a common market in which coal and steel products from the Member States could move freely in order to meet the needs of all Community inhabitants, without discrimination on grounds of nationality. Capital and workers in both sectors should also circulate freely. These rules were to be implemented by Community institutions, which would exercise the powers previously held by the states in those sectors: namely a High Authority and a special Council (of Ministers), the decisions of which would be binding on all Member States. Ambitious despite its restricted scope, the ECSC Treaty instituted a European Assembly and a European Court of Justice. The avowed intentions of the founders of the ECSC were, indeed, that it should be an experiment, which could gradually be extended to other economic spheres, culminating in a "European Federation". For this reason, the duration of the ECSC Treaty was limited to fifty years. On 23 July 2002, when it expired, the specific rules concerning the coal and steel sectors were integrated in the Community law and their particular resources, programmes and international obligations were taken over by the European Community[1]. The coal and steel sectors, previously covered by the ECSC Treaty, are dealt with respectively in the chapters on energy and industry.

The Treaty establishing the **European Atomic Energy Community (EAEC**, but more commonly known as **Euratom**) was signed in Rome on 25 March 1957 and came into force on 1 January 1958. Its aim was to create a common market for nuclear materials and equipment, establish common nuclear legislation, introduce a common system for supplies of fissile materials and establish a system for supervising the peaceful use of nuclear energy and common standards for nuclear safety and for the health and safety protection of the population and workers against ionising radiation. The key elements in this Treaty were, however, the coordination of the Member States' research programmes and a joint research programme, implemented in a Joint Research Centre, which was to develop technology and stimulate nuclear production in Europe [see sections 18.2.4. and 18.3.]. Although it was very much in the spotlight at the time of its establishment, Euratom has experienced many ups and downs as a result both of disillusionment as regards nuclear energy's economic prospects and of the ambition of some Member States to develop their own nuclear industry, and not purely for civil purposes. Nevertheless, the EAEC Treaty is still in force. The subjects concerning it are examined mainly in the chapters on research and energy.

Signed at the same time as the Euratom Treaty on the Capitol Hill in Rome on 25 March 1957, the Treaty establishing the **European Economic Community (EEC)** was likewise brought into force on 1 January 1958. Although the EEC and EAEC treaties are sometimes referred to as the "Treaties of Rome", the "Treaty of Rome" is obviously the EEC Treaty. The essential task, which the Treaty of Rome assigned to the Community institutions, was **the creation of a common market** between the Member States. That involved: (a) the achievement of a customs union entailing, on

---

[1] Decision 2002/234, OJ L 79, 22.03.2002, Decisions 2002/595 and 2002/596, OJ L 194, 23.07.2002 and Decisions 2003/76 and 2003/77, OJ L 29, 05.02.2003.

the one hand, the abolition of customs duties, import quotas and other barriers to trade between Member States and, on the other hand, the introduction of a Common Customs Tariff (CCT) vis-à-vis third countries [see chapter 5]; and (b) the implementation, *inter alia* through common policies, of **four fundamental freedoms**: freedom of movement of goods, of course, but also freedom of movement of salaried workers, freedom of establishment and freedom to provide services by independent persons and companies and, finally, freedom of capital movements [see chapter 6].

Although in the preamble to the EEC Treaty the Member States declared that they were determined to lay the foundations of an ever closer union among the peoples of Europe, the Treaty itself constituted the charter for a common market. It set the objectives to be attained so as to arrive at that stage of European integration. However, through its Article 235 (Art. 308 TEC), it gave Member States **the possibility to act in the fields not provided by it** by taking unanimously the measures required to attain one of its objectives. This allowed the Member States to implement a large number of common or, so called, Community policies without amending the Treaty.

Nevertheless, the EEC Treaty had a serious fault: although it had set a timetable for the abolition of customs barriers to trade, it had not done the same for the removal of trade barriers of equivalent effect. This vacuum was covered by **the Single European Act**, which came into force on 1 July 1987. Supplementing the EEC Treaty, the Single Act committed the Community to adopt measures with the aim of progressively establishing the internal market over a period expiring on 31 December 1992. At the same time it consecrated the European Council, European cooperation on foreign policy and social and economic cohesion between Member States. Lastly, it served as a legal base for numerous common policies, notably, social, environmental, research and technology.

2.2. The Treaty of Maastricht

The integrationists in the original six Member States were, already before the completion of the single market, pushing their new partners to step into the next integration stage, that of the economic and monetary union, and even to sketch the final stage, that of political union. The defenders of the intergovernmental method were, however, reticent. They had joined the Community in order to reap the benefits of the single market and had accepted the cessions of sovereignty necessary to that end. But they were reticent to make any more concessions to the Community method of integration and its evolutionary properties.

The compromise solution found in Maastricht, in December 1991, was to split the integration venture in half. Hence, the so-called Treaty of Maastricht, which was signed on 7 February 1992, was in fact made up of two separate but interrelated Treaties: the **Treaty on the European Union (TEU)**; and the **Treaty establishing the European Community (TEC)**.

These two Treaties separated the European construction into three pillars or edifices [see section 3.1.], distinguished mainly on the basis of the decision-making process: the main pillar or edifice, which is the European Community and where the common work of the participants is regulated by the TEC and where the Community method prevails; the pillar or edifice of justice and home affairs; and the pillar or edifice of the common foreign and security policy (CFSP). The method of construction of the two new pillars or edifices was based on intergovernmental cooperation, since the TEU required unanimity for decision-making and, hence, any Member State could veto a common action.

Thus, since the putting into effect of the Treaty of Maastricht in 1992, we speak of the **European Community/Union (EC/EU)**, in order to keep in mind that they are two different organisations and legal entities.

2.3. The Treaty of Amsterdam

The Treaty signed on 17 June 1997 at Amsterdam, only six years and a half after the signature of the Treaty of Maastricht, did not bring fundamental changes to the integration process, but it marked some progress in several policy areas. The most important development was the transfer, under the European Community's wing, thus entailing the Community decision-making method, of policies related to the free movement of persons, notably concerning visas, asylum and immigration [see section 8.1.]. In particular, it made the Union's **institutional structure** more efficient by extending the co-decision procedure (Parliament/Council) and qualified majority voting in the Council [see section 4.3.]. Another important objective of the Amsterdam Treaty was to place employment and **social protection** at the heart of the Union [see sections 13.3. and 13.5.3.].

Under its European Union wing, the Amsterdam Treaty strengthened the common foreign and security policy by making the European Council (heads of State or government) responsible for defining common strategies to be implemented by the Union and the Member States and by designating a High Representative for the CFSP (the Secretary General of the Council) and a Policy Planning and Early Warning Unit under his responsibility [see section 8.2.].

2.4. The Treaty of Nice

The Treaty that was signed in Nice on 26 February 2001, only three years and a half after the signature of the Treaty of Amsterdam, did not aspire to give a fresh impetus to the European integration process, but only to prepare the institutions of the European Community/Union to function with the representatives of twelve new Member States[1].

---

[1]   OJ C 325, 24.12.2002.

The Treaty of Nice extended the qualified majority voting to new subjects, thereby boosting the role of the European Parliament in the codecision process with the Council. It reinforced and facilitated the enhanced cooperation of some Member States, in cases where an agreement cannot be reached by normal decision-making procedures. The Protocol on the enlargement of the European Union, adopted at Nice, redefined the weighting of the votes of each Member State in the Council and introduced a population element by specifying that decisions taken by qualified majority on the basis of a Commission proposal should gather at least 72% of the total votes of the members, representing at least 62% of the total population of the Union[1]. As regards the composition of the Commission, the same protocol provides that after the enlargement of the Union each Member State will have one Commissioner until such time as the 27th Member State joins the European Union, but thereafter the number of Commissioners will be smaller than the number of Member States.

The Treaty of Nice came into force on 1 February 2003. Under the heading of the city in which it was signed, the Treaty of Nice, as the repealed Treaties of Maastricht and Amsterdam, includes in fact two Treaties: the Treaty on the European Union (**TEU**) and the Treaty establishing the European Community (**TEC**). The existence of two separate Treaties for the Community and the Union, their frequent modifications, the new numbering of their articles and the technocratic language of their texts are daunting and hardly likely to mobilise the public opinion in favour of European integration [see sections 10.1. and 10.4.]. **This book follows the numbering of the articles of the TEU and the TEC** adopted in Nice and actually in force, except when referring to past legislation based on previous versions of the Treaties.

2.5. The Treaty of Lisbon: a virtual Constitution

The Treaty of Nice was conceived by the governments of the Fifteen as a transitory Treaty, allowing the European Community/Union (EC/EU) to function temporarily after the accession of ten new members. Consequently, the heads of state or government of the enlarged Union **signed the Constitutional Treaty on 29 October 2004**, in Rome[2]. However, the negative referendums in France and in the Netherlands, in 29 May 29 and 1 June 2005, pronounced the death of the Constitutional Treaty. Still, the political leaders of Europe, aware of the need of reforming the institutions to allow them to function correctly in the enlarged Union, agreed to reform the existing treaties.

The **Treaty of Lisbon**, signed by the heads of State or government of the 27 Member States, on 13 December 2007, maintained all the important elements of the stillborn constitutional Treaty, setting aside certain secon-

---

[1] Decision 2007/4, OJ L 1, 04.01.2007.
[2] OJ C 310, 16.12.2004.

dary or emblematic elements, which bothered particularly eurosceptics, notably the title of "Constitution" that for some concealed the transformation of the Union into a Super-State.

The most important reforms proposed by the defunct Constitution are taken over by the Treaty of Lisbon. First of all, **the European Union will absorb the European Community**, which will cease to exist as such. Under the name of the city where they were signed, there will still be found two Treaties having the same rank: the Treaty on the European Union (TEU) and the Treaty on the Functioning of the European Union (TFEU), which will replace the Treaty establishing the European Community (TEC), thus ending the confusion between "the Community" and the "Union". The treaty of Lisbon emphasises the voluntary nature of the integration process [see section 1.1.2], by explicitly recognising the possibility for a Member State to withdraw from the Union (Article 49 A, Lisbon = Article I-60, Constitution).

Under the new Treaty, the European Union becomes more democratic. The **powers of the European Parliament** are increased considerably [see section 4.1.3]. The "co-decision procedure" of the Parliament and the Council is renamed "ordinary legislative procedure" [see section 4.3] and is extended to several new fields, including justice and home affairs, some aspects of the common trade and agricultural policies, as well as the EU budget (Article 9 A, Lisbon = article I-20, Constitution). Thus, the Parliament will have the functions of a lower chamber, representing the citizens of the Union, while the Council will play the role of a Senate, representing the governments of the Member States.

In parallel with its strengthened role, the composition of the **European Parliament** is also adapted to the new circumstances of the enlarged Union. The number of MEPs is capped at 751 (750 plus the president of the Parliament) and Seats will be distributed among countries according to "degressive proportionality", i.e. MEPs from more populous countries will each represent more people than those from smaller countries [see section 4.1.3]. The **European Council** will be headed by a permanent president, elected by the European Council for two and a half years [see section 4.1.1]. The **European Commission** will have a new role to play in external relations, since its vice-president, responsible for external relations will become the EU high representative for foreign and security policy and will chair the "foreign affairs Council" [see section 4.1.2].

The standard system of voting in the Council of Ministers will be **"qualified majority voting"**, which, from 2014, will be based on the double majority of States and population. Decisions in the Council of Ministers will need the support of 55% of Member States representing a minimum of 65% of the EU's population, thus facilitating decision-making in the enlarged Union [see sections 4.1.4 and 4.3]. Following the path of the Constitutional Treaty; the Treaty of Lisbon extends the ordinary legislative procedure to practically all aspects of justice and home affairs (JHA), thus abolishing the so-called third pillar of the Union [see section 8.1].

Like the draft Constitution, the Treaty of Lisbon does not extend qualified majority voting to the **common foreign and security policy (CFSP)**.
Unanimity will continue to be the rule for decision-making on CFSP matters, thus preventing this policy from becoming really common and effective [see section 8.2.1]. Nevertheless, the fact that the new **High Representative for Foreign Affairs and Security Policy** will be Vice-President
of the Commission will help the EU work more effectively and consistently on the world scene [see section 4.1.2]. In addition, the Treaty of Lisbon (like the draft Constitutional Treaty) **strengthens the European Security and Defence Policy** (ESDP) and allows Member States which have
made more binding commitments to one another in this area to establish
permanent structured cooperation within the Union framework [see section 8.2.3].

The negative Irish vote in the referendum of 12 June 2008, which denied the ratification of the treaty of Lisbon, risks to bring to a standstill the
development of the Union. The existing Treaty of Nice will remain the basis for the work of the EU until the ratification of the Treaty of Lisbon by
all Member States.

2.6. The treaties as instruments of progress

The frequency and vigour of the amendments of the European treaties
show that their authors, i.e. the governments of the Member States, do not
consider them as sacred and unalterable, but they use them as perfectible
instruments of the multinational integration process. Given that the problems of European states change continually under the pressure of internal
and external factors, the common policies must develop regularly in order
to face them successfully. This is the reason why the Treaties, which are
the primary source of European law and hence the legal basis of common
policies, have to be modified frequently.

In fact, **the Treaty of Lisbon is only a ring** - certainly not the last - in
the chain of treaties that move forward European economic and political
integration. The integration process is evolutionary and the Treaties are the
means of progress [see section 1.1.2]. But, together with the progress of the
integration process, grow eurosceptic objections to its extension, particularly in the political field. It is normal that in any social group (family,
tribe, nation, group of nations…) there should be differences of opinion as
to the management of its affairs. The way to settle this problem found by
the democratic system of governance is the majority rule, whereby the minority has to follow decisions taken by the majority. This rule has henceforth to be applied in the signing and ratification of European treaties. The
unanimity rule for the ratification of the European treaties should be replaced by a rule of three thirds majority, similar to that in force for the ratification of the amendments to the Constitution of the United States [see the
European perspectives in the conclusions].

Bibliography on European Treaties

- AALT Willem Heringa, KIIVER Philipp. *Constitutions compared: an introduction to comparative constitutional law.* Antwerpen: Intersentia, 2007.
- CENTRE FOR EUROPEAN POLICY STUDIES. *The Treaty of Lisbon: Implementing the institutional innovations*: joint study. Brussels: Egmont - The Royal Institute for International Relations, 2007.
- CHRISTIANSEN Thomas, *Constitutionalising the European Union.* Lanham: Palgrave MacMillan, 2007.
- CRAIG Paul. "The Treaty of Lisbon: process, architecture and substance, in *European Law Review*, v. 33, n. 2, April 2008, p. 137-166.
- EGMONT - CENTRE FOR EUROPEAN POLICY STUDIES (CEPS). The Treaty of Lisbon: implementing the institutional innovations: joint study. Brussels: Egmont - The Royal Institute for International Relations, 2007.
- ERK Jan. "Real constitution, formal constitution and democracy in the European Union" in *Journal of Common Market Studies*, v. 45, n. 3, September 2007, p. 633-652.
- FITOUSSI Jean-Paul, LE CACHEUX Jacques (eds.). *Reforming the European Union.* Basingstoke: Palgrave Macmillan, 2007.
- KINNEGING Andreas (ed.). *Rethinking Europe's Constitution.* Nijmegen: Wolf Legal Publishers, 2007.
- MOUSSIS Nicolas. "Le traité de Lisbonne: une Constitution sans le titre", in *Revue du Marché commun et de l'Union européenne*, n°516, mars 2008, p. 1-8.
- SAURON Jean-Luc. *Comprendre le Traité de Lisbonne: texte consolidé intégral des traités, explications et commentaires.* Paris: Gualino, 2007.

DISCUSSION TOPICS

1. Which were the principal goals of the Treaties of Rome?
2. Which were the new goals set by the Treaty of Maastricht?
3. Which were the new goals set by the Constitutional Treaty and the Reform treaty?
4. Is the signing and ratification of a treaty necessary for the passage from one integration stage to the next?
5. Discuss the advantages and disadvantages of a Constitutional treaty for the Member States of the European Union.

Chapter 3

EUROPEAN LAW AND FINANCES

I n the previous chapter we explained that two different Treaties - the Treaty on the European Union and the Treaty establishing the European Community - actually institute and govern two different organisations. In the first part of this chapter, we analyse these two organisations: the European Union and the European Community. We see when and how the European Union covers the European Community, when each of these organisations should be treated separately and when they should be joined together under the name of **European Community/Union (EC/EU)**.

3.1. European Community and European Union

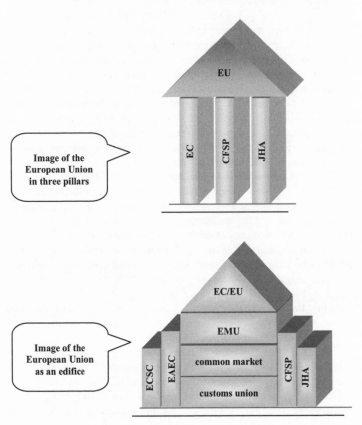

Image of the European Union in three pillars

Image of the European Union as an edifice

One often hears about **the three "pillars"** of the European Union, the first being the European Community (EC), the second the common foreign and security policy (CFSP) and the third justice and home affairs (JHA). We should say, however, that the image of the EU as three pillars minimises the place of the Community, which is preponderant, since it contains all common policies instituted in the framework of the three original Treaties and all the legislation adopted on their bases since 1952.

The European Union is better visualised **as an on-going construction.** In this image, the European Community constitutes the main edifice, solid and functional, thanks to the existence within it of a great number of common policies, which are at various stages of development. Next to it, the CFSP and especially the JHA are still at the stage of foundations, built following the plans drafted under the Treaty on the European Union. Their edifices need to be patiently built with common legal acts. Moreover, the Treaty of Amsterdam has transferred into the Community edifice many subjects, which were originally under the JHA wing. In this wing, intergovernmental cooperation is presently confined to police and judicial cooperation in criminal matters [see section 8.1.2.]. It would be absurd to represent this cooperation as a pillar of the European construction.

A closer look at the metaphorical image of the European construction shows that **the main edifice, that of the Community**, is divided horizontally in floors. The floor of the common market is built on the foundations of the customs union. Apart from the four fundamental freedoms (free movement of goods, persons, services and capital), the common market floor consists of numerous horizontal and vertical compartments, which contain the common policies that constitute the bulk of this book. The compartments of coal, steel and nuclear energy, built with the Community method provided by the ECSC and Euratom Treaties, are also found on these first floors of the Community edifice.

The floor of **economic and monetary union (EMU)** was built above the floor of the common market and, therefore, inside the Community edifice [see chapter 7]. The Treaty on European Community has drawn the architectural plans and the "memorandum of understanding" that the builders (European institutions and Member States) need to respect in order to succeed in the construction of the EMU. Some of the contractors (Member States), who have advanced faster than others, find themselves already in the "penthouse" of the Community edifice, which shelters the single currency, and have started setting up common policies inside it. The others, including the new Member States will continue to work inside the lower floors, until the time that they are ready and/or willing to join the pioneers in the top floor of the collective edifice.

The "European Community" exists thus and grows under the roof of the "European Union". It is correct to speak about the "**Community**" in respect of everything that happened and that was built up until the 1st November 1993, when the "European Union" came into being. It is even correct to speak about the "Community" for measures taken after that date by following the Community procedure on the basis of the EC Treaty (but also the ECSC and EAEC Treaties). The term **"European Union"** should, however, be used for designating the organisation of European countries, which have decided to create an ever closer union among their peoples, covering relations much broader than the economic relations governed by the original Community. It must be noted, in this context, that the European Community has an international legal personality, which includes the capacity to conclude agreements, whereas the Union does not have such a personality. All this will change with the coming into force of the **Treaty of Lisbon**, since it abolishes the European Community altogether and it bestows legal personality to the European Union alone, thus ending the absurdity of the "three pillars" of the EU and the confusion between the "Community" and the "Union" [see section 2.5].

3.2. The competences of the European Community/Union

When the member states of a multinational integration scheme adopt a fundamental or secondary common policy [see section 1.1.2], they implicitly recognise that it has an added value in relation to their previously independent national policies in a certain field. Certainly, as common policies advance, national policies lose some of their independence in terms of goals and means, since segments of national sovereignty are blended into a new concept of **"shared sovereignty"** that is intended to serve better the various national interests. But, this loss of independence is circumscribed by two means: the continuing influence of the member states in the development of a common policy after its inception, through the common institutions in which they participate [see chapter 4]; and the possibility left to the member states to choose the means that suit them best to attain the common goals of a common policy, by virtue of the principles of subsidiarity and proportionality explained below.

The **principle of subsidiarity** means that the Community must not undertake or regulate what can be managed or regulated more efficiently at national or regional levels. This principle, implying multi-level governance [see section 1.1.1.] must be exercised in a spirit of cooperation between the various levels of power. According to the Treaties (Art. 5 TEC and Art. 2 TEU), the European Community/Union must act within the limits of the powers conferred upon it by the Treaties and of the objectives assigned to it therein. In areas which do not fall within its exclusive competence, the Community must take action, in accordance with the principle of subsidiarity, only if and in so far as the objectives of the proposed action cannot be sufficiently achieved by the Member States and can therefore, by reason of the scale or effects of the proposed action, be better achieved by the Community. Any action by the Community must not exceed that which is necessary to achieve the objectives of the Treaties. Article 308 of the EC

Treaty enables the Council, by unanimity and after consulting the European Parliament, to introduce the provisions needed to attain a common objective, but does not make it possible to create new powers for the Community. An interinstitutional agreement sets out the procedures for implementing the principle of subsidiarity[1].

The **principle of proportionality** implies that, if a Community action proves to be necessary to attain the objectives of the Treaty, the Community institutions must further examine whether legislative action is required or whether other sufficiently effective means can be used (financial support, encouragement of cooperation between Member States by a Recommendation, inducement to take action by a Resolution, etc.).

In many areas where common policies have not been agreed, the "**open method of coordination**", established by the Lisbon European Council (23 and 24 March 2000), is used as non-binding means of spreading best practice and achieving greater convergence of national policies. This method involves setting common objectives, translating these objectives into national policy strategies and periodic monitoring on the basis, inter alia, of commonly agreed and defined indicators. The intergovernmental cooperation achieved through this method does not obligate the Member States to follow the objectives set in common, but may through the learning process lead to real common policies.

The **Treaty of Lisbon** (like the defunct Constitutional Treaty) does not depart from current practice on the question of transfer of sovereign rights from the Member States to the Union, but it defines in detail the principles which govern this transfer and guarantees that these principles should not be infringed. These principles are: the principle of conferral, under which the Union shall act within the limits of the competences conferred upon it by the Member States in the Treaties (Article 3b, Lisbon = Article I-11, Constitution); and the principles of subsidiarity and proportionality, which henceforth are submitted to the control of national parliaments (Article 8 C, Lisbon = Article III-259, Constitution). Competences not conferred upon the Union in the Treaties remain with the Member States.

3.3. The Community legal system

Common policies, which are the essence of multinational integration, are based on **common legislation**. Inherent in the concept of a common policy [see section 1.1.2.] is its **binding force on the member states**. The latter must give the common institutions the legal means to implement common policies and to enforce their decisions on all the parties concerned and on their citizens. Hence, common policies are shaped by legal acts agreed by the common institutions, implemented by the member states and/or the common institutions and controlled by the common institutions

---

[1]　Interinstitutional agreement, OJ C 329, 06.12.1993.

[see chapter 4]. The national laws of the member states are harmonised in a great number of fields in the context of common policies. A special law, based on the treaties and called *acquis communautaire*, is thus built to bring into being common policies, a law that is superimposed and takes **precedence over national law**, even the constitutional law, of the Member States, whether national legislation predates or postdates Community legislation. In fact, according to the Court of Justice, the Member States have definitively transferred sovereign rights to the Community they created, and they cannot subsequently go back on that transfer through unilateral measures[1], unless they decide to break away from the EC/EU. If they do not opt for such a radical measure, they cannot contravene European legislation, to the making of which they have contributed, by invoking their national, even their constitutional law. This is another feature of the multinational integration process, which distinguishes it from intergovernmental cooperation, where decisions may have political consequences but do not carry a legal binding force on the participating states. A multinational integration process, such as that of the EC/EU, could not function, if each Member State could circumvent the common legislation by bringing into play its national - including its constitutional - law.

The legal acts, which substantiate the common policies, may be undertaken by the competent institutions with legal effect only if they are empowered to do so by the European Treaties (principle of conferral or of attribution of powers). Article 249 of the EC Treaty provides for five forms of legal act, each with a different effect on the Member States' legal systems. Some are directly applicable in place of national legislation, while others permit the progressive adjustment of that legislation to Community provisions.

The **regulation** has a general scope, is binding in all its elements and is directly applicable in each Member State. Just like a national law, it gives rise to rights and obligations directly applicable to the citizens of the European Union[2]. Regulations enter into force on a date which they lay down or, where they do not set a date, on the twentieth day following their publication in the Official Journal of the European Union. The regulation substitutes European law for national law and is therefore the most effective legal instrument provided for by the EC Treaty. As "European laws", regulations must be complied with fully by those to whom they are addressed (individuals, Member States, European institutions).

The **directive** binds any Member State to which it is addressed with regard to the result to be achieved, while allowing the national authorities competency as to the form and methods used. It is a sort of Community framework law and lends itself particularly well to the harmonisation of national laws. It defines the objective or objectives to be attained by a

---

[1] Judgment of 15 July 1964, case 6/64, Costa/ENEL, ECR 1964, p. 1160.

[2] See on this subject, notably, the judgments of the Court of Justice of 14.12.1971, case 43/71, Politi, ECR 1971, p. 1049 and of 7.2.1973, case 39/72, Commission v Italy, ECR 1973, pp. 114-115.

common policy and leaves it to the Member States to choose the forms and instruments necessary for complying with it. Since the Member States are only bound by the objectives laid down in directives, they have some discretion, in transposing them into national law, in taking into account of special national circumstances. They must, however, "ensure fulfilment of the obligations arising out of the Treaty or resulting from action taken by the institutions of the Community" (Art. 10 TEC). Although they are generally published in the Official Journal, Directives take effect by virtue of being notified to the Member States to which they are addressed. The latter are obliged to adopt the national measures necessary for implementation of the Directive within time-limits set by it, failing which they are infringing Community legislation.

The **decision** is binding on the addressees it indicates, who may be one, several, or even all the Member States or one or more natural or legal persons. This variety of potential addressees is coupled with a variety in the scope of its contents, which may extend from a quasi regulation or a quasi directive to a specific administrative decision. It takes effect on its communication to the addressees rather than on its publication in the Official Journal. In any case, according to the Court of Justice, a decision can produce direct effects creating for the individuals rights that national jurisdictions must safeguard[1].

The above legal acts are normally used, on the basis of the Treaty and following the Community method [see section 4.3.], for harmonising or approximating national legislations. Their effects are binding on the Member States, the Community institutions and, in many cases, the citizens of the Member States. This is the case of laws or decisions which must apply uniformly in all Member States. However, the objectives of the common policies are also sought by **non-binding concerted action**, taking the form of coordination of national policies, mechanisms for exchanging information, bodies for cooperation, Community programmes and/or financial support.

Therefore, in addition to the above binding acts, which form the Community law, the Council and the Commission can adopt **Recommendations** suggesting a certain line of conduct or outlining the goals of a common policy and **opinions** assessing a current situation or certain facts in the Community or the Member States. Furthermore, the Council and the European Parliament adopt **Resolutions**, which are also not binding, suggesting a political desire to act in a given area. These instruments enable the Community institutions to suggest guidelines for coordination of national legislations or administrative practices in a non-binding manner, i.e. without any legal obligations for the addressees - Member States and/or citizens.

---

[1]   Judgment of 6 October 1970, case 9/70, Grad, ECR 1970, p. 838 and judgment of 12 December 1990, joined cases 100/89 and 101/89, ECR 1990, p. I-4647.

While Resolutions and opinions are published in the "C" series (communications) of the **Official Journal of the European Union (OJ)**, binding acts and recommendations are published in the "L" series (legislation) of the OJ, in order to stress their political importance. The same is true for the **common positions** and **joint actions** of the common foreign and security policy and of justice and home affairs (Art. 12 and 31 of TEU) [see sections 8.1. and 8.2.1.]. They are published in the L series of the OJ, although they do not have a legal binding force on the Member States, since the Court of Justice of the European Communities (CJEC) does not have jurisdiction on their interpretation and implementation. They embody, however, political commitments for joint behaviour and/or action.

The stillborn **Constitutional Treaty** renamed the legal instruments of the Union. These would have been: European laws (instead of regulations), European framework laws (instead of directives), European regulations (non legislative acts for the implementation of legislative acts), European decisions, recommendations and opinions (Art. I-33). The **Treaty of Lisbon** has not followed this suggestion of the draft Constitutional Treaty and, therefore, the legal instruments of the Union remain in their traditional form, which differentiates them from national legal instruments.

3.4. The Community finances

The conventional international organisations such as the UN or the OECD are financed by contributions from their member countries. In most instances their financial requirements amount to staff and operational expenditure. If they are entrusted with operational tasks, their financing is generally provided on an "à la carte" basis by those member countries which agreed on those tasks. It is virtually never a question, in such organisations, of financial transfers or even of financial compensation. The European Community, on the other hand, although it is not a federation in the formal sense, pursues many federating common policies, which call for a transfer of resources from the national to the supranational level.

Some common policies of the European Community/Union are clearly in the interest of the stronger and wealthier Member States. This is the case notably of the internal market, competition and taxation policies, because they open the markets of the poorer and less developed Member States to their products and services. Therefore, some other policies are needed to **balance the benefits of the integration process**, by operating capital transfers in favour of the poorer Member States: e.g. agricultural, regional and social policies. These transfers of capital are also in the interest of the wealthier Member States, since they allow their poorer partners to buy more of their products and services. This balance of the benefits of the Member States, which distinguishes, inter alia, a multinational integration scheme from a free trade area one, is organised by the Community budget.

The implementation of many common policies requires, indeed, not only legal but also some financial means. Certainly, not all common policies need common financing. For example, competition and taxation policies are based almost exclusively on legal measures. But the implementation of most common policies is based on a mixture of legal and financial measures. Common regional, education, aid to development policies, e.g., would be seriously restrained without Community financing of their common programmes. There could be no common agricultural or fisheries policies, in the sense that we know them, without common support of prices and/or incomes [see sections 21.4.2, 21.4.3 and 22.3.]. It is a political value judgment whether there should be more or less common financing of this or that common policy and this judgment is subject to a long debate carried out every year among the budgetary authorities of the Community - i.e. politicians from the Member States sitting in the Council and the European Parliament - on the basis of technical reports and proposals provided by the Commission. The result of this multinational political debate is recorded in the **Community budget**.

The transfer of customs revenue to the Community budget was a spill-over effect [see section 1.1.1.] of the realisation, provided for in the Treaty, of a genuine customs union[1]. However, since the realisation of the customs union in 1968, the importance of customs duties was continually diminishing inasmuch as they were being progressively abolished or reduced under the General Agreement on Tariffs and Trade (GATT) and the various tariff concessions granted to the least developed countries [see section 23.4. and chapter 24]. For that reason it was decided, in 1970, to use a proportion of the **value added tax (VAT)** as an additional source of Community financing. That tax, which has a uniform basis of assessment takes fairly accurate account of the economic capacity of the citizens of the Member States, as it is levied at the consumption level [see section 14.2.1.]. The "**uniform base**", which was adopted for calculating the proportions of the VAT yield which countries must pay to the EU, is made up of all taxable supplies of goods and provisions of services in the Union[2].

Since 2001, the system of the European Communities' own resources is based on the following elements[3]:

- the **maximum ceiling** on own resources is fixed at 1.27 % of gross national income (GNI) of the EC/EU (+/- 70% of the resources);
- **traditional own resources** - essentially customs and agricultural duties - minus 25% retained by the Member States as collection costs (+/- 15% of the resources);
- 0.5% of the maximum call-in rate from **VAT resources**, aiming at correcting the regressive aspects of the system for the least prosperous Member States (+/- 15% of the resources);

---

[1] Decision 70/243, OJ L 94, 28.04.1970.
[2] Decision 88/376, OJ L 185, 15.07.1988.
[3] Decision 2007/436, OJ L 163, 23.06.2007.

- **technical adjustments** aiming at the correction of budgetary imbalances in favour of the United Kingdom and originating in the famous battle cry of Margaret Thatcher of 30 November 1979: "I want my money back".

However, **Community expenditures** still represent little more than one percent (actually 1.03%) of the EU-27 gross national income (GNI). More than 90% of the receipts of the European Union are redistributed to the Member States and serve to finance the objectives of the various common policies (redistributive function of the Community budget). Thus, out of a total € 129.1 billion in commitment appropriations of the 2008 budget[1], the most important commitments were: € 58.0 billion (45% of the total) for sustainable growth, including competitiveness, research, energy and transport networks, education and training; € 46.9 billion (36.3%) for regional growth and employment; € 55.0 billion (42.6%) for natural resources, including agriculture, rural development and the environment; € 1.3 billion (1%) for citizenship, freedom, security and justice. € 7.3 billion (5,7%) were allotted to EU actions outside the Member States, including pre-accession aid for candidate and potential candidate countries, the neighbourhood policy and aid to development and humanitarian efforts around the world.

Each year, the European Commission prepares the preliminary draft budget, and submits it to the Council in April or early May, taking account of the multi-annual financial perspective in force and the budget guidelines for the coming year. The **budgetary authority**, consisting of the Council and the European Parliament, amends and adopts the draft budget, the latter having the final word, as it may reject the budget, in which case a system of provisional twelfths applies until the two branches of the budgetary authority reach an agreement. However, the budgetary powers of the Council go beyond those of the Parliament, whose powers differ according to the type of expenditure. For "**compulsory expenditure**" (CE), i.e. expenditure resulting from the Treaties and the decisions adopted pursuant thereto (roughly 50% of appropriations, made up chiefly of those relating to the common agricultural policy), the Parliament may propose modifications provided that they do not increase the total volume of the budget. The **Treaty of Lisbon** abolishes the current distinction between "compulsory" expenditure and "non-compulsory" expenditure, with the result that the European Parliament and the Council will have equal powers for the whole budget (Article 9A, Lisbon).

The **management of the Community budget** is entrusted to the Commission (Art. 274 TEC) and is exercised according to a Financial Regulation, which sets the principles and ground rules governing the establishment and implementation of the budget and financial control, ensuring more efficient and effective management and control of European taxpayers' money[2]. Article 280 of the EC Treaty stipulates that the Member States must coordinate their action aimed at protecting the financial interests of

---

[1] 2008 budget, OJ L 71, 14.03.2008.

[2] Regulation 1605/2002, OJ L 248, 16.09.2002 and Regulation 2342/2002, OJ L 357, 31.12.2002 last amended by Regulation 1525/2007, OJ L 343, 27.12.2007.

the Community against fraud and must take the same measures to counter fraud affecting the financial interests of the Community as they take to counter fraud affecting their own financial interests.

Bibliography on European law and finances

* BARNARD Catherine. *The substantive law of the EU: the four freedoms.* Oxford: Oxford University Press, 2007.
* BAUDENBACHER Carl (et al.). *European integration through interaction of legal regimes.* Oslo: Universitetsforlaget, 2007.
* BENEDETTO Giacomo, HOYLAND Bjorn. The EU annual budgetary procedure: the existing rules and proposed reforms of the Convention and the Intergovernmental Conference 2002-04, in *Journal of Common Market Studies*, v. 45, n. 3, September 2007, p. 565-587.
* BERRY Elspeth, HARGREAVES Sylvia. *European Union law*: textbook Edition, 2nd ed. Oxford: Oxford University Press, 2007.
* CHALMERS Damia (et al.). *European Union law: Text and materials.* 2nd ed. Cambridge: Cambridge University Press, 2007.
* DEMARET Paul (et al.). *European legal dynamics = Dynamiques juridiques européennes.* Rev. and updated ed. of "30 years of European legal studies at the College of Europe = 30 ans d'études juridiques européennes au Collège d'Europe". Bruxelles: PIE - P. Lang, 2007.
* EUROPEAN COMMISSION. *A Europe of results- Applying Community Law*, Luxembourg: EUR-OP*, 2007.
* HOUSE OF LORDS, European Union Committee. *Funding the European Union: report with evidence.* London: Stationery Office, 2007.
* NÚÑEZ FERRER Jorge. *The EU budget: the UK rebate and the CAP - phasing them both out?* Brussels: Centre for European Policy Studies, 2007.
* THOMSON Robert (et al.). "The paradox of compliance: infringements and delays in transposing European Union directives", in *British Journal of Political Science*, v. 37, n. 4, October 2007, p. 685-709.

DISCUSSION TOPICS

1. Comment the imagery of the European Union in three pillars and as an edifice.
2. Discuss the importance of the principles of subsidiarity and proportionality.
3. Compare the legal system of the Community to that of a national state.
4. Consider the Community finances from the point of view of multinational integration.
5. Discuss the interaction between national and Community administrations in the fight against fraud.

Chapter 4

THE STRUCTURE AND FUNCTIONS OF EUROPEAN INSTITUTIONS

In the first part of this chapter is analysed the structure and the role of the institutions or organs of the European Union. In the second part is examined their interaction which leads to the formation and enforcement of European law. In the third part of the chapter we make some suggestions for a drastic reform of the institutions in view of the enlargement of the EC/EU and its evolution towards a political union.

4.1. The European Institutions

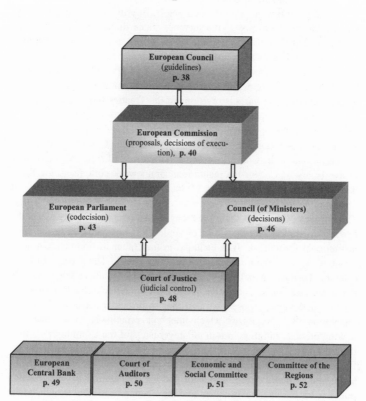

Common policies, which are the essence of the multinational integration process, are the fruit of intensive negotiations among the parties, which participate in this process. In order to be acceptable to all parties (member states), the conception of a common policy must try to satisfy or, at least, not harm the national interests of the parties and, therefore, the governments of all member states must participate in the decision-making process. Their participation, however, may be direct or indirect. Decisions on fundamental common policies, requiring new transfers of national sovereignties to the shared or supranational sovereignty, are taken by the participating governments (in intergovernmental conferences) and are outlined in treaties, signed by those governments and ratified by them after authorisation by the national parliaments [see chapter 2]. Decisions on secondary common policies, i.e. those needed to attain the goals set in the treaty, including policy guidelines and legal acts based on the treaty, are taken by the **common institutions** set up by the treaty, according to procedures and following the legal forms agreed in this treaty [see sections 3.3. and 4.3.]. In contrast to an organisation based on intergovernmental cooperation, where the governments are the main actors, in a multinational integration process the governments of the member states direct the play from the backstage, but they leave the stage to the actors, that is their representatives, appointed by them and/or by their citizens.

The principal actors of European integration are called **"institutions"** by the European Treaties. However, the qualification of an organ as institutional is changing in various revisions of the Treaties following the development of the European Community/Union. According to the EC Treaty (Nice version) the basic institutional structure of the European Union consists of five institutions: the European Parliament, the Council of Ministers, the Commission, the Court of Justice and the Court of Auditors. According to the Treaty of Lisbon the institutional framework comprises: the European Parliament, the European Council, the Council of Ministers, the European Commission and the Court of Justice of the European Union. The European Council is therefore recognised by the new Treaty as a fully-fledged institution, but the Court of Auditors is not included in the basic institutional framework. It is included in the "other institutions and advisory bodies", as is the European Central Bank (ECB). The Treaty of Lisbon (like the Treaty of Nice) recognises the status of "advisory bodies" to the Economic and Social Committee and to the Committee of the Regions.

For analytical purposes, we consider as principal actors of European integration the five organs which intervene principally in the decision-making process and therefore in the governance of the Community/Union: the European Council, which sets the goals of the common policies; the European Commission, which makes the proposals for the decisions to be taken and is mainly responsible for the implementation of the common policies; the European Parliament and the Council of Ministers, which take the decisions; and the Court of Justice, which controls the legality of these decisions.

4.1.1. The European Council

The European Council is made up of the **Heads of State** (the President of the French Republic and the Presidents of the Republics of Cyprus, Latvia and Lithuania, responsible for foreign and European affairs) **or of Government** (the Prime Ministers of the other Member States) of the EU and the President of the European Commission. Begun on an informal basis as "Summit meetings" in the early 1960s, the European Council is now explicitly provided for in Article 4 of the Treaty on European Union (Nice). This Article provides that the European Council shall meet at least twice a year, under the chairmanship of the Head of State or Government of the Member State which holds the Presidency of the Council [see section 4.1.4]. Departing from the letter of the Treaty, the Seville European Council (21-22 June 2002) has agreed that it shall meet in principle four times a year (twice every six months) and that, in exceptional circumstances, it may hold an extraordinary meeting.

The European Council is the architect of European construction. It provides the Union with the necessary impetus for its development; it defines the general political guidelines thereof and resolves the most important problems of the construction. The European Council is above all **a forum for free and informal exchanges of views** between the responsible leaders of the Member States. Its strength is its spontaneity and its informality, which bring about a sort of *"esprit de corps"* on the part of Europe's political leaders. Being a venue where package deals can be struck, the European Council often acts as an appeal body for politically and economically important business which is deadlocked at ministerial level.

It should be noted, however, that the Heads of State or Government **do not adopt legal acts formally binding** the Member States [see section 3.3.]. Their deliberations result in the publication of declarations containing guidelines and general directives for future Community action. These declarations have undeniable political value, but no legal binding force. They give the political impetus necessary for common policies, but the latter are constructed with Community provisions adopted subsequently in accordance with the procedures laid down in the Treaties. The situation is quite different in the sphere of the common foreign and security policy where the European Council, in addition to adopting common strategies, can decide upon joint actions or common positions, which bind politically, if not legally, the Member States [see section 8.2.1.].

The **Treaty of Lisbon** (following the stillborn Constitution) establishes a permanent President of the European Council, who will take on the work currently assigned to rotating Presidencies. He or she will be elected by qualified majority, for a term of two and a half years, renewable once (Article 9b, Lisbon = Article I-22, Constitution). The President would have the freedom of time and spirit to conduct the necessary discussions and negotiations with the twenty-seven heads of government should be able to facilitate cohesion and consensus and drive forward the work of the Euro-

pean Council. In addition, the President of the European Council will ensure the external representation of the Union on issues concerning common
foreign and security policy, without prejudice to the responsibilities of the
High Representative of the Union for Foreign Affairs and Security Policy.

4.1.2. The European Commission

From the very beginning of the Community until 2004, the European
Commission, usually referred to simply as **the Commission**, was made up
of two nationals from each "big" and one national from each "small"
Member State. Hence, the Treaty of Nice - adopted at a time when the
European Community/Union numbered fifteen Member States, five of
which were considered as big (Germany, France, the UK, Italy and Spain)
- stated that "the Commission shall consist of 20 Members, who shall be
chosen on the grounds of their general competence and whose independence is beyond doubt" (Article 213 TEC). Anticipating the enlargement of
the EC/EU, this Treaty provided, however, that the number of members of
the Commission could be altered by the Council, acting unanimously. In
fact, in the Act of Accession of the ten new Member States (article 45), it
was agreed (not without difficulties) that any State acceding to the Union
should be entitled to have one of its nationals as a member of the Commission and that a new Commission composed of one national of each Member State should take up its duties on 1 November 2004, after the European
elections of June 2004.

Thus, actually, the Commission is composed of 27 members (Commissioners), who are proposed by the government of each Member State and
are appointed, for a period of five years, by the Council, acting by a qualified majority and by common accord with the nominee for President. The
members of the Commission may not, during their term of office, engage
in any other occupation, whether gainful or not. They must not take instructions from any government and all governments must respect this
principle and not seek to influence the members of the Commission in the
performance of their tasks (Art. 213 TEC).

The Heads of State or Government, acting by a qualified majority,
nominate the President of the Commission and the nomination must be approved by the European Parliament. The President and the other Members
of the Commission are subject as a body to a vote of approval by the European Parliament (Art. 214 TEC). The Parliament examines every Commissioner as to his or her programme and ideas and may put forward objections as to his/her suitability for his/her particular responsibilities inside the
Commission, but may not reject his/her appointment. Hence, in case of objections expressed by the Parliament for certain members of the Commission, its President has the option of either assigning other responsibilities to

the members in question or of risking the rejection of the body by the Parliament[1].

The **Treaty of Lisbon** (copying the draft Constitutional Treaty) provides that the current composition of the Commission – one Commissioner per Member State – should be maintained until November 2014. From then on, the Commission shall comprise a number of Commissioners corresponding to two thirds of the number of Member States. The members of the Commission shall be chosen according to a system based on equal rotation among the Member States, guaranteeing equal treatment and reflecting the demographic and geographical range of all the Member States (article 9 D, Lisbon = article I-26, Constitution). The President of the Commission shall be proposed to the European Parliament by the European Council, acting by a qualified majority. The proposal of the European Council should take into account the elections to the European Parliament, thus respecting the will of the majority of the citizens of the Union, since the personality proposed to head the Commission should have the same political orientations as the political group which carried the European elections. The Parliament shall elect the candidate, acting by a majority of its component members. If he or she does not obtain the required majority, the European Council, acting by a qualified majority, shall within one month propose a new candidate who shall be elected by the European Parliament following the same procedure.

The Commission is the driving force for European integration. Under the Community decision-making process provided for in the European Community Treaty [see section 4.3.], it alone **has the initiative to make proposals** with a view to Community decision-making. No other body and no individual State can replace the Commission in this task. It alone can amend its proposal, with the sole exception of there being unanimity in the Council to do so. The **power of initiative**, which is held by the Commission, is particularly important for the development of the common policies and therefore for the progress of the multinational integration process. However, the **Treaty of Lisbon** gives the citizens (at least one million citizens who are nationals of a significant number of Member States) the possibility to influence the initiatives of the Commission (Article 8 B, Lisbon).

In its proposals, the Commission is entrusted with the task of defining the common interest in each policy, legal measure or action that it proposes and the representatives of the Member States can only unanimously substitute it in this role. This means that even if only one state believes that the amendment to the proposal of the Commission, promoted by the majority, is contrary to its interests, the proposal cannot be adopted by the Council with qualified majority voting. In most cases, however, in the course of the deliberations and negotiations within the Council, the Commission amends

---

[1] See e.g. Decision 2004/642, OJ L 294, 17.09.2004 and Decision 2004/753, OJ L 333, 09.11.2004.

its proposal repeatedly in order to encourage concessions here and there and thus reach agreement.

It should be stressed, however, that the Commission **only proposes legal acts or actions** of the EC/EU. The decisions are taken, usually in tandem, by the European Parliament and the Council with the codecision procedure or, in some cases, by the Council alone, i.e. by the representatives of the Member States. The Commission does not legislate. On the one hand, it proposes legal or administrative measures. On the other hand, it implements the acts and decisions taken by the Member States themselves through their representatives in the Parliament and the Council. The slogan concerning "the laws made by the technocrats of Brussels" is a myth well cultivated by europhobic media [see section 10.1.].

The Commission is also the **guardian of the Treaties** and of the "acquis communautaire" (i.e., all the Community's legislation) [see section 3.3.]. One of its main tasks is to ensure fulfilment of the obligations of the Member States and/or proper application by them of the provisions of the Treaties and of secondary legislation (Art 226 TEC). For that purpose it has investigative power, which it exercises at its own initiative or in response to a request from a government or a complaint from an individual. If, following its investigation, the Commission considers that there is **infringement of Community legislation**, it invites the State concerned to submit its comments within a given period. If the Member State fails to conform to the reasoned opinion, the Commission refers the matter to the Court of Justice, which arbitrates the dispute and, more often than not, sanctions the irregularity as noted by the Commission and requires the recalcitrant Member State to conform to the Community legal order.

The Commission is also the **executive body** of the Community and plays, therefore, an **administrative role**. The Treaties confer upon the Commission extensive powers of execution to ensure the attainment of the objectives set out in them: good functioning of the single market, control of the rules of competition, supply of fissile materials, etc. But the Commission's powers are constantly increased by the powers conferred to it by the legislator, i.e. the European Parliament and the Council for the implementation of common policies (Art. 202 TEC)[1]. It is the Commission which implements the decisions of the legislative bodies (the Council and the Parliament) and manages the Community budget [see section 3.4.] and in particular the various Community Funds[2] [see section 12.3.] and the research and technological development programmes [see section 18.2.2.].

Finally, the Commission plays a **representative role** by ensuring the representation of the European Union in third countries and in many international organisations. The role of the Commission is particularly important in the conduct of the common commercial policy and of the aid to de-

---

[1] Decision 1999/468, OJ L 184, 17.07.1999 and Regulation 1882/2003, OJ L 284, 31.10.2003.
[2] Regulation 1105/2003, OJ L 158, 27.06.2003.

velopment policy. Acting on behalf of the Community on instructions from the Council, the Commission negotiates tariff agreements, formerly in the context of the General Agreement on Tariffs and Trade (GATT) and now of the World Trade Organisation (WTO) [see section 23.4.], trade and partnership agreements with third countries, association agreements and even, in practice, the agreements on the accession of new member states to the European Union. In order to carry out its representative role, the Commission has its own representations in more than 160 countries with which the EC/EU has diplomatic relations and in international organisations such as the Organisation for Economic Cooperation and Development (OECD), the WTO and the Council of Europe.

The **Treaty of Lisbon** (like the draft Constitutional Treaty) confirms all the above tasks of the Commission. It asserts that Union legislative acts may only be adopted on the basis of a Commission proposal, except where the Treaties provide otherwise. The Commission shall promote the general interest of the Union and take appropriate initiatives to that end. It shall ensure the application of the Treaties, and of measures adopted by the institutions pursuant to them. It shall oversee the application of Union law under the control of the Court of Justice of the European Union. It shall execute the budget and manage programmes. It shall exercise coordinating, executive and management functions, as laid down in the Treaties. With the exception of the common foreign and security policy, and other cases provided for in the Treaties, it shall ensure the Union's external representation (Article 9 D, Lisbon = Article I-26, Constitution).

The Treaty of Lisbon extends the role of the Commission in the field of common foreign and security policy (CFSP), since the **High Representative of the Union** for Foreign Affairs and Security Policy, who shall be one of the Vice-Presidents of the Commission, will have the power of proposal and will, thus, have a strong voice in the development of the Union's common foreign and security policy, which should be conducted and carried out as mandated by the Council (Article 9 E, Lisbon = Article I-28, Constitution). Indeed, the High Representative of the Union will play a dual role, one in the Commission, as its Vice-President, and one in the Foreign Affairs Council, as its President.

4.1.3. The European Parliament

The number of Members of the European Parliament has increased with the successive enlargements of the Community/Union. After the 2004 enlargement, **the number of seats was increased to 732, which were allocated as follows:**
99 to Germany;
78 each to: France, Italy and the United Kingdom;
54 each to: Spain and Poland;
35 to Romania;
27 to the Netherlands;

24 each to: Belgium, the Czech Republic, Greece, Hungary and Portugal;
19 to Sweden;
18 to Austria and Bulgaria;
14 each to: Denmark, Slovakia and Finland;
13 each to: Ireland and Lithuania;
9 to Latvia;
7 to Slovenia;
6 each to: Cyprus, Estonia and Luxembourg; and
5 to Malta.

Thanks to its direct election by the peoples of the Union, the European Parliament is the only real multinational legislative assembly in the world and plays an increasingly important role in the European integration process. Although under the original Treaties the Parliament's role was purely advisory, it has kept growing, particularly in the legislative and budgetary fields, with each amendment of the Treaties. It has to be said, moreover, that the national parliaments rarely exercise their legislative and budgetary powers to the full, subject as they are to the will of the parties which support the governments submitting legislative drafts to them. The European Parliament is not subjected to such constraints. At present **the EP exercises four functions**: legislative, political, supervisory and budgetary.

The European Parliament's first task under the Treaties establishing the original Communities, that of **consultation**, whereby Parliament gives its opinion on Commission proposals, was strengthened by the Single Act of 1987 which introduced a procedure of cooperation with the Council in many Community decisions. The **legislative function** of the Parliament was considerably increased with the Treaties of Amsterdam and Nice. Article 192 (TEC) provides, in fact, for the participation of the European Parliament in the process leading up to the adoption of Community acts through exercise of its powers under the procedures laid down in Articles 251 and 252 (co-decision and cooperation) [see section 4.3.]. Furthermore, the Parliament has the right to give or withhold its **assent** as regards the conclusion of certain international agreements, the accession of new Member States and the structural and cohesion funds. The assent procedure may be regarded as a joint decision-making power of the Parliament in defining, implementing and monitoring the Community's foreign policy.

The **political function** of the Parliament is also essential. As it represents 456 million citizens (EU-25) and is the European forum par excellence, the Parliament is the virtual contractor for European construction. It often calls upon the other protagonists, the Commission and the Council, to develop or alter existing common policies or to initiate new ones. Indeed, the Treaty gives it the right to request that the Commission submit any appropriate proposals on matters on which it considers a Community act is required (Art. 192 TEC). Should the Commission or the Council fail to act as required for the purpose of implementing the Treaty, the Parliament may initiate proceedings against them before the Court of Justice (Art. 232 TCE) [see section 4.1.5.].

The **monitoring function** of the Parliament is exercised in particular vis-à-vis the Commission. The President and the other members of the Commission are subject as a body to a vote of approval by the European Parliament (Art. 214 TEC). The Commission has to account to the European Parliament, defend its position before parliamentary commissions and in plenary sessions. The Parliament may, at the request of a quarter of its members, set up a temporary Committee of Inquiry to investigate alleged contraventions or maladministration in the implementation of Community law (Art. 193 TEC). In case of a serious maladministration, the Parliament may pass a motion of censure against the Commission by a two-thirds majority of its members and thus compel it to resign (Art. 201 TEC), as it has threatened to do in March 1999.

The European Parliament appoints an **Ombudsman** empowered to receive complaints from any citizen of the Union or any natural or legal person residing or having its registered office in a Member State and concerning instances of maladministration in the activities of the Community institutions or bodies, with the exception of the Court of Justice and the Court of First Instance acting in their judicial role[1]. In cases where the Ombudsman establishes that mismanagement has occurred, he refers the matter to the institution concerned, which has three months in which to inform him of its views. The Ombudsman must then forward a report to the European Parliament and the institution concerned and inform the person lodging the complaint of the outcome of such inquiries (Art. 195 TEC).

As regards **budgetary functions**, the Parliament has to give its agreement to any major decision involving expenditure to be borne by the Community budget. It is effectively the Parliament which, at the end of a conciliation procedure with the Council, adopts or rejects the budget proposed by the Commission. Thus, it exercises a democratic control on the own resources of the Community [see section 3.4.].

According to the **Treaty of Lisbon** (following the draft Constitutional Treaty), the European Parliament shall be composed of representatives of the Union's citizens, who shall not exceed 750 in number, plus the President. Representation of citizens should be degressively proportional, with a minimum threshold of 6 deputies per Member State, in order to make sure that, even in the least populous Member States, all the major shades of political opinion would have a chance of being represented in the European Parliament. It follows that, since the number of EMPs would never exceed the total of 750 and, since the smaller Member States would always be allocated at least 6 EMPs each, the larger Member States would have to hand down a number of their seats to the acceding Member States.

The Treaty of Lisbon (like the draft Constitutional Treaty) **enhances significantly the functions** of the European Parliament. According to it, the Parliament shall, jointly with the Council, exercise legislative and

---

[1] Decision 94/114, OJ L 54, 25.02.1994, Decision 94/262, OJ L 113, 04.05.1994 and Decision 2002/262, OJ L 92, 09.04.2002.

budgetary functions (Article 9 A, Lisbon). The new Treaty extends the co-decision procedure [see section 4.3], renamed "ordinary legislative procedure", to a large number of fields, with the notable exception of the common foreign and security policy. The Parliament thus would have the functions of a House of Representatives, representing the citizens of the Union, while the Council would play the role of a Senate, representing the governments of the Member States. Concerning the budget of the Union, the Treaty of Lisbon abolishes the distinction between "compulsory" expenditure and "non-compulsory" expenditure. Hence, the Parliament would exercise the same budgetary functions as the Council [see section 3.4].

4.1.4. The Council

The **Council** is composed of a representative of each Member State at ministerial level, authorised to commit the government of that Member State (Art 203 TEC). While it is usually referred to broadly as "the Council" or "the Council of Ministers", it actually consists of nine specialised **configurations** regrouping several related areas, e.g. general affairs and external relations or economic and financial affairs[1]. Each Council configuration is composed of the ministers with responsibility in the matter, but several ministers may participate as full members of the same Council configuration, e.g. the ministers responsible for health and social policy. Although Commission proposals are discussed inside the specialised Council configurations, decisions agreed by all the Member States can be taken without a debate (as "points A" in the agenda) by any Council whatsoever, and this is often the **"General Affairs and External Relations Council"**, composed of the Ministers of Foreign Affairs. This is the principal Council configuration and holds separate meetings (with separate agendas and possibly on different dates) dealing, respectively, with: (a) preparation for and follow-up to the European Council, institutional and administrative questions, horizontal dossiers which affect several of the Union's policies; and (b) the whole of the Union's external action, namely common foreign and security policy, foreign trade, development cooperation and humanitarian aid.

The **Council Presidency** changes every six months to another country in alphabetical order, and it is therefore the Minister of the country holding the Presidency who chairs each Council meeting[2]. The rotation of the Presidency has the advantage of giving each country a chance to prove its efficiency in promoting common policies, on the basis of Commission proposals, thus encouraging emulation among the Member States in the advancement of European integration. In order to obviate the problem of differing priorities of twenty-five presidencies in the enlarged Union, its

---

[1] Decision 2004/338, OJ L 106, 15.04.2004.
[2] Concerning the order of the Presidencies see Decision 2007/5, OJ L 1, 04.01.2007.

legislative work is henceforth based on a three-year strategic programme adopted by the European Council.

The Council is assisted by a General Secretariat, consisting of "Eurocrats" of all the nationalities of the Union, separate from their counterparts in the Commission but organised in a similar way. The Council is also assisted by many working parties of national civil servants, which examine the proposals of the Commission and report to the **Permanent Representatives Committee (COREPER)**, which is responsible for preparing the work of the Council and for carrying out the tasks assigned to it by the Council" (Art. 207 TEC). The Coreper sits in two parts. Coreper Part 1, which is composed of the Deputy Permanent Representatives, examines technical questions on the whole. Coreper Part 2, which is composed of the Ambassadors themselves, deals with political questions on the whole. The European Commission participates in all the meetings of the working parties of national experts, of the Coreper and of the Council itself to explain its positions and assist the Presidency in reaching agreement on its proposals. After examining an issue Coreper either submits a report to the Council, preparing the ground for its discussions by drawing attention to the political aspects which deserve particular attention, or, if unanimous agreement has been reached between the Permanent Representatives and the Commission representative, Coreper recommends that the Council adopt the prepared text "as **an 'A' item**", i.e. without discussion. In both cases the Council's work is facilitated thanks to Coreper's intervention.

On the basis of the original Treaties, the Council was the only legislative authority of the Community and this was the main reason for the then existing democratic deficit of the Community [see section 9.5.]. Subsequent amendments of the Treaties have joined, ever more closely, the European Parliament in the decision-making process, thus making the Council one of the two legislative authorities [see section 4.3.] and reducing, consequently, the democratic deficit. Going a step further, the **Treaty of Lisbon** (following the draft Constitutional Treaty) specifies that the Council shall, jointly with the European Parliament, exercise legislative and budgetary functions (Article 9 C, Lisbon = Article I-23, Constitution). Hence, the legislative functions of the Council will come close to those of an Upper House or Senate, representing the governments of the Member States and sharing these functions with the European Parliament, representing directly the peoples of the Union.

The **Treaty of Lisbon** stipulates that the Presidency of all Council configurations, other than that of Foreign Affairs, is to be held by Member State representatives on the basis of a system of equal rotation, defined by a European Council decision adopted by a qualified majority. The new Treaty separates the Foreign Affairs Council, which shall elaborate the Union's external action, from the General Affairs Council, which shall ensure consistency in the work of the different Council configurations (Article 9 C, Lisbon).

4.1.5. The Court of Justice

In a community of states the common rules adopted by the decision-making bodies might be interpreted and applied differently from country to country, if only national courts controlled them. Therefore, the general task assigned to the Court of Justice and to the Court of First Instance is to ensure that Community **law is observed in a uniform manner** in the interpretation and application of the Treaty, of the legal acts and of the decisions adopted by the Council and the Parliament or by the Commission (Art. 220 to 245 TEC). The judgments of the Court of Justice, many important ones of which are referred to in the footnotes of this book, consolidate the European law to which are subject the governments, the national courts, the parliaments and the citizens of the Member States. Although European law is a statute law passed by legislative bodies, it is often amended by them in accordance with the case law of the Court of Justice. The Court plays therefore an important role in the European integration process by clarifying ambiguous legal provisions, adopted sometimes under the pressure of reaching agreement between law-makers of different cultures concerned about various national interests.

The **Court of Justice of the European Communities (CJEC)** consists, in fact, of two bodies, the Court of Justice proper and the Court of First Instance. **The Court of Justice**, often called European Court of Justice (ECJ) consists of one judge per Member State. It sits in chambers or in a Grand Chamber, in accordance with the rules laid down in its Statutes. It is assisted by Advocates-General (Art. 221 TEC). The **Court of First Instance** comprises at least one judge per Member State, which means that it may include judges of the same nationality. The number of Judges is determined by the Statute of the Court of Justice, which may provide for the Court of First Instance to be assisted by Advocates-General (Art. 224 TEC).

The **Court of First Instance (CFI)** is the common law judge for all direct actions, i.e. proceedings against a decision (Article 230 TEC), action for failure to act (Article 232 TEC) and action for damages (Article 235 TEC), with the exception of those the statute reserves for the Court of Justice and those which are attributed to a specialised chamber. The judgments of the CFI may be subject to appeals, confined to points of law, to the Court of Justice (Art. 225 TEC).

Being the supreme court of the Communities, the **Court of Justice** not only gives a coherent and uniform interpretation of European law, but it ensures that all the Member States and their citizens comply with it. Apart from the tendency of governments to interpret European law in the interest of their nations, it is new law and not always well known. The national judges, who are the judges of first instance of the rules and behaviour relative to European law, may turn to the Court of Justice by means of a **referral for a preliminary ruling** to ask it to adopt a position on the interpretation or evaluation of the validity of the provisions of European acts. Although they are normally optional, referrals for a preliminary ruling are obligatory where judicial remedy under national law is no longer possible, i.e. when the court, which has to apply the Community law, is taking its decisions in the final instance. Through its preliminary rulings, the Court plays the role of a legal council whose opinions are binding on the parties concerned. The referral for a preliminary ruling is appreciated by the national courts and stimulates the cooperation between them and the ECJ.

Disputes falling within the unlimited jurisdiction of the Court are made up in particular of cases relating to non-compliance or to the interpretation of the Community's rules of competition. Hearing an appeal by undertakings (firms, businesses) penalised by the Commission for infringing competition law, the Court gives a ruling on the merits of the Commission's decision and on the appropriateness of the penalty imposed on the undertaking.

According to the **Treaty of Lisbon** (emulating the draft Constitutional Treaty), the Court of Justice of the European Union includes the Court of Justice, the General Court and specialised courts. Hence, the term "Court of Justice of the European Union" will officially designate the two levels of jurisdiction taken together. The supreme body will be called the "Court of Justice" while the Court of First Instance will be renamed "General Court", but their actual composition and tasks will not be changed (Article 9 F, Lisbon, Article I-29, Constitution).

4.2. Other institutions and advisory bodies

As mentioned at the beginning of this chapter, the institutions of the EC/EU are evolving along with the evolution of European integration. Of the institutions and advisory bodies that we consider in this section, only the European Economic and Social Committee was provided for in the original Treaties. New institutions and bodies have been created to cover new needs, notably the Committee of the Regions and the European Central Bank. Apart from the main institutions, examined above, the **Treaty of Lisbon** considers as institutions the European Central Bank and the Court of Auditors.

4.2.1. The European Central Bank

In the framework of the economic and monetary union that it has launched, the Treaty of Maastricht has established a **European system of central banks (ESCB)** and a **European Central Bank (ECB)** [see section 7.2.4.]. The two organs are closely associated. They act within the limits of the powers conferred upon them by the EC Treaty and by the Statute of the ESCB and of the ECB annexed thereto (Art. 8 TEC). The ESCB is composed of the ECB and of the national central banks and is governed by the decision-making bodies of the ECB which are the Governing Council and the Executive Board. (Art 107 TEC). The Governing Council is composed of the Governors of the central banks of all the Member States of the EC/EU, whereas the President, the Vice-President and the other members of the Executive Board of the ECB are appointed by common accord of the governments of the Member States, which have adopted the euro[1] [see section 7.2.3]. Neither the ECB, nor a national central bank, nor any member of their decision-making bodies may seek or take instructions from Community institutions or bodies, from any government of a Member State or from any other body (Art. 108 TEC). The objectives of the ESCB are, primarily, to maintain price stability and, without prejudice to this objective, to support the general economic policies in the Community (Art. 105 TEC). The basic tasks of the ESCB are: to define and implement the monetary policy of the Community, to conduct foreign-exchange operations, to hold and manage the official foreign reserves of the Member States and to promote the smooth operation of payment systems. The ECB, which has legal personality, has the exclusive right to authorise the issue of banknotes within the Community's eurozone (Art. 106 TEC).

The **Treaty of Lisbon** states that the European Central Bank, together with the national central banks, shall constitute the European System of Central Banks (ESCB). The European Central Bank, together with the national central banks of the Member States whose currency is the euro, which constitute the Eurosystem, shall conduct the monetary policy of the Union (Article 245a, Lisbon – Article I-30, Constitution).

4.2.2. The European Court of Auditors

The Court of Auditors consists of one national from each Member State. The Members of the Court of Auditors are chosen from among persons who belong or have belonged in their respective countries to external audit bodies or who are especially qualified for this office. They are appointed for a term of six years by the Council, acting by a qualified majority after consulting the European Parliament. They are completely independent in the performance of their duties (Art. 247 TEC).

The Court of Auditors examines the accounts of all revenue and expenditure of the Community, particularly the annual budget managed by the Commission, and of all bodies set up by the Community. It examines in particular whether all revenue has been received and all expenditure incurred in a lawful and regular manner and must report on any cases of irregularity. The audit must be based on records and, if necessary, performed on the spot in the other institutions of the Community, on the premises of any body which manages revenue or expenditure on behalf of the Community and in the Member States, including on the premises of any natural or legal person in receipt of payments from the budget (Art. 248 TEC). The Court of Auditors must provide the European Parliament and the Council

---

[1]   Decision 98/345, OJ L 154, 28.05.1998.

with a statement of assurance as to the reliability of the accounts and the legality and regularity of the underlying transactions. The annual and the specific reports of the Court of Auditors are acknowledged to be a valuable input to Parliament's debates on the discharge to be given to the Commission for its execution of the budget.

The Treaty of Lisbon does not modify the structure and the functions of the Court of Auditors, stating simply that provisions relating to it are set out in the Treaty on the Functioning of the European Union (Article 9, Lisbon = Article I-31, Constitution).

4.2.3. The Economic and Social Committee

The European Economic and Social Committee (EESC) is the official body which enables the Community institutions to evaluate and take into account in the conception of common policies the **interests of the various economic and social groups**. Its 344 members are proposed by the governments of the Member States (Germany, France, Italy and the United Kingdom proposing 24 each; Spain and Poland 21; Romania 15; Belgium, Bulgaria, the Czech Republic, Greece, Hungary, Netherlands, Portugal, Austria and Sweden 12 each; Denmark, Ireland, Lithuania, Slovakia and Finland 9 each; Estonia, Latvia and Slovenia 7 each, Cyprus and Luxembourg 6 each and Malta 5) and are appointed for a term of four years by the Council after consulting the Commission. They must provide a wide representation of the various categories of economic and social life (Art. 257-262 TEC) and divide voluntarily into three groups: the Employers' Group (known as "Group I"), which is made up of representatives of industry, banking or financial institutions, transport operators' federations, etc.; the Workers' Group (known as "Group II"), mainly composed of representatives of trade union organisations; and the Various Interests Group (known as "Group III"), which comprises representatives of agriculture, skilled trades, small and medium-sized enterprises, the professions, consumer associations and organisations representing various interests, such as families or ecological movements.

The Committee **must be consulted** by the Council or by the Commission in certain areas provided for by the Treaty establishing the European Community. The Committee **may be consulted** by these institutions in all cases where they consider it appropriate. Furthermore, the EESC may issue an **opinion at its own initiative** when it considers such action appropriate (Art. 262 TEC). Whether they are requested by the Commission or the Council or issued at its own initiative, the Committee's Opinions are not binding on the institutions, a shortcoming that weakens their significance. This is a flaw of the role of the Committee that should also be corrected [see section 4.4.]. However, the Committee plays the role of a forum in which the interests of the various socio-professional categories, rather than national arguments, are expressed officially and assessed. The opinions of the EESC on the proposals of the Commission reflect the concerns of economic and societal groups and provide valuable indications of the opposing arguments, of the divergences of interests and of the possibilities of reaching agreement at Community level. In this limited way the Committee influences decisions and makes its contribution to the formulation of common policies, a contribution that could be greater if better exploited.

The **Treaty of Lisbon** does not modify the structure and the functions of the Court of Auditors, stating simply that provisions relating to it are set out in the Treaty on the Functioning of the European Union (Article 9, Lisbon = Article I-31, Constitution).

4.2.4. The Committee of the Regions

The Treaty establishing the European Community officially acknowledges the regional diversity and the role played by regions in the governance of the Community through the Committee of the Regions made up of **representatives of regional and local bodies** (Art. 263-265 TEC). The 344 members of the Committee and an equal number of alternate members (with the same national distribution as the members of the EESC) [see section 4.2.3] are proposed by the governments of the Member States and appointed for four years by the Council, acting by qualified majority.

The Committee of the Regions **must be consulted** by the Council or the Commission on matters relating notably to employment guidelines, legislation on social matters, environment, education, vocational training, culture, public health, European networks and the Structural Funds. It **may be consulted** in all other cases considered appropriate by one of the two institutions, in particular those which concern cross-border cooperation. It can also issue an **own-initiative opinion** when it considers that specific regional interests are at stake (Art. 265 TEC). The Committee of the Regions thus involves regional and local authorities in the decision-making process and expresses their views on all common policies concerning them. Yet again, these views could have a greater impact on these policies than they now have, if a way was found to make the decision-making organs to take them more seriously into consideration [see section 4.4.].

The **Treaty of Lisbon** simply states that the European Parliament, the Council and the Commission shall be assisted by an Economic and Social Committee and a Committee of the Regions acting in an advisory capacity (Article 9, Lisbon). It does not envisage any changes to their structure and functions.

4.3. The Community's decision-making process

The Treaties establishing the Communities defined the objectives to be attained, laid down the rules to be implemented, set out timetables to be met and established an institutional framework which provides the Community with an original method of decision-making and legislation. The

Community method implies a decision-making process entailing: (a) a single and supranational source of the right of initiative; (b) usually co-decision of the European Parliament with the Council, deciding by qualified majority; and (c) control of the decisions by a supranational judicial authority, the European Court of Justice. The Community method is, indeed, an **original combination** of: **technocratic proposals** emanating from the Commission, worked out with the technical advice of experts from all the Member States; **and legislative acts and** political decisions taken by the Council, representing the governments of the Member States, usually in tandem with the European Parliament, representing the peoples of the Union.

The Community method does not imply legislation by the European Commission. The Community Treaties authorise the Commission to propose legislative acts and to execute the legislative and other decisions taken by the legislative bodies. The rhetoric about the "decisions taken by the technocrats of Brussels" (meaning the Commission) is maliciously erroneous. The fact is that the technocrats propose the Community measures; but it is the political institutions representing the democratically elected governments (the Council of Ministers) and the citizens of the Member States (the European Parliament) that take the decisions. Except in a few areas, such as competition, where the Treaties give it full competence, the Commission may only adopt acts implementing the decisions of the legislative bodies.

The Treaties attribute, however, **the initiative for the Community's decision-making procedure** to the Commission [see section 4.1.2.]. It prepares all proposals for Council Regulations, Directives and Decisions. The Commission's role is political in so far as it chooses and prepares the ground on which the construction of the Community is undertaken, but otherwise its role is technocratic as its proposals are based on technical considerations and/or scientific grounds. Using an "impact assessment method", the Commission analyses the direct and indirect implications of a proposed measure (e.g. concerning businesses, trade, employment, the environment and health). The results of each assessment are made public[1]. Moreover, the Commission is responsible for defining in its proposals the common interest or the interest of the Community. To make sure that its proposal is adopted, the Commission must take into consideration the often-divergent interests of the Member States and endeavour to detect and express the common interest. If it does not succeed in this definition or if it does not itself amend its proposal, taking into consideration the positions of the other Community organs, all the Member States together, in total agreement within the Council, must find a different definition of the common interest inherent in a proposal of a common policy or a common measure (Art. 250 TEC); something that happens very rarely.

---

[1] COM (2002) 276, 5 June 2002.

When adopted by the Commission, a proposal is submitted, depending on the form of the procedure examined below, either to the European Parliament and to the Council for decision or to the first for opinion and to the second for decision and, very often, to the Economic and Social Committee and to the Committee of the Regions for an opinion. **Detailed discussions** begin within the working party of competent national experts, who prepare the Council's decision, the relevant Parliamentary Committee and the groups of experts of the Economic and Social Committee and of the Committee of the Regions. The interest groups at national and Community levels, alerted in good time of this preparatory work, lobby these various technical and political experts and, if the issue is important, public opinion. The Commission has published general principles and **minimum standards for consultation** of interested parties[1]. They enable all those affected by a proposal to express their opinions and, thus, to participate in the legislative process. A database of information on the different bodies consulted gives an overview of the way civil society consultation is organised at European level[2]. The general public has access to the different stages of the legislative process through the Internet-based EUR-Lex service[3].

The interaction of these actors, representing all the Member States and all the interests concerned tends to confirm or redefine the common interest of the proposal formulated by the Commission. As, more often than not, a common policy cannot fully satisfy all national interests, negotiations have to take place within and between the main actors in order to find the common denominator that best satisfies most national interests. The text ultimately adopted by the legislative bodies takes into account all national, professional and other interests voiced at various points of the lengthy preparatory work.

It goes without saying that **the Community interest may not harm an "essential interest"** of a Community State, but the definition of an "essential interest" is inevitably subjective. Each Member State has a natural tendency to exaggerate its own problems and minimise those of the others. In other words, the Community decision-making process risks frequently to come to a deadlock, and it has to be emphasised that it is through the joint mediation efforts of the Commission and the Council Presidency that the deadlock can on most occasions be avoided. On the one hand, the majority has to be persuaded to make the necessary concessions to accommodate the minority and, on the other hand, the Member State upholding an extreme or isolated position has to be persuaded that the general advantages of an agreement are more important than its individual interests. Even though they first and foremost assert the interests of their respective governments, the members of the Council usually respect the objectives and needs of the EC as a whole. This is what distinguishes the Council from an

---

[1]   COM (2002) 277, 5 June 2002.

[2]   http://europa.eu.int/comm/civil_society/coneccs/index_en.htm.

[3]   http://europa.eu.int/eur-lex/en/index.html.

intergovernmental conference, where national interests prevail over the common interest [see section 4.1.4.].

The European Parliament is ever more involved in the Community decision-making process under two procedures, co-decision and cooperation with the Council of Ministers. Article 251 (TEC), defines the **co-decision procedure** of the Council with the European Parliament. This procedure was introduced by the EC Treaty at Maastricht and was largely extended by the Amsterdam and Nice amendments of the TEC. It is now applied to practically all important matters covered by this Treaty.

In the co-decision procedure, the Council acting by a qualified majority adopts "common positions", which may be accepted, rejected or amended by the Parliament. If the Council does not agree with the amendments proposed by the Parliament, a **conciliation committee**, composed of equal numbers of representatives of the two institutions, must bring together the different points of view. The Commission can act as an arbitrator between the two decision-making bodies, by accepting in its amended proposal some of the amendments proposed by the Parliament. In the rare cases where a compromise solution is not found, the Parliament may reject the proposed act by absolute majority of expressed votes. Thus, the Parliament has the final word in this legislative procedure. Regulations, Directives and Decisions adopted under the Article 251 procedure are signed both by the President of the European Parliament and the President of the Council. The co-decision procedure has worked well so far. Indeed decisions have been taken fairly quickly as a result of a good working relationship between the institutions, based on the interinstitutional agreement on the Rules of Procedure of the Conciliation Committee, concluded on 21 October 1993.

Article 252 (TCE) defines the **cooperation procedure,** where the Parliament is involved in the legislative process by means of its two readings and the proposal of amendments to the Council's common position. In this procedure, the Commission plays an arbitration role, since it may adopt some or many of the amendments of the Parliament in its own amended proposal; but the Council has the final word, since it may unanimously reject the amended proposal of the Commission. However, this procedure is now limited to a few subject matters.

At present, where the treaties do not provide otherwise, the Council takes decisions by a simple majority of its members. This is rarely the case, however, as in the vast majority of instances the treaties provide that decisions are taken either by unanimity or by qualified majority. Unanimity is undemocratic, because the vote of the smallest country weighs as much as that of the largest and any country can block a decision wished by all its other partners. Therefore, the successive amendments of the Treaties have extended qualified majority voting, notably in the areas where there is participation of the Parliament in the decision-making process. **Qualified majority** is calculated on the basis of votes allocated to each Member State under Article 205 (TEC), as modified by the Accession Act of the ten new Member States. According to the latter, the total number of votes in the

Council is 321 and is distributed to the twenty-five Ministers in a weighted manner, so that the influence of a Member State in the decision-making process is more or less related to the size of its population. Actually, **the votes of the Council members are weighted as follows**:

- Germany, France, Italy and the United Kingdom 29 each;
- Romania 14;
- Spain and Poland 27 each;
- Netherlands 13;
- Belgium, the Czech Republic, Greece, Hungary and Portugal 12 each;
- Austria, Bulgaria and Sweden 10 each;
- Denmark, Finland, Ireland, Lithuania and Slovakia 7 each;
- Cyprus, Estonia, Latvia, Luxembourg and Slovenia 4 each; and
- Malta 3.

As a rule, Community decisions taken by qualified majority on the basis of a Commission proposal must gather at least **72% of the total votes of the members, representing at least 62% of the total population** of the Union (on the basis of data supplied by Eurostat)[1]. The same conditions apply to Article 34 of the EU Treaty, but the 232 votes in favour should, in any case, be cast by at least two-thirds of the members. Whilst the qualified-majority voting system of the Treaty of Nice technically opened the door to enlargement, the weighing of the votes in the Council in no way improves the efficiency and transparency of the decision-making process, a fact which gives cause for serious concern as to how it may operate in a Union of 27 or more Member States.

Responding to this concern, the **Treaty of Lisbon** (copying the draft Constitutional Treaty), firstly, generalises qualified majority voting in the normal legislative process. Secondly, it abandons the weighting of the votes in the Council and, thus, simplifies greatly the system of qualified majority. As from 1 November 2014, a qualified majority shall be defined as at least **55% of the members** of the Council, comprising at least fifteen of them and representing Member States comprising at least **65% of the population of the Union**. A blocking minority must include at least four Council members, failing which the qualified majority shall be deemed attained (Article 9 C, Lisbon). The new voting system respects the equality of Member States as each one has one vote in respect of the first criterion, whilst their different population sizes are taken into account in meeting the second criterion. Moreover, the new system, which defines once and for all the criteria of qualified majority, would prevent, during subsequent enlargements, long negotiations on the allocation of votes to Member States and the definition of the qualified majority threshold.

So as to prevent one or two Member States from blocking further progress of the Union in certain fields, the Treaty of Nice has reinforced and facilitated **enhanced cooperations**, which aim at safeguarding the values

---

[1] Decision 2004/701, OJ L 319, 20.10.2004.

and serving the interests of the Union as a whole by asserting its identity as a coherent force on the international scene (Art. 27a to 28 and 40 to 45 (TEU) and 11 (TEC). **In connection with the EC Treaty**, the veto possibility is removed. Member States which intend to establish enhanced cooperation between themselves must address a request to the Commission, which should submit a proposal to the Council to that effect or inform the Member States concerned of the reasons for not doing so. The assent of the European Parliament is required for an enhanced cooperation in a field coming under the co-decision procedure (Art 11 TEC). **In connection with the common foreign and security policy**, enhanced cooperation is possible for the implementation of a joint action or common position, except in the sphere of the security and defence policy (Art 27b TEU). The Council should act by qualified majority, but the 232 votes in favour of the decision should be cast by at least two-thirds of the members (Art. 23.2 TEU). It should be said that, until now, enhanced cooperations have either been inscribed in the Treaty (participation in the euro-zone) or have been consecrated by it a posteriori (Schengen cooperation agreement) [see section 9.2.]

According to the **Treaty of Lisbon** (copying again the draft Constitutional Treaty), enhanced cooperation shall aim to further the objectives of the Union, protect its interests and reinforce its integration process. Such cooperation shall be open at any time to all Member States (Article 10, Lisbon = Articles I-44 and III-416 to III-423, Constitution). The decision authorising enhanced cooperation shall be adopted by the Council, acting unanimously, as a last resort, if it has established that the objectives of such cooperation cannot be attained within a reasonable period by the Union as a whole, and if at least one third of the Member States participated in it. Special conditions concern the permanent structured cooperation provided in Article 28 A of the Treaty of Lisbon [see section 8.2.3].

4.4. Prospects of European governance

Thanks to the Community method of making and implementing decisions [see section 4.3], the often conflicting national interests are passed through the successive **filters of three institutions**, each defending different but complementary interests: the Commission, the common interest; the Council, the interests of the Member States; the Parliament, the interests of the citizens of the Union. Community policies thus rarely - if ever - can promote the interests of some Member States at the expense of those of some others. In the absence of such filters, an intergovernmental cooperation scheme wishing to serve equally all national interests would have to give equal weight to the positions defended by each one of the participating governments and this would lead to a standstill. If it gave policy leadership to a few Member States, namely the bigger ones, intergovernmental cooperation would lead to conflicts of interests and hence to secessionist tendencies.

"**European governance**" - i.e., the rules, processes and behaviour of the actors that affect the way in which powers are exercised at European level - has worked relatively well up to now, since it has made possible all the achievements of the common policies examined in this book. Therefore, the role of the existing institutions should not be radically changed, nor should new institutions be added, because the rules of the functioning of the protagonists of European integration might be altered, with unknown consequences. However, European governance has already reached its limits of efficiency, even after the improvements brought about by the Treaty of Lisbon. It is doubtful that it could function efficiently in a union of twenty-seven - and soon more - Member States, which could in addition have the ambition to deepen their political union. In order to enable the Union to better face internal and external challenges, a drastic reform of the institutions is needed.

The structure of the **European Commission**, in particular, should be democratised in parallel with the reinforcement of its role, because its technocratic character, useful as it is, engenders its remoteness from the citizens of the Member States. The Commission is already the executive body of the Community, since it proposes the legislation to the legislative bodies, executes their decisions and controls their implementation by the Member States. It thus plays the role of a "proto-government" of the Union, which has not full democratic legitimacy, since the Commissioners are not elected but are appointed by the governments of the Member States. The solution to this problem would be to entrust the citizens themselves with the election of the members of the Commission at the occasion of European elections. At the same time as they would choose the members of the European Parliament, the voters of each country could elect the Commissioner having the nationality of this country from a short list of candidates prepared by the national parliament. With this system of election in two phases, the national parliaments would play an important role in selecting (by successive votes) two or three personalities capable of assuming European functions, but the Commissioner for each nationality would finally be elected by the citizens of each nation (with the simple majority of the votes cast).

The **president of the Commission** and the **vice-president,** who would also be the High Representative of the Union for Foreign Affairs and Security Policy (according to the Treaty of Lisbon), should be chosen from among these elected personalities by the European Council, acting by qualified majority, and be elected by the European Parliament (as provided for in the Treaty of Lisbon). The big difference between the system proposed here and the actual system or the one set forth in the Treaty of Lisbon is that the president and the vice-president of the Commission would first be elected by their respective countrymen and then would be chosen by the majority of the representatives of the peoples of the Union. They would not come out of the sole inspiration of the heads of State or government and would thus have a double democratic legitimacy, national and European. With such a system of democratic designation of the Commissioners, the citizens would have an important incentive to elect strong personalities as members of the European executive organ, hoping that their compatriot could qualify for a top job, including that of the president and vice-president of the Commission. Moreover, the citizens would feel that they participate in the governance of the Union, since they would elect directly not only the members of one branch of the legislative authority (the European Parliament), but also the members of the executive authority (the European Commission).

The **European Parliament** should play an important role not only in the investiture of the executive authority of the Union, but also in its monitoring. In addition to the legality of the actions of the Commissioners, the Parliament should permanently control their independence in respect of their country of origin and their efficiency in the implementation of their pre-approved work programme. The political role of the European Parliament would thus resemble that of a national parliament, which controls the government of its country. At the same time, the legislative power of the Parliament - through the ordinary legislative procedure - should be extended to all legislative fields, including that of foreign and security policy, which could thus, little by little, become a real common policy and propel the Union on the world scene.

The roles of the **European Economic and Social Committee (EESC) and the Committee of the Regions** [see sections 4.2.3. and 4.2.4.] should be boosted. In order to ensure that the members of the EESC are in principle chosen for their competence rather than for their political allegiance, they should be co-opted by the members of the professional and other organisations that they would represent in Brussels without government intervention in their appointment. In order to bring the Committee of the Regions closer to the local and regional populations that it should represent, its members should be chosen directly by them at **European elections**, at the same time as that of European MPs and the Commissioners.

Bibliography on the European institutions

- AMERICAN CHAMBER OF COMMERCE TO THE EUROPEAN UNION. Guide to the Council of the European Union. Bruxelles: AmCham EU, 2007.
- BEACH Derek, MAZZUCELLI Colette (eds.). Leadership in the big bangs of European integration. Basingstoke: Palgrave Macmillan, 2007.
- BIÈVRE Dirk de, NEUHOLD Christine (eds.). *Dynamics and obstacles of European governance.* Cheltenham: Edward Elgar, 2007.
- CHALMERS Damian, TOMKINS Adam. *European Union public law: text and materials.* Cambridge: Cambridge University Press, 2007.
- COMMITTEE OF THE REGIONS. *The regional and local authorities at the heart of Europe: The Committee of the Regions celebrates the 50th anniversary of the Rome Treaties.* Luxembourg: EUR-OP*, 2007.

- EUROPEAN COMMISSION. *EU agencies: whatever you do, we work for you*. Luxembourg: EUR-OP*, 2007.
- HEARD-LAUREOTE Karen. *European Union Governance: efficiency and legitimacy in European Commission Committees*. London: Routledge, 2007.
- LEEUW Magdalena Elisabeth. "Openness in the legislative process in the European Union", in *European Law Review*, v. 32, n. 3, June 2007, p. 295-318.
- PANKE Diana. "The European Court of Justice as an agent of Europeanization?: Restoring compliance with EU law", in *Journal of European Public Policy*, v. 14, n. 6, 2007, p. 847-866.
- TRONDAL Jarle. "Contending decision-making dynamics within the European Commission", in *Comparative European politics*, v. 5, n. 2, July 2007, p. 158-178.

DISCUSSION TOPICS

1. Discuss the similarities and dissimilarities between the institutions of the European Union and those of a federal state like Germany or Belgium.
2. Explain the role of the European Commission in the Community decision-making process.
3. Discuss the functions of the European Parliament and of the Council (of Ministers) in comparison with the functions of national parliaments and upper houses or senates.
4. Consider the role of the European Court of Justice in the European integration process.
5. Discuss the past and the potential future evolution of the functions of the European institutions.

Part II: Integration stages

Although the multinational integration process is continuous, it can be distinguished into **four large stages**: customs union, common market, economic and monetary union, political union. In the isolationist period, usually following a devastating war, like the Second World War, states erect **high protection barriers against foreign trade** and therefore against international competition. These may be customs barriers (tariffs, quotas and measures having equivalent effect), fiscal barriers (higher levels of taxation for goods largely manufactured outside the country), administrative barriers (complicated bureaucratic procedures for imports) or technical barriers (concerning, for example, environment or human health protection) serving in one way or another to discourage or even prohibit imports [see section 6.2.]. This is the zero point in the scale of multinational integration.

Such a protectionist system leads to **great dissatisfaction on the part of consumers**, whose choice is very restricted, and on the part of the most dynamic and/or less protected businessmen, who find their field of activity limited by the barriers. Dissatisfied citizens, as consumers and voters, and progressive businessmen, as influential interest groups, press the political elite to reduce external protection. Under the sine qua non condition that the later were susceptible to such pressures and were sincerely seeking the maximisation of national interests - two prerequisites that exclude authoritarian regimes - they would normally start discussing the possibilities of trade liberalisation with like-minded elite in neighbouring countries [see section 1.1.2.]. If the economic and political elite of several states would agree on the desirability of mutual trade liberalisation, they would still have the option to pursue it either within a framework of bilateral or multilateral intergovernmental cooperation or in the framework of a multinational integration process.

A **free trade area** is based on intergovernmental cooperation. In such an area, member countries abolish import duties and other customs barriers to the free movement of goods manufactured in the territory of their partners. However, each country retains its own external tariff and its customs policy vis-à-vis third countries. It also retains entirely its national sovereignty. Compared to isolationism, trade liberalisation is a common policy of a group of states, but, since without concessions of sovereignty, there can be no spillover from this unique common policy to other policy areas [see section 1.1.1.], a free trade area should be placed at a low level of multinational integration, before the beginning of the evolutionary process.

By contrast, in a **customs union**, which is the first stage of the evolutionary multinational integration process, free movement concerns not only products manufactured in the territory of the partners, but all products, irrespective of origin, situated in the territory of the member countries. Furthermore, the latter lose their customs autonomy and apply a common external customs tariff to third countries. In order to manage the common customs tariff, the members of a customs union must have a common commercial policy. In addition, trade liberalisation has in this case spillover or multiplicative effects on other common policies. There is therefore, already at this stage some concession of segments of national sovereignty to the common institutions that run the customs union [see chapter 5].

If the implementation of these initial common policies linked with the customs union gave satisfactory but not optimal results, it would reveal the necessity for more common policies inside a **common market** and would consequently have a multiplier effect on the process. In fact, if the members would like to turn a customs union into a real internal market, they would need to ensure not only the free movement of goods and services, but also the free movement of production factors, namely labour and capital. In order to obtain these fundamental freedoms of a common market, the member states would need to develop a great number of common policies, calling for further sharing of national sovereignties [see chapter 6].

However, even if all the freedoms of a common market were achieved, the single market would still not resemble a genuine internal market, if currency fluctuations and the exchange risk could create new barriers to trade, restrict the interpenetration of the financial markets and impede the establishment of businesses in places where the factors of production would appear to be most propitious for their activities. In order to optimise the conditions of trade, investment and production, the member states of a common market would need, therefore, to move forward to the next stage of economic integration, viz. **economic and monetary union (EMU)**. This would imply a single monetary policy, necessary for the management of a single currency, and the convergence of national economic policies, with a view to achieving economic and social cohesion.

Even before that integration stage was wholly completed, the member states of a multinational integration scheme would have developed so many economic and political links between themselves that they would feel the need to step forward into the final integration stage, that of political union, by harmonising their justice and home affairs policies, in order to protect efficiently their area of freedom, security and justice, and their foreign policies, so that the economic giant that they had created through economic integration would have a voice commensurate with its size in the international arena [see section 2.3.and chapter 8].

Chapter 5

CUSTOMS UNION

Diagram of the chapter

A customs union is a stage of multinational integration, during which the member states agree, by treaty, to refrain from imposing any customs duties, charges having equivalent effect or quantitative restrictions on each other and to adopt an external common customs tariff in their relations with third countries. The common customs tariff implies, not only a common customs policy, but also a common foreign trade policy [see chapter 23]. Furthermore, the freedom of movement is applicable in a customs union regardless of the origin of goods, thus eliminating customs controls at internal borders.

The founders of the European Economic Community had, from the start the goal not only of setting up a customs union, but also a common market in which goods, services and capital could be traded freely. In economic integration, they foresaw not only a formula offering economic advantages, but also the means to set up the conditions for political union in Europe. In order to achieve this, **a sound foundation** was required. Customs union was, accurately enough, such a foundation; it allowed for unprecedented trade growth in the participating Member States and the construction upon it of the entire European edifice. In fact, all the common policies examined in this book would be unthinkable were they not based on customs union.

5.1. Intra-Community trade

Before the Community treaties came into force, every European country protected its national production with **customs tariffs**, preventing the import of goods at prices lower than those of the national production, and **quantitative restrictions**, preventing the import of certain products in quantities exceeding those which were necessary to satisfy local demand not covered by national production. Thus, a country would import the quantities and qualities not normally supplied by its internal production. As industry was well protected, it saw no need to make large-scale efforts to modernise or reduce production costs. The European consumer, faced with a limited choice and high prices for low quality goods, was the main victim of this **protectionism**. The customs union, limited initially to the coal and steel sectors governed by the ECSC Treaty but rapidly extended to all products and services, thanks to the EEC Treaty [see section 2.1.], aimed at correcting this situation.

5.1.1. The abolition of customs barriers to trade

According to article 23 of the EC Treaty, the Community is based upon a customs union which covers all trade in goods and which involves the prohibition between Member States of customs duties on imports and exports and of all charges having equivalent effect, and the adoption of a common customs tariff in their relations with third countries. The customs union of the EC **covers "all trade in goods"**. This means that products coming from a third country can move freely within the Community if the import formalities have been complied with and any customs duties or charges having equivalent effect, which are payable, have been levied in the importing Member State (Art. 24 TEC).

Articles 13 and 14 of the Treaty of Rome provided that **customs duties and charges having equivalent effect** to customs duties on imports were to be progressively abolished during the twelve-year transitional period from 1 January 1958 to 31 December 1969. Although the Treaty gave the Member States the option of varying the rate of reduction of customs duties according to product (should a sector have difficulties), the reduction was constant and problem-free. The rate of tariff dismantling was even accelerated by two Council decisions, and completed on 1 July 1968, 18 months ahead of schedule. This demonstrates that tariff dismantling caused no major problems to the industries of the Member States, as any country's objection would have prevented the change of schedule provided by the Treaty. The States which acceded to the Community later on had a five-year transitional period to eliminate customs duties in intra-Community trade. This was also problem-free. Certainly, many of the previously protected industries were obliged to renovate or shut down, but many new industries were created or expanded on sound premises.

The accelerated completion of the tariff union meant that, as of 1 July 1968, intra-Community trade was freed of customs duties and quantitative restrictions on imports and exports. However, **other trade obstacles,** such as charges having equivalent effect to customs duties and measures having equivalent effect to quantitative restrictions, were far from gone. The proper functioning of the tariff union required the removal of these obstacles too by the end of the transitional period. Indeed, the Treaty of Rome expressly noted the necessity of "reducing formalities imposed on trade as much as possible" (Art 10 EEC). In reality, as soon as tariff disarmament was accomplished, the "formalities war" was stepped up between Member State administrations anxious to protect national production and at the same time prevent the decrease of their own functions and powers. Of course, every form, every stamp required for cross-border trade had a reason: tax collection, statistics, and customs checks aimed at preventing the import of products not conforming to national regulations, etc. But each stamp meant time and money to the Community's businesses.

A great number of those **trade barriers were hidden in regulations**, such as consumer or environment protection standards, which varied from one State to another [see section 6.1.]. Their restrictive effects were often more damaging than customs duties and quantitative restrictions. Indeed, while customs barriers raised the price of imports or quantitatively limited them, various regulations could completely block the import of a product. Fortunately, such extreme cases were rather limited. However, as seen in the chapter on the common market, the elimination of non-customs barriers to trade proved to be much more difficult and took three times as long as did the elimination of customs barriers.

Despite the non-completion of the customs union by 1968, **the economic results of the free circulation of goods** achieved by it were indisputable. From 1958 to 1972, while trade between the six founding Member States and the rest of the world had tripled, intra-Community trade had been multiplied by nine. Such exceptional trade growth was a key factor in economic development and the raising of the standard of living in all member countries of the original EEC. The stimulating effect of the wider market created a feeling of business confidence, which resulted in investment growth. Consumers emerged as the overall winners; supply was much more diverse and products cheaper than before tariff dismantling. The welfare objective of European integration was undoubtedly well pursued through the customs union. The task of the common institutions was, therefore, to eliminate the remaining problems and increase the benefits of the customs union.

5.1.2. Elimination of internal borders

The good results of the customs union **spurred the completion of the common market**, examined in the next chapter, itself needed for the completion of the customs union. Indeed, the customs union and the common market, which were the goals of the Treaty of Rome, both suffered from the same problems and finally benefited from the same remedies. Heartened by the evident benefits of the customs union, the Community institutions under the leadership of the Commission waged a "war of attrition on formalities", which, thanks to the Single European Act of 1987 [see section 2.1.], reached a successful conclusion on December 31, 1992.

Since January 1, 1993, no customs formalities are required for trade within the Community. Hence, all checks and all formalities in respect of goods moving within the Community have been eliminated[1]. The Community henceforth forms **one single border-free area** for the purposes of the movement of goods under cover of the TIR (international road transport) and ATA (temporary admission of goods) carnets[2]. This saves a great deal of time for economic operators and thus helps cut the cost of transporting goods within the Community.

5.1.3. Veterinary and plant health legislation

Veterinary and plant health legislation is important not only for intra-Community trade, but also for the protection of the environment and of human health. It is in the interest of all Member States to strengthen their common legislation in these fields and, at the same time, not to upset intra-Community trade of foodstuffs.

The **plant health arrangements,** which came into force on 1 June 1993, have made it possible to remove all physical obstacles to trade of plants and plant products[3]. These arrangements include the rules applicable to the intra-Community trade of plants and plant products imported from third countries, the standards for the protection of the environment and human health against harmful or undesirable organisms and the protective measures against the introduction into the Community of organisms harmful to plants or plant products and against their spread within the Community. The Community Plant Variety Office supervises the protection of plant varieties in the Community[4].

In the **veterinary field**, the efforts of the Community are mainly geared towards **protecting the health of animals and consequently human health,** while allowing the smooth operation of the internal market. Since January 1, 1992, veterinary checks at intra-Community frontiers have been abolished and are instead carried out at the point of departure[5], while measures were taken to monitor zoonoses and zoonotic agents and

---

[1]   Regulation 450/2008, OJ L 145, 04.06.2008.
[2]   Regulation 719/91, OJ L 78, 26.03.1991 repealed by Regulation 2913/92, OJ L 302, 19.10.1992.
[3]   Directive 2000/29, OJ L 169, 10.07.2000 last amended by Directive 2007/71, OJ L 169, 29.06.2007.
[4]   Regulation 2100/94, OJ L 227, 01.09.1994 last amended by Regulation 15/2008, OJ L 8, 11.01.2008.
[5]   Directive 89/662, OJ L 395, 30.12.1989 and Directive 2004/41, OJ L 157, 30.04.2004.

thus prevent outbreaks of food-borne infections and intoxications[1]. At the same time, the Community has switched from a system characterised by a policy of systematic preventive vaccination against foot and mouth disease, which could act as an obstacle to the free movement of animals and products, to a policy of non-vaccination and slaughter in the event of an infection source appearing.

Although the elimination of controls at internal frontiers was necessary for the free circulation of animals and animal products in the internal market, it brought about other problems. The epizootic disease of bovine spongiform encephalopathy (BSE - **"mad cow disease"**), which first appeared in the United Kingdom in 1996 and then spread to several other countries, is indicative of the importance of veterinary questions for the customs union. Despite the prohibition of exports of bovine animals over the age of 6 months, of meat and specified meat products from the United Kingdom, the certification of animals and animal products in tandem with increased veterinary checks in the consigning Member State[2], the consumers' concerns spread in all the Member States and the beef market collapsed in the whole Community [see sections 11.2. and 21.4.2.].

Similar problems were created after the detection, in Belgium in June 1999, of **contamination by dioxins** of certain animal products intended for human or animal consumption. The protective measures, taken under the safeguard clause, obliged all Member States to ensure the withdrawal from the market and destruction of any poultry or egg products or food products containing poultry-related products which had come from suspect farms[3]. These cases demonstrate the fact that in a customs union the market problems of a single Member State are **in reality problems of the single market**. Therefore, the measures taken in order to face the problems of a country concern all the members of the Union.

5.1.4. Customs cooperation

The abolition of administrative procedures on crossing the internal frontiers of the Community heightens the **risk of fraud**, if all the Member States do not apply equivalent control measures. Administrative cooperation must encourage a comparative level of checks, thus ensuring the uniform application of Community law at every point of the EU external borders and guaranteeing mutual trust and equal conditions of competition. The efficiency of a customs union depends, indeed, as much on homogeneous rules as on the quality of its operational structures.

Customs officials make up an important **human network** of the EU. Since they collect customs duties, which must be transferred to the Community budget [see section 3.4.], and guard the external frontiers against il-

---

[1] Directive 2003/99, OJ L 325, 12.12.2003.
[2] Directives 96/90 and 96/91, OJ L 13, 16.01.1997.
[3] Decision 1999/449, OJ L 175, 10.07.1999 and Decision 1999/601, OJ L 232, 02.09.1999

licit trading, the customs officers of the Member States **act in fact in the name of the Community** and must apply the Community law. They must be open to cooperation both among themselves and with the Commission in the spirit of Article 10 of the EC Treaty.

Article 29 of the EU Treaty urges the Council to take measures in order to strengthen cooperation between customs authorities and police forces, both directly and through the European Police Office (Europol). In fact, such measures are taken both in the context of the customs union and of justice and home affairs cooperation [see section 8.1.]. Thus, the Council Regulation on the **mutual assistance** between the Member States' administrations and on their collaboration with the Commission aims to step up fraud prevention, ensure the proper application of customs and agricultural regulations, providing *inter alia* for the administration of a computerised "customs information system" (CIS)[1]. The **Naples II Convention** on Mutual Assistance and Cooperation between Customs Administrations aims to crack down on the proliferation of illicit trafficking in breach of national and Community provisions by making customs cooperation faster and more effective[2].

5.2. Trade with non-member countries

Apart from removing obstacles to intra-Community trade, a customs union includes the harmonisation of customs regulations on trade with non-member countries. The efforts aimed at implementing such regulations in the European Union take two solid forms. On the one hand, the Community has established, and manages, a **Common Customs Tariff (CCT)**; on the other hand, Community rules fit into an international context, whose evolution they must follow. Thus, arrangements agreed previously in the context of GATT and, henceforth, of the World Trade Organisation must be transposed into Community law [see section 23.4.].

Customs union requires more than just having a common customs tariff. This tariff must also be applied according to identical rules throughout all Member States. Failure to do this could result in different values attributed to goods for customs purposes or different rules on the release of goods for circulation according to the importing Member State. The **Community Customs Code (CCC)**, which groups together all the provisions of the Community's customs legislation, aims precisely at removing the risk of different interpretations of EU rules in trade between the Member States and third countries [see section 5.2.3.][3]. The common customs legislation grouped together in the customs code is an attribute of the customs union.

---

[1]   Regulation 1468/81, OJ L 144, 02.06.1981 and Regulation 515/97, OJ L 82, 22.03.1997.

[2]   OJ C 24, 23.01.1998.

[3]   Regulation 450/2008, OJ L 145, 04.06.2008.

5.2.1. The Common Customs Tariff

A customs union is characterised by the existence of **a single external tariff** applied by all Member States to imports coming from third countries. Such imports only have to clear customs once and can then move freely within the common customs area. Reaching an agreement among the original Member States on a single external tariff required a complex striking of balances and compromises, given the different national interests, stemming from the different products that each country wished to protect. The common customs tariff adopted by the European institutions in 1968 is, therefore, a major achievement of European integration.

For the member countries, the CCT meant both the loss of **customs revenue**, which, since 1975, has been a resource of the Community budget, and the option of carrying out an independent customs or trade policy [see sections 3.4. and 23.1.]. No member country can unilaterally decide on or negotiate tariff matters; **all changes to the CCT are decided by the Council** following negotiation (if necessary) and proposal by the Commission. All bilateral (between the EU and non-member countries) and multilateral (in the past inside GATT and now inside WTO) negotiations are carried out by the Commission.

As of 1968, **the Member States are not entitled to unilaterally carry out customs policy**, i.e. suspend customs duties or change CCT. Only the Council can waive the normal application of CCT by means of regulations adopting various tariff measures. Such measures, whether required under agreements or introduced unilaterally, involve reductions in customs duties or zero-rating in respect of some or all imports of a given product in the territory of the Community. They take the form of Community tariff quotas, tariff ceilings or total or partial suspension of duties.

The most important tariff concessions were granted by the Community in the context of the **General Agreement on Tariffs and Trade (GATT)**. In the course of several international negotiations, namely: the "Dillon Round" (1960-62), the "Kennedy Round" (1964-67) and the "Tokyo Round" (1973-79), substantial reductions of customs duties were made on most industrial products. The "Uruguay Round", which was launched on 20 September 1986 and was concluded on 15 December 1993, has achieved major tariff reductions on the part of the 117 participating countries in the sectors of industry, agriculture and services. It has also imposed new rules and disciplines to international trade, rules that the EU has incorporated into Community law [see section 23.4.].

Since 1995, the customs tariff of the European Union takes account of the outcome of the **GATT Uruguay Round of negotiations** [see section 23.2.]. In principle, for each item and sub-item of the tariff nomenclature, both the autonomous rates and the conventional rates resulting from the GATT negotiations are indicated. Several technical annexes to the CCT set out the specific import regimes, such as the import regime for certain agricultural products or the regime for pharmaceutical substances which may benefit from exoneration on duties.

5.2.2. The Community Customs Code

A customs union, without borders, presupposes that the customs relations of the Member States with the rest of the world be regulated in the same way. The common customs legislation is, in fact, applicable to the jurisdictions of all Member States as internal law. For this purpose, the **Community Customs Code (CCC)** groups together and presents all of the provisions of customs legislation governing the Community's trade with third countries in the light of its undertakings within the World Trade Organisation[1] [see section 23.4.]. It aims to guarantee the clarity of Community customs regulations and remove the risk of divergent interpretations or legal vagueness.

The Code contains, first of all, **the basic rules of common customs legislation**: customs territory of the European Union, customs value, goods origin, etc. The definition of the **customs territory** of the Community includes inter alia the coastal Member States' territorial sea, a matter of particular importance to the fishing and offshore activities of Member States. **Value for customs purposes** can sometimes have a greater impact on trade than customs duties. The Community Customs Code specifies the method by which such value is determined, the customs clearance criteria for goods finished or processed out of their country of origin, and the conditions under which goods are temporarily exempt of import duties. The **rules of origin** determine to what extent products coming from third countries may be exempt of duty by determining the degree of processing or transformation they have undergone. These rules are important for the proper application of preference systems and several provisions of the commercial policy of the European Union [see sections 23.2.1. and 24.5.].

Common customs regulations, uniformly applicable in the Community's trade relations with other countries, involve setting up **various customs procedures** with economic impact. The Community Customs Code harmonised the legislative, regulatory and administrative provisions relative to customs warehouses procedures, free zones procedures, and usual forms of handling, which can be undertaken in customs warehouses and free zones[2]. Thus, it includes provisions on: the customs treatment of goods entering the Community's customs territory and on the temporary storage of these goods; goods brought into the customs territory of the Community until such goods have received a destination for customs purposes[3]; returned goods in the customs territory of the Community; and ad-

---

[1]   Regulation 450/2008, OJ L 145, 04.06.2008.
[2]   Ibid.
[3]   OJ L 367, 31.12.1988.

mission to free circulation of goods[1]. **Transit systems** (Community transit, common transit and TIR) are at the heart of the customs union and the common commercial policy, but these systems are subject to fraud [see details below]. A common transit procedure exists between the EC countries and the EFTA countries[2]. The EU implements the principles of the revised Kyoto Convention on the simplification and harmonisation of customs procedures[3].

The CCC governs also the **export procedures** of Community goods, the deferred payment of customs duties on imports or exports, the refund or remittance of these duties and the post-clearance collection of export duties not imposed on goods entered for a customs procedure. For Community exports, the Commission has adapted the model certificate of origin to the overall frame recommended by the UN[4]. A Community system of relief from customs duties exists[5].

5.3. *Appraisal and outlook*

The first ten years of the European Economic Community were the years of glory for customs union. The removal of customs duties and quantitative restrictions on imports and exports and the introduction of a common customs tariff, in July 1968, were important achievements of the young Community. They ruled out any "national preference" and gave rise to the "Community preference" for the products of the Member States. They provided formidable stimulus to intra-Community trade and, as expected by the EEC Treaty, were the foundation for the common market and all the common policies examined in this book.

The realisation of the customs union has also had important effects for the consumers of the member countries. It **contributed to the material wellbeing of the Member States' citizens**, through a remarkable increase of better quality goods at lower prices. Tangible manifestations of the customs union are the products from all over the continent, which are available at affordable prices in local stores in all the Member States. The customs union has also greatly facilitated the travel of the citizens inside the countries of the EC/EU.

What the Treaty had not foreseen was the perseverance of the national administrations, which quickly found obstacles other than those of customs to hinder trade between Member States, protect national production in an arbitrary way and, at the same time, defend their own functions and very

---

[1] Regulation 450/2008, OJ L 145, 04.06.2008.
[2] Convention and Decision 87/415, OJ L 226, 13.08.1987, OJ L 226, 13.08.1987.
[3] Decision 2003/231, OJ L 86, 03.04.2003 and Decision 2004/485, OJ L 162, 30.04.2004.
[4] Regulation 2454/93, OJ L 253, 11.10.1993 last amended by Regulation 214/2007, OJ L 62, 01.03.2007.
[5] Regulation 918/83, OJ L 105, 23.04.1983, last amended by Regulation 274/2008, OJ L 85, 27.03.2008.

existence (as in the case of the restructuring of customs administrations brought about by the abolition of customs controls).

As will be explained in the next chapter, the customs union was finally completed, together with the completion of the single market in 1992. The most striking manifestation of the customs union was the disappearance of customs checks at the borders between Member States. The abolition of customs checks at internal borders was achieved thanks to the abolition of customs administrative documents, which burdened intra-Community trade every year, a far-ranging reform of indirect taxation, examined in the chapter on taxation [see section 14.2.2.] and the entry into force of a series of provisions reorganising fiscal, veterinary, phytosanitary, sanitary and safety checks and the collection of statistical data. The most meaningful aspect of this process is the lightening of the administrative burden of companies carrying out intra-Community sales and purchases and, therefore, the encouragement of intra-Community transactions.

In addition to the internal environment of the Union, **the international environment of customs and commerce** has been profoundly modified in the 1990s. The opening up of free international trade to the Central and Eastern European countries as well as those of the former Soviet Union and the entry into force of the new GATT agreements have been powerful catalysts in the globalisation of trade. At the same time, however, there has been a growing globalisation of illicit traffic in all areas, such as drugs, arms, nuclear material and protected animal species. From a customs viewpoint, this requires strengthened cooperation and mutual assistance between the customs' administrations of Community countries and those of third countries, notably those of other European countries.

Therefore, the abolition of customs formalities at internal borders must be counterbalanced by the **reinforcement of measures at external frontiers.** Customs checks at the Community's external frontiers have to be strengthened for illegal imports from third countries and customs cooperation must ensure that differences in regulations do not give rise to fraud or problems for consumers. National security problems (crime, drugs, terrorism, firearms traffic) will have to be settled jointly and by a detailed exchange of information between the police and security forces of the Member States in the context of police and judicial cooperation in criminal matters [see section 8.1.2.]. Common policies are necessary regarding citizens of non-member countries circulating freely within the Member States, once they have crossed the borders of one of them [see section 8.1.4.]. It is obvious that the customs union has had and continues having important spillover or multiplicative effects [see section 1.1.1.] on a great number of common policies in other economic and even political fields.

Bibliography on Customs Union

- CADOT Olivier (et al.). "Rules of origin for preferential trading arrangements: implications for the ASEAN Free Trade Area of EU and US experience", in *Journal of Economic Integration*, v. 22, n. 2, June 2007, p. 288-319.
- EUROPEAN COMMISSION. *Community Programmes Customs 2013 and Fiscalis 2013.* Luxembourg: EUR-OP*, 2006.
  - Customs blueprints: pathway to modern customs. Luxembourg: EUR-OP*, 2007.
- GORMLEY Laurence. *EU law of free movement of goods and customs union.* Oxford: Oxford University Press, 2007.
- HAYS Thomas. *Parallel importation under European Union law.* London: Sweet & Maxwell, 2007.
- JOERGES Christian, GODT Christine. "Free trade: the erosion of national, and the birth of transnational governance", *European Review: Interdisciplinary Journal of the Academia Europaea*, v. 13, suppl. 1, May 2005, p. 93-117.
- JOVANOVIC Miroslav. *The economics of international integration.* Cheltenham: Edward Elgar, 2006.
- NOWAK-LEHMANN Felicitas (et al.). "The impact of a customs union between Turkey and the EU on Turkey's exports to the EU", in *Journal of Common Market Studies*, v. 45, n. 3, September 2007, p. 719-743.
- VALETTE Marie-Françoise. "Le nouveau schéma européen de préférences tarifaires généralisées: sous le signe du développement durable et de la bonne gouvernance", in *Revue du Marché commun et de l'Union européenne*, n. 506, mars 2007, p. 163-171.
- VRINS Olivier, SCHNEIDER Marius. *Enforcement of intellectual property rights through border measures: law and practice in the EU.* Oxford: Oxford University Press, 2006.

* The publications of the Office for Official Publications of the European Communities (EUR-OP*) exist generally in all official languages of the EU.

DISCUSSION TOPICS

1. Which are the main attributes of a customs union?
2. Consider the inferences of the increasing membership of the Community customs union and the decreasing one of the EFTA.
3. What was more important for multinational integration: trade liberalisation among the Member States or the common customs policy towards third countries?
4. The "mad cow disease" (BSE) demonstrated the effects of the customs union on the common agricultural policy and on the consumer protection policy. Outline the interactions between the three policies and the lessons to be drawn from this disastrous experience.
5. Can fraud prevention in a customs union be dealt with national measures or does it require a common policy?

Chapter 6

COMMON MARKET

Diagram of the chapter

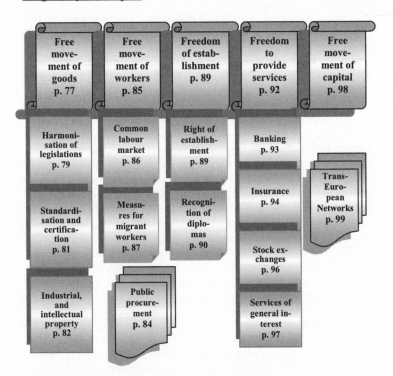

The creation of a single European economic area based on a common market was **the fundamental objective of the Treaty of Rome** [see section 2.1.]. Article 2 of that Treaty set out that objective as follows: "The Community shall have as its task, by establishing a common market and progressively approximating the economic policies of Member States, to promote throughout the Community a harmonious development of economic activities, a continuous and balanced expansion, an increase in stability, an accelerated raising of the standard of living and closer relations between the States belonging to it". It is obvious that the common market was not an end in itself, but a means to achieve economic and political goals.

It is useful to define here the concepts of "common market", "single market" and "internal market" which are used almost synonymously but which have significant nuances of meaning. The **common market** is a stage in the multinational integration process, which, in the words of a Court of Justice ruling, aims to remove all the barriers to intra-Community trade with a view to the merger of national markets into a **single market** giving rise to conditions as close as possible to a genuine **internal market**[1]. It is worth noting that the Treaty establishing the European Community ignores the concept of the "single market". It refers generally to the stage of the "common market" and to the end result of it, the "internal market", which according to its Article 14 comprises "an area without internal frontiers in which the free movement of goods, persons, services and capital is ensured in accordance with the provisions of this Treaty". The Community had to clear many obstacles during the common market stage in order to reach the goal of a single market by the end of 1992, a goal set, in 1985, by the then President of the Commission, Jacques Delors.

The establishment of the common market first required the **elimination of all import and export duties** existing between Member States before the foundation of the Community. We saw in the previous chapter how the Member States effectively removed the customs barriers and how immediately after tariff dismantling, they began erecting other barriers between them, in particular technical barriers which, in some cases, were even more difficult to overcome [see sections 5.1. and 6.1.]. In the first section of this chapter, we shall look at how the Member States decided to complete the common market and what measures they decided to take to eliminate technical obstacles to trade and to open up public procurement.

The creation of a common market resembling an internal market implies not only the liberalisation of trade among the participating member states, it also necessitates the **free movement of production factors**. Hence, in order to speak about a common market, we need to have between the Member States that make it up the existence of **four fundamental freedoms**: freedom of movement of goods, thanks to the elimination of all trade barriers; freedom of movement of workers, thanks to the elimination of all restrictions to their entrance and residence in other Member States; freedom of establishment of persons and companies in the territory of any Member State and of the provision of services by them in the host country; and freedom of capital movements for business or personal purposes. It appears that the **keyword of the common market is freedom**.

6.1. Completion of the internal market

In January 1985, the President of the Commission, **Jacques Delors**, forcefully declared that in order to achieve the main objective of the EEC Treaty, the creation of a single market, all internal European borders should be eliminated by the end of 1992. Therefore, in June 1985 the Commission forwarded to the European Council a **"white paper"** on

---

[1]   Judgment of May 5 Gaston Schul, , case 15/81, ECR 1982, p. 1409

completing the internal market[1]. The Milan European Council (28-June 1985) welcomed the programme established in the white paper and decided, by a majority of its members, to call an intergovernmental conference with the brief of drawing up a draft Treaty covering, on the one hand, political cooperation and, on the other, the amendments to the EEC Treaty required for the completion of the internal market. The Commission's proposals for a "single framework" for the amendment of the EEC Treaty and for political cooperation were finalised in the form of a **"Single European Act"** by the Ministers for Foreign Affairs meeting in Intergovernmental Conference on 27 January 1986 [see section 2.1.]. By making significant changes to the Community decision-making process (qualified majority voting in the Council acting in cooperation with the European Parliament) [see section 4.3.], the Single Act not only succeeded in removing the technical barriers to trade, thus creating the Single Market, but has had important spillover effects [see section 1.1.1.] on many common policies, such as transport, taxation and environment protection.

6.2. Free movement of goods

Tariff disarmament completed thanks to the customs union, in July 1968, had eliminated customs barriers to intra-Community trade. But there still remained technical obstacles to trade and the EEC Treaty had not fixed a timetable for their elimination. **Technical barriers to trade result from national regulations** obliging the producers of industrial products and foodstuffs to satisfy certain criteria or to meet certain standards and technical specifications. This legislation is necessary for various reasons: standardising industrial production, guaranteeing the safety of workers, protecting the health of consumers and preventing or reducing environmental pollution, etc. The problem for the common market was not the existence of national regulations, but the differences between them and also the fact that those regulations could be used to protect the national market from products from other Member States which were subject to different standards. The impetus given by the Single European Act to the efforts of the Commission helped to eliminate this problem and thus establish the single market.

The free movement of goods within the Community established by Articles 25 to 28 (TEC) is in actual fact safeguarded by the **infringement procedure** provided in Article 226 of the EC Treaty [see section 4.1.2.]. The Commission invokes those procedures whenever it records an infringement of Community provisions attributable to any authority whatsoever of a Member State (including judicial authorities[2]). It may consider a

---

[1] COM(85)310 final.

[2] See Judgment of 30 September 2003, case C-224/01 Gerhard Köbler v Republic of Austria; ECR 2003.

case as a matter of routine in the light of information provided by Members of the European Parliament or published in the press or in the official journal of a Member State. Usually, however, a **complaint** is brought before it by a company, an association or even another Member State in respect of draft standards or technical rules of a Member State. Article 30 (TEC) allows some restrictions on imports on grounds of public morality, public policy or public security, but specifies that they must not constitute disguised restrictions on trade between Member States[1]. According to the Court of Justice, willing to ensure the survival of a company cannot be a justification founded on this Article[2].

The adoption of the directives establishing the single market solved the major problem in the free movement of goods. A supplementary problem is the not complete or correct **transposition of the directives** relating to the realisation of the single market[3]. A Council Regulation reiterates the obligations of the Member States to take all necessary measures to facilitate the free movement of goods in the Community and establishes an early warning mechanism in the event of an obstacle or the risk of an obstacle to the free movement of goods, as well as a specific mechanism enabling the Commission to request a Member State to take the measures necessary to remove such an obstacle[4]. The Member States have all agreed on the principle that penalties be applicable for breaches of the internal market law[5].

6.2.1. Harmonisation of legislations

The removal of technical obstacles to trade in **industrial products** is normally based on Article 94 of the EC Treaty (Art. 100 EEC), which provides for the **approximation of** such **provisions** laid down by law, regulation or administrative action that directly affect the functioning of the common market. On this legal basis, the Commission has for many years been trying to align national regulations with Community standards agreed upon in Council directives. Such alignment is not, however, as easy as it seems at first sight. As technical regulations relate to production systems and consequently investments already made, and as their harmonisation sometimes entails the need for industrialists in some Member States to change their production systems by means of new investment expenditure, the removal of technical obstacles to trade used to be the subject of interminable discussions. Each member country tried to persuade its partners that its own technical regulations were the best and should be adopted by the Community.

---

[1] See in this context the Judgment of the Court on German beer, case 178/84, ECR 1987, p. 1227.
[2] Judgment of 28 March 1995, case C-324/93, ECR 1995, p. 1-0563.
[3] COM (95) 500, 07.06.1995.
[4] Regulation 2679/98, OJ L 337, 12.12.1998 and COM (2001) 160, 22 March 2001.
[5] OJ C 188, 22.07.1995, p. 1-3.

The **harmonisation directives** have harmonised the national regulations in fields as diverse as motor vehicle equipment, foodstuffs and proprietary medicinal products. Thus, considerable progress has been made in the motor vehicle sector, in particular as a result of the entry into force of the EC type-approval for motor vehicles and their trailers[1]. In the foodstuffs sector a body of Community inspectors is responsible for evaluating and checking the control systems in the Member States[2]. Directives have been adopted in the particularly sensitive areas of food additives, colourings and sweeteners[3]. The harmonisation work relating to pharmaceutical products has culminated in the creation of the single market in medicinal products and in the establishment of a European Agency for the Evaluation of Medicinal Products[4].

The laborious procedures involved in the approximation of laws leads to results which are **very useful for economic integration**. Indeed, once the standards are the same in all member countries, type approval of a product granted in any member country is recognised by all the others. The manufacturers need only guarantee that all examples of a product will conform to the prototype that has been approved in the directive. Items which do not conform may not be sold anywhere in the common market, including the producer's home market. Conversely, no Member State may apply more stringent national rules to oppose the import or use of products which meet Community requirements. But, the harmonisation of legislations is also very useful for consumers, since it guarantees them the quality and safety of products circulating in the large market.

However, whilst some problems were being resolved through the harmonisation of legislations, the Member States, tempted by protectionism, in particular during the gloomy economic climate of the 1970s, were adopting new legislation and **creating further technical obstacles to trade**. The Community institutions' laborious work to remove those obstacles therefore resembled the endless tasks of the Danaides, punished by Greek gods to carry water eternally in leaky jars. For that reason, the Commission considered a fresh approach to the problem. For that it relied upon the case law of the Court of Justice. In its judgment of 20 February 1979 in the **"Cassis de Dijon" case** (concerning the sale in Germany of blackcurrant liqueur produced in France), the Court of Justice gave a very broad definition of the obstacles to free trade which were prohibited under Article 30 et seq. of the EEC Treaty (Art. 28 to 31 TEC)[5]. It stated that any product lawfully manufactured and marketed in a Member State should in principle be admitted to the market of any other Member State.

Even if they are applicable without distinction to domestic and imported products, national regulations may not create obstacles unless they

---

[1] Directive 92/53, OJ L 225, 10.08.1992.

[2] Regulation 882/2004, OJ L 165, 30.04.2004 and Regulation 301/2008, OJ L 97, 09.04.2008.

[3] Directives 94/34, 94/35 and 94/36, OJ L 237, 10.09.1994.

[4] Regulation 726/2004, OJ L 136, 30.04.2004.

[5] Judgment of 20 February 1979, Case 120/78, ECR 1979, p. 649.

are necessary to satisfy mandatory requirements and are directed towards an objective of general interest which is such as to take precedence over the requirements of the free movement of goods, that is one of the basic rules of the Community. In plain language, a country must not bar the way to competing products from another Member State solely because they are slightly different from domestic products. If it does so, the Commission will take proceedings against it as far as the Court of Justice, where it stands every chance of being condemned on the basis of existing case law. According to another Court judgment, **national provisions must not discriminate** against the traders to whom they apply or have the effect of discriminating between the marketing of national products and that of products from other Member States[1].

In parallel with the application of the "Cassis de Dijon" principle, the Commission secured, in 1983, the adoption by the Council of a **procedure for the provision of information** by the Member States on any new technical standards and regulations that they envisage. This procedure was codified in 1998[2], while its field of application was extended to information society services in the new Member States[3]. Thanks to the information procedure, the Commission is notified by the competent authorities of any new technical standards or regulations that they envisage and can thus notify the other Member States and request amendments before their entry into force. This is an example of shared sovereignty: the Member States have agreed to lose their independence of action in the field of standardisation, but have gained in exchange the right of surveying the actions of their neighbours [see section 1.1.2.].

6.2.2. Common standardisation and certification policy

As regards the existing rules and standards, at the instigation of the Commission, the Council adopted, in 1985, a **new approach to technical harmonisation and standards**[4]. In cases where full harmonisation of technical standards cannot be applied, because divergences are too great between the essential aims of different national laws, legislative harmonisation is confined to the adoption of the **essential safety requirements** (or other requirements in the general interest) with which products must conform, in order to enjoy free movement throughout the EU. Member States must notify the Commission of any measure that they may take for some reason, which may obstruct the free movement of a model or type of product that is lawfully manufactured or marketed in another Member State[5].

---

[1] Judgment given on 24 November 1993, Joined Cases C-267/91 and C-268/91, Keck and Mithouard, ECR 1993, p. I-6097.
[2] Directive 98/34, OJ L 204, 21.07.1998 amended by Directive 2006/96, OJ L 363, 20.12.2006.
[3] Decision 2004/299, OJ L 98, 02.04.2004 and Decision 2004/330, OJ L 117, 22.04.2004.
[4] OJ C 136, 04.06.1985, p. 1-9.
[5] Decision 3052/95, OJ L 321, 30.12.1995.

The key to the implementation of the new approach to technical harmonisation is the **common standardisation policy**, i.e. the establishment of standards that determine the specifications for industrial production. The standards are adopted by European bodies, which have the task of elaborating technical specifications that meet the essential requirements laid down by the technical harmonisation Directives, while ensuring that those standards are the result of agreement of all parties concerned: producers, users, consumers, administrations, etc. These bodies are: the European Committee for Standardisation (CEN), the European Committee for Electrotechnical Standardisation (CENELEC) and the European Telecommunication Standards Institute (ETSI). No mandatory nature is attributed to these technical specifications, which have the status of voluntary standards. Industrialists are not obliged but have an interest, if they want to market their products in all the common market, to manufacture them in accordance with the Community directives and hence with Community standards. On the other hand, the national authorities are obliged to recognise that products manufactured in conformity with harmonised standards are presumed to conform to the essential requirements laid down in that Directive. The Community contributes to the financing of European standardisation[1].

In order to be able to exercise their positive effects, European standards must, however, also be **certified and recognised by the relevant national bodies**. Reciprocal recognition of certificates of conformity with rules and standards is therefore essential to the free movement of goods. Hence, the Community laid down the guiding principles for the European policy on the mutual recognition of tests and certificates[2], provided for the setting up of the European Organisation for Testing and Certification (EOTC) and adopted conformity assessment procedures and the rules for the affixing and use of the CE conformity marking, intended for use in the technical harmonisation Directives for the marketing of industrial products [see also sections 17.3.6 and 19.2.1.][3]. In order to control the respect of these procedures and rules, the Community set out rules on the inspection and verification of good laboratory practice (GLP)[4]. The **principle of mutual recognition** enables, especially in sectors which have not been harmonised at Community level, the competent authorities of importing Member States to recognise technical specifications, standards and rules applicable in other Member States and the validity of tests carried out by approved laboratories in other Member States offering adequate guarantees of reliability and efficiency.

A **single "CE" marking** is used in order to facilitate controls on the Community market by inspectors and to clarify the obligations of economic operators in respect of marking under the various Community regu-

---

[1] Decision 1673/2006, OJ L 315, 15.11.2006.
[2] OJ C 10, 16.01.1990, p. 1-2.
[3] Decision 93/465, OJ L 220, 30.08.1993.
[4] Directive 2004/9, OJ L 50, 20.02.2004.

lations[1]. The aim of the CE marking is to symbolize the conformity of a product with the levels of protection of collective interests imposed by the total harmonization directives and to indicate that the economic operator has undergone all the evaluation procedures laid down by Community law in respect of his product. Consumers who see the **Community marking CE** (Communitas Europaea) on a product thus have an indication (not necessarily the proof) that it has been manufactured in conformity with Community standards.

6.2.3. Protection of intellectual and industrial property

The internal market has become the appropriate environment for achieving economies of scale in the analogue or digital exploitation of intellectual property, which accounts for more than 5% of the Community's gross domestic product (GDP). Community-wide protection of **intellectual and industrial property** helps to ensure the maintenance and development of creativity in the interests of authors, performers, producers, consumers, culture, industry and the public at large. Hence, intellectual property has been recognised as an integral part of property and one of the keys to added value and competitiveness [see also sections 10.3. and 23.4.].

Therefore, a Directive concerns the **legal protection of copyright and related rights** in the framework of the internal market, with particular emphasis on the information society[2]. It provides a secure environment for cross-border trade in copyright-protected goods and services and facilitates the development of electronic commerce in the field of new and multimedia products and services. Another directive establishes measures and procedures to ensure the **enforcement of intellectual property rights**, including industrial property rights[3]. It requires the Member States to apply effective, dissuasive and proportionate remedies and penalties against anyone engaging in counterfeiting and piracy so as to create a level playing field for rightholders in the EU. It includes procedures covering evidence, the protection of evidence and provisional measures such as injunctions and seizure. Remedies available to rightholders include the destruction, recall or permanent removal from the market of illegal goods, as well as financial compensation, injunctions and damages.

Directive 89/104 **protects on the territory of the Community every trade mark** in respect of goods or services which is the subject of registration or of an application in a Member State for registration as an individual trade mark, a collective mark or a guarantee or certification mark, or which is the subject of a registration or an application for registration in the Benelux Trade Mark Office or of an international registration having effect in a

---

[1]   Decision 93/465, OJ L 220, 30.08.1993.
[2]   Directive 2001/29, OJ L 167, 22.06.2001.
[3]   Directive 2004/48, OJ L 157, 30.04.2004.

Member State[1]. Member States remain free to fix the provisions of procedure concerning the registration, the revocation and the invalidity of trade marks acquired by registration.

Companies that wish to adapt their activities to the scale of the Community have at their disposal the legal instrument of the **Community trade mark**, enabling their products or services to be distinguished by identical means throughout the entire Community[2]. A Community trade mark may consist of any signs capable of being represented graphically, particularly words, including personal names, designs, letters, numerals, the shape of goods or of their packaging, provided that such signs are capable of distinguishing the goods produced by one firm from those produced by other firms. The Community trade mark provides uniform protection throughout the Community, which can be obtained by means of a single procedure. This protection enables the proprietor to prevent any other person from using the mark for the same products or services or for similar products if there is a danger of confusion. The Community trade mark is granted (registered) for a period of 10 years, which is renewable, by the Office for Harmonisation in the Internal Market (OHIM) based in Alicante. Its protection on all the territory of the Union is reinforced by the existence of quasi-judicial bodies - the Boards of Appeal of the Office for Harmonisation in the Internal Market - whose decisions may be challenged before the Court of Justice.

As regards industrial property, a Directive seeks to guarantee effective legal protection for **industrial designs** (in machinery, tools, electronic equipment, etc.), by defining a "design", by establishing the conditions governing its protection and the scope of protection including the exclusive right to use the design[3]. The **Community Design** provides uniform protection throughout the Community for registered designs managed by the Office for Harmonisation in the Internal Market (Trademarks and Designs) in Alicante[4].

6.3. Public procurement

In the context of the single market the award of contracts concluded in the Member States on behalf of the State, regional or local authorities and other bodies governed by public law entities is subject to the respect of the principles of the Treaty and in particular to the principles of freedom of movement of goods, of freedom of establishment and of freedom to provide services and to the principles deriving therefrom, such as the principles of equal treatment, of non-discrimination, of mutual recognition, of proportionality and of transparency. The application of these principles to

---

[1] Directive 89/104, OJ L 40, 11.02.1989 and Decision 92/10, OJ L 106, 11.01.1992.
[2] Regulation 40/94, OJ L 11, 14.01.1994 and Regulation 422/2004, OJ L 70, 09.03.2004.
[3] Directive 98/71, OJ L 289, 28.10.1998.
[4] Regulation 2868/95, OJ L 303, 15.12.1995.

public procurement was established in the early 1970s[1]. Nevertheless, the opening up of the public sector to Community competition was achieved only in the 1990s through Directives 92/50 relating to the coordination of procedures for the award of public service contracts, 93/36 coordinating procedures for the award of public supply contracts and 93/37 concerning the coordination of procedures for the award of public works contracts.

These Directives were replaced in 2004 by a single Directive on the coordination of procedures for the award of **public works contracts, public supply contracts and public service contracts**, which have a value exclusive of VAT equal to or greater than certain thresholds (generally, EUR 162,000 for public supply and service contracts and EUR 6,242,000 for public works contracts)[2]. Directive 2004/18 draws up provisions of Community coordination of national procedures for the award of such contracts so as to guarantee the opening-up of public procurement to competition. To ensure development of effective competition in the field of public contracts, contract notices drawn up by the contracting authorities of Member States must be advertised throughout the Community. Verification of the suitability of tenderers, in open procedures, and of candidates, in restricted and negotiated procedures with publication of a contract notice must be carried out in transparent conditions. For this purpose, non-discriminatory criteria must be indicated which the contracting authorities may use when selecting competitors and the means which economic operators may use to prove they have satisfied those criteria. Contracts must be awarded on the basis of objective criteria which ensure compliance with the principles of transparency, non-discrimination and equal treatment and which guarantee that tenders are assessed in conditions of effective competition. Consequently, the directive allows the application of two award criteria only: "the lowest price" and "the most economically advantageous tender". In order to guarantee equal treatment, the criteria for the award of the contract should enable tenders to be compared and assessed objectively.

Similar principles and rules apply to the procurement procedures of entities operating in the **water, energy, transport and postal services sectors (public utility sectors)**, which were originally covered by Directive 93/38 and now by Directive 2004/17[3]. Specific rules guaranteeing the opening up to competition of public procurement contracts above a certain value (EUR 499,000 in the case of supply and service contracts and EUR 6,242,000 in the case of works contracts), awarded by entities operating in these sectors, were necessary because of: (a) the variety of ways in which national authorities can influence the behaviour of these entities, including participation in their capital and representation in the entities' administrative, managerial or supervisory bodies; and (b) the closed nature of the

---

[1] Directive 71/304, OJ L 185, 16.08.1971, repealed by Directive 2007/24, OJ L 154, 14.06.2007.

[2] Directive 2004/18, OJ L 134, 30.04.2004 and Directive 2005/75, OJ L 323, 09.12.2005.

[3] Directive 2004/17, OJ L 134, 30.04.2004.

markets in which they operate, due to the existence of special or exclusive rights granted by the Member States concerning the supply to, provision or operation of networks for providing the service concerned. The contracting entities in these sectors, which, by virtue of the existence of exclusive government-regulated networks or concession rights, could formerly not resist political pressure to "buy national", are now obliged to call for tenders throughout the Community. Since particular competition rules apply to telecommunications, shipping and air transport [see sections 17.3.6, 20.3.3 and 20.3.4.], the public procurement contracts in these sectors are not included in the scope of Directive 2004/17.

6.4. Free movement of workers

The freedom of movement of salaried and non-salaried workers allows EU citizens to seek, within the Union, **better living and working conditions** than are available to them in their region of origin. It therefore boosts greatly the chances of improving the standards of living of the individual. At the same time, freedom of movement reduces social pressure in the poorest regions of the European Union and allows the living conditions of those remaining to improve. In the EU in general it facilitates the adjustment of the labour supply to the variations in the demand of undertakings and opens the way for more coherent and more effective economic policies at a European level. Thus, freedom of movement of workers contributes to the attainment of the objectives of the common market as well as to the flexibility and efficiency of the labour market.

Free movement is not restricted to workers. Article 18 of the EC Treaty, which has direct effect [see section 3.3.], gives every citizen of the Union the **right to move and reside freely** within the territory of the Member States. A citizen of the European Union who no longer enjoys a right of residence as a migrant worker in the host Member State can, as a citizen of the Union, enjoy a right of residence there by direct application of Article 18(1) EC[1]. The same right is enjoyed by his spouse, their descendants under the age of 21 and their dependent relatives in the ascending line. This right contributes to a concrete and practical expression of European citizenship [see sections 9.1 and 9.2]. Freedom of movement may contribute to the attainment of the objectives of the common market, while giving more flexibility and thus greater efficiency to the labour market. The challenge to the Union now is, however, to create a real European mobility area, in which freedom of movement becomes not only a legal entitlement but also a daily reality for people across Europe. This calls for a complex interaction of common policies, some of which are explained be-

---

[1] Judgment of 17 September 2002, Case C-413/99, Baumbast and R v Secretary of State for the Home Department, ECR 2002, p. I-07091.

low and some in the chapter on social progress [see sections 13.3, 13.4.2. and 13.5.].

6.4.1. The common labour market

The **EEC Treaty** had the objective, as regards workers, of creating a common labour market, which meant the free movement of labour within the Community and the abolition of any discrimination based on nationality between workers of the Member States as regards employment, remuneration and other conditions of work and employment. Under Article 39 of the EC Treaty (Art. 48 EEC), freedom of movement of workers entails the right, subject to limitations justified on grounds of public policy, public security or public health to accept offers of employment actually made, **to move freely** within the territory of Member States for this purpose, **to stay** in a Member State for the purpose of employment and **to remain** in the territory of that Member State after having been employed in it. The Community legislation that materialised those principles was completed in 1968 and, thus, freedom of movement of workers was achieved, from the legal point of view, at the same time as customs union. This freedom was extended to all the workers in the European Economic Area in 1994 [see section 25.1.].

Nowadays, **all persons residing legally in a Member State** have equal rights of movement and residence in the other States of the Union [see sections 6.5.1 and 9.2.]. Therefore, a directive replaced a range of complex legislation relating to different categories of beneficiaries, including salaried and non salaried workers[1]. For periods of residence of longer than three months, Member States may only require Union citizens to register with the competent authorities in the place of residence. The worker can continue to reside, in the country in which he or she has settled after the termination of his or her employment. In fact, the worker and his or her family members who have resided in a host Member State during a continuous period of five years have a right of permanent residence in that State. The members of the family enjoy the right of residence even after the worker's death.

A directive implementing the **principle of equal treatment** between persons irrespective of racial or ethnic origin, provided in Article 13 of the EC Treaty, seeks to prohibit discrimination throughout the Community in different areas such as employment, education, social security, health care and access to goods and services[2]. It defines the concepts of direct and indirect discrimination, gives right of redress to victims of discrimination, imposes an obligation on the employer to prove that the principle of equal treatment has not been breached, and offers protection against harassment and victimisation in all the Member States.

---

[1]   Regulation 1612/68, OJ L 257, 19.10.1968 and Directive 2004/38, OJ L 158, 30.04.2004
[2]   Directive 2000/43, OJ L 180, 19.07.2000.

The Community has set up a general framework for **combating discrimination** on grounds of religion or belief, disability, age or sexual orientation as regards employment and occupation[1]. A Community action programme to combat discrimination (2001-06) aims to promote measures to combat all forms of discrimination except that based on sex, which is the subject of specific Community action[2] [see section 13.5.5.]. The objective is to change practices and attitudes by mobilising the players involved and fostering the exchange of information and good practice. In particular, the programme seeks to set up databases and promote the networking of those involved. With a Green Paper, the Commission invited interested parties to participate in an extensive debate on the future approach to combating discrimination in the enlarged Union[3].

6.4.2. Measures in favour of migrant workers

Adequate protection by European **provisions in the field of social security** is necessary for the effective use of the right of the citizens of one Member State to stay and work in another State of the Union. Without such protection, persons moving across borders to work or to look for a job, would risk losing all or part of their rights acquired or in the process of being acquired under national legislation (concerning, for example pensions, health insurance, unemployment benefits or family benefits). Article 42 of the EC Treaty (Art. 51 EEC) provides for the adoption of the measures necessary for that purpose through arrangements to secure for migrant workers and their dependents: (a) aggregation, for the purpose of acquiring and retaining the right to benefit, of all periods taken into account under the laws of several countries, and (b) payment of benefits to persons resident in the territories of Member States. The system required by the Treaty was in fact adopted in 1958, but it has undergone many changes and improvements since then.

On the basis of Regulations 1408/71 and 574/72, **pensions of similar nature** acquired in the various Member States may be aggregated, but the person concerned may not obtain total benefits in excess of the highest pension he or she would have obtained if he or she had spent his or her whole insurance career under the legislation of any one of the States in which he or she had been employed[4]. This legislation covers also students moving within the Community, taking account of their specific situation and of the special features of the schemes under which they are insured. Civil servants and persons treated as such have equal treatment as regards general statutory pension rights and special schemes for civil servants pre-

---

[1] Directive 2000/78, OJ L 303, 02.12.2000.

[2] Decision 2000/750, OJ L 303, 02.12.2000.

[3] COM (2004) 379, 28 May 2004.

[4] Regulation 1408/71, OJ L 149, 05.07.1971 and Regulation 574/72, OJ L 74, 27.03.1972, last amended by Regulation 629/2006, OJ L 114, 27.04.2006.

vailing in the Member States[1]. The supplementary pension rights of employed and self-employed persons moving within the European Union are equally guaranteed[2]. Rights and obligations comparable to those applying to EU citizens are granted to nationals of third countries who are legally resident in the Community and who satisfy the other conditions laid down in Regulations 1408/71 and 574/72[3].

The **unemployed person** who leaves for another Member State to seek employment receives, for a maximum period of three months from the date of departure, the benefits of the country in which he or she was last employed, to be paid for by that country. Repayments in respect of health care provided for members of the family resident in a Member State other than that in which the worker is employed and insured are made entirely to the institutions of the country of residence. Family allowances are granted under the legislation of, and at the rate laid down in, the country of employment. According to the Court of Justice, such allowances are not subject to requirements as to minimum period of residence[4].

Similar arrangements cover **self-employed persons** and their families[5] as well as employed persons or self-employed persons pursuing activities in the territories of two or more Member States[6]. Concerning health insurance, any insured person staying temporarily in a Member State other than the one in which he or she is insured, for tourist or employment purposes, may be admitted to hospital or receive refunds in respect of urgent medical care in the host State on presentation of the **European health insurance card** ("European card")[7]. This card replaced all paper forms needed for health treatment in another Member State provided for by Regulations 1408/71 and 574/72 giving entitlement to reimbursement of health care costs during a temporary stay in a Member State other than the competent State or the State of residence. The European card simplified access to care in the country visited, while providing a guarantee for the bodies financing the health system in that country that the patient is fully insured in his or her country of origin and that they can therefore rely on reimbursement by their counterparts.

For the effective functioning of a common labour market, it is also necessary that potential migrant workers have at their disposal adequate information regarding the number and nature of jobs available in the Community and the qualifications required. This is the task of the **European Employment Service (EURES)**, a network of some 400 "Euroadvisers" from the national employment services, employer organisations, trade un-

[1] Regulation 1606/98, OJ L 209, 25.07.1998.

[2] Regulation 1223/98, OJ L 168, 13.06.1998.

[3] Regulation 859/2003, OJ L 124, 20.05.2003.

[4] Judgment given on 10 March 1993, Case C-111/91, Commission v Luxembourg, ECR 1993, I-840.

[5] Regulation 1390/81, OJ L 143, 29.05.1981 and Regulation 1408/71, OJ L 149, 05.07.1971 last amended by Regulation 629/2006, OJ L 114, 27.04.2006.

[6] Regulation 3811/86, OJ L 355, 16.12.1986.

[7] Decisions 2003/751, 2003/752 and 2003/753, OJ L 276, 27.10.2003.

ions, regional administrations and universities, specially trained to deal with the needs of transnational job-seekers and job-providers[1].

6.5. Freedom of establishment and recognition of qualifications

Freedom of establishment means the free movement of self-employed persons. For them, as for salaried workers, the basic principle is equality of treatment of all Community citizens, i.e. the abolition of discriminations based on nationality. **Freedom of establishment includes** the right to take up and pursue activities as self-employed persons and to set up and manage undertakings, in particular companies or firms within the meaning of the second paragraph of Article 48 (TEC), i.e., companies established under the conditions laid down for its own nationals by the law of the country where such establishment is effected. The freedom of establishment of companies extends to what is known as freedom of secondary establishment, i.e. the setting up of agencies, branches or subsidiaries (Art. 43 TEC).

6.5.1. Right of establishment

Whereas freedom to provide services chiefly concerns the pursuit of an economic activity by a person in another Member State without having the principal or secondary place of business in that State, **right of establishment entails permanent installation** in a Member State in order to pursue an economic activity in that State. In fact, the situation of the person who establishes himself is characterised by the fact that he creates a permanent link with the country of establishment, unlike somebody who provides services in a country other then that of his permanent establishment. Through its judgment of 21 June 1974 in the Reyners case (Dutch legal practitioner wishing to pursue his profession in Belgium), the Court established the **direct effect** [see section 3.3.] of Treaty provisions concerning the freedom of establishment. It held that any individual may, on the basis of Article 52 of the EEC Treaty (43 TEC), demand directly the same treatment as is applied to nationals[2]. Therefore, no special Community legislation is required.

The right for citizens of EU Member States to work or pursue activities as self-employed persons in the Member States means the **right to enter and to reside** in the member country in which they wish to work or pursue those activities. This right is extended to their spouses, children and other members of their families, including the registered partner if the legislation of the host Member State treats registered partnership as equivalent to mar-

---

[1] Decision2003/8, OJ L 5, 10.01.2003.

[2] Judgment of 21 June 1974, Case 2/74, ECR 1974, p. 631.

riage[1]. For periods of residence of longer than three months, Member States may only require Union citizens to register with the competent authorities in the place of residence. The self-employed person can continue to reside, in the country in which he or she has settled after the termination of his or her employment. In fact, the self-employed person and his or her family members who have resided in a host Member State during a continuous period of five years have a right of permanent residence in that State. The members of the family enjoy the right of residence even after the self-employed person's death. A residence requirement can be justified only if it is based on objective considerations independent of the nationality of the persons concerned and proportionate to the legitimate aim of the national provisions[2].

Under Article 46 (TEC), the principle of freedom of establishment does not concern national provisions providing for special treatment for foreign nationals on **grounds of public policy, public security or public health**. The Directive on the right of citizens of the Union and their family members to move and reside freely within the territory of the Member States contains an enumeration of the circumstances, which cannot be invoked as grounds for refusal of entry or expulsion and a series of rules concerning the procedure, which must be followed where nationals of Member States may be refused entry or expelled[3]. According to the Court of Justice, Community law precludes the automatic expulsion without right of appeal of the national of a Member State following a criminal conviction which takes account neither of the personal conduct of the person convicted nor of the risk he represents to public order[4].

6.5.2. Recognition of professional qualifications

The abolition, between Member States, of obstacles to the free movement of persons and services is one of the objectives of the Community (Art. 3 TEC). For nationals of the Member States, this includes, in particular, the right to pursue a profession, in a self-employed or employed capacity, in a Member State other than the one in which they have obtained their professional qualifications. After the elimination of apparent discriminations, in accordance with the letter and the spirit of the Treaty, there could remain other obstacles to the freedom of establishment, i.e. the numerous requirements of the Member States with regard to the training of employed and self-employed persons, and the detailed arrangements for pursuing industrial and commercial activities. Even though these requirements were not in themselves discriminatory, they could impede the

---

[1]   Directive 2004/38, OJ L 158, 30.04.2004.
[2]   Judgement of 23 March 2004, Case C-138/02 *Brian Francis Collins* v *Secretary of State for Work and Pensions*, ECR 2004.
[3]   Directive 2004/38, OJ L 158, 30.04.2004.
[4]   Judgment of 29 April 2004, Joined Cases C-482/01 and C-493/01, Orfanopoulos and others, ECR 2004.

free establishment, if they differed from country to country and obliged the interested person to **take a new examination** for the recognition of his or her professional competence. That is why Article 47 of the EC Treaty empowers the Council and the Parliament to issue directives for the mutual recognition of diplomas, certificates and other evidence of formal qualifications and for the coordination of national provisions concerning the taking up and pursuit of activities as self-employed persons. Such directives have in fact been adopted for certain professions, notably those of nurses, doctors, architects and lawyers; but they have been abolished by the general directive on the recognition of professional qualifications examined below.

However, the free provision of services within the Community should be as simple as within an individual Member State. This is the objective of the Directive on the **recognition of professional qualifications**[1]. Directive 2005/36 applies to all nationals of a Member State, including those belonging to the liberal professions, wishing to pursue a regulated profession in a Member State other than that in which they obtained their professional qualifications, on either a self-employed or employed basis. It establishes rules according to which a Member State which makes access to or pursuit of a regulated profession in its territory contingent upon possession of specific professional qualifications (the host Member State) should recognise professional qualifications obtained in one or more other Member States (the home Member State) and which allow the holder of the said qualifications to pursue the same profession there, for access to and pursuit of that profession.

According to this directive, **"regulated profession"** is a professional activity or group of professional activities, access to which or the pursuit of which is subject to the possession of specific professional qualifications; in particular, the use of a professional title. **"Professional qualifications"** are qualifications attested by evidence of formal qualifications, an attestation of competence and/or professional experience. "Evidence of formal qualifications" means diplomas, certificates and other evidence issued by an authority in a Member State. "Aptitude test" is a test limited to the professional knowledge of the applicant, made by the competent authorities of the host Member State with the aim of assessing the ability of the applicant to pursue a regulated profession in that Member State. The aptitude test must take account of the fact that the applicant is a qualified professional in the home Member State or the Member State from which he comes.

The recognition of professional qualifications by the host Member State allows the beneficiary to gain access in that Member State to the same profession as that for which he is qualified in the home Member State and to pursue it in the host Member State under the same conditions as its nationals. It also allows the free provision of services in case the service provider moves to the territory of the host Member State to pursue, **on a**

---

[1] Directive 2005/36, OJ L 255, 30.09.2005.

temporary and occasional basis, the regulated profession. However, the exercise of a regulated profession is subject to the professional and disciplinary rules of the host Member State relating to professional qualifications.

6.6. Freedom to provide services

Article 49 (TEC) provides that restrictions on "freedom to provide services" within the Community shall be "abolished in respect of nationals of Member States who are established in a State of the Community other than that of the person for whom the services are intended". Any discrimination concerning the provision of services on the basis of nationality is prohibited directly by this Article (without the need of specific Community legislation). Under Article 50 (TEC), **services shall be considered as such** where they are normally provided for remuneration, in so far as they are not governed by the provisions relating to freedom of movement for goods, capital and persons. This Article specifies, however, that the provisions on the free movement of services **cover all activities of an industrial or commercial character** or of craftsmen and the activities of the professions. It appears that the freedom of establishment and the freedom to provide services cannot be clearly distinguished in all situations and that they often go together, since a person or company seeks establishment in another Member State in order to provide services in that state. This is why the two freedoms are usually considered as **one: the freedom of establishment and provision of services**.

Services constitute the engine of economic growth of the EU, since they account for 70% of GDP and employment in most Member States. They therefore are a linchpin for smooth operation of the EU's internal market. Their liberalisation was originally based on **the principle of mutual recognition**, according to which, if a service is lawfully authorised in one Member State it must be open to users in the other Member States without having to comply with every detail of the legislation of the host country, except those concerning consumer protection. However, numerous barriers in the Member States prevented providers, particularly small and medium-sized enterprises (SMEs), from extending their operations beyond their national borders and from taking full advantage of the internal market. Since the barriers in the internal market for services affected operators who wished to become established in other Member States as well as those who provided a service in another Member State without being established there, it was necessary to remove barriers both to the freedom of establishment for providers in Member States and to the free movement of services between Member States and to guarantee recipients and providers the legal certainty necessary for the exercise in practice of those two fundamental freedoms of the EC Treaty.

This is the aim of the "**services directive**", which establishes a general legal framework facilitating the exercise of the freedom of establishment for service providers and the free movement of services, while maintaining a high quality of services[1]. That framework is based on a dynamic and selective approach consisting in the removal, as a matter of priority, of barriers which may be dismantled quickly and, for the others, the launching of a process of evaluation, consultation and complementary harmonisation of specific issues, which will make possible the progressive and coordinated modernisation of national regulatory systems for service activities, in order to achieve a genuine internal market for services by 2010. Directive 2006/123 does not affect terms and conditions of employment, including maximum work periods and minimum rest periods, minimum paid annual holidays, minimum rates of pay as well as health, safety and hygiene at work, which Member States apply in compliance with Community law. This Directive does not deal with services of non-economic general interest (education and health), social services provided for by the State, audiovisual services, including cinematographic services, gambling, activities connected with the exercise of official authority, private security services, services provided by notaries and bailiffs and services of temporary work agencies.

Financial services - banks, insurance companies and stock exchanges - which are closely monitored by the official authorities, are particularly important, as they constitute a vast market and are indispensable for the proper functioning of the other economic sectors. The freedoms of establishment and provision of services in the common market required that those services be liberalised from the protectionist measures applied by most Member States. This liberalisation, however, should reconcile two contradictory requirements, viz. the need to maintain very stringent criteria for control and financial security and the need to leave the branch concerned enough flexibility for it to be able to meet the new and ever-more complex requirements of its customers throughout the European market, particularly since the introduction of the euro. The Financial Services Committee helps define the medium- and long-term Community strategy for financial services issues examined below[2] [see sections 6.6.1, 6.6.2 and 6.6.3].

6.6.1. Banking

All restrictions on freedom of establishment and freedom to provide services in respect of self-employed activities of **banks and other financial institutions** have been abolished since the 1970s. The laws, regulations and administrative provisions of the Member States relating to the taking up and pursuit of the business of credit institutions have been coor-

---

[1]   Directive 2006/123, OJ L 376, 27.12.2006.
[2]   Decision 2003/165, OJ L 67, 12.03.2003.

dinated within a single regulatory framework[1]. The right of access is based on the mutual recognition of supervision systems, i.e. application of the principle of supervision of a credit institution by the Member State in which it has its head office, and the issue of a **"single bank licence"** which is valid throughout the Community. The single licence authorises a bank established in a Member State to open branches without any other formalities or to propose its services in the partner countries. The principle of reciprocity governs the opening in the Community of subsidiaries of banks from non-member countries. Directive 2006/48 gives a definition of the **own funds** of credit institutions, a definition which is vital to the harmonisation necessary for mutual recognition. It also establishes a minimum level for the **solvency ratio** for credit institutions and the method of calculating the ratio to be observed between own funds and risk assets and off-balance-sheet items.

In the European internal market, the transparency, performance and stability of cross-border payment systems should match the properties of the best domestic payment systems. To this effect, a Directive harmonises the legal frame of payment services in the EU, including the conditions of information as well as the rights and obligations of the parts and purports to develop the infrastructures, procedures, common rules and standards needed for a **pan-European payment system**[2] [see section 6.7]. A Commission notice supplementing this Directive provides a framework allowing banks to set in place cooperation arrangements aimed at making cross-border credit transfers more efficient without unduly restricting competition, particularly concerning market access and price competition[3].

A Directive on **deposit-guarantee schemes** is designed to protect depositors in the event of an authorised credit institution failing[4]. It stipulates that there must be a guarantee scheme in all Member States, financed by the banking sector and covering all deposits up to EUR 20 000 per depositor (EUR 15 000 in Spain, Portugal, Greece and Luxembourg). The scheme covers depositors not only in institutions in the Member State which authorise them, but also those in branches of such institutions set up in other Member States.

A clear regulatory framework for **electronic money** in the single market aims to enhance business and consumer confidence in this new form of payment, while ensuring that equal competitive conditions prevail for traditional credit institutions and other companies which issue electronic money[5]. Electronic money institutions are included within the general scope of the provisions of the banking coordination directives [see also sections 14.2.1. and 17.3.5.].

---

[1]   Directive 2006/48, OJ L 177, 30.06.2006 and Directive 2007/64, OJ L 319, 05.12.2007.
[2]   Directive 2007/64, OJ L 319, 05.12.2007.
[3]   OJ C 251, 27.09.1995.
[4]   Directive 94/19, OJ L 135, 31.05.1994 and Directive 2005/1, OJ L 79, 24.03.2005.
[5]   Directive 2000/46, OJ L 275, 27.10.2000.

6.6.2. Insurance

The laws, regulations and administrative provisions relating to the taking-up and pursuit of the business of **direct insurance other than life insurance** have been coordinated[1] and the effective exercise of freedom to provide insurance services in the Community is a reality[2]. Community arrangements cover major industrial and commercial risks and provide adequate protection for minor consumers. Also coordinated are the legislations of the Member States concerning **credit insurance** and **suretyship insurance**, on the one hand,[3] and **legal expenses insurance**[4], on the other.

The coordination of the provisions of the Member States and the freedom to provide services **in the field of life assurance** offer policy-holders the choice between all the different types of contract available in the Community, while guaranteeing them adequate protection. The freedoms of establishment and provision of services are implemented through the mutual recognition of authorisations and prudential control systems, thereby making it possible to grant a single authorisation valid throughout the Community[5]. The coordination of the basic rules of prudential and financial supervision provides for single authorisation valid throughout the Community, along with the checking of all of a broker's activities by the Member State of origin.

A **single authorisation system** enables an insurance company with its registered office in a Community Member State to open branches and operate services in all the Member States without the need for authorisation procedures in each country[6]. This system is designed to ensure the free movement of insurance products within the Community and give European citizens the opportunity to take out insurance with any Community insurer, thus finding the coverage best suited to their needs at the lowest cost, while enjoying an adequate level of protection.

The approximation of the laws of the Member States relating to insurance against **civil liability in respect of the use of motor vehicles**, and to the enforcement of the obligation to insure against such liability affords adequate protection for the victims of road accidents, irrespective of the Member State in which the accident occurred[7]. The Community legislation imposes compulsory cover for all passengers of the vehicle, covering the entire territory of the Community, including cases where the passenger is the owner, the holder of the vehicle or the insured person himself[8]. Thanks to this legislation and to the Multilateral Guarantee Agreement between na-

---

[1] First Council Directive 73/239, OJ L 228, 16.08.1973 and Directive 2005/68, OJ L 323, 09.12.2005.

[2] Directive 88/357, OJ L 172, 04.07.1988 and Directive 2005/14, OJ L 149, 11.06.2005.

[3] Directive 87/343, OJ L 185, 04.07.1987.

[4] Directive 87/344, OJ L 185, 04.07.1987.

[5] Directive 2002/83, OJ L 345, 19.12.2002 and directive 2005/68, OJ L 323, 09.12.2005.

[6] Directive 92/49, OJ L 228, 11.08.1992 and Directive 2005/68, OJ L 323, 09.12.2005.

[7] Directive 2000/26, OJ L 181, 20.07.2000 and Directive 2005/14, OJ L 149, 11.06.2005.

[8] Directive 90/232, OJ L 129, 19.05.1990 and Directive 2005/14, OJ L 149, 11.06.2005.

tional insurers' bureaux signed in Madrid on March 1991, Member States do not need to make any checks on insurance against civil liability in respect of vehicles which are normally based in a Member State or in certain third countries[1].

6.6.3. Stock exchanges and financial services

Community law on stock exchanges and other securities markets is directed towards widening the range of investments at Community level while protecting investors. The conditions for the admission of securities to official stock exchange listing are coordinated and the **single market in securities** is a reality[2]. Investment services in the securities field can be freely conducted, although monitored throughout the EU financial area by the Directive on markets in financial instruments[3]. This directive establishes a comprehensive regulatory framework governing the organised execution of investor transactions by exchanges, other trading systems and investment firms and makes sure investors enjoy a high level of protection when employing investment firms, wherever they are located in the EU. An investment firm in any Member State can carry out its activities anywhere in the European Union on the basis of a single authorisation (called a "European passport) issued by the Member State of origin. The conditions governing authorisation and business activity have been harmonised for this purpose. Prudential supervision, based on uniform rules, is carried out by the authorities of the home Member State, but in cooperation with the authorities of the host Member State. Investment firms have right of access to all the regulated markets in the EU. Common standards pertain to the prudential supervision of financial conglomerates (credit institutions, insurance undertakings and investment firms) in order to create a level playing field and legal certainty for the financial establishments concerned.

The equity capital of investment firms and credit institutions must be adequate to safeguard market stability, guarantee an identical level of **protection against bankruptcy** to investors throughout the European Union and to ensure fair competition between banks, which are subject to specific prudential provisions, and investment societies on the securities market. In order to fulfil these objectives, a Directive lays down minimum initial capital requirements and sets the equity capital, which must permanently be held in order to cover position, settlement, exchange and interest rate risks[4]. All Member States must provide for minimum compensation for investors in the event of the failure of an investment firm, authorised to provide services throughout the Union[5]. In cases of insolvency, collateral se-

[1]   Commission Decision 2003/564, OJ L 192, 31.07.2003.
[2]   Directive 2001/34, OJ L 184, 06.07.2001 and Directive 2005/1, OJ L 79, 24.03.2005.
[3]   Directive 2004/39, OJ L 145, 30.04.2004 and Directive 2007/44, OJ L 247, 21.09.2007.
[4]   Directive 2006/49, OJ L 177, 30.06.2006.
[5]   Directive 97/9, OJ L 84, 26.03.1997.

curity is provided[1]. The directive setting up common rules for collateral pledged to payment and securities settlement systems aims to limit credit risk and improve the functioning and stability of the European financial markets[2].

In order to combat fraudulent use of privileged stock exchange information, ensure the integrity of European financial markets and enhance investor confidence in those markets a directive prohibits **insider dealing and market manipulation (market abuse)**[3]. Member States must prohibit any person who possesses inside information (as defined in the directive) from using that information by acquiring or disposing of for his own account or for the account of a third party, either directly or indirectly, financial instruments to which that information relates. "Market manipulation" means notably transactions or dissemination of information, which give false or misleading signals as to the supply of, demand for or price of financial instruments or which employ fictitious devices or any other form of deception or contrivance.

6.6.4. Services of general interest

The **services of general interest** indicate "market" and "non-market" activities, considered to be of general interest by the public authorities, and subjected for this reason to specific public service obligations. Article 86 of the EC Treaty specifies that undertakings entrusted with the operation of (market) services of general economic interest are subject to the rules contained in the Treaty, in particular to the rules on competition, in so far as the application of such rules does not obstruct the performance of the particular tasks assigned to them (postal, telecommunications, transport, electricity, broadcasting, etc.). However, advantages granted to operators of these services must not enable them to compete unfairly at the expense of other companies[4]. The evolutionary concept of **"universal service"**, developed by the Community institutions, refers to a set of general interest requirements, which should be satisfied to make sure that all citizens have access to certain essential services of high quality at prices they can afford[5]. It is sensitive to national diversity and takes into consideration the special features of the European model of society [see section 13.1.].

Article 16 of the EC Treaty specifies that, without prejudice to Articles 73, 86 and 87 (TEC), and given the place occupied by services of general economic interest in the **shared values of the Union**, the Community and the Member States must take care that such services operate on the basis of principles and conditions which enable them to fulfil their missions. A Protocol to the EC Treaty inserted at Amsterdam asserts that **public service**

---

[1]   Directive 98/26, OJ L 166, 11.06.1998.

[2]   Directive 2002/47, OJ L 168, 27.06.2002.

[3]   Directive 2003/6, OJ L 96, 12.04.2003.

[4]   COM (2002) 636, 27 November 2002.

[5]   COM (2000) 580 and COM (2001) 598, 17 October 2001.

broadcasting is directly related to the democratic, social and cultural needs of each society and to the need to preserve media pluralism. Therefore, the provisions of the Treaty are without prejudice to the competence of Member States to provide for the funding of public service broadcasting, provided that certain conditions are met, notably that such funding does not affect trading conditions and competition in the Community [see section 10.2.].

6.7. Free movement of capital

Freedom of capital movement is another essential element for the proper functioning of the large European internal market. The liberalisation of payment transactions is a vital **complement to the free movement of goods, persons and services**. Borrowers - individuals and companies notably SMEs - must be able to obtain capital where it is cheapest and best tailored to their needs, while investors and suppliers of capital must be able to offer their resources on the market where there is the greatest interest. That is why it is important that the member states of a common market free capital movements and allow payments to be made in the currency of the member state in which the creditor or beneficiary is established. Obviously, all these conditions must pre-exist before the passage to the stage of an economic and monetary union, involving the circulation of a single currency.

To this end, a 1988 Directive ensures the **full liberalisation of capital movements**[1]. Under this Directive, all restrictions on capital movements between persons (natural or legal) resident in Member States were removed in the beginning of the nineties. Monetary and quasi-monetary operations (financial loans and credits, operations in current and deposit accounts and operations in securities and other instruments normally dealt in on the money market) in particular were liberalised.

However, the EC Treaty, which replaced the EEC Treaty in 1992, went even further than the 1988 Directive in the liberalisation of capital movements. The principle of the free movement of capital and payments is now expressly laid down in the Treaty. Article 56 (TEC) declares, in fact, that all restrictions on the movement of capital between Member States and between Member States and third countries are prohibited. It thus extends the **liberalisation of capital movements to and from third countries**. Article 59, however, authorises temporary safeguard measures to be taken where they are justified on serious political grounds or where capital movements to and from third countries cause serious difficulties for the functioning of economic and monetary union. In addition, Article 58 authorises Member States to take all requisite measures to prevent infringements of national

---

[1]   Directive 88/361, OJ L 178, 08.07.1988 and OJ L 1, 03.01.1994.

law and regulations, in particular in the field of taxation and the prudential supervision of financial institutions.

On the basis of these provisions and of those liberalising banking, stock-exchange and insurance services [see sections 6.6.1. to 6.6.3.], the Community **financial market has been completely liberalised** since January 1, 1993. European businesses and individuals have access to the full range of options available in the Member States as regards banking services, mortgage loans, securities and insurance. They are able to choose what is best suited to their specific needs or requirements for their daily lives and for their professional activities in the large market. The Member States must, however, dissuade the exploitation of the financial market for illegal purposes, notably laundering money generated by criminal or terrorist activities[1].

Directive 2007/64 harmonises the legal frame of payment services in the EU, including the conditions of information as well as the rights and obligations of the parts[2]. By removing existing legal obstacles, it enables the payments sector to develop the infrastructures, procedures, common rules and standards needed for a **pan-European payment system**, where improved economies of scale and competition will help to reduce the cost of payments and enhance safety and efficiency, as compared with the different national systems.

6.8. Trans-European Networks

A common policy on infrastructure trans-European networks (TENs) is needed for the good functioning of the common market. Indeed, the integration of national markets through the completion of the internal market can only have full economic and social impact, if businesses and citizens enjoy trans-European **transport, telecommunications and energy networks**, which optimise the use of the various legal instruments governing the operation of this market. With a view to enabling citizens, economic operators and regional and local authorities to derive full benefit from the setting up of an area without internal frontiers, the Community strives to promote the interconnection and inter-operability of national networks and access to these networks. It takes account in particular of the need to link island, landlocked and peripheral regions with the central regions of the Community (Art. 154 TEC). To speed up the implementation of networks, and to encourage public-private partnerships, the complex national rules and procedures are streamlined in the case of TENs, by having one approval procedure instead of requiring a series of different approvals for each element of the project.

---

[1]   Directive 2005/60, OJ L 309, 25.11.2005.
[2]   Directive 2007/64, OJ L 319, 05.12.2007.

Article 155 (TEC) provides that, in order to foster the **completion of trans-European networks**, the Community:

- establishes a series of guidelines identifying projects of common interest and providing the objectives, the priorities, the general lines of Community action and coordination with national decisions:

- adopts measures designed to harmonise technical standards;

- supports the financial efforts made by the Member States for projects of common interest, by carrying out feasibility studies and granting loan guarantees or interest rate subsidies. These decisions are taken by the Council and the European Parliament pursuant to the procedure of Article 251 (TEC);

- contributes to the financing of specific projects in the area of transport infrastructure through the Cohesion Fund.

The **financial instruments**, which facilitate the realisation of these networks, are notably the Cohesion Fund [see section 12.1.2], certain actions provided for under the Structural Funds Regulations, the loans of the European Investment Bank and the loan guarantees of the European Investment Fund [see section 12.3.]. A Council Regulation lays down the legal rules for the granting of Community financial assistance in the field of trans-European networks[1]. It defines the types of aid, the project selection criteria and the procedures for examining, assessing and monitoring applications for funding. It encourages public-private partnerships and risk-capital participation. The Community support to TENs can take the form of contributions to feasibility studies, interest-rate subsidies, loan guarantees and, in duly justified cases, direct grants to investments.

6.9. Appraisal and outlook

It took nearly a quarter of a century after the removal of customs duties and quantitative restrictions between Member States to complete *in tandem* customs union and common market. However delayed, the **achievement of a single market** is a great step forward in the process of European integration. Free movement reduces the manufacturing and transport costs of goods, facilitates exports and the realisation of important economies. The reduction of administrative and financial costs of intra-Community trade and the realisation of economies of scale tend to liberate the dynamism and the creativity of European businesses and to give them a solid base from which to tackle international competitiveness. In a global economy characterised by fierce competition, particularly between multinational companies, the economies and the companies of small and medium European countries would certainly be much worse off than they are today, if it was not for the large internal market, which is their safe haven and springboard for external markets. This is why, business interest groups back the multi-

---

[1] Regulation 2236/95, OJ L 228, 23.09.1995 and Regulation 680/2007, OJ L 162, 22.06.2007.

national integration process [see section 1.1.2]. On its part, the Community helps businesses and particularly SMEs striving to adapt to the conditions of the single market [see section 17.2.].

The common market has also boosted the welfare of the citizens of the Member States. European consumers, previously confined to their respective national markets, now enjoy a huge choice of high quality goods and services at prices dictated by free competition. The free movement of workers, freedom to provide services and freedom of establishment for self-employed persons constitute **fundamental rights**, guaranteeing the citizens of the Community the right to pursue an occupation in any Member State. The citizen of a Member State, be he or she worker, businessman or tourist, can no longer be regarded as an alien in another Member State, but as an EU citizen, and no discrimination against him or her is permitted [see section 9.1.].

The implementation of the fundamental freedoms of the common market allows the **production factors of work and capital to operate** without hindrance. Businesses can manufacture and sell their products in accordance with a system of free competition in the Member State in which conditions are most advantageous to them. They can set themselves up wherever they wish in the common market and can call on a multitude of services and sources of capital, which exist in all the Member States. The liberalisation of capital movements contributes to a better allocation of resources within the Union. Public procurement in all Member States is open to tenders from all Community companies. In banking and insurance sectors, where obstacles to cross-border trade were particularly pronounced, the increase in cross-border competition is reflected in a growing number of branches and outlets in other Member States of the Union.

All this **does not mean that all is well in the best possible single market**. The priority is now to make it work efficiently. This implies, in particular, adequate implementation of the measures taken for the completion of the internal market in every Member State, effective opening-up of public contracts, further mutual recognition of standards, more transparent rules for the internal market and simplification of the taxation system. These requirements for the proper functioning of the common market are not met uniformly and constantly in all Member States. Hence, the common market is not yet a completely integrated internal market.

Bibliography on the Common Market

- BOGUSZ Barbara (et al. eds.). *The regulation of sport in the European Union.* Cheltenham: Edward Elgar, 2007.
- BROBERG Morten, HOLST-CHRISTENSEN Nina. Free movement in the European Union: cases, commentaries and questions. Copenhagen: DJØF Publishing, 2007.

- EUROPEAN COMMISSION. *Services of general interest, including social services of general interest: a new European commitment.* Luxembourg: EUR-OP*, 2007.

  - *A single market for 21st century Europe.* Luxembourg: EUR-OP*, 2007.

  - *Handbook on implementation of the Services Directive.* Luxembourg: EUR-OP*, 2007.

- MALLINSON Roland. "Trade marks in the European Union: one right, one law, one decision - or not?" in *European Intellectual Property Review,* v. 29, n. 10, October 2007, p. 432-438.

- PARRISH Richard, MIETTINEN Samuli. *The sporting exception in European Union law.* The Hague: T.M.C. Asser Press, 2007.

- RUBALCABA Luis. *The new service economy: challenges and policy implications for Europe.* Cheltenham: Edward Elgar, 2007.

- SPAVENTA Eleanor. *Free movement of persons in the European Union: barriers to movement in their constitutional context.* The Hague: Kluwer Law International, 2007.

- TRIANDAFYLLIDOU Anna, GROPAS Ruby (eds.). *European immigration: a sourcebook.* Aldershot: Ashgate, 2007.

---

* The publications of the Office for Official Publications of the European Communities (EUR-OP*) exist generally in all official languages of the EU.

DISCUSSION TOPICS

1. Could the common market be built on a free trade area agreement or did it presuppose a customs union? Reflect on the evolution of the multinational integration process.

2. Why has the completion of the common market been retarded and how has it been brought about? Consider the role of the common institutions in the completion of the common market.

3. The EFTA countries participating in the EEA agreement apply the fundamental freedoms of a common market. Do they still form a free trade area or have they moved to the stage of the common market?

4. Why does the realisation of the fundamental freedoms of a common market necessitate common policies and harmonisation of the legislation of the member states?

5. What is the "acquis communautaire" of the common market and how does it affect other common policies?

Chapter 7

ECONOMIC AND MONETARY UNION

Diagram of the chapter

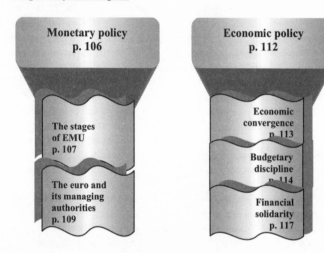

Economic and monetary union (EMU) is **an advanced stage of multinational integration** involving a common monetary policy and closely coordinated economic policies of the member states. EMU has to be based on a common market in goods and services, but is itself necessary for the proper functioning of the common market, as exchange rate variations between Member States' currencies hinder trade and investments.

In the early 1970s, the original six members of the European Economic Community tried already to establish an EMU and failed. The reasons were both external - the collapse of the international monetary system - and internal - the non-completion of the stage of the common market. This failure served, however, as a learning experience. The Member States of the European Community understood that they could not rush the multinational integration process, that they should complete the common market stage, adopt many accompanying common policies and commit themselves by treaty to the goal of EMU. The economic and monetary union initiated by the Maastricht Treaty [see section 2.2.] and completed for most Member States with the circulation of the euro is an evidence of the continuity of the multinational integration process [see section 1.1.2.].

7.1. The need for EMU

During the stage of the customs union, exchange rate variations are still possible and, to a certain extent, desirable, because the member states conserve the autonomy of their economic policies and can, by means of those variations, adjust their economies to the new conditions of competition prevailing between themselves and with the rest of the world. During the stage of the common market, however, the **exchange rate variations become more and more inconvenient** for the partners. While equal conditions of competition should prevail in a common market, the devaluation of the currency of a Member State could provide a competitive advantage to its industries, whereas the revaluation of the currency of another Member State could handicap its exports. In fact, **the devaluation** of the currency of a country which is a member of a common market could have an equivalent effect to imposing customs tariffs on all imported products and subsidising that country's exports. Conversely, **the revaluation** of a member country's currency would mean restricting its exports and encouraging its imports, factors which could get in the way of business expansion in countries with strong currencies.

A single market without a single currency is exposed to monetary and economic problems. On the **monetary level**, because of the possibility of upward or downward change in the value of certain currencies of the member states, there is an exchange risk in the event of credit sales to a business in a partner country, and this greatly restricts credit exports in member states. Indeed, an exchange rate adjustment, even a moderate one, may substantially alter the contractual obligations of firms operating in the different member states and at the same time affect the relative wealth of citizens and the purchasing power of consumers.

Currency fluctuations can penalise both investors who have financed their **foreign investments** by exporting capital from their countries and those who have had recourse to the resources of the host country. In the first case, devaluation of the currency of the country in which the investment took place or revaluation of the currency of the investor's country erodes the repatriated capital and profits. In the second case, devaluation in the investor's country or revaluation in the host country means higher amortisation and therefore a greater investment cost than expected. These risks could hinder businesses from investing in partner countries or from borrowing in them capital needed for their investments. Exchange risks, thus, would limit interpenetration of financial markets and therefore economic growth in a single market without a single currency.

From the **economic point of view**, if the common market were divided into autonomous markets as a result of divergent economic policies followed by the member states, the anticipated advantages, in particular economic growth and economic stability, would be greatly reduced. In reality, the interdependence of the economies of members of a common market accelerates the **transmission of cyclical fluctuations** and of the effects of measures intended to deal with them. Attainment of the economic objectives of a member state depends to a large extent on economic conditions in the other member states. An unfavourable economic situation in one member state leads to a reduction in its imports from the other members of the common market, which are affected in turn. On the other hand, a favourable economic situation in one member country has positive effects on the economies of the others and feedback effects on the former. If there were no coordination of economic policies, the differences in economic development - which would take the form of high interest rates in some member states and low rates in others and, conversely, of low exchange rates in the former and high exchange rates in the latter - could result in undesirable capital movements, that is to say from the poorest to the richest countries.

Negative effects can also ensue from **divergences in national short-term economic policies**. If, for example, a member state wished to pursue a deflationary policy by raising interest rates, whilst another member state followed an expansionist policy with low interest rates, capital would emigrate, for short-term investments, from the second country to the first and prevent the attainment of the objectives of both. Even if they pursued the same objectives, but by different means, two member states of a common market without a single currency could bring about undesirable movements of capital. If, for example, in order to pursue a deflationary policy, a state imposed quantitative restrictions on credit, whilst another raised interest rates, capital from the first might go to short-term investment in the second, causing balance of payments problems in the first and inflationary pressures in the second.

The semi-integration, or imperfect integration, which characterises a common market, generates situations that are unstable and in the long term intolerable for member states' economic policies. Those policies are no longer sufficient for regulating short-term economic situations because, firstly, some of their causes lie abroad and, secondly, some economic policy instruments are already beyond the control of the national authorities, including customs duties, import restrictions and export incentives [see sections 5.2. and 23.1.].It can be seen that the increasing interpenetration of the economies in a common market leads to a **dwindling of the independence of national short-term economic policies.** This means that the economies of the member states of a common market cannot be managed effectively by national authorities, i.e. the appropriate ministries and the central banks of those states. It becomes manifest that the loss of autonomy of the national economic and monetary policies of the member states of a common market needs to be counterbalanced by the establishment of a common economic and a single monetary policy. Hence, the member states of a common market that want to complete it need to pass to the next stage of multinational integration, which is that of economic and monetary union.

If economic conditions in the common market are to resemble those in an internal market, it is first and foremost necessary to eliminate exchange rate adjustments, which disrupt trade and investment by affecting in an unpredictable way their profitability. To this end, the member states of a common market must agree the full and **irreversible conversion of their currencies** at fixed parities or, better, **adopt a single currency**. In either case, they need to establish a monetary union within which transaction costs (the costs of foreign-exchange transactions or the costs of exchange rate cover) would disappear altogether. The second possibility, however, which was rightly preferred by the EU, has some additional advantages. The single currency permits a genuine comparison of prices of goods and services within the single market. It is one of the main exchange and reserve currencies in the world and it allows Europeans to pay for their imports from third countries in their own currency, without the intermediation of the dollar.

In other words, the single currency is a necessary attribute of a genuine single market. This is the reason why, in view of the completion of the single market, the Member States of the Community decided, in December 1991, in Maastricht to pursue the path of economic and monetary union. By greatly facilitating the functioning of the single market, the single currency should provide a stable macroeconomic environment, which would be of considerable benefit to businesses. Under *ceteris paribus* conditions, this environment should normally foster trade, improve the allocation of resources, encourage savings and investments, thus enhancing economic growth.

7.2. The single monetary policy

The Treaty of Rome did not provide for the monetary organisation of the Community because that Treaty aimed at the realisation of the first two stages of European integration: the customs union and the common. Moreover, at the time of drafting the EEC Treaty an international monetary organisation existed, namely the Bretton Woods system, which ensured the convertibility of all the currencies of the Western World at fixed parities. This system warranted monetary stability, which is indispensable in a common market.

It was just at the time when the Bretton Woods system collapsed, **in early 1971**, that the Member States of the Community **began their effort to organise their monetary affairs** in an economic and monetary union. Acting on a proposal from the Commission based on the "Werner Report", the Council and the Representatives of the Governments of the Member States expressed their political will to establish economic and monetary union in accordance with a phased plan beginning retroactively on 1 January

1971[1]. At the conclusion of that process the Community was to have constituted a single currency area within the international system, possessing such powers and responsibilities in economic and monetary matters as would enable its institutions to administer the union.

With hindsight, that initial effort looks like a headlong rush without sound foundations, as it was not based on a real common market. However, that initial effort enabled the Members States to acquire precious experience and devise instruments and mechanisms that were, in 1979, transferred to the European Monetary System (which tried with variable success to stabilise the exchange rates of the common market countries), have been improved over time and were used for the second effort at establishing an economic and monetary union in the 1990s. This second effort had a better foothold than the first. The common market stage had been completed [see section 6.1], the Member States had developed closer links through common policies and had engaged themselves in the Maastricht Treaty to advance to the stage of economic and monetary union [see section 2.2.].

7.2.1. The stages of EMU

The Treaty establishing the European Community, signed at Maastricht in 1991 [see section 2.2.], provided for the introduction of a single monetary policy based upon **a single currency managed by a single and independent central bank**. According to the Treaty, the primary objective of the single monetary policy and exchange rate policy should be to maintain price stability and, without prejudice to this objective, to support the general economic policies in the Community, in accordance with the principle of an open market economy with free competition. These activities of the Member States and the Community should entail compliance with the following guiding principles: stable prices, sound public finances and monetary conditions and a sustainable balance of payments (Art. 4 TEC).

The 1971 experience served the EU to prepare successfully the changeover to the single currency. Although economic and monetary union was envisaged as a single process, there were, in fact, **three stages involved**. The **first stage**, marking the beginning of the whole process, came with the entry into force of the Directive on the complete liberalisation of capital movements in July 1990 [see section 6.7.]. The central objectives of this stage were greater convergence of economic policies and closer cooperation between central banks, incorporating greater consistency between monetary practices in the framework of the European Monetary System[2].

As provided for in Article 118 of the EC Treaty, the **composition of the basket of the ecu** was "frozen" on 1 November 1993, the date of the entry into force of the Maastricht Treaty, on the basis of the composition of the basket (in amounts of each national currency) defined on 21st Septem-

---

[1]   OJ C 28, 27.03.1971, p. 1-4.
[2]   Decision 64/300, OJ L 77, 21.05.1964 and Decision 90/142, OJ L 78, 24.03.1990.

ber 1989 at the occasion of the entry into the basket of the peseta and the escudo. The European Council, meeting in Madrid on 15 and 16 December 1995, decided that, as of the start of stage three, **the name given to the European currency should be the euro,** a name that symbolises Europe and should be the same in all the official languages of the European Union, taking into account the existence of different alphabets, i.e. the Latin and the Greek.

The **second stage** of economic and monetary union began on 1st January 1994 and ended on 31 December 1998. During that stage, the Treaty on the European Community compelled each Member State to endeavour to avoid excessive public deficits and initiate steps leading to independence of its central bank, so that the future monetary union encompassed only countries which were well managed economically. Regulation 3605/93 laid down detailed rules and definitions for the application of the excessive deficit procedure (EDP), including the definition of public debt, as well as rules for the reporting of data by the Member States to the Commission, which fulfils the role of statistical authority in the context of the EDP[1]. In the process leading to the **independence of central banks**, the Treaty prohibited them from granting governments overdraft facilities or any other type of credit facility and from purchasing public sector debt instruments directly from them (Art. 101 TEC). Regulation 3605/93 clarified certain implications of this prohibition[2].

Together with the prohibition on the direct monetary financing of public deficits and in order to submit public borrowings to market discipline, the Treaty provided that public authorities should not have privileged access to financial institutions, unless this was based on prudential considerations (Article 102 TEC). The Treaty sought, thus, to institutionalise a sort of **market-induced budgetary control**. To this effect, Council Regulation 3604/93 defined the terms "privileged access", "financial institutions", "prudential considerations" and "public undertakings"[3].

In **preparation for the move to the third stage**, the Treaty required a high degree of convergence assessed by reference to **four specific criteria** [see also section 7.3.1.]: (a) a rate of inflation which is close to that of the three best performing Member States in terms of price stability; (b) a government budgetary position without a deficit that is excessive, meaning a government deficit not exceeding 3% of GNP and total government debt not greater than 60% of GNP (subject to an appraisement by the Council deciding by qualified majority); (c) the durability of convergence achieved by the Member State being reflected in the long-term interest rate levels; and (d) the observance of the normal fluctuation margins provided for by the Exchange Rate Mechanism of the European Monetary System for at least two years (Art. 121 TEC and Protocol on the excessive deficit procedure).

---

[1]   Regulation 3605/93, OJ L 332, 31.12.1993 and Regulation 2103/2005, OJ L 337, 22.12.2005.
[2]   Ibid.
[3]   Regulation 3604/93, OJ L 332, 31.12.1993.

Following the procedure and the timetable set out in the EC Treaty, the Council meeting at the level of Heads of State or Government on 3 May 1998, decided that 11 Member States **satisfied the necessary conditions for the adoption of the single currency** on 1 January 1999: Belgium, Germany, Spain, France, Ireland, Italy, Luxembourg, the Netherlands, Austria, Portugal and Finland. In July 2000, the Council agreed that Greece also fulfilled the convergence criteria and could therefore adopt the single currency. The Council had previously stated that Sweden did not at that stage fulfil the necessary conditions for the adoption of the single currency, because it did not participate in the mechanism of the European Monetary System. It did not examine whether the United Kingdom and Denmark fulfilled the conditions, because, in accordance with the relevant Treaty provisions, the United Kingdom notified the Council that it did not intend to move to the third stage of EMU on 1 January 1999 and Denmark notified the Council that it would not participate in the third stage of EMU. Member States benefiting from an "opt-out" and those which do not meet the criteria from the outset participate nevertheless in all the procedures (multilateral surveillance, excessive deficit...) designed to facilitate their future participation. The Governors of their central banks are members of the ECB General Council [see section 4.2.1]. Slovenia adopted the single currency on 1 January 2007[1]. Since 1 January 2008, the eurozone comprises 15 Member States, including Cyprus[2] and Malta[3].

7.2.2. The euro and its supervising authorities

Stage three of EMU began on 1 January 1999 with the irrevocable fixing of conversion rates between the currencies of the participating countries and against the euro[4]. The ecu was replaced by the euro, and this became a currency in its own right, the currency of those Member States which participate fully in the single monetary policy (Art. 123 TEC). Since that date, monetary policy and the foreign exchange rate policy have been conducted in euros, the use of the euro has been encouraged in foreign exchange markets and new tradeable public debt had to be issued in euros by the participating Member States. The participating Member States have a single monetary policy and a single currency - the euro[5]. They are monitored by the **European Central Bank (ECB)**, which replaced the European monetary Institute (provisional institution of the second stage) and formed together with the central banks of the Member States, the **European System of Central Banks (ESCB).** Neither the ECB nor national central banks may seek or take instructions from governments or Community institutions (Art. 108 TEC). The president, the vice-president and the

---

[1] Decision 2006/495, OJ L 195, 15.07.2006.
[2] Decision 2007/503, OJ L 186, 18.07.2007.
[3] Decision 2007/504, OJ L 186, 18.07.2007.
[4] Regulation 2866/98, OJ L 359, 31.12.1998 and Regulation 1478/2000, OJ L 167, 07.07.2000.
[5] Regulation 974/98, OJ L 139, 11.05.1998 and Regulation 2169/2005, OJ L 346, 29.12.2005.

other members of the Executive Board of the ECB were appointed by decision taken by common accord of the governments of the Member States, which adopted the single currency, after their appointments were endorsed by the European Parliament[1].

All central banks, including those not participating in the single monetary policy, are members of the ESCB from the start of the third stage. The **primary objective of the ESCB** is to maintain price stability. In addition, the ESCB must support the general economic policies in the Community with a view to contributing to the achievement of the objectives of the common policies referred to in Article 2 (TEC). The **basic tasks to be carried out through the ESCB** are: to define and implement the monetary policy of the Community; to conduct foreign exchange operations consistent with the provisions of Article 111 (TEC); to hold and manage the official foreign reserves of the Member States; and to promote the smooth operation of payment systems (Art. 105 TEC). However, exchange policy with regard to the currencies of third countries (US dollar, Japanese yen, etc.) is determined by the Council after consultation of the ECB (Article 111 TEC).

The **ECB** can adopt regulations and take decisions necessary for carrying out the tasks entrusted to the ESCB (Art. 110 TEC). National authorities must consult the ECB regarding draft legislation within its field of competence[2]. The ECB has powers to: apply minimum reserves and specify the remuneration of such reserves; impose fines and periodic penalty payments on firms for infringing its regulations or decisions[3]; and collect statistical information in order to carry out its tasks[4]. The ECB has the **exclusive right to authorise the issue of euro bank notes** within the Community. The ECB and the national central banks may issue such notes[5]. Member States may issue euro coins subject to approval by the ECB of the volume of the issue (Art. 106 TEC). The ECB must be consulted on any proposed Community act and may submit opinions to Community institutions or to national authorities on matters within its field of competence (Art. 105 TEC). A Council decision defines the scope and conditions of consultation of the Bank by national authorities concerning draft legislation within its field of competence[6].

The Amsterdam European Council of 16 and 17 June 1997 adopted a Resolution laying down the firm commitments of the Member States, the Commission and the Council regarding the implementation of the **Stability and Growth Pact** [see section 7.3.2.]. In this Pact Member States are committed to: respecting the medium term budgetary objective of "close to balance or in surplus" set out in their stability or convergence programmes;

---

[1] Recommendation 98/318, OJ L 139, 11.05.1998 and Decision 98/345, OJ L 154, 28.05.1998.
[2] Decision 98/415, OJ L 189, 03.07.1998.
[3] Regulation 2531/98, OJ L 318, 27.11.1998 and regulation 134/2002, OJ L 24, 26.01.2002.
[4] Regulation 2533/98, OJ L 318, 27.11.1998.
[5] Decision ECB/1998/6, OJ L 8, 14.01.1999.
[6] Decision 98/415, OJ L 189, 03.07.1998.

correcting excessive deficits as quickly as possible after their emergence; to make public, on their own initiative, recommendations made in accordance with Article 104 (TEC); and not seeking an exemption from the excessive deficit procedure unless they are in severe recession characterised by a fall in real GDP of at least 0,75%.

The Amsterdam European Council also agreed two Regulations that form part of the Stability and Growth Pact for ensuring budgetary discipline in the third stage of EMU. These Regulations set out a framework for **effective multilateral surveillance** and give precision to the excessive deficit procedure. The first concerns the continuity of contracts, the replacement of references to the ecu in legal instruments by references to the euro at a rate of one for one, the conversion rates and rounding rules[1]. In addition to this Regulation, the Directive on consumer protection in the indication of prices of products offered to consumers [see section 11.3.] sets down requirements concerning conversion rates, rounding rules, and the clarity and legibility of price displays[2]. The second Regulation provided for the conditions in which the currencies of the participating Member States would be replaced by the euro from 1 January 1999[3].

A Regulation on denominations and technical specifications of euro coins intended for circulation provided that the first series of euro currency would consist of eight coins (1 cent, 2 cent, 5 cent, 10 cent, 20 cent, 50 cent, 1 euro and 2 euro)[4]. In parallel with the introduction of the euro on 1 January 2002, bank charges for cross-border payments in euro were brought into line with those applying at national level[5]. A Council Framework Decision aims at increasing protection against counterfeiting in connection with the introduction of the euro[6], while two Regulations lay down the measures necessary to this effect[7]. Europol centralises and processes all information designed to facilitate the investigation, prevention and combating of euro counterfeiting[8]. The Pericles programme concentrates on promoting convergence of national measures so as to guarantee equivalent levels of protection of the euro against counterfeiting[9].

At the starting date of the third stage, on 1 January 1999, the **exchange rate mechanism (ERM)** has replaced the European Monetary System, in order to link currencies of Member States outside the euro area to the euro and help to ensure that they orient their policies to stability, foster convergence and thereby help them in their efforts to adopt the euro. However,

---

[1] Regulation 1103/97, OJ L 162, 19.06.1997 and Regulation 2595/2000, OJ L 300, 29.11.2000.
[2] Directive 98/6, OJ L 80, 18.03.1998.
[3] Regulation 974/98, OJ L 139, 11.05.1998 and Regulation 2169/2005, OJ L 346, 29.12.2005.
[4] Regulation 975/98, OJ L 139, 11.05.1998 and Regulation 423/1999, OJ L 52, 27.02.1999.
[5] Regulation 2560/2001, OJ L 344, 28.12.2001.
[6] Framework Decision 2000/383/JHA, OJ L 140, 14.06.2000 and Framework Decision 2001/888, OJ L 329, 14.12.2001.
[7] Regulations 1338/2001 and 1339/2001, OJ L 181, 04.07.2001.
[8] Decision 2005/511, OJ L 185, 16.07.2005.
[9] Decisions 2001/923 and 2001/924, OJ L 334, 21.12.2001 and Decision 2006/75, OJ L 36, 08.02.2006.

the voting rights of these Member States in the Council are suspended for all questions relating to the single currency. A central rate against the euro is defined for the currency of each Member State outside the euro area participating in the exchange rate mechanism. Accordingly, central rates are set for the "pre-in" currencies with a standard fluctuation band against the euro of 15% in either direction. Intervention at the margins will in principle be automatic and unlimited, with very short-term financing available, but the European Central Bank and the central banks of the other participants could suspend intervention if this were to conflict with their primary objective. On the other hand, formally agreed fluctuation bands narrower then the standard one and backed up in principle by automatic intervention and financing may be set at the request of the non-euro area Member State concerned[1].

At 00.00 on 1 January 2002, the national currencies of the twelve Euro-zone States ceased to exist. National notes and coins could be used in most countries for a further eight weeks at the most, but it was no longer possible to make payments in the old national currency units by card, cheque or transfer. After this short period of dual circulation, during which the old notes and coins were exchanged for the new ones, old banknotes can be exchanged for a period of ten years only at central banks. The European institutions and the governments of the participating Member States had carefully planned and therefore succeeded the tremendous enterprise of the changeover to the euro. What these authorities had not foreseen and hence neglected was the attempt by many providers of goods and services to profit from the rounding possibilities offered by the new currency. This uncontrolled profiteering has increased inflationary pressures in economies already depressed from the unstable international environment. Most vulnerable were the consumers accustomed to banknotes with a large number of zeros, like the Italians and the Greeks, who underestimated the price increases in euro. The responsible authorities should now do their best to keep prices down. They should also ensure the practical preparation of the new Member States for the future enlargement of the euro area[2].

7.3. The common economic policy

The Treaty of Rome had considered it desirable that the Member States **regard their economic policies as a matter of common concern**. Article 103 stipulated that they should consult each other and the Commission on the measures to be taken in the light of the prevailing circumstances. Pursuant to that provision of the Treaty, the Council set up an **Economic Policy Committee**[3]. That Committee, which consists of one representative for each Member State and a Commission representative,

---

[1] Resolution of the European Council, OJ C 236, 02.08.1997, p. 5-6.

[2] COM/2005/0545, 4 November 2005.

[3] Decision 2000/604, OJ L 257, 11.10.2000.

has the task of preparing the meetings of the **Economic and Financial Affairs (ECOFIN) Council**. It is also responsible for the exchange, on a reciprocal and continuing basis, of information on decisions or measures envisaged by the Member States which could have a considerable effect on the economies of the other Member States or on the internal or external equilibrium of the Member State concerned or which could give rise to a considerable gap between the development of the economy of a country and the jointly defined medium-term objectives.

7.3.1. Economic convergence in the European Union

In contrast to monetary policy, Member States **retain ultimate responsibility for economic policy** within the economic and monetary union. They are, however, required to act in such a way as to respect the principle of an open market economy where competition reigns, to regard their economic policies as a matter of common concern and to conduct them with a view to contributing to the achievement of the objectives of the Community (Art. 98 and 99 TEC). Thus, the common economic policy complements the single monetary policy.

Since the second stage of EMU, i.e. since the 1st January 1994, economic policies of the Member States are coordinated at Community level. A Council Decision of 1990 is directed towards the attainment of progressive convergence of economic performance of the Member States[1]. To this effect the **Economic and Financial Affairs Council (ECOFIN)**, acting by a qualified majority on a recommendation from the Commission, formulates, each year in the spring, a draft for the **broad economic policy guidelines (BEPGs)** of the Member States and of the Community, and reports its findings to the European Council. This discusses a conclusion on the broad guidelines of the economic policies of the Member States and of the Community. On this basis, the Commission recommends and the Council, acting on a qualified majority endorses the BEPGs, which lay down the common objectives in terms of inflation, public finance, exchange rate stability and employment (Art. 99 TEC)[2]. The BEPGs are at the centre of economic policy coordination in the European Union. They must be concise, concentrate on the main challenges facing the Union, with particular focus on the euro area, where coordination is most needed, and help to ensure that measures adopted in all Community economic coordination processes are consistent.

The Council, on the basis of reports submitted by the Commission[3], monitors economic developments in each of the Member States and in the Community as well as the consistency of economic policies with the broad guidelines (Art 121 TEC). This **multilateral monitoring** is based on con-

---

[1] Decision 90/141, OJ L 78, 24.03.1990.
[2] See for example the Recommendation of the Commission for 2003, COM (2003) 170, 8 April 2003 and Council Recommendation OJ L 195, 01.08.2003.
[3] See e.g., COM/2004/0020.

vergence programmes presented by each Member State which specifically aim at addressing the main sources of difficulty in terms of convergence (Art. 99,3 TEC). It also involves a review of budgetary policies, with particular reference to the size and financing of deficits, if possible prior to the drafting of national budgets [see section 7.3.2.]. Multilateral monitoring aims at obtaining from the Member States reciprocal engagements for an autonomous coordination of their policies.

Where it is established that the economic policies of a Member State are not consistent with these guidelines, the Council may, acting by a qualified majority, make the necessary recommendations to the Member State concerned. It may decide to make its recommendations public (Art. 99,4 TEC). **Where a Member State is in difficulties** or is seriously threatened with severe difficulties caused by exceptional occurrences beyond its control, the Council may, acting unanimously on a proposal from the Commission, grant, under certain conditions, Community financial assistance to the Member State concerned (Art. 100 TEC).

The move to the third stage of economic and monetary union has brought the economies of the Member States adopting the euro closer together. They share a single monetary policy and a single exchange rate. Economic policies and wage determination, however, remain a national responsibility, subject to the provisions of Article 104 (TEC) and of the Stability and Growth Pact. In order to ensure further convergence and the smooth functioning of the single market, non-participating Member States must be included in the coordination of economic policies. This is particularly true for those Member States which participate in the exchange rate mechanism (ERM 2) [see section 7.2.4.].

The **Lisbon strategy for growth and employment** [see section 13.3.2.] calls for synergy and complementarity between the Member States' own programmes and the Community programmes. The Community contributes to the overall economic and employment policy agenda with particular emphasis on a number of key actions with high added value, including: support for knowledge and innovation in Europe; reform of State aid policy; completion of the internal market for services; and support for efforts to deal with the social consequences of economic restructuring[1].

7.3.2. Budgetary discipline and the single currency

Budgetary policy is perhaps the area in which differences between Member States are still at their strongest. This stems from the fact that the budget is the most characteristic manifestation of national sovereignty in economic terms. The budget is in fact the main instrument of orientation of the economy in general and of individual government policies, such as regional, social, industrial policies, etc. Through its expenditure side the budget has a direct influence on public investment and an indirect influ-

---

[1]   COM/2005/0330, 20 July 2005.

ence, through aids of all sorts, on private investment. Through its revenue side the budget acts on savings and on the circulation of currency. Clearly, although it is difficult, coordination of budgetary policies is extremely important for economic convergence sought by the Treaty on European Union and for participation of a Member State in the third stage of EMU.

From the third stage of EMU, which began on 1 January 1999, the budgetary policies of the Member States are constrained by three rules: overdraft facilities or any other type of credit facility from the ECB or national central banks to public authorities (Community, national or regional) are prohibited (Art. 101 TEC); any privileged access of public authorities to the financial institutions are banned (Art. 102 TEC)[1]; neither the Community nor any Member State is liable for the commitments of public authorities, bodies or undertakings of a Member State (Art. 103 TEC). Implementing the new arrangements for economic policy coordination, the Council looks closely into actual and prospective developments in Member States' budgetary policies.

The Commission should monitor the development of the budgetary situation and the level of government debt in the Member States with a view to identifying gross errors. In particular it should examine compliance with **budgetary discipline** on the basis of the following two criteria [see also section 7.2.3.]: a) whether the ratio of the planned or actual government deficit to Gross Domestic Product exceeds a reference value (3% of GDP), unless either the ratio has declined substantially and continuously and reached a level that comes close to the reference value or, alternatively, the excess over the reference value is exceptional and temporary and the ratio remains close to the reference value; b) whether the ratio of government debt to gross domestic product exceeds a reference value (60% of GDP), unless the ratio is sufficiently diminishing and approaching the reference value at a satisfactory pace (Art. 104 TEC and Protocol on the excessive deficit procedure).

If a Member State does not fulfil the requirements under one or both of these criteria, the Commission shall prepare a report, taking into account all relevant factors. The Council shall, acting by a qualified majority on a recommendation from the Commission, decide whether an **excessive deficit** exists. Where the existence of an excessive deficit is decided, the Council shall make recommendations to the Member State concerned. If there is no effective action in response to its recommendations within the period laid down, the Council may, first, make its recommendations public and, then, decide by qualified majority certain measures to be taken by the recalcitrant Member State (Art. 104 TEC).

In view of the difficulties encountered by many Member States in respecting the criteria of the **Stability and Growth Pact (SGP)**, mentioned above [see section 7.2.4], the European Council meeting in Brussels (22-23 March 2005) agreed on the revision of the Regulations which provide for

---

[1] Regulations 3603/93, 3604/93 and 3605/93, OJ L 332, 31.12.1993.

prevention and correction of excessive deficits. Regulation 1466/97 introduced three principal changes to the **preventive arm of the SGP**[1]: (a) the medium-term budgetary objectives will take into account the diversity of economic and budgetary positions and their sustainability, ranging from a deficit of 1% of GDP to a position of balance or in surplus for euro area and the exchange rate mechanism (ERM-II) countries; (b) those countries that have not yet reached their medium-term budgetary objective should pursue an annual improvement of 0.5% of GDP in cyclically adjusted terms (with an extra effort being made in economic good times); (c) Member States that have implemented major structural reforms with a verifiable impact on the long-term sustainability of public finances will be allowed to deviate temporarily from the medium-term budgetary objective.

The purpose of Regulation 1467/97 (**corrective arm of the SGP**) is to speed up and clarify the implementation of the excessive deficit procedure, in particular as regards the sanctions to be imposed on Member States which fail to take appropriate measures to correct an excessive deficit[2]. The amendments introduced in June 2005 entail: a new definition of "severe economic downturn"; clarification of "other relevant factors", under the condition that the general government deficit remains close to the 3% ceiling and that the excess is temporary; extension of the deadlines for correcting any excessive deficit, in order to give a country more time to take effective and more permanent action rather than resort to one-off measures; asking Member States in an excessive deficit situation to achieve a minimum annual budgetary effort of at least 0.5% of GDP in structural terms. The economic policy strategy allows a flexible response to changing economic conditions in the short run whilst safeguarding and strengthening the productive capacity of the economy over the medium term. Member States are required to compile and transmit to the Commission data on their quarterly government debt[3].

7.3.3. Financial solidarity

The main Community instrument of financial solidarity is the **European Investment Bank** (EIB). According to Article 267 (TEC) the task of the EIB is to contribute, by having recourse to the capital market and utilising its own resources, to the balanced and steady development of the Community and the implementation of its policies. Thanks to its high credit rating, the Bank borrows on the best terms on the capital markets world-wide and on-lends to the Member States and their financial institutions - which distribute these global loans to SMEs. Since the EIB is a bank, it does not grant interest-rate reductions, but the financial institutions in the Member States and notably those whose vocation is regional devel-

---

[1]   Regulation 1466/97, OJ L 209, 02.08.1997 and Regulation 1055/2005, OJ L 174, 07.07.2005.
[2]   Regulation 1467/97, OJ L 209, 02.08.1997 and Regulation 1056/2005, OJ L 174, 07.07.2005.
[3]   Regulation 1222/2004, OJ L 233, 02.07.2004.

opment can borrow from the Bank and on-lend at more favourable terms. Some of the loans do have interest-rate subsidies attached, funded by the Community budget [see section 3.4.].

The EIB is a major source of finance for new industrial activities and advanced technology in sectors such as the motor vehicle industry, chemicals, pharmaceuticals, aeronautical engineering and information technologies. It also contributes to the establishment of trans-European telecommunications, transport and energy networks [see section 6.8.], reinforcement of industrial competitiveness [see sections 17.1. and 17.2.3.], environmental protection and cooperation in the development of third countries [see section 23.1.]. However, the main priority of the EIB is to contribute to the development of the least favoured regions of the European Union [see sections 12.1.1. and 12.3.]. These contributions account for around 70% of its financings in the Community.

Established in 1994, the **European Investment Fund (EIF)** is the specialist venture capital arm of the EIB Group. The EIF's tripartite share ownership structure - European Investment Bank (60%), European Commission (30%) and members of the banking sector (28 financial institutions) - facilitates the development of synergies between Community organs and the financial community, enhancing the catalytic effects of the EIB Group's action in support of small and medium enterprises (SMEs). The EIF's main objective is the financing of innovative and jobs creating SMEs through venture capital, in the Union and in the12 applicant countries [see section 17.2.3.]. Acting as a "fund of funds", it acquires stakes in public or private sector venture capital funds with a view of strengthening the ability of European financial institutions to inject equity capital into SMEs, especially those in the growth phase.

7.4. Appraisal and outlook

As happened with the first attempt at establishing an economic and monetary union in Europe, in 1971, the launch of the euro coincided with a highly adverse international economic and monetary situation: the terrorist attacks in New York and Madrid, the sizeable devaluation of the dollar, wars in Afghanistan and Iraq on Europe' doorstep and high energy prices, probably related to these wars. In this global situation, the economies of the eurozone have run into unexpected difficulties, largely due to outside factors: the strong competition in world markets from companies working with undervalued currencies; the equally strong competition from countries practicing social dumping, i.e. countries with no social protection and therefore extremely cheap labour force; high prices of imported oil; and last but not least, the precarious situation in the Middle East. In this adverse global situation, the euro has shielded the economies of the eurozone from competitive devaluations, galloping inflation and an increase in the prices of imports, more than 60% of which come from other euro countries. It is highly probable that if European economies had not the shield of the euro, they would have been in a much worse situation than the one in which they found themselves when the euro became the strongest currency in the world.

Despite the adverse global situation, the second effort at creating a European economic and monetary union was an unquestionable success, particularly in view of the great challenge of the changeover to the single currency. Not only was the physical introduction of the euro a historic event, it also represented an unprecedented strategic, logistical and practical challenge. From one day to the next, automatic cash dispensers (ATMs), instead of national currency, had to supply euro banknotes. Several million coin-operated machines and several hundred thousand ATMs had to be recalibrated. Some 15 billion euro banknotes and 50 billion euro coins replaced, in the space of a few weeks, a broadly equivalent quantity of national notes and coins in twelve countries with a combined population of some 310 million.

Citizens and businesses were certainly faced with formidable problems in adapting their habits to the new currency. For the former the problems were mainly psychological. They had to forsake their sentimental attachment to a national currency, in some cases very prestigious, as the Deutsche Mark and in some cases very old, like the Greek Drachma born more than 26 centuries ago. Consumers had to familiarise themselves with the euro and make the necessary effort to construct for themselves a new scale of values. Traders had to display prices and give change in euros. Businesses had to adapt their equipment, prepare to use a new currency and make the most of the increased competition within the single market resulting from greater price transparency. Despite these difficulties and the Cassandras' catastrophic prophesies, the euro was circulated successfully, thanks to an exemplary planning and cooperation of national and European authorities.

Moreover, in spite of the great advance of multinational integration brought about by the EMU, national sovereignties have not suffered unduly. The Member States, which have moved to the third stage of EMU, have undoubtedly **lost the autonomy of their monetary policy**, since they are no longer at liberty to use the two main levers of this policy - exchange rates and interest rates (a freedom which they had already lost to a large extent, due to the interdependence of the European economies). At the same time, however, they lost responsibility for the parity of their currency and the equilibrium of their balance of payments, while enjoying shared responsibility for the parity of the euro against the currencies of third countries and the equilibrium of the collective balance of payments of the eurozone countries. However, balance of current payments constraints exist for the zone as a whole. Therein lies the importance of the close coordination of economic policies.

The most direct "static gain" of the EMU is the ending, within the unified market, of all transaction costs inherent in the use of several currencies, costs representing between 0.3 and 0.4% of the GDP of the Union.

Travellers, who previously lost important amounts in the exchange of their currency for those of the countries they visited, should particularly welcome these gains. "Dynamic gains", which cannot be measured directly, could take two forms: those resulting from heightened productivity and those generated by the elimination of the uncertainties concerning the long-term evolution of exchange rates.

Supported by progress achieved by the Member States in economic convergence (sound public finances, very low inflation, exchange rate stability) and the mechanisms for closer coordination of economic policies put in place as part of the introduction of the euro, economic and monetary union has already made the European Union a pole of stability in a world tormented by constant financial crises. In addition, the euro allows a **better balance of the international monetary system**, dominated for half a century by the dollar, which serves as a reference currency for almost 60% of world trade, whereas American exports represent around 12% of world exports. Its economic and commercial weight (16% of world exports) entitles the Union to play an important role in the necessary review of the international monetary and financial system.

As a matter of fact, the economic and monetary union suffers from a disequilibrium between its strong monetary wing and its feeble economic one. The euro area is a monetary union working under a single monetary policy and **coordinated but decentralised economic policies**. While monetary policy management is the exclusive responsibility of the European Central Bank, economic and budgetary policies are a national prerogative. However, in an integrated monetary and economic zone, overspending and deficient restraint of inflation rates in some countries inflict a collective cost borne by all the countries sharing the same currency. There is a need, therefore, to reinforce existing economic, in particular fiscal, policy coordination mechanisms within the euro area.

Bibliography on the EMU

* AARLE BAS van, WEYERSTRASS Klaus (eds.). *Economic spillovers, structural reforms and policy coordination in the euro area.* Berlin: Springer, 2008.
* AGRAA Ali (ed.). *The European Union: economics and policies,* 8th ed. Cambridge: Cambridge University Press, 2007.
* COUNCIL OF THE EUROPEAN UNION, EUROPEAN COMMISSION. Economic and monetary union: Legal and political texts. Luxembourg: EUROP*, 2007.
* DE GRAUWE Paul. *Economics of monetary union.* Oxford: Oxford University Press, 2007.
* HANCKÉ Bob (et al. eds.). *Beyond varieties of capitalism: conflict, contradictions, and complementarities in the European economy.* Oxford: Oxford University Press, 2007.
* MAES Ivo. *Half a century of European financial integration: from the Treaty of Rome to the 21st century.* Bruxelles: Fonds Mercator, 2007.

- NEYER Ulrike. *The design of the Eurosystem's monetary policy instruments*. Heidelberg; New York: Physica-Verlag, 2007.
- PAGANETTO Luigi (ed.). *The political economy of the European Constitution*. Aldershot: Ashgate, 2007.
- ROY Joaquin, GOMIS-PORQUERAS Pedro (eds.). *The €uro and the dollar in a globalized economy*. Aldershot: Ashgate, 2007.
- TILLY Richard, WELFENS Paul, HEISE Michael. *50 years of EU economic dynamics: integration, financial markets and innovations*. Berlin: Springer, 2007.

DISCUSSION TOPICS

1. Why does a common market need a single currency in order to become a genuine internal market?
2. Why did the first attempt of the Community to create an economic and monetary union fail?
3. How does the common economic policy interact with the single monetary policy in an EMU?
4. Why is budgetary discipline indispensable in an EMU and how is it secured?
5. How does economic policy coordination affect the national sovereignty of member states participating in an EMU?

Chapter 8

TOWARDS A POLITICAL UNION

Diagram of the chapter

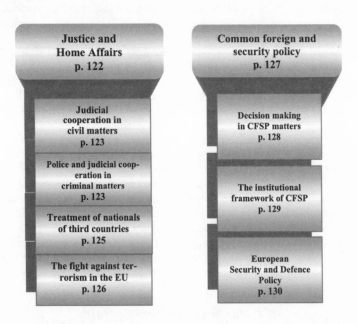

Justice and Home Affairs p. 122	Common foreign and security policy p. 127
Judicial cooperation in civil matters p. 123	Decision making in CFSP matters p. 128
Police and judicial cooperation in criminal matters p. 123	The institutional framework of CFSP p. 129
Treatment of nationals of third countries p. 125	European Security and Defence Policy p. 130
The fight against terrorism in the EU p. 126	

Political union is the last stage of the multinational integration process. It involves **common home and judicial policies and a common foreign and security policy**. According to the definition given above [see section 1.1.2.], a common policy entails a set of decisions, measures, rules and codes of conduct adopted by the common institutions set up by a group of states and implemented by the common institutions and the member states. A common policy does not exclude national policies, which continue to exist in all areas not covered by the decisions and rules agreed by the common institutions. Its development, however, requires the implementation by all the participating states of the common home and foreign policies agreed by the common institutions and the monitoring of this implementation by the common institutions. As long as these requirements are not met in certain sectors, political union, even though provided in a Treaty, is deficient or inexistent. In its place there may only exist intergovernmental political cooperation, leaving practically all freedom of action to the participants [see section 1.1.2].

At the same time as they were preparing the economic and monetary union stage, **at Maastricht in 1991**, europhilic nations were also projecting their political union. They, of course, encountered the opposition of their eurosceptic partners. The compromise solution that was found there and then was the division of the European Union into **two Treaties** (that of the European Community and that of the European Union) and into **three construction pillars**: the European Community - the first and main pillar; common foreign and security policy (CFSP); and justice and home affairs (JHA). The first and by far the more important Treaty (although coming second under the general heading of the Maastricht and now the Nice Treaties) and the first pillar were to direct and regulate the first three stages of European integration: the customs union, the common market and the projected economic and monetary union using the Community method of decision-making by the common institutions. The second Treaty and the second and third pillars were intended to direct and manage the stage of political union using the intergovernmental cooperation method.

It was soon apparent that this method was leading nowhere towards the construction of the second and third pillars of the Union and, therefore, the progress of political integration. The disappointment was most felt in the area of the third pillar, where there were matters of common interest to be regulated urgently: the free circulation of citizens and residents of the Member States, a common immigration policy and a common protection of the external borders of the Union from all sorts of illegal trafficking. These needs led to the revision of the European Union Treaty, at Amsterdam in 1997. Most of the justice and home affairs pillar was placed under the Community orbit, i.e. under the Community decision-making procedure.

8.1. Justice and home affairs

The common values underlining the objective of **an area of freedom, security and justice** are long-standing principles of the modern democracies of the European Union. The declared objective of the Union is to provide citizens with a high level of safety within an area of freedom, security and justice by developing **common action** among the Member States in the fields of police and judicial cooperation in criminal matters and by preventing and combating racism and xenophobia. The means that disposes the Union to this effect are: closer cooperation between police forces, customs authorities and other competent authorities in the Member States; closer cooperation between judicial and other competent authorities of the Member States; and approximation, where necessary, of rules on criminal matters in the Member States (Art. 29 TEU).

Whereas questions relating to the free movement of persons, asylum, immigration, the crossing of external borders and judicial cooperation depended on intergovernmental cooperation in the Maastricht version of the TEU [see section 2.2.], the Amsterdam revision of the TEU has integrated them into the Community framework [see section 2.3.]. This fact has important implications concerning notably the decision-making process [see section 4.3.] and the competence of the Court of Justice in both litigation and interpretation [see section 4.1.5.]. It also gives the citizens of the Member States, who are crossing internal borders without police controls, the sentiment of belonging to a union[1] [see section 9.2.]. Only **police cooperation and judicial cooperation in criminal matters** are now governed by an **intergovernmental framework** [see section 8.1.2.].

The European Council of Brussels (4-5 November 2004) adopted the so-called **Hague five-year programme** for strengthening freedom, security and justice in the EU. Its objective is to improve the common capability of the Union and its Member States to guarantee fundamental rights, to regulate migration flows, to fight organised cross-border crime and repress the threat of terrorism. The European Agency for the Management of Operational Cooperation at the External Borders (Frontex) strives to improve the integrated management of the external borders of the Member States[2].

The **Treaty of Lisbon** extends the community method to virtually all aspects of the field of justice and home affairs, thus abolishing the so-called third pillar of the Union [see section 3.1.]. The European Parliament and the Council, acting in accordance with the ordinary legislative procedure [see section 4.3], shall adopt measures developing notably: a common policy on visas and other short-stay residence permits; an integrated management system for external borders; a common policy on asylum; a common immigration policy (Articles 62 to 63a, Lisbon).

8.1.1. Judicial cooperation in civil matters

Judicial cooperation in civil matters is important since in a genuine European area of justice, individuals and businesses should not be prevented or discouraged from exercising their rights by the incompatibility or complexity of legal and administrative systems in the Member States. The main objective in this area is legal certainty and equal access to justice for all EU citizens, ensuring that people will not be treated unevenly according to the jurisdiction dealing with their case. The rules may be different provided that they are equivalent. The European Council of Tampere (15 and 16 October 1999), therefore, endorsed the principle of **mutual recognition of judicial decisions and judgments**, which is the cornerstone of judicial cooperation in both civil and criminal matters.

A Regulation on **jurisdiction and the recognition and enforcement of judgments** in civil and commercial matters, which replaced the 1968 Brussels Convention, lays down provisions concerning general jurisdiction and special jurisdiction in matters relating to insurance, consumer con-

---

[1] Decisions 1999/435 and 1999/436, OJ L 176, 10.07.1999.
[2] Regulation 2007/2004, OJ L 349, 25.11.2004 last amended by Regulation 863/2007, OJ L 199, 31.07.2007.

tracts, individual contracts of employment and some exclusive jurisdictions[1]. It also contains rules on prorogation, examination, admissibility, enforcement of judgments, authentic instruments and court settlements. Another Regulation established a general framework for activities aiming to **facilitate the implementation of judicial cooperation** in civil matters[2].

8.1.2. Police and judicial cooperation in criminal matters

Police and judicial cooperation in criminal matters (PJCCM) means that criminal behaviours should be approached in the same way throughout the Union. Article 29 of the TEU declares that the Union's objective is to provide citizens with **a high level of safety** within an area of freedom, security and justice. The Union is set to achieve this objective by preventing and combating crime, organised or otherwise, in particular terrorism, trafficking in persons and offences against children, illicit drug or arms trafficking, corruption and fraud. In the areas of PJCCM, Member States must inform and consult one another within the Council with a view to coordinating their action. To that end, they must establish collaboration between the relevant departments of their administrations (Art. 34 TEU).

In police and judicial cooperation in criminal matters the Council may, acting unanimously on the initiative of any Member State or of the Commission: (a) adopt **common positions** defining the approach of the Union to a particular matter; (b) adopt **framework decisions** for the purpose of approximation of the laws and regulations of the Member States, which are binding on the latter as to the result to be achieved but leave to the national authorities the choice of form and methods; (c) adopt **decisions** for any other purpose, which are binding but do not entail direct effect and must be implemented by the necessary measures adopted by the Council acting by a qualified majority; and (d) establish **conventions**, which, once adopted by at least half of the Member States, enter into force for those Member States, and may be implemented by measures adopted within the Council by a majority of two-thirds of the Contracting Parties (Art. 34 TEU).

The Council must consult the **European Parliament** before adopting any of the above measures and must give it adequate time to deliver its opinion, but is free to take or not take account of this opinion (Art. 39 TEU). Hence, the Parliament has a consultative role, but no co-decision or cooperation role in the field of PJCCM [see section 4.3.]. The competence of the **Court of Justice** of the European Communities is limited in giving preliminary rulings on the validity and interpretation of framework decisions and decisions, and on the validity and interpretation of the measures implementing them.

Judicial cooperation in criminal matters includes: cooperation between the competent ministries and judicial authorities of the Member

---

[1]   Regulation 44/2001, OJ L 12, 16.01.2001 and Regulation 2245/2004, OJ L 381, 28.12.2004.
[2]   Regulation 743/2002, OJ L 115, 01.05.2002.

States in relation to proceedings and the enforcement of decisions; facilitation of the extradition between Member States; compatibility of rules applicable in the Member States; prevention of conflicts of jurisdiction between Member States; and the progressive establishment of common rules relating to the constituent elements of criminal acts and to penalties in the fields of organised crime, terrorism and illicit drug trafficking (Art. 31 TEU).

Police cooperation is organised both directly and through the **European Police Office (Europol)**. The Council should notably: enable Europol to coordinate specific investigative actions by the competent authorities of the Member States and assist them in investigating cases of organised crime; promote liaison arrangements between prosecuting/investigating officials; and establish a research, documentation and statistical network on cross-border crime (Art 30 TEU). The **Europol Convention** was signed on 26 June 1995[1]. Europol's remit includes the fight against terrorism[2] and against serious forms of international crime[3]. The tasks of Europol include also the exchange and analysis of information and intelligence relating to illicit drug trafficking, trafficking in nuclear substances, clandestine immigration networks, traffic in human beings and illicit vehicle trafficking[4].

Member States which intend to **establish enhanced cooperation** between themselves in the field of PJCCM may be authorised to make use of the institutions, procedures and mechanisms laid down by the Treaties (including the Community decision-making process and Court competence) provided that the cooperation proposed respects the powers of the European Community and aims at developing more rapidly an area of freedom, security and justice (Art. 40 TEU).

8.1.3. Common treatment of nationals of third countries

The **abolition of checks at internal borders** of the Community is effective both for the citizens of the Member States and for third country nationals, once they have crossed the external frontiers of a Member State. In other words, freedom of movement applies to all those within the territory of the Community. This is why the Member States must have common rules for the crossing of their borders by foreigners and for the treatment of foreigners within their territory. This common need has led to the adoption of common policies in the fields of visas, immigration, the right of asylum, the status of refugees and extradition. Thus, the Member States have established a Community Code on the rules governing the movement of persons across borders (Schengen Borders Code)[5] [see section 9.2]. A Directive determines: (a) the terms for conferring and withdrawing long-term resident

---

[1] Council Act OJ C 316, 27.11.1995 and Decision, OJ C 362, 18.12.2001.

[2] Decision, OJ C 26, 30.01.1999, p. 22.

[3] Decision, OJ C 362, 18.12.2001, p. 41.

[4] Joint Action 96/748/JHA, OJ L 342, 31.12.1996.

[5] Regulation 562/2006, OJ L 105, 13.04.2006.

status granted by a Member State in relation to third-country nationals legally residing in its territory, and the rights pertaining thereto; and (b) the
terms of residence in Member States other than the one which conferred
long-term status on them for third-country nationals enjoying that status[1].

The **framework programme on solidarity and management of migration flows** for the period 2007-2013 is designed to improve management of migratory flows at the level of the European Union and to
strengthen solidarity between Member States[2]. The programme is assisted
by four funds: the External Borders Fund; the European Refugee Fund; the
European Fund for integration of third-country nationals; and the European
Return Fund.

8.1.4. The fight against terrorism inside the EU

The **common policy for the fight against terrorism** has two wings:
one in the realm of justice and home affairs policy; and one attached to the
European security and defence policy [see section 8.2.3]. In the light of the
attacks in the United States on 11 September, the Council decided to set up
within Europol a team of counter-terrorist specialists, whose remit includes
the following tasks: to collect in a timely manner all relevant information
and intelligence concerning the current threat; to analyse the collected information and undertake the necessary operational and strategic analysis.

A framework decision aims to approximate the **definition of terrorist offences** in all Member States, including those offences relating to terrorist groups, and to provide for penalties and sanctions for natural and legal persons who have committed or are responsible for such offences[3]. A
Directive aims at the prevention of the use of the financial system for the
purpose of money laundering and terrorist financing[4] [see section 6.7]. On
the other hand, a regulation obliges the Member States to incorporate in
new passports a digital photograph and fingerprints of the holder. It also
harmonises security standards for the production of passports and other
travel documents issued by the Member States[5]. The **Judicial Cooperation
Unit, Eurojust**, brings together Member States' magistrates (prosecutors,
judges or police officers) specialising in counter-terrorism in order to examine any measure whereby current investigations into terrorism can be
properly coordinated[6].

---

[1] Directive 2003/109, OJ L 16, 23.01.2004.
[2] COM/2005/123, 06.04.2005.
[3] Decision 2002/475, OJ L 164, 22.06.2002.
[4] Directive 2005/60, OJ L 309, 25.11.2005.
[5] Regulation 2252/2004, OJ L 385, 29.12.2004.
[6] Decision 2002/187, OJ L 63, 06.03.2002 and Decision 2003/659, OJ L 245, 29.09.2003.

8.2. Common foreign and security policy

According to the European Union Treaty, the **objectives of CFSP** are: to safeguard the common values, fundamental interests, independence and integrity of the Union; to strengthen the security of the Union in all ways; to preserve peace and strengthen international security, in accordance with the principles of the UN Charter, the Helsinki Final Act and the Paris Charter; to promote international cooperation; to develop and consolidate democracy and the rule of law, as well as respect for human rights and fundamental freedoms (Art. 11 TEU). However, in order to pursue these ambitious objectives, the TEU gives the common institutions some means dependent on an **intergovernmental cooperation method**: defining the principles of and general guidelines for the common foreign and security policy; deciding on common strategies; adopting joint actions; adopting common positions; and strengthening systematic cooperation between the Member States in the conduct of policy (Art. 12 TEU).

In the framework of their **systematic cooperation** the Member States must inform and consult one another within the Council on any matter of foreign and security policy of general interest in order to ensure that their combined influence is exerted as effectively as possible (Art. 16 TEU) [see chapter 25]. The diplomatic and consular missions of the Member States and the Commission delegations in third countries and their representations in international organisations must step up cooperation by exchanging information, carrying out joint assessments and contributing to the implementation of the CFSP (Art. 20 TEU).

Member States must **coordinate their action in international organisations** and at international conferences. All the Member States or those participating in such fora must uphold the common positions and keep each other informed of any matter of common interest. Member States which are permanent or temporary members of the United Nations Security Council must keep the other Member States fully informed and ensure the defence of the positions and the interests of the Union (Art. 19 TEU).

According to the **Treaty of Lisbon** (which imitates again the Constitutional Treaty), the Union's competence in matters of common foreign and security policy shall cover all areas of foreign policy and all questions relating to the Union's security, including the progressive framing of a common defence policy that might lead to a common defence (Article 10 C, Lisbon = Article I-16, Constitution). But this so-called "common policy" will still be conducted by intergovernmental cooperation [see the European perspectives in the conclusions].

8.2.1. Decision-making in CFSP matters

There are several departures from the Community method [see section 4.3.] concerning decision-making in CFSP matters. Whereas in Community decision-making only the Commission has the right to propose and hence the responsibility to define the common interest and ensure the coherence of action, in CFSP all the Member States and the Commission have the power to propose. The risks are inconsistency of the proposed action with the other policies of the EC/EU and disregard of the interests of the Member States in the minority, which cannot block the proposal. There are also two independent executive organs of the policy, since the Commission entrusts one of its members with the responsibility of the external relations of the Community and the Council appoints its Secretary General as High Representative for CFSP. Here again there is a risk of incoherence in the management of policy instruments and resources. Finally and most importantly, instead of the classical forms of Community acts [see section 3.3.], CFSP decisions take special forms, are usually taken by the Council acting unanimously and are not subjected to the control of the Court of Justice.

It transpires that the CFSP method is an improved intergovernmental cooperation method, but not much more than that. Probably, the most useful improvement is the definition by the European Council of **common strategies** in areas where the Member States have important interests in common. Since the definition of common strategies depends on the identification of common interests by the majority of the Member States, common strategies are a useful framework to find strategic answers to international crises and to increase the Union's efficiency by permitting decisions to be taken **by majority voting** (subject to the remark above). Common strategies set out their objectives, duration and the means to be made available by the Union and the Member States. On the basis of the general guidelines defined by the European Council, the Council takes the decisions necessary for defining and implementing the CFSP, usually by unanimous voting. It recommends common strategies to the European Council and implements them (Art. 13 TEU).

Common positions adopted by the Council define the approach of the Union to a particular matter of a geographical or thematic nature. Member States must ensure that their national policies conform to the common positions (Art 15 TEU). Article 3 of the Union Treaty contains an obligation to ensure the consistency of the Union's activities. Therefore, a common position adopted on the basis of Article 12 (TEU), while respecting the division of responsibilities set out in the Treaty, has to be compatible with the guidelines governing the EU's economic relations with a third country and with the objectives and priorities of its external policies, although it is the European Community that is responsible for adopting practical measures [see introduction to Part VI].

Joint actions adopted by the Council address specific situations where operational action by the Union is deemed to be required. They lay down their objectives, scope, the means to be made available to the Union, if necessary their duration, and the conditions for their implementation. Joint actions commit the Member States to the positions they adopt and in the conduct of their activity. Whenever a Member State plans to adopt a national position or take national action pursuant to a joint action, it must provide information in time to allow, if necessary, for prior consultations within the Council. Member States may take the necessary measures as a matter of urgency having regard to the general objectives of the joint action, and inform the Council immediately of any such measures (Art. 14 TEU).

8.2.2. The institutional framework of CFSP

Subject to the requirement laid down in Article 3 of the EU Treaty for the Council and the Commission **to ensure consistency in external relations**, and in accordance with their respective responsibilities under the Treaties, the Presidency, the Secretary-General/High Representative and the Commissioner for external relations, must cooperate closely in order to ensure overall continuity and coherence of action by the Union in external relations [see introduction to Part VI].

The Secretary-General of the Council, who is the **High Representative for the CFSP**, assists the Council in the matters coming within the scope of the CFSP, by contributing, in particular, to the formulation, preparation and implementation of policy decisions and, at the request of the Presidency, by conducting political dialogue with third parties (Art. 26 TEU). More specifically, according to the Helsinki European Council (10-11 December 1999), the High Representative of the Union **has the following tasks**:

- assist the Presidency in coordinating work in the Council to ensure coherence on the various aspects of the Union's external relations;
- contribute to preparing policy decisions and formulating options for the Council on foreign and security policy matters, so that it constantly focuses on the major political issues requiring an operational decision or political guidance;
- contribute to the implementation of foreign and security policy decisions in close coordination with the Commission, Member States and other authorities responsible for effective application on the ground.

The Presidency represents the Union in all matters falling within the CFSP. It is responsible for the implementation of common measures and expresses the position of the Union in international organisations and conferences. The Commission is closely involved in those tasks of the Presidency. The latter is assisted by the High Representative for the CFSP and may be assisted by the next Member State to hold the Presidency (Art. 18 TEU). The Presidency must consult the European Parliament on the main aspects and the basic choices of the CFSP and must ensure that its views are duly taken into consideration (Art. 21 TEU).

The **Treaty of Lisbon**'s principal amendment to the CFSP provisions of the Treaty on European Union is the reinforcement of the role of the **High Representative of the Union** for Foreign Affairs and Security Policy; repeating the role of the Union Minister for Foreign Affairs of the stillborn Constitution. Like the Union Minister, the High Representative of the Union will wear two hats, being both one of the Commission's Vice-Presidents and the President of the Foreign Affairs Council. This association of the Commission and the Council in the person of the High Representative of the Union can be beneficial for the common foreign and security policy. Exercising the right of initiative of the Commission, the High Representative shall contribute to the development of the CFSP, which he or she shall carry out as mandated by the Council. The same would apply to the common security and defence policy (Article 9 E, Lisbon). He or she shall have responsibilities incumbent on the Commission in external relations and for coordinating the CFSP with other aspects of the Union's external action. By presiding over the Foreign Affairs Council, the High Representative of the Union shall contribute by his proposals to the preparation of common foreign and security policy and ensure implementation of decisions adopted by the European Council and the Council of Ministers. The High Representative shall represent the EU in matters concerning the common foreign and security policy, conduct political dialogue on the Union's behalf and express the Union's position in international organisations and at international conferences and forums (Article 13a, Lisbon).

8.2.3. European security and defence policy

Common foreign and security policy covers all questions related to the security of the European Union, including the **progressive framing of a European security and defence policy (ESDP)**, which might in time lead to a common defence, should the European Council so decide. It shall in that case recommend to the Member States the adoption of such a decision in accordance with their respective constitutional requirements. The progressive framing of a common defence policy will be supported, when considered appropriate, by cooperation between the Member States in the field of armaments (Art. 17 TEU). The language used here gives an indication of the Member States' extreme caution in venturing into the field of common defence involving, in the long term, the integration of their Armed Forces. According to the Brussels European Council (October 1993) this policy must be aimed in particular at reducing risks and uncertainties which could impair the territorial integrity and political independence of the Union and of its Member States, their democratic nature, their economic stability and the stability of the neighbouring regions.

To assume their responsibilities across the full range of conflict prevention and crisis management tasks defined in the EU Treaty, the so-called **Petersberg tasks**, the Member States, at the Helsinki European Council (10-11 December 1999), have decided to **develop more effective military capabilities** and establish new political and military structures for these tasks. In this connection, the objective is for the Union to have an autonomous capacity to take decisions and, where NATO as a whole is not engaged, to launch and then to conduct EU-led military operations in response to international crises. For this purpose, a "common European **headline goal**" was set: to deploy 60 000 men in less than 60 days and to sustain them for at least one year, for the purpose of EU-led conflict prevention and crisis management tasks (Petersberg tasks). Although the goal was attained in 2003, the capability development mechanism (CDM) presents several problems, such as command and control arrangements for operational headquarters, the principles and framework for capability requirements and coordination and synergy with NATO. The "2010 headline goal" is the capability to deploy forces on the ground no later than 10 days after the decision to launch the operation.

To pursue the headline goal of the European Security and Defence policy (ESDP), the following permanent **political and military bodies** have been established within the Council:
(a) a standing **Political and Security Committee (PSC)** in Brussels, composed of national representatives of senior/ambassadorial level, deals with all aspects of the CFSP, including the common European security and defence policy. In the case of a military crisis management operation, the PSC will exercise, under the authority of the Council, the political control and strategic direction of the operation[1];
(b) the **Military Committee (MC)**, composed of the chiefs of defence or their military delegates and a Chair appointed by the Council on the Committee's recommendation, gives military advice, makes recommendations to the PSC and provides military direction to the Military Staff[2];
(c) the **Military Staff (MS)**, composed of military personnel seconded from Member States to the General Secretariat of the Council, provides military expertise and support to the ESDP, including the conduct of early warning, situation assessment and strategic planning for Petersberg tasks including identification of European national and multinational forces[3].

According to the Helsinki European Council, all Member States (defence ministers) are entitled to participate fully and on an equal footing in all decisions and deliberations of the Council and Council bodies on EU-led operations, but the commitment of national assets by Member States to such operations will be **based on their sovereign decision**. Russia, Ukraine and other European States engaged in political dialogue with the Union and other interested States may be invited to take part in the EU-led operations. A "European capability action plan", agreed by the Council on

[1] Decision 2001/78, OJ L 27, 30.01.2001.
[2] Decision 2001/79, OJ L 27, 30.01.2001.
[3] Decision 2001/80, OJ L 27, 30.01.2001 and Decision 2008/298, OJ L 102, 12.04.2008.

19 November 2001, should incorporate all the efforts and investments, developments and coordination measures executed or planned at both national and multinational level with a view to improving existing resources and gradually developing the capabilities necessary for the Union's activities. The Council established a mechanism, called "Athena" having the necessary legal capacity for the financing of EU operations with military or defence implications[1].

Article 17 of the EU Treaty does not rule out the development of **closer cooperation between two or more Member States** on a bilateral level, in the framework of the Western European Union (WEU) and the Atlantic Alliance, provided such cooperation does not run counter to or impede multilateral cooperation. Thus, on 5 November 1993, France, Germany and Belgium took the important initiative of placing under common command certain units of their armies. The **Eurocorps**, which is placed under the authority of a "Joint Committee" made up of the Heads of Staff and political directors of the three countries, could be used autonomously by these three countries, or else placed at the disposal of NATO and the WEU.

The same Article 17 (TEU) underlines that the policy of the Union does not prejudice the specific character of the security and defence policy of certain Member States, respects the obligations of certain Member States under the **North Atlantic Treaty Organisation (NATO)** and is compatible with the common security and defence policy established within that framework. For the Member States concerned, this means that the actions and decisions they undertake within the framework of EU military crisis management will respect at all times all their Treaty obligations as NATO allies. In the case of an EU-led operation using NATO assets and capabilities, non-EU European allies will, if they wish, participate in the operation, and will be involved in its planning and preparation in accordance with the procedures laid down within NATO.

The **European Defence Agency (EDA)** was set up in 2004 in order to develop projects and programmes aimed at supporting the development of European security and defence policy[2]. Subject to the Council's authority and open to participation by all willing Member States, the Agency aims at developing defence capabilities in the field of crisis management, promoting and enhancing European armaments cooperation, strengthening the European defence industrial and technological base (DTIB), creating a competitive European defence equipment market and promoting research aimed at leadership in strategic technologies for future defence and security capabilities.

The European Council met in extraordinary session on 21 September 2001 in order to analyse the international situation following the terrorist attacks in the United States and to impart the necessary impetus to the ac-

---

[1] Decision 2004/197, OJ L 63, 28.02.2004 and Decision 2005/68, OJ L 27, 29.01.2005.

[2] Joint action 2004/551/CFSP, OJ L 245, 17.07.2004, last amended by Joint Action 2008/299, OJ L 102, 12.04.2008.

tions of the European Union. Stating that terrorism is a real challenge to the world and to Europe, the European Council has decided that **the fight against terrorism** will, more than ever, be a priority objective of the European Union.

In the light of the **terrorist attacks in Madrid** on 11 March 2004, the Brussels European Council (25-26 March 2004) decided to revise the EU's action plan to combat terrorism, setting the following objectives: deepen the international consensus and enhance international efforts to combat terrorism; reduce the access of terrorists to financial and other economic resources; maximise capacity within EU bodies and Member States to detect, investigate and prosecute terrorists and prevent terrorist attacks; protect the security of international transport and ensure effective systems of border control; enhance the capability of the European Union and of Member States to deal with the consequences of a terrorist attack; address the factors which contribute to support for, and recruitment into, terrorism. Moreover, the European Council declared that in the spirit of the solidarity clause laid down in Article I-43 of the draft Treaty establishing a Constitution for Europe, the Member States and the acceding States shall act jointly in a spirit of solidarity mobilise all the instruments at their disposal, including military resources, if one of them is the victim of a terrorist attack.

According to the **Treaty of Lisbon** (following the defunct Constitutional Treaty), those Member States whose military capabilities fulfil higher criteria and which have made more binding commitments to one another in this area with a view to the most demanding missions shall establish permanent structured cooperation within the Union framework (Article 28 A.6, Lisbon = Articles I-41.6 and III-312, Constitution). Such cooperation shall be governed by Article 28 E and by the **Protocol on permanent structured cooperation**. The latter specifies that such cooperation shall be open to any Member State which undertakes to: (a) proceed more intensively to develop its defence capacities through the development of its national contributions and participation, where appropriate, in multinational forces, in the main European equipment programmes, and in the activity of the Agency in the field of defence capabilities development, research, acquisition and armaments (European Defence Agency), and (b) have the capacity to supply by 2010 at the latest targeted combat units for the missions planned, structured at a tactical level as a battle group capable of carrying out the tasks referred to in Article 28 B of the Treaty on European Union, within a period of 5 to 30 days, in particular in response to requests from the United Nations Organisation, and which can be sustained for an initial period of 30 days and be extended up to at least 120 days.

8.3. Appraisal and outlook

The two wings of the last storey of the European edifice are built at uneven pace. The wing of internal affairs has much advanced, while the wing of external affairs is far behind. This is due to the different methods used for the construction of each one. The perception of the need for a **common policy in internal affairs** has led to the effective disbanding of the so-called third pillar of the Union and to the placement of most subjects concerning it inside the principal edifice of the Community managed by the Community decision-making procedure. Thus, much progress was made since the entry into force of the Treaty of Amsterdam and particularly since the programme set by the Tampere European Council for the creation of an **area of freedom, security and justice**. The achievements of the common policy include: reinforcement of the rights of citizens and their families to move and reside freely in the territory of the Union; foundations of a common immigration and asylum policy; consolidation of the integrated management of external borders; better access to justice, notably through application of the principle of mutual recognition in the civil and commercial spheres; introduction of a European arrest warrant; and cooperation through legislation to combat cross-border crime and terrorism. In the aftermath of the terrorist attacks of 11 September 2001, Member States reinforced their **counter-terrorism** machinery in addition to enhancing international cooperation. They also assessed their counter-terrorism capacity, adopting new laws and allocating additional financial or personnel resources to strengthen their machinery. Nowadays, the greatest challenge of the Union in this area is tackling the root causes of **illegal migration** by its aid to development policy, notably through the promotion of economic growth, good governance and the protection of human rights in countries of origin [see section 24.1].

To safeguard its area of freedom, security and justice, the Union must also develop a capacity to act and be regarded as a significant partner on the international scene. This is the objective of the foreign policy of the Union. The Treaty on the EU invites the Union to "assert its identity on the international scene", but it does not give it the instruments to pursue this goal effectively. Certainly, some progress has been made. The **common foreign and security policy** (CFSP) has been given in Amsterdam more coherent instruments and a more effective decision-making procedure. Common strategies and "constructive abstention" give the possibility to the European Council and the Council to act by qualified majority, even if some Member States do not agree with a common policy. Through the recent development of the European security and defence policy (ESDP) and the strengthening of its capabilities, both civil and military, the Union has established crisis-management structures and procedures which enable it to launch and carry out military crisis-management operations.

But there is still much confusion in the external activities of the Union and its Member States are **still not speaking with a single voice** in the scene of world affairs. It is no wonder, therefore, that the Member States of the Union were radically divided when their supposedly common foreign and security policy was tested for the first time: the March 2003 war and occupation of Iraq under American aegis, without the consent of the Security Council of the United Nations. The prevailing intergovernmental co-operation, even if improved by the Constitutional Treaty, cannot lead to a really common policy. The very term "common foreign and security policy" is misleading. The citizens hear "common policy" and do not see anything resembling that. If the Treaty called for a cooperation in foreign and security policy, the citizens would at least understand better what is meant by it. Now, they rightly believe that they are derided when their political leaders speak about a common policy and at the first test of such a policy hide behind their national interests (real or imaginary), in order to undermine it. The truth is that a common policy cannot be achieved with intergovernmental cooperation.

To assume its responsibilities as a global power, the EU should **rule out the use of unanimity** and hence of the veto in the common foreign and security policy. This policy should be given the necessary resources (budget, efficient procedures, network of external delegations, etc.). The actual functions of the High Representative for the CFSP and of the Commissioner for External Relations should be merged into the tasks of the Minister for Foreign Affairs (envisaged by the Constitutional Treaty), ensuring coherent single representation of collective EU external interests, a leading role in crisis management and consistency with other common policies such as trade and aid to development. The Commissioner/High Representative for External Relations should be proposed by the European Council and named by the European Parliament [see section 4.4.]. Finally, the two wings of the foreign and security policy should back each other and make a coherent whole, because a foreign policy that cannot be enforced cannot be respected.

The same considerations apply to the common defence policy. The Community decision-making method should be applied to the European security and defence policy (ESDP), thus making it really common and truly European. The ESDP should be based on a common armament policy, which could rationalise, boost and make more competitive the armaments industries of the Member States. This could mean, inter alia, that the single market and common commercial policy could be applied to the defence industries. This integration could alleviate the current deficiencies of European military capabilities in the field of intelligence, logistics, communications and air transport systems. Effective public procurement and standardisation of armaments industries could help restructure, rationalise and strengthen European defence. When Europe realised its full defence potential, it would be ready to assume its role as a global player.

Bibliography on JHA and CFSP

- CAPE Ed (et al. eds.). *Suspects in Europe: procedural rights at the investigative stage of the criminal process in the European Union*. Antwerpen: Intersentia, 2007.
- CULLEN Peter, BUONO Laviero, FICHERA Massimo. "Creating an area of criminal justice in the EU: putting principles into practice", in *ERA-Forum: scripta iuris europaei*, v. 8, n. 2, June 2007, p. 169-287.

- EDER Franz, MANGOTT Gerhard, SENN Martin (eds.). Transatlantic discord: combating terrorism and proliferation, preventing crises. Baden-Baden: Nomos, 2007.
- EUROPEAN COMMISSION. The role of Eurojust and the European Judicial Network in the fight against organised crime and terrorism in the European Union. Luxembourg: EUR-OP, 2007.
- HOUSE OF LORDS. EUROPEAN UNION COMMITTEE. *Current developments in European defence policy*: report with evidence. London: Stationery Office, 2007.
- KIRCHNER Emil, SPERLING James. *EU security governance*. Manchester; New York: Manchester University Press, 2007.
- MONAR Jörg. "The EU's approach to post-September 11: global terrorism as a multidimensional law enforcement challenge", in *Cambridge review of international affairs*, v. 20, n. 2, June 2007, p. 267-283.
- PALADINI Luca. "The contribution of the Security Policy to the coherence of the European Union's external action", in *Studi sull'integrazione europea*, v. II, n. 1, 2007, p. 111-142.
- SPENCE David (ed.). *The European Union and terrorism*. London: John Harper, 2007.
- VAN SLIEGERT Elies, PADFIELD Nicola. "The European Arrest Warrant: between trust, democracy and the rule of law", in *European constitutional law review: EuConst*, v. 3, n. 2, 2007, p. 244-268.

DISCUSSION TOPICS

1. Discuss the treatment of the common justice and home affairs policy in the Treaties of Maastricht and Amsterdam.
2. Should nationals of third countries be treated in the same way by all member states of a common market?
3. Comment on the development of the common foreign and security policy through the stages of the customs union, the common market and the economic and monetary union.
4. Compare the Community decision-making process, explained in section 4.2., to decision-making concerning the common foreign and security policy.
5. Do you perceive a spillover of economic into political integration in the case of the EC/EU or do you consider that the two processes develop independently from each other?

Part III: Policies concerning the citizens

European citizens are present at and are taking part both wittingly or unwittingly in, an experience that will leave its mark on the history of the planet for a long time: the gradual and free unification of nations, which until very recently were hostile to each other. The **keyword of the multinational integration experience is freedom**: freedom of movement of persons, of goods, of services and of capital [see chapter 6]; freedom based on human rights, democratic institutions and the rule of law [see section 8.1.], but, also and above all freedom of States and their people to belong or not to the Union. Economic and political freedom is the water of the mortar for the construction of the European edifice. The citizens who love these freedoms should normally be conscious or unconscious supporters of European integration, if only they realised the effects of this integration on their professional and everyday lives. As we will see in the next chapter, however, most citizens of the Union are unaware of the benefits of European integration.

The fact is that **all Europeans take part** in one way or another in the construction of Europe: the housewife filling her basket with products from the four corners of the European Union; the motorist choosing the car which suits him without regard to its origin; the worker employed by a Community firm in his country or the firm's country; the businessman rushing across borders to conclude deals with foreign partners; the student studying in a partner country; the young person participating in an exchange programme; the pensioner from a northern country who takes his vacations or his residence in a country of Southern Europe; the citizen of one of those countries who aspires to come into contact with the lifestyle and culture of his neighbours. They all participate in the construction of the large European edifice without realising it. Why? Because all these activities, which were difficult or unthinkable at the time of economic protectionism and which now appear so natural, bring the citizens of the Member States close to each other and to the process of European integration.

Each time the citizens choose a product or service from a partner country, they unknowingly contribute their grain of sand to the mortar necessary to cement the European edifice [see section 3.1.]. The citizens are not aware of the importance of these acts because they find them as natural as the air they breathe. In fact, they have become as essential to their daily lives as that air. They should, however, realise that their lives would be very different if they did not enjoy the freedom of choice made possible by European integration.

The title of this part of the book is misleading, since it limits the policies concerning the citizens to only three fields. In reality, measures of great importance to the individual in areas such as employment, social protection, the fight against poverty and health care are part of social policy and are dealt with in the Chapter on social progress. That Chapter also tackles the major issues of education and training, security at work and public health. Other measures of concern for the citizens are covered by the common policies on justice and home affairs, environment protection, etc. Thus, the following pages look at measures of interest to the individual not touched upon in other parts of this book, notably the rights of citizens, information, audiovisual and cultural activities and protection of consumers' interests.

Chapter 9

CITIZENS' RIGHTS AND PARTICIPATION

Diagram of the chapter

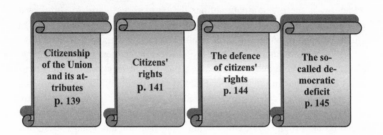

| Citizenship of the Union and its attributes p. 139 | Citizens' rights p. 141 | The defence of citizens' rights p. 144 | The so-called democratic deficit p. 145 |

In their great majority citizens ignore the many rights that they have acquired thanks to European integration, some of which are founded directly on the EC and EU Treaties, but most are based on the policies and the legislation derived from them. This ignorance is due to a deficient information of the general public, which the European institutions are trying unsuccessfully to develop, but which should be boosted by correct information from government sources and, of course, the media [see chapter 10]. A good cooperation between Community and national information sources is also necessary for an efficient protection of the health, safety and economic interests of European consumers [see chapter 11].

9.1. Citizenship of the Union and its attributes

The Treaty of Nice (following the Treaty of Amsterdam) establishes the **citizenship of the Union**, which is complementary to national citizenship. Every person holding the nationality of a Member State is a citizen of the Union. Citizens of the Union, thus defined, enjoy the rights conferred by the Treaty and are subject to the duties imposed thereby (Art. 17 TEC). Every citizen of the Union is, in the territory of a third country in which the Member State of which he or she is a national is not represented, entitled to protection by the diplomatic or consular authorities of any Member State, on the same conditions as the nationals of that State (Art. 20 TEC). Two Decisions specify the **right to diplomatic protection**[1]. This right is not negligible, as there are many cases where one Member State is not repre-

---

[1] Decision 95/553/EC, OJ L 314, 28.12.1995.

sented in a third country. It includes assistance in the event of death, illness or serious accident, arrest, detention or assault as well as help and repatriation in the event of difficulty. In practical terms, EU nationals whose passport or travel document is lost, stolen or temporarily unavailable in a country where their own Member State has no representation, may obtain an **emergency travel document**, from the diplomatic or consular representation of another Member State[1].

In addition, every citizen of the Union residing in a Member State of which he or she is not a national has the **right to vote and to stand as a candidate** at European and municipal elections in the Member State in which he resides, under the same conditions as nationals of that State (Art. 19 TEC). A Community directive lays down arrangements for the exercise of the right to vote and to stand as a candidate **in elections to the European Parliament** in the Member State of residence[2]. While including provisions to ensure freedom of choice and to prevent individuals from voting or standing for election in two constituencies at once, the Directive is based on the principles of equality and non-discrimination and is designed to facilitate the exercise by the citizens of the Union of their right to vote and to stand for election in the Member State where they reside.

The Directive laying down detailed arrangements for the exercise of the right to vote and stand as candidates in **municipal elections** ensures the same rights to Union citizens in elections by direct universal suffrage at local government level[3]. Member States may, however, reserve for their own nationals the posts of mayor and deputy mayor, which involve participation in an official authority or in the election of a parliamentary assembly.

Article 6 of the TEU states that the Union is founded on the principles of liberty, democracy, respect for **human rights and fundamental freedoms**, and the rule of law. The EC Treaty explicitly acknowledges that human rights include economic and social rights, and lays down the principle of equal rights for citizens without discrimination based on sex, racial or ethnic origin, religion or belief, disability, age or sexual orientation (Art. 13 TEC). The Council, acting by a four-fifths majority of its members and with the assent of Parliament, can declare that a clear danger exists of a Member State committing a serious breach of fundamental rights and address to that Member State appropriate recommendations. The **European Union Agency for Fundamental Rights** provides the relevant institutions, bodies, offices and agencies of the Community and its Member States with assistance and expertise relating to fundamental rights[4].

---

[1] Decision 96/409/CFSP, OJ L 168, 06.07.1996.

[2] Directive 93/109, OJ L 329, 30.12.1993.

[3] Directive 94/80, OJ L 368, 31.12.1994 and Directive 96/30, OJ L 122, 22.05.1996.

[4] Regulation 168/2007, OJ L 53, 22.02.2007.

9.2. Citizens' rights

Protection of fundamental rights is a founding principle of the Union and an indispensable prerequisite for its legitimacy. Article 6 of the EU Treaty states that "the Union shall respect fundamental rights, as guaranteed by the European Convention for the Protection of Human Rights and Fundamental Freedoms signed in Rome on 4 November 1950 and as they result from the constitutional traditions common to the Member States, as general principles of Community law". Moreover, the **Charter of fundamental rights of European citizens** was officially proclaimed at the Nice European Council (7-9 December 2000) by the European Parliament, the Council and the Commission[1]. It is divided into chapters dealing with the universal values of human dignity, freedom, equality, solidarity, citizenship and justice. It is designed to make more visible and explicit to the European Union's citizens the fundamental rights, which are already derived from a variety of international and Community sources, such as the European Convention on Human Rights, the Community Treaties and the case-law of the Court of Justice. Alongside the standard civil and political rights and the rights of citizens deriving from the Community Treaties, the charter incorporates fundamental social and economic rights, such as the rights of workers to collective bargaining, to take strike action and to be informed and consulted. The charter is likely to become mandatory through the Court of Justice's interpretation of it as belonging to the general principles of Community law[2].

With the emergence of information systems spanning the entire internal market, the European Union has increasingly to concentrate on the **protection of the personal data** of its citizens [see also sections 17.3.5. and 17.3.6.]. Thus a Directive aims at the development of the information society and the service sector in the EU, while guaranteeing individuals a high level of protection with regard to the processing of personal data (safe harbour privacy principles)[3]. Accordingly, it imposes obligations on data controllers such as public authorities, companies and associations, and establishes rights for data subjects, such as the right to be informed of processing carried out, the right of access to data and the right to ask for data to be corrected. In any event, the Directive prohibits the processing of sensitive data, such as data revealing racial or ethnic origin, political opinions, religious or philosophical beliefs, or state of health, except in certain circumstances that are exhaustively listed, in particular when the data subject has given his explicit consent or where a substantial public interest requires such processing (e.g. medical or scientific research). Community institutions and bodies must also protect the fundamental rights and freedoms of individuals, and in particular their right to privacy with respect

---

[1]   Solemn proclamation, OJ C 364, 18.12.2000.

[2]   COM(2000) 644, 11 October 2000.

[3]   Directive 95/46, OJ L 281, 23.11.1995.

to the processing of personal data[1]. An independent supervisory body, the European Data Protection Supervisor, monitors the application of the relevant rules[2].

In addition to the fundamental rights, as defined in the Charter of the Union and in the European Convention for the Protection of Human Rights and Fundamental Freedoms signed in Rome on 4 November 1950, the citizens of the European Union have many rights, some of which they are not even aware of because they appear obvious. Their self-evident nature is a consequence of the existence of the Union and the membership of their State of origin to it. The Court of Justice has established that Community law, independent from the legislation of the Member States, can create obligations and rights for individuals[3]. These rights are so numerous that it would be tedious to list them all here. Almost all **the provisions of Community law examined in this book create rights** and obligations for the citizens of the EU's Member States, particularly as regards professional activities. The weight of this law is growing as European integration marches forward. It is superimposed on national law and in many cases simply replaces it [see section 3.3.]. It therefore has growing influence over the professional and day-to-day lives of European citizens.

Some Community policies influence not only the professional life, but also the **everyday life of citizens**. Thus, important measures for the citizens in the fields of employment, vocational training, security at work and public health have their origin in the Community social policy. Furthermore, obligations imposed on industrialists by the Community policies of environment and consumers' protection have important effects on the quality of life of citizens. The citizens have the right to purchase goods in any one country of the Union at the conditions prevailing in that country and to take them to their country of origin without paying customs duties or any tax supplements [see section 5.1.2.]. They have the right to use any banking, insurance, telecommunications and audiovisual service offered in the large European market. They have the right to be treated by the administrative or judicial authorities of a country of the Union in the same way as the nationals of that country, i.e. without any discrimination on grounds of nationality (Art 12 TEC). This right covers a wide range of situations and human relations such as financial, contractual, family or student, which fall within the scope of Community law[4].

The Nice Treaty confers on every citizen of the Union a primary and individual **right to move and reside freely** within the territory of the Member States, subject to the limitations and conditions laid down in the Treaty and to the measures adopted to give it effect (Art. 2 TEU and Art. 18 TEC). Therefore, Directive 2004/38 replaced various instruments of Community law concerning freedom of movement and residence with a

---

[1]   Regulation 45/2001, OJ L 8, 12.01.2001.
[2]   Decision 1247/2002, OJ L 183, 12.07.2002.
[3]   Judgment of 5 February 1963, case 26/62, van Gend en Loos, ECR 1963, p. 1.
[4]   Judgment of 12 May 1998, Case C-85/96, ECR 1998, p. I-2691.

single text, aimed at reinforcing this fundamental entitlement of EU citizens by means of more flexible conditions and formalities and better protection against expulsion[1]. By virtue of this Directive, EU citizens enjoy right of residence provided that they satisfy certain conditions, notably if they themselves and the members of their families have sickness insurance covering all the risks in the host Member State. The directive facilitates considerably the freedom of movement and right of residence of family members of EU citizens, including the registered partner if the legislation of the host Member State treats registered partnership as equivalent to marriage. In addition, family members enjoy enhanced legal protection, notably in the event of the death of the EU citizen on whom they depend or the dissolution of the marriage, subject to certain conditions. The right of residence in any Member State has been teamed up with a number of practical measures such as the introduction of national driving licences based on a Community model[2].

Many EU countries signed, on June 19, 1990, the **Schengen Convention** for the abolition of border checks at the frontiers between them, the reinforcement of controls at external borders and the cooperation among their administrations[3]. A Protocol annexed to the Treaty of Amsterdam integrates the Schengen "acquis" - i.e., the existing legislation - into the framework of the European Union[4] and allows the signatories to the Schengen Convention (the Member States of the Union minus the United Kingdom and Ireland plus Norway and Iceland[5]) to initiate between them, within the legal and institutional framework of the Union, cooperation in the areas covered by the Convention. Ireland participates in all aspects of the Schengen *acquis* with the exception of those elements linked to border controls, notably cross-border surveillance and hot pursuit[6]. The new Member States apply the Schengen *acquis* in full[7]. The United Kingdom participates in cooperation in police, judicial and criminal matters, drug trafficking and the Schengen information system[8]. A Community Code establishes rules governing the movement of persons across borders as well as rules governing border control of persons crossing the external borders of the Member States of the European Union (**Schengen Borders Code**)[9]. Community rules on local border traffic at the external land borders of the Member States ease their crossing for border residents possessing a local border traffic permit[10].

The **second generation Schengen information system (SIS II)** constitutes an essential tool for the application of the provisions of the Schen-

---

[1] Directive 2004/38, OJ L 158, 30.04.2004.
[2] Directive 2006/126, OJ L 403, 30.12.2006.
[3] Schengen Convention, OJ L 239, 22.09.2000.
[4] Decisions 1999/435 and 1999/436, OJ L 176, 10.07.1999.
[5] Agreement, OJ L 149, 23.06.2000.
[6] Decision 2002/192, OJ L 64, 07.03.2002.
[7] Decision 2007/801, OJ L 323, 08.12.2007.
[8] Decision 2000/365, OJ L 131, 01.06.2000 and Decision 2004/926, OJ L 395, 31.12.2004.
[9] Regulation 562/2006, OJ L 105, 13.04.2006.
[10] Regulation 1931/2006, OJ L 29, 03.02.2007.

gen acquis[1]. It contributes to maintaining a high level of security within the area of freedom, security and justice of the European Union by supporting the implementation of policies linked to the movement of persons that are part of the Schengen acquis, as integrated into Treaty establishing the European Community. SIS II includes a computerised central system (Central SIS II) and national applications. A Regulation lays down provisions on the technical architecture of SIS II, the responsibilities of the Member States and of the management authority, on general data processing, the rights of the persons concerned and liability[2]. Some new functions were introduced in the SIS II, including in the fight against terrorism[3] [see section 8.1.4].

9.3. The defence of citizens' rights

Citizens should be conscious of their rights, some of which were mentioned above, to be able to defend them when they think that a Member State is not respecting them. They should also know that they are entitled to **defend their rights** acquired through Community law. They can do so by taking their case to the national courts, which can either issue a ruling or turn to the Court of Justice for a preliminary ruling[4], or by simply and inexpensively lodging a complaint with the Commission or a petition with the European Parliament (Art. 21 and 194 TEC). The Parliament has a Committee on Petitions which examines the complaints of citizens, mainly relating to social security, the recognition of professional qualifications or environment protection[5]. If the complaint concerns instances of mismanagement in the activities of the Community institutions or bodies, the citizen may address himself or herself to the **Ombudsman** appointed by the European Parliament (Art. 21 and 195 TEC) [see section 4.1.3.][6].

Regardless of whether they are lodged with it or with the Parliament, the Commission is obliged to examine the **grievances of citizens**, which number around one thousand per year. Sometimes they are not justified and the Commission must explain to the citizen why this is the case. Not infrequently, however, they are justified and the Commission must address the Member State in question and ask it for explanations. If it does not get a good answer it must formally ask the Member State to correct its legislation or administrative practices which are causing injury to one or several

---

[1] Regulation 2424/2001 and Decision 2001/886/JHA, OJ L328, 13.12.2001 amended by Regulation 1988/2006 and Decision 2007/533, OJ L 205, 07.08.2007.

[2] Regulation 1987/2006, OJ L 381, 28.12.2006.

[3] Decision 2005/211, OJ L 68, 15.03.2005, Decisions 2006/228 and 2006/229, OJ L 81, 18.03.2006 and Decision 2006/631, OJ L 256, 20.09.2006.

[4] Judgment of 25 July 2002, Case C-50/00 P, Unión de Pequeños Agricultores v Council, ECR 2002, p. I-6677.

[5] Resolution, OJ C 175, 16.07.1990, p. 214.

[6] Decision 94/114, OJ L 54, 25.02.1994, Decision 94/262, OJ L 113, 04.05.1994 and Decision 2002/262, OJ L 92, 09.04.2002.

citizens either of the State in question or of another Member State. If the Member State does not come into step with Community law as requested by the Commission, the latter must take the State to the Court of Justice, which will give a final ruling on the obligations of the Member State. According to the Court, the Member States are obliged to compensate for damage caused to individuals by violations of Community law attributable to them[1]. The citizens of the European Union therefore have powerful means at their disposal to obtain justice under Community law.

It goes without saying that if they are to defend these rights, they must be aware of them. The fact is that the vast majority of the citizens of the Member States are not **aware of their rights as citizens** of the European Union. The task of informing them therefore falls both to national and Community authorities, which are not very active in this area. The **information deficit**, examined in the following chapter [see section 10.1.2.], weakens the defence of citizens' rights. On the contrary, the multinational human networks, which are growing in number and influence in the Union, may, among other things, defend the rights of citizens of different Member States.

9.4. The so-called democratic deficit

Numerous critics of European integration point out at the "democratic deficit" as cause of the indifference of the citizens of the Union, insinuating that the citizens do not participate in the Community decision-making process, which is therefore undemocratic and causes the estrangement of the citizens from European institutions. They overlook the fact that European **citizens have almost the same influence** on the shaping of European law as they have on the shaping of national law. They indirectly influence it through the choice of the political parties, which make up the national governments and which therefore are involved in all European decisions adopted by the Council of Ministers. In addition, citizens have a direct say in the election of the members of the European Parliament, which has an important participation in the legislative process, thanks to improvements brought by successive European Treaties [see section 4.1.3].

The fact is that the legislative and control powers of the European Parliament have greatly increased since the early days when it had a purely consultative role in the legislative process and when, as a consequence, the democratic deficit at European level was substantially greater than that at the national level. Now, most decisions are taken jointly by the Council, representing the democratically elected governments of the Union, and by the European Parliament, representing directly the citizens of the Union [see sections 2.5, 4.1.3 and 4.3.]. It follows that the **"democratic deficit" is another myth** propagated by eurosceptic circles. Paradoxically, these same circles are among the most vehement detractors of the extension of

---

[1] Judgment of November 19, 1991 in the joint cases C-6/90 and C-9/90, Francovich, ECR 1991, p. I-5357.

the codecision procedure to the common foreign and security policy, which would practically eliminate the remnants of the democratic deficit.

Furthermore, the viewpoints of European citizens concerning various common policies are also expressed by the **national parliaments**, which manifest a growing interest in European integration. Indeed, the Conference of European Affairs Committees (COSAC) of the national parliaments may examine any legislative proposal or initiative which might have a direct bearing on the rights and freedoms of individuals and may address to the European institutions any contributions which it deems appropriate on the legislative activities of the Union.

Article 191 of the EC Treaty states that **political parties at European level** are important as a factor for integration within the Union and that they contribute to forming a European awareness and to expressing the political will of the citizens of the Union. A regulation aims to establish a long-term framework for European political parties and their financing from the Community budget, while also laying down minimum standards of democratic conduct for such parties[1]. In accordance with this regulation, a political party at European level must satisfy certain conditions, notably: it must be represented, in at least one quarter of Member States and it must observe in its programme and in its activities, the principles on which the European Union is founded, namely the principles of liberty, democracy, respect for human rights and fundamental freedoms, and the rule of law.

Far from being detached from the European integration process, national parliaments and the political parties, which dominate them, **are instrumental in** its launching, development and monitoring. The experience to date proves that practically all major parties in the great majority of the Member States are in favour of the general objectives of European integration. This is demonstrated by the fact that there is little or no change of national behaviour towards European policies when there is a change of a parliamentary majority and, therefore, of a government in a Member State. Instead of showing public misgivings about the democratic legitimacy of European integration, the overall evidence brings out **an extraordinary political consensus** on the main elements of the common policies that determine it.

The **Treaty of Lisbon** (following the draft Constitutional Treaty) defines, for the first time, the democratic foundations of the Union, which are based on **three principles**: those of democratic equality, representative democracy and participatory democracy (Article 8, Lisbon). The Treaty of Lisbon aims also at the democratisation of the functioning of the Union through the **reinforcement of the role of national parliaments**, which should contribute actively to the good functioning of the Union: (a) through having draft legislative acts of the Union forwarded to them in accordance with the Protocol on the role of national Parliaments in the European Union; (b) by seeing to it that the principle of subsidiarity is respected

---

[1]   Regulation 2004/2003, OJ L 297, 15.11.2003.

in accordance with the procedures provided for in the Protocol on the application of the principles of subsidiarity and proportionality [see section 3.2]; (c) by taking part, within the framework of the area of freedom, security and justice, in the evaluation mechanisms for the implementation of the Union policies in that area and through being involved in the political monitoring of Europol and the evaluation of Eurojust's activities [see sections 8.1.2 and 8.1.4]; (d) by taking part in the revision procedures of the Treaties; (e) by being notified of applications for accession to the Union; and (f) by taking part in the inter-parliamentary cooperation between national parliaments and with the European Parliament (Article 8 C, Lisbon).

9.5. Appraisal and outlook

Given that the economic activities of the Member States are guided by European law, the **activities of individual citizens are influenced** and governed to a large extent by the common policies which dictate that law. Regulations on the right of entry and residence in the Member States, freedom of movement of workers, freedom of establishment of and provision of services by individuals and businesses, vocational training, protection of the environment and of the consumer, to mention but a few, are all the outcome of the various common policies.

The Union also contributes to the elevation of the standard of living of its citizens. There are certainly still important differences in prosperity between the various regions of the Union, which this endeavours to iron out [see chapter 12]. However, a **European social model** exists already and guarantees, not only fundamental human rights and the democratic and pluralistic principles, but also fundamental rights of workers: training adapted to the technical progress, fair pay allowing decent living conditions and social protection covering the hazards of life, illness, unemployment and old age [see section 13.5.]. This social model, which is defended by the majority of political parties in the Member States, places the European Union in the vanguard of social progress in the world.

Citizens are aware that the multinational integration process provides **a guarantee of peace and prosperity** in Western Europe and therefore support the idea of the Community in principle. But, citizens are largely unaware of the extent to which they are surrounded by the workings of the Union in their daily and professional lives. They hardly understand the rights that emanate from the citizenship of the Union and they ignore the rights that derive from European legislation. Ignorance brings indifference and indifference is more dangerous for the European construction than the so-called democratic deficit, which is shrinking while indifference is expanding. The European institutions and the Member States should, therefore, permanently strive to ensure an easy access of the citizens to **simple and factual information about their rights** and generally about the common policies that establish those rights.

Bibliography on citizens' rights

- BELL Mark, CHOPIN Isabelle, PALMER Fiona (eds.). *Developing anti-discrimination law in Europe: the 25 EU Member States compared.* European Commission. Luxembourg: EUR-OP, 2007.
- EUROPEAN COMMISSION. *The EU, what's in it for me?: a no-nonsense guide for UK citizens to what the European Union delivers.* Luxembourg: EUR-OP, 2007.
- EUROPEAN UNION. *Charter of fundamental rights of the European Union.* Luxembourg: EUR-OP, 2007.
- GIORGI Liana (et al. eds.). *Democracy in the European Union: towards the emergence of a public sphere.* Abingdon: Routledge, 2006.
- HARVÁTH Enikö. *Mandating identity: citizenship, kinship laws and plural nationality in the European Union.* The Hague: Kluwer Law International, 2007.
- HENRARD Kristin. *Equal rights versus special rights?: Minority protection and the prohibition of discrimination.* Luxembourg: EUR-OP, 2007.
- HOLZHACKER Ronald (ed.). "Democratic legitimacy and the European Union", in *Journal of European integration*, v. 29, n. 3, July 2007, p. 255-385.
- MARTINELLI Alberto (ed.). *Transatlantic divide: comparing American and European society.* Oxford: Oxford University Press, 2007.
- SOMEK Alexander. "Solidarity decomposed: being and time in European citizenship", in *European Law Review*, v. 32, n. 6, December 2007, p. 787-818.
- TSADIRAS Alexandros. "The position of the European Ombudsman in the Community system of judicial remedies", in *European Law Review*, v. 32, n. 5, October 2007, p. 607-626.

DISCUSSION TOPICS

1. What are the advantages and disadvantages of European integration for the citizens of the Member States?
2. What rights and obligations do the common policies create for the citizens of the Member States?
3. What is the practical significance of the principles of liberty, democracy, respect for human rights and the rule of law, inscribed in the EC Treaty?
4. Can European citizens adequately defend their rights?
5. Discuss the existence and the importance of the so-called democratic deficit of the EU, comparing the structure and functions of European institutions to those of the Member States.

Chapter 10

INFORMATION, AUDIOVISUAL AND CULTURAL POLICIES

Diagram of the chapter

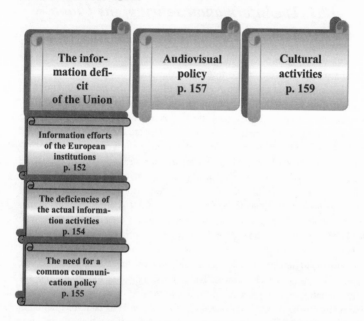

The info-
mation defi-
cit
of the Union

Audiovisual
policy
p. 157

Cultural
activities
p. 159

Information efforts
of the European
institutions
p. 152

The deficiencies of
the actual informa-
tion activities
p. 154

The need for a
common communi-
cation policy
p. 155

The point was made in the previous chapter that the citizens are silent, but indispensable, actors in the construction of Europe. The
EC/EU could not have been built by the political elite, without the implicit
consent of the citizens involved in the process. In fact, European citizens
are generally in favour and consider as evident the fundamental principles
and ideals the Union stands for, notably peace among their previously antagonistic nations, respect for human rights and the rule of law, economic
development and social protection. The **public opinion survey known as
"Eurobarometer"**, which is conducted each spring and autumn under the
auspices of the Commission, shows that, at the end of 2004, the EU citizens (from the 25 Member States) were largely convinced that EU membership was a "good" rather than a "bad thing" (56% vs. 13%). 50% of the
citizens had a positive image of the EU, compared to 15% who had a bad
image. Almost one out of two respondents (47%) declared that the Union
gives them a feeling of hope. 52% of the respondents in the 25 countries

had confidence in the European Commission and 57% had confidence in the European Parliament. The European public is even largely in favour of projects which are subject to controversy among the EU institutions and the governments of the Member States, such as a European constitution (63% vs. 10%), the common defence (74% vs. 15%) or the foreign policy (67% vs. 19%).

10.1. The information deficit of the Union

Although they are well disposed towards European integration, most citizens either ignore its achievements or take them for granted. In the Eurobarometer surveys, three fourths of the citizens say that they are not well informed about the institutions and policies of the European Union. It is interesting to note that two out of three citizens who claim to be well informed have a positive image of the EU as against one out of three who admit to being ill informed. However, the latter are the vast majority in the 25 countries (55%). Three out of four citizens would like to be better informed about the EU and 85% support the notion that children should be taught in school about the way European Union institutions work. Civic education on EU institutions is even the first priority theme for the very large majority of Europeans. Apparently, the citizens are aware that something important is happening in Europe, in which they cannot participate for lack of general knowledge and day-to-day information and they call for better access to European affairs for themselves and their children.

The information deficit, acknowledged by the citizens themselves, means that they are ill informed about the reasons, the goals and the achievements of European policies, laws and measures. Ignorance brings disregard for the obscure phenomenon. At best, citizens take for granted or fail to see that the EC/EU is behind the many rights that they have acquired thanks to European integration, some of which we examined in the previous chapter [see section 9.2.], particularly the right to a peaceful, liberal and law secured existence. For uninformed Europeans, the peaceful coexistence and emulation of different European nations is self-evident and not to be attributed to unfamiliar Treaties, policies or common legislation. Uninterested citizens tend to forget the tariffs and other barriers hindering trade and therefore limiting their choice of goods and services from other European countries, in the pre-integration years [see section 5.1.1]. They do not recall the erstwhile controls at borders, the restrictions on movement, establishment and work in neighbouring countries, the limited amounts at their disposal when travelling abroad, the general restrictions on capital movements, the snags of dealing in several currencies, etc. Young Europeans tend even to disregard the bloody wars fought by their forefathers with nations that they themselves now consider friendly and allied to their own nation.

Instead of a democratic deficit, which as we explained in the previous chapter is largely overstated [see section 9.4.], we should rather speak about **an information deficit** in European affairs. The information deficit originates from the early days of the customs union and the common market, when the issues of European unification were too technical to really interest the public and the threat of the communist block was considered a sufficient justification of this unification. Now that the communist threat has disappeared and the evolutionary integration process generates, every day, new common policies and laws affecting all sectors of the economy and society of the Member States, the citizens are bewildered about their impact on their lives. Furthermore, in order to judge the common enterprise on its real advantages and disadvantages, they need to have matter-of-fact information on the benefits and drawbacks already drawn and those expected from it, as well as on the real management difficulties that it is facing. Responsible for the information deficit are the institutions, which shy away from the development of a common information and communication policy, the governments of the Member States, which prefer to present the accomplishments of the Union as their own, and the media, which find more interesting to criticise the problems of the Union than present its achievements. Let us examine one by one these various factors of the information deficit of the Union.

The information deficit is partly due to the European institutions, notably the Commission, the Council and the Parliament, which do not join their forces to build a common communication policy. In their defence, it may be said that they are not encouraged - if they are not discouraged - by the governments of the Member States, which do not feel that they have a common interest in setting up a common information policy. In order to assume the political credit of modernisation, governments, when proposing innovating laws to national parliaments, transposing in effect Community directives, or when changing their administrative practices to comply with European law, rarely take the trouble to explain to the general public that they are thus fulfilling their Community obligations.

Paradoxically, however, the providers of information themselves, the mass communication media, have their share of responsibility in the information deficit of the Union. In fact, the **media** can play an important role in the multinational integration process by shaping public opinion and by exerting pressure on the political decision makers for or against common policies. They may also ignore or report incorrectly important issues of the integration process and, thus, leave the public ignorant or lead it astray as to the advantages and disadvantages of particular common policies or the integration process in general. If the majority of the media adopt attitudes different from the majority of the political elite of a nation, concerning the issue of integration or particular aspects of it, this may lead to a different stance of the majority of the public from that of the majority of the political elite of the nation. We may thus have the following antidemocratic phenomenon: the popular media transforming the political consensus existing among the democratically elected leaders of a nation, concerning the major political issues discussed at European level [see section 9.4.], into a public opinion dissent on those issues, orchestrated by non-elected opinion leaders (media tycoons, trendy journalists, popular television speakers, etc.) and/or a vociferous minority (party, movement or union)[1].

In contrast to eurosceptic media, which systematically provide disinformation rather than information, unbiased mass media **rarely report the decisions of the EC/EU;** probably because they are too technical, too detailed and often quite difficult to understand for the general public and sometimes for the journalists themselves. Instead of bringing forward the need and/or the common interest of measures in discussion, the media (particularly the popular ones) tend to highlight the usual and comprehensible disagreements in the deliberations of the Council, stemming from different socioeconomic structures, cultural traditions and vested interests. Moreover, the media of a country tend to present as right the national points of view and as wrong those of the other Member States. When a compromise solution is found within the framework of the co-decision procedure of the Council and the Parliament (as happens with 95% of the technocratic proposals of the Commission, after thorough deliberation and many amendments introduced by the political bodies), and a Community measure (regulation, directive or decision) is adopted, the same media tend either to ignore it or to summarise its content in small print and in a language difficult to understand for the average citizen. Furthermore, as a compromise solution is halfway between the best possible solution and no solution at all, even an unprejudiced journalist can easily disregard or belittle the achievement that it represents and emphasize its shortcomings. The resulting information in such a case is half-right or half-wrong, according to one's standpoint. But, again, it should be said, in the journalists' discharge, that they need clear, simple and interesting press releases on which to work; and these can only be provided by the European institutions. We thus have a vicious circle: the governments do not mandate the European institutions to set up a common information and communication policy; hence the institutions do not provide interesting factual information to the media; and these, on their turn, do not report to the public the activities of the institutions worthy of note.

10.1.1. Information efforts of the European institutions

At present each of the three main European institutions has its own means and instruments to carry out its information policy. While preserving full autonomy, the Parliament and the Commission have established an Inter-Institutional Group on Information (IGI) to coordinate their policies. They carry out jointly some priority information campaigns on subjects of topical interest, such as the euro (before its circulation), the new enlargement of the Union or the debate on the future of Europe. The Commission

---

[1]   The best example is the bitter opposition of the media tycoon Rupert Murdoch to the will of the Labour government of the UK to adopt the euro.

Representations and the European Parliament External Offices in the Member States are co-operating locally on an ad-hoc basis. Although it shares some means of communication with the Commission and the Parliament, such as the Europa server and the Europe by Satellite (EBS) - a television news instrument offering live coverage of the institutions' work and news summaries - the Council has a separate information and communication policy from the other institutions. As it has few budgetary resources for this purpose, it operates its own relations with the press and media. In general, except for a limited co-operation between the Commission and the Parliament, the three main European institutions have independent and heterogeneous information activities.

Although in its White Paper on a **"European communication policy"**[1] the Commission acknowledges that the success of this much needed policy depends on the involvement of all the key players – the other EU institutions and bodies, the national, regional and local authorities in the Member States, European political parties and the civil society – it does not propose a legal instrument involving the Member States in the European communication policy. Instead of proposing a European Parliament and Council decision or regulation, which would engage all European institutions and Member States to participate in the communication effort, it proposes an inter-institutional agreement – European Parliament, Commission, Council - on Communicating Europe in Partnership[2]. Instead of proposing a common civic education for young Europeans, it calls for "identification of aspects of school education where joint action at EU level could support Member States (sic)"[3]. Instead of asking each Minister participating in a Council session, which would have adopted an important measure, to comment in his or her own words the common press release, it encourages each Member State to nominate a high-level contact person as "national communication director" in matters relating to communication on EU issues. The cooperation and the development of synergies between the institutions are certainly better than the separate communication activities of the institutions, but they cannot replace a common communication policy with the participation of the member states; and the existing Inter-Institutional Group on Information cannot play the role of a European Press Agency, suggested below [see section 10.1.3].

As a matter of fact, **the Commission is the main provider of information on the EC/EU.** Major European affairs and problems, which occasionally attract television attention, are presented and commented in the press room of the Commission by its President, the competent Commissioner or a spokesperson. Rarely is press attention focussed on the European Parliament and almost never on the Council of Ministers. Although it practically monopolises Community information, the Commission is not a secretive organisation and is even a good provider of information, as far as

---

[1] COM/2006/35.

[2] COM/2007/569.

[3] COM/2007/568.

its activities are concerned. Its Representations in the capitals and other major cities of the Member States are open to the interested public. Its Europa server on the Internet gives free and user-friendly access to more than 60 databases, each of which contains several hundred thousand documents in the 21 official languages of the European Union[1]. All the documents listed in the footnotes of this book are accessible at the Eur-lex database. The addresses of the general and of some of the most interesting free sites of Europa are the following:

- **(Europa gateway)** http://europa.eu/index_en.htm;
- **(information for citizens)**
  http://ec.europa.eu/youreurope/index_en.html;
- **(European legislation)** http://eur-lex.europa.eu/en/index.htm;
- **(common policies)** http://europa.eu/scadplus/scad_en.htm;
- **(books, publications)**
  http://www.libeurop.be/our_books.php?lang=en;
- **(Bulletin of the EU)** http://europa.eu/bulletin/en/welcome.htm;
- **(Who's Who in the institutions)**
  http://europa.eu/whoiswho/public/index.cfm;

Moreover, the Commission does not make any secret of its intentions concerning legislation in preparation. All its proposals are communicated directly to the press the day of their adoption and are published in the very informative monthly *Bulletin of the European Union*, available in paper and electronic form. In case of preparation of new policies or changes in existing policies, the Commission publishes **Green Papers** (reflection documents inviting a debate on the options of a policy before the preparation of proposals) and **White Papers** (general documents announcing a programme of actions)[2]. A White Paper usually presents the points of view of interested parties (organisations, associations, institutions…) at national and Community level on a Green Paper, along with the conclusions and intentions of the Commission.

10.1.2. The deficiencies of the actual information activities

A cursory view of the information activities of European institutions gives the impression of a flood of documentation - coming mainly from the Commission - rather than of an information drought. But floods can be more harmful than droughts, if the soil is not prepared to receive the overflow. In this case, the soil is totally unprepared, because the citizens do not and never will make an effort to get the existing information, but rightly expect that they will be automatically informed, through their familiar media, about European affairs and decisions that are of interest to them. When they say in Eurobarometer surveys that they want to be informed about the institutions and policies of the EU, they mean that this information should

---

[1]   Regulation 1/1958, OJ 17, 06.10.1958 and Regulation 1791/2006, OJ L 363, 20.12.2006.
[2]   The index provides references to several Green and White Papers.

come to them, not that they should go after it. Useful as they are to interested persons (researchers, interest groups and other specialists), the Commission publications and Internet sites are ignored and are therefore useless for the large majority of citizens.

Indeed, information by the Commission suffers from two inherent defects. Firstly, it is addressed to a few initiated persons rather than to the average citizen, who does not read sophisticated publications or surf in the Europa server of the Commission. Secondly, information by the Commission reflects mainly its own proposals rather than the policies decided upon by the governments of the Member States and the Parliament of the peoples of the Union. Therefore, journalists and through them the public get the - partly right - impression that, through its information activities, the Commission defends its own policies rather than the common policies of the Member States.

The result of information deficiency, combined with disinformation on the part of eurosceptic media, is **the indifference or, worse, the dissatisfaction of citizens**, who quite sincerely believe that, instead of progressing in the field of European unification, the European Union is a theatre of infighting among European politicians; that it is totally unable to monitor global phenomena - such as globalisation, climate change and international conflicts - and that it is even responsible for some of their national problems, such as unemployment and the cost of living. It is this mismatch between high expectations and totally or partly false perceptions of the public that endangers European unification. The indifference and/or dissatisfaction of citizens, demonstrated in European elections, opinion polls and referendums, must be recognised as a major failure of the integration process and a grave danger for its future.

10.1.3. The need for a common communication policy

It is strange that, whereas the citizens themselves recognize their problem of understanding the European institutions and decisions, the political leaders ignore it or underrate it. If they ever examine seriously the Eurobarometers or other opinion surveys in their countries, they will understand that the citizens do not ask for a direct participation in the decision making process of the Union, but for a clear information as to how and why decisions are taken and as to what bearing they have on their lives. If this demand of the citizens was taken seriously into consideration, a common information and communication policy, covering all other common policies, could easily be conceived and implemented.

By **common information and communication policy** we mean a policy with a common set of guidelines, decisions, rules, measures and codes of conduct adopted by the European institutions and implemented by the European institutions and the governments of the Member States [see section 1.1.2]. Although the Treaties do not explicitly call for such a policy, the Commission could, on the basis of the abovementioned Helsinki mandate of the European Council, take the initiative to propose it to the other institutions, as it usually does concerning all policies and measures. Thereafter, the Council and the European Parliament, with their own committees and experts, could work on the proposals of the Commission to make them acceptable to all parties concerned. The ensuing common communication policy should entail two basic elements: a common information and communication strategy of the European institutions and the governments of the Member States and a structure to carry it out, with at its head a European Press Agency.

The common strategy should encourage and give guidelines to the European institutions and the governments of the Member States to participate, together with regional and local authorities, in the common information tasks, in respect of the specific national and regional information needs. Coordination between the information services of the European institutions and the governments of the Member States should be assigned to a **European Press Agency (EPA)**, i.e. an inter-institutional body, based in Brussels, depending from and representing all the European institutions: not only the three decision-making institutions of the Union, the Commission, the Council and the European Parliament, but also the European Ombudsman, the European Court of Justice, the Economic and Social Committee and the Committee of the Regions. The European Press Agency should have a budget sufficient to allow it to carry out its tasks. It should subsidise the "Euronews" TV channel, which broadcasts European news, to permit it to transmit in all the official languages of the EU. In addition, it should subsidise national and regional media to diffuse, on prime time, five minutes of European news provided by the EPA.

The attention of ordinary citizens should be attracted primarily to the activities and decisions of the main institutions, which have an effect on their professional and everyday lives. Press-conferences should present both the important proposals of the Commission and the major decisions of the Council and the Parliament. In the latter case, apart from the spokesmen of the institutions, it would be interesting to have the president of the Council and the chairman of the relevant parliamentary committee present a fresh decision to the press. Such a presentation should explain the problem addressed, the consequences of inaction, the reasons calling for common action in preference to individual action by the Member States, the main objectives aimed at by the decision and the most important means provided for attaining them. But, this common presentation should only be the basis of the information campaign on important decisions. On this basis should be built nationally oriented information by the ministers and the members of the competent parliamentary committee involved in a decision, addressed to the national media both in Brussels and at home.

It would, indeed, be quite reasonable that, upon adopting an important European law or measure, the responsible ministers give an accurate account to the journalists of their countries of the reasons of this law or measure, its goals and its effects on the professional or daily lives of the citizens of their states. Thus, each minister participating in the Council, which would have taken an important decision, would present in his or her own words and language the decision taken and/or circulate a press-release to national and regional media, based on the common press-release prepared by the European Press Agency. If he or she had voted against the measure taken, he or she should explain his or her disagreement, but also the reasoning having prevailed among his or her colleagues in the Council.

Journalists, commentators and politicians of the opposition could, of course, criticise the measure taken and eventually blame the responsible minister for not having well defended national interests. In this way, citizens would have the double benefit of having a first-hand account of the reasons and objectives of a European measure, together with the arguments for and against it. They would thus be incited to think about the measure and take a stand on it, as they do about national measures and options. They would also come to know who and how represent them in Brussels. Eurosceptic media would, then, hopefully, avoid spreading false information about European decisions. In any case, they would not be able to claim that decisions are taken in secret by the "Eurocrats of Brussels", pointing at the Commission, when the citizens would be able to see for themselves that their own representatives, Ministers and European MPs, take part in the decision-making process in Brussels and can be appraised for their negotiating skills or called to account for any harm to national interests, actually or supposedly brought about by a common measure co-authored by them.

10.2. Audiovisual Policy

The audiovisual sector, which covers programme production and distribution ("software") and equipment manufacturing ("hardware"), has a great potential for growth and job creation in Europe. The European film and television programme industry, which plays a strategic role in the development of the audiovisual sector, is, in addition, **a prime vector of European culture** and a living testimony to the traditions and identity of each country. It must, therefore, illustrate the creative genius and the personality of the peoples of Europe; but, to do this, it must be competitive in an open, worldwide market[1].

In contrast to the information policy, the Member States of the Union have felt the need for a common audiovisual policy. A Protocol, annexed to the TEC in Amsterdam, asserts that **public broadcasting** in the Member States is directly related to the democratic, social and cultural needs of each society and to the need to preserve media pluralism [see also section 6.6.4.]. Member States may therefore provide for the funding of public service broadcasting in so far as such funding is granted to broadcasting organisations for the fulfilment of the public service remit as conferred, defined and organised by each Member State, and such funding does not affect trading conditions and competition in the Community.

---

[1] COM (94) 96, 6 April 1994.

The audiovisual sector in Europe took on a totally new face at the end of the 1980s, with the rapid growth in broadcasting by cable and telecommunications satellites and the emergence of the first European direct broadcasting satellites. However, **national markets in the Member States were too narrow** to be able to offer at competitive rates the equipment and programmes required by the new technologies and the proliferation of channels. This was a handicap for the European audiovisual sector, which was expected to be one of the principal service sectors in the 21st century.

Scattered and confined in their smallish national markets, European producers found themselves in conditions of uneven competition in the international arena as far as the costs were concerned. Europe should unify its audiovisual market to enable European producers to participate profitably in this technological revolution. Otherwise, it had to rely on powerful American and Japanese audiovisual industry, capable of covering cheaply international markets. American movies and serials and Japanese cartoons can defy world competition, because their cost is amortised on the large national market. European producers were doomed to disappear or be confined in their national markets.

At the same time a "technological revolution" was underway with the introduction of **high definition television (HDTV)** that gives to the image an almost perfect quality and makes it possible for the image to be accompanied by four sound channels, thus permitting, for example, a stereophonic sound and the simultaneous transmission of dialogues in two languages at the choice of the spectator. To prepare this revolution, the **Community's strategy on new technologies in the audiovisual sector** sought the cooperation between the Member States for the promotion of the European standard for HDTV, the aid for technological development and the aid to audiovisual operators for launching services using the new technology[1]. A single regulatory framework now covers the converging telecommunications, information technology and audiovisual sectors, including digital television[2] [see section 17.3.6.].

A particular regulatory framework was also necessary to permit the free provision of audiovisual services in the European space. To this end, a Directive concerning the exercise of television broadcasting activities (**"television without frontiers"**) aimed at the free movement of television programmes within the Community through the freedom to pick up and retransmit programmes from another Member State. It consequently lays down the principle that compliance with the rules is to be enforced by the broadcasting State, without interference from the country of retransmission of the programme. The Directive introduced minimum harmonisation of advertising (breaks, duration, advertising for certain products, ethical rules), sponsorship, protection of minors and right of reply, while promoting the production and distribution of European audiovisual works. It

---

[1]   Decision 89/337, OJ L 142, 25.05.1989 and Decision 89/630, OJ L 363, 13.12.1989.
[2]   Directive 2002/21, OJ L 108, 24.04.2002.

stipulates that the Member States must ensure, "where practicable" and by appropriate means, that broadcasters reserve a majority proportion of their transmission time, excluding certain types of programme, for European works. The Directive also specifies that at least 10% of airtime or of the programming budgets should be earmarked for European works by independent producers. The 1989 Directive was amended in 1997 in order to clarify certain definitions of terms such as "television advertising" and "European works", to introduce rules on teleshopping and broadcasting for self-promotional purposes and to strengthen the protection of minors, in particular by making it compulsory for unencoded programmes likely to be unsuitable for minors to be preceded by a sound or visual warning[1].

The "**MEDIA 2007**" programme of support for the European audiovisual sector (2007-2013) aspires to strengthen the audiovisual sector economically to enable it to play its cultural roles more effectively[2]. It aims, in particular, to (a) preserve and enhance European cultural and linguistic diversity and its cinematographic and audiovisual heritage; (b) increase the circulation and viewership of European audiovisual works inside and outside the European Union; (c) strengthen the competitiveness of the European audiovisual sector in the framework of an open and competitive European market favourable to employment. Upstream of audiovisual production it helps the acquisition and improvement of skills in the audiovisual field and the development of European audiovisual works. Downstream of audiovisual production it supports the distribution and promotion of European audiovisual works. In general it aspires to strengthen the structure of the European audiovisual sector, particularly SMEs and to reduce the imbalances in the European audiovisual market between high audiovisual production capacity countries and countries or regions with low audiovisual production capacity and/or a restricted geographic and linguistic area. The Community participates in the **European Audiovisual Observatory** aimed at boosting the competitiveness of European audiovisual industry[3].

10.3. Cultural activities

Culture was brought fully into the action scope of the Community through the Treaty of Maastricht [see section 2.2.]. The common cultural policy **does not aim at any harmonisation of the cultural identities** of the Member States, but, on the contrary, at the conservation of their diversity. Article 151 (TEC) states, in fact, that the Community should contribute to the flowering of the cultures of the Member States, while respecting their national and regional diversity and at the same time bringing the common cultural heritage to the fore. Its action aims at encouraging coop-

---

[1] Directive 89/552, OJ L 298, 17.10.1989 and Directive 2007/65, OJ L 332, 18.12.2007.
[2] Decision 1718/2006, OJ L 327, 24.11.2006.
[3] Decision 1999/784, OJ L 307, 02.12.1999 and Decision 2004/2239, OJ L 390, 31.12.2004.

eration between Member States and, if necessary, supporting and supplementing their action in the following areas: improvement of the knowledge and dissemination of the culture and history of the European peoples; conservation and safeguarding of cultural heritage of European significance; non-commercial cultural exchanges; artistic and literary creation, including in the audiovisual sector.

In order to achieve these objectives, **four means are employed**: cooperation between Member States; consideration for cultural aspects under other Community policies, including competition policy, concerning in particular aid to promote culture and heritage conservation (Art. 87 TEC); cooperation between the Community and its Member States with third countries and the competent international organisations; specific measures to support action taken by Member States which may take two forms: incentive measures, excluding any harmonisation of the laws and regulations of the Member States [see section 6.2.1.], adopted unanimously by the Council acting under the co-decision procedure after consultation of the Committee of the Regions; and recommendations unanimously adopted by the Council. The departure from the normal co-decision procedure [see section 4.3.] denotes that a Member State may not be forced by a qualified majority in the Council to take an action that it considers to be harmful to its cultural identity.

The **Culture Programme** (2007 to 2013) aims to enhance the cultural area shared by Europeans and based on a common cultural heritage through the development of cultural cooperation between the creators, cultural players and cultural institutions of the countries taking part in the Programme, with a view to encouraging the emergence of European citizenship[1]. The Programme is open to the participation of non-audiovisual cultural industries, in particular small cultural enterprises, where such industries are acting in a non-profit-making cultural capacity. The specific objectives of the Programme are: (a) to promote the transnational mobility of cultural players; (b) to encourage the transnational circulation of works and cultural and artistic products; and (c) to encourage intercultural dialogue. Another programme of Community action provides financial support to organisations active at European level in the field of culture[2]. The year 2008 was designated as the **"European Year of Intercultural Dialogue"** to contribute to giving expression and a high profile to a sustained process of intercultural dialogue which will continue beyond that year[3].

The European Union must strike a balance between the objectives arising from the completion of the internal market and those relating to the **protection of the national heritage**. In fact, a Council Regulation subjects the **export outside the Community of cultural goods** of artistic, historical or archaeological value to an export licence issued by the Member State on

---

[1] Decision 1903/2006, OJ L 378, 27.12.2006.
[2] Decision 792/2004, OJ L 138, 30.04.2004.
[3] Decision 1983/2006, OJ L 412, 30.12.2006.

whose territory it is lawfully located[1]. In the same vein, a Directive provides for the return of cultural objects unlawfully removed from the territory of a Member State unlawfully removed from the on or after 1 January 1993[2]. It notably establishes a judicial procedure for the return of cultural objects and cooperation between the competent authorities of the Member States.

A rigorous, effective system for the **protection of copyright and related rights** is one of the main ways of ensuring that European cultural creativity and production receive the necessary resources and of safeguarding the independence and dignity of artistic creators and performers [see also sections 6.2.4 and 23.4.]. Therefore, **copyright** is protected at European Union level by a Directive that harmonises the term of copyright at 70 years after the death of the author in the case of literary, artistic, cinematographic or audiovisual works[3]. For the last two categories, calculation of the term of protection begins after the death of the last of the persons to survive from among the principal director, the author of the screenplay, the author of the dialogue and the composer of the music. The same Directive harmonises at 50 years the term of protection of the main **related rights** (those of performers, producers of phonograms or of films and broadcasting organisations). It also provides collective and obligatory management of the rights for cable retransmission through collective societies representing the various categories of rightholders.

10.4. Appraisal and outlook

Information is a key instrument of any policy making, let alone multinational policy-making. Citizens rightly distrust the common policies, which they do not understand for lack of proper information. The role of information has been underestimated and largely neglected in the EC/EU, with the result of a growing estrangement of the European public from European policies, which become ever more complicated as they advance and, hence, increasingly difficult to understand. As we saw above, three fourths of European citizens believe that they are ill informed about European affairs. This information deficit is endangering European unification. The more ignorant the citizens are about the institutions, the goals and the mechanisms of the integration process, the more easily **public opinion may be misled** about particular issues or the general thrust of the process.

The lack of generalised information combined with a sharp disinformation on the part of eurosceptic media is an explosive mixture placed under the foundations of European unification, because it separates citizens in two categories: the apathetics and the dogmatics. The vast silent majority is indifferent, because it finds living and working conditions generally ac-

---

[1]   Regulation 3911/92, OJ L 395, 31.12.1992 and Regulation 974/2001, OJ L 137, 19.05.2001.
[2]   Directive 93/7, OJ L 74, 27.03.1993 and Directive 2001/38, OJ L 187, 10.07.2001.
[3]   Directive 2006/116, OJ L 372, 27.12.2006.

ceptable in Europe, compared with other parts of the world, but does not credit the EC/EU with a significant role in shaping those conditions. On the other hand, a minority, which is systematically irritated against the deeds or supposed misdeeds of the European institutions (notably that of usurping national sovereignty), underestimates or even denies all the achievements of the Union in terms of peace, relative prosperity and unob-structed movement of goods, services, labour and capital. This situation is harmful, not only to the progress of European integration, but also to the good functioning of its democratic institutions [see section 4.3.] that are debased in the eyes of the citizens by some activists with dubious motives.

The states which participate in the integration process have, conse-quently, a common interest in developing **a common information and communication policy about this process.** This means using simple lan-guage, which can be used by the mass media, to put forward the reasons for European policies, the consequences of inertia and the benefits of common action in the interests of all participants. This would not be propaganda, but information necessary in a democratic community con-cerned with encouraging participation of all its members in communal life. This factual information is necessary in order to bring the citizens closer to the institutions of the Union and thus bridge the information and the de-mocratic gaps. Priority should be given to information on issues close to the daily lives of citizens, such as price stability and employment as well as on issues of major political interest, such as the future of Europe and the place of the Union in the world. The Commission should take the initiative to propose a common communication policy with common goals, common means and multi-level implementation: European, national, regional and local.

Likewise, the European institutions - the Commission, the Council and the Parliament - should encourage the Member States to introduce the **teaching of the history, the institutions and the goals of European inte-gration** in the high schools. This, again, would not be indoctrination dan-gerous for the democracy, but rather a civic education, necessary for the correct functioning of the democratic institutions at European level. The proper functioning of democratic institutions depends on well-informed and educated citizens. As revealed by public opinion surveys, practically all the citizens in all the Member States demand with insistence better in-formation for themselves and better education for their children. They are right, because the two go together. The civic education of the young about the basic facts of European unification should, indeed, be the trunk on which would grow and be constantly developed, by the institutions and the Member States, the branches and leaves of the European information tree relating to all common policies and activities.

The cultural activities of the Union rightly emphasise the **cultural di-versity of the nations that make it up** rather than trying to promote a common culture; but the national cultural identities should not overshadow the common cultural heritage of European peoples. Consciousness of a common cultural heritage is part of the process of an ever closer union among the peoples of Europe. The proper historical dimension, in particular, could contribute to a better mutual understanding of the cultures of European peoples. History lessons taught from the national angle, accentuate the divisions, the wars and the hatreds among European nations rather than their common cultural heritage. The Ministers of Education should one day agree on a textbook of European history and culture, which could make young Europeans understand that the national cultural particularities, which make up Europe's cultural wealth, are all parts of the same European civilisation of Greek-Roman origin.

In this respect, an effective **European audiovisual policy**, which is still in its inception phase, can enhance not only the common European cultural identity, but also the various national identities that enrich it. Certain Community measures could improve the industry's competitiveness, such as support systems for the distribution of non-domestic European works, the encouragement of private investment in European audiovisual production on foreign markets, the organisation of a pan-European prize-giving ceremony by the audiovisual profession and, last but not least, the launching of digital television in a competitive environment. Digital cinema, facilitating the circulation of European audiovisual works, could promote European cinema, which is in constant decline in recent years.

Bibliography on information, audiovisual and cultural policies

- AIM Research Consortium (ed.). *Comparing the logic of EU reporting: transnational analysis of EU correspondence from Brussels*. Dortmund: AIM, 2007.
- EUROPEAN COMMISSION. *Communicating Europe in Partnership*. COM (2007) 569. Luxembourg: EUR-OP*, 2007.
- FETZER Thomas. "Turning Eurosceptic: British trade unions and European integration (1961-1975)", in *Journal of European Integration History*, v. 13, n. 2, 2007, p. 85-101.
- MAALOUF Amin. *A rewarding challenge: how language diversity could strengthen Europe*. Luxembourg: EUR-OP, 2007.
- MARCUSSEN Martin, TORFING Jacob (eds.). *Democratic network governance in Europe*. Basingstoke: Palgrave MacMillan, 2007.
- PSYCHOGIOPOULOU Evangelina. *The integration of cultural considerations in EU law and policies*. Leiden: M. Nijhoff, 2008.
- RAMSBROCK Annelie (et al. eds.). *Conflicted memories: Europeanizing contemporary histories*. Oxford: Berghahn Books, 2007.
- RUVALCABA GARCIA Aldonza. *How television failed to integrate Europe*. Genève: Institut européen de l'Université de Genève, 2007.
- TANS Olaf (et al. eds.). *National parliaments and European democracy: a bottom-up approach to European constitutionalism*. Groningen: Europa Law, 2007.
- TSAKATIKA Myrto. "Governance vs. politics: the European Union's constitutive 'democratic deficit'", in *Journal of European Public Policy*, v. 14, n. 6, 2007, p. 867-885.

DISCUSSION TOPICS

1. Consider the lack of a common information policy and its consequences on public awareness of the European integration process.
2. Discuss the relative importance of the democratic deficit and the information deficit of the European integration process.
3. Do the media that you are familiar with tend to give an objective and adequate view of the European integration process?
4. Is there a need for a common audiovisual policy of the EU?
5. Should the goal of a European cultural policy be a cultural uniformity or the defence of the particular cultures of the nations participating in the integration process?

Chapter 11

CONSUMER POLICY

Diagram of the chapter

Consumer information p. 166	Protection of health and physical safety p. 167	Protection of economic and legal interests p. 169

A common policy to protect consumers and users of products and services is essential for the functioning of the single market in the interest of the citizens. The aim of the common consumer policy is to ensure that the European Union's consumers draw maximum benefit from the existence of the internal market and play an active role in it. The single market must serve their maximum wellbeing and give them **a free choice of goods and services** of the best possible quality and at the best possible price, without consideration for their origin or for the nationality of their supplier [see section 6.1.]. Furthermore, within the single market consumers must enjoy a similar level of protection to that provided within a national market. For these reasons, the goods and services offered in the single market should be safe and the consumers should dispose of the necessary information so as to make the good choices.

Article 153 (TEC), gives the Community the task of contributing to the **protection of health, safety and economic interests** of consumers, as well to the promotion of their right to information, education and to organise themselves in order to safeguard their interests. The attainment of those objectives should be pursued through: (a) measures adopted pursuant to Article 95 (harmonisation of legislations) in the context of the completion of the internal market [see section 6.2.1.]; and (b) measures which support, supplement and monitor the policy pursued by the Member States. In order to help achieve the objectives of consumer protection, a Council Resolution demands that allowance be made for consumers' interests in **other Community policies**[1]. Obviously, the common consumer policy should interact with other common policies, notably in the fields of agriculture,

---

[1]   OJ C 3, 07.01.1987, p. 1-2.

fisheries, environment protection and the harmonisation of legislations necessary for the internal market.

According to the Commission, the EU **Consumer Policy strategy 2007-2013** has three main objectives[1]:

- to empower EU consumers, i.e., to give them real choices, accurate information, market transparency and the confidence that comes from effective protection and solid rights;
- to enhance EU consumers' welfare in terms of price, choice, quality, diversity, affordability and safety;
- to protect consumers effectively from the serious risks and threats that they cannot tackle as individuals.

The **programme of Community action** in the field of consumer policy (2007-2013) aims to complement, support and monitor the policies of the Member States and to contribute to protecting the health, safety and economic and legal interests of consumers, as well as to promoting their rights to information, to education and to organise themselves in order to safeguard their interests[2].

11.1. Consumer information

Consumer information seeks to ensure that consumers are able to **compare the prices** for the same product within a country and are as well informed as possible on price differences between the Member States. The **indication of the prices** of the products represents an important means of information and protection of consumers. A Community Directive imposes the indication of the price per unit of measurement of all products sold in the shops, thereby giving the consumer a clear idea of the unit cost of the product in question and enabling him or her to compare different products and to make the best choice[3]. The selling price and the unit price must be unambiguous, easily identifiable and clearly legible. They must relate to the final price of the product and must refer to the quantity declared in accordance with national and Community provisions.

Labelling of products is also an important way of achieving better information and transparency for the consumer and ensuring the smooth operation of the internal market[4]. The language requirements, the trade name, the stated quantity of the ingredients and other provisions are specified in the Directive on the labelling, presentation and advertising of foodstuffs[5]. Harmonised rules apply to nutrition and health claims made in commercial

---

[1]   COM/2007/99.
[2]   Decision 1926/2006, OJ L 404, 30.12.2006.
[3]   Directive 98/6, OJ L 80, 18.03.1998.
[4]   OJ C 186, 23.07.1992, p. 1-3 and OJ C 110, 20.04.1993, p. 1-2.
[5]   Directive 2000/13, OJ L 109, 06.05.2000 and Directive 2003/89, OJ L 308, 25.11.2003.

communications, whether in the labelling, presentation or advertising of foods to be delivered as such to the final consumer[1].

11.2. Protection of health and physical safety

The effort to complete the internal market proved the effective trigger of a genuine policy to protect the health and physical safety of consumers. In the 1980s the Community placed the wellbeing of its citizens high on its list of priorities by adopting **general legislation guaranteeing the safety of individuals** in their capacity as users of products, regardless of the origin of the latter. This is the aim of a Directive on the approximation of the laws of the Member States concerning products which, appearing to be other than they are, endanger the health or safety of consumers[2]. This Directive prohibits the marketing, import and either manufacture or export of **dangerous imitations of foodstuffs**.

A major Directive in the context of the single market was adopted in 1988 dealing with **toy safety**[3]. It sets the basic safety requirements that must be met by all toys manufactured in the Community or imported from third countries. The European standardisation committees then adopt harmonised standards and manufacturers respecting these are covered by a presumption that their toys meet the basic safety requirements defined in the Directive [see section 6.2.3.].

Since it is difficult to adopt Community legislation for every product, it is necessary to establish at Community level a general safety requirement. This general legal instrument is provided by a Directive on **general product safety**[4]. The purpose of this Directive is to ensure that products placed on the market, which are intended for consumers or likely, under reasonably foreseeable conditions, to be used by consumers even if not intended for them, are safe. Producers are obliged to place only safe products on the market, conforming to the specific rules of national law of the Member State in whose territory the product is marketed drawn up in conformity with the Treaty and in accordance with Directive 98/34 laying down a procedure for the provision of information in the field of technical standards and regulations [see section 6.2.2.]. Distributors are required to act with due care to help to ensure compliance with the applicable safety requirements, in particular by not supplying products which they know or should have presumed, on the basis of the information in their possession and as professionals, do not comply with those requirements. Where producers and distributors know or ought to know that a product that they have placed on the market poses risks to the consumer they must immediately

---

[1] Regulation 1924/2006, OJ L 404, 30.12.2006 and Regulation 109/2008, OJ L 39, 13.02.2008.

[2] Directive 87/357, OJ L 192, 11.07.1987.

[3] Directive 88/378, OJ L 187, 16.07.1988 and Directive 93/68, OJ L 220, 30.08.1993.

[4] Directive 2001/95, OJ L 11, 15.01.2002, repealing Directive 92/59, OJ L 228, 11.08.1992 from 15 January 2004.

inform the competent authorities of the Member States thereof. Member States must ensure that producers and distributors comply with their obligations, establish or nominate authorities competent to monitor the compliance of products with the general safety requirements and lay down the rules on penalties applicable to infringements of the national provisions adopted. The Commission must promote and take part in the operation in a European network of the authorities of the Member States competent for product safety. This network must be coordinated with other Community procedures, in particular the **Community Rapid Information System (RAPEX)**, which is described in Annex II of the directive and is essentially aimed at a rapid exchange of information in the event of a serious risk.

Regulation 178/2002 lays down the general principles and procedures in matters of **food law and food safety** and establishes the European Food Safety Authority[1]. Whilst ensuring the effective functioning of the internal market, it aims at ensuring a high level of protection of human health and consumers' interest in relation to food, taking into account in particular the diversity in the supply of food including traditional products. It establishes common principles and responsibilities, the means to provide a strong science base, efficient organisational arrangements and procedures to underpin decision-making in matters of food and feed safety. The **European Food Safety Authority** must provide scientific advice, independent information and scientific and technical support for the Community's legislation.

The Community legislation governing **food hygiene**[2], health issues related to the marketing of **products of animal origin**[3] and the organisation of **official controls** on such products[4] has been recast in 2004. Henceforth, a distinction is made between aspects of food hygiene and matters to do with animal health and official controls, thus providing scope for defining clearly the responsibilities of food business operators and the competent authorities in the Member States. A key point of the new legislation is that every operator involved in the food chain will bear primary responsibility for food safety, with a single, transparent hygiene policy being applicable to all foodstuffs and all operators (from the farm to the table), together with effective instruments to guarantee food safety and manage any future crisis in the sector. Administrative measures with criminal sanctions and financial penalties may be imposed on any Member State which fails to comply with Community feed and food law[5]. In 2005, rigorous Community measures were taken for the control of **avian influenza**, including provision of contingency plans in the event of human contamination[6].

---

[1]   Regulation 178/2002, OJ L 31, 01.02.2002 and Regulation 1642/2003, OJ L 245, 29.09.2003.
[2]   Regulation 852/2004, OJ L 157, 30.04.2004.
[3]   Regulation 853/2004, OJ L 157, 30.04.2004.
[4]   Regulation 854/2004, OJ L 157, 30.04.2004 and Regulation 882/2004, OJ L 165, 30.04.2004.
[5]   Regulation 882/2004, OJ L 165, 30.04.2004.
[6]   Directive 2005/94, OJ L 10, 14.01.2006.

The food safety policy of the Community is based on the **precaution-ary principle**. This principle means that where, following an assessment of available information, the possibility of harmful effects on health is identi-fied but scientific uncertainty persists, provisional risk management meas-ures necessary to ensure the high level of health protection may be adopted, pending further scientific information for a more comprehensive risk assessment. According to the Court of Justice, when there is uncer-tainty regarding the risk to human health or safety, the Community institu-tions are empowered to take protective measures without having to wait until the reality and seriousness of those risks becomes fully apparent[1].

In accordance with the precautionary principle, a Directive aims at monitoring the deliberate release into the environment and on the placing on the market of **genetically modified organisms (GMOs)** as or in prod-ucts[2]. Products containing GMOs must be clearly labelled and the public must be informed and consulted prior to the release and placing on the market of GMOs and products containing GMOs. Member States must es-tablish public registers of all locations where GMOs are grown and have agreed deadlines for phasing out antibiotic resistance markers in GMOs which could have adverse effects on human health and the environment. Genetically modified micro-organisms may be used solely under condi-tions of contained use[3]. A Regulation provides a framework for the **trace-ability of products** consisting of or containing GMOs, and food and feed produced from GMOs, with the objectives of facilitating accurate labelling, monitoring the effects on the environment and, where appropriate, on health, and the implementation of the appropriate risk management meas-ures including, if necessary, withdrawal of products[4]. Another Regulation lays down Community procedures for the authorisation and supervision of genetically modified food and feed and lays down provisions for the **label-ling** of genetically modified food and feed[5].

11.3. Protection of economic and legal interests

With the opening up of the markets, the economic interests of the con-sumers had to be protected uniformly in the single market. Thus, the Direc-tive on **liability for defective products** seeks to ensure a high level of consumer protection against damage caused to health or property by a de-fective product and at the same time to reduce the disparities between na-tional liability laws which distort competition and restrict the free move-ment of goods. It establishes the principle of objective liability or liability

---

[1] Judgments of 5 May 1998, Cases C-180/96 and C-157/96, ECR 1998 I-2265.
[2] Directive 2001/18, OJ L 106, 17.04.2001 and Decisions 2002/811, 2002/812 and 2002/813, OJ L 280, 18.10.2002.
[3] Directive 90/219, OJ L 117, 08.05.1990, Directive 98/81, OJ L 330, 05.12.1998 and Decision 2001/204, OJ L 73, 15.03.2001.
[4] Regulation 1830/2003, OJ L 268, 18.10.2003.
[5] Regulation 1829/2003, OJ L 268, 18.10.2003.

without fault of the producer in cases of damage caused by a defective product. In the aftermath of the "mad cow" crisis, its scope was extended to primary agricultural products (such as meat, cereals, fruit and vegetables) and game products[1]. "Producer" is taken to mean: any participant in the production process; the importer of the defective product; any person supplying a product whose producer cannot be identified. The injured person does not need to prove the negligence or fault of the producer, but only the actual damage; the defect in the product; and the causal relationship between damage and defect. The producer's liability is not altered when the damage is caused both by a defect in the product and by the act or omission of a third party. However, when the injured person is at fault, the producer's liability may be reduced. "Damage" means: damage caused by death or by personal injuries; damage to an item of property intended for private use or consumption other than the defective product, with a lower threshold of 500 euros. The injured person has three years within which to seek compensation.

Going a step further, the Directive on certain aspects of the sale of consumer goods and associated guarantees introduced the **principle of the conformity of the product** with the contract[2]. The Directive is concerned both with commercial guarantees and with the legal guarantee, which includes all legal protection of the purchaser in respect of defects in the goods acquired, resulting directly from the law, as a collateral effect of the contract of sale. The seller is liable to the consumer for any lack of conformity which exists when the goods are delivered to the consumer and which becomes apparent within a period of two years unless, at the moment of conclusion of the contract of sale, the consumer knew or could not reasonably be unaware of the lack of conformity. When a lack of conformity is notified to the seller, the consumer is entitled to ask (in a logical sequence) for the goods to be repaired or replaced free of charge or for an appropriate reduction to be made to the price or to have the contract rescinded. On top of the legal guarantee, the commercial guarantee offered by a seller or producer should be legally binding under the conditions laid down in the guarantee document and the associated advertising.

A Directive seeks to protect consumers, traders and the public in general against **misleading advertising** and its unfair consequences[3]. When a user considers that an advertising text or presentation has misled him or her, he or she can launch proceedings against the manufacturer. The Directive on misleading advertising introduced a uniform regulatory framework on **comparative advertising**, defined as the advertising that explicitly or by implication identifies a competitor or goods or services offered by a competitor. Such advertising is allowed under certain conditions, namely: it must not be misleading within the meaning of the Directive; it must ob-

---

[1] Directive 85/374, OJ L 210, 07.08.1985 and Directive 1999/34, OJ L 141, 04.06.1999.

[2] Directive 1999/44, OJ L 171, 07.07.1999.

[3] Directive 84/450, OJ L 250, 19.09.1984 codified by Directive 2006/114, OJ L 376, 27.12.2006.

jectively compare material, relevant, verifiable and representative features of goods and services, including prices; and it must neither create confusion in the market place between trade marks or trade names nor discredit or denigrate a competitor's marks, goods, services or activities. The Court of Justice has given useful indications about the meaning of "misleading advertisement"[1]

Directive 2005/29 approximates the laws of the Member States on **unfair commercial practices**, including unfair advertising, which directly harm consumers' economic interests and thereby indirectly harm the economic interests of legitimate competitors[2]. It covers those practices (actions or omissions) which by deceiving the consumer prevent him from making an informed and thus efficient choice. Aggressive commercial practices, which are also prohibited by this Directive, cover those practices - such as harassment, coercion, the use of physical force and undue influence - which significantly impair the consumer's freedom of choice.

A number of Directives concern **contractual relations**. The Community is concerned in particular with the protection of consumers in respect of contracts negotiated away from business premises (**door-to-door sales**). A Directive grants consumers seven days in which to reconsider and renounce any agreement on a door-to-door sale[3]. The trader must inform the consumer in writing of the right of renunciation at his or her disposal.

In the same spirit, a Directive lays down minimum consumer protection rules concerning **distance contracts** regardless of the technology used (e.g. mail-order, telephone, fax, computer, television, etc.) and regardless of the product or service marketed, with the exception of financial services[4]. The underlying purpose of the Directive is to provide consumers with information in advance and to ensure that transactions are transparent. When any offer of goods or services is made, and when a sales contract is drawn up, the identity of the supplier and the commercial nature of the proposal must be clearly stated (at the beginning of the call in the case of a telephone communication). Other details, which must be made clear, include the price of the proposed product or service, the technical characteristics, the arrangements for payment and the conditions governing withdrawal from the contract. The consumer's agreement must be obtained before any goods or services, for which payment is required, are supplied. The consumer is entitled to a period of seven working days in which to withdraw from the contract without penalty. A supplier who fails to fulfil his or her obligations must reimburse any sums paid.

A special directive concerning the **distance marketing of consumer financial services** provides for common rules for selling contracts by phone, fax or Internet. It is designed to offer consumers much-needed pro-

---

[1] Judgment of 19 September 2006, Case C-356/04, Lidl Belgium GmbH & Co., ECR 2006, p. I-8501.
[2] Directive 2005/29, OJ L 149, 11.06.2005.
[3] Directive 85/577, OJ L 372, 31.12.1985 and OJ L 1, 03.01.1994.
[4] Directive 97/7, OJ L 144, 04.06.1997 and Directive 2007/64, OJ L 319, 05.12.2007.

tection and rights and to increase their confidence in e-commerce, both within individual Member States and across borders[1] [see also Directive 2007/64 in section 6.7]. Its main features are: the prohibition of abusive marketing practices seeking to oblige consumers to buy a service they have not solicited ("inertia selling"); rules to restrict other practices such as unsolicited phone calls and e-mails ("cold calling" and "spamming"); an obligation to provide consumers with comprehensive information before a contract is concluded; and a consumer right to withdraw from the contract during a cool-off period, except in cases where there is a risk of speculation.

Another Directive concerns **unfair terms in contracts** concluded between a consumer and a professional[2]. It establishes, in particular, a distinction between contractual terms negotiated among the parties and terms which the consumer has not negotiated expressly. A non-negotiated clause is to be regarded as unfair where it creates a significant imbalance, to the detriment of the consumer, between the rights and obligations of the parties to the contract. The Directive establishes the principle that consumers are not bound by unfair terms in contracts, and makes Member States responsible for implementing appropriate and effective means of ensuring that professionals cease to use such terms.

Uniform protection in the European Union is provided to all consumers who use credit to finance their purchases. The Directive on **credit agreements for consumers** establishes common rules on consumer credit aimed at harmonising certain aspects of the laws, regulations and administrative provisions on consumer credit in the internal market[3]. The directive covers personal loans of between EUR 200 and 75 000 repayable after more than a month. It does not apply to mortgages or to deferred debit cards. It provides for the application of a single Community formula for calculating the annual percentage rate of charge for consumer credit.

A Council Directive on **package travel, including package holidays and package tours**, protects millions of tourists against possible corrupt practices by the organisers of these popular holidays[4]. Contract clauses must be recorded in writing and the consumer must receive a copy of them. The information supplied cannot be misleading: brochures placed at the disposal of the consumer must contain clear and precise information on prices, means of transport, type of accommodation, its situation, category and so on. In principle, prices cannot be revised, unless express provision is made for this in the contract. Even when surcharges are possible, they are subject to certain conditions. If the organiser cancels the package, the consumer has the right either to another package of equivalent or higher quality, or to reimbursement of all sums already paid, without prejudice to any compensation. The consumer also has the right to compensation if the organiser does not supply a large part of the service agreed upon. Finally,

---

[1]   Directive 2002/65, OJ L 271, 09.10.2002 and directive 2007/64, OJ L 319, 05.12.2007.

[2]   Directive 93/13, OJ L 95, 21.04.1993.

[3]   Directive 2008/48, OJ L 133, 22.05.2008.

[4]   Directive 90/314, OJ L 158, 23.06.1990.

the organiser or the travel agency must give proof of sufficient guarantees to ensure repayment of the sums paid or the repatriation of the consumer in the event of insolvency or bankruptcy.

Still in the field of tourism and of cross-border vacations, a Directive protects purchasers of **timeshare rights** to one or more immovable properties[1]. The purchaser must be provided with a description relating, in particular, to the property itself, its situation, details of any communal services to which the purchaser will have access and the conditions governing such access, the period of enjoyment, the price and an estimate of the charges payable. The contract and the document describing the property covered by the contract must be drawn up in the official language (or one of the languages) of the Member State in which the purchaser resides or, if he or she so wishes, in the language (or one of the languages) of the Member State of which he or she is a citizen. In addition, the vendor must provide the purchaser with a certified translation of the contract in the official Community language (or one of the languages) of the Member State in which the property is situated. In any case, the purchaser is entitled to withdraw within 10 days without giving any reason. Any advance payment by the purchaser before the end of that cooling-off period is prohibited.

11.4. Appraisal and outlook

The European Union shows a growing interest in the protection of the physical safety and of the economic interests of its citizens. This is a natural evolution since the single market has increased not only the choice of goods and services from the partners, but also the risks to consumers of all the Member States from defective products, notably foodstuffs, produced in one of them. Those risks were amply demonstrated during the mad cow crisis, which originated in the United Kingdom in 1996, and the scandal of dioxin-contaminated foodstuffs of Belgian origin, in 1999 [see section 5.1.3.]. While on these occasions, the Community consumer protection legislation proved its usefulness at preventing the spread of diseases and contaminations, it also revealed its limits, concerning its implementation by the Member States. With the increasing number of economic transactions between individuals and businesses from different Member States, there is also a growing need for their protection from dishonest business practices through uniform measures, supplementing the different national measures. Moreover, consumer representatives should be given the support they need to be effective in increasingly complex and technical debates, and the consumer's voice should be heard more systematically in the decision-making process.

---

[1] Directive 94/47, OJ L 280, 29.10.1994.

Bibliography on consumer protection policy

- BOOM Willem van, LOOS Marco (eds.). *Collective enforcement of consumer law: securing compliance in Europe through private group action and public authority intervention*. Groningen: European Law Publishing, 2007.
- EUROPEAN COMMISSION. *EU consumer policy strategy 2007-2013: Empowering consumers, enhancing their welfare, effectively protecting them*; COM (2007) 99. Luxembourg: EUR-OP*, 2007.
  - Your rights as a consumer: how the European Union protects your interests. Luxembourg: EUR-OP*, 2007.
- FAIRGRIEVE Duncan, HOWELLS Geraint. "Rethinking product liability: a missing element in the European Commission's third review of the European Product Liability Directive", in *The Modern Law Review*, v. 70, n. 6, November 2007, p. 962-978.
- FELCE Jon. "European Union law: packing it in", in *European Food and Feed Law Review*, v. 2, n. 6, 2007, p. 386-391.
- GORMLEY Laurence (ed.). "Special issue on competition law and the consumer in the EU", *European Business Law Review*, v. 17, n. 1, 2006, p. 1-104.
- KARSTEN Jens. "Passengers, consumers, and travellers: the rise of passenger rights in EC transport law and its repercussions for Community consumer law and policy", in *Journal of Consumer Policy*, v. 30, n. 2, June 2007, p. 117-136.
- LANDO Ole." Liberal, social and 'ethical' justice in European contract law" in *Common Market Law Review*, v. 43, n. 3, June 2006, p. 817-833.
- SHEARS Peter. "The EU product liability directive: twenty years on", in *The Journal of Business Law*, November 2007, p. 884-908.
- TWIGG-FLESNER Christian (ed.). *The yearbook of consumer law 2008*. Oxon: Ashgate Publishing, 2007.

DISCUSSION TOPICS

1. Discuss the need for a consumer protection policy in the context of a common market.
2. Outline the respective responsibilities of national and Community authorities in tackling problems endangering public health.
3. What are the lessons to be drawn from the mad cow and dioxin crises?
4. Is there a need for a common legislation concerning contractual relations in a common market?
5. Compare the objectives of the Directives on general product safety and on liability for defective products.

Part IV: Horizontal policies

In **Part IV we examine the horizontal policies of the Union**, that is to say the objectives set, the means employed and the measures taken in common by the Member States of the Union in order to support and supplement their policies in five broad areas of their economic and socio-political activities: regional development, social progress, taxation, competition and environmental protection. All these common policies were launched during the stages of the customs union and the common market and are being continuously developed in order to further the higher goals set for the stages of economic and monetary union and political integration.

The **common regional policy** by means of the Structural Funds aims to help the poorer regions of the Community to face the increased trade and competition from the more developed regions imposed by the single market and the economic and monetary union. Such a union, implying abandonment of the use of exchange rate adjustment as a means of balance of the national economy, would be to the detriment of the poorer Member States without an efficient common regional policy revolving around sufficient capital transfers from the richer to the poorer regions of the EU. The common regional policy aims, therefore, at the economic and social cohesion of the Union.

The acceleration in the process of European integration since the middle of the 1980s has resulted in major progress in the **common social policy**, spanning fields such as vocational training, social protection and worker health and safety. This process is stepped up in the economic and monetary union, which takes out of governments' hands many economic and monetary instruments and hence their ability to tackle their social problems alone. Therefore, the Amsterdam Treaty identified the promotion of a high level of employment as a Community objective and introduced a coordinated strategy for employment.

The **common taxation policy** has gone beyond the Treaty requirements of fiscal neutrality. The Member States succeeded in replacing their various cumulative multi-stage turnover taxes with a uniform value added tax, the structures of which have been closely harmonised. The abolition of tax frontiers, made possible by the approximation of VAT rates and excise duties, made a vital contribution to the final completion of the single market. As economic and monetary union advances, approximation is also required for company and savings taxes.

The **common competition policy** plays the role of economic regulator in the common market. It prevents market compartmentalisation, abolished in the single market, from being restored by means of agreements between large companies. It also prevents multinational companies from exploiting their dominant position or monopolising a market by acquisition of independent firms. As regards State interventionism, the role of the common competition policy is to confine it to aid which fits in with the common objective of adjusting the structures of the European Union's production mechanism to internal and external changes.

The **common environment policy** is vital for the quality of life of the citizens of the Union. In a European economy, which faces strong international competition, the challenge of policy-makers is to take measures that make it possible to painlessly achieve the objective of growth, which is compatible with the essential requirements of the environment. The EU follows, indeed, a coherent programme for sustainable growth. However, the EU cannot work alone for the protection of the environment of the globe. Using its economic power, it should lead the way to a better international coordination in this area.

Chapter 12

REGIONAL DEVELOPMENT POLICY

Diagram of the chapter

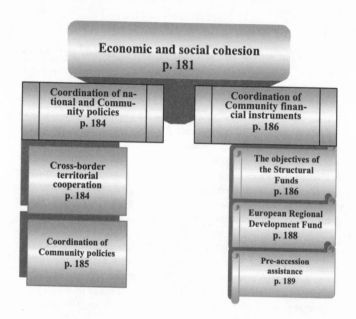

The main objective of the common regional policy is the reduction of existing regional disparities and the prevention of further regional imbalances in the EU by transferring Community resources to problem regions using the financial instruments of the Community known as the Structural Funds. The common regional policy of the EU does not seek to supersede national regional policies. In accordance with the principle of subsidiarity [see section 3.2.], the Member States, through their own regional policies, are the first ones who must solve the problems in their regions by promoting infrastructures and financially supporting job-creation investments. However, the common regional policy coordinates national regional policies by formulating guidelines and establishing certain principles in order to **avoid competition for regional aid between Member States**. It coordinates also the various policies and financial instruments of the EU to give them a "regional dimension" and thus more impact on regions most in need of care.

The **Committee of the Regions** set up by the Treaty of Maastricht in order to enhance the role of regional authorities in the institutional system of the Union [see section 4.2.4.], plays an important role in the forecasting of regional tendencies and in the management of structural interventions of the EU. In the enlarged Union, where the unequal distribution of wealth among regions would be greatly increased, the democratic legitimacy and the role of the Committee of the Regions should also be increased [see section 4.4.].

12.1. The need for a common regional policy

By assisting the problem regions build up their infrastructure networks, the Member States and the Union can help them to both develop their markets for the benefit of all and better balance the European economy in the light of future changes. Of course, each Member State carries out its own regional policy, which generally aims at favouring the development of the national territory's less prosperous regions by means of **transferring resources from wealthier regions**. The means normally used by Member States to remedy regional problems are of two types: firstly, improving the infrastructure and the social and cultural development of backward regions, and secondly, various premiums, subsidies and tax incentives for attracting private investment in these regions. The general objective of these measures is to create or re-establish a better distribution of economic activities and population over the national territory. To do this, certain governments also try to discourage investments in highly developed regions. The advantages of such measures are twofold: favouring the transfer of resources towards poor regions while halting the disproportionate expansion of congested regions.

Certainly, it is primarily up to the national authorities to solve the problems of their regions, namely by promoting infrastructures or giving incentives to businesses to attract their investments in disadvantaged regions. The scale of the effort required to stimulate economic activity in the least advanced regions means that public funds must be used in conjunction with private investment. **Regional aid**, when judiciously applied, is a vital instrument to regional development and to continued and balanced expansion within the European Union. But given the possibility of competition inside a single market between the various regions in order to attract Community and foreign investments (including those from partner countries), the advantages granted can go beyond compensation for material difficulties faced by investors in the areas to be promoted. Thus, part of the aid granted would merely serve a reciprocal neutralisation. The national regional actions would simply be more expensive and grant unwarranted profits to benefiting undertakings [see also section 15.5.]. Therefore, the prime objective of EU regional policy is to **coordinate national regional**

policies by formulating guidelines and setting priorities at European level, which effectively help close the gap between regions.

In addition, the EU has a common interest in regional development through structural change. The very essence of economic integration is **the optimisation of the market mechanism** at a European scale. But a market policy based on some sort of spontaneous balance between the various economic parameters essentially benefits rich regions. Indeed, prior to the creation of the common market, economic activities had developed in a national context; certain activities usually grouped in certain regions were protected from international competition by customs barriers. With the opening of borders, European and foreign (American, Japanese...) companies wanting to set up business in the EU market are normally attracted in European regions where infrastructure is most developed, where labour is most qualified, and where the economic environment is most adapted to their activities. Economic concentration invites more concentration. The common regional policy strives to make up for this tendency in order to achieve **a better-balanced growth within the common market**. Its goals and mechanisms are coordinated and interact with those of other common policies, notably social, enterprise, environment, agricultural and fisheries policies.

12.1.1. The classification of EU regions

Economic, social and territorial disparities at both regional and national level have **increased in the enlarged European Union**. At the dawn of the 21st century, gross domestic product (GDP) per head in the lagging regions of the Union averaged 66% of the EU15 average, which stood at EUR 20,213 per head. The enlargement to ten new countries in 2004 and to two more in 2007 reduced the EU average GDP per head to EUR 16,500. The population living in regions with GDP per head of less than 75% of the present EU average was increased from 71 million to 174 million, or from 19% of the EU15 total to 36% of the EU27 total. Three groups of countries can be distinguished in the EU of 27 in terms of GDP per head. The first group with GDP per head 20% above the new average was formed by the EU15 Member States, apart from Greece, Portugal and Spain. These three cohesion countries plus Cyprus, the Czech Republic, Slovenia and Malta formed the second group, with GDP per head between 68% (the Czech Republic) and 95% (Spain) of the EU 27 average. The remaining 8 countries formed the third group, with GDP per head only 40% of the EU27 average.

The identification of the priority regions and areas at Community level are based on the **common classification of territorial units for statistics (NUTS)**[1]. On this basis, Regulation 1083/2006, laying down general provisions on the Structural Funds, identifies three categories of regions covered

---

[1] Regulation 1059/2003, OJ L 154, 21.06.2003 and Regulation 176/2008, OJ L 61, 05.03.2008.

by priority objectives: (a) the Convergence objective; (b) the Regional competitiveness and employment objective; and (c) the European territorial cooperation objective[1] [see section 12.3.1].

The regions eligible for funding from the Structural Funds under the **Convergence objective** are regions corresponding to level 2 of the common classification of territorial units for statistics (NUTS level 2) whose gross domestic product (GDP) per capita, measured in purchasing power parities and calculated on the basis of Community figures for the period 2000 to 2002, is less than 75% of the average GDP of the EU-25 for the same reference period. These regions are to be found both in the new and the old Member States. The latter are the regions suffering from the statistical effect linked to the reduction in the Community average following the enlargement of the European Union. These regions would have been eligible for Convergence objective status had the eligibility threshold remained at 75% of the average GDP of the EU-15. They benefit for that reason from substantial **transitional aid** in order to complete their convergence process. This aid is to end in 2013 and is not to be followed by a further transitional period. In addition, the Member States eligible for funding from the Cohesion Fund under the convergence objective are those whose gross national income (GNI) per capita, measured in purchasing power parities and calculated on the basis of Community figures for the period 2001 to 2003, is less than 90 % of the average GNI of the EU-25 and which have a programme for meeting the economic convergence conditions referred to in Article 104 of the EC Treaty. In reality the Convergence objective for 2007-2013 applies to 100 regions, including 16 granted transitional "phasing-out" status – accounting for just over 35% of the EU27 population[2].

The regions eligible for funding from the Structural Funds under the **Regional competitiveness and employment (RCE) objective** are those not eligible under the convergence objective or the transitional support objective. The NUTS level 2 regions totally covered by Objective 1 in 2006 under Article 3 of Regulation 1260/1999 whose nominal GDP level per capita will exceed 75% of the average GDP of the EU15 are eligible, on a transitional and specific basis, for financing by the Structural Funds under the Regional competitiveness and employment objective. Hence the RCE objective applies in principle to the rest of the Union, or to 155 regions with 61% of EU27 population, while another 13 regions are classified as "phasing-in" (almost 4% of the EU population).

A **European territorial cooperation objective** covers regions having land or sea frontiers, the areas for transnational cooperation being defined with regard to actions promoting integrated territorial development and support for interregional cooperation and exchange of experience. These are NUTS level 3 regions of the Community along all internal and certain

---

[1] Regulation 1083/2006, OJ L 210, 31.07.2006 and R. 1989/2006, OJ L 411, 30.12.2006.
[2] COM/2006/281.

external land borders and all NUTS level 3 regions of the Community along maritime borders separated, as a general rule, by a maximum of 150 kilometres. For the purpose of interregional cooperation, cooperation networks and exchange of experience, the entire territory of the Community shall be eligible.

12.1.2. Economic and social cohesion of the Union

The wider European market reinforces the polarisation of pre-existing economic activities and thus **accelerates the agglomeration and concentration process**. If measures were not taken at national and European level, the completion of the internal market would tend further to widen existing inequalities in the distribution of economic activities throughout the territory of the EU. That is why, the objective of economic and social cohesion, implying the desire to reduce disparities between the various regions of the Community, was introduced by the Single European Act [see section 2.1.]. On top of the single market, **the achievement of economic and monetary union** promises enhanced prospects for the developed and the less favoured regions alike. The reduction of trans-frontier transaction costs and the elimination of exchange rate risk may promote regional specialisation and intra-Community trade in goods and services. The weaker regions can benefit from this specialisation by exploiting more fully their comparative advantages. Furthermore, increased capital mobility in EMU, supported by the single currency and the tendency towards quasi-uniform inflation rates, tends to equalise interest rates for any given level of risk, which should favour the less developed regions where capital is often relatively scarce and capital costs, therefore, relatively high.

At the same time, however, Member States participating in the euro-zone **lose certain fiscal and monetary policy options** as well as the ability to adjust the exchange rate. Exchange rate flexibility is important in that, in principle, it enables a country, through devaluation, to offset a loss in international competitiveness in a relatively painless manner. As such, it facilitates short-term adjustment to general, or country-specific economic shocks. The removal of the possibility of exchange rate adjustment, therefore, represents a more important loss to the least developed countries of the euro-zone, which are the ones that must carry out the most important structural changes. Those countries must invest most, while spending least so as to conform to the Maastricht criteria and to the requirements of the Stability Pact [see section 7.2.4. and 7.3.2.].

In addition, those countries could **lose the advantage of lower labour costs.** As long as markets were protected by customs and other barriers, salaries in certain countries were much lower than in others, compensating for the lower productivity of a labour force that was not very qualified. But in a common market, and even more in an economic and monetary union, freedom of movement for workers, better information on respective situations, and trade union demands tend to align revenues towards the levels already attained in the more prosperous regions. This may be a positive outcome from a social point of view but it is one which engenders inflationist tendencies and creates difficulties for businesses in areas where productivity is low. If these businesses have to shut down, the workers lose their jobs and their revenue increase is merely an illusion.

From both an economic and social point of view, neither the weakest member countries nor the European Union can tolerate a substantial part of their patrimony being left to underdevelopment because of economic integration. The prosperity of certain areas of the union cannot be paid for by the decline or stagnation of other areas. Wide **disparities are intolerable in a community**, if the term is to have any meaning at all. Furthermore, disparities do not just imply a poorer quality of life for the disadvantaged regions, but indicate a failure to take advantage of economic opportunities that could benefit the Union as a whole.

For all these reasons, the Treaty on the European Union states in its Article 2 that the strengthening of **economic and social cohesion is a fundamental objective of the Union**. Article 158 of the EC Treaty provides that, in order to strengthen its economic and social cohesion, the Community is to aim at reducing disparities between the levels of development of the various regions and the backwardness of the least favoured regions or islands, including rural areas. Article 159 of the Treaty requires this action to be supported by the Structural Funds, the European Investment Bank (EIB) and the other existing Financial Instruments. Although all Community policies can contribute to reinforcing economic and social cohesion, as is stated in Article 159 (TEC), a major role is, certainly, played by the Structural Funds (Art. 161 TEC).

Initially the **"Structural Funds"** included the European Regional Development Fund (ERDF), the European Social Fund (ESF), the European Agricultural Guidance and Guarantee Fund (EAGGF) - Guidance Section, and the Financial Instrument for Fisheries Guidance (FIFG). After the reforms of the common agricultural and the common fisheries policies, in 2005, the instrument providing aid for rural development, namely the European Agricultural Fund for Rural Development (EAFRD) [see section 21.5.1], and that of the fisheries sector, namely the European Fisheries Fund (EFF) [see section 22.4] have been integrated into the instruments under the common agricultural policy and the common fisheries policy. They must be coordinated with the instruments under the cohesion policy, but are not included in those instruments. The Structural Funds should take complementary action over and above that of the EAFRD and of the EFF to promote the economic diversification of rural areas and of areas dependent on fisheries. However, the exclusion of the agricultural and fisheries instruments means that the Funds providing assistance under the cohesion policy are nowadays limited to the European Regional Development Fund (ERDF), the European Social Fund (ESF) and the Cohesion Fund. Hence, the Cohesion Fund is now fully integrated into the programming of structural assistance, a fact that should increase the coherence in the intervention of the various Funds.

The greater regional diversity of the Union [see section 12.1.1] and the expansion of its land and sea borders after the enlargements of 2004 and 2007 have increased the importance of transnational and interregional cooperation in the Community. Therefore, the cohesion policy of the Community was completely revised in 2006. Regulation 1083/2006, repealing Regulation 1260/1999, lays down the **general rules** governing the European Regional Development Fund (ERDF), the European Social Fund (ESF) and the Cohesion Fund[1]. Regulation 1083/2006 defines the objectives to which the Structural Funds and the Cohesion Fund are to contribute, the criteria for Member States and regions to be eligible under those Funds, the financial resources available and the criteria for their allocation. Community **strategic guidelines** on economic, social and territorial cohesion serve as an indicative framework for the Member States for the preparation of the national strategic reference frameworks and operational programmes for the period 2007 to 2013[2]. The European Neighbourhood and Partnership Instrument and the Instrument for Pre-Accession Assistance established by Regulation 1085/2006[3] are closely aligned to Structural Fund and Rural Development practices.

Article 161 (TEC) and a Protocol annexed to the Treaty of Maastricht [see section 2.2.] have provided for the creation of the **Cohesion Fund**. Assistance from the Cohesion Fund shall be given to actions in the following areas, according to the investment and infrastructure needs specific to each Member State receiving assistance[4]: (a) trans-European transport networks, in particular priority projects of common interest as identified by Decision 1692/96[5]; and (b) the environment within the priorities assigned to the Community environmental protection policy under the policy and action programme on the environment [see section 16.2]. Assistance from the Fund may be suspended if the Council has decided in accordance with Article 104(6) of the Treaty that excessive government deficit exists in a beneficiary Member State, and has established that the Member State concerned has not taken effective action in response to a Council recommendation.

---

[1] Regulation 1083/2006, OJ L 210, 31.07.2006 and R. 1989/2006, OJ L 411, 30.12.2006.
[2] Decision 2006/702, OJ L 291, 21.10.2006.
[3] Regulation 1085/2006, OJ L 210, 31.07.2006.
[4] Regulation 1084/2006, OJ L 210, 31.07.2006.
[5] Decision 1692/96, OJ L 228, 09.09.1996, last amended by Decision 884/2004, OJ L 167, 30.04.2004.

12.2. Coordination of national and Community policies

On the basis of Article 87(3)(a) and (c) of the EC Treaty, State aid granted to promote the economic development of certain disadvantaged areas within the European Union may be considered to be compatible with the common market by the Commission. It ensues that the European Commission determines the compatibility or incompatibility of a given national regional aid with the common market. Article 88 (TEC) states that the Commission shall, in cooperation with the Member States, keep **under constant review all systems of aid** existing in those States. It must be informed, in sufficient time to enable it to submit its comments, of any plans to grant or alter aid. The Member States notify the Commission of proposed levels of regional aid and the latter either approves or amends them, often to lower levels. The Member State concerned must not put its proposed measures into effect until the procedure initiated by the Commission has resulted in a final decision. If the State concerned does not comply with this decision within the prescribed time, the Commission or any other interested State may refer the matter to the Court of Justice directly, which happens quite often.

The important political and economic developments in the beginning of the 21st century, notably the accelerated process of integration following the introduction of the single currency, the enlargement of the European Union on 1 May 2004 and 1 January 2007 created the need for a comprehensive review of the **criteria applied by the Commission** when examining the compatibility of national regional aid with the common market under Article 87(3a) and (3c) of the EC Treaty. These criteria are codified in the **Guidelines on national regional aid** for 2007-2013[1]. According to these guidelines, regional aid should, in general, be granted under a multi-sectoral aid scheme which forms an integral part of a regional development strategy with clearly defined objectives. Regional **aid for large investment projects**, while covered by the regional aid guidelines, is also subject to specific rules, because it might be granted to large firms which are little affected by region-specific problems, but which possess considerable bargaining power vis-à-vis the authorities granting aid and may cause unjustified distortions in competition[2].

12.2.1. Cross-border territorial cooperation

In view of the difficulties encountered by the Member States in carrying out and managing cross-border, transnational and interregional cooperation, the new legislative framework [see section 12.1.2], provides for the creation of a Community-level cooperation instrument allowing the

---

[1]   OJ C 54, 04.03.2006, p. 13-44.
[2]   Communication from the Commission OJ C 70, 19.03.2002, p. 8-20.

creation of cooperative groupings with their own legal personality, called **"European groupings of territorial cooperation" (EGTC)**[1]. An EGTC is an optional cooperation instrument at Community level. The objective of an EGTC should be to facilitate and promote cross-border, transnational and/or interregional cooperation, with the exclusive aim of strengthening economic and social cohesion. An EGTC may be made up of members belonging to one or more of the following categories: (a) Member States; (b) regional authorities; (c) local authorities; and (d) bodies governed by public law. The decision to establish an EGTC should be taken at the initiative of its prospective members. An EGTC may act on behalf of its members, and notably the regional and local authorities of which it is composed.

An EGTC should carry out the tasks given to it by its members in accordance with Regulation 1082/2006. Its tasks are defined by the convention agreed by its members, but should be limited to the facilitation and promotion of **territorial cooperation** to strengthen economic and social cohesion. Specifically, the tasks of an EGTC should be limited primarily to the implementation of territorial cooperation programmes or projects co-financed by the Community through the European Regional Development Fund, the European Social Fund and/or the Cohesion Fund. However, an EGTC may carry out actions of territorial cooperation which are at the sole initiative of the Member States and their regional and local authorities with or without a financial contribution from the Community.

12.2.2. Coordination of Community policies

The general Regulation on the Structural Funds specifies that the Commission and the Member States must ensure that the operations of the Funds are consistent with other Community policies and operations[2]. Indeed, several **common policies favour by their nature the process of integration and cohesion**. Thus, the common social policy has an important impact on labour law, health and security at work, free movement of workers and equal opportunities for men and women in the poor regions of the Union. Community research programmes develop research capabilities in weaker Member States strengthening their scientific and technological base and accelerating innovation and economic development. The common agricultural policy has also a positive cohesion effect, with the cohesion countries receiving net transfers through it.

Since any economic activity is of necessity localised in one area, the majority of the Community's measures, be it in agriculture, industry, transport or research, have an impact at regional level. The Community's regional policy consequently attempts to ensure consistency between regional objectives and those of other common policies by the European Spatial Development Perspective (ESDP)[3]. A Community framework for

---

[1] Regulation 1082/2006, OJ L 210, 31.07.2006.

[2] Regulation 1083/2006, OJ L 210, 31.07.2006 and R. 1989/2006, OJ L 411, 30.12.2006.

[3] OJ C 36, 09.02.1979, p. 10-11.

cooperation supports awareness-raising on sustainable urban development and urban environment, through development and transfer of good practices and cooperation between actors involved in sustainable development[1].

12.3. Coordination of Community financial instruments

The coordination of the financial instruments of the Community is ensured by the Regulation laying down general provisions on the European Regional Development Fund, the European Social Fund and the Cohesion Fund[2]. According to article 9.4 of this Regulation, the Commission and the Member States shall ensure the coordination between the assistance from these Funds, the European Agricultural Fund for Rural Development (EAFRD), the European Fisheries Fund (EFF) and the interventions of the EIB and of other existing financial instruments, notably the European Investment Fund (EIF). Such coordination should also cover the preparation of complex financial schemes and public-private partnerships. The Commission is assisted by a Coordination Committee of the Funds set up by Article 103 of the Regulation.

In order to maximise the stimulus provided by the budget resources deployed, making use of appropriate financial instruments, the Community assistance provided in the form of grants may be combined in an appropriate way with loans and guarantees of the **European Investment Bank (EIB)** [see section 7.3.3.]. The latter is the longest standing regional development instrument, for the Treaty of Rome called upon it to ensure a balanced and smooth development of the common market in the interests of the Community (Art. 267 TEC). Almost 75% of EIB financing in the Community contribute to regional development, although they pursue other objectives such as those of promoting SMEs and trans-European networks [see section 6.8.]. The EIB notably supplies long-term capital for the financing of infrastructure projects in the fields of transport, energy and telecommunications.

12.3.1. The objectives and methods of the Structural Funds

The action taken by the Community under Article 158 of the EC Treaty is designed to strengthen the economic and social cohesion of the enlarged European Union in order to promote its **harmonious, balanced and sustainable development**. This action is taken with the aid of the Structural Funds, the European Investment Bank (EIB) and other existing financial

---

[1] Decision 1411/2001, OJ L 91, 13.07.2001 and Decision 786/2004, OJ L 138, 30.04.2004.
[2] Regulation 1083/2006, OJ L 210, 31.07.2006 and R. 1989/2006, OJ L 411, 30.12.2006.

instruments. It is aimed at reducing the economic, social and territorial disparities which have arisen in the enlarged Union, particularly in countries and regions whose development is lagging behind and in connection with economic and social restructuring and the ageing of the population. According to the Regulation laying down general provisions on the European Regional Development Fund, the European Social Fund and the Cohesion Fund, the action taken under the Funds shall incorporate, at national and regional level, the Community's priorities in favour of sustainable development by strengthening growth, competitiveness, employment and social inclusion and by protecting and improving the quality of the environment[1]. To that end, the ERDF, the ESF, the Cohesion Fund, the EIB and the other existing Community financial instruments should each contribute towards achieving the **following three objectives**:

(a) **the Convergence objective**, which is aimed at speeding up the convergence of the least-developed Member States and regions by improving conditions for growth and employment through the increasing and improvement of the quality of investment in physical and human capital, the development of innovation and of the knowledge society, adaptability to economic and social changes, the protection and improvement of the environment, and administrative efficiency. This objective constitutes the priority of the Funds. The ERDF, the ESF and the Cohesion Fund contribute, each in accordance with the specific provisions governing it, towards achieving this objective.

(b) the **Regional competitiveness and employment objective**, which is aimed at strengthening the competitiveness and attractiveness of regions, as well as employment by anticipating economic and social changes, including those linked to the opening of trade. The means employed towards those aims are: the increasing and improvement of the quality of investment in human capital, innovation and the promotion of the knowledge society, entrepreneurship, the protection and improvement of the environment, and the improvement of accessibility, adaptability of workers and businesses as well as the development of inclusive job markets. The least-developed regions, which are eligible under the Convergence objective, are not eligible under this objective. The ERDF and the ESF contribute, each in accordance with the specific provisions governing it, towards achieving the regional competitiveness and employment objective. The Cohesion Fund may also intervene, under certain conditions, in Member States eligible for its support.

(c) the **European territorial cooperation objective**, which is aimed at strengthening cross-border cooperation through joint local and regional initiatives, strengthening transnational cooperation by means of actions conducive to integrated territorial development linked to the Community priorities, and strengthening interregional cooperation and exchange of experience at the appropriate territorial level. Only the ERDF contributes to-

---

[1] Regulation 1083/2006, OJ L 210, 31.07.2006 and R. 1989/2006, OJ L 411, 30.12.2006.

wards achieving this objective, but the Cohesion Fund may also intervene, under certain conditions, in Member States eligible for its support.

The objectives of the Funds are pursued in the framework of a **multiannual programming system** organised in several stages comprising the identification of the priorities, the financing, and a system of management and control[1]. The Council establishes at Community level concise **strategic guidelines** on economic, social and territorial cohesion defining an indicative framework for the intervention of the Funds, taking account of other relevant Community policies. The Member States present a **national strategic reference framework** which ensures that assistance from the Funds is consistent with the Community strategic guidelines on cohesion. Each national strategic reference framework constitutes a reference instrument for preparing the programming of the Funds for the period 1 January 2007 to 31 December 2013. The national strategic reference framework is prepared by each Member State in **partnership** (i.e. close cooperation) with the Commission and appropriate authorities and bodies such as: (a) the competent regional, local, urban and other public authorities; (b) the economic and social partners; (c) any other appropriate body representing civil society and non-governmental organisations.

The activities of the Funds in the Member States take the form of **operational programmes** within the national strategic reference framework. An operational programme is a document submitted by a Member State and adopted by the Commission setting out a development strategy with a coherent set of priorities to be carried out with the aid of a Fund, or, in the case of the Convergence objective, with the aid of the Cohesion Fund and the ERDF. According to the **principle of additionality**, the contributions from the Structural Funds must not replace public or equivalent structural expenditure by a Member State. In particular, the assistance co-financed by the Funds must target the European Union priorities of promoting competitiveness and creating jobs, including meeting the objectives of the Integrated Guidelines for Growth and Jobs (2005 to 2008)[2].

12.3.2. European Regional Development Fund

Article 160 of the EC Treaty provides that the **European Regional Development Fund (ERDF)** is intended to help to redress the main regional imbalances in the Community. The ERDF has been reformed five times since its creation in 1975, demonstrating both the Community's growing commitment to regional development and its increased experience on this matter. Nowadays, the **ERDF is governed** by the general Regulation 1083/2006[3] and by the special Regulation 1080/2006[4], which estab-

---

[1] Regulation 1083/2006, OJ L 210, 31.07.2006 and R. 1989/2006, OJ L 411, 30.12.2006.
[2] Decision 2005/600, OJ L 205, 06.08.2005 and Decision 2007/491, OJ L 183, 13.07.2007.
[3] Regulation 1083/2006, OJ L 210, 31.07.2006 and R. 1989/2006, OJ L 411, 30.12.2006.
[4] Regulation 1080/2006, OJ L 210, 31.07.2006.

lishes its tasks, the scope of its assistance and the rules on eligibility for assistance. Pursuant to these Regulations, the ERDF contributes to the financing of assistance which aims to reinforce economic and social cohesion by redressing the main regional imbalances through support for the development and structural adjustment of regional economies, including the conversion of declining industrial regions and regions lagging behind, and support for cross-border, transnational and interregional cooperation. In so doing, the ERDF must give effect to the priorities of the Community, and in particular the need to strengthen competitiveness and innovation, create and safeguard sustainable jobs, and ensure sustainable development.

The ERDF **contributes towards the financing of**:

(a) **productive investment** which contributes to creating and safeguarding sustainable jobs, primarily through direct aid to investment in small and medium-sized enterprises (SMEs);

(b) investment in **infrastructure**;

(c) development of **endogenous potential** by measures which support regional and local development, including support for and services to enterprises, in particular SMEs, creation and development of financing instruments such as venture capital, loan and guarantee funds, local development funds, interest subsidies, networking, cooperation and exchange of experience between regions, towns, and relevant social, economic and environmental actors;

(d) **technical assistance** which, either at the initiative of the Commission or at the initiative of the Member State, may finance the preparatory, management, monitoring, evaluation, information and control activities of operational programmes together with activities to reinforce the administrative capacity for implementing the Funds.

12.3.3. Pre-accession assistance

In order to improve the efficiency of the Community's External Aid, a new framework for programming and delivery of assistance was adopted at the same time as the 2006 reform of the Structural Funds. The Regulation establishing an **Instrument for Pre-Accession Assistance (IPA)** constitutes one of the general instruments directly supporting European External Aid policies[1]. In the interest of coherence, assistance for candidate countries as well as for potential candidate countries is granted in the context of a coherent framework, taking advantage of the lessons learned from earlier pre-accession instruments, but this assistance is also **consistent with the development policy** of the Community in accordance with Article 181a of the EC Treaty [see sections 24.4 and 25.2].

The Community assists candidate countries and potential candidate countries in their progressive alignment with the standards and policies of the European Union, including where appropriate the acquis communautaire, with a view to membership. A distinction is however made between

---

[1] Regulation 1085/2006, OJ L 210, 31.07.2006.

candidate countries (Croatia, Turkey, The former Yugoslav Republic of Macedonia) and **potential candidate countries** (Albania, Bosnia, Montenegro, Serbia, including Kosovo). In general, assistance for candidate countries as well as for potential candidate countries supports a wide range of institution-building measures. On the one hand it supports them in their efforts to strengthen democratic institutions and the rule of law, reform public administration, carry out economic reforms, respect human as well as minority rights, promote gender equality, support the development of civil society and advance regional cooperation as well as reconciliation and reconstruction. On the other hand, Community assistance contributes to sustainable development and poverty reduction in all these countries. Assistance for candidate countries additionally focuses on the adoption and implementation of the full acquis communautaire and prepares candidate countries for the implementation of the Community's agricultural and cohesion policy.

12.4. Appraisal and outlook

The common regional policy has grown in importance since the Treaty made it an **essential instrument of economic and social cohesion**, itself necessary for the progress of economic and monetary union, implying the convergence of the Member States' economies. Indeed, the regional policy of the Union promotes the concept of European solidarity by completing and guiding the action of the Member States in view of a balanced European integration, profitable not only to the poor regions, but also to the rest of the Union.

In view of the new objective of economic and monetary union that it set, **the Treaty of Maastricht** provided both a frame of reference and support for the common regional policy, notably by establishing economic and social cohesion as a fundamental objective of the Union, creating the Cohesion Fund, setting up the Committee of the Regions and promoting trans-European infrastructure networks. By signing and ratifying this Treaty, the Member States acknowledged that the objectives of the EMU and of economic and social cohesion should be pursued in parallel. As seen in the Chapter on economic and monetary union, such union, implying the abandonment of the use of exchange rate adjustment as a means of rebalancing the national economy, would not be feasible without an efficient regional policy revolving around sufficient capital transfers from the richer to the poorer regions of the EU [see sections 7.2.3. and 7.4.]. The problem for the least-favoured regions is, in particular, to ensure that the effort to stabilise the budget does not choke off the investment in basic infrastructure, education and training which those regions require.

The efforts of the Union to develop its poorest regions are proving to be successful. The gross domestic product (GDP) per head of poorer regions is converging towards the Community average. Between 1986 and

1996, GDP per head in the 10 poorest regions increased from 41% of the EU average to 50%, and in the 25 poorest regions it rose from 52% to 59%. GDP per head in the four Cohesion countries went up from 65% of the EU average to 77% in 1999. The Cohesion Fund enabled the beneficiary countries (Spain, Greece, Ireland and Portugal) to sustain a substantial level of public investment in the areas of the environment and transport, while complying with the goals of reducing expected budget deficits through the convergence programmes drawn up in the context of economic and monetary union. The GDP per capita (Purchasing Power Parities at US$) of Greece rose from 6726 in 1984 to 32764 in 2007, that of Portugal from 5715 to 26982, that of Spain from 7621 to 37657 and that of Ireland from 12332 to 52927. In 2007, Greece had reached 90% of the EU27 GDP per capita average (24600 €), Portugal stood at 74%, Spain at 103% and Ireland at 147%. Ireland had even the highest per capita income of the EU countries, out of Luxembourg. The structural and cohesion policies have largely contributed to these results. But it is not only the poorest Member States which have benefited. Indeed, the capital transfers carried out in the framework of an efficient regional policy are not just an offering to the less fortunate in the Union. They are also in the economic interest of the more prosperous States, since they develop markets for their products and help to stimulate growth in all the territory of the Union. Estimates show that almost 40% of all funding that flows into the poorest Member States returns to the richer ones in the form of purchase of know-how or capital equipment.

The big question is how the Structural Funds of the Union will cope with the **accession of 12 Member States**, most of which have a per capita GDP far below that of the EU15. The Convergence regions (including those in phasing-out) are characterised by low levels of GDP and employment, as well as high unemployment. Their total share in EU27 GDP in 2002 was only 12.5% compared to a 35% population share. Therefore, since 2006, the complete overhaul of the Structural Funds and of the Cohesion Fund is geared more to the structural problems of the poorest regions of old and new Member States. It remains to be seen if the new common regional policy will substantially reduce the regional diversity of the Union. The fact is that real needs persist throughout the EU requiring continued investment, in order to raise growth potential in line with the Lisbon objectives [see section 13.3.2].

Bibliography on regional policy

- BACHTLER John, MÉNDEZ Carlos. "Who governs EU cohesion policy?: Deconstructing the reforms of the structural funds", in *Journal of Common Market Studies*, v. 45, n. 3, September 2007, p. 535-564.
- BELLOUBET-FRIER Nicole (et al. eds.) "Les transferts territoriaux de compétences en Europe", in Numéro thématique de: *Revue française d'administration publique*, n. 121-122, avril-juin 2007.
- CRESPO Nuno, FONTOURA Maria Paula. "Integration of CEECs into EU market: structural change and convergence", in *Journal of Common Market Studies*, v. 45, n. 3, September 2007, p. 611-632.
- ESTEVADEORDAL Antoni (et al.). "The new regionalism" in Special issue of: *Economie internationale: la revue du CEPII*, n. 109, 2007.
- EUROPEAN COMMISSION. *New funds, better rules: Overview of new financial rules and funding opportunities 2007-2013*. Luxembourg: EUR-OP, 2007.
- HASHI Iraj, WELLENS Paul, WZIATEK-KUBIAK Anna. *Industrial competitiveness and restructuring in enlarged Europe: how accession countries catch up and integrate in the European Union*. Basingtoke: Palgrave Macmillan, 2007.
- KORRES George (ed.). *Regionalisation, growth, and economic integration*. Heidelberg: Physica-Verlag, 2007.
- KÖSLER Ariane, ZIMMEK Martin (eds.) *Global voices on regional integration*. Bonn: Zentrum für Europäische Integrationsforschung, 2007.
- TIESSEN Ulrich, GREGORY Paul. "Modeling structural change: an application to the new EU Member States and accession candidates", in *Eastern European Economics*, v. 45, n. 4, July-August 2007, p. 5-35.
- ULLTVEIT-MOE Karen Helene. "Regional policy design: an analysis of relocation, efficiency and equity", in *European Economic Review*, v. 51, n. 6, August 2007, p. 1443-1467.

DISCUSSION TOPICS

1. What is the need for a common regional policy in the stages of the common market and of the economic and monetary union?
2. What is the meaning of economic and social cohesion in the EU?
3. Which are the two wings of the common regional policy and how do they complement each other?
4. Outline the objectives and methods of the Structural Funds of the EU.
5. Discuss the role of the common regional policy within an enlarged Union containing a large number of poor regions.

Chapter 13

SOCIAL PROGRESS POLICIES

Diagram of the chapter

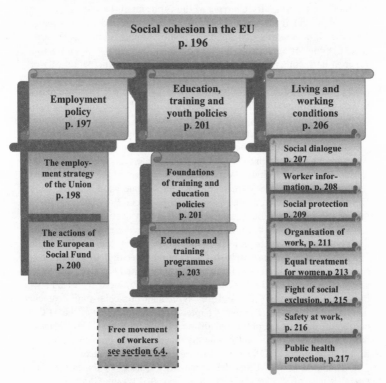

Given the varied economic structures of the Community Member States, their social problems were from the outset - and still are to some extent - quite different. It would not have been possible at the start - and that still holds true - to entrust the common social policy with the task of solving all the Member States' social problems. Such a solution depends to a great extent upon economic policy, which is still to a large degree in the hands of the individual governments. But as European integration advances and the Member States delegate significant economic and monetary policy instruments to the European Union, the latter **commits itself increasingly to the advancement of social progress** for all the peoples who make it up.

As we will see below, the Treaty of Rome aimed mainly at the free movement of workers [see section 6.4.] and relied above all on the functioning of the common market to improve living and working conditions in all Member States [see section 6.1.]. In line with the reform of the Structural Funds, which constituted the financial side of economic and social cohesion, the European Council, despite the opposition of Mrs. Thatcher, who was then Prime Minister of the United Kingdom, agreed in December 1989 on the **Community Charter of the fundamental rights of workers**, which represented the legal side of social cohesion and stressed particularly the alignment of social standards in the Member States: social protection; freedom of association and of collective bargaining; equal treatment for men and women; information, consultation and participation of workers; the protection of health and safety at the workplace; and the protection of children and adolescents, the elderly and the disabled. The Commission, which had proposed the Charter, proposed immediately after its adoption by the majority of heads of State of Government, a series of Community laws in order to implement it. But due to the unanimity rule required and the negative position of the United Kingdom, very few social measures were adopted before the completion of the internal market, which they should in principle follow in step. In order to get out of the impasse, eleven (out of the then twelve Member States), on the one hand, and the United Kingdom, on the other, signed at Maastricht a Social Protocol allowing the former to adopt alone the social measures that they deemed useful.

However, the anomaly of a common policy where one Member State did not share the others' objectives was corrected at Amsterdam, in June 1997, when **the Labour British Government decided to accede** to the social provisions of the new Treaty and to accept the Directives that had already been agreed under the Social Agreement. Protocol N° 14 on social policy annexed to the TEC and the Agreement on social policy attached thereto were repealed. The new Chapter 4 on Social Policy of the TEC incorporates most of the provisions of the Maastricht Social Agreement, notably: the objectives of the Community Charter of the Fundamental Social Rights of Workers and the measures to achieve those objectives.

It should be noted that the Community Charter of the Fundamental Social Rights of Workers of 1989 was surpassed by the **Charter of Fundamental Rights of the European Union** solemnly proclaimed in Nice, on 7 December 2000, by the European Parliament, the Council and the Commission[1] [see section 9.2.]. The **Treaty of Lisbon** declares that the Union recognises the rights, freedoms and principles set out in the Charter of Fundamental Rights of the European Union of 7 December 2000, as adapted at Strasbourg, on 12 December 2007[2], which shall have the same legal value as the Treaties (Article 6, Lisbon). This means that the Member States and the European institutions have to respect the principles of the Charter under the control of their courts and of the Court of Justice of the European Union. However, a Protocol appended to the Treaty affirms that the Charter does not extend the ability of the Court of Justice of the Euro-

---

[1]   Solemn Declaration, OJ C 364, 18.12.2000.
[2]   Charter and Explanations, OJ C 303, 14.12.2007.

pean Union, or any court or tribunal of Poland or of the United Kingdom, to find that the laws, regulations or administrative provisions, practices or action of Poland or of the United Kingdom are inconsistent with the fundamental rights, freedoms and principles that it reaffirms.

13.1. The need for a common social policy

The objectives of the common social policy are very close to those of the common regional policy. The latter is directed towards improving the lot of the least-favoured regions of the European Union, the social policy that of its poorest citizens. Both seek to **even out the economic and social imbalances** in the Union and to ensure that the advantages ensuing from the functioning of the common market are shared amongst all the countries and all the citizens. Several of their measures are complementary, and their financial instruments are closely coordinated in order to put them into effect.

A Community social policy, which was necessary for the social cohesion of the Community as early as the stage of the progressive implementation of the common market, was provided for in vague terms in the EEC Treaty. Although its signatories stated that they were resolved to ensure social progress by common action and affirmed as the essential objective the improvement of the living and working conditions of their peoples, they remained entirely independent in the field of social policies. They placed their faith above all in the automatic improvement of social conditions, relying on the **knock-on effect that economic integration would produce**. They were not wrong in that, but they were not completely right either.

It is certain that the progressive integration of the economies in itself promotes the convergence of the social conditions of the States of the Community. The most characteristic social features of the Community during the first forty years of its existence have been the moderate growth of the population, increased life expectancy and shorter working life, the widespread extension of compulsory education and the mass entry of women into economic activities. In addition to those general phenomena there have been structural changes within sectors and sectoral movements from agriculture to industry and from the latter to the service industries. Thus, it is not by chance that the problems of employment, social security and the vocational training of certain categories of workers (the young, the old and women) are priorities in every Member State. It is, therefore, true that the closer the economic conditions become in a multinational integration scheme, the more the **social problems of the member states become similar** and more similar, not to say common, solutions become necessary. Likewise, the free movement of workers and transnational trade union contacts have promoted a degree of **upward levelling** of wages, social benefits and social protection.

Increased prosperity brought about largely by European integration, did not, however, resolve all the Community's social problems. It even made some of them more acute or gave rise to new ones, viz. problems of disadvantaged regions and categories of persons who do not participate fully in the general progress; problems of structural unemployment; problems relating to the distribution of income and wealth; contradictions between economic and social values and, on occasion, dramatic changes in lifestyle with negative consequences for the behaviour of young people. Since the Treaty on the European Community actually calls for a social model based on the market economy, democracy and pluralism, respect of individual rights, free collective bargaining, equality of opportunity for all, social welfare and solidarity, it instructs the common institutions to strive to attain those objectives.

13.2. Social cohesion in the European Union

Economic and social cohesion is an objective of the Community (Art. 2 and 3 TEC). Whereas the common regional policy deals mainly with economic cohesion, the common social policy tries to strengthen social cohesion. Article 136 of the EC Treaty declares that the Community and the Member States, having in mind fundamental social rights such as those set out in the European Social Charter signed at Turin on 18 October 1961 and in the 1989 Community Charter of the Fundamental Social Rights of Workers, have as their objectives the promotion of employment, improved living and working conditions, so as to make possible their harmonisation while the improvement is being maintained, proper social protection, dialogue between management and labour and the development of human resources. This last goal entails effectual education and training policies. Article 136 states also that the objectives of social progress and cohesion that it sets should ensue not only from the functioning of the common market, which will favour the harmonisation of social systems, but also from the procedures provided for in the Treaty and from the approximation of provisions laid down by law, regulation or administrative action (particularly in the context of the single market). However, the measures taken by the Community and the Member States to attain the objectives of Article 136 must take account of the diverse forms of national practices, in particular in the field of contractual relations, and the need to maintain the competitiveness of the Community economy.

To attain social cohesion in the Union **minimum social standards are needed**, having regard to differing national systems and needs, and to the relative economic strengths of the Member States. The establishment of a framework of basic minimum standards guarantees acceptable social and physical security conditions to all the workers in the Union. At the same time, it provides a bulwark against reducing social standards to increase the competitiveness of the businesses of one Member State and, hence, against using low social standards as an instrument of unfair economic competition. These basic standards should not over-stretch the economically weaker Member States, but they should not prevent the more developed Member States from implementing higher standards.

The **effort to complete the single market** at the end of the 1980s was to mean a fresh start for the Community's social policy and its financial instrument, the European Social Fund (ESF) [see section 13.3.3]. The Single European Act and, later on, the Maastricht Treaty stated that "in order to promote its overall harmonious development, the Community shall develop and pursue its actions leading to the strengthening of its economic and social cohesion" (Art. 158 TEC). The Structural Funds, and especially the **European Social Fund** (ESF), represent the main instruments for promoting social cohesion within the Union [see section 12.1.2.]. As we saw under the heading of coordination of financial instruments in the chapter on regional development, the ESF contributes to the attainment of the Objectives set out set out in the context of the Community structural policy [see section 12.3.1.].

The **social policy agenda,** proposed by the Commission and approved by the Nice European Council in December 2000, provides the roadmap for employment and social policy, translating the policy objectives of the Lisbon strategy for economic and social renewal into concrete measures[1] [see section 13.3.2.]. A high level of social cohesion is central to the Lisbon agenda. Strategies which strive for gender equality, for the eradication of poverty and social exclusion and for the modernisation of social protection systems, in particular pension and healthcare systems, play a key role in this agenda. In short, the Union aims at social progress and cohesion through the specific policies for employment, education and professional training, as well as through the promotion and improvement of living and working conditions, including social protection and social inclusion. These are the subjects examined in the following parts of this chapter.

13.3. Common employment policy

Unemployment became a matter of serious concern for all the countries of the Community around the mid-1970s. Until then employment problems in the Community merely consisted of structural and regional imbalances in a general context of full employment. A series of very variable economic factors led to the **rapid deterioration of the employment situation** in the Community, viz.: the inflation and economic recession of the late 1970s and early 1980s, resulting from monetary and energy crises [see sections 7.2.1. and 19.1.1.], lively competition from recently industrialised countries in Asia with cheap labour, a degree of saturation of demand in Europe for industrial goods and the evolution of the economy and of Euro-

---

[1] COM (2000) 379 and COM (2003) 312, 2 June 2003.

pean companies towards a post-industrial stage. Many jobs thus became superfluous and disappeared. Others were created, but required new qualifications which most of the unemployed did not possess. At the same time, women, most of who had previously stayed at home, joined the labour market in force [see section 13.5.5.].

Averaging more than 10% of the active population of the Member States (with important differences between them), in the beginning of the 21st century, the unemployment rate of the European Union is seen as **its gravest social problem**. The economic and social costs of this unemployment are enormous. They include not only the direct expenditure on providing social security support for the unemployed, but also: the loss of tax revenue which the unemployed would pay out of their income if they were working; the increased burden on social services; rising poverty, crime and ill-health. Special concern focuses on the lack of prospects for new entrants to the labour market, especially young people and women and for people excluded from regular work [see section 13.5.6.]. Under the pressure of these problems was endorsed the employment strategy of the Union.

13.3.1. The employment strategy of the Union

The EU Treaty sets among the objectives of the Union, mentioned in Article 2 (TEU), that of promoting "economic and social progress and a high level of employment". The **Title on Employment** of the EC Treaty urges the Member States and the Community to work towards developing a coordinated strategy for employment and particularly for promoting a skilled, trained and adaptable workforce and labour markets responsive to economic change (Art. 125 TEC). To this end, Member States must regard promoting employment as a matter of common concern and must coordinate their action in this respect within the Council (Art. 126 TEC). The Community must encourage cooperation between the Member States, support and, if necessary, complement their action (Art. 127 TEC). The European Council should each year consider the employment situation of the Community and adopt conclusions thereon, on the basis of which the Council should draw up employment guidelines, consistent with the broad guidelines of economic policies [see section 7.3.1.], which the Member States should take into account in their employment policies (Art 128 TEC). The Council, under the co-decision procedure with the Parliament [see section 4.3.], may adopt incentive measures designed to encourage cooperation between Member States and to support their action in the field of employment through initiatives aimed at developing exchanges of information and best practices (Art 129 TEC). Indeed, a Council decision aimed at: fostering cooperation in the field of employment as regards analysis, research and monitoring; identifying good practices and promoting exchanges and transfers of information and experience; and developing an active information policy[1].

The Cologne European Council (3 and 4 June 1999) adopted a **European Employment Pact** aimed at a sustainable reduction of unemployment. The European Employment Pact embodies a comprehensive overall approach bringing together all the Union's employment policy measures, which support and mutually reinforce one another. In the broad economic policy guidelines (BEPGs), the Member States and the Community agree annually on the main elements of their economic policy [see section 7.3.1.]; in the employment guidelines the Member States and the Community agree annually on the main elements of the coordinated employment strategy; in the macroeconomic dialogue (within the framework of the ECOFIN Council), information and opinions of the relevant Community institutions and the social partners are exchanged in an appropriate manner concerning the question of how to design macroeconomic policy in order to increase and make full use of the potential for growth and employment [see section 7.3.1].

The Lisbon European Council (23 and 24 March 2000) agreed to a **strategic goal** to be pursued over the first decade of the 21st century, with the aim of boosting employment, economic reform and social cohesion within the framework of a knowledge-based economy. The three key elements of this strategy are geared to: preparing the transition to a knowledge-based economy and society by means of policies tailored more to the needs of the information society and research and development, stepping up the process of structural reform to boost competitiveness and innovation, while completing the internal market; modernising the European social model, investing in people and combating social exclusion; and sustaining a healthy economic outlook and favourable growth prospects by applying an appropriate macroeconomic policy mix. Implementation of the Lisbon strategic goal involves: fixing guidelines for the Union combined with specific timetables for achieving the goals in the short, medium and long terms; translating these European guidelines into national and regional policies; and periodic monitoring, evaluation and peer review.

The Community **Programme for Employment and Social Solidarity**, called **Progress** (2007-2013) supports financially the implementation of the objectives of the European Union in the fields of employment and social affairs, thereby contributing to the achievement of the Lisbon Strategy goals in those fields[2]. The Progress Programme is divided into the following five sections: employment; social protection and inclusion; working conditions; antidiscrimination and diversity; and gender equality.

The **European Globalisation Adjustment Fund (EGF)** provides support for workers made redundant as a result of major structural changes in world trade patterns due to globalisation where these redundancies have a significant adverse impact on the regional or local economy[3]. The EGF

---

[1] Decision 98/171, OJ L 63, 04.03.1998.

[2] Decision 1672/2006, OJ L 315, 15.11.2006.

[3] Regulation 1927/2006, OJ L 406, 30.12.2006.

provides specific, one-off support to facilitate the re-integration into employment of workers in areas, sectors territories, or labour market regions suffering the shock of serious economic disruption. It also promotes entrepreneurship, for example through micro-credits or for setting up cooperative projects.

13.3.2. The actions of the European Social Fund

According to Article 146 (TEC) the **European Social Fund (ESF)** aims to: (a) render the employment of workers easier and to increase their geographical and occupational mobility within the Community; and (b) facilitate their adaptation to industrial changes and to changes in production systems, in particular through vocational training and retraining. The ESF is administered by the Commission, which is assisted in this task by a Committee composed of representatives of the governments, trade unions and employers' organisations (Art. 147 TEC).

Regulation 1083/2006 establishes the framework for action by the Structural Funds and the Cohesion Fund for the period 2007 to 2013 and lays down, in particular, their objectives, principles and rules concerning partnership, programming, evaluation and management[1] [see section 12.1.2]. **The ESF is therefore governed** by Regulation 1083/2006 and by Regulation 1081/2006, which establishes its tasks, the scope of its assistance, specific provisions and the types of expenditure eligible for assistance[2].

The main task of the ESF is to contribute to the priorities of the Community as regards strengthening economic and social cohesion by improving employment and job opportunities, encouraging a high level of employment and more and better jobs. In order to better contribute to the implementation of the objectives and targets agreed at the Lisbon and Göteborg European Councils [see sections 13.3.2 and 16.2], the ESF must support actions in line with measures taken by Member States on the basis of the guidelines adopted under the European Employment Strategy, as incorporated into the Integrated Guidelines for Growth and Jobs, and the accompanying recommendations [see section 13.3.2].

With a view to better anticipating and managing change and increasing economic growth, employment opportunities for both women and men, and quality and productivity at work under the **Convergence and Regional competitiveness and employment objectives** [see section 12.3.1], assistance from the ESF focuses, in particular, on improving the adaptability of workers and enterprises, enhancing human capital and access to employment and participation in the labour market, reinforcing the social inclusion of disadvantaged people, combating discrimination, encouraging economically inactive persons to enter the labour market and promoting partnerships for reform. In addition to these priorities, in the least developed regions and Member States, under **the Convergence objective** and with a view to increasing economic growth, employment opportunities for

---

[1] Regulation 1083/2006, OJ L 210, 31.07.2006 and R. 1989/2006, OJ L 411, 30.12.2006.
[2] Regulation 1081/2006, OJ L 210, 31.07.2006.

both women and men, and quality and productivity at work, the ESF helps to expand and improve investment in human capital and to improve institutional, administrative and judicial capacity, so as to prepare and implement reforms and enforce the acquis.

13.4. Education, vocational training and youth policies

The problems of employment and vocational training are related, as very often the jobs offered require qualifications, which those seeking employment lack. That is why **employment and vocational training policies are also linked**. In fact, training is an instrument of active labour market policy. At the same time, measures promoting vocational training or retraining promote the employment or re-employment of workers in sectors where qualified labour is needed. Many workers cannot secure employment without becoming specialised, but they cannot acquire specialisation through experience until they have found a job. Breaking this vicious circle through vocational training is vital as workers should be able to change more frequently jobs throughout their working lives in the future.

Vocational training is not only a basic human right, enabling workers to realise their full potential, but also a **prerequisite for technological progress** and regional development. Indeed, a skilled, adaptable and mobile workforce is an essential component in the competitiveness, productivity and quality of companies, since it allows industries and regions to adapt rapidly to the requirements of technology and market trends and thus to become or remain competitive. Unemployment is in fact rife especially in the traditional industries in decline (steel, shipbuilding, textiles...), whilst the new industries (information technology, telecommunications, aerospace...) are badly in need of qualified labour. The new qualifications can help the European economy to effect the necessary structural changes in the information society and enable it better to face competition from the newly industrialised countries. The EU's education and training policies aim therefore to develop human resources throughout people's working lives, starting with basic education and working through initial training to continuing training.

13.4.1. The foundations of training and education policies

Underlying the common education policy is the collection and dissemination of information on the programmes and projects of the various higher education establishments in the Member States. An **Education Information Network** in the European Community, under the name of EURYDICE, is available to users with responsibilities in the field of education, such as the Community institutions, national authorities and officials responsible for higher education in the Member States[1]. The Eurydice network is the chief instrument for providing information on national and Community structures, systems and developments in the field of education. The network assists the drawing up of comparative analyses, reports and surveys on common priority topics determined inter alia in the Education Committee and in the Advisory Committee on Vocational Training[2].

An organ of the common policy on professional training is the **European Centre for the Development of Vocational Training (CEDEFOP)**, located in Thessaloniki[3]. Cedefop's programme of work focuses on two priority areas, namely qualifications and vocational training systems. The former is essentially concerned with the transparency of qualifications and new occupations at European level and the impact of new forms of work organisation and qualifications on training systems. The latter is concerned with strategies for the optimum combination of types and phases of training with a view to achieving a lifelong learning process and with improved teacher training.

As agreed at the Lisbon European Council (23 and 24 March 2000) [see section 13.3.2.], the *e***Learning initiative** is designed to make good the shortcomings in Europe in the use of new information and communications technologies, thereby accelerating the pace of change in education and training systems and helping Europe to move towards a knowledge-based society[4]. The key objectives are focused on: improving infrastructure, notably equipping all schools in the Union; training the population at all levels by making schools, training centres and other places of learning accessible to all; development of high-quality multimedia services and content; and networking of schools (European Schoolnet). Moreover, a Council Resolution invited the Commission to promote the **involvement of young people** in the development, execution and evaluation of Community youth activities and programmes[5]. The Commission mobilises Community programmes and instruments to achieve these objectives.

In the framework of the Lisbon strategy, the **European Institute of Innovation and Technology (EIT)** was established, in March 2008, to contribute to the development of the Community's and the Member States' innovation capacity, by involving higher education, research and innovation activities at the highest standards[6]. Following the example of the Massachusetts Institute of Technology (MIT), the EIT aims at the transfer of the outcome of its higher education, research and innovation activities to the business context and their commercial application, as well as at the support of the creation of start-ups, spin-offs and small and medium-sized enterprises (SMEs).

A Council decision seeks to promote mobility and flexibility in Europe's labour market, by improving transparency and facilitating the mu-

---

[1] Resolution, OJ C 329, 31.12.1990, p. 23-24 and Council Conclusions, OJ C 336, 19.12.1992, p. 7.
[2] Decision 2004/223, OJ L 68, 06.03.2004.
[3] Regulation 337/75, OJ L 39, 13.02.1975 and Regulation 2051/2004, OJ L 355, 01.12.2004.
[4] COM (2000) 318, 24 May 2000.
[5] Resolution, OJ C 42, 17.02.1999, p. 1-2.
[6] Regulation 294/2008, OJ L 97, 09.04.2008.

tual recognition of diplomas, qualifications and competences within a single EU-level framework known as **"Europass"**, taking the form of a structured, personalised portfolio incorporating a set of pre-existing documents with separate characteristics: "Europass-CV", "Europass-Mobility" (for periods of learning in other countries), "Europass-Diploma supplement" (for higher education), "Europass-Certificate supplement" (for vocational training), "Europass-Language portfolio" (for linguistic skills)[1].

The **European Training Foundation (ETF)**, established in Turin, supports the reform of vocational education and training and management training in over 40 partner countries and territories, divided into four main geographical blocs (Mediterranean region, western Balkans, eastern Europe and central Asia, candidate/acceding countries), and provides technical assistance to the Commission for the Tempus programme[2] [see section 13.4.2.].

Sporting activities are covered in a declaration to the final act of the Amsterdam Treaty, which contains two essential principles: that sport has a role in forging identity, which amounts to saying that national identities in this field should be respected; and that sports associations should be listened to by the bodies of the European Union when important questions affecting sport are at issue, which gives them a consultative function in these matters [see section 6.4.1.]. A Commission White paper aims to encourage debate on specific problems, to enhance the visibility of sport in EU policy-making and to raise public awareness on the needs and specificities of the sector[3].

13.4.2. Education and training programmes

The Maastricht Treaty [see section 2.2.] has consecrated Community action in the fields of education, vocational training and youth. Article 149 (TEC) specifies that the Community contributes to the development of **quality education** by encouraging cooperation between Member States and, if necessary, by supporting and supplementing their action in the fields of: developing the European dimension in education, particularly through the teaching and dissemination of languages; mobility of students and teachers; cooperation between educational establishments; exchanges of information and experience; exchanges of young people and socio-educational instructors; and the development of distance education. Incentive measures, excluding any harmonisation of the laws and regulations of the Member States, are adopted by the Council acting in accordance with the procedure referred to in Article 251 (co-decision with the European Parliament). Community action must, however, fully respect the responsibility of the Member States for the content of teaching, the organisation of education systems and vocational training and their cultural and linguistic diversity. An Internet portal brings together the measures taken by the

---

[1] Decision 2241/2004, OJ L 390, 31.12.2004.
[2] Regulation 1360/90, OJ L 131, 23.05.1990 and Regulation 1648/2003, OJ L 245, 29.09.2003.
[3] COM/2007/391, 11.07.2007.

European Union to promote language learning and linguistic diversity[1]. The Commission promotes a framework strategy for multilingualism[2]. It is evident that the EU not only **respects the cultural diversity** of its Member States but also encourages it [see section 10.3.].

According to Article 150 of the EC Treaty, the Community implements a **vocational training policy**, which supports and supplements the action of the Member States and which aims to: facilitate adaptation to industrial changes, in particular through vocational training and retraining; improve initial and continuing vocational training in order to facilitate vocational integration and reintegration into the labour market; facilitate access to vocational training and encourage mobility of instructors and trainees; stimulate cooperation between educational or training establishments and firms; and develop exchanges of information and experience on issues common to the training systems of the Member States. This Article is the foundation of the common training policy.

Twenty years after the flagship programme for university education, Erasmus, was launched in 1987, the EC/EU adopted the **"Lifelong learning programme"**, which fosters interchange, cooperation and mobility between education and training systems within the Community[3]. Its overall objective is that European education and training systems become a world quality reference in accordance with the Lisbon strategy, while contributing to the development of the Community as an advanced knowledge-based society, with sustainable economic development, more and better jobs and greater social cohesion. The implementation of the Lifelong Learning Programme has been allocated a **budget of € 6,970 million** for the period 2007-2013.

The action programme is divided up into **six sub-programmes**, four of which are sectoral. They are all structured in the same way and address the teaching and learning needs of all participants as well as of the institutions and organisations providing or facilitating education and training in each respective sector. All the actions incorporate mobility, language and new technology.

The **Comenius** programme covers pre-school and school education up to the end of upper secondary education, and the institutions and organisations providing such education (€ 1,047 million). Its two specific objectives are to: develop understanding among young people and educational staff of the diversity of European cultures and its value; help young people acquire the basic life-skills and competences necessary for their personal development, for future employment and for active European citizenship. Comenius should involve at least three million pupils in joint educational activities, over the period of the programme.

The **Erasmus programme** addresses formal higher education and vocational education and training at tertiary level, whatever the length of the

---

[1]   http://europa.eu/languages/en/home.
[2]   COM/2005/596, 22 November 2005.
[3]   Decision 1720/2006, OJ L 327, 24.11.2006.

course or qualification may be and including doctoral studies (€ 3,114 million). Unlike the previous programmes, vocational education and training at tertiary level comes under Erasmus now and not Leonardo da Vinci. The two specific objectives of Erasmus are to: support the achievement of a European Area of Higher Education; and reinforce the contribution of higher education and advanced vocational education to the process of innovation.

The **Leonardo da Vinci programme** addresses vocational education and training, other than at tertiary level (€ 1,725 million). Its specific objectives are to: support participants in training in the acquisition and the use of knowledge, skills and qualifications to facilitate personal development, employability and participation in the European labour market; support improvements in quality and innovation; and enhance the attractiveness of vocational education and training and mobility. Leonardo should contribute to 80,000 placements in enterprises per year.

The **Grundtvig programme** addresses all forms of adult education (€ 358 million). It aims to: respond to the educational challenge of an ageing population in Europe; and help provide adults with pathways to improving their knowledge and competences. It should support the mobility of 7,000 individuals involved in adult education per year.

The **transversal programme** mainly addresses activities which extend beyond the limits of the sectoral programmes (€ 369 million). It covers four key activities in the field of lifelong learning, i.e.: policy cooperation and innovation; the promotion of language learning; the development of innovative information and communication technologies (ICT)-based content, services, pedagogies and practices; and the dissemination and exploitation of results of actions supported under the programme or previous programmes, and exchange of good practice.

The **Jean Monnet Programme** targets specific issues of European integration in the academic world and the support needed for institutions and associations active in education and training at European level (€ 170 million). It covers three key activities: the Jean Monnet action, in which institutions from third countries can also participate; operating grants to designated institutions which pursue objectives of European interest; and operating subsidies to other European institutions and associations in the field of education and training. The institutions, which receive operating grants, are: the College of Europe , the European University Institute in Florence, the European Institute of Public Administration (EIPA) in Maastricht, the Academy of European Law (ERA) in Trier, the European Agency for Development in Special Needs Education in Middelfart, and the International Centre for European Training (CIFE) in Nice.

The "**Youth in Action Programme**", with a budget of € 885 million for the period 2007-2013, has five general objectives which complement EU activities such as training, culture, sport and employment[1]. The general

---

[1]   Decision 1719/2006, OJ L 327, 24.11.2006.

objectives of the programme are: (a) to promote young people's active citizenship in general and their European citizenship in particular; (b) to develop solidarity and promote tolerance among young people, in particular in order to reinforce social cohesion in the EU; (c) to foster mutual understanding between young people in different countries; (d) to contribute to developing the quality of support systems for youth activities and the capabilities of civil society organisations in the youth field; and (e) to promote European cooperation in the youth field. The programme supports small-scale projects promoting the active participation of young people. The projects can be local, regional, national or international, including the networking of similar projects in different participating countries. The programme is open to the EU and EFTA Member States, EU candidate countries, the countries of the western Balkans, Switzerland, subject to the conclusion of a bilateral agreement, and to third countries (or partner countries) that have signed cooperation agreements with the EU relevant to the youth field.

The **Trans-European Mobility programme for University Studies (TEMPUS III)** (2000-2006) is designed to promote, in line with the general guidelines and objectives of the Phare and Tacis programmes [see sections 25.2. and 25.4.], the development of higher education systems in the eligible countries (independent States of the former Soviet Union, non-associated countries of Central Europe, Mongolia and Mediterranean countries) through cooperation with partners in the EU Member States[1]. Joint European projects (JEPs), involving at least one Member State University, a partner in another Member State and a university in a beneficiary country, are the main instruments of the programme.

13.5. Common measures for the improvement of living and working conditions

The concern of the European Union for the living and working conditions of its citizens is not new, but its commitment in this respect has grown apace with economic integration. In article 117 of the EEC Treaty the States of the Community agreed on "the need to **promote improved working conditions and an improved standard of living for workers**, so as to make possible their harmonisation while the improvement is being maintained". They expected such a development to ensue, in the first place, from the functioning of the common market, which would favour the harmonisation of social systems and, to the extent necessary, from the approximation of national provisions.

In Article 136 of the EC Treaty the Member States declare having as **their objectives** the promotion of employment, improved living and working conditions, proper social protection, dialogue between management

---

[1]   Decision 1999/311, OJ L 120, 08.05.1999 and Decision 2002/601, OJ L 195, 24.07.2002.

and labour, the development of human resources with a view to lasting employment and the combating of social exclusion. Under Article 137 of the EC Treaty, the Community **supports and complements the activities of the Member States** tending to improve, in particular: the working environment so as to protect workers health and safety, the working conditions, the information and consultation of workers, the integration of persons excluded from the labour market and the equality of opportunities between men and women. The Council and the Parliament adopt, by means of Directives, minimal requirements for the gradual implementation of these objectives. These subjects are examined below.

13.5.1. The social dialogue in the EU

The social dialogue which was under way from the beginning of the Community, was consecrated first by the Single European Act and then by the Treaty on European Union, which commits the Commission to develop the **dialogue between management and labour at European level** by submitting to them its guidelines for proposals in the social field (Art. 138 TEC). Social dialogue at European level covers the negotiations between European social partners themselves and between them and the organs of the European Union. This dialogue contributes to the improvement of mutual understanding between the social partners and to the stimulation and/or acceptance of economic and social policies implemented at European level.

At general European level the social partners are represented by the European Trade Union Confederation (ETUC), the Union of Industries of the European Community (UNICE) and the European Centre of Public Enterprises (CEEP). The **Tripartite Social Summit for Growth and Employment** is intended to ensure that there is continuous consultation between the Council, the Commission and the social partners on economic, social and employment matters[1] [see also section 13.3.1] The summit consists of representatives, at the highest level, of the Council Presidency, the two subsequent Presidencies, the Commission and the social partners. Since 1995, the Commission and the social partners have set up, in Florence, the European Centre for Industrial Relations (ECIR)[2].

The dialogue between social partners may lead to common opinions and/or, should the partners so desire, to **contractual relations, including agreements**. Such agreements may be implemented either in accordance with the procedures and practices specific to management and labour in each Member State or, in matters concerning working conditions, at the joint request of the signatory parties, by a Council decision on a proposal from the Commission (Art. 139 TEC). Thus, the social partners negotiated and signed, on 14 December 1995, a collective agreement, that entitles

---

[1]   Decision 2003/174, OJ L 70, 14.03.2003.
[2]   COM (95) 445, 25 December 1995.

both male and female workers to unpaid **parental leave** of at least three months' duration and to time off work in the event of an unforeseen family emergency. At the request of the social partners, a 1996 Directive, which originally excluded the United Kingdom but in 1998 was extended to it, lays down minimum requirements concerning parental leave and absence by dint of "force majeure"[1].

13.5.2. Worker information, consultation and participation

In addition to the social dialogue, the 1989 Social Charter, now incorporated in the EC Treaty (Art. 136 and 137), stipulates that information, consultation and participation for workers must be **developed along appropriate lines**, taking account of the practices in the various Member States. Such information, consultation and participation must be implemented in due time, particularly in the following cases:

- when technological changes which, from the point of view of working conditions and work organisation, have major implications for the work-force, are introduced into undertakings;
- in connection with restructuring operations in undertakings or in cases of mergers having an impact on the employment of workers;
- in cases of collective redundancy procedures; and
- when workers, especially transboundary ones, are affected by the employment policies of the company where they are employed.

A general framework for minimum requirements relating to the right of employees to be informed and consulted is applicable to undertakings and establishments operating **within a single Member State** and with at least 50 or 20 employees respectively[2]. The emphasis is on fostering social dialogue and ways of ensuring information for employees and effective consultation of their representatives at the earliest possible stage of the company decision-making process. Employers must inform employees about: the recent and foreseeable development of the company's activities and its economic and financial situation; the situation, structure and reasonably foreseeable developments of employment within the company; decisions which may lead to substantial changes in work organisation or in contractual relations (consultation between the employer and employees entails dialogue and exchange of views, including efforts to reach prior agreement on the decision in question).

The information and consultation of workers **in multinational companies** is pursued by Directive 94/45 - extended in 1998 to the United Kingdom - providing for the establishment of a **European Works Council** or a procedure for the purposes of informing and consulting employees in European-scale undertakings[3]. The companies or groups of companies

---

[1]   Directive 96/34, OJ L 145, 19.06.1996 and Directive 97/75, OJ L 10, 16.01.1998.
[2]   Directive 2002/14, OJ L 80, 23.03.2002.
[3]   Directive 94/45, OJ L 254, 30.09.1994 and Directive 97/74, OJ L 10, 16.01.1998.

concerned are those with more than 1000 employees in total in the Community and with at least two establishments in different Member States, each employing at least 150 people. The Directive also covers undertakings or groups of undertakings with headquarters outside the territory of the Member States, in so far as they meet the above criteria. The Directive provides for the establishment, at the initiative of the company or group management or at the written request of at least 100 employees or their representatives in at least two Member States, of a "special negotiating body" with the task of concluding an agreement between the management and the employees' representatives, on the scope, composition, powers and term of office of the European committee to be set up in the undertaking or group, or the practical arrangements for an alternative procedure for the information and consultation of employees.

In parallel with the regulation on the statute for a European company, with the Latin designation *Societas Europaea* (SE) [see section 17.2.1.], the Council adopted a directive supplementing this statute with regard to the involvement of employees[1]. The rules relating to **employee involvement in the SE** seek to ensure that the creation of an SE does not entail the disappearance or reduction of practices of employee involvement existing within the companies participating in the establishment of an SE. Therefore, when the management or administrative organs of the participating companies draw up a plan for the establishment of an SE, they must as soon as possible after publishing the draft terms of merger or creating a holding company or after agreeing a plan to form a subsidiary or to transform into an SE, take the necessary steps (including providing information about the identity of the participating companies, concerned subsidiaries or establishments, and the number of their employees) to start negotiations with the representatives of the companies' employees on arrangements for the involvement of employees in the SE. For this purpose, a **special negotiating body** representative of the employees of the participating companies and concerned subsidiaries or establishments must be created in accordance with the provisions laid down in the directive. The special negotiating body and the competent organs of the participating companies must determine, by written agreement, arrangements for the involvement of employees within the SE. Member States must lay down standard rules on employee involvement which must satisfy the provisions of the directive.

13.5.3. Social protection

Article 136 (TEC) names proper social protection and improved living and working conditions among the objectives of the Community and the Member States. **Social protection in the strict sense** usually means social security, while **social protection in a broad sense** includes social security

---

[1] Regulation 2157/2001 and directive 2001/86, OJ L 294, 10.11.2001 and Regulation 885/2004, OJ L 168, 01.05.2004.

among other social rights of the citizens. In fact, under the heading "solidarity", the Charter of Fundamental Rights of the European Union[1] [see section 9.2.] mentions several rights, such as: the workers' right to information and consultation within the undertaking; the protection in the event of unjustified dismissal; fair and just working conditions; protection of young people at work; and, of course, social security and social assistance.

Concerning this last subject, namely social protection in the strict sense, the Charter of Fundamental Rights declares that the Union recognises and respects the entitlement to social security benefits and social services providing protection in cases such as maternity, illness, industrial accidents, dependency or old age, and in the case of loss of employment, in accordance with the rules laid down by Community law and national laws and practices. The Charter acknowledges that everyone residing and moving legally within the European Union is entitled to social security benefits and social advantages in accordance with Community law and national laws and practices. According to the subsidiarity principle, however, the Member States must apply Community law if and where it exists. Concerning social security, Community provisions concern only the implementation of the principle of equal treatment for certain categories of workers, i.e. immigrants [see section 6.4.2.] and women [see section 13.5.5.]. For the rest, social security is covered by the national law of each Member State.

In fact, the Member States have preferred coordination rather than harmonisation of social protection and particularly social security legislation. On these subjects the Council decides alone (without the Parliament) and by unanimity, which means that any Member State may veto the adoption of Community legislation (Art 137 TEC). Therefore, a regulation aims to coordinate national social security systems so as to eliminate obstacles to freedom of movement, thereby allowing EU citizens to move freely within the Community, whether for purposes of study, leisure or work, without losing any social security rights or protection to which they are entitled[2].

The Community has already made headway when the term "social protection" is taken in its broadest sense to cover social security and the right to work. An important Community measure for the social protection of employees, particularly those of multinational companies, is the Directive on the approximation of the laws of the Member States relating to **collective redundancies**[3]. Employers who envisage such redundancies have to hold consultations with workers' representatives on the possibilities of avoiding or reducing such redundancies. Moreover, the employer has to notify any proposed collective redundancy to the competent official authority and may not implement it before the expiry of a period of 30 days which the authority uses to try to find solutions to the problems that have

---

[1]   Solemn declaration, OJ C 364, 18.12.2000.

[2]   Regulation 883/2004, OJ L 166, 30.04.2004.

[3]   Directive 98/59, OJ L 225, 12.08.1998.

arisen and/or to lessen the impact of the redundancies. This Directive is particularly important for workers employed by multinational companies which operate in one or more EU countries, as it prevents multinational companies from taking advantage of differences between national laws.

In the same vein, a Directive on the approximation of the laws of the Member States aims at safeguarding employees' rights in the event of **transfers of undertakings**, businesses or parts of businesses[1]. Before any such amalgamation, the workers' representatives have to be informed of the reasons for it and of its consequences for the employees and of the measures envisaged in their favour. In principle, the workers' rights and obligations are transferred to the new employer for at least a year and agreement on the conditions of the take-over has to be reached in consultation with the work force. Failing agreement between the employer or employers and the workers, an arbitration body gives a final ruling on the steps to be taken in favour of the workers. A representation scheme not dependent on the employer's will is necessary for compliance with the Directive[2].

But the workers' interests also need to be protected **in the event of the insolvency** of their employer, especially where assets are not sufficient to cover outstanding claims resulting from contracts of employment or employment relationships, even where the latter are privileged. To prevent such situations, a Council Directive obliges Member States to set up guarantee institutions independent of the employers' operating capital so that their assets are inaccessible to proceedings for insolvency[3]. In such an eventuality, those institutions must settle the claims of employees arising prior to the insolvency of the employer, including contributions under social security schemes.

A Directive on the **protection of young people at work** prohibits work by children (less than 15 years of age or still subject to compulsory full-time schooling), with the exception of certain cultural, artistic or sporting activities. Children of at least 14 years of age may take up combined work/ training schemes, in-plant work-experience schemes and certain light work[4]. The Directive asks Member States to strictly regulate work done by adolescents of more than 18 years of age, by imposing specific rules in respect of working time, daily rest periods, weekly rest periods and night work, and laying down technical, health and safety standards.

13.5.4. The organisation of work

Social protection in the EU covers also **atypical work**, i.e. other forms of work than that for an indefinite period, such as work for a specific duration, interim work, temporary work and seasonal work. These different

---

[1] Directive 2001/23, OJ L 82, 28.03.2001.
[2] Judgments given on 8 June 1994, Cases C-382/92 and C-383/92, Commission v United Kingdom, ECR 1994, p. I-2435.
[3] Directive 80/987, OJ L 283, 20.10.1980 and Directive 2002/74, OJ L 270, 08.10.2002.
[4] Directive 94/33, OJ L 216, 20.08.1994 and Directive 2007/30, OJ L 165, 27.06.2007.

forms of work enable companies to organise their work and their production in such a way as to improve productivity and thus become more competitive. Similarly, they enable workers to adapt the hours they work to suit their personal and family circumstances. But in a single market, certain essential conditions must be determined both to avoid distortions of competition and to protect the workers who opt for or accept (for want of something better) these new forms of work. These two objectives are contained in the Directives on atypical work. Thus a Directive guarantees satisfactory health and safety conditions of workers with a fixed-duration employment relationship (whose duration is fixed by objective criteria) or a temporary employment relationship (between the employer - a temporary employment agency - and the employee)[1]. Another Directive, based on a framework agreement on fixed-term work concluded between the social partners, ensures compliance with the principle of non-discrimination *vis-à-vis* employment of indefinite duration[2].

Contract duration is but one of the areas where there have been changes in the organisation of work in Europe. Alongside traditional work practices of indefinite time, recent years have seen the growth of **new forms of work**: homeworking (out-workers), part-time work, job sharing, job splitting, being "on call", distance working, etc. These new work forms have arisen as a result of new technologies, to accommodate companies' needs for flexibility and to meet the personal and family demands of many workers. However, they can obscure the situation of these workers if there is no written proof of the essential points of the employment relationship. Therefore, a Directive provides for the drawing up of a written declaration **regarding an employment relationship**[3]. It stipulates that an employer shall notify an employee of the essential aspects of the contract or employment relationship by written declaration.

A Directive concerning certain aspects of the **organisation of working time** lays down a basic set of minimum provisions covering more particularly: the maximum weekly working time (48 hours), the minimum daily rest period (11 uninterrupted hours), the minimum period of paid leave (4 weeks), conditions relating to night work and the maximum period of such work (8 hours), and breaks in the event of prolonged periods of work[4]. Although, in theory, most workers in the European Union enjoy better organisation of working time than is embodied in the European Directive, this is intended to exercise a pressure on the Governments of the Member States to better enforce the relative legislations. Another Directive aims to prevent part-time workers from being treated less favourably than full-time workers, concerning particularly employment conditions and continuing training[5].

---

[1]   Directive 91/383, OJ L 206, 29.07.1991 and Directive 2007/30, OJ L 165, 27.06.2007.

[2]   Directive 1999/70, OJ L 175, 10.07.1999.

[3]   Directive, 91/533, OJ L 288, 18.10.1991.

[4]   Directive 2003/88, OJ L 299, 18.11.2003.

[5]   Directive 97/81, OJ L 14, 20.01.1998 and Directive 98/23, OJ L 131, 05.05.1998.

13.5.5. Equal treatment for men and women

Article 141 of the EC Treaty (ex-Art. 119 EEC) stipulates that each Member State shall ensure the application of the principle that men and women should receive **equal pay for equal work**. This principle means: (a) that pay for the same work at piece rates shall be calculated on the basis of the same unit of measurement; and (b) that pay for work at time rates shall be the same for the same job. The original Community's concern for equality of the sexes - compared to its non-commitment in other important issues - stemmed from the fact that competition between Community countries could be distorted by the employment in some of them of women who were paid less than men for the same job. Moreover, unequal conditions of employment and remuneration between the sexes could be eliminated only through Community action, as no country could go it alone with a reform, which would be likely to alter conditions of competition to its detriment, in particular in industries employing large numbers of women. In any case, the EC Treaty places the achievement of equal treatment between men and women among the tasks of the Community (Art. 2 TEC).

The original Member States did not hasten to take the legislative and administrative measures necessary in order to implement the principle of non-discrimination based on the sex, as they were invited to do by Article 119 (EEC). However, the Court of Justice in three famous judgments bearing the name of Gabrielle Defrenne, air hostess of Sabena, established that, although Article 119 had a horizontal direct effect and could be evoked in national courts, it needed **interpretation by the Community legislative authority**, particularly concerning indirect or disguised discriminations and equal working conditions other than payment[1].

The opinion of the Court was followed by the Commission in its proposals and finally by the Council, which adopted a Directive on the approximation of the laws of the Member States relating to the **application of the principle of equal pay** for men and women[2]. The purpose of this Directive is to eliminate any discrimination on grounds of sex as regards all aspects and conditions of pay. It calls on the Member States to "cleanse" their legal provisions of all discriminatory aspects and to repeal all collective or contractual provisions that were at variance with the principle of equal pay. A Commission code of practice on the implementation of equal pay for work of equal value for women and men, drawn up in close collaboration with the social partners, aims to provide concrete advice for employers and collective bargaining partners at business level to ensure that the principle of equality is applied to all aspects of pay[3].

Equal pay was only one battle won in the war against discrimination against women, which was based on historical and cultural causes and was

---

[1] Judgments of: 25 May 1971, ECR 1971, p. 445; 8 April 1976, ECR 1976, p. 455; and 15 June 1978, ECR 1978, p. 1365.

[2] Directive 2006/54, OJ L 204, 26.07.2006.

[3] COM (96) 336, 17 July 1996.

reinforced in practice by the education system, inadequate vocational guidance and the demanding role imposed on women as wives and mothers.
Therefore, the abovementioned Directive on the **implementation of the
principle of equal treatment** of men and women in matters of employment and occupation prohibits any indirect discrimination, i.e. the ways in
which women are disadvantaged in relation to men in spite of apparently
equal treatment, viz.: individual or collective contracts concerning employment and working conditions[1]. A specific Directive provides for the
equal treatment between men and women engaged in an activity, including
agriculture, in a self-employed capacity, and on the protection of self-
employed women during pregnancy and motherhood[2]. It should be noted
that the Directives on the equal treatment of men and women complete Directive 2000/78 laying down a general framework for combating discrimination on the grounds of religion or belief, disability, age or sexual orientation as regards employment and occupation [see section 6.4.1].

The principle of equal opportunity means, among other things, that
there should be no discrimination based on sex especially as regards: the
scope and the conditions governing the right to any work regime; the calculation of contributions; the calculation of benefits and the conditions
governing the duration and preservation of pension rights. Two Directives
concern, indeed, the implementation of the principle of equal treatment for
men and women in matters of social security[3] and in occupational social
security schemes[4].

However, according to the Court, the principle of non-discrimination
applies indifferently to both men and women. Indeed, in its "Barber"
judgment the Court of Justice held that any sex discrimination in the granting or calculation of an occupational pension, notably the differentiation of
the age of pension according to the sex, is prohibited by Article 119
(EEC)[5]. As the Barber judgment had important financial implications for
the professional schemes of social security, the Council amended the 1986
Directive in order to bring it into line with Article 119 of the EEC Treaty
as interpreted by the Court in this judgment[6]. According to the Court, however, different treatment of **stable relationships between two persons of
the same sex** and marriages or stable relationships outside marriage between persons of opposite sex in matters of social security, does not constitute discrimination directly based on sex[7].

Measures must be taken in all Member States to improve the **health
and safety protection of women workers** who are pregnant, have just

1   Directive 2006/54, OJ L 204, 26.07.2006.
2   Directive 86/613, OJ L 359, 19.12.1986.
3   Directive 79/7, OJ L 6, 10.01.1979.
4   Directive 86/378, OJ L 225, OJ L 225, 12.08.1986 and Directive 96/97, OJ L 46, 17.02.1997.
5   Judgment given on 17 May 1990, Case C-262/89, Barber v Guardian Royal Exchange, ECR
    1990, p.1889.
6   Commission proposal, OJ C 379, 14.12.1996.
7   Judgment of 17 February 1998, Case C-249/96, ECR 1998 I-621.

given birth or are breast-feeding[1] [see also section 13.5.7.]. These measures on the one hand prohibit the dismissing of the women workers in question and their exposure to specific agents or working conditions which could endanger their health and safety, and on the other ensure the preservation of the rights derived from the employment contract and of maternity leave of at least fourteen consecutive weeks. In addition, according to the ECJ, the non-recruitment of pregnant women or the laying off of women who have a bad health condition after having given birth are discriminatory and cannot be tolerated[2]. The dismissal would be illegal even if the worker was recruited for a fixed period and because of her pregnancy was unable to work during a substantial part of the term of the contract[3].

13.5.6. Action to combat social exclusion

Social exclusion represents one of the major challenges facing the European Union. The challenge cannot be addressed merely by offering better assistance to those who are excluded or at risk of exclusion from work, but also requires active measures to tackle the obstacles to social inclusion. Article 137 (TEC) gives the Community a specific role in **supporting and complementing the activities of the Member States** as regards the integration of persons excluded from the labour market. In compliance with the principle of subsidiarity however, initiatives to combat poverty and social exclusion are primarily the preserve of the Member States' local, regional and national authorities. The European Union can only complete and stimulate the work of the Member States in these fields by promoting the exchange of information, the comparison of experiences, the transfer of know-how and the demonstration of the validity of the projects based on partnerships. Thus, the Community action against social exclusion is mainly centred on vocational training [see section 13.4.2.].

A Community action programme, covering the period from 1 January 2002 to 31 December 2006, encourages cooperation between Member States to combat poverty and social exclusion[4]. The objectives of the **social exclusion action programme** are, in particular, to improve understanding of social exclusion and poverty, to organise discussions on policies pursued and mutual lessons, and to develop the capacity of actors to address social exclusion and poverty effectively, by promoting innovative approaches and supporting networks of all those involved at EU, national and regional levels.

Building on the momentum created and the results achieved in 2003 by the "European Year of People with Disabilities", the Commission introduced a multiannual action plan through to 2010, aimed at mainstreaming

---

[1] Directive 92/85, OJ L 348, 28.11.1992 and Directive 2007/30, OJ L 165, 27.06.2007
[2] Judgments of 8 November 1990, ECR 1990, I-3941 and I-3979.
[3] Judgment of 4 October 2001, Case C-109/2000, ECR 2001, p. I-06993.
[4] Decision 50/2002, OJ L 10, 12.01.2002 and Decision 786/2004, OJ L 138, 30.04.2004.

disability issues in the **relevant Community policies** and implementing specific measures in key areas with a view to enhancing the economic and social integration of people with disabilities[1]. Thus, a Regulation establishes rules for the protection of and provision of assistance to disabled persons and persons with reduced mobility travelling by air[2].

13.5.7. Safety and health at work

Despite the limited competences that assigned the EEC Treaty to the European Community, Directives were adopted concerning the protection of workers, notably from the major accident hazards of certain industrial activities[3] [see section 16.3.5.] and exposure to asbestos[4]. After the 1987 Single Act [see section 2.1.] had increased the Community's authority as regards the health and safety of the work force, the Commission set up a mutual information system for legislative and administrative acts of the Member States concerning health and security of workers at the place of work[5]. At the instigation of the Commission, the Council adopted, in 1989, a **Framework Directive** on the introduction of measures to encourage improvements in the safety and health of workers at the workplace[6]. This Directive lays down three main principles: the employer's general obligation to guarantee the workers' health and safety in all work-related aspects, in particular by preventing professional risks, by keeping the work force informed and by training; the obligation of every worker to contribute to his own health and safety and that of others by using the work facilities correctly and respecting the safety instructions; the absence or limited liability for employers for things caused by abnormal unforeseen circumstances or exceptional events. By laying down the main principles concerning health and safety at work in the Community, the framework Directive is the foundation on which all other directives aiming at the improvement of the working environment to protect workers' health and safety (Art. 137 TEC) are superimposed.

This is particularly the case as regards the specific Directives laying down **minimum requirements notably on**:
- workplaces[7];
- work equipment and machinery[8];
- personal protective equipment[9];
- work using display screens[1];

---

[1] COM/2007/738.
[2] Regulation 1107/2006, OJ L 204, 26.07.2006.
[3] Directive 96/82, OJ L 10, 14.1.1997 and Directive 2003/105, OJ L 345, 31.12.2003.
[4] Directive 83/477, OJ L 263, 24.09.1983 and Directive 2003/18, OJ L 97, 15.04.2003.
[5] Decision 88/383, OJ L 183, 14.07.1988.
[6] Directive 89/391, OJ L 183, 29.06.1989 and Directive 2007/30, OJ L 165, 27.06.2007
[7] Directive 89/654, OJ L 393, 30.12.1989 and Directive 2007/30, OJ L 165, 27.06.2007
[8] Directive 89/655, OJ L 393, 30.12.1989 and Directive 95/63, OJ L 335, 30.12.1995.
[9] Directive 89/656, OJ L 393, 30.12.1989 and Directive 2007/30, OJ L 165, 27.06.2007.

- exposure at work to carcinogenic agents[2];
- safety and/or health signs in the workplace[3];
- exposure to the risks arising from physical agents (noise)[4].

These Directives guarantee the right to safety at work for the workers in all Member States, including those which previously had not high safety standards. Workers having an interim or specific duration work relation must enjoy the same health and safety conditions as the other workers of an undertaking[5]. As seen above, a directive aims at improving the health and safety of pregnant workers and workers who have recently given birth or are breastfeeding[6] [see section 13.5.5.]. The Council recommends that the Member States recognise, in the context of their policy on preventing occupational hazards and accidents, the right of self-employed workers to health and safety protection, and their duties in this area[7].

The **new Community strategy on health and safety at work** aims at a global approach to well-being at work, taking account of changes in the world of work and the emergence of new risks, especially of a psycho-social nature. According to the Commission, the strategy should be based on: consolidating a culture of risk prevention, including psychological and social risks such as stress, harassment, depression and alcoholism; combining a variety of political instruments, such as social dialogue and corporate social responsibility; and building partnerships between all players in the field of health and safety[8].

13.5.8. Public health protection

Public health was brought fully into the action scope of the European Union by a special title of the Maastricht Treaty, which, as amended at Amsterdam to heed the "mad cow" and dioxin lessons [see sections 5.1.3. and 11.2.], states that a **high level of human health protection** shall be ensured in the definition and implementation of all Community policies and activities. Article 152 (TEC) invites the Community to contribute towards ensuring a high level of human health protection by encouraging co-operation between the Member States and by fostering cooperation with third countries and the competent international organisations.

Health threats such as communicable disease pandemics and bioterrorism are a growing concern, while the health impact of climate change raises new threats. On the other hand, new technologies are revolutionising the way health is promoted and illness is prevented and treated. To address

---

[1] Directive 90/270, OJ L 156, 21.06.1990 and Directive 2007/30, OJ L 165, 27.06.2007.
[2] Directive 2004/37, OJ L 158, 30.04.2004.
[3] Directive 92/58, OJ L 245, 26.08.1992 and Directive 2007/30, OJ L 165, 27.06.2007
[4] Directive 2003/10, OJ L 42, 15.02.2003 and Directive 2007/30, OJ L 165, 27.06.2007.
[5] Directive 91/383, OJ L 206, 29.07.1991.
[6] Directive 92/85, OJ L 348, 28.11.1992.
[7] Recommendation 2003/134, OJ L 53, 28.02.2003.
[8] Commission communication, COM (2002) 118, 11 March 2002.

these challenges, a White Paper of the Commission sets out a **strategic framework for work on health** at the EU level in the coming years[1]. The Strategic Approach for the EU 2008-2013 "Together for Health" puts forward an overarching framework which will focus on four principles and three strategic objectives for improving health in the EU.

The second **programme of Community action in the field of health** (2008-13) aims to protect and improve public health in the European Union by complementing, supporting and adding value to the policies of the Member States[2]. Its specific objectives are: to improve citizens' health security, to promote health, including the reduction of health inequalities, and to generate and disseminate health information and knowledge. An independent European agency named the **European Centre for Disease Prevention and Control** has the mission to identify, assess and communicate current and emerging threats to human health from communicable diseases[3].

13.6. Appraisal and outlook

The common social policy makes an important contribution to European integration, notably in helping achieve the **social cohesion** necessary among the Member States. It is interesting to note in the following paragraphs that each of the four wings of this policy makes a different contribution to the integration process. They, nevertheless, reinforce each other and interact with other common policies, notably the economic and monetary, industrial, research and development ones, in fostering the social cohesion necessary in an economic and monetary union.

The **freedom of movement of workers** was essential for the completion of the common market and, therefore, was examined under that heading [see section 6.4.]. By virtue of the Community regulations adopted in their favour, migrant workers and self-employed persons from any Member State enjoy fair conditions compared with nationals of the host country with regard to access to employment, social security, the education and vocational training of their children, living and working conditions and the right to exercise union rights. The common labour market is handicapped, however, by the existence of different languages, customs and working methods and, although the EU is taking measures to overcome these hurdles to the free movement of workers, it will certainly need much time before it encompasses a really homogeneous labour market.

The **common employment policy** is striving to ensure that the national employment policies and the common policies of the EU, notably in the economic and monetary field, work together in a consistent manner so as to boost economic reforms and employment while maintaining price stabil-

---

[1]   COM/2007/630.
[2]   Decision 1350/2007, OJ L 301, 20.11.2007.
[3]   Regulation 851/2004, OJ L 152, 30.04.2004.

ity. The coordinated employment strategy aims to harness structural reforms and modernisation to improve the efficiency of the labour market, while maintaining a non-inflationary growth dynamic. The employment guidelines, agreed by the Council, help the Member States to devise their own employment strategies, while pursuing common goals, such as: improving employability, with the emphasis on suitable training; developing entrepreneurship; encouraging the adaptability of the work force; and strengthening equal opportunities policies for women and men. The Lisbon agenda has shifted the focus of the European employment strategy from the fight against unemployment towards the wider priority of more and better jobs in an inclusive society and has helped employment creation in the EU [see section 13.3.2.]. However, performance varies considerably among the Member States and reforms are not pursued in a sufficiently comprehensive way by all of them, whether in terms of creating and maintaining employment or improving vocational skills and the quality of jobs.

The **common education and training policies** complement the common employment policy by encouraging the adaptation of the work force to the new conditions of the industrial and service sectors in Europe and in the rest of the world. The cooperation and exchange of experiences through the Community programmes helps the Member States develop the European dimension in education, the teaching of languages, the vocational training and retraining needed in the information society and in the global economy. While helping achieve the objectives of the Lisbon Strategy, these programmes build networks of teachers, instructors and young people who participate actively in the European integration process [see section 9.4.].

The **common policy for the improvement of living and working conditions** is aimed at the convergence of social protection systems and through it at the social cohesion of the Union. Community directives fixing common minimum standards guarantee the rights, the physical safety and health of workers, particularly the women and the young, in all Member States. The establishment of a framework of basic minimum standards provides a bulwark against using low social standards as an instrument of unfair economic competition. However, economic and social developments in European countries make it necessary to modernise social protection systems in order to attain four main objectives: creating more incentives to work and provide a secure income; safeguarding pensions with sustainable pension schemes; promoting social inclusion; and ensuring the high quality and sustainability of health protection.

Bibliography on social policy

*   ALBER Jens (et al.). Handbook of quality of life in the enlarged European Union. London: Routledge, 2008.
*   BUCHS Milena. *New governance in European social policy: the open method of coordination*. Basingstoke: Palgrave Macmillan, 2007.

- BURCHELL Brendan (et al.). *Working conditions in the European Union: the gender perspective.* European Foundation for the Improvement of Living and Working Conditions. Luxembourg: EUR-OP*, 2007.
- COUNTOURIS Nicola. *The changing law of the employment relationship: comparative analyses in the European context.* Aldershot: Ashgate, 2007.
- EUROPEAN COMMISSION. *Ten years of the European Employment Strategy (EES).* Luxembourg: EUR-OP, 2007.
- HARTLAPP Miriam. "On enforcement, management and persuasion: different logics of implementation policy in the EU and the ILO", in *Journal of Common Market Studies*, v. 45, n. 3, September 2007, p. 653-674.
- IMMERGUT Ellen (et al. eds.). *The handbook of West European pension politics.* Oxford: Oxford University Press, 2007.
- KVIST Jon, SAARI Juho (eds.). *The europeanisation of social protection.* London: Policy Press, 2007.
- MATHERS Andy. *Struggling for a social Europe: neoliberal globalization and the birth of a European social movement.* Aldershot: Ashgate, 2007.
- SHAW Jo, HUNT Jo, WALLACE Chloë, *Economic and social law of the European Union.* Basingstoke: Palgrave Macmillan, 2007.

DISCUSSION TOPICS

1. Discuss the development of the common social policy through the stages of customs union, common market, economic and monetary union, as outlined in the Treaties of Rome, Maastricht and Amsterdam.
2. What are the lessons to be drawn concerning the development of common policies from the momentary conflict between the common social policy and the national social policy of the UK?
3. How does the EU go about its social cohesion?
4. Consider the education, training and youth programmes of the EU in relation with employment qualifications, cultural identities and the building of human networks.
5. What is the significance of social protection in the EU context?

Chapter 14

TAXATION POLICY

Diagram of the chapter

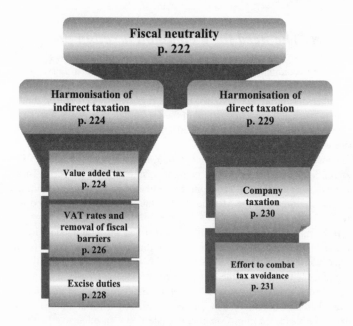

The EEC Treaty was very cautious as regards tax harmonisation. What it wanted above all was the introduction and observance of **the rule of fiscal neutrality in Community trade**, i.e. equal tax treatment for domestic production and imports from other member countries. Beyond that, the Treaty merely invited the Commission to examine how turnover taxes could be harmonised. The Treaty did not call for any harmonisation or other Community action with regard to direct taxes.

The fiscal objectives of the Treaty were attained rapidly. Cumulative multi-stage taxes, which did not guarantee fiscal neutrality, were replaced by **a new turnover tax, the value added tax**, and the structures of that tax were harmonised in all Community Member States, old and new. The principle of fiscal neutrality was thus guaranteed, but at the price of maintaining tax barriers, which were necessary for the collection of VAT and excise duties in the country of destination of goods.

However, in the single market goods must be able to move completely freely, and to achieve this, tax has to be imposed on them either in the country of origin or in that of destination. This led, at the end of the 1980s, to the **alignment of VAT and excise duties**. At the same time the harmonisation of direct taxes has begun, especially concerning those on companies and savings, in order to make the growth of companies and capital movement independent of tax considerations. Inside the economic and monetary union, tax harmonisation should progress at the same pace as economic integration.

14.1. The need for a common taxation policy

Having economic and social structures which differed in many ways, the States which were to form the European Economic Community also had rather **dissimilar tax systems**, both as regards financial policy, that is to say in particular the composition of the tax burden as between direct and indirect taxes, and the technical organisation of taxation. In the short term there was no question of making a single fiscal territory of the European Community. But pending such unification, some urgent measures in the taxation field were needed for the common market to work properly. These measures were centred on achieving fiscal neutrality and equal conditions of competition among the Member States, the two subjects discussed below.

If the member states of a common market had absolute freedom in the fiscal field, they could very quickly **replace the customs barriers to trade by tax barriers**. They could in fact, while lowering their customs duties in accordance with the timetable laid down by the Treaty, raise their domestic taxes in such a way that the total burden on imports remained unchanged. It was therefore necessary that indirect taxes, in particular turnover tax, have no influence on intra-Community trade flows. In other words, **fiscal neutrality** between domestic production and imports from the partner countries was needed. To secure fiscal neutrality in a common market the turnover tax of the country of origin or of the country of destination would have to be imposed on all goods.

If the rule of **the tax of the country of origin** were adopted, there would be a danger of creating trade flows based artificially on the difference in the taxes rather than on the difference in comparative costs, but there would be pressure on the Member States to approximate the rates of their taxes, and fiscal frontiers could be removed, as imported goods would already have paid taxes at the rate of the country of origin. If, on the other hand, the system of the **tax of the country of destination** were applied, production could be concentrated where the comparative economic advantages were greatest rather than where taxation would be lower, as all products in competition on a market, whether of domestic origin or imported, would be uniformly subject to the tax on consumption in force on that market. However, under that system the tax barriers would have to be maintained in order to levy the taxes of the country of destination on imported goods and the Member States would not be encouraged to approximate the rates of their taxes. This was the price, which the founding Member States, in light of the low level of integration of their economies, paid in opting for the system of taxation in the country of destination.

Just behind the harmonisation of the structures of all indirect taxes came, of course, the harmonisation of their rates. It is obvious that in order to create completely impartial conditions of competition in the common market **a common system of taxes on consumption is needed**, comprising not only the same structures, but also very approximate rates or, indeed, the same rates wherever possible. In effect, the different rates of taxes could have a different influence on the consumption of various products in the common market and could distort the conditions of competition between the undertakings of the Member States. Where the tax burden on a product is lower in one country than in another, if the other conditions of competition are equal in both countries, the undertakings which manufacture the product in the first country are in a much more **favourable competitive position** than their counterparts in the second country, as they can have increased demand and high profits in their principal market.

Moreover, there are grounds for questioning whether, in spite of the harmonisation of tax structures and the alignment of indirect taxation, fiscal neutrality exists, when some states have much more recourse than others to **direct taxation**. It is true that such states tax the products of their partners less than do those which have more recourse to indirect taxes, but the terms of trade and productivity offset to a large extent the fiscal disparities of member states' companies. Moreover, states clearly apply certain categories of tax on the basis of historic habit, sociological structure and economic conditions. Some mainly apply indirect taxes, which are easily collected, whilst others have greater recourse to direct taxation, which is fairer from the social viewpoint. The member states of a common market need to have sufficient autonomy in the tax field so as to have enough room for manoeuvre to act in the light of their economic situations.

In fact, the requirements for tax harmonisation increase together with progress in economic integration. Whilst fiscal neutrality in a customs union is ensured by the harmonisation of the structures of turnover tax and excise duties, in a common market and even more so **in an economic and monetary union** gradual harmonisation of the levels of those taxes and even of direct taxation are also necessary, to ensure fair competition throughout the single market. The long-term goal is to reach a taxation framework conducive to enterprise, job creation and environment protection in the Union[1]. Tax harmonisation may have spillover effects [see section 1.1.1.] on the development of the common enterprise, employment and environment policies.

---

[1]   COM (96) 546, 22 October 1996.

14.2. Harmonisation of indirect taxation

Indirect taxes are **those on turnover, production or consumption of goods and services** - regarded as components of cost prices and selling prices - which are collected without regard to the realisation of profits, or indeed income, but which are deductible when determining profits. Customs duties are a form of indirect taxation. That is why, following the removal of customs barriers in a common market, Member States could be tempted to replace them with fiscal barriers, i.e. with internal taxes. That danger was foreseen in the EEC Treaty, Articles 95 to 98 of which contained provisions to obviate it, together with Article 99, which called upon the Commission to consider how the legislation of the various Member States concerning turnover taxes, excise duties and other forms of indirect taxation could be harmonised in the interest of the common market. Indeed, the Commission, assisted by two committees of experts, examined the harmonisation of indirect taxation and proposed the adoption by all Member States of a system of turnover taxes which did not distort conditions of competition either within a country or between Member States. Such a system was the tax on value added.

14.2.1. Value added tax

When it was **adopted for the first time, in France in 1954, value added tax (VAT)** was regarded as merely another tax on turnover or on consumption and did not attract the attention of other countries. It was only since 1962, with the publication of two reports ordered by the Commission recommending its adoption by all Member States, that its interest for the Community was understood. Acting on the basis of Commission proposals, the Council adopted on 11 April 1967 two Directives on the harmonisation of the legislation of Member States concerning turnover taxes[1]. Those two Directives laid the groundwork for the common value added tax system and a third one, adopted in 1969, introduced it in the tax systems of the Member States[2].

According to Article 2 of the first Directive of 1967, **VAT is a general tax on consumption**, i.e. a tax on all expenditure on goods and services. The tax is levied at each stage of an economic activity on the value added at that stage. It is paid by all those involved in the production and distribution of a product or service, but it is not an element in the costs of those intermediaries and does not appear as an item of expenditure in their accounts, as it is not they who bear the tax, but the end consumer.

The tax is proportional to the price of the products and services irrespective of the number of transactions, which have taken place at the stages preceding that to which it is applied. At the time of each transaction, the

---

[1] Directive 67/227, OJ 71, 14.04.1967 and Directive 2008/8, OJ L 44, 20.02.2008
[2] Directive 69/463, OJ L 320, 20.12.1969.

amount of VAT, calculated on the price of the good or service, is reduced by the amount of the taxes previously paid on the cost of the various components of the cost price. The total sum which changes hands at each stage in the production or distribution includes the VAT paid up to that point, but the amount of the tax is recovered at each sale, except for the final sale to the **final consumer**, who purchases the product or service for his private use. The tax is paid to the State by the vendor in each transaction. However, the latter does not bear the burden of the VAT, as his purchaser has advanced the full amount of the VAT to him. Tax paid at previous stages, on deliveries made or services rendered to the taxable person, and the tax paid on imports, is deductible from the turnover tax of that taxable person. Given this **deductibility of taxes already paid**, VAT is neutral from the point of view of domestic competition, i.e. it does not favour vertically integrated undertakings, as did the cumulative multi-stage taxes. But VAT is also neutral from the point of view of international competition, since it cannot favour domestic products. Calculation of the tax paid is easy, as it appears on all invoices and documents accompanying the product.

The **sixth directive** on the harmonisation of turnover taxes established a package of common rules making it possible to define the scope of the tax and the method of determining tax liability, i.e. the territorial application of the tax, the taxable persons, the taxable transactions, the place of applicability of such transactions, the chargeable event, the taxable amount, the detailed procedures for applying rates of taxation, the exemptions and the special schemes[1]. In Community jargon all these rules are known as **"the uniform basis of assessment of VAT"**, and that basis is particularly important in that VAT is a basic source of revenue for the Community [see section 3.4.]. Moreover, Directive 77/388 harmonised the laws on turnover tax structures of the Member States in the fields of the **provision of services**, agricultural production, small undertakings and exempt activities and operations linked with importation, exportation and international trade in goods. Subject to Council approval, a Member State may introduce into its legislation special measures for derogation from the common system of value-added tax, either in order to simplify the procedure for charging the tax or to prevent certain types of tax evasion or avoidance, or in the form of an agreement with a non-member country or an international organisation. Regulation 1777/2005 lays down implementing measures for Directive 77/388[2].

A directive amending the sixth directive put in place uniform taxation rules for radio and television broadcasting services and for certain electronically supplied services, making it as easy and straightforward as possible to comply with these rules, particularly in the fields of supply, electronic networks, services linked to software and computers in general, and of information, cultural, arts, sports, science, education and leisure ser-

---

[1] Directive 77/388, OJ L 145, 13.06.1977 last amended by Directive 2008/8, OJ L 44, 20.02.2008

[2] Regulation 1777/2005, OJ L 288, 29.10.2005.

vices[1]. These rules allow Member States to subject to VAT services provided electronically and radio and television broadcasting services supplied on subscription or pay-per-view basis in the European Union and to exempt these services from VAT if they are provided for consumption outside the Union [see also sections 6.6.1. and 17.3.5.]. Another directive amended the rules for the application of VAT and harmonised the rules on the place of **taxation of natural gas and electricity**[2]. Supplies to dealers are taxable at the place of their business or fixed establishment for which the goods are supplied, whereas supplies to end consumers are taxable at the place of consumption of gas and electricity, which is usually the place where the customer's meter is located.

14.2.2. VAT rates and removal of fiscal barriers

The export refunds and import taxes, which accompanied intra-Community trade, and the resultant controls, constituted the so-called "**fiscal frontiers**". To remove those barriers to trade, it was vital that cross-border trade be treated in the same way as purchases and sales within a State. The Commission actually proposed that as from 1 January 1993 all sales of goods and services should be taxed at the rate of the country of origin[3]. But the Council did not follow the Commission's lead. In conclusions of 9 October 1989, adopted unanimously (necessary condition in order to counter the proposal of the Commission) [see section 4.3.], it considered that conditions could not be fulfilled for a system of taxation in the country of origin and that it was therefore necessary to continue, for a limited period, to levy VAT and excise duty in the State of consumption.

The Directive on the common system of value added tax stipulates that, during the operational period of the transitional VAT arrangements (where the VAT rate is that of the country of destination and not that of the country of origin), the Member States shall apply **a standard VAT rate of at least 15%**[4]. However, the standard VAT rate varies between 15 and 25% in the twenty-seven Member States. In fact, in January 2008 the standard VAT rate was:

- **15,** in Luxembourg and Cyprus;
- **16,** in Spain;
- **17.5,** in the United Kingdom;
- **18,** in Estonia, Latvia, Lithuania and Malta;
- **19,** in Germany, Greece, Romania, the Netherlands, the Czech Republic and Slovakia;
- **19.6,** in France;
- **20,** in Italy, Hungary, Bulgaria, Austria and Slovenia;

---

[1] Directive 2002/38, OJ L 128, 15.05.2002 and Directive 2006/58, OJ L 174, 28.06.2006.
[2] Directive 2003/96, OJ L 283, 31.10.2003 and Directive 2004/74, OJ L 157, 30.04.2004.
[3] Commission proposal, OJ C 250, 19.09.1987, p. 2.
[4] Directive 2006/112, OJ L 347, 11.12.2006 and Directive 2008/8, OJ L 44, 20.02.2008.

- **21,** in Portugal, Belgium and Ireland;
- **22,** in Poland and Finland; and
- **25,** in Denmark, Sweden and Hungary.

All the higher VAT rates existing in several Member States have been abolished, leading to a significant fall in consumer prices in some sectors, such as automobiles. The Member States however enjoy the option of applying, alongside the normal rate, one (or two) **reduced rates**, equal to or higher than 5%, applicable only to certain goods and services of a social or cultural nature. Examples include foodstuffs, pharmaceuticals, passenger transport services, books, newspapers and periodicals, entrance to shows, museums and the like, publications and copyright, subsidised housing, hotel accommodation, social activities and medical care in hospitals. The preservation of the zero and extra-low rates (below 5%) is authorised on a transitional basis, along with reduced rates on housing other than subsidised housing, catering and children's clothes and shoes.

The common system of VAT dispensed with customs procedures[1]. Intra-Community trade in goods between taxable bodies is subject to taxation in the country of destination. In the case of sales between companies subject to VAT, i.e. the vast majority, the vendor exempts the deliveries made to clients in other Member States. In his VAT return, he indicates, in a separate box, the total of his exempted intra-Community sales. In another return (usually quarterly), he lists the VAT number of his customers in the other Member States and the total amount of his sales to each of them during the period in question. The purchaser applies VAT to his purchase in another Member State, termed an "acquisition". He must declare the total amount of these acquisitions in a separate box in his normal VAT return and can request the deductibility of this VAT in the same return.

Individuals travelling from one Member State to another pay VAT there where they purchase the goods and are no longer subject to any VAT-related taxation or any border formality when they cross from one Member State to another. In return, the system of travellers' allowances (tax free sales in ports, airports, etc.) was abolished in intra-Community travelling[2].

14.2.3. Excise duties

In a fiscally integrated Community a number of major **special taxes on consumption** (**excise duties**), i.e. taxes on the consumption of certain products, yielding substantial revenue to the States, must be maintained alongside VAT. Excise duties make it possible to impose a much larger tax burden on a small number of products than that borne by the vast majority of goods that are only subject to VAT, which has very few, and fairly low, rates. If the various excise duties in the Community States were abolished,

---

[1] Directive 91/680, OJ L 376, 31.12.1991 and OJ L 384, 30.12.1992.
[2] Directive 94/4, OJ L 60, 03.03.1994 and Directive 98/94, OJ L 358, 31.12.1998.

the resultant losses of revenue would have to be offset by increasing VAT rates, which would be certain to have an inflationary effect on their economies. Thus, for example, manufactured tobacco products and mineral oils bear, without major drawbacks, very high taxes, which on average yield more than 10% of the tax revenue of the EU States. Moreover, within the overall context of a tax scheme, excise duties constitute **flexible components**, which can easily be manoeuvred if further tax revenue is needed. As they are separate taxes, excise duties can easily be adapted to the various economic, social and structural requirements. Lastly, they can be levied specifically in order to reduce consumption of certain products, such as tobacco products and alcoholic drinks, for public health reasons, and petroleum products for reasons of environment linked energy savings and reduction of energy dependence.

But if some excise duties had to be maintained in the Community two conditions had to be met so as **not to disturb the common market**: their structures had to be harmonised, so as to remove taxation indirectly protecting national production; and their rates had to be harmonised so as to eliminate, in trade between Member States, taxation and tax refunds as well as frontier controls, which disturbed the free movement of goods within the common market.

Taking account of these conditions, a Directive defines the **general arrangements** for the holding and movement of products subject to excise duty[1]. In contrast to the harmonised VAT system, the general arrangements for excise duties are definitive. The taxable event takes place at the stage of manufacture in the Community or of import into the Community from a third country. The tax is payable when the product is put up for consumption and must be acquitted in the country of actual consumption. The Member States have the option of introducing or maintaining taxation on other products and services, provided however that this taxation does not give rise to border crossing formalities in trade between the Member States.

Excise duties are paid by the consignee in the country of destination and the appropriate provisions are taken to this effect. For commercial operations, the Community system is similar to that applied within a state. The movement of products subject to suspended excise duty is run through interconnected bonded warehouses and is covered by an accompanying document, which has been harmonised at Community level. The payment of the excise due in the Member State of destination can be assumed by a fiscal representative established in this State and designated by the consignor. The appropriate provisions are taken to enable the exchange of information between all the Member States concerned by the movement of goods subject to excise with a view to ensuring effective fraud control[2]. Individuals can purchase the products of their choice in other Member

---

[1]   Directive 92/12, OJ L 76, 23.03.1992 and Directive 2004/106, OJ L 359, 04.12.2004.
[2]   Decision 1152/2003, OJ L 162, 01.07.2003.

States, inclusive of tax, for their personal use. Denmark, Finland and Sweden are, however, authorised by the Council to continue restricting the quantities of certain alcoholic drinks and tobacco products which individuals purchase in other Member States and import for their own consumption. Following these general guidelines, seven specific directives harmonise the structures and minimum excise duty rates on manufactured tobaccos, mineral oils, spirits and alcoholic beverages.

14.3. Harmonisation of direct taxation

Taxes on the revenue of undertakings (firms, companies, businesses) and private individuals, which are not incorporated in cost prices or selling prices and the rate of which is often progressive, may be regarded as direct taxes. The two important categories of direct taxes are **income tax and capital gains tax**. Article 92 of the EC Treaty prohibits, as regards such taxes, countervailing charges at frontiers, i.e. the application of remissions and repayments in respect of exports to other Member States. Derogations may not be granted unless the measures contemplated have been previously approved for a limited period by the Council. Apart from that provision, the EC Treaty does not deal with direct taxes and does not call for them to be harmonised.

Whilst the harmonisation of indirect taxes was necessary from the outset to avoid obstacles to trade and to free competition and later to make the removal of fiscal frontiers possible, the harmonisation of direct taxes was not considered indispensable at the common market stage. It gradually became clear, however, that the free movement of capital and the rational distribution of production factors in the Community required a **minimum degree of harmonisation of direct taxes**. In effect, the convergence of Member States' economic policies [see section 7.3.1.] necessitates a coordination of the fiscal instruments used by them. Likewise, the global competitiveness of European businesses requires that the taxation of companies operating in several Member States does not place them at a disadvantage in relation to their competitors restricting their activities to the purely national level. The Commission had tabled proposals to this end in 1969, right after the realisation of the customs union. The Council needed 21 years of debate (!) before it could approve these proposals, vital for transnational cooperation and company mergers in the single market.

14.3.1. Company taxation

The first Directive concerning business taxation, adopted by the Council in July 1990 relates to the taxation system applicable to the **capital gains generated upon the merger**, division, transfer of assets, contribution of assets or exchange of shares between two companies operating in

different Member States[1]. National regulations consider this type of operation as a total or partial liquidation of the company making the contribution
and subject it to capital gains tax. This is usually set in an artificial manner,
since it compares the market value of the good in question (the company
itself, a building, land or a share package) to the value entered in the balance sheet, traditionally underestimated. Such a calculation is unjust, inso-
far as no liquidation is taking place in effect, but two companies from different Member States are forming closer links. The Community solution
consists of not taxing the capital gain at the time when the merger or contribution of assets takes place but rather when it is collected. This solution
encourages the formation of "European companies", which usually result
from the merger of companies originally established in different Member
States.

The second Council Directive of July 1990 relates to the common fiscal system applicable to **parent companies and subsidiaries** situated in
different Member States[2]. There can be little doubt that the decision by a
company to set up a subsidiary in another Member State of the Community
would be adversely affected by the fact that the dividends of the latter
would be subject, on the one hand, to corporation tax in the country where
it had its domicile and, on the other, to a non-recoverable withholding tax,
in the Member State where the subsidiary would be domiciled. The Directive abolishes withholding taxes on dividends distributed by a subsidiary to
its parent company established in another Member State.

A **code of conduct on business taxation** engages the Member States
not to bring in any tax rules which constitute harmful tax competition and
to phase out existing rules including withholding taxes on interest and royalty payments between companies forming part of a group[3]. A group
within the framework of the Council has the task to assess the tax measures
that may fall within the scope of the code and to oversee the provision by
the Member States of information on those measures[4]. A Commission notice clarifies the application of the State aid rules to measures relating to
direct business taxation[5].

A common system of taxation is applicable to interest and royalty
payments made between **associated companies in different Member
States**[6]. Therefore, interest or royalty payments arising in a Member State
are exempted from any taxes imposed on those payments in that State,
whether by deduction at source or by assessment. For budgetary reasons,
Greece, Spain and Portugal may apply transitional measures in introducing
the new system.

---

[1] Directive 90/434, OJ L 225, 20.08.1990 and Directive 2006/98, OJ L 363, 20.12.2006.
[2] Directive 90/435, OJ L 225, 20.08.1990 and Directive 2006/98, OJ L 363, 20.12.2006.
[3] Resolution, OJ C 2, 06.01.1998, p. 2-5.
[4] Council conclusions, OJ C 99, 01.04.1998, p. 1-2.
[5] Commission notice, OJ C 384, 10.12.1998.
[6] Directive 2003/49, OJ L 157, 26.06.2003 and directive 2004/66, OJ L 168, 01.05.2004.

14.3.2. Effort to combat tax avoidance

The most important and urgent problems for the Community in the area of direct taxation were posed by **international tax avoidance**. In addition to the substantial budgetary losses for States and the fiscal injustice, international tax avoidance generates abnormal capital movements and distortions of conditions of competition. Therefore, a 1977 Directive instituted a **mutual assistance by the competent authorities** of the Member States in the field of direct taxation (income tax, company tax and capital gains tax) and certain excise duties and taxation of insurance premiums[1]. That Directive introduced a procedure for the systematic exchange of information directed towards enabling them to effect a correct assessment of direct taxes in the Community. It permits the Member States to coordinate their investigative action against cross-border tax fraud and to carry out more procedures on behalf of each other. A regulation lays down a set of conditions and procedures to assist administrative authorities in preventing fraud and distortions of competition in movements of excisable products[2].

However, the liberalisation of capital movements as from 1 July 1990 [see section 6.7.], has **increased the risk of tax evasion**. In fact, Community residents can nowadays freely transfer their savings to bank accounts in any Member State without the corresponding income necessarily being declared to the tax authorities of the State of residence. Since, in several Member States, there is no "withholding tax" on bank interest paid to nonresidents, investments would flow towards those States, thus avoiding any taxation. Such capital movements, motivated purely by tax considerations, would be contrary to the optimum allocation of resources, which is the objective of establishing a common financial area [see section 6.6.].

In order to lessen the risk of tax distortion, evasion and avoidance, it was necessary to intensify the exchange of information between tax authorities and to remove the encouragement to invest in a Member State, which applies a more favourable tax scheme than the Member State of the investor, by introducing in all the Member States a relatively low withholding tax. These objectives are aimed at by the Directive ensuring a minimum of effective **taxation of savings income** in the form of interest payments within the Community[3]. Under the terms of the Directive, each Member State should automatically provide the other Member States with information on savings income of their residents. However, Belgium, Luxembourg and Austria may, for a transitional period (until the end of 2009), instead apply a non-final withholding tax to the interest on savings of nonresidents. This should be applied at a rate of 15% for the first three years, after which it should rise to 20%, and the percentage of revenue transferred to the Member State of residence of the saver by the Member State of the paying agent should be 75%. In order to preserve the competitiveness of

[1] Directive 77/799, OJ L 336, 27.12.1977 and Directive 2006/98, OJ L 363, 20.12.2006.
[2] Regulation 2073/2004, OJ L 359, 04.12.2004.
[3] Directive 2003/48, OJ L 157, 26.06.2003 and decision 2004/587, OJ L 257, 04.08.2004.

European financial markets, the European institutions entered into discussions with key third countries, such as the USA, Switzerland, Liechtenstein, Monaco, Andorra and San Marino, to promote the adoption of equivalent measures in those countries, notably effective exchange of information. Agreements have been reached with the European countries, notably Switzerland[1], Liechtenstein[2], Andorra[3] and San Marino[4].

14.4. Appraisal and outlook

The aim of creating a unified fiscal area in the European Union is ambitious, even if unification means the harmonisation of national tax laws rather than the creation of a federal tax system. Fiscal unification could only be achieved progressively, in line with the convergence of the national economies. It was, however, urgent for the common market to harmonise turnover tax structures and consequently to **achieve fiscal neutrality**, i.e. equal tax treatment of domestic products and products imported from the Member States. That was to a large extent achieved with the adoption of the VAT system by all the original Member States at the beginning of the 1970s and by the new Member States after their accession. Such a close harmonisation of turnover taxes as that resulting from the adoption by all Member States of the value added tax with a uniform basis of assessment was not called for by the Treaty of Rome. The Member States therefore went beyond what was required of them by the Treaty.

Twenty years later, under pressure from the completion of the single market which required the abolition of fiscal frontiers, the Member States also agreed to harmonise their excise duties, thus proving that when the political will exists, the technical problems of multinational integration can always be overcome. Indeed, the harmonisation of VAT rates and of excise-duty structures and rates, achieved in 1992, meant a great deal of **upheaval in the tax revenue of the Member States** that rely heavily on revenue from indirect taxation. However, despite the reservations and the predictions of impending disaster among some fiscal experts, they have been able to carry out this harmonisation without major upset. This fact tends to demonstrate that the multinational integration process brings about dynamic effects that are sometimes overlooked by conservative considerations [see section 1.1.2.].

The harmonisation of indirect taxation is very important, not just for the smooth operation of the internal market but also for the **convergence of economic conditions in the Member States** [see section 7.3.1.]. The VAT and excise duties arrangements enable companies to sell, purchase and invest in all the Member States without being subject to controls or formali-

---

[1]   Decisions 2004/911 and 2004/912, OJ L 385, 29.12.2004.

[2]   Decision 2004/897, OJ L 379, 24.12.2004.

[3]   Decision 2005/356, OJ L 114, 04.05.2005.

[4]   Decision 2005/357, OJ L 114, 04.05.2005.

ties arising from the crossing of borders. Individuals can purchase goods in all the Community countries and, without restriction, bring them back for their personal consumption without any checks or taxation on border crossing. The trans-European computerised networks ensure the imposition of goods and services in all the Member States in accordance with Community tax legislation.

Some very important areas of direct taxation, such as personal income tax, are not directly targeted by the harmonisation process, and the propensity to align the rates and the progressivity effect is markedly less. **As EMU advances**, however, a procedure for the coordination of national fiscal policies will have to be introduced to enable these policies to converge progressively in parallel with the convergence of economic policies. Such coordination should not necessarily aim at uniform tax rates, but should strive to reduce the continuing distortions in the single market, to get tax structures to develop in more employment and environment-friendly way and to prevent losses of tax revenue. Indeed, all Member States have common problems, notably that of capital evasion to fiscal paradises and even that of competition among themselves in order to attract capital while penalising their work forces. If they would put together part of their sovereignty in the fiscal field so as to take common measures, Member States could better face international competition and avoid seeing the money market forces obstruct their common goals.

Bibliography on taxation policy

* ANDERSSON Krister, EBERHARTIGER Eva, OXELHEIM Lars. *National tax policy in Europe: to be or not to be?* Berlin: Springer, 2007.
* BARENFELD Jesper. "A common consolidated corporate tax base in the European Union: a beauty or a beast in the quest for tax simplicity?" in *Bulletin for International Taxation*, v. 61, n. 7, July 2007, p. 258-271.
* CATTOIR Philippe. *A history of the "tax package": the principles and issues underlying the community approach.* European Commission. Luxembourg: EUR-OP*, 2007.
* CERIONI Luca. "A hypothesis for radical tax reform in the European Union: the implications of the abolition of corporate income taxes", in *European Taxation*, v. 47, n. 8-9, August-September 2007, p. 377-388.
* EUROPEAN COMMISSION. *Fiscal blueprints: a path to a robust, modern and efficient tax administration.* Luxembourg: EUR-OP*, 2007.
* EUROSTAT. *Taxation trends in the European Union: main results.* Luxembourg: EUR-OP, 2007.
* OESTREICHER Andreas, SPENGEL Christoph. "Tax harmonization in Europe: the determination of corporate taxable income in the Member States", in *European Taxation*, v. 47, n. 10, October 2007, p. 437-451.
* SCHWARZ Jonathan. "The need and scope for coordination of tax policies in the European Union", in *Bulletin for International Taxation*, v. 61, n. 7, July 2007, p. 272-276.

- SØRENSEN Karsten Engsig. "Towards a more comprehensive examination of the compatibility of indirect taxes with the internal market", in *Intertax*, v. 35, n. 4, April 2007, p. 246-255.
- WEBER Denis (ed.). *The influence of European law on direct taxation: recent and future developments*. The Hague: Kluwer Law International, 2007.

DISCUSSION TOPICS

1. What is the significance of fiscal neutrality in a common market?
2. What was the interest for multinational integration of the adoption by all Member States of the value added tax?
3. How were "fiscal frontiers" removed inside the common market?
4. Outline the harmonisation of indirect taxation in the EU.
5. Discuss the need for harmonisation of direct taxation at the stages of the common market and of the economic and monetary union.

Chapter 15

COMPETITION POLICY

Diagram of the chapter

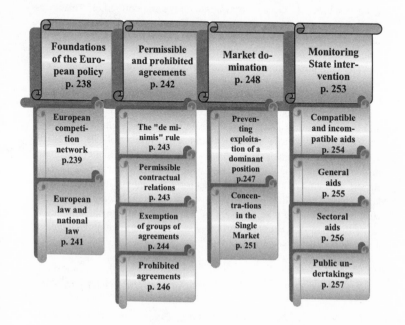

Foundations of the European policy p. 238	Permissible and prohibited agreements p. 242	Market domination p. 248	Monitoring State intervention p. 253
European competition network p.239	The "de minimis" rule p. 243	Preventing exploitation of a dominant position p.247	Compatible and incompatible aids p. 254
European law and national law p. 241	Permissible contractual relations p. 243	Concentrations in the Single Market p. 251	General aids p. 255
	Exemption of groups of agreements p. 244		Sectoral aids p. 256
	Prohibited agreements p. 246		Public undertakings p. 257

The essence of the single market is the possibility of undertakings to compete on equal terms on the markets of all the Member States. Therefore, the common competition policy is **essential to the achievement and maintenance of the single market** [see section 6.1.]. It ensures the competitive conduct of undertakings (firms, companies, businesses) and protects the interests of consumers by enabling them to procure goods and services on the best terms. It promotes economic efficiency by creating a climate favourable to innovation and technical progress [see section 17.1.]. It prevents anti-competitive practices on the part of companies, which might choke off the competitive dynamics generated by the completion of the single market.

Common competition rules, necessary for preserving a level playing field for all undertakings in the internal market, may go against national interests and have to be complied with by all governments, which accounts for the **need for a neutral and respected referee placed above the clash of national interests**. The EC Treaty allocates that role to the European

Commission. This is indeed one of the few areas in which the Commission has autonomous, supranational power and, in addition to its initiative role, it has the responsibility of taking primary decisions [see section 4.1.2.]. Under the control of the Court of Justice, the Commission establishes Community law on competition, which provides a framework for and orientates national laws [see section 3.3.]. In effect, the national competition authorities put into effect their own national competition law which, in many respects, takes its cue from Community competition law. This means that in many areas the implementation of Community rules can be assigned to Member States' authorities and courts, thus relieving the Commission from routine work.

The common competition policy affects virtually all the **other common policies**, which must comply with its rules [see section 1.1.2]. This is true in particular of industrial policy, as regards structural and sectoral measures, regional policy, as regards State aid for the poor regions, energy and transport policies, as regards the major public and multinational undertakings in those sectors, and agricultural and fisheries policies, as regards common market organisations. A proactive competition policy facilitates business activity, wide dissemination of knowledge, a better deal for consumers and efficient economic restructuring throughout the internal market[1]. Since competition policy is impacting upon the economic performance of Europe, it is a key element of a coherent and integrated policy to foster the competitiveness of Europe's industries and to attain the goals of the Lisbon strategy [see section 13.3.2].

15.1. The need for a common competition policy

Before the opening up of borders to intra-Community trade and competition, prices in some sectors in most countries were artificially maintained at a level that allowed marginal undertakings to survive. **The consumer bore the cost of protecting non-profitable businesses**. In other sectors, unprofitable businesses were supported by aids of all kinds, and it was therefore the taxpayer that kept them alive. Hence, both consumers and taxpayers had a great interest in seeing the unprofitable undertakings disappear from the market thanks to the fair play of competition. This common interest of the citizens of the Member States is a major driving force of the multinational integration process [see section 1.1.2.].

National rules alone cannot ensure competition in a common market. They must be completed by Community rules to cover the cases, which affect trade between the Member States and where, therefore, there is Community competence. In contrast to national competition policies, the common competition policy has **a market integration objective**. It must ensure the unity of the common market by preventing undertakings from di-

---

[1]   COM (2004) 293, 20 April 2004.

viding it up amongst themselves by means of protective agreements. It must obviate the monopolisation of certain markets by preventing major companies from abusing their dominant position to impose their conditions or to buy out their competitors. Lastly, it must prevent governments from distorting the rules of the game by means of aids to private sector undertakings or discrimination in favour of public undertakings.

The very essence of the large market of the European Union is the liveliness of competition. The large market actually enables undertakings to produce on a large scale, to put in hand modern methods of production and to reduce their costs, to the **benefit of consumers**. Thanks to the common market, consumers have a choice between domestic products and products from partner countries, imported free of quantitative restrictions and customs duties [see section 5.1.]. Their choice naturally turns towards better-quality products, taking into account their price, irrespective of their origin. Consumers are therefore the judges of the performance of businesses in the large market. The least viable firms are obliged to modernise or shut down.

The increase of competition as a result of the creation of the common market involves the upheaval of supply conditions, the **renunciation of traditional habits and behaviour** and, in some instances, the loss of monopoly profits. Such developments cannot leave businessmen indifferent. Their attitude may be positive or negative. In most cases, they will endeavour to preserve or even increase their share of the market by reducing their cost prices through restructuring, investment outlay and rationalising production and distribution methods [see section 17.1.]. Such an approach is in the interest both of consumers, who benefit from plentiful supply on the best possible conditions, and of the businessmen themselves, as they learn to live with the common market and to cope better with international competition. Vertical agreements between producers and local distributors can be used pro-competitively to promote market integration.

In order to ensure that undertakings operating in the internal market enjoy the same conditions of competition everywhere, efforts have to be made to combat not only unfair practices on the part of undertakings, but also **discriminatory measures on the part of States**. Economic integration and the increasing liberalisation of international trade greatly weaken the classical methods of commercial protection, viz. high customs duties and quantitative restrictions on imports as well as technical barriers to trade. For that reason, States have more frequent recourse to **aids as an instrument of economic policy**, especially given that increased competition and more rapid technological change reveal structural weaknesses in several sectors and regions. Some aids are doubtless justified on the grounds of social policy or regional policy, while others are necessary to direct businesses towards the requisite adjustments at an acceptable social cost. But the Member States' aid policies are often aimed at artificially ensuring the survival of sectors undergoing structural difficulties. Such aid measures run counter to the changes to the production structures inherent in technological progress and their social cost is often greater than the sums allo-

cated to them, as they block production factors which could be better employed elsewhere. In addition, such uncoordinated measures at European
level lead to spiralling aid, as each country finds itself obliged to follow in
its neighbour's footsteps whenever the latter supports an economic activity.
All these reasons necessitate European control of national aids.

One of the most intricate problems in the field of competition is posed
by **public undertakings** and undertakings controlled by the public authorities. Member States use them as instruments for attaining various economic, political and social objectives such as directing investment towards
certain sectors or regions, administering certain unprofitable public services, handling certain economic activities regarded as strategic, acting as
the nation's standard bearer in the arena of international competition and
employ persons who do not find jobs in the private sector. In return for the
manifold services they render to governments, the latter tend to discriminate in favour of public undertakings. The various privileges, which are
granted to them, can distort conditions of competition vis-à-vis undertakings in the private sector of their own nationality and those of their partners
in the common market. It is this latter aspect of relations between Member
States and their public undertakings that is of particular concern for the
European institutions.

15.2. Foundations of the European policy

Protectionist agreements, concentrations, national aids and discrimination in favour of public undertakings are incompatible with the common
market. They **must be controlled by the European institutions** on the basis of European criteria, because the Member States' competition policies,
even when they are stringent, are not efficacious at European level. Therefore, Article 3 of the EC Treaty, given over to the principles of the Community, provided for the institution "of a system ensuring that competition
in the internal market is not distorted", and the whole chapter on competition allocated to the Community the task of organising intra-Community
trade, free from tariff barriers, on the basis of the law of supply and demand.

The competition rules of the Treaty are interpreted and applied through
Council regulations and Commission regulations as well as through general communications and individual decisions of the Commission. Regulation N° 17 of 1972, first Regulation implementing Articles 85 and 86 of the
EEC Treaty[1], was replaced by Regulation 1/2003 on the implementation of
the rules on competition laid down in Articles 81 and 82 of the EC Treaty
(which have the same content as Articles 85 and 86 EEC)[2]. Whereas Regulation 17/62 was based on prior notification and centralised Commission

---

[1] Regulation 17, OJ 13, 21.02.1962 and Regulation 3385/94, OJ L 377, 31.12.1994.
[2] Regulation 1/2003, OJ L 1, 04.01.2003 and Regulation 411/2004, OJ L 68, 06.03.2004.

authorisation of agreements, Regulation 1/2003 is based on ex post control and on a **decentralised application of the competition rules** of Articles 81(1), 81(3) and 82 by the national authorities and courts, thus relieving the Commission of the examination of trivial cases and the industry of the costs connected with notification. On the basis of this regulation, agreements, decisions and concerted practices caught by Article 81(1) of the Treaty, which do not satisfy the conditions of Article 81(3), are prohibited, no prior decision to that effect being required. This is also the case concerning an abuse of a dominant position referred to in Article 82 of the Treaty. On the contrary, agreements, decisions and concerted practices, which satisfy the conditions of Article 81(3) of the Treaty [see section 15.3.2.], are not prohibited, no prior decision to that effect being required.

15.2.1. European competition network

Council Regulation No 17 of 1962 laid down a system of supervision requiring restrictive practices affecting trade between Member States to be notified to the Commission in order for them to qualify for an exemption[1]. The Commission thus had the exclusive power to authorise restrictive practices meeting the conditions of Article 81 (3) (formerly Article 85(3)) of the EC Treaty. This system of centralised authorisation was necessary and proved very effective in establishing a "competition culture" in Europe at a time when the interpretation of Article 81 (restrictive practices) and Article 82 (abuse of a dominant position) was still uncertain and when the Commission was making an effort to integrate national markets which were still very heterogeneous. During the forty years of the existence of Regulation 17/62, however, a great number of individual decisions were made by the Commission applying the exemption criteria of Article 81(3) of the Treaty. National competition authorities and national courts are therefore nowadays well aware of the conditions under which the benefit of Article 81.3 can be granted. Individual exemption decisions taken by the Commission are thus no longer indispensable to ensure a uniform application of Article 81(3) of the Treaty. Moreover, a system of notifications, entailing a great scrutiny workload for the Commission, is no longer workable in a Union of 27 Member States.

Therefore, at the proposal of the Commission, Regulation 1/2003 replaced its absolute powers in the field of competition by a network of competition authorities, called the **European Competition Network (ECN)**, which is a key plank of the new enforcement system. Formed by the Commission and the competition authorities of the Member States, this network of public authorities applies the Community competition rules in close cooperation, providing for an allocation of cases according to the principle of the best-placed authority, the objective being that each case should be handled by a single authority. In addition, the Commission con-

---

[1] Regulation 17/62, OJ 13, 21.02.1962 and Regulation 1/2003, OJ L 1, 04.01.2003.

sults an Advisory Committee on Restrictive Practices and Dominant Positions, composed of representatives of the competition authorities of the Member States.

The Commission may continue to adopt so called "block" exemption regulations by which it declares Article 81(1) of the Treaty inapplicable to categories of agreements, decisions and concerted practices. It may still adopt individual decisions prohibiting serious cartels affecting trade between the Member States and having the effect of restricting competition. Where the Commission, acting on a complaint or on its own initiative, finds that there is an infringement of Article 81 or of Article 82 of the Treaty, it may by decision require the undertakings and associations of undertakings concerned to bring such infringement to an end. For this purpose, it may impose on them any behavioural or structural remedies which are proportionate to the infringement committed and necessary to bring the infringement effectively to an end.

On their side, **national competition authorities and courts** are empowered to apply Community law. They have the power to apply not only Article 81(1) and Article 82 of the Treaty, which have direct applicability by virtue of the case-law of the Court of Justice, but also Article 81(3) of the Treaty. This means that national competition authorities are empowered to withdraw the benefit of a Community block exemption regulation [see section 15.3.3.]. National competition authorities may take the following decisions: requiring that an infringement be brought to an end, ordering interim measures, accepting commitments, imposing fines, periodic penalty payments or any other penalty provided for in their national law. National courts may apply Community competition rules in lawsuits between private parties, acting as public enforcers or as review courts. They can apply Article 81 of the EC Treaty in three types of proceedings: contractual liability proceedings (disputes between parties to an agreement); non-contractual liability proceedings (disputes between a third party and one or more parties to the agreement); and applications for injunctions. In any case, national courts may ask the Commission for information or for its opinion on points concerning the application of Community competition law.

Compliance with Articles 81 and 82 of the Treaty and the fulfilment of the obligations imposed on undertakings and associations of undertakings under Regulation 1/2003 is enforceable by means of fines and periodic penalty payments. The rules on periods of limitation for the imposition of fines and periodic penalty payments were laid down in Regulation 2988/74[1], which also concerns penalties in the field of transport. The imposition or non-imposition of a fine, and the amount thereof, depend in particular on the gravity of the infringement, its duration and the size of the undertakings involved. An intentional infringement usually leads to a heavier fine than when undertakings are simply guilty of negligence. Practices

---

[1]   Regulation 2988/74, OJ L 319, 29.11.1974.

that have already in the past been frequently punished by the Commission also carry heavier fines, as the earlier decisions of the Commission and of the Court of Justice should have alerted undertakings to the unlawful nature of such behaviour. The Commission may also impose on undertakings and associations of undertakings fines where, intentionally or negligently, they supply incorrect or misleading information, do not supply information within the required time-limit or refuse to submit to inspections.

Commission action in the area of competition is controlled, from the legal standpoint, by the **Court of Justice**, which can rescind or amend any formal Commission decision, i.e. negative clearances, decisions granting or refusing an exemption, orders to put an end to infringements, etc. [see section 4.1.5.]. The Court may also confirm, reduce, repeal or increase the fines and penalty payments imposed by the Commission. Any natural or legal person in respect of whom a decision has been taken may institute proceedings before the Court, as may any other person directly and individually concerned by a decision of which he is not the addressee. The Commission's competition policy is controlled, from the political standpoint, by the **European Parliament** [see section 4.1.3], which adopts positions on its guidelines and scrutinises its annual report on competition.

15.2.2. European law and national law

In the field of competition, national competence and Community competence are autonomous and parallel, the latter being defined by the criterion of the effect of trade among Member States. In a concrete case there may be juxtaposition of the validity of European law and national law. In any case, **European law takes precedence over national law** [see section 3.3.]. National authorities may take action against an agreement, pursuant to national law, even where the position of that agreement with regard to Community rules is pending before the Commission. They can also apply the Community competition law. However, the decision resulting from **a national procedure may not run counter to the Commission's decision**. Where the latter precedes the national decision, the competent authorities of the Member State are obliged to observe its effects. Where, on the other hand, the Commission's decision post-dates the national decision and is at variance with its effects, it is for the national authorities to take appropriate measures in conformity with it.

The **Member States cannot oppose Commission decisions**, whereas the Commission can request the competent authorities of the States concerned to proceed with any verification it deems necessary or to collect fines or penalty payments it has imposed. National courts can apply the Community law or refer matters of Community law to the Court of Justice of the European Communities for a preliminary ruling. Appeal courts are obliged to request a preliminary ruling where a decision on the point at issue is necessary to enable them to deliver their judgment.

15.3. Permissible cooperations and prohibited agreements

Article 81 of the EC Treaty declares that all agreements between undertakings, decisions by associations of undertakings and concerted practices which may affect trade between Member States and which have as their object or effect the prevention, restriction or distortion of competition within the common market shall be **prohibited as incompatible with the common market**. In particular, this article prohibits agreements which: (a) directly or indirectly fix purchase or selling prices or any other trading conditions; (b) limit or control production, markets, technical development, or investment; (c) share markets or sources of supply; (d) apply dissimilar conditions to equivalent transactions with other trading parties, thereby placing them at a competitive disadvantage; (e) make the conclusion of contracts subject to acceptance by the other parties of supplementary obligations which, by their nature or according to commercial usage, have no connection with the subject of such contracts. Prohibited agreements shall be automatically void.

However, under **paragraph 3 of Article 81**, the Commission may declare the provisions of paragraph 1 of that Article inapplicable in the case of any agreement or category of agreements between undertakings, any decisions by associations of undertakings and any concerted practice or category of concerted practices, on the following conditions: that they contribute to improving the production or distribution of goods or to promoting technical or economic progress, while allowing consumers a fair share of the resulting benefit, and that they do not afford such undertakings the possibility of eliminating competition in respect of a substantial part of the products in question. On the basis of Regulation 1/2003, agreements, decisions and concerted practices, caught by Article 81(1) of the Treaty, which satisfy the conditions of Article 81(3) of the Treaty, are not prohibited, no prior decision to that effect being required. These conditions can, however, be controlled at any time by the European competition network [see section 15.2.1.].

It ensues that not all agreements between Community undertakings are prohibited - far from it. Most are even desirable with a view to improving the structures of European industry, as we see in the relevant chapter [see section 17.2.4.]. In parallel with the elimination of situations incompatible with the system of competition and market unity, the Commission has in fact always pursued a policy of encouraging cooperation between undertakings where, in its opinion, such cooperation is compatible with the common market and can produce favourable economic effects.

Over the years, the Commission has endeavoured to specify, in a double series of measures, some of which were individual and some general or sectoral (e.g., air transport or telecommunications) [see sections 17.3.6. and 20.3.5.], those agreements **not covered by the prohibition** in Article 85 paragraph 1 (present Art. 81 TEC) [see section 15.3.2.] and those which, although covered by the prohibition, were **likely to be exempted from it** [see sections 15.3.1. and 15.3.3.]. Individual exemption decisions do not lend themselves to ill-considered generalisation, as the conditions for exemption can only be specific on a case-by-case basis. However, some types of clearly defined agreements are covered by group exemptions.

15.3.1. The "de minimis" rule

In a notice on **agreements of minor importance (de minimis)**, the Commission quantifies, with the help of market share thresholds, what is not an appreciable restriction of competition under Article 81 of the EC Treaty[1]. The Commission holds the view that an agreement between undertakings, even if it affects trade between Member States, does not appreciably restrict competition within the meaning of Article 81(1) of the EC Treaty if :(a) the aggregate market share held by the parties to the agreement does not exceed 10% on any of the relevant markets affected by the agreement, where the agreement is made between undertakings **which are actual or potential competitors** on any of these markets; or (b) the market share held by each of the parties to the agreement does not exceed 15% on any of the relevant markets affected by the agreement, where the agreement is made between undertakings which **are not actual or potential competitors** on any of these markets. In these cases the Commission will not institute proceedings either upon application or on its own initiative.

Agreements entered into by SMEs whose annual turnover and balance-sheet total do not exceed EUR 40 million and 27 million respectively and which have a maximum of 250 employees are rarely capable of appreciably affecting trade between Member States and are not, in principle, investigated by the Commission. However, there exists a "blacklist of hardcore restrictions" - such as price-fixing, market-sharing or territorial protection - which, because of their nature are regarded as typically incompatible with Article 81(1) of the EC Treaty and hence liable to be caught by the ban on agreements, even if the parties' market shares are below the above-mentioned thresholds.

15.3.2. Permissible contractual relations

Agreements between undertakings are not regarded as restricting competition and, therefore, do not need to be notified to the Commission where their purpose is a **form of authorised cooperation,** such as: the joint carrying out of comparative studies, the joint preparation of statistics and models, the joint study of markets, cooperation on accounting, joint financial guarantees, the joint execution of research and development contracts, the joint use of means of production, storage and transport and, under cer-

---

[1] Commission notice, OJ C 368, 22.12.2001, p. 13.

tain conditions, the joint performance of orders, joint selling, joint after-sales and repair service and joint advertising[1].

In order to lift any doubts the Commission specified in two communications the characteristics of very common contractual relations concerning exclusive representation and subcontracting, which do not fall under the prohibition of Article 81, paragraph 1, provided that they do not establish absolute territorial protection. Thus, the Commission considers that an **exclusive representation** contract concluded between a "commercial agent", who does not accept any liability for the financial risks involved in the transactions and he in fact acts only as a simple middleman for a "principal", is not covered by Article 81 paragraph 1[2]. **Subcontracts** are also allowed according to the Commission[3] [see also section 17.2.4.]. Subcontracting usually involves, for a small undertaking, known as the "subcontractor", performance of an order for a large undertaking, known as the "principal", in accordance with the directives of the latter. The Commission considers that the obligation to supply only to the latter manufactured objects or work executed does not restrict competition within the meaning of Article 81 of the EC Treaty (former Article 85).

15.3.3. Exemption of categories of agreements

Whereas the contractual relations mentioned above are not prohibited by Article 81, paragraph 1, the contractual relations mentioned below are in principle prohibited but can be exempted from the prohibition. Indeed, under paragraph 3 of Article 81, the Commission may declare the **provisions of paragraph 1 inapplicable** in the case of certain agreements or categories of agreements which contribute to improving the production or distribution of goods or to promoting technical or economic progress, while allowing consumers a fair share of the resulting benefit. A Council Regulation empowers the Commission to apply Article 81(3) of the Treaty by regulation to certain categories of agreements, decisions and concerted practices falling within the scope of Article 81(1)[4]. Another Council Regulation lays down the conditions under which the Commission may declare by way of regulation that the provisions of Article 81(1) do not apply to certain categories of agreements and concerted practices[5].

The instrument of the **"block-exemption" regulation** is used by the Commission to discharge a class of similar agreements whose pro-competitive benefits outweigh their anti-competitive effects. These Commission Regulations identify clearly-defined categories of agreements which automatically benefit from the exemption provision of Article 81, paragraph 3, provided that they do not seal off markets by preventing ac-

---

[1]   OJ C 75, 29.07.1968, p. 3-6.
[2]   OJ 139, 24.12.1962.
[3]   Communication of the Commission, OJ C 1, 03.01.1979, p. 2-3.
[4]   Regulation 2821/71, OJ L 285, 29.12.1971.
[5]   Regulation 19/65, OJ 36, 06.03.1965 and Regulation 1215/1999, OJ L 148, 15.06.1999.

cess and parallel trade. These block exemption Regulations are particularly useful for SMEs and were in many respects specifically designed for their benefit.

Following a 1997 Green Paper[1] and a communication of the Commission on the application of the Community competition rules to vertical restraints, Regulation No 17/62 and Regulation 19/65 have been amended with the aim of creating a single block exemption covering all vertical agreements or restraints[2]. Indeed, the general **exemption for certain vertical agreements** has replaced three regulations, one on exclusive distribution, one on exclusive purchasing and one on franchise agreements. Such agreements are concluded between firms operating at different (vertical) levels of the production or distribution chain - in practice all industrial distribution and supply agreements between firms whose market shares do not exceed 30% - and govern the conditions under which distribution firms may acquire from producers, sell or re-sell final or intermediate goods or services. Above the 30% threshold, agreements are not presumed to be unlawful but may require an individual examination. The Commission has issued guidelines intended, first, to clarify how the provisions of the block exemption should be interpreted and, second, to explain the general criteria applicable when examining agreements not covered by the block exemption or when withdrawing the benefit of the exemption regulation[3].

The Commission is favourable to **joint ventures of a cooperative character**, particularly when they can introduce more quickly into Europe a new technology, the development costs of which are very high. Under certain conditions cooperative joint ventures concerning specialisation agreements, research and development agreements, patent licensing agreements and know-how licensing agreements enjoy a block exemption[4].

15.3.4. Prohibited agreements

We shall not attempt, here, to describe all the forms of horizontal agreements which are prohibited by the rules of competition of the Treaties. Each case differs depending on the product concerned, the market involved and the imagination of the executives of the participant undertakings. We shall confine ourselves to **a few characteristic cases** of agreements incompatible with the common market, as emerging from Commission decisions. The Commission judges the advantages and disadvantages of an agreement or category of agreements not on the basis of purely legal criteria, but also using the criterion of the general interest of the producers and consumers in a sector. In addition, it applies the "de minimis" rule,

---

[1] COM (96) 721, 22 January 1997.
[2] Regulations1215/1999 and 1216/1999, OJ L 148, 15.06.1999.
[3] Commission notice, OJ C 291, 13.10.2000.
[4] Regulation 151/93, OJ L 21 of 29.01.1993 and OJ C 43, 16.02.1993.

discussed above, to agreements that infringe the rules of competition but the economic impact of which is insignificant.

The sharing of markets is particularly restrictive of competition and at variance with the objectives of the common market, as agreements based on the principle of reciprocal respect of national markets for the benefit of the participants established there have the effect of obstructing intra-Community trade in the products concerned. Through the system of fixing supply quotas on the basis of the total sales of members of the agreement, those members waive the freedom to apply an independent sales policy, but have, on the other hand, the possibility of applying a prices policy shielded from the competition of their partners. The following are celebrated cases of penalised market-sharing agreements: the case of the Community quinine producers, who had decided amongst themselves, by gentleman's agreements, on price regulation and quotas covering all their sales on the internal market and abroad[1]; and the case of the major sugar undertakings, which controlled intra-Community trade in sugar for human consumption[2].

Agreements on the fixing of prices or of other conditions of transactions seriously limit competition, because they prevent purchasers from benefiting from the competitive behaviour that producers would have shown had the agreement not existed. As they are coupled with reciprocal respect for national markets, they are also likely to have an adverse effect on intra-Community trade. The Commission has therefore prohibited: concerted practices for the purpose of the application by the participating undertakings, on the same dates and in respect of the same categories of product (colorants), identical rates of price increases[3]; horizontal price fixing agreements and horizontal exclusive dealing agreements[4]; and concerted methods for calculating a price supplement, as was the case of a price cartel in the stainless steel sector[5]. It should be noted that many cases of prohibited cartels combine **market sharing and fixing of prices**, notably: the one concerning the world market for graphite electrodes[6] and the cartel of industrial tube producers.

Restrictions on access to the market by new entrants are also prohibited. Access to the market can be impeded where a large number of retailers on this market are tied by an obligation to sell only the products of the manufacturer with whom they have a contract or vertical arrangements having a similar exclusionary effect on third parties. This is why, the Commission condemned the exclusivity conditions imposed by Unilever as part of its terms for supplying freezer cabinets to its Irish retailers[7]. In other

---

[1] Decision 69/240, OJ L 192, 05.08.1969.
[2] Decision 73/109, OJ L 140, 26.05.1973.
[3] Decision 69/243, OJ L 195, 07.08.1969.
[4] Decision 95/551, OJ L 312, 23.12.1995.
[5] Decision 98/247/ECSC, OJ L 100, 01.04.1998.
[6] Decision 2002/271, OJ L 100, 16.04.2002.
[7] Decision 98/531, OJ L 246, 04.09.1998.

cases, new competitors can be prevented from entering the market through a horizontal agreement or concerted practice, as in the aforementioned case of the Dutch crane-hire market[1].

The most complicated cases are those of **exclusive distribution agreements,** which are covered by a category exemption, but not where they provide for absolute territorial protection **which prevents parallel imports**. This is the case of agreements, which stand in the way of the distributor re-exporting the products in question to other Member States or of such products being imported from other Member States in the concessionaire's area and being distributed there by persons other than the concessionaire. Commission policy on the matter was clearly set out in its decision of 23 September 1964 in the "Grundig-Consten" case[2], essentially upheld by the Court of Justice in its judgment of 13 July 1966[3]. The Commission continues to fight against distribution systems which impede parallel trade, such as that of DaimlerChrysler, which instructed the members of its German distribution network for Mercedes passenger cars not to sell cars outside their respective territories and to oblige foreign consumers to pay a deposit of 15% to DaimlerChrysler when ordering a car in Germany[4].

15.4. Market domination

We shall see in the relevant chapter that, from the point of view of the Community's industrial and enterprise policies, concentrations of small and medium-sized undertakings into larger units are in principle desirable and should be encouraged, as they lead to economies of scale, the rationalisation of the production and distribution of products in the common market and promote technical progress [see section 17.2.1.]. But **if the concentration exceeds certain limits**, which vary from sector to sector, it may result in the formation of monopolies or, more often, oligopolies and the consequent restrictions of competition and intra-Community trade. This occurs in particular where an undertaking, which dominates a sector by virtue of its size and economic strength, acquires the smaller undertakings in competition with it one by one.

15.4.1. Preventing the exploitation of a dominant position

Article 82 of the EC Treaty (ex Art. 86 EEC) stipulates that "**any abuse by one or more undertakings of a dominant position** within the common market or in a substantial part of it shall be prohibited as incom-

---

[1] Decision 95/551, OJ L 312, 23.12.1995.
[2] Decision 64/566, OJ 161, 20.10.1964, p. 2545.
[3] Joined cases 56 and 58/64, ECR 1966, p. 299.
[4] Decision 2003/792, OJ L 300, 18.11.2003.

patible with the common market in so far as it may affect trade between Member States". Apart from the fact that this Article does not prohibit the obtaining of a dominant position, but only abuse thereof, it leaves several issues obscure, although they are now clarified by various standard Commission decisions and judgments of the Court of Justice.

First, **domination of a given market** cannot be defined solely on the basis of the market share held by an undertaking or of other quantitative elements, but must also be looked at in the light of its ability to exercise an appreciable influence on the functioning of the market and on the behaviour of other firms. In its judgment of 14 February 1978 in the case of "United Brands Company v. Commission" the Court upheld and enlarged the definition of the dominant position adopted by the Commission as early as its decision of 9 December 1971 in the "Continental Can Company" case[1]. It thus stated that the dominant position referred to in Article 86 (EEC)"relates to a position of economic strength enjoyed by an undertaking which enables it to prevent effective competition being maintained on the relevant market by giving it the power to behave to an appreciable extent independently of its competitors, customers and ultimately of its consumers".

The definition of **the relevant market** or of the market in question is also of great importance, as the more strictly that market is defined in time and space, the greater the likelihood that a dominant position can be identified in the common market. In its judgment of 13 February 1979 in the "Hoffman-La Roche v. Commission" case, the Court of Justice felt, in common with the Commission[2], that each group of vitamins constitutes a separate market and that one product can belong to two separate markets if it can be used for several purposes[3]. The Court held that actual competition must be able to exist between products that belong to the relevant market, which presupposes an adequate degree of interchangeability or substitutability between such products. The Commission's notice on the relevant market is an analytical tool which makes it possible to calculate firm's market shares[4].

As regards the concept of the **distortion of trade between Member States,** which is the same for Articles 81 and 82 (TEC), the Commission and the Court of Justice agree that a concentration in which an undertaking occupies a dominant position in the common market or in a substantial part of it will always be of importance for trade between Member States. In its judgment of 13 July 1966 in the "Grundig-Consten" case the Court opined that the concept of damage to trade between Member States should be seen as a question of "whether the agreement is capable of constituting a threat... to freedom of trade between Member States in a manner which might harm the attainment of the objectives of a single market between

---

[1]   Decision 72/21, OJ L 7, 08.01.1972.

[2]   Decision 76/642, OJ L 223, 16.08.1976.

[3]   Judgment of 13 February 1979, case 85/76, ECR 1979, p. 461.

[4]   OJ C 372, 09.12.1997, p. 5-13.

States"[1]. It goes without saying that abuse of a dominant position is judged all the more harshly because it tends to compartmentalise the relevant market and make economic interpenetration more difficult. That was the case with British Leyland, which refused to issue type-approval certificates for left-hand-drive "Metro" vehicles in order to prevent the re-importation of such vehicles from other Member States[2].

Lastly, as regards the concept of **abuse of a dominant position**, Article 82 is more explicit, as it stipulates that "abuse may in particular, consist in: (a) ... imposing unfair purchase or selling prices or other unfair trading conditions; (b) limiting production, markets or technical development ...; (c) applying dissimilar conditions to equivalent transactions with other trading parties ..." and "(d) making the conclusion of contracts subject to acceptance by the other parties of supplementary obligations" which have no connection with such contracts. We note that the concept of abuse of a dominant position is similar to the concept of restriction or distortion of competition given by article 81 TEC [see section 15.3.].

Generally speaking, an undertaking in a dominant position **may abuse its power on the market in one of the following ways**:

- by setting the prices on the dominated market, (as in the case of Deutsche Telekom AG (DT) concerning the prices for access to its fixed telecommunications network[3]);

- by imposing discriminatory commercial fees on service providers (as in the case of the Aéroports de Paris concerning groundhandling, catering, cleaning and freight handling services[4];

- by "tying" the products or services of the dominated market to other products or services (as in the case of Microsoft Corporation concerning the position of Windows on the market for PC operating systems[5]);

- by imposing on its customers agreements for the exclusive purchase of products (such as the vitamins in the Hoffmann-La Roche case[6]) or services (as in the case of the company operating Frankfurt airport[7]);

- by restricting competition from imports (as in the case of Irish Sugar plc[8]); or

- by attempting to eliminate competition by "predatory pricing", i.e. by selling below cost for a short period of time until the competitors are driven out of the market (as in the case of Deutsche Post AG concerning the market for business parcel services[9]) and in the case of

---

[1] Joined Cases 56 and 58/64, Consten-Grundig v Commission, ECR 1966, p. 299.
[2] OJ L 207, 02.08.1984 and case 226/84, British Leyland PLC v Commission, ECR 1986, p. 3263.
[3] Decision 2003/707, OJ L 263, 14.10.2003.
[4] Decision 98/513, OJ L 230, 18.08.1998.
[5] Case COMP/C-3/37.792, 24.03.2004 and case T-201/04, ECR 2007.
[6] Decision 76/142, OJ L 223, 16.08.1976.
[7] Decision 98/190, OJ L 72, 11.03.1998.
[8] Decision 97/624, OJ L 258, 22.09.1997..
[9] Decision 2001/354, OJ L 125, 05.05.2001.

Wanadoo Interactive, a subsidiary of France Télécom, concerning access to the Internet by the general public[1].

It is certain that the Commission and the Court regard it as an abuse where an undertaking in a dominant position strengthens that position by means of a concentration or of **the elimination of competitors**, with the result that competition, which continued in spite of the existence of the dominant position, is virtually eliminated as regards the products concerned in a substantial part of the common market. The Commission accordingly imposed heavy fines on British Sugar plc for implementing a series of abuses designed to eliminate a smaller competitor from the retail sugar market[2]. On 24 March 2004, the Commission fined Microsoft Corporation EUR 497 million, because it used the near-monopoly position enjoyed by its Windows product on the market for PC operating systems to restrict competition on other software markets: work group server operating systems; and the market in media players[3].

15.4.2. Concentrations in the Single Market

Concentrations are arrangements whereby one or more companies acquire control of other companies and thus change the structure of the companies involved and of the market they operate in. The most **important forms of concentrations** of undertakings are the holding of a company in the authorised capital of another company or of other companies, the total or partial acquisitions by a company of the assets of other companies and, lastly, the merger of two or more companies which are legally independent into a new company. Concentrations allow economies of scale to be obtained, production and distribution costs to be reduced, profitability to be improved and technical progress to be speeded up. All of that facilitates the international competitiveness of Community undertakings and may provide consumers with part of the benefits of economic integration. It is, however, obvious that where the concentration in an industry exceeds certain limits it can lead to monopoly or oligopoly structures, which restrict competition and jeopardise consumers' interests.

Cross-border mergers of limited liability companies, involving the takeover of one by the other or the founding of a new company, encounter many legislative and administrative difficulties in the Community, due to various types of limited liability company governed by the laws of different Member States. Therefore, Directive 2005/56 facilitates the **cross-border merger of limited liability companies** as defined therein, notably a company with share capital and having legal personality, possessing separate assets which alone serve to cover its debts[4]. The laws of the Member States are to allow the cross-border merger of a national

---

[1]   Case COMP/38.233, 16.07.2003.
[2]   Decision 88/518, OJ L 284, 19.10.1988.
[3]   Case COMP/C-3/37.792, 24.03.2004.
[4]   Directive 2005/56, OJ L 310, 25.11.2005.

limited liability company with a limited liability company from another Member State if the national law of the relevant Member States permits mergers between such types of company. In order to facilitate cross-border merger operations, each company taking part in a cross-border merger, and each third party concerned, remains subject to the provisions and formalities of the national law which would be applicable in the case of a national merger. The directive includes provisions aimed at preserving workers' participation rights in the event of cross-border mergers [see sections 13.5.2 and 17.2.1].

Directive 2005/56 is without prejudice to the application of the legislation on the control of concentrations between undertakings. As mentioned above, Article 86 of the EEC Treaty **prohibited abuse of a dominant position, but not its existence or creation**. This means that the EEC Treaty did not request authorisation by the Commission for a concentration operation, which could lead to a dominant position. The EC Treaty has not altered this situation. However, the Commission undertook to **fill the legislative vacuum in the EEC Treaty** on the basis of Article 3 thereof. In the Commission's view, since that Treaty had the objective of ensuring the functioning of an undistorted system of competition, the exploitation of a dominant position should be regarded as abusive if it in practice prevented the functioning of undistorted competition. A concentration of undertakings that results in the **monopolisation of a market** should therefore be dealt with as abuse of a dominant position within the meaning of Article 86 of the EEC Treaty. For the first time in 1971 the Commission translated that interpretation into fact by adopting a Decision applying Article 86 (EEC) in the case of the concentration of an undertaking occupying a dominant position, namely Continental Can Cy, with a competing undertaking[1]. The Commission considered that Continental Can Cy had abused its dominant position by **taking control of one of its potential main competitors**, thus strengthening the said dominant position in such a way that competition in a substantial part of the common market was virtually eliminated with regard to the products concerned. The judgment delivered by the Court of Justice on 21 February 1973 confirmed the correctness of the Commission's approach to the application of Article 86 (Art. 82 TEC) to abuse of the dominant position by the concentration[2]. More recently, the Court has ruled that any merger, which created or strengthened a **collective dominant position** enjoyed by the parties concerned, was likely to prove incompatible with the system of undistorted competition envisaged in the Treaty[3].

Thus, with the support of the Court of Justice, the Commission could exercise an *a posteriori* **control of concentrations** of undertakings, one of which had already achieved a dominant position. However, knowing that "prevention is better than cure", the Commission wanted a preventive pol-

[1] Decision 72/21, OJ L 7, 08.01.1972.
[2] Case 6/72, Europemballage Corporation v Commission, ECR 1973, p. 215.
[3] Judgment of 31 March 1998, Joined Cases C-68/94 and C-30/95, ECR 1998 I-1375.

icy in the field of concentrations. Already in 1973, it had submitted to the Council a proposal for a regulation on the control of mergers. It took sixteen years of discussions in the Council for the **Regulation on the control of concentrations between undertakings** finally to be adopted in December 1989. Still, this Regulation provided a high threshold for obligatory notification of concentrations and the Commission, after some new discussions, succeeded, in June 1997, to persuade the Council to reduce it[1].

According to this Regulation, compulsory notification covers mergers involving undertakings whose aggregate world-wide **turnover** exceeds 2.5 billion euro (general threshold), and the turnover in each of at least three Member States exceeds 100 million euro. The system whereby a merger is referred to the national authorities by the Commission or vice versa is simplified, with the aim of ensuring both that the authority best placed to examine the situation is given charge of the file, in accordance with the subsidiarity principle [see section 3.2.], and that multiple notifications are avoided. Thus, the Commission only takes action on mergers if they have a Community dimension and on restrictive practices only if they affect trade between Member States. In these cases its position, its experience and its powers of inquiry place it at the best level to assess the factors involved. Moreover, the Commission can authorise a national anti-cartel office to investigate a concentration, which may have significant effects on a local market. The Commission has to base its decision principally on criteria of competition, but may also **take into consideration other factors**, such as economic and technical progress.

To ensure the effective application of the principle of compulsory notification, the Commission has adopted a Regulation covering, among other points, time limits and hearings, the form, content and other **provisions relating to notifications**[2]. According to this Regulation, notifications relating to Regulation 139/2004 on the control of concentrations between undertakings and to Article 57 of the EEA Agreement must be submitted in the manner prescribed by "Form CO" or, under certain conditions in "Short Form", while reasoned submissions for a pre-notification referral must take the "form RS". The three forms are set out in the Annexes of the Regulation of the Commission.

The procedures established for dealing with notifications enable the Commission to make effective use of its powers in this area. The Commission grants authorisation, within the space of a month, to the vast majority of operations which do not create or reinforce a dominant position in the common market or a substantial part of it[3]. In a large number of cases the authorisation of the Commission is granted subject to compliance with

---

[1]   Regulation 4064/89, OJ L 395, 30.12.1989 repealed by Regulation 139/2004, OJ L 24, 2901.2004.

[2]   Regulation 802/2004, OJ L 133, 30.04.2004.

[3]   See, for example, Commission Decision 95/404, OJ L 239, 07.10.1995, (Swissair/Sabena).

conditions and obligations[1]. Only when serious doubts exist as to the operations' compatibility with the common market does it decide to open a detailed investigation as provided for in the second part of the procedure.

15.5. Monitoring State intervention

Competition in the common market can be distorted not only by the behaviour of undertakings, but also by State intervention. The **arguments adduced by governments for intervening** in economic activities are numerous, but they all have a socio-political ring: to prevent the closure of undertakings which might give rise to collective redundancies, which are unacceptable in social and regional terms. At national level, undertakings experiencing difficulties make public opinion and the official authorities aware of their predicament, especially when they are big companies, regarded as "flagship undertakings" and/or they occupy a large number of workers whose jobs are endangered.

The social and regional consequences of structural changes should indeed be attenuated, but the changes themselves should **not be opposed by artificially ensuring the survival** of obsolete industries or sectors in decline. The question should be asked, on a case-by-case basis, whether aid is really needed, rather than a radical change in production structures and methods, and whether aid for an industry in difficulty in one Member State of the EU might not harm the interests of the same industries established in the other Member States, which will be placed in a less favourable position and will press their governments to redress the situation. Unilaterally conceived State initiatives cannot, therefore, but trigger reciprocation from partner countries and lead to costly operations for everyone. In order to avoid retaliation from partner countries and squandered resources, therefore, a "code of good conduct" is needed for the Member States in this area.

In fact, as other forms of protectionism recede, the importance of State aids as an anti-competitive mechanism tends to grow. Beyond their negative effect on competition, State aids can also have **serious implications for economic cohesion** within the EU [see section 12.1.2.]. Large and well developed Member States are able to outbid less developed Member States on the periphery of the Union in the aid race. Indeed, the four largest Member States account for 88% of all aid granted in the Union.

Aid of a regional character was examined in the chapter on regional development [see section 12.2.1.]. The following paragraphs look at other State operations: general aid, sectoral aid, national monopolies and public undertakings.

---

[1] See, for example, Commission Decision 97/816, OJ L 336, 08.12.1997 (Boeing/McDonnell Douglas).

15.5.1. Compatible and incompatible aids

Article 87 of the EC Treaty (ex Art. 92 EEC) stipulates that "any aid granted... which distorts or threatens to distort competition by favouring certain undertakings or the production of certain goods shall, in so far as it affects trade between Member States, **be incompatible with the common market".** Given the high degree of integration of the Community's economy, most national subsidies are likely to be considered trade-distorting, even for products which are not exported to other Member States, if they compete on their home market with imports from other Member States. The Commission has devised a mechanism for fixing and revising the reference rates used to calculate the grant equivalent of aid[1]. The form of the aid is irrelevant: for example outright grants, soft loans, tax concessions, guarantees, the supply of goods or services at less than cost are all subject to Community State aid control. However, under the **"de minimis" rule**, aid of less than EUR 100 000 over three years is judged not to affect trade between Member States and thus need not be notified to the Commission[2].

Paragraph 2 of Article 87 considers that the following shall be **compatible with the common market**, provided that aid is granted without discrimination related to the origin of the products concerned: aid having a social character granted to individual consumers and aid to make good the damage caused by natural disasters or exceptional occurrences. Paragraph 3 of Article 87, for its part, stipulates that the following **may be considered to be compatible** with the common market: aid to promote the economic development of areas with economic or social problems; aid to promote the execution of an important project of common European interest or to remedy a serious disturbance in the economy of a Member State; aid to facilitate the development of certain economic activities or of certain economic areas, where such aid does not adversely affect trading conditions; aid to promote culture and heritage conservation[3]; and such other categories of aid as may be specified by decision of the Council.

The Council has empowered the Commission to adopt block exemption regulations for certain **categories of horizontal aid** (in favour of SMEs, research and development, environment protection, employment and training) and for aid below a given threshold[4]. A Commission decision of 22 July 1998 clarifies the circumstances in which public funding for training may be caught by the competition rules on State aid and sets the criteria which it applies in ascertaining whether such aid is compatible with the common market. A Commission notice of 11 November 1998 sets out the criteria it applies when examining or reviewing Member States' measures relating to direct business taxation[5].

---

[1] OJ C 31, 03.02.1979.
[2] Regulation 69/2001, OJ L 10, 13.01.2001.
[3] Point inserted at Maastricht.
[4] Regulation 994/98, OJ L 142, 14.05.1998.
[5] OJ C 384, 10.12.1998, p.3.

So that the Commission may adopt a position on the possible application of one of the above derogations from the incompatibility of aid, the Member States are obliged, under Article 88 paragraph 3 of the EC Treaty (ex Art. 93) to **inform it in sufficient time**, through a detailed questionnaire, of any plans to grant new aid or alter existing aid. Such aid may not be granted by Member States until the Commission has taken a final decision on it. In case the Member States fail to fulfil their obligation to notify proposals to grant aid, the Commission reserves the right to take a provisional decision requiring them to recover, with interest, any aid paid illegally pending a final decision by it on the compatibility of the aid with the common market[1]. In order to increase legal certainty and transparency in the Commission's decision-making process, a Council Regulation lays down detailed rules for the application of Article 88 of the EC Treaty[2].

15.5.2. General aids

Aid from which any undertaking whatsoever can benefit, without regard to its geographical location or to the sector to which it belongs, is regarded as general aid. Owing to this lack of a specific character, such aid cannot lay claim to an exemption provision provided for in the Treaty. The Commission has to be able to verify, prior to their being granted, that general aids are in **response to genuine economic or social needs**, that they lead to an improvement in the structures of beneficiary undertakings and that they do not give rise to problems at Community level. The Commission tries to prevent aid that does not pursue clearly defined objectives. For that reason, it requires Member States, when applying general aid arrangements, either to notify it in advance of the relevant regional or sectoral programmes or, if there are no such programmes, to inform it of significant individual cases.

The Commission systematically prohibits **State export aid** within the Community and normally prohibits aid, which does not have a **counterpart in the Community interest**. Aid on which no time limit is placed and which is required to support current activities (**"operating aid"**) is just as unacceptable as aid for intra-Community exports. According to the Court of Justice, State **participation in the capital of undertakings** is likely to be considered State aid coming within the scope of Article 92 *et seq.* of the EEC Treaty (Art. 87 *et seq.* TEC).

However, certain general aids are granted to achieve **legitimate objectives** and may be approved by the Commission under certain conditions, specified in its communications. In addition to regional development aids [see section 12.2.1.], this is generally the case for research and development aids[3], aids in favour of small and medium-sized enterprises[1], envi-

---

[1] OJ C 156, 27.06.1995, p. 5.
[2] Regulation 659/1999, OJ L 83, 27.03.1999.
[3] OJ C 45, 17.02.1996, p. 5-14 and OJ C 111, 08.05.2002, p. 3.

ronmental protection aids[2], aids for rescuing and restructuring firms in difficulty[3], vocational training aids[4] and aids for employment[5].

15.5.3. Sectoral aids

The Commission's policy on sectoral aids involves examining whether the problems facing certain industries may justify the granting of State aid while ensuring that such aid does not unduly delay the necessary changes, does not distort competition to an extent counter to the common interest and is in line with the attainment of the Community's objectives, or at least will not hinder that goal.

The symbiosis of national economies in the common market is reflected by very similar economic developments in the Member States, even though their economic structures are not homogeneous. The difficulties justifying intervention by a Member State are often to be found in some or all of its partners. A **"Community framework"** encompassing national measures may therefore be elaborated when the conditions in a sector so dictate. Such a framework should include guidelines for the objectives to be attained at Community level and a description of how to achieve that. The framework for aids to sectors in crisis could generally be based on the criterion of "overcapacity", for which the definition and implementing provisions should take account of the features of the specific market in question such as progress in production technologies and the degree of globalisation. Community frameworks have existed in the past for aids to shipbuilding[6], maritime transport[7], the steel industry[8], the synthetic fibres industry[9] and the motor vehicle industry[10].

In February 2002 the Commission considered that the specific sectoral frameworks should be integrated into a multisectoral framework[11]. It has therefore approved the recasting of the rules applicable to regional aid to **large investment projects**, including in steel, the motor vehicle and synthetic fibres sectors[12] [see section 12.2.1.]. Under this framework no advance notification of aid below certain thresholds for large investment projects is required, provided that aid is granted in accordance with a regional aid scheme approved by the Commission. The framework is aimed at set-

---

[1] Regulation 70/2001, OJ L 10, 13.01.2001 and Regulation 1040/2006, OJ L 187, 08.07.2006.
[2] Commission decision, OJ C 37, 03.02.2001, p. 3-15.
[3] OJ C 244, 01.10.2004, p. 2.
[4] Regulation 68/2001, OJ L 10, 13.01.2001 and Regulation 1040/2006, OJ L 187, 08.07.2006.
[5] Regulation 2204/2002, OJ L 337, 13.12.2002 and Regulation 1040/2006, OJ L 187, 08.07.2006.
[6] Regulation 1540/98, OJ L 202, 18.07.1998.
[7] COM (96) 81 and OJ C 205, 05.07.1997.
[8] Decision 2496/96, OJ L 338, 28.12.1996.
[9] OJ C 96, 30.03.1996, p. 11-14 and OJ C 368, 22.12.2001, p.10.
[10] OJ C 279, 15.09.1997, p. 1-8 and OJ C 368, 22.12.2001, p. 10.
[11] Communication from the Commission, OJ C 70, 19.03.2002, p. 8-20.
[12] Communication from the Commission OJ C 70, 19.03.2002.

ting up a quicker, simpler and more transparent system of controlling public authority support for major investment projects in the European Union. The new system enhances Member States' responsibility as regards implementation of the State aid rules and guarantees proper control of State aid levels in an enlarged and more heterogeneous Community.

15.5.4. Public undertakings

While remaining neutral with regard to the legal position on ownership in the Member States, the EC Treaty stipulates, in **Article 86**, that "in the case of public undertakings and undertakings to which Member States grant special or exclusive rights, Member States shall neither enact nor maintain in force any measures contrary to the rules contained in this Treaty ...". Such undertakings therefore **have the same obligations as private firms,** including those laid down in Article 12 (prohibition of discrimination on grounds of nationality) and 81 to 89 inclusive (rules of competition). Article 86, paragraph 3 (TEC) confers on the Commission the task of ensuring the application of these provisions and the power to address directives or decisions to Member States where necessary.

However, Article 86(2) allows exceptions to the rules of competition of the Treaty **in favour of public utility undertakings**, entrusted with the operation of services of general economic interest (water, energy, transport and telecommunications) or having the character of a revenue-producing monopoly, so as not to obstruct the performance, in law or in fact, of the particular tasks assigned to them. Nevertheless, the development of Community trade must not be affected by aid to these undertakings to such an extent as would be contrary to the interests of the Community.

Indeed, governments grant certain public enterprises **statutory monopoly protection**. Such exclusive monopoly rights are awarded for various public policy reasons, such as ensuring security of supply, providing a basic service to the whole population or avoiding the costs of duplicating an expensive distribution network. Such practices are common, notably for utilities (energy and water), postal services, telecommunications and to some extent in broadcasting, transport (air and maritime), banking and insurance. Member States must, therefore, not take measures, which could lead their public enterprises enjoying monopoly rights to infringe Community rules on competition or the free movement of goods and services.

In any case, greater **transparency of the financial relations** between States and their public undertakings is needed, in order to enable the Commission to decide whether transfer of public funds to those undertakings are compatible with the rules laid down in the Treaty. That is precisely the aim of a Commission Directive, which obliges Member States to supply the Commission, at the latter's request, with information on public funds made available directly or indirectly to public undertakings, thus covering not only "active transfer" of public funds, such as the provision of capital and the covering of losses, but also "passive transfers", such as the forgoing by the State of income of profits or of a normal return on the funds used[1].

The Commission recognises that the operation of **services of general economic interest** - in the sense of Article 86(2) of the EC Treaty - must not be prejudiced. However, it is examining on a sector-by-sector basis whether less restrictive practices are possible, how to limit statutory monopoly rights to the essential activities and whether competing services could use existing networks or new technologies would permit the construction of alternative networks.

Commission directives have paved the way for liberalisation in the **satellite telecommunications** sector, thus helping the development of trans-European networks in this sector and facilitating the European information society. The Commission Directive on free competition on the Community markets in **telecommunications terminal equipment** (modems, telex and telefax terminals, private satellite stations, etc.) prohibits any exclusive rights to import, market, connect, bring into service and maintain such equipment[2] [see section 17.3.6.]. Similarly, the Commission Directive on competition in the markets for **electronic communications networks and services** aims at: the abolition of existing exclusive and special rights; the prohibition of the granting of new rights in the electronic communications sector; and the guarantee of the right of firms to benefit from freedom of establishment and freedom to supply services within an undistorted competitive framework[3]. In any case, according to the Court, the regulatory prerogatives enjoyed by national telecommunications organisations must be dissociated from their commercial activities[4].

15.6. Appraisal and outlook

Competition policy has traditionally been seen as a prerogative of the nation-state. The EC/EU is the first group of states to practice a policy, which tries to deal with the impact that distortions of competition have on trade. The basic objective of the common competition policy is to prevent the unity of the common market from being called into question by measures that have the effect of giving preference to certain economic operators (businesses, companies) and of restoring the partitioning of domestic markets. In fact, whatever means are used to **correct the rigours of competition**, the usual effect consists in raising prices to restore business profitability, at the expense of the consumer or the taxpayer.

The administrative practice developed gradually by the Commission and confirmed by the case-law of the Court of Justice has made it possible to interpret and improve the rules of the Treaty in order to establish a range

---

[1] Directive 80/723, OJ L 195, 29.07.1980 and Directive 93/84, OJ L 254, 12.10.1993.
[2] Directive 88/301, OJ L 131, 27.05.1988 and Directive 94/46, OJ L 268, 19.10.1994.
[3] Directive 2002/77, OJ L 249, 17.09.2002.
[4] Judgment given on 27 October 1993, Joined Cases C-46/90 and C-93/91, Lagauche and Others, ECR 1993, p. I-5267.

of principles of fair behaviour which, while not hindering free enterprise, indicates to economic operators the rules to be complied with to ensure that free trade and equal opportunity are guaranteed within the common market. The practices of businesses directed towards impeding imports or exports, fixing production or sales quotas and generally sharing the market are accordingly actively proceeded against. Agreements, which have the effect of concentrating demand on specific producers, and exclusive distribution agreements which prevent traders and consumers from purchasing products in any Member State, are also prohibited. Companies which practice the prohibited restrictions of competition, thus jeopardising the unity of the common market, have to expect to have heavy fines imposed on them.

Legal proceedings are also brought against undertakings which **abuse a dominant position** by refusing to supply a long-standing customer, by applying discriminatory prices, unlawful practices which cause or could cause damage to customers or consumers or, lastly, by absorbing one another thus eliminating competition in a market. The **control of concentrations** does not mean the prohibition of concentrations. Just as concentrations are dangerous when they strengthen the dominant position of major undertakings, so are they desirable when they strengthen the competitive position of small and medium-sized enterprises. Refraining from a strictly legal approach to problems of competition, the Commission conducts in fact two parallel policies: a policy for the elimination of abuse by major companies and a policy of encouragement of cooperation and concentration between SMEs [see sections 17.1.4 and 17.2.4.].

As regards State aids, the role of the Community competition policy is to ensure that aid to undertakings does not constitute the resurgence of protectionist measures in a new form. The common competition policy is thus not only pivotal to the good functioning of the single market, but also a complement to Community sectoral policies - in particular in the industrial, energy, agriculture and transport sectors - aimed at improving production structures. Through its effect on the structure of markets, competition policy influences the competitiveness of the European economy and hence helps to orient the Union's macroeconomic framework towards better employment conditions.

Bibliography on competition policy

* BUELENS Christian (et al.). *The economic analysis of state aid: some open questions*. Luxembourg: EUR-OP*, 2007.
* EHLERMANN Claus-Dieter, ATANASIU Isabela (eds.). *European competition law annual 2006: Enforcement of prohibition of cartels*. 11th ed. Oxford: Hart, 2007.
* EUROPEAN COMMISSION. *25th Annual Report from the Commission to the European Parliament on the community's anti-dumping, anti-subsidy and safeguard activities (2006)*. Luxembourg: EUR-OP*, 2007.

- GERSTER Cornelia, KLEINE Juliana, NASS TØNNESSEN. *State aid rules in the European Union.* Brussels: European Association of Public Banks, 2007.
- HOLMES Marjorie, DAVEY Lesley (eds.). A practical guide to national competition rules across Europe. The Hague: Kluwer Law International, 2007.
- KOKKORIS Ioannis. *Competition cases from the European Union.* London: Sweet & Maxwell, 2007.
- LINDRUP Garth (ed.). *Butterworths competition law handbook.* London: Lexis Nexis Butterworths, 2007.
- MARSDEN Philip (et al. eds.). *Current competition law*: Volumes I-V. London: British Institute of International and Comparative Law, 2007.
- NEMITZ Paul (ed.). *The effective application of EU state aid procedures: the role of national law and practice.* The Hague: Kluwer Law International, 2007.
- RILEY Alan. "The EU Reform Treaty and the competition protocol: undermining EC competition law", in *European Competition Law Review*, v. 28, n. 12, December 2007, p. 703-707.

DISCUSSION TOPICS

1. What is the significance of a common competition policy in a multinational integration scheme?
2. Discuss the respective roles of the Commission and of national authorities in the common competition policy.
3. Give some examples of permissible business cooperations and of prohibited agreements in the EU.
4. How does the EU try to prevent the domination of its internal market by large companies?
5. Which State interventions are considered incompatible with the common market?

Chapter 16

ENVIRONMENT POLICY

Diagram of the chapter

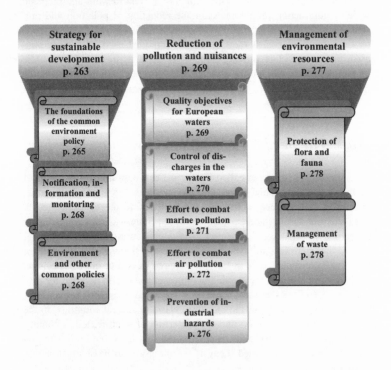

Up to the end of the 1960s no European country had a clearly defined environment policy. Student unrest in France and Germany in May 1968, the United Nations Conference on the Human Environment, held in Stockholm in June 1972, and the publication in the same period of the report by the Club of Rome on "the limits of growth" alerted European public opinion to the **ecological problems of economic development** and questioned the hierarchy of the values extolled by the consumer society.

The Governments of the Community States were obliged hastily to design measures against pollution and nuisances so as to **open a safety valve to an ecological movement** likely to swing the pendulum to the other extreme, to impose "zero growth", to block technological progress and with it, perhaps, economic and social progress. But all the Member States had to act together, as any country which took measures on its own against pollution or nuisances, or measures more stringent than its neighbours, would be likely to penalise its industry, which would have to bear the cost. Having done so, it would be forced to block the placing on its market of more pollutant, noisy or dangerous products from its more lax partners, which would bring the risk of technical barriers to trade [see section 6.2.].

The Summit Conference of Heads of State and Government held in Paris in 1972 opened the way to the implementation of a common policy on environmental protection. The Commission went to work and prepared wide-ranging action programmes for the reduction of pollution and nuisances and for the management of environmental resources. In record time by Community standards the Community provided itself with many concrete measures, a fact proving that, when there is pressure from public opinion, political will and the absence of deep-rooted national policies, the European institutions are capable of **legislative work comparable to that of an individual State**.

16.1. The need for a common environment policy

In the mosaic of States called Europe the **common market in terms of pollution** was established before the common market in goods. Polluted air and water moved freely across borders well before the idea emerged to open them to foreign goods. Each European State was thus immediately concerned by what was happening in its neighbouring countries with regard to the environment. It must not be forgotten that virtually every large lake and large watercourse in Europe is shared by two or more States, that the Mediterranean and the North Sea represent a common heritage for several European States and that those seas, lakes and rivers are used as common dumping grounds for the industrial waste of several countries. In the field of nature conservation and the protection of wildlife, too, a country that protected migratory birds or endangered species would be wasting its time if its neighbours killed them. If the mess was to be stopped, action therefore had to be taken together.

Not only neighbourliness, but also the comparable socio-economic development of the European countries, argued in favour of Community action to protect the environment. The **phenomena common to all European States** of the expansion of industrial activities, the increase in the urban population within megalopoles and the drift away from increasingly large tracts of territory originally used and maintained by agriculture required comparable measures and means to be utilised in the Member States to cope with them.

Common environmental problems **needed common solutions**. Short of seriously affecting the competitive capacity of its economy, no European State could hope to resolve its environmental problems by acting on its own. The fight against pollution in fact imposes certain expenditure on industrialists to adapt their products or their manufacturing processes. Such expenditure is all the greater, the more stringent are the standards laid down by the public authorities. If a State of the Union imposed stringent and **costly anti-pollution measures** on its industry, it might penalise it vis-à-vis its competitors from other States which were less attentive to the damage caused by pollution or which had different ideas as to how to apportion expenditure for the fight against pollution. Competition would therefore be distorted in the common market. It was therefore necessary for the same rules to be imposed on all European producers.

The free **movement of goods** within the common market would also be affected if each Member State laid down different standards for products put on sale on its market [see section 6.2.]. The country, which laid down more stringent standards than its neighbours, for example, on restrictions on the noise of certain engines or on the exhaust emissions of motor vehicles, would impede imports of related products from other countries. Protection against pollution and noise could thus quickly deteriorate into protection against foreign products. In other words, national environment policy could be used to thwart the internal market in a very subtle manner. On the other hand, environmental policy can make a huge contribution to growth, jobs and quality of life, with environmental measures having a positive impact on job creation, public health and healthcare costs, energy security and energy efficiency.

Lastly, it has to be said that the **European institutions are better placed than governments** to have a long-term view of environmental problems and requirements. Even when they are certain of remaining in office for fairly long time, national governments, being preoccupied with short-term problems, are rarely in a position to plan long-term strategies in this non-profit-making sector. Its relative detachment from the day-to-day problems peculiar to each Member State and its right of initiative with regard to the harmonisation of legislation make it possible for the European Commission to conceive a long-term programme against pollution [see section 4.1.2.]. Let us not forget, however, that in the case of the common environment policy, as in any other common policy, the "Eurocrats" of Brussels (the Commission), assisted by national technocrats (scientific and administrative committees), only propose the measures considered scientifically and technically necessary to protect the environment. It is the politicians in the European Parliament and the Council who take the final decisions [see section 4.3.], taking into consideration the industrial and political cost of precautionary measures proposed.

16.2. Common strategy for sustainable development

Sustainable development is a key objective set out in the Treaty, for all European Community policies (Art. 3 TEC). It aims at the continuous improvement of the quality of life on Earth of both current and future generations, by combating the abusive exploitation of natural resources and of human beings. Consequently, it is based on the principles of democracy, solidarity, the rule of law and respect for fundamental rights including freedom and equal opportunities for all. It seeks to promote a dynamic economy respecting the environment, human values, cultural diversity, full employment, a high level of education, health protection, social and territorial cohesion in a peaceful and secure world.

Concerning the environment, in particular, the European Union's environment programme now aims at a development, which takes into account the present economic and social needs without jeopardising, through resource misuse, the **development possibilities of future generations**[1]. This means that short term economic gains at the expense of the environment should be replaced by a more sustainable model of economic and social development, which may constitute the basis for greater efficiency and competitiveness, both at a Union level and internationally.

The Göteborg European Council (15-16 June 2001) approved a **European Union strategy for sustainable development**, proposed by the Commission[2], based on: coordinated development of common policies addressing the economic, environmental and social dimensions of sustainability; a set of headline objectives to limit climate change and increase use of clean energy; and the steps to implement the strategy and review its progress at every spring meeting of the European Council (Cardiff process launched in 1998).

The **sixth Community environment action programme (6EAP)** sets out environmental objectives for the years 2001 to 2010 focuses on four priority issues[3]:

1. **tackling climate change** by reducing greenhouse gases according to the objectives of the Kyoto Protocol [see section 16.3.4.], i.e. achieving the Community's target of reducing emissions by 8% by 2008 to 2012 (compared to 1990 levels) and by 20 to 40% by 2020, through structural changes and stronger efforts on energy-saving and the establishment of an EU-wide emissions trading scheme;

2. **nature and biodiversity**, i.e. protecting and restoring the structure and functioning of natural systems and halting the loss of biodiversity notably through: the implementation of environmental legislation; protection, conservation and restoration of landscapes; completion of the Natura 2000 network to avert the threats to the survival of many species and their habitats in Europe; new initiatives for protecting the marine environment; and a thematic strategy for protecting soils[4];

3. **environment and health**, i.e. achieving a quality of the environment which does not endanger human health, necessitating *inter alia:* a fundamental overhaul of the Community's risk-management system for chemicals[5], a strategy for reducing risks from pesticides, protec-

---

[1] COM (2001) 31, 24 January 2001.
[2] COM (2001) 264, 15 May 2001.
[3] Decision 1600/2002, OJ L 242, 10.09.2002.
[4] COM(2001) 162, 27 March 2001.
[5] See Commission White Paper, COM (2001) 88, 13 February 2001.

tion of water quality in the Union, noise abatement and a thematic strategy for air quality;

4. **sustainable management of natural resources** by decoupling resource use from economic growth, in particular through: improved resource efficiency; taxation of resource use; increased recycling and waste prevention with the aid of an integrated product policy.

The **Financial Instrument for the Environment (LIFE+)** supports the implementation of the 6th EAP, including the thematic strategies, and finance measures and projects with European added value in Member States[1]. It also finances operational activities of NGOs that are primarily active in protecting and enhancing the environment at European level. The new programme is divided into three strands:

- **LIFE+ Nature and Biodiversity**, which focuses on the implementation of the EU directives on the conservation of habitats and of wild birds, as well as further strengthening the knowledge needed for developing, assessing, monitoring and evaluating EU nature and biodiversity policy and legislation [see also section 16.4];
- **LIFE+ Environment Policy and Governance**, which covers the other 6EAP priorities including climate change, environment and health and quality of life, and natural resources and wastes, as well as strategic approaches to policy development, implementation and enforcement;
5. **LIFE+ Information and Communication**, which aims at disseminating information and raising awareness on environmental issues, including forest fire prevention.

16.2.1. The foundations of the common environment policy

The legal basis of environment policy was considerably enlarged by the Single Act of 1987 [see section 2.1.] and **firmly established by the Maastricht Treaty** [see section 2.2.]. As revised at Amsterdam, Article 2 of that the EU Treaty sets the achievement of balanced and sustainable development among the objectives of the Union. The common environment policy has now the **following objectives**: preserving, protecting and improving the quality of the environment; protecting human health; rationalising the utilisation of natural resources; promoting measures at international level to deal with regional or world-wide environmental problems (Art. 174 TEC).

According to Article 175 (TEC), the Council acting under the **co-decision procedure** with the European Parliament [see section 4.3.] and after consultation of the Economic and Social Committee and of the Committee of the Regions takes the measures necessary for the implementation of the objectives of Article 174. Still, **the unanimity of the Council** acting after consultation of the European Parliament and the ESC is needed for:

---

[1] Regulation 614/2007, OJ L 149, 09.06.2007.

provisions primarily of a fiscal nature; measures concerning town and country planning; and measures significantly affecting a Member State's energy supply.

The Member States finance and implement environment policy. However, without prejudice to the principle that the polluter pays, if a measure involves costs deemed disproportionate for the public authorities of a Member State, notably a cohesion State [see section 12.1.2.], the Council, in the act adopting that measure, lays down appropriate provisions in the form of temporary derogations and/or financial support from the Cohesion Fund (Art. 175 TEC).

The common environment policy is based on the **precautionary and preventive action** principles, on the principle that environmental damage should to the extent possible be **rectified at source** and on the principle that **the polluter should pay** (Art. 174 TEC).

Indeed, the European Union's work on the environment is marked more and more by an integrated, **preventive approach** taking account of human activities and their consequences for the environment as a whole. The pro-active policy of voluntary prevention is manifested in the Directive on **the assessment of the effects of certain public and private projects** on the environment and on natural resources, which takes into account the commitments entered into under the international "Espoo" Convention on Environmental Impact Assessment in a Transboundary Context, particularly concerning the types of project for which impact assessment is compulsory[1]. According to this Directive, the promoter of the project, whether it be industrial, agricultural or relating to infrastructure, has to supply detailed information on its possible consequences for air, water, soil, noise, wild animals and their habitats, etc. Member States should ensure that members of the public concerned have access to a review procedure before a court of law or another independent and impartial body to challenge the substantive or procedural legality of decisions[2]. Another Directive imposes an assessment, including the preparing of an environmental report, during the preparation of a plan or programme and before its adoption or submission to the legislative procedure[3]. The authorities and the public affected or having an interest in the decision-making process can express their opinion on the environmental effects of a draft plan or programme.

The "polluter pays" principle, which is mentioned in Article 174, paragraph 2, of the EC Treaty, means that the cost incurred in combating pollution and nuisances in the first instance falls to the polluter, i.e. the polluting industry. Given, however, that the polluting industry can pass the cost of the prevention or elimination of pollution on to the consumer, the principle amounts to saying that **polluting production should bear**: **the expenditure** corresponding to the measures necessary to combat pollution (investment in apparatus and equipment for combating pollution, imple-

---

[1]   Directive 85/337, OJ L 175, 05.07.1985 and Directive 2003/35, OJ L 156, 25.06.2003.

[2]   Directive 2003/35, OJ L 156, 25.06.2003.

[3]   Directive 2001/42, OJ L 197, 21.07.2001.

mentation of new processes, operating expenditure for anti-pollution plant, etc.); **and the charges** whose purpose is to encourage the polluter himself to take, as cheaply as possible, the measures necessary to reduce the pollution caused by him (incentive function) or to make him bear his share of the costs of collective purification measures (redistribution function).

Based on the "polluter pays" principle, an important directive establishes a framework of **environmental liability** with regard to the prevention and remedying of environmental damage, including transboundary damage, but excluding damage caused by *force majeure* or expressly authorised activities[1]. It aims at preventing environmental damage to water resources, soil, fauna, flora and natural habitats and at making the polluters pay whenever damage cannot be avoided. Risky or potentially risky activities include activities releasing heavy metals into water or the air, installations producing dangerous chemicals, landfill sites and incineration plants. Member States are required to ensure that all environmental damage is restored, which entails assessing the gravity and extent of the damage and determining the most appropriate restoration measures to be taken. If the costs of implementing the prevention and restoration measures were not borne directly by the operator who caused the pollution, the competent authority must make sure that they are recovered from the operator. Member States are also required to promote the development of financial security products and encourage operators to take out financial security cover.

Another means for the prevention of pollutions is the **"eco-label"**, which guides the consumers towards "clean" products [see section 11.1.] and incites the industrialists to produce them, thus contributing to the efficient use of resources planned and to a high level of environmental protection[2]. The scheme functions on a voluntary basis and may be applied to a product belonging to product groups for which ecological criteria have been set by the Commission in accordance with the regulation.

16.2.2. Notification, information and monitoring

The **European Environment Agency**, which is established near Copenhagen, provides the Commission and the national authorities with the technical, scientific and economic information necessary for the framing and implementation of measures and legislation relating to the environment[3]. Being a Community body open to third countries because of the multinational character of problems and work concerning the environment, the Agency acts as a European network for monitoring and obtaining information on the environment. The **European pollutant release and transfer register** ("the European PRTR") aims to contribute to the prevention and reduction of pollution by providing data for policy-makers as well as facilitating public participation in decision-making[4].

---

[1] Directive 2004/35, OJ L 143, 30.04.2004.
[2] Regulation 1980/2000, OJ L 237, 21.09.2000.
[3] Regulation 1210/90, OJ L 120, 11.05.1990 and Regulation 933/1999, OJ L 117, 05.05.1999.
[4] Regulation 166/2006, OJ L 33, 04.02.2006.

In any event, the Commission receives information on the legislative or administrative intentions of the Member States. It verifies the transposition by the Member States of Community legislation into national law and initiates proceedings against States which either fail to implement Community provisions on the environment in full or correctly or do not give notification of domestic measures on the environment. The Commission has an important ally in the matter, namely **the citizens in the Member States**, who are concerned at environmental damage and make a growing number of complaints to it each year [see section 9.3.]. When it receives a complaint from an individual citizen or association, the Commission carries out an inquiry to verify the facts, and if it considers that Community law has been infringed it initiates the procedure provided for in Article 226 of the EC Treaty [see section 4.1.2.]. A Directive, implementing the UN Aarhus Convention, guarantees freedom of access to and dissemination of information on the environment held by public authorities and sets the basic conditions under which information on the environment should be made available to the public[1]. The latter, through pressure that it can exercise on national authorities can contribute a great deal to improving the respect of Community legislation.

16.2.3. Environment and common policies

Article 6 of the EC Treaty, stipulates that environmental protection requirements must be integrated into the **definition and implementation of other Community policies**. This is meant to ensure environmental protection in all its forms by means of prior analysis of the potential problems in this sector and of the adoption of measures which integrate environmental requirements into the planning and performance of economic and social activities. In fact, many environmental issues such as climate change, acidification and waste management can only be tackled by an interplay between the main economic public and private actors, not only by legislative means, but also by an extended and integrated mix of other instruments, such as standards, certification systems, voluntary schemes or economic instruments. Therefore, the sustainable protection of the environment depends to a large extent on the common policies pursued in the fields of industry, energy, transport, agriculture and tourism, which are in turn dependent on the capacity of the environment to sustain them.

The Commission has set out a long-term Community strategy for the progressive **integration of environmental issues with economic policy**, including the incorporation of the objectives of environmental integration into the broad economic policy guidelines (BEPGs) [see section 7.3.1.][2] and the removal of subsidies which are harmful to the environment..

---

[1] Directive 2003/4, OJ L 41, 14.02.2003.
[2] COM (2000) 576, 20 September 2000.

In the related field of **civil protection**, a Solidarity Fund is destined to provide rapid financial assistance to the population of the regions hit mainly by major natural disasters[1]. A Community action programme aims at organising the levels of preparedness in each Member State and at achieving closer Community cooperation for the protection of the population, the environment and property in the event of a natural or technological disaster[2]. The Council has established a **Civil Protection Financial Instrument** to support and complement the efforts of the Member States for the protection, primarily of people but also of the environment and property, including cultural heritage, in the event of natural and man-made disasters[3]. A **Community Mechanism** facilitates reinforced cooperation between the Community and the Member States in civil protection assistance intervention in the event of major emergencies, or the imminent threat thereof[4].

16.3. Reduction of pollution and nuisances

The efforts of the Community environment policy to combat pollution and nuisances are more specifically directed towards: the fixing of quality objectives for European waters, the control of discharges into the aquatic environment of the European Union, efforts to combat sea and air pollution, the prevention of industrial accidents and efforts to combat noise pollution. These various groups of activity are examined in succession below.

16.3.1. Quality objectives for European waters

Water is an element indispensable not only to human life, but also to many of man's activities, from fishing to industry, by way of agriculture. **Water plays an essential role in the natural ecological balance** by procuring a substantial proportion of the oxygen necessary for life. In addition, seas, lakes and rivers are of great value for recreational activities and leisure, which are indispensable for town-dwellers. The Commission considers that appropriate water pricing has a key role to play in the development of sustainable water policies[5].

The physical interdependence of the various surroundings that make up the aquatic ecosystem, such as surface fresh water, groundwater and seawater, **necessitates the coherent management of these resources**. The fact that watercourses often cross several countries and that lakeshores also extend across the territories of several countries dictates the common management of these resources. Comparable, and sometimes common, man-

---

[1] Regulation 2012/2002, OJ L 311, 14.11.2002 and Decision 2007/930, OJ L 202, 03.08.2007.

[2] Decision 1999/847, OJ L 327, 21.12.1999 and Decision 2005/12, OJ L 6, 08.01.2005.

[3] Decision 2007/162, OJ L 71, 10.03.2007.

[4] Decision 2007/779, OJ L 314, 01.12.2007.

[5] COM (2000) 477, 26 July 2000.

agement of water is indispensable, *inter alia*, to prevent distortions of competition between major water-using undertakings. Therefore, Directive 2000/60 establishing a framework for Community action in the field of water policy lays down a basis for coordinating the Member States' policies and measures to protect inland surface waters, transitional waters, coastal waters and groundwater[1]. The **principal objectives of this policy** are to:

- prevent further deterioration and protect and enhance the state of aquatic ecosystems;
- promote sustainable use of water based on the long-term protection of available water resources;
- ensure the progressive reduction of pollution of groundwater and prevent further pollution thereof;
- provide a sufficient supply of good quality surface water and groundwater as needed for sustainable, balanced and equitable water use; and
- protect territorial and marine waters.

To achieve these objectives, the EU States lay down quality objectives or quality standards so as to manage water rationally and limit water pollution. Supplementing Directive 2000/60 on water policy, a decision establishes a list of 33 substances or groups of substances, some of which are identified as "priority hazardous substances", discharges of which must be halted, and others as "priority substances under review"[2]. Quality objectives lay down the **pollution or nuisance levels not to be exceeded** in a given surrounding or part thereof. European directives fix certain mandatory values, which must not be exceeded, and some guide values, which Member States endeavour to comply with. A Directive establishes **specific measures** in order to prevent and control groundwater pollution[3].

16.3.2. Control of discharges into the aquatic environment

To attain and maintain the water-quality objectives described above, strict methods must be used to **reduce pollution caused by certain dangerous substances** discharged into the European aquatic environment, i.e. inland surface water, groundwater, internal coastal waters and territorial sea waters. Some toxic substances discharged into the water are, of course, chemically or biologically diluted and decomposed until their toxicity disappears, but others are persistent, i.e. they retain their chemical composition, and therefore their danger to the environment and to man, for a lengthy period, which can, in some cases, be several years.

For this reason a Community Directive contains provisions on the collection, processing and discharge of **urban waste water** and biodegradable water from some industrial sectors, and on the disposal of sludges[4]. In par-

---

[1]   Directive 2000/60, OJ L 327, 22.12.2000.
[2]   Decision 2455/2001, OJ L 331, 15.12.2001.
[3]   Directive 2006/118, OJ L 372, 27.12.2006.
[4]   Directive 91/271, OJ L 135, 30.05.1991 and Directive 98/15, OJ L 67, 07.03.1998.

ticular, the Directive stipulates that as a general rule, waste water which enters into collection systems must, before disposal, be subjected to secondary treatment in accordance with a timetable adjusted to the size of the population covered and the type and situation of the collection water. Another Directive concerns the protection of waters against pollution caused by nitrates from agricultural sources[1].

A Directive on pollution caused by certain dangerous substances discharged into the aquatic environment of the Community is directed towards curbing the process of the deterioration of that environment by **prohibiting or restricting the discharge of toxic substances**[2]. The latter are divided into two lists: a "black list" grouping particularly toxic, persistent and bioaccumulable substances, and a "grey list" which mainly concerns substances whose harmful effects are limited to one locality and depend on the properties of the receiving waters. The "black list" is constantly amended in the light of the development of scientific and technical knowledge of the toxicity of the various substances[3]. Whether substances from the first list or the second list are involved, the Directive provides for authorisations granted for all discharges into Community waters, issued by the competent authority of the Member State concerned for a limited period.

16.3.3. Effort to combat marine pollution

The marine environment is a precious asset, since oceans and seas cover 70% of the Earth's surface and contain 90% of its biosphere. Of all forms of pollution, sea pollution is one of the most dangerous because of its consequences for fundamental biological and ecological balances, the degree of degradation already reached, the diversity of sources of pollution and the difficulty of monitoring compliance with measures adopted. Apart from the accidental spillage of hydrocarbons in the sea, the **main sources of sea pollution are land-based ones**, i.e. the discharge of effluent from land and discharges of waste at sea. Therefore, the measures taken to control discharges into the aquatic environment, examined above, combat marine pollution.

In June 1978 the Council set up an action programme of the European Communities on the control and reduction of **pollution caused by hydrocarbons** discharged at sea[4]. In order to implement this action programme the Commission set up under its aegis an Advisory Committee on the Control and Reduction of Pollution Caused by Hydrocarbons Discharged at Sea[5]. International standards for ship-source pollution are incorporated into Community law and ensure that persons responsible for environmental dis-

---

[1] Directive 91/676, OJ L 375, 31.12.1991.
[2] Directive 2006/11, OJ L 64, 04.03.2006.
[3] Directive 86/280, OJ L 181, 04.07.1986 and Directive 91/692, OJ L 377, 31.12.1991.
[4] Resolution, OJ C 162, 08.07.1978, p. 1-4.
[5] Decision 80/686, OJ L 188, 22.07.1980 and Decision 87/144, OJ L 57, 27.02.1987.

asters resulting both from the pollution caused by accidents involving ships carrying substances harmful to the marine environment and from deliberate discharges by ships, including tank-cleaning and waste oil disposal at sea, are subject to **adequate penalties**[1].

It should be noted that the Community effort to combat marine pollution is based on voluntary measures and cooperation between the Member States. Thus, a **Community framework for cooperation** in the field of accidental marine pollution from harmful substances, whatever their origin, aims at the prevention of the risks and at efficient mutual assistance between Member States in this field, including compensation for damage in accordance with the polluter-pays principle[2] [see also section 20.3.4.].

The Commission advocates an **integrated maritime policy** for the European Union embracing *inter alia* a European maritime space without barriers; a European network for maritime surveillance; a strategy to mitigate the effects of climate change on coastal regions; and reduction of CO2 emissions and pollution by shipping[3]].

16.3.4. Effort to combat air pollution

Industrial and household activities depend much on the **burning of fossil fuels**. Such burning causes the emission into the air of sulphur dioxide (SO_2), due to the presence of certain quantities of sulphur in the fuel and of very fine particles of partly burned carbon and hydrocarbons which are highly pollutant for the air and highly toxic for human health. Since several of the most industrialised regions of the European Union are situated in frontier areas, **sulphur dioxide and suspended particulate matter** are carried from one European region to another according to wind direction. The European States therefore have to act in unison to prevent air pollution and at the same time to prevent the effects on the functioning of the common market resulting from barriers to trade in fuels and on the conditions of competition between industries using such fuels.

The framework Directive 96/62 defines the basic principles of a **common strategy on air quality objectives for ambient air**[4]. These are: the establishment of air quality objectives based on limit values and alert thresholds for the principal harmful substances; the assessment of air quality in the Member States on the basis of common methods and criteria; the maintenance and improvement of air quality; and the measures to be taken where there is a risk of the limit values being exceeded. The most polluting substances that the EU endeavours to reduce are: ozone in ambient air (tropospheric ozone), sulphur dioxide, carbon dioxide, carbon monoxide, lead and its compounds.

---

[1]   Directive 2005/35, OJ L 255, 30.09.2005.
[2]   Decision 2850/2000, OJ L 332, 28.12.2000 and decision 787/2004, OJ L 138, 30.04.2004.
[3]   COM/2007/575.
[4]   Directive 96/62, OJ L 296, 21.11.1996.

In order to attain and maintain air quality standards, a whole gamut of measures to limit the **emission of sulphur dioxide and other pollutants** is, of course, required. Therefore, a Directive set limit values not to be exceeded and guide values to be used as reference points for air quality with regard to sulphur dioxide and suspended particulates[1]. Community Directives limit the sulphur content of certain liquid fuels[2], the emissions of sulphur and other pollutants from industrial plants[3], from large combustion plants[4] and from internal combustion engines installed in non-road mobile machinery[5].

A major source of air pollution addressed by the Community is pollution by emissions from motor vehicles. **Carbon monoxide** resulting from the incomplete combustion of organic substances used in fuel was tackled first owing to its adverse consequences for human health and the environment. A 1970 Directive concerning the harmonisation of legislation on measures against air pollution by motor vehicle emissions obliged Member States to introduce three types of test to control gas emissions from positive-ignition engines of motor vehicles[6]. The technical controls of vehicles laid down by that Directive led to a significant reduction in emissions of carbon monoxide and unburned hydrocarbons by each vehicle. However, that effect was to a large extent neutralised by the increase in the number of vehicles in circulation in the Community States. For that reason the 1970 Directive was adapted to technical progress on several occasions in order to reduce the permissible levels of carbon monoxide emissions.

Another first-category air pollutant is **lead** and its compounds. A large proportion of the total quantity of this element in the air comes from emissions from petrol-engine vehicles. A 1982 Directive fixed a limit value for lead in the air[7]. Compliance with that limit required very costly measures for the Member States motor-vehicle industry. In order to prevent barriers to trade and the upheaval of conditions of competition, it was necessary to proceed in stages with the approximation of the laws of the Member States concerning the **lead content of petrol**, allowing the European motor vehicle industry and the petrol production and distribution industry time to adapt to the new conditions. New Directives, repealing the former ones, concern the quality of petrol and diesel fuels[8] and limit values for sulphur dioxide, nitrogen dioxide and oxides of nitrogen, particulate matter and lead in ambient air[9].

---

[1] Directive 1999/30, OJ L 163, 29.06.1999 and Decision 2001/744, OJ L 278. 23.10.2001.

[2] Directive 93/12, OJ L 74, 27.03.1993, Directive 1999/32, OJ L 121, 11.05.1999 and Directive 2005/33, OJ L 22.07.2005.

[3] Directive 84/360, OJ L 188, 16.07.1984 and Directive 91/692, OJ L 377, 31.12.1991.

[4] Directive 2001/80, OJ L 309, 27.11.2001.

[5] Directive 97/68, OJ L 59, 27.02.1998 and Directive 2004/26, OJ L 146, 30.04.2004.

[6] Directive 70/220, OJ L 76, 06.04.1970 and Directive 2003/76, OJ L 206, 15.08.2003.

[7] Directive 82/884, OJ L 378, 31.12.1982 repealed by Directive 1999/30, OJ L 163, 29.06.1999.

[8] Directive 98/70, OJ L 350, 28.12.1998 and Directive 2003/17, OJ L 76, 22.03.2003.

[9] Directive 1999/30, OJ L 163, 29.06.1999.

Whereas it is a pollutant in the lower atmosphere (troposphere), with adverse effects on vegetation, ecosystems and the environment as a whole, **ozone** is a natural element in the upper atmosphere (stratosphere), produced by photochemical reaction. The **stratospheric ozone layer** is vital to mankind, as it filters a large proportion of the sun's ultraviolet rays. A reduction in that layer could lead to a large increase in the number of skin cancers or considerable damage to agriculture on the planet. Emissions of **carbon dioxide** (CO_2) and of chemicals such as chlorofluorocarbons (CFCs) and halons contribute to the **"greenhouse effect"** and hence to global warming. Effective combating of this phenomenon requires concerted action at international level. Therefore, the European Union is signatory of the Vienna **Convention for the protection of the ozone layer** and the Montreal Protocol on substances that deplete the ozone layer, the objective of which is to stabilise greenhouse gas concentrations in the air at a level avoiding dangerous climate change[1]. Particular reference should be made to the Protocol on Substances that Deplete the Ozone Layer and therefore on the control of greenhouse gas emissions, signed at Montreal in 1987 and amended several times[2]. An EC regulation is intended to implement the commitment agreed by the parties to the Montreal Protocol, and provides for measures designed to help speed up the process of regeneration of the ozone layer[3].

During the United Nations Conference on Environment and Development, the so-called "Earth Summit", held in Rio de Janeiro from June 3 to 14, 1992, the United Nations **Framework Convention on Climate Change (UNFCCC)** was signed by the European Community and its Member States. The European Community adhered to the Convention in 1994[4]. The ultimate objective of the UNFCCC and of its Kyoto Protocol, which sets mandatory limits on greenhouse gas emissions for individual countries, is to achieve, in accordance with the relevant provisions of the Convention, the stabilization of greenhouse gas concentrations in the atmosphere at a level that would prevent dangerous anthropogenic interference with the climate system. The Convention enjoys near universal membership, with 192 countries having ratified it. The European Community accepted the commitments of the Kyoto Protocol[5] and all its Member States have ratified it. In contrast, although the United States have signed both the Convention and the Protocol, the Bush administration did not ratify the Kyoto Protocol, so as not to accept a binding commitment to reduce US greenhouse gas emissions.

[1] Vienna Convention, Montreal Protocol and Decision 88/540, OJ L 297, 31.10.1988.
[2] UN Convention, amendment to the Montreal Protocol and Decisions 94/68 and 94/69, OJ L 33, 07.02.1994, amendment to Montreal Protocol and Decision 2002/215, OJ L 72, 14.03.2002.
[3] Regulation 2037/2000, OJ L 244, 29.09.2000 last amended by Regulation 1366/2006, OJ L 264, 25.09.2006.
[4] Decision 94/69, OJ L 33, 07.02.1994.
[5] Decision 2002/358, OJ L 130, 15.05.2002.

The **Kyoto Protocol** sets legally binding targets for industrialised countries to reduce their greenhouse-gas emissions relative to the base year (1990) by 2008-2012, calculated as an average of these years. These 5 years are known as the first commitment period. The Kyoto Protocol suggests various means of attaining these objectives: stepping up or introducing national policies to reduce emissions (greater energy efficiency, promotion of sustainable forms of agriculture, development of renewable energy sources, etc.), as well as cooperation mechanisms, namely emission permits and joint implementation. Whereas, the Parties to Annex I to the Framework Convention (industrialised countries) have undertaken to reduce their greenhouse gas emissions by at least 5% below 1990 levels during the period 2008 to 2012, the European Union, although it is responsible for only 14% of global greenhouse gas emissions, has committed itself to reducing its greenhouse gas emissions by 8% during the first commitment period.

In order to honour EU Kyoto commitments, Directive 2002/3 established **long-term objectives**, target values, an alert threshold and an information threshold for concentrations of ozone in ambient air in the Community, designed to avoid, prevent or reduce harmful effects on human health and the environment as a whole[1]. Directive 2001/81 set up **national emission ceilings** for certain atmospheric pollutants, taking the years 2010 and 2020 as benchmarks[2]. Directive 2003/87 established a **Community greenhouse gas emission trading scheme** (one of the flexible mechanisms recommended in the Kyoto protocol), according to which each Member State must draw up a national plan indicating the allowances (entitlements to emit greenhouse gases) it intends to allocate to each polluting installation[3]. With effect from 1 January 2008, each such installation must be in possession of an appropriate permit issued by the competent authorities for a five-year period. A decision set up a **mechanism** for implementing the Kyoto Protocol by **monitoring Community greenhouse gas emissions** by sources and removals by sinks of greenhouse gases (i.e. forests, which remove carbon dioxide from the atmosphere)[4]. Directive 2008/1, concerning **integrated pollution prevention and control**, lays down measures designed to prevent or, where that is not practicable, to reduce emissions in the air, water and land from polluting industrial activities, including measures concerning waste, in order to achieve a high level of protection of the environment taken as a whole[5].

---

[1] Directive 2002/3, OJ L 67, 09.03.2002.
[2] Directive 2001/81, OJ L 309, 27.11.2001.
[3] Directive 2003/87, OJ L 275, 25.10.2003 and Directive 2004/101, OJ L 338, 13.11.2004.
[4] Decision 280/2004, OJ L 49, 19.02.2004.
[5] Directive 2008/1, OJ L 24, 29.01.2008.

16.3.5. Prevention of industrial and chemical hazards

National and Community rules against pollution cannot in themselves prevent serious industrial accidents which are catastrophic for the environment, like those in Seveso in Italy in 1976 and Bhopal in India in 1984. For that reason, rules should be taken concerning controls on land-use planning when new installations are authorized and when urban development takes place around existing installations. Therefore, Directive 96/82 aims at the **prevention of major accidents which involve dangerous substances** and the limitation of their consequences for man and the environment, with a view to ensuring high levels of protection throughout the Community in a consistent and effective manner[1]. It provides for: definition, by each establishment covered, of a major-accident prevention policy; submission, by each establishment where dangerous substances are present in large quantities, of safety reports demonstrating that the major accident hazards have been identified, that the design, construction, operation and maintenance of the installation are sufficiently safe and that the emergency plans have been drawn up; taking account, in land-use policies, of the objectives of preventing major accidents, limiting the consequences and improving the procedures for consulting and informing the public.

Independently of accident hazards control, a framework Directive aims at an **integrated pollution prevention and control (IPPC)**[2]. Its across-the-board approach involves the various media (air, water, soil) by applying the principle of the best environmental option, in particular in order to avoid transferring pollution from one medium to another. It provides that the operators of certain polluting plants submit requests for operating permits to the competent authority in the Member States, with the issuing of a permit being conditional on compliance with basic obligations such as not to exceed emission limit values set by the Directive. The Community has established a scheme for greenhouse gas **emission allowance trading** within its territory ("Community scheme")[3]. The scheme aims both to achieve a pre-determined emission reduction and to decrease the resulting costs. It is based on granting authorised emissions allowances, purchasing emissions permits from companies which have not used up their full allowance and imposing fines in the event of misuse of this scheme.

A European **pollutant emission register (EPER)**, introduced in 2003, contains data concerning emissions of 50 pollutants from some 20 000 industrial facilities across the EU. Both the public and industry may use EPER data to compare the environmental performance of individual facilities or industrial sectors in different countries and to monitor the progress made in meeting environment targets set in national and international agreements and protocols[4].

---

[1]   Directive 96/82, OJ L 10, 14.01.1997 and Directive 2003/105, OJ L 345, 31.12.2003.

[2]   Directive 2008/1, OJ L 24, 29.01.2008..

[3]   Directive 2003/87, OJ L275, 25.10.2003 and Directive 2004/101, OJ L 338, 13.11.2004.

[4]   Decision 2000/479, OJ L 192, 28.07.2000.

Major pollution of water, air and soil is caused by **chemical products discharged in the form of by-products or industrial waste**. The problems here are identifying the dangerous substances and monitoring their utilisation and disposal. This is why, under the Directive on the approximation of the laws relating to the classification, packaging and **labelling of dangerous substances** each Member State undertook to act as a representative of its European Community partners when authorising the introduction of a new chemical product into the whole Community market[1]. For that purpose, the producer or importer has to provide the State into whose market the product is first introduced with a **"base set"**. That dossier is composed of a whole range of information on the physico-chemical properties of the new product concerned, its possible effects on health and the environment, the uses for which it is intended, the quantities produced, the proposed classification and labelling and a general evaluation of the dangers. That information is forwarded to the Commission, which sends it to each Member State and to the advisory Scientific Committee on Health and Environmental Risks (SCHER), which examines the toxicity and ecotoxicity of chemical compounds[2]. Businesses are authorised to place on the market only "EC" labelled and, accordingly controlled, dangerous substances[3] [see section 6.2.3.].

16.4. Management of environmental resources

The Community environment programme is not confined to the effort to combat pollution and nuisances, but also seeks to make an active contribution to improving the environment and the quality of life through the rational management of space, the environment and natural resources. The measures provided for in that section of the Community environment programme can be grouped under the headings of the **protection of flora and fauna** in Europe and the **management of waste** in the Community. The nature and biodiversity component of the **financial instrument LIFE+** [see section 16.2] finances notably: site and species management and site planning, including the improvement of the ecological coherence of the Natura 2000 network; and the development and implementation of species and habitats conservation action plans[4].

---

[1] Directive 67/548, OJ L 196, 16.08.1967 and Directive 2004/73, OJ L 152, 30.04.2004.
[2] Decision 2004/210, OJ L 66, 04.03.2004.
[3] Directive 96/56, OJ L 236, 18.09.1996.
[4] Regulation 614/2007, OJ L 149, 09.06.2007.

16.4.1. Protection of flora and fauna

Species of wild flowers and the animal populations form **part of European heritage**. Apart from the fact that they represent non-renewable genetic assets, they participate in many natural functions which ensure overall ecological balances, such as the regulation of the development of undesirable organisms, the protection of the soil against erosion and the regulation of aquatic ecosystems. The genetic assets represented by all present-day animal and plant species constitute a resource of ecological, scientific and economic interest of inestimable value for the future of mankind. However, industrialisation, urbanisation and pollution are threatening a growing number of wild species and undermining the natural balances resulting from several million years of evolution.

A Community Directive aims to **protect natural and semi-natural habitats** and wild fauna and flora[1]. It provides for the establishment of a European ecological network of special conservation areas, "Natura 2000", made up of sites which are home to types of natural habitats of species of interest to the Community. The Member States must take appropriate steps to avoid their deterioration or any other disturbances affecting the species.

A significant means of protecting wildlife threatened with extinction is to restrict and **control rigorously international trade in plants and animals** belonging to such species and products made from them. Therefore, the Community implements the Convention on International Trade in Endangered Species of Wild Fauna and Flora (CITES), which aims at protecting 2.000 species through the stringent control of international trade. However, the relevant Community Regulation covers a wider field than the Convention, dividing the species into four classes to be given protection, ranging from statistical monitoring of trade to a total trading ban, depending on the degree of the threat of extinction[2]. Special attention is given to re-exportation, control of commercial activities involving such specimens and definition of the infringements, which Member States are required to penalise.

16.4.2. Management of waste

As the penalty paid for economic development and urbanisation, the accumulation of **waste destroys the environment** and is at the same time proof of regrettable profligacy. Waste of all kinds, i.e. household waste, industrial waste, sewage sludge from waste water, agricultural waste and waste from the extractive industries, accounts for some 3 billion tons each year in the EU.

Included amongst "waste" are **toxic substances** and substances which are hazardous for man and the environment, as they can pollute the water

---

[1] Directive 92/43, OJ L 206, 22.07.1992 and Directive 97/62, OJ L 305, 08.11.1997.
[2] Regulation 338/97, OJ L 61, 03.03.1997 and Regulation 1332/2005, OJ L 215, 19.08.2005.

table by percolation, contaminate micro-organisms and appear in the food chain through complex and little-known means. But "waste" also includes scrap metal, paper, plastics and waste oils, which can be recycled, which is important in a Europe becoming increasingly poor in raw materials.

In view of the close interdependence of waste management and many industrial and commercial activities, the lack of a Community design for waste management is likely to affect not only environmental protection, but also the completion of the internal market by creating distortions of competition and unjustified movements of investment, or even the partitioning of the market. The objectives of a **Community strategy on waste management** are: (a) prevention, by encouraging the use of products which create less waste; (b) increasing its value, through the optimisation of collection and sorting systems; (c) the laying down of stringent standards for final disposal, as contained in the Council Directives on new municipal waste-incineration plants and on existing municipal waste-incineration plants[1]; and (d) rules governing the carriage of dangerous substances, so as to ensure safe and economic carriage and the restoration of contaminated areas, taking into account the civil liability of the polluter. The principle of producer responsibility is a key component in future Community legislation on waste management[2].

The "framework Directive" for Community waste policy obliges the Member States to take measures to ensure that waste is eliminated without endangering human health and without damaging the environment, and in particular without giving rise to risk to water, air or soil, fauna or flora, without causing discomfort through noise or smell and without affecting areas or landscapes[3]. It also aims to set up an integrated and appropriate network of waste disposal plants, to encourage disposal as close as possible to the waste production site, thus reducing the dangers inherent in waste transport, and to promote clean technologies and products which can be recycled and reused.

A directive aims at preventing or reducing as far as possible the adverse **effects of landfills** on the environment, particularly pollution of surface water, groundwater, soil and air, and on the global environment, including the greenhouse effect, and the resulting risks to human health during the whole lifecycle of the landfill[4]. An accompanying decision on the acceptance of waste at landfills lays down the procedures for characterising waste, for checking that it complies with the acceptance criteria and for on-site verification that it is identical to the waste described in the accompanying documents[5].

---

[1] Directive 2000/76, OJ L 332, 28.12.2000.

[2] COM (96) 399, 30 July 1996 and resolution, OJ C 76, 11.03.1997, p. 1-4.

[3] Directive 2006/12, OJ L 114, 27.04.2006.

[4] Directive 1999/31, OJ L 182, 16.07.1999.

[5] Decision 2003/33, OJ L 11, 16.01.2003.

16.5. Appraisal and outlook

Thanks to the Treaty of Maastricht environment protection has gradu-
ated to the status of a common policy and falls into the **priority objectives
of the Union**. Environmental constraints must be integrated into the definition and implementation of other common policies. The uniform application in all Member States of environmental standards is, in fact, indispensable not only for the preservation of Europe's environment, but also for
the good functioning of the internal market and for economic and social
cohesion [see section 12.1.2].

It is very difficult to evaluate the specific results of the European
measures in this area, first because the quality of the environment is a
highly subjective notion and therefore difficult to define, and secondly because the policy to combat pollution is a **Sisyphean task**. The quality objectives that it lays down are incessantly thrust aside by economic development and urbanisation. It is true that the annual reports of the Commission to the Parliament and the Council on the implementation of the European Community's environment programme show that significant progress
has been achieved on phasing out ozone-depleting substances, reducing
emissions of certain pollutants into the atmosphere and surface waters, improving water quality and reducing acidification. But, the state of the environment overall remains a cause for concern, particularly in respect to
growing consumption of natural resources, chemical risks, soil degradation, global warming and biodiversity losses.

Moreover, serious problems and excessive delays in the enforcement
and implementation of the environment directives exist in many Member
States, which also have a bad record on producing the necessary reports
and information in general. To make the Union a highly eco-efficient
economy, the environmental dimension of the Lisbon Process [see section
13.3.2.] should be strengthened, so as to give equal attention to economic,
social and environmental considerations in policy-making and decision-
taking processes. In any case, a permanent vigilance is required of citizens,
who can lodge complaints with the Commission whenever they observe
that European standards are not being complied with by an undertaking or
by public or private works in their country or a neighbouring country.
Likewise, mechanisms are needed for handling complaints and carrying
out environmental investigations outside the courts [see section 9.3.].

However, the European Union cannot work in isolation in this field.
Even if it were to succeed in significantly reducing and preventing pollution in its territory, it would still be open to water and air pollution from
the other countries of Europe and the other regions of the world. For that
reason the Union must play a leading role in international negotiations and
take more visible action in the framework of **international organisations**
such as the Council of Europe and the United Nations. Thus, the accession
to the Union of **Central and Eastern European countries** must go hand-
in-hand with increased consideration of environmental constraints, which

have been tragically neglected in the past. The European Environment Agency, which is open to the other countries of Europe, plays an important part in this area.

The environmental interdependence of all the countries in the world is particularly marked with regard to the **greenhouse effect** and its climatic consequences for the globe. The EU is set to achieve and even overachieve its Kyoto target. By 2010, total EU-27 GHG emissions are projected to be about 10.7% below base-year levels. The projected decline is 13.2% when the effect of the Kyoto mechanisms and carbon sinks are accounted for and it could reach 16.7% if the additional domestic policies and measures currently under discussion were to be implemented on time and would deliver as estimated. Yet, the EU's climate policy does not stop in 2012. Many of the EU policies that are already in place will have an important impact beyond the Kyoto Protocol's first commitment period. The **Sixth Community Environment Action Programme** (2002-2012) [see section 16.2] envisages that further reductions are required to achieve the Kyoto objectives and therefore, more concrete policies and measures are necessary. In spring 2007, the European Council endorsed the EU's independent commitment to reduce GHG emissions by at least 20% by 2020 compared to 1990 levels even if no international agreement is reached. The EU would be prepared to increase this reduction to 30%, provided that such an agreement would indeed materialize.

However, the European Union cannot curb the greenhouse phenomenon alone. **At the international level**, the EU should aim at promoting sustainable development and the effective participation of all players, ensuring greater consistency, better implementation of environmental standards and greater integration of environmental concerns into states' internal policies. It should summon other industrialised countries and, particularly, the United States, as the biggest emitter of greenhouse gases, to comply with standards agreed in international fora. It should also take the initiative to call for international **environmental governance**, based on coherent international, regional, sub-regional and national institutional environmental architecture topped by a World Environment Organisation, capable of responding to current challenges.

Bibliography on environment policy

- ECKSTEIN Anne. *The European Union and the environment: review of EU legislation to 31 December 2006*. Brussels: European Information Service, 2007.
- ENGLE Eric. "Ecotaxes and the European Union", in *European environmental law review*, v. 16, n. 11, November 2007, p. 298-303.
- EUROPEAN COMMISSION. *The Montreal Protocol*. Luxembourg: EUR-OP, 2007.
  - *Europe's environment: the fourth assessment*. Luxembourg: EUR-OP, 2007.

- *Greenhouse gas emission trends and projections in Europe 2007: tracking progress towards Kyoto targets.* Luxembourg: EUR-OP, 2007.
- EUROPEAN ENVIRONMENT AGENCY. *The pan-European environment: Glimpses into an uncertain future.* Luxembourg: EUR-OP*, 2007.
- HARRISON Kathryn, McINTOSH SUNDSTROM Lisa (eds.). "The comparative politics of climate change", in *Global environmental politics*, v. 7, n. 4, November 2007, p. i-139.
- KNILL Christoph, LIEFFERINK *Duncan. Environmental politics in the European Union: policy-making, implementation and patterns of multi-level governance.* Manchester: Manchester University Press, 2007.
- KULESSA Margareta. "The climate policy of the European Union", in *Intereconomics*, v. 42, n. 2, March-April 2007, p. 64-95.
- PERKINS Richard, NEUMAYER Eric. "Implementing multilateral environmental agreements: an analysis of EU directives", in *Global environmental politics*, v. 7, n. 3, August 2007, p. 13-41.

DISCUSSION TOPICS

1. Compare the efficiency of various national environment protection policies with that of a common European policy.
2. How does the common environment protection policy interact with other common policies?
3. Discuss the "polluter pays" and "prevention" principles of the common environment policy.
4. Consider the significance of the efforts of the EU to restrain fresh water and marine pollution.
5. Assess the effectiveness of the measures taken by the EU States at curbing atmospheric pollution and global warming.

Part V. Sectoral Policies

In **Part V we consider the sectoral policies of the Union**, that is to say, the policies concerning big sectors of the economies of the Member States, industry, research, energy, transports and agriculture. We will see that in the last three sectors the Treaties required explicitly the development of common policies, whereas for industry they asked for no policy as such, but the whole multinational integration process was geared towards the restructuring and competitiveness of European industry. Common research and energy policies were partially defined in the sectoral Treaties, notably that on Euratom. The various legal foundations of the five main sectoral policies certainly account for their dissimilar development; but so do as well the different requirements that the Member States set for those policies during the stages of the customs union, the common market and more recently the economic and monetary union.

Whilst, the EEC Treaty made no call for a common or Community **industrial policy**, it chiefly regulated the common market in industrial products (free trade, rules of competition, approximation of laws, tax provisions...). It assumed that the abolition of protectionist measures and the opening-up of the markets, thanks to the common market would provide sufficient impetus for the restructuring of sectors and undertakings. We saw that this assumption was partly invalidated because of national protectionism, which persisted until the early 1990s by means of technical barriers to trade [see section 6.1.]. Now that the single market has become a reality, small and medium-sized enterprises (SMEs) must adjust to the new conditions of heightened competition. The new **enterprise policy** of the Community shores up their efforts. The common enterprise policy, however, aims to help SMEs in both the industrial and service sectors adjust to the new conditions of the large internal market. This is also the goal of common sub-sectoral policies, notably in declining or fast growing industrial sectors, which need to be freed from old protectionist practices so as to better face the new conditions of competition in Europe and the world.

A common **research policy** is also a vital rung on the ladder of the European Union's industrial development. It is essential for the definition of industrial strategy, for technical progress in high-technology sectors, for the mastery of the Community's energy problems and, finally, for the adaptation of businesses to the post-industrial information society.

Research is a key feature of the common **energy policy**, the aim of which is to reduce Europe's dependence on imported energy and raise the competitiveness of European industry through the development of cheap, safe and clean energies. Due to its foundation on the ECSC and Euratom sectoral Treaties [see section 2.1.], the common policy is well advanced in the sectors of coal and nuclear energy and very little in the oil and gas sectors.

Unlike most other Community policies, **transport policy** was specifically mentioned in the EEC Treaty, even with the specification that it should be a common policy. We will note that diverging national interests have impeded progress of the transport policy during the first thirty years of the Community's existence; but the completion of the single market, which has resulted in strong growth in demand for transport services for both goods and persons, went in step with a large-scale liberalisation in the areas of road haulage, sea and air transport.

By contrast, the **common agricultural policy** (CAP) covered a great deal of ground during the first years of the Community. However, of all the policies examined in this book, the CAP has been the most controversial and the most versatile, since it is reformed every five years or so to respond both to internal and external requirements. The CAP presents, indeed, a good example of the constant adaptation of a common policy to new societal needs and to the changing European and international competition and trade requirements.

The **fisheries policy**, initially a part of the common agricultural policy, gives a good illustration of how a common policy can develop. It starts out with a few isolated measures addressing a particular situation or shared problems in a sector and, little by little there is a realisation that if the common achievements are to be safeguarded, other measures are required leading to a full-grown common policy. Thanks to this policy and despite the growing depletion of fishing resources in the waters of the Union and worldwide, there is a single market for fisheries products.

Chapter 17

INDUSTRIAL AND ENTERPRISE POLICIES

Diagram of the chapter

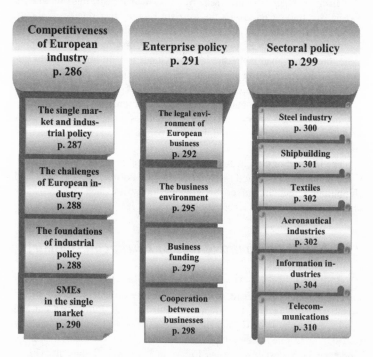

Competitiveness of European industry p. 286	Enterprise policy p. 291	Sectoral policy p. 299
The single market and industrial policy p. 287	The legal environment of European business p. 292	Steel industry p. 300
The challenges of European industry p. 288	The business environment p. 295	Shipbuilding p. 301
The foundations of industrial policy p. 288	Business funding p. 297	Textiles p. 302
SMEs in the single market p. 290	Cooperation between businesses p. 298	Aeronautical industries p. 302
		Information industries p. 304
		Telecommunications p. 310

The Treaty establishing the European Economic Community organised the achievement of customs union in great detail with regard to the industrial products of the Member States, but **made no call for an industrial policy as such**. In fact the founding fathers of the EEC had hoped that the liberalisation of trade and increased competition inside the common market could, on their own, bring about the structural changes that Community industry needed. As was explained in the chapter on the common market, this hope was tardily realised because of the tardy completion of the single market [see section 6.1.]. However, an important part of the common industrial policy, concerning the harmonisation of legislations, standardisation and public procurement, was dealt with in the chapter on the common market [see section 6.2.].

In the absence of a specific structural policy for the industrial sector, a large part of the present chapter is devoted to **enterprise policy**. In the run-up to the completion of the single market, in the early 1990s, the Community has, in fact, paid close attention to small and medium-sized enterprises (SMEs), which account for almost 99% of the industrial fabric of the Community and for 70% of total employment in the private sector of the Member States and which face problems of integration in the single market. The enterprise policy, however, covers not only industrial firms but also firms in other economic sectors, in particular craft, tourism and the distributive trade. Concerning the **tourism sector**, in particular, it should be noted that, despite the common interest in developing a common policy for the promotion of European tourism, the Council, has done nothing more, until now, than invite the Member States to help implement the co-operation approach between tourism stakeholders through the open method of coordination, i.e. without using Community legal instruments[1]. However, a Commission communication introduces a renewed EU tourism policy, outlining the Commission's future initiatives on the principal aspects of European policy-making and the ways partnerships amongst concerned stakeholders should evolve[2].

The last part of this chapter deals with sectoral industrial policy, that is, Community policy for industries in decline in Europe, such as steel and shipbuilding, and "infant" or fast growing industries, such as information and telecommunications technologies.

17.1. The competitiveness of European industry

Whilst the European Treaties did not make provision for a Community industrial policy, they **dealt primarily with the industrial sector** of the Member States. In fact, the Treaties establishing the European Coal and Steel Community (ECSC) and the European Atomic Energy Community (EAEC) constituted sectoral policies in the relevant industrial sectors, while the Treaty establishing the European Economic Community (EEC) chiefly regulated the common market in industrial products [see section 2.1.]. But the ECSC and EAEC (Euratom) Treaties were more precise than the EEC Treaty or even the EC Treaty. They included provisions both on the attainment of the common market and on the structural policy of the sectors to which they related, and they gave powers to the Community institutions to formulate such policies.

Certainly, the customs union enhanced the ability of European industry to compete both on its own market and globally. As from 1968, with the introduction of the **Common Customs Tariff** and by virtue of its uniform duties, the Community had available to it a valuable instrument for conducting an effective commercial policy and for pressing on towards the liberalisation of international trade [see section 5.2.1.]. That instrument has

---

[1]   COM (2001) 665 and Council resolution, OJ C 135, 06.06.2002.
[2]   COM (2006) 134, 17.03.2006.

been used successfully by the Commission, which has negotiated, on be-half of the Community, the reduction of the customs protection of the major commercial powers within the framework of the General Agreement on Tariffs and Trade (GATT) [see section 23.4.].

However, the easing of international protectionism did not suffice to redress the competitive situation of Community industry. To be able to measure up to the American and Japanese multinational companies, European industries had to find the **dimension most appropriate to the new conditions of competition** and improve their productivity by seeking new products and new production methods. Only the large European market could offer them those conditions of competitiveness.

17.1.1. The single market and industrial policy

The completion of the single European market, topped by the single currency, presents businesses with an opportunity to **benefit from economies of scale**, to cut their administrative and financial costs, to gain easier access to public procurement in other Member States and to cooperate more closely with each other across borders. Thus, the single market represents an essential base for business to look, think and act strategically beyond national borders. Certainly, the tendency of multinational enterprises to acquire a dominant position in the single market under the guise of achieving a sufficient critical size must be monitored by the competition authorities, [see section 15.4.2.], allowing, however, European companies to pursue business strategies, which may safeguard their competitiveness at world level,.

Several objectives of the Community industrial policy were attained through the completion of the single market. Thus, since the beginning of the1990s, **European standardisation** provides manufacturers with technical specifications recognised as giving a presumption of conformity to the essential requirements of Community directives [see section 6.2.3.]. European standards are not only required for the purpose of removing technical barriers to trade; increasingly they are also becoming a key element for the promotion of industrial competitiveness by lowering costs for producers and enabling the emergence of new markets, particularly for developing new technologies. At the same time, greater standardisation of products places a premium on product innovation, manufacturing excellence, design and reliability rather than on the more traditional factors of competitiveness like proximity to markets, distribution systems and customer loyalty.

Very important for European industrial competitiveness is also **public procurement**, which is now opened up thanks to the legislation of the single market [see section 6.3.]. Its importance for industry is threefold. Firstly, the vast size of public procurement - 16% of GDP - means that access to the public markets is very important for all firms. Secondly, public procurement may enhance technological capability by increasing the marketable demand of high technology products. Thirdly, public procurement being concentrated on a relatively small group of industries, these industries need a competitive market for public procurement in order to develop the necessary products and skills to be successful internationally.

17.1.2. The challenges of European industry

Although European industry now benefits from the advantages of a single large market, it is faced with new challenges. **Globalisation of economies and markets**, which enables greater economies of scale to be reaped and better specialisation for distinctive market segments, entails the intensification of international competition. In the context of this globalisation, European businesses must be able to face international competition. Although it has not deteriorated, apparent labour productivity in Community manufacturing still lags a good way behind that of the US and Japanese industry. Economic operators and public authorities in Europe must therefore pay more attention to the factors influencing productivity: technological development, investment in R&D, the rate of capacity utilisation, the cost and skill of the labour force, management skills and the organisation of production.

Apart from globalisation of markets and competition, European industry must prepare to face the challenge of the **new industrial revolution**, the one resulting from the development of information and communications technologies. These reduce the traditional distinctions between electronics, information technology, telecommunications and the audiovisual sectors [see sections 17.3.5 and 17.3.6.]. This revolution has far-reaching effects on production structures and methods. It spells changes in the way companies are organised, in managerial responsibilities and relations with workers, particularly concerning the organisation of work. There is therefore a need for structural adjustment and the steady shifting of resources towards the most productive outlets. In general, business competitiveness depends increasingly on the **ability to innovate**, notably by the development of new products and services.

17.1.3. The foundations of industrial policy

With the entry into force, in November 1993, of the Treaty of Maastricht [see section 2.2.], industrial competitiveness became one of the stated objectives of European integration. Article 3 of the EC Treaty states, in fact, that the action of the Community includes, *inter alia*, the **strengthening of the competitiveness of Community industry**. The Title on Industry of the TEC announces that the Community and the Member States must ensure the existence of the conditions necessary for the competitiveness of the Community's industry. For this purpose, in accordance with a system of open and competitive markets, **their action aims at**: speeding up the adjustment of industry to structural changes; encouraging an environment favourable to initiative and to the development of undertakings throughout the Community, particularly small and medium-sized undertakings; encouraging an environment favourable to cooperation between undertakings; and fostering better exploitation of the industrial potential of innovation and research and technological development policies (Art. 157 TEC).

This article forms the legal basis for Community action in the fields of industry and business. It specifies however that it does not provide a basis for the introduction by the Community of any measures that could lead to a distortion of competition. The objectives set out above may be **pursued by the following means**: the mutual consultation of the Member States and, where necessary, the coordination of their action, in liaison with and upon initiative of the Commission; the coordination with other Community policies and activities; and specific measures in support of action taken in the Member States decided by the Council acting unanimously on a proposal from the Commission after consultation of the European Parliament and the Economic and Social Committee. The unanimity rule required for specific measures in the industrial sector denotes the reluctance of the Member States to weaken national policies in favour of a common industrial policy. Hence, most industrial policy is carried out not at EU level but under the competence of the Member States.

Yet, industrial competitiveness depends on policies such as competition, the internal market, research and development, education, trade and sustainable development. Therefore, the common industrial policy must ensure that other common policies contribute to the competitiveness of Europe's industry. It therefore covers a very wide field, while many of its instruments are the instruments of other policy fields[1]. The **common industrial strategy is based on three principles**: consistent recourse to all common policies with a bearing on industrial activity, in particular that of protection of the environment[2]; improved access of Community businesses to non-Community markets and to measures against unfair trading practices and in favour of international industrial cooperation[3] [see sections 23.2.2. and 23.4.].

Following the Lisbon objectives [see section 13.3.2], the **competitiveness and innovation framework programme** (CIP, 2007-2013) aims to contribute to the competitiveness and innovative capacity of the Community as an advanced knowledge society, with sustainable development based on robust economic growth and a highly competitive social market economy with a high level of protection and improvement of the quality of the environment[4]. It has the following objectives: to foster the competitiveness of enterprises, in particular of SMEs; to promote all forms of innovation including eco-innovation; to accelerate the development of a sus-

---

[1] COM (2002) 714, 11 December 2002.
[2] Resolution, OJ C 331, 16.12.1992, p. 5-7.
[3] Resolution, OJ C 178, 15.07.1992, p. 1-3.
[4] Decision 1639/2006, OJ L 310, 09.11.2006.

tainable, competitive, innovative and inclusive information society; to promote energy efficiency and new and renewable energy sources in all sectors, including transport. These objectives are pursued through the implementation of three programmes: (a) the Entrepreneurship and Innovation Programme; (b) the Information and Communications Technologies (ICT) Policy Support Programme; and (c) the Intelligent Energy-Europe Programme. The framework programme should contribute to closing the gap between research and innovation and promote all forms of innovation, but it does not cover research, technological development and demonstration activities carried out in accordance with Article 166 of the Treaty [see section 18.4].

17.1.4. SMEs in the single market

As was seen above, Article 157 (TEC) states, among other things, that the Community and the Member States shall encourage "an environment favourable to initiative and to the development of undertakings throughout the Community, particularly small and medium-sized undertakings". This is the base of the common enterprise policy, a policy in favour of small businesses, known in Community jargon as **small and medium-sized enterprises (SMEs)**. But what are the SMEs?

Until the mid-1990s, different definitions of SMEs were used in Community policies (competition, Structural Funds, R&D, tendering for public procurement, etc.). This diversity could give rise to doubts among public authorities and even to confusion among the businessmen concerned. Therefore, the Commission adopted a recommendation concerning the **definition of micro, small and medium-sized enterprises** used in Community policies[1]. An enterprise is considered to be any entity engaged in an economic activity, irrespective of its legal form. The category of micro, small and medium-sized enterprises (SMEs) is made up of enterprises which employ fewer than 250 persons and which have an annual turnover not exceeding EUR 50 million, and/or an annual balance sheet total not exceeding EUR 43 million. Within the SME category, a small enterprise is defined as an enterprise which employs fewer than 50 persons and whose annual turnover and/or annual balance sheet total does not exceed EUR 10 million. A microenterprise is defined as an enterprise which employs fewer than 10 persons and whose annual turnover and/or annual balance sheet total does not exceed EUR 2 million. However, the Commission recommends to remove from the SMEs category non-autonomous enterprises, i.e. those which have holdings entailing a controlling position (partner enterprises) or those that are linked to other enterprises.

This definition serves as a reference for Community programmes, policy and legislation concerning SMEs and thus provides an overall framework, which can increase the coherence, effectiveness and visibility

---

[1] Recommendation 2003/361, OJ L 124, 20.05.2003.

of all measures to assist these enterprises. It should be noted that with this definition, the Union (Fifteen) numbers some 17 million SMEs, providing over 75% of its employment, accounting for 50% of investment and representing 60% of its wealth.

In addition to quantitative and easily verifiable criteria, SMEs are often also identified by **qualitative criteria**, focusing chiefly on the ownership of their capital, their management and their methods of financing. A SME is often a family business, whose management and ownership are in the hands of the same person(s). Day-to-day running of a SME falls upon the company head, enabling flexibility and rapidity in the decision-making process and a personalised relationship with staff, suppliers and customers. Finally, a SME is heavily dependent on self-financing due to difficult access to the financial markets and it often suffers from limited availability of financial resources.

Of course, SMEs have **their weak points, which are notably**: (a) the difficulty to face the complicated administrative and legal environment created by the completion of the internal market and the globalisation of production; (b) lack in management training for many businessmen and/or lack of willingness to delegate part of the management to qualified associates; and (c) funding difficulties, despite the increase and the differentiation of sources of financing in the large market. It is clearly more difficult and relatively more costly for SMEs than for large firms to have access to world technological capital, to avail themselves of the most sophisticated management techniques and business services and to find their proper place in the global economy and even in the EU's single market.

Small and, above all, medium-sized businesses, must, first and foremost, **rely on their own efforts to achieve success** in the single market. In order to succeed they must make the effort to adapt to their new environment by abandoning some of their family-style management habits and/or their production and marketing methods and cooperate with each other in order to overcome some of the handicaps which are attributable to their size, in particular with regard to supply and the distribution of their products over a number of Member States. In so doing SMEs must, however, **be assisted** by their trade organisations, their governments and the European institutions. That is why a common enterprise policy is needed to provide a framework for and coordinate the efforts deployed by the Member States to assist their SMEs, without distorting competition by favouring certain undertakings or the production of certain goods within the meaning of Article 87 of the EC Treaty [see section 15.5.1.].

17.2. Enterprise policy

The **European Charter for Small Enterprises,** endorsed by the Feira European Council (19 and 20 June 2000), states that the situation of small business in the European Union can be improved by action to stimulate entrepreneurship, to evaluate existing measures, and when necessary, to make them small-business-friendly, and to ensure that policy-makers take due consideration of small business needs. In this Charter the Member States pledged themselves to: strengthen the spirit of innovation and entrepreneurship; achieve a regulatory, fiscal and administrative framework conducive to entrepreneurial activity; ensure access to markets on the basis of the least burdensome requirements that are consistent with overriding public policy objectives; facilitate access to the best research and technology; improve access to finance and performance continuously, so that the EU will offer the best environment for small business in the world; listen to the voice of small business; and promote top-class small business support. The Charter commits the Member States to work along ten lines of action in order to achieve these objectives. The Charter has political rather than legal value, since it cannot be called upon in courts, but SME policy has become a key element of the renewed Lisbon partnership for growth and jobs and SMEs' concerns have been placed at the heart of Community and national policies by applying the "think small first" principle.

The **Entrepreneurship and Innovation Programme,** which is part of the "Competitiveness and Innovation Programme (2007-13)" [see section 17.1.3], specifically targets SMEs, from hi-tech "gazelles" (companies with high growth potential) to the traditional micro-businesses and family firms which make up a large majority of European enterprises[1]. It facilitates SMEs' access to finance and investment during their start-up and growth phase and brings together activities to promote entrepreneurship, industrial competitiveness and innovation. Part of the **"Action Programme for reducing administrative burdens in the European Union"**, which is meant to identify and suppress unnecessary administrative burdens, is the website http://ec.europa.eu/enterprise/admin-burdens-reduction/[2].

17.2.1. The legal environment of European business

The objectives pursued by the Community through its efforts at harmonisation in the area of **company law and accounting** are: the mobility of firms in order to allow them to benefit from the advantages of a unified market; the equality of the conditions of competition between firms established in different Member States; the promotion of commercial links between the Member States; the stimulation of cooperation between firms across borders and the facilitation of cross-border mergers and acquisitions. Appropriate Community measures are needed to provide for legal structures which facilitate cross-border establishment and investment, and to smooth discrepancies between national systems of company law which discourage or penalise these activities.

---

[1] Decision 1639/2006, OJ L 310, 09.11.2006.
[2] COM (2007) 23, 24.01.2007.

By virtue of the freedom of establishment laid down by the EC Treaty, undertakings formed in accordance with the law of one Member State do not encounter administrative problems in establishing themselves in the territory of another Member State [see section 6.5.1.]. The same cannot be said of **the real economic and legal problems of establishment**, which cannot disappear by the sole virtue of the provisions of the Treaty. Indeed, as the common market develops, companies see a constant increase in the transnational dimension of their relations with third parties, be they shareholders, employees, creditors or others. That development multiplies the danger of conflict between the various national measures, which guarantee the rights of those people. It is accordingly understandable that the Community's first effort of structural policy concerned **the coordination of the company law** of the Member States by means of Council Directives, based on Article 54.3.g. of the EEC Treaty (Art.44.2.g TEC), which provides for coordination of the safeguards which are required by Member States of Community companies for the protection of the interests of members and others. On the basis of this article, a number of directives harmonised several aspects of the company law of the Member States.

The first Directive lays down a **system of disclosure** applicable to all companies in order to coordinate safeguards for the protection of the interests of members and others and to facilitate public access to information on companies[1]. It obliges Member States to keep a register of companies, which anyone may examine, and to ensure that certain information is published in a national gazette. Also to protect the interests of members and others, the second Directive provides for the harmonisation of the standards and procedures relating to the **formation of public limited liability companies** and the maintenance and alteration of their capital. An amendment to this Directive aims to ensure that this type of company does not make use of a subsidiary for the acquisition of its own shares[2]. The third Directive introduces into the legal systems of all member countries the procedure for **the merger of public limited liability companies**, with the transfer of the assets and liabilities of the acquired company to the acquiring company[3]. The sixth Directive regulates **the hiving-off process**, i.e. the division of an existing company into several entities[4]. The eleventh Directive imposes measures in respect of disclosure in the Member State in which a branch is situated, in order to ensure the protection of persons who through **the intermediary of the branch** deal with a company who is governed by the law of another Member State[5]. The twelfth Directive deals with **single-member private companies** and allows, under certain conditions, the limitation of liability of the individual entrepreneur throughout

---

[1] Directive 68/151, OJ L 65, 14.03.1968 and Directive 2003/58, OJ L 221, 04.09.2003.
[2] Directive 77/91, OJ L 26, 30.01.1977 and Directive 2006/68, OJ L 264, 25.09.2006.
[3] Directive 78/855, OJ L 295, 20.10.1978 and Directive 2007/63, OJ L 300, 17.11.2007.
[4] Directive 82/891, OJ L 378, 31.12.1982 and Directive 2007/63, OJ L 300, 17.11.2007.
[5] Directive 89/666, OJ L 395, 30.12.1989 and OJ L 1, 03.01.1994.

the Community[1]. A Directive establishes requirements in relation to the exercise of certain **shareholder rights**[2].

More than 31 years after the Commission proposal for the creation of the **European company** (a record in Community legislation), the Council finally adopted the two legislative instruments necessary for its creation, the regulation on the statute for a European company and a directive supplementing this statute with regard to the involvement of employees[3]. These legal provisions, which will enter into force together on 8 October 2004, will make it possible for a company to be set up within the territory of the Community in the form of a public limited-liability company, with the Latin name *Societas Europaea* **(SE)**. An SE is entered in a register in the Member State where its registered office is situated. Every registered SE is publicised in the Official Journal of the European Union. An SE must take the form of a company with share capital of at least EUR 120 000. The rules relating to **employee involvement in the SE** seek to ensure that the creation of an SE does not entail the disappearance or reduction of practices of employee involvement existing within the companies participating in the establishment of an SE [see section 13.5.2.].

The **Statute for the European company** provides enterprises with an optional new instrument, which makes cross-border enterprise management more flexible and less bureaucratic and may help improve the competitiveness of European enterprises. The SE makes it possible to operate Community-wide while being subject to Community legislation directly applicable in all Member States. Several options are available to enterprises from at least two Member States wishing to form an SE: a merger, a holding company, the creation of a subsidiary, or transformation into an SE. The statute allows a public limited-liability company, which has its registered office and head office within the Community, to transform itself into an SE without going into liquidation. An SE may itself set up one or more subsidiaries in the form of SEs. The registered office of an SE may be transferred to another Member State under certain conditions, but without winding up of the SE or creating a new legal person. Subject to the Regulation on the statute of SEs, an SE should be treated in every Member State as if it were a public limited-liability company formed in accordance with the law of the Member State in which it has its registered office.

The statute for a **European cooperative society (SCE)** is modelled on that of the European company, with the changes required by the specific characteristics of cooperative societies[4]. It allows the creation of a new legal entity for the organisation of economic operations in two or more Member States in the form of a cooperative society. It is supplemented by

---

[1]   Directive 89/667, OJ L 395, 30.12.1989 and OJ L 1, 03.01.1994.

[2]   Directive 2007/36, OJ L 184, 14.07.2007.

[3]   Regulation 2157/2001 and directive 2001/86, OJ L 294, 10.11.2001 and Regulation 885/2004, OJ L 168, 01.05.2004.

[4]   Regulation 1435/2003, OJ L 207, 18.08.2003.

a Directive providing arrangements for the involvement of employees in a SCE[1].

The harmonisation of company law and the creation of European companies facilitate the interpenetration of markets and the concentration of companies at European level. But it is also necessary for Community undertakings to be able **to cooperate easily amongst themselves**, which is by no means straightforward. The various forms provided for by national laws for cooperation between domestic undertakings are not adapted to cooperation at common market level, owing specifically to their attachment to a national legal system, which means that cooperation between undertakings from several countries must be subject to the national law governing one of the participating undertakings. Economic operators, however, do not readily accept attachment to a foreign legal system, both for psychological reasons and owing to ignorance of foreign laws. Such legal barriers to international cooperation are particularly important where the parties involved are SMEs.

It was therefore necessary to introduce a legal instrument covered by Community law, which would make adequate cooperation between undertakings from different Member States possible. This is the purpose of the **"European Economic Interest Grouping" (EEIG)**, an instrument for cooperation on a contractual basis created by a Council Regulation in 1985[2]. The EEIG is not an economic entity separate from and independent of its members, behaving autonomously and trying to make profits for itself. It is a hybrid legal instrument offering the flexibility of a contract and some of the advantages of company status, including notably legal capacity. It serves as an economic staging post for the economic activity of its members. It enables them, by virtue of pooled functions, to develop their own activity and thus increase their own profits. Each member of the Grouping remains entirely autonomous both in economic and legal terms. That is a pre-condition for the existence of the European Economic Interest Grouping and distinguishes it from any other form or stage of merger. The Grouping ensures the equality of its members. None of them could give the others or the Grouping itself binding directives. Lastly, the Grouping may not seek profit for itself, may provide services only to its members and must invoice them at the cost price. These services can consist of marketing, the grouped purchase of raw materials or the representation of its members' interests.

17.2.2. The business environment

In the run-up to the completion of the single market the Community has endeavoured in particular to remove any obstacles to cross-border business activity, so as to help companies take advantage of new commer-

---

[1] Directive 2003/72, OJ L 207, 18.08.2003.
[2] Regulation 2137/85, OJ L 199, 31.07.1985 and OJ L 1, 03.01.1994.

cial opportunities on partner countries markets and, in general, to improve the environment in which Union business operates. Nevertheless, because of the complex nature of certain European provisions and **inadequate knowledge of the European legislation** concerned [see section 3.3.], businessmen often regard that legislation as an impediment to the entrepreneurial spirit. The European Union should therefore ensure that the impact of its legislation on enterprises, in particular SMEs, is not in conflict with the common objective of seeing enterprises reach their full development in the single market.

The European institutions try, indeed, to take into account the problems and conditions which are specific to SMEs when drawing up and implementing common policies (regional, social, research, environment, etc.). All proposals presented by the Commission to the Council and the Parliament are accompanied by an **impact assessment describing their likely effects on businesses**, in particular small and medium-sized enterprises, and on job creation. Through the "impact assessment method", the Commission analyses the direct and indirect implications of a proposed measure (e.g. concerning businesses, trade, employment, the environment and health). The results of each assessment are made public[1]. The impact assessment also gives details of the consultations that have taken place with the trade organisations concerned by the proposal[2]. The Community's legislative authorities are thus kept fully informed of the implications of a proposal on business and employment [see section 4.3.].

It is advisable, however, to ensure that Member States do not complicate matters when transposing Community legislation into national law. Therefore, the Council recommended to the Member States to implement programmes of **administrative simplification** covering both new legislative proposals and existing legislation and to examine the impact of all proposed legislation or rules on the administrative burden on enterprises[3]. In a resolution on realising the full potential of SMEs, the Council called on the Member States and the Commission to examine how the business environment for SMEs could be improved by removing the structural impediments resulting from the legal, financial and administrative framework[4]. At the invitation of the Amsterdam European Council, the Commission set up in July 1997 a **Business Environment Simplification Task Force (BEST)**, consisting of independent experts, which has the job of proposing concrete measures to improve the quality of legislation and reduce the constraints on SME development.

In order to improve the European business environment, a directive aims at combating **late payment in commercial transactions** in the public as well as the private sector[5]. This directive obliged the Member States to

[1]   COM (2002) 276, 5 June 2002.
[2]   Resolution, OJ C 331, 16.12.1992, p. 3-4.
[3]   Recommendation, OJ L 141, 02.06.1990, p. 55-56 and resolution, OJ C 331, 16.12.1992, p. 3.
[4]   Resolution, OJ C 18, 17.01.1997, p. 1-5.
[5]   Directive 2000/35, OJ L 200, 08.08.2000.

limit the deadline for payment at thirty days from the invoice date, unless otherwise specified in the contract and it harmonised the interest on late payments at seven percentage points above the European Central Bank rate. It also provided for retention of title by the seller until the time of payment of the purchase price and accelerated recovery procedures for undisputed debts with a maximum 90 days between the lodging of the creditor's action and the time when the writ of execution becomes enforceable.

It is also necessary to improve the quality and flow of information on the internal market and other fields of Community policy directed towards enterprises, in particular SMEs. The **Euro-Info-Centre (EIC) network** is designed to respond to SMEs' requests for information covering in particular the internal market (legal, technical and social aspects of Community trade) and the possibility of benefiting from Community funding. The EICs have three major objectives: to provide information about all single market issues and opportunities of interest to enterprises; to assist and advise businesses on participation in European activities; and to act as a channel of communication between enterprises and the Commission.

17.2.3. Business funding

Many European SMEs experience financing problems. They have less equity capital than their counterparts in the United States or Japan and they are more dependent than large firms on direct institutional finance (bank overdrafts, short and long-term loans), which is more expensive. The Commission noted that the situation could be improved easily by providing them with effective advice regarding both their management methods and their relations with their financial backers[1]. It also suggested improving coordination and communication between the various European, national, regional and local programmes aimed at strengthening the financial position of SMEs. The risk capital action plan (RCAP), adopted by the Cardiff European Council in June 1998, encourages venture capital investments by the structural funds and other capital markets, particularly in the seed and start-up phases, which have traditionally been the weakest links of the financing cycle in Europe[2].

The **European Investment Bank (EIB)** through its Global Loans and the **European Investment Fund (EIF)** are the financial institutions of the Community in support of SMEs [see section 7.3.3.]. The EIF's activity is centred upon two areas, venture capital and guarantees. EIF's venture capital instruments consist of equity investments in venture capital funds and business incubators that support SMEs, particularly those that are early stage and technology-oriented. EIF's guarantee instruments consist of providing guarantees to financial institutions that cover credits to SMEs. Both instruments implemented by the EIF for SMEs are complementary to the

---

[1] COM (93) 528.

[2] COM (2001) 605, 25 October 2001 and COM (2002) 563, 16 October 2002.

Global Loans provided by the European Investment Bank to financial intermediaries in support of SME financing. EIF's instruments are implemented in the context of the multiannual programme for enterprise and entrepreneurship (2001-05) [see section 17.2.].

SMEs are particularly interested in the possibility of Community funding under the common regional policy. The Regulation on the **European
Regional Development Fund**[1] provides for a series of measures to support
local development initiatives and the activities of SMEs [see sections
12.3.1. and 12.3.3.]. It supports notably:

- productive investment which contributes to creating and safeguarding
  sustainable jobs, primarily through direct aid to investment primarily
  in small and medium-sized enterprises (SMEs);
- measures which support regional and local development, including
  support for and services to enterprises, in particular SMEs;
- aid to R&TD, notably in SMEs, and to technology transfer,
  improvement of links between SMEs, support for the provision of
  business and technology services to groups of SMEs and fostering of
  entrepreneurship and innovation funding for SMEs through financial
  engineering instruments;
- aid and services to SMEs to adopt and effectively use information and
  communication technologies (ICTs) or to exploit new ideas;
- aid to SMEs to promote sustainable production patterns through the
  introduction of cost-effective environmental management systems and
  the adoption and use of pollution-prevention technologies;
- tourism, including promotion of natural assets as potential for the
  development of sustainable tourism.

The Business and Innovation Centres (BICs), set up by the Commission and public and private regional partners are designed to promote business creation and expansion by providing a comprehensive programme of
services (training, finance, marketing, technology transfer, etc.) to SMEs
which are developing innovative technology-based projects [see section
12.2.3.][2].

17.2.4. Cooperation between businesses

The opening up of markets as a result of economic integration in the
Community is bringing with it faster structural change and greater competitive pressures on businesses. In many situations, cooperation or partnership between small businesses in different regions or countries of the
Community can **help to meet the challenge of the wider market** and to
compete with larger ones, especially if the arrangements concerned are
based on complementarity resulting in mutual benefits. Moreover, cooperation can foster the modernisation and diversification of SMEs. There are
different forms of cooperation, e.g. joint ventures, syndicates, agreements

---

[1]   Regulation 1083, 2006, OJ L 210, 31.07.2006.
[2]   Special report No 5/93, OJ C 13, 17.01.1994, p. 1-11.

covering non-financial links (the granting/purchasing of licences, the transfer of know-how, marketing, etc.) or the acquisition of holdings. It may be formal, i.e. based on a contract, e.g. via a European economic interest grouping [see section 17.2.1.], or informal. Before taking part in any form of cooperation, firms must of course consider whether that cooperation is legal, since cooperation agreements sometimes give rise to problems in connection with the provisions of the Treaties concerning competition [see section 15.3.]. Such cases are, however, rare. As stated in the chapter on competition, the Commission is in favour of cooperation between SMEs and agreements of minor importance [see section 15.3.1.][1].

While cooperation between Community firms is regarded as desirable and is generally authorised, it still has to overcome problems of a technical and psychological nature. SMEs investing in other Member States prefer to create subsidiaries rather than joint ventures, or to enter into looser cooperation agreements without the obligation to create a new legal entity. The **Business to Europe (B2Europe)** initiative of the Commission is a means of strengthening the links between the various Community networks and providing businesses with a range of services which answer their needs, including cooperation between them in various countries of the Union.

17.3. Sectoral policy

Sectoral industrial policy is largely linked with commercial policy. The **commercial policy measures** that have the greatest consequences for industrial sectors are manipulations of the customs tariff, anti-dumping measures, trade agreements and various export incentives. By virtue of customs union, most of those measures are already in the hands of the European institutions [see sections 23.3. and 23.5.]. Other sectoral policy measures are the **incentives used by governments** to modernise and guide national industries, such as grants to certain research bodies, to documentation centres and centres for the dissemination of knowledge, to productivity centres and to vocational training centres. Some such measures are already centralised at European level. The others **require Community coordination**, inasmuch as they may disturb conditions of competition on the single market.

Also still in the hands of governments are the most direct and best-known sectoral measures, i.e. **aids of every kind**: grants, loans, interest rate subsidies, etc. Aids for the improvement of certain sectors and aids to "infant industries" are characteristic examples of sectoral measures. The main grounds for them are employment promotion, regional development or even national prestige where important undertakings, regarded as "flagship companies", are involved [see section 15.5.3.]. Since sectoral aids and the conditions under which they are granted vary greatly from one EU

---

[1] OJ C 231, 12.09.1986, p. 2-4.

State to another, they may affect trade between Member States and distort or threaten to distort competition. Therefore, the objective of industrial policy should be to create the conditions that allow better control of such aids. Moreover, the effectiveness of the Community's policies to promote greater cohesion could be improved by a progressive reduction in aid intensities in the central and more prosperous regions.

It is for that reason that Articles 87 and 88 of the EC Treaty provide for Commission control of the aids which States grant directly or indirectly to certain undertakings or the production of certain goods. Such **aids must be notified to the Commission**, which has the power to authorise them or prohibit them in accordance with the criteria laid down in the Treaty or under secondary legislation [see section 15.5.]. Thus, although the most powerful instrument of sectoral industrial policy is still in the hands of the governments, the Commission may prevent such national aids from distorting conditions of competition or running counter to the objectives of the EU's industrial policy.

The best way to prevent individual sectoral measures by governments that are harmful to the common interest and at the same time to restructure European industry is the **common sectoral policy**. This has developed in the most vulnerable sectors at international level, either because the markets are saturated (steel, shipbuilding, textiles) or because they are not yet well developed at European level (aeronautics, information industries, telecommunications). We shall examine Community policy in those sectors below.

17.3.1. Steel industry

The **Community rules for State aid** to the steel industry provide a framework for reasonable intervention without distortion of the competition conditions in the common steel market[1].Nowadays, the **steel market is closely monitored**, on the one hand, by way of information that steel companies must communicate to the Commission concerning their investments[2] and, on the other, in the framework of the Strategic Research Agenda (SRA) of the European Steel Technology Platform (ESTEP). The "external aspect of steel", entails a few tariff quotas and the prior statistical monitoring of imports from Central and Eastern European countries to ensure that they do not harm the Community steel industry [see section 23.5.]. Since the ECSC Treaty expired in July 2002, the regulatory framework on steel products came into line with the European policy applied to the whole of manufacturing[3].

In a resolution adopted on 14 March 2002, the European Parliament deplored the **American protectionist decision** to impose extraordinary tar-

---

[1] Decision 2496/96, OJ L 338, 28.12.1996.
[2] Decision 3010/91, OJ L 286, 16.10.1991.
[3] COM (1999) 453, 5 October 1999.

iffs of up to 30% on steel imports in violation of World Trade Organisation (WTO) rules and backed the Commission in its decision to take a case immediately to the WTO and take all necessary measures to safeguard the EU steel industry in line with WTO rules [see section 25.7.]. As the severe American restrictions threatened to deflect a large amount of steel products away from the United States and on to the Community market and thus to cause serious harm to Community producers, the Commission introduced prior Community surveillance to all the products concerned by the above US measures[1]. Following the conditions laid down by the WTO safeguard agreement, the Commission imposed indeed provisional safeguard measures against imports of seven American steel products[2]. The Council established additional customs duties on imports of certain products originating in the USA and applied concession suspensions not only to steel products but also to other products with a view to offsetting the effects of the safeguard measures taken by the United States in March 2002[3]. The WTO ruled the American safeguard action incompatible with its rules and the US government repealed it on 5 December 2003. The EU countermeasures were lifted as of the following day[4].

17.3.2. Shipbuilding

The multilateral negotiations launched in 1989 under the auspices of the OECD between the main producing countries (European Union, Japan, South Korea, Norway, United States), which together account for more than 70% of world shipyard output, led to an agreement in July 1994 on the elimination of all obstacles to normal conditions of competition in the sector as from 1 January 1998. Consequently, a Council Regulation on aid to shipbuilding implements the provisions of the **OECD Agreement on respecting normal competitive conditions** in the commercial shipbuilding and repair industry, although this agreement, pending its ratification by the USA, has still not entered into force [see section 23.5.][5]. Hence, problems continue. Community inquiries reveal that South Korea is distorting competition on the world market in shipbuilding through dumping practices. The Council has authorised the Commission to initiate WTO proceedings against South Korea in May 2001 and introduced a temporary defence mechanism for the Community shipbuilding industry to counter unfair trade practices by the Republic of Korea in world shipbuilding markets until the conclusion of dispute settlement proceedings at the WTO[6] [see

---

[1] Regulation 76/2002, OJ L 16, 18.01.2002 and Regulation 1337/2002, OJ L 195, 24.07.2002.
[2] Regulation 560/2002, OJ L 85, 28.03.2002 and Regulation 2142/2003, OJ L 321, 06.12.2003.
[3] Regulation 1031/2002, OJ L 157, 15.06.2002 repealed by Regulation 2168/2003, OJ L 326, 13.12.2003.
[4] Regulation 2168/2003, OJ L 326, 13.12.2003.
[5] Regulation 3094/95, OJ L 332, 30.12.1995 and Regulation 2600/97, OJ L 351, 23.12.1997.
[6] Regulation 1177/2002, OJ L 172, 02.07.2002 last amended by Regulation 502/2004, OJ L 81, 19.03.2004.

section 23.5.]. In any case, the Community Regulation prohibits contract-related aid (operating aid) as from 31 December 2000 [see section 15.5.3.][1]. The Commission concentrates its efforts on defending European industry against unfair trade practices by shipbuilders in third countries and on improving its competitiveness by encouraging research and supporting closer industrial cooperation[2].

17.3.3. Textiles and clothing industries

On the internal level, the Commission **monitors national aids** and applies a policy aiming at preventing such aids from giving rise to distortions of competition within the Community or having the effect of transferring labour problems and structural difficulties from one country to another[3] [see section 15.5.3].

The **external aspect** of the common textiles policy aims at organising international trade in textiles in order to provide breathing space for the Community industry without frustrating the industrialisation hopes of the developing countries. Such organisation was sought within the framework of the General Agreement on Tariffs and Trade (GATT) through the arrangement on international trade in textiles, commonly known as the "Multifibre Arrangement" (MFA). However, the **agreement on textiles and clothing**, concluded within the framework of the Uruguay Round aims at the progressive liberalisation of textile and clothing products within the World Trade Organisation [see section 23.5.]. In this context, the Commission proposes to strengthen the protection of intellectual property rights and measures to tackle fraud and counterfeiting in the fields of the internal market and commercial policy [see section 23.2.2.], to promote the harmonisation of customs duties under the WTO's Doha Development Agenda, and to remove non-tariff barriers to trade in order to boost access to markets[4].

17.3.4. Aeronautical and aerospace industries

In a communication entitled " Europe and space: Turning to a new chapter", which was adopted in agreement with the **European Space Agency (ESA)**, the Commission defined the objectives of a Community strategy for space: strengthening the foundation for space activities so that Europe preserves independent and affordable access to space; enhancing scientific knowledge; and exploiting the benefits of space-based tools for markets and society[5]. This strategy aims to establish the right political and

---

[1]   Regulation 1540/98, OJ L 202, 18.07.1998.
[2]   COM (97) 470 and COM (1999) 474.
[3]   Communication from the Commission OJ C 70, 19.03.2002.
[4]   COM (2003) 649, 29 October 2003.
[5]   COM(2000) 597, 27 September 2000.

regulatory conditions for space activities, to catalyse joint R & D efforts and to bring together all the players around common political objectives in projects of Europe-wide interest.

A Framework Agreement between the European Community and the European Space Agency aims at the coherent and progressive development of an **overall European Space Policy**[1]. In particular, this policy seeks to: link demand for services and applications using space systems in support of the Community policies with the supply of space systems and infrastructure necessary to meet that demand; and secure Europe's independent and cost-effective access to space and the development of other fields of strategic interest necessary for the independent use and application of space technologies in Europe.

A key element of the European space policy is the development of a **global navigation satellite systems (GNSS)** at European level offering a service meeting the needs of civilian users[2] [see also section 18.2.6]. The European satellite radio-navigation policy is presently implemented through the Galileo and EGNOS programmes. **Galileo** is the first European space programme to be financed and managed by the European Union in association with the European Space Agency. It is expected to contribute to the development of numerous applications in areas that are associated, directly or indirectly, with Community policies, such as transport (positioning and measurement of the speed of moving bodies), insurance, motorway tolls and law enforcement (surveillance of suspects, measures to combat crime). **EGNOS** is a tripartite programme between the European Community, the ESA and Eurocontrol aiming at augmenting the American GPS and Russian GLONASS signals for reliability purposes on a broad geographical area. It is independent from and complementary to Galileo.

In view of the fact that substantial private sector participation is a fundamental element for the success of Galileo in its deployment and operational phases and the need to ensure that essential public interests related to the strategic nature of the European satellite radio-navigation programmes are adequately defended and represented, a Regulation set up a Community agency, called the **European GNSS Supervisory Authority**, to manage the public interests relating to the European GNSS programs[3]. This is the licensing authority vis-à-vis the private concession holder responsible for implementing and managing the Galileo deployment and operating phases. It is entrusted with the responsibility of managing the agreement with the economic operator charged with operating EGNOS. It should coordinate Member States' actions in respect of the frequencies necessary to ensure the operation of the system and hold the right to use all these frequencies wherever the system is located. The Council, acting unanimously, may give the necessary **instructions to the European GNSS Supervisory Authority** and the concession holder of the system in

---

[1] Framework Agreement and Decision 2004/578, OJ L 261, 06.08.2004.
[2] COM (1998) 29, 21 January 1998.
[3] Regulation 1321/2004, OJ L 246, 20.07.2004 and R. 1942/2006, OJ L 367, 22.12.2006.

the event of a threat to the security of the European Union or of a Member State arising from the operation or use of the system, or in the event of a threat to the operation of the system, in particular as a result of an international crisis[1].

17.3.5. Information industries

The economic and social development of nations depends, increasingly, on the use of information and knowledge, with the aid of the enormous progress made in **information and communications technologies (ICTs)**. Harnessing the opportunities opened up by the digitalisation of information in all its forms, these technologies are transforming dramatically many aspects of economic and social life, such as working methods and relations, the organisation of businesses, the focus of education and training, and the way people communicate with each other. The **information society** is the dawning of a multimedia world (sound - text - image) representing a radical change comparable with the first industrial revolution. It goes hand in hand with the "non-physical" economy, based on the creation, circulation and exploitation of knowledge. The conditions of access to information, to the networks carrying it (broad band networks called "information highways") and to the services facilitating the use of the data (including high value-added services, databases, etc.) are vital components of the Union's future competitiveness. ICTs are also the vehicle for a growing number of societal services such as health, education, transport, entertainment and culture. Since they are amongst the highest growth activities, and they are also highly skilled activities, these technologies have a high potential for employment creation.

The problem is that, although there is a strong demand for information in Europe, the suppliers could be anywhere in the world since the delivery is instantaneous. Indeed, **the United States and Japan have a head-start** as suppliers of information, because they each have a single system of standards and a single national language. Europe, thus, has to overcome large handicaps in this field. It should be noted that under the Information Technology Agreement, concluded in March 1997 under the auspices of the World Trade Organisation, tariffs on information technology products of countries accounting for 92% of world trade were eliminated as of January 2000, a fact which intensifies further investment competition[2] [see section 23.4.].

A multiannual Community programme aims to stimulate the development and use of **European digital content (*e*Contentplus programme)** on the global networks and to promote linguistic diversity in the information society[3]. It proposes action over a period of four years (2005-2008)

---

[1] Joint Action 2004/552, OJ L 246, 20.07.2004.
[2] Decision 97/359, OJ L 155, 12.06.1997 and Regulation 2216/97, OJ L 305, 08.11.1997.
[3] Decision 456/2005, OJ L 160, 23.06.2005.

aimed at making digital content in Europe more accessible, usable and exploitable, by facilitating the creation and diffusion of information, in areas of public interest, at Community level. The online availability of Europe's rich and diverse cultural heritage will make it usable for all citizens for their studies, work or leisure and will give innovators, artists and entrepreneurs the raw material that they need for new creative efforts. The seventh Framework Research and Development programme seeks, inter alia, to boost hardware and software technologies and applications at the heart of the creation of the information society and to harness the knowledge-based society for the benefit of the citizens[1] [see section 18.2.6]. In the context of the Lisbon strategy [see section 13.3.2.], a European Information Society for growth and employment initiative (**i2010**) promotes an open and competitive digital economy[2].

By guaranteeing recognition of **electronic signatures** throughout the European Union, a Directive on a common framework for electronic signatures was the first step towards establishing a European framework for development of electronic commerce [see also section 6.6.1.][3]. This framework is provided by the so-called **electronic commerce directive**[4]. This Directive harmonises certain legal aspects, such as determining the place of establishment of service providers, the transparency obligations for providers and for commercial communications, the validity of electronic contracts and the transparency of the contractual process, the responsibility of Internet intermediaries, on-line dispute settlements and the role of national governments. It clarifies the application of key internal market principles (freedom of establishment of service providers and free movement of services) to information society services, affirming the country-of-origin principle by which service providers must comply with the legislation of the Member State of origin.

The action plan "*e*Europe**"** of the Commission, which was endorsed by the Feira European Council (19-20 June 2000), seeks to remove the key barriers to the uptake of the Internet in Europe, aiming in particular at: providing a cheaper, faster and more secure Internet; investing in skills; giving the public access to the Internet and encouraging its use[5]. A new programme called "Safer Internet plus" (2005-2008) aims to promote safer use of the Internet and new online technologies, in particular for children, and to combat illegal and unwanted content[6].

In the framework of the "*e*Europe" action plan, a regulation lays down the conditions for designating the registry responsible for the organisation, administration and management of the **Internet ".eu" country code top-level domain (ccTLD)** and establishes the general policy frame-

---

[1] Decision 2002/834, OJ L 294, 29.10.2002.
[2] COM/2005/229, 01.06.2005.
[3] Directive 1999/93, OJ L 13, 19.01.2000.
[4] Directive 2000/31, OJ L 178, 17.07.2000.
[5] Decision 2256/2003, OJ L 336, 23.12.2003 and Decision 2113/2005, OJ L 344, 27.12.2005.
[6] Decision 854/2005, OJ L 149, 11.06.2005.

work within which the Registry functions[1]. Domain names and the related addresses are essential elements of the global interoperability of the World Wide Web (www), since they allow users to locate computers and websites on the Web. TLDs are also an integral part of every Internet e-mail address. The ".eu" TLD should promote the use of, and access to, the Internet networks and the virtual market (electronic commerce) place based on the Internet, by providing a complementary registration domain to existing country code TLDs and should in consequence increase choice and competition. The establishment of the ".eu" TLD registry, which is the entity charged with the organisation, administration and management of the ".eu" TLD, should contribute to the promotion of the European Union image on the global information networks and bring an added value to the Internet naming system in addition to the national ccTLDs. A Commission Regulation laid down public policy rules concerning the implementation and functions of the .eu top level domain and the principles governing registration[2].

17.3.6. Telecommunications

Digital technologies, developed by the information industry, allow the integrated transmission of sound, text and image in one communication system and project Europe into the information era, radically changing the modes of consumption, production and organisation of work. On the other hand, advanced **communications technologies and services** are a vital link between industry, the services sector and market as well as between peripheral areas and economic centres. These services are therefore crucial for consolidation of the internal market, for Europe's industrial competitiveness and for economic and social cohesion in Europe. They can also contribute to social progress and to cultural development. The common policy on telecommunications is developing since the 1990s around four axes: the creation of a single market of telecommunications equipment and services; the liberalisation of telecommunication services; the technological development of the sector with the assistance of Community research; and the balanced development of the regions of the Union by means of trans-European telecommunication networks.

The **regulatory framework for telecommunications terminal equipment** follows and affects the new approach to standardisation, testing and certification that we have examined in the chapter on the common market [see section 6.2.3.]. A Council Decision and a Resolution on standardisation in the field of information technology and telecommunications pursue the objective of creating a **European market in telecommunications equipment**[3]. Such standardisation of information technology and telecommunications prevents distortions of competition and ensures ex-

---

[1] Regulation 733/2002, OJ L 113, 30.04.2002.
[2] Regulation 874/2004, OJ L 162, 30.04.2004 and Regulation 1654/2005, OJ L 266, 11.10.2005.
[3] Decision 87/95, OJ L 36, 07.02.1987 and resolution, OJ C 117, 11.05.1989, p. 1.

changes of information, the convergence of industrial strategies and, ultimately, the creation and exploitation of a vast European information technologies and telecommunications (IT&T) market. European standards are used in many Community policies, above all those connected with the single market, *e*Europe [see section 17.3.5.], general product safety and environment protection. A Directive establishes a single market for radio equipment and telecommunications terminal equipment and prescribes the mutual recognition of their conformity based on the principle of the manufacturer's declaration[1].

European institutions and standardisation bodies endeavour to ensure the coherence with the regulatory framework applicable to information equipment in order to meet the challenge of interoperability. The Commission collates requirements with regard to standardisation on the part of users and establishes the priorities of a work programme, which is entrusted to the CEN (European Committee for Standardisation) and the CENELEC (European Committee for Electrotechnical Standardisation), with the participation of the CEPT (European Conference of Postal and Telecommunications Administrations). In addition to the European Telecommunication Standards Institute (ETSI), private organisations representing industry and consumers are involved in the pre-standardisation process and in the effective application of harmonised standards in the Member States, including for public contracts.

The creation of a single market in telecommunications services necessitated the progressive **liberalisation of telecommunications markets**, which were traditionally State monopolies. Telecommunications services had to be liberated and conditions of free provision of services by the networks had to be defined. To pursue this objective, which represents the second axis of the Community policy in this sector, the Commission adopted a Directive based on Article 90 of the EEC Treaty (Art. 86 TEC), requiring Member States to introduce arrangements ensuring free competition on the Community market in telecommunications terminal equipment (modems, telex terminals, receive-only satellite stations, etc.)[2] [see section 15.5.4.]. This Directive gives users the possibility of connecting terminal equipment, which they are able to procure freely without being obliged to apply to a single national telecommunications authority. Through its successive amendments, the Directive entitles suppliers of telecommunications services to use capacity on cable television networks for all telecommunications services, primarily data communications, "closed" corporate networks and multimedia services. It also requires Member States to abolish the exclusive and special rights remaining in telecommunications, the restrictions on the installations used for mobile networks and the obstacles to direct interconnection between such networks. Last but not least, the

---

[1] Directive 1999/5, OJ L 91, 07.04.1999.
[2] Directive 2002/77, OJ L 249, 17.09.2002.

Commission Directive provided for the complete liberalisation of voice telephony and telecommunications infrastructures on 1 January 1998.

Liberalisation of telecommunications services cleared the way for the **creation of the single telecommunications market**. This is the aim of the "telecoms package", adopted in 2002. The package constitutes a single regulatory framework covering the converging telecommunications, media and information technology sectors. It is made up of a framework Directive and four specific Directives concerning access, authorisation, universal service and protection of privacy. National regulatory authorities must contribute to the development of the internal market by cooperating with each other and with the Commission to ensure the consistent application, in all Member States, of the provisions of those Directives.

Directive 2002/21 established a harmonised **regulatory framework** for electronic communications networks and services across the EU[1]. This Directive covers all electronic communications networks and services within its scope, namely: transmission systems and, where applicable, switching or routing equipment and other resources which permit the conveyance of signals by wire, by radio, by optical or by other electromagnetic means, including satellite networks, fixed (including Internet) and mobile terrestrial networks, electricity cable systems, networks used for radio and television broadcasting, and cable television networks. It sets out a number of principles and objectives for regulators to follow, as well as a series of tasks in respect of management of scarce resources such as radio spectra and numbering.

The aim of **the "access directive"** is to lay down a framework of rules that are technologically neutral, but which may be applied to specific product or service markets in particular geographical areas, to address identified market problems between access and interconnection suppliers[2]. It covers, in particular, access to fixed and mobile networks, as well as access to digital broadcasting networks, including access to conditional systems and other associated facilities such as electronic programme guides and application programme interfaces. The directive provides legal certainty for market players by establishing clear criteria on their rights and obligations and for regulatory intervention. It indicates clearly what obligations concerning access and interconnection can be imposed in which circumstances, whilst at the same time allowing for sufficient flexibility to allow regulatory authorities to deal effectively with new market problems that hinder effective competition.

The aim of the **"authorisation directive"** is to implement an internal market in electronic communications networks and services through the harmonisation and simplification of authorisation rules and conditions in order to facilitate their provision throughout the Community[3]. According to the Directive, "general authorisation" means a legal framework established

[1] Directive 2002/21, OJ L 108, 24.04.2002.
[2] Directive 2002/19, OJ L 108, 24.04.2002.
[3] Directive 2002/20, OJ L 108, 24.04.2002.

by the Member State ensuring rights for the provision of electronic communications networks or services and laying down sector specific obligations that may apply to all or to specific types of electronic communications networks and services. The general authorisation system should apply to all such services and networks regardless of their technological characteristics and should limit administrative barriers to entry into the market to a minimum.

The aim of the "**universal users**" directive is to ensure universal service provision for public telephony services in an environment of greater overall competitiveness, with provisions for financing the cost of providing a universal service in the most competitively neutral manner and for ensuring a maximum of information transparency[1]. It also establishes the rights of users and consumers of electronic communications services, with corresponding obligations on undertakings. It aims to ensure the interoperability of digital consumer television equipment and the provision of certain mandatory services, such as leased lines. Finally, it lays down harmonised rules for the imposition of "must carry" obligations by Member States on network operators.

The **protection of privacy** directive translates the principles set out in Directive 95/46 [see section 9.2.] into specific rules for the telecommunications sector[2]. In fact, publicly available electronic communications services over the Internet open new possibilities for users but also new risks for their personal data and privacy, in particular with regard to the increasing capacity for automated storage and processing of data relating to subscribers and users. Therefore, the Directive on privacy and electronic communications harmonises the provisions of the Member States required to ensure an equivalent level of protection of fundamental rights and freedoms, and in particular the right to privacy, with respect to the processing of personal data in the electronic communication sector and to ensure the free movement of such data and of electronic communication equipment and services in the Community. However, another Directive harmonises Member States' provisions concerning the obligations of the providers of publicly available electronic communications services or of public communications networks with respect to the **retention of certain data** which are generated or processed by them, in order to ensure that the data are available for the purpose of the investigation, detection and prosecution of serious crime, as defined by each Member State in its national law[3].

The Regulation on **roaming on public mobile telephone networks** introduces a common approach to ensuring that users of public mobile telephone networks when travelling within the Community do not pay excessive prices for Community-wide roaming services[4].

---

[1] Directive 2002/22, OJ L 108, 24.04.2002.

[2] Directive 2002/58, OJ L 201, 31.07.2002 and Directive 2006/24, OJ L 105, 13.04.2006.

[3] Directive 2006/24, OJ L 105, 13.04.2006

[4] Regulation 717/2007, OJ L 171, 29.06.2007.

17.4. Appraisal and outlook

Generally speaking, the EU intervenes in the industrial sector only to create an environment conducive either to the expansion of undertakings throughout the internal market (enterprise policy) or to the activity of certain industrial branches which present common problems, to enable them to cope better with increased competition at European and world levels (sectoral policy).

Although disparities remain between Member States' industrial structures, we are nonetheless in the presence of a parallel development of the various parameters in the secondary sector. **The completion of the single market**, in 1992, provided a fillip to the restructuring of European industry. The removal of the physical, technical and fiscal barriers to intra-Community trade gave rise to strengthened trade and therefore bolstered competition within the Community. Thanks to the removal of border controls and technical trade barriers, businesses can now supply a single product for the whole of the single market. Manufacturers no longer have to produce for fifteen separate markets. This situation increases competition enormously in the internal market. Greater competition results in the alignment of national suppliers' prices on those of foreign suppliers, who penetrate markets that had previously been protected. In the short term that squeezes the profit margins of undertakings which had been protected and/or enjoyed monopoly situations. Some of them are even forced to leave the market.

The elimination of the least competitive producers enables, however, those firms which survive to **expand on the market**. They are thus able to: better exploit and maximise their production capabilities, or even increase them (economies of scale); strengthen their domestic efficiency by restructuring and concentrating their activities and by improving allocation of human, technical and financial resources; improve their organisation and the quality and variety of their products, and innovate both as regards the production process and the products offered. This competitive pressure has already caused the wind of change to sweep the Union's industrial fabric.

Entrepreneurship and a well-functioning internal market are vital to growth and job creation. The regulatory environment should encourage entrepreneurial activity and make it as simple as possible to set up new businesses. Creation of a favourable business environment implies the **elimination of superfluous and niggling regulation**. The internal market must be made as unbureaucratic as possible. Both the Union and the Member States must therefore facilitate market entry and exit for businesses of all sizes, improve access to finance and know-how, improve regulation and reduce administrative burdens. The regulatory framework should be clear and predictable, while regulation should be limited to what is strictly necessary for achieving clearly-defined objectives. The common enterprise policy aims at this end, but it is not certain that the national policies follow suit. Member States should transpose faster Community legislation on the internal market and related subjects into national legal and administrative practice. On the other hand, company law and corporate governance practices need to be modernised in the wake of corporate governance scandals and in view of the growing trend for European companies to operate cross-border in the internal market, the continued integration of European capital markets, the rapid development of new information and communication technology and the enlargement of the EU to new Member States, most of which have not a long-established business culture.

Bibliography on industrial policy

- AYDIN Umut. "Promoting industries in the global economy: subsidies in OECD countries, 1989 to 1995", in *Journal of European Public Policy*, v. 14, n. 1, 2007, p. 115-131.
- DANNREUTHER Charles. "A zeal for a zeal?: SME policy and the political economy of the EU", in *Comparative European politics*, v. 5, n. 4, December 2007, p. 377-399.
- ELIASSEN Kjell, FROM Johan (eds.). *The privatisation of European telecommunications*. Aldershot: Ashgate, 2007.
- EUROPEAN COMMISSION. *Small and medium-sized enterprises: key for delivering more growth and jobs - A mid-term review of Modern SME policy*. Luxembourg: EUR-OP*, 2007.
    - *EU industrial structure 2007: challenges and opportunities*. Luxembourg: EUR-OP*, 2007.
- KRONENBERG Jakub. *Ecological economics and industrial ecology: a case study of the integrated product policy of the European Union*. London: Routledge, 2007.
- MAYER Thierry, OTTAVIANO Gianmarco. *The happy few: the internationalisation of European firms*. Brussels: Bruegel, 2007.
- ORGANISATION FOR ECONOMIC COOPERATION AND DEVELOPMENT. Business and the environment: policy incentives and corporate responses. Paris: OECD, 2007.
- SERGI Bruno (et al. eds.). *Industries and markets in Central and Eastern Europe* Aldershot: Ashgate, 2007.
- TROUILLE Jean-Marc. "Re-inventing industrial policy in the EU: a Franco-German approach", in *West European Politics*, v. 30, n. 3, May 2007, p. 502-523.

The publications of the Office for Official Publications of the European Communities (EUR-OP) exist generally in all official languages of the EU.

DISCUSSION TOPICS

1. How does the common industrial policy interact with other common policies?
2. How can the common market affect the restructuring and competitiveness of European industry?
3. What are the advantages and disadvantages of SMEs in the large single market?
4. How does the EU support the advent of the information society?
5. Outline the common strategy in the telecommunications sector.

Chapter 18

RESEARCH AND TECHNOLOGY POLICY

Diagram of the chapter

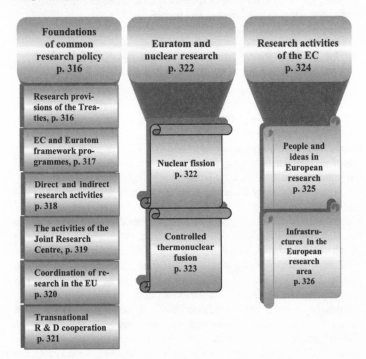

Economic and social progress and the competitiveness of European States at world level come about through efficacious scientific research and technological development. European research, however, is handicapped in the international arena as a result of the **fragmentation of research policies pursued in the Member States** of the Union and the resulting dispersion of efforts. The common research and development policy is therefore essential for European integration. The aim of that policy is to coordinate national research policies and to define and implement research programmes of European interest, i.e. programmes geared to the large market, of interest to all Member States and necessitating technical and human resources which Member States cannot put together individually. At world level, only the coordinated research of the Member States can allow the European Union to play a leading role in vast international programmes such as the one on global change.

Common research policy is closely **linked to the common industrial policy**, which we have just examined, and to the common energy policy, which we shall examine in the next chapter. Indeed, research is essential for the definition of industrial strategy, especially in high-technology sectors, by offering a common reference basis for technology forecasting and development. It is also necessary for the promotion of **reliable energy sources**, which reduce Europe's dependence on imported oil, particularly for the development of thermonuclear fusion.

18.1. The need for a common research policy

Although the challenges facing the European nations change over time, and with them the scientific and technical research priorities, certain immutable reasons militate in favour of a **common approach to research problems**. The common research policy must define the economic, social, political and even military objectives of research, draw up an inventory of the resources available in terms of human resources, laboratories and funds, set the priorities and apportion the work among the laboratories of the Member States. In this way it can be ensured that no important sector is neglected, that duplication is avoided and that the Union's human, material and financial resources are put to best use. Labour distribution can also ensure that Europe's smallest countries, which would otherwise be excluded owing to a lack of resources, can participate in research and development.

Europe is experiencing a massive transformation of its economy and society. Traditional industrial structures are undergoing rapid change. The problems that are observed in the structures of the traditional European industries, like textiles, shipbuilding and steel, are notably the results of the movement of production to countries with low wage levels induced by the globalisation of markets and economies [see sections 17.1. and 17.3.]. The transfer of European traditional industrial production to other countries can be offset only by new industries with a high level of technology.

Europe's industrial competitiveness, its jobs, its quality of life and the sustainability of growth depend on it being at the leading edge of the development and utilisation of **information society technologies**. Advances in information processing and communications are opening up exciting new possibilities [see sections 17.3.5. and 17.3.6.]. However, the increasing diversity and complexity of systems is also presenting new challenges for their development and use. Continuous efforts are required, in research, technological development and demonstration to tackle the universal issues such as access, ease of use, cost-effectiveness and interoperability and standardisation. They should also address the social changes brought about by the introduction and more widespread use of new information and communications technologies.

Innovation requires constant and organised interdependence between the upstream phases linked to technology, and the downstream phases linked to the market, such as the development of new business concepts, new means of distribution, marketing or design. This means that, in order to have **industrially efficient innovation**, the needs of the market should be taken into account, particularly by modernising the approaches and practices of marketing, and synergies in research and technological development (R & D) should be facilitated by trans-European cooperation. These considerations are particularly pertinent for SMEs, which are innovative by their nature, but which do not exploit efficiently their R & D potential because of their structural and financial handicaps [see section 17.1.4.].

Society is making increasing demands for better living conditions, better safety, and better use of scarce resources including secure and economic energy supplies and services. Availability of a sufficient and economic energy supply must be assured to promote industrial competitiveness and to maintain the quality of life for Europe's citizens [see section 19.1.]. At the same time, the environmental impact of energy production and use must be reduced. Indeed, rising population and per-capita use of resources, globalisation of economic markets and natural variability in earth systems are causing or exacerbating major environmental problems [see section 16.3.]. R & D in the fields of **energy, environment and sustainable development** is essential for the social well-being of Europe's citizens and the implementation of policies formulated at Community level or deriving from international environmental commitments - in particular, the implementation of the Kyoto Protocol [see section 16.3.4.].

The promotion of scientific and technological excellence is an essential prerequisite for Europe to succeed in the competitive environment of international research and scientific development. Access to **major research infrastructures**, in particular, is indispensable for researchers working at the forefront of science. The ability of European research teams to remain competitive with teams elsewhere in the world depends on their being supported by state-of-the-art infrastructures. As most of the major research infrastructures in Europe are operated by national authorities, principally for the benefit of their national researchers, access to these infrastructures is often restricted largely or even entirely to national research teams. The result is that researchers do not always have the opportunity to access the infrastructures most appropriate for their work. European R & D should therefore make available major research infrastructures in all Member States to competent multinational teams of researchers.

18.2. The foundations of the common research policy

Contrary to the Euratom treaty, concerning nuclear research, the EEC treaty did not give the Community Institutions any powers to finance or even coordinate Member States' research in the other sectors of the economy. This is now changed with the new provisions of the **EC Treaty** [see section 2.2.], the new concepts of the framework programme [see section 18.2.2.] and of direct and indirect actions [see section 18.2.3.] and, above all, the new missions of the Joint Research Centre [see section 18.2.4.]. These are the main subjects of this part of the chapter.

18.2.1. Research provisions of the Community Treaties

Article 163 of the **EC Treaty** (Maastricht version) **consecrated research and technological development as a policy of the Community**, stating that the latter shall aim to strengthen the scientific and technological foundations of Community industry and boost its competitiveness at international level and shall promote the research activities deemed necessary by virtue of other Community policies. To this end, it adds, the Community shall in all the Member States encourage undertakings, including small and medium-sized enterprises, research centres and universities, in their research and technological development activities of high quality. Through its support for their cooperation efforts, the Community aims to enable undertakings to draw full benefit from the potential of the internal market, in particular through the opening up of national public contracts, the definition of common standards and the removal of legal and fiscal obstacles to cooperation.

The Community and the Member States coordinate their research and technological development activities (Art. 165 TEC). In pursuit of the objectives detailed in Article 163 (TEC), the Community conducts the following **priority activities**, complementing the R & D activities in the Member States (Art. 164 TEC):

(a) implementation of research, technological development and demonstration programmes, by promoting cooperation with and between undertakings, research centres and universities;
(b) promotion of cooperation in the field of Community research, technological development and demonstration with third countries and international organisations;
(c) dissemination and optimisation of the results of activities in Community research, technological development and demonstration; and
(d) stimulation of the training and mobility of researchers in the Community.

The **Euratom Treaty** gives an even more important place to the development of (nuclear) research, devoting its first Chapter to it [see section 2.1.]. Article 4 makes the Commission responsible for promoting and facilitating nuclear research in the Member States and for complementing it by carrying out a European Atomic Energy Community research and training programme. For purposes of coordinating and complementing research undertaken in Member States, the Commission calls upon Member States, persons or undertakings to communicate to it their programmes relating to the research which it specifies in the request. By its opinions the Commission should discourage unnecessary duplication and should direct research towards sectors which are insufficiently explored, of which it should publish at regular intervals a list. (Art. 5 EAEC).

18.2.2. EC and Euratom R & D framework programmes

A two-phased **decision-making process** exists for Community research programmes. Every five years, the Council acting under the co-decision procedure with the European Parliament [see section 4.3.] adopts a multiannual research and technological development **framework programme**. By laying down the objectives, the priorities and the overall funds for Community action and their apportionment in broad terms, the framework-programme constitutes a "guide" for decisions on specific programmes to be taken during the five years covered. In addition, the framework programme has the desired characteristic of making visible, for scientific establishments, undertakings or Member States, the medium-term research possibilities afforded by the Community. By providing clear indications of the specific measures that the Community intends to undertake, it allows the various European research operators better to programme their efforts and Community research to take its proper place in the concert of European cooperation actions. The framework programmes are implemented through **specific programmes** [see sections 18.3. and 18.4.] adopted by the Council, acting by a qualified majority, after consultation of the European Parliament and the Economic and Social Committee (Art. 166 TEC).

The **Seventh Framework Programme** of the European Community for research, technological development and demonstration activities (2007-2013), with a budget of EUR 50.5 billion, is organised in four specific programmes, corresponding to four major objectives of European research policy[1]. Under the **"Cooperation" programme**, support is given to the whole range of research activities carried out in transnational cooperation, from collaborative projects and networks to the coordination of research programmes[2]. International cooperation between the European Union and third countries is an integral part of this programme, which disposes of a budget of EUR 32.4 billion [see section 18.2.6]. The **"Ideas"** **programme**, with a budget of EUR 7.5 billion, provides that the European Research Council may support investigator-driven frontier research carried out by individual teams competing at European level, in all scientific and technological fields, including engineering, socioeconomic sciences and the humanities[3]. [see section 18.4.1] The **"People" programme**, with a budget of EUR 4.75 billion, reinforces the activities supporting training and career development of researchers, referred to as 'Marie Curie' actions,

---

[1]   Decision 1982/2006, OJ L 412, 30.12.2006.

[2]   Decision 2006/971, OJ L 400, 30.12.2006.

[3]   Decision 2006/972, OJ L 400, 30.12. 2006.

with a better focus on the key aspects of skills and career development and strengthened links with national systems[1] [see section 18.4.1]. Under the **"Capacities" programme**, disposing of a budget of EUR 4.1 billion, key aspects of European research and innovation capacities are supported, notably, research infrastructures, research for the benefit of small and medium-sized enterprises, and regional research-driven clusters[2] [see section 18.4.2]. Through these four specific programmes, the aim is to allow for the creation of European poles of excellence.

The **Euratom framework programme** disposes of a budget of EUR 2.75 billion and is organised in two specific programmes[3]. The first programme consists of **fusion energy research**, aimed at developing the technology for a safe, sustainable, environmentally responsible and economically viable energy source. This programme, with a budget of EUR 1947 million, also includes **nuclear fission** and radiation protection and aims to promote the safe use and exploitation of nuclear fission and other uses of radiation in industry and medicine[4]. The second programme, with a budget of EUR 517 million, covers the **activities of the Joint Research Centre** in the field of nuclear energy[5]. Its objective is to provide scientific and technical support to the policy-making process.

18.2.3. Direct and indirect research activities

Community research policy does not necessarily mean the "communitarisation" of all programmes or the joint financing of all research and technological development (R & D) activities in the Member States. In application of the subsidiarity principle [see section 3.2.], a distinction has to be made between various forms of research. With regard to **fundamental research and basic research**, which necessitate very large investment and highly specialised researchers and whose results can be expected only in the fairly distant future, it is in the interest of the EU countries to pool their efforts in **direct actions** financed entirely by the European Union and bringing together researchers of several nationalities.

For the **development of leading-edge technology** (nuclear, information, aeronautical and aerospace technologies, etc), on the other hand, **indirect actions** promoting the coordination of research carried out in the Member States is better suited to ensure industrial success, the transnational restructuring of undertakings, the opening up of public contracts, and even the grouping of purchases by public electricity, telecommunications and transport services. European R & D is therefore distinguished into direct actions and indirect actions.

---

[1] Decision 2006/973, OJ L 400, 30.12. 2006.
[2] Decision 2006/974, OJ L 400, 30.12. 2006.
[3] Decision 2006/970, OJ L 460, 30.12.2006.
[4] Decision 2006/976, OJ L 400, 30.12. 2006.
[5] Decision 2006/977, OJ L 400, 30.12. 2006.

Direct actions are research activities proper pursued by the Commission in the research establishments of the **Joint Research Centre (JRC)** and paid for entirely from the Community budget [see sections 3.4. and 18.2.4.]. The European dimension of its research is one of the fundamental strengths of the JRC. Its activities are characterised by a multidisciplinary approach based on the broad span of its capabilities. This multidisciplinarity is reflected in the diversity of subjects covered by its institutes and helps it meet Europe's scientific challenges as they rise. The JRC, however, must carry out its activities in close cooperation with the scientific community and enterprises in Europe.

The second form taken by Community R & D, **indirect research**, which absorbs more than 80% of the financial resources of Community R & D, is conducted in research centres, universities or undertakings, with financial assistance from the Commission and on conditions laid down by the rules governing participation in the various programmes, notably the participation of at least two partners from different Member States. Community financial assistance covers, as a general rule, 50% of the total cost of research work.

The Commission, with the assistance of the Advisory Committees on Management and Coordination (ACMC)[1], prepares the research programmes on indirect action which are adopted by the Council. The Commission then publishes in the Official Journal of the European Union calls for tenders for researchers from the Member States, specifying the research objectives written into the European programme. The tenders are appraised by the Commission and the Committees on the basis of criteria determined in advance and aimed at ensuring the best possible results. There are no national quotas for research assistance. The rules for the participation of undertakings (companies, firms), research centres and universities in actions under the seventh framework programmes of the European Community[2] and of the European Atomic Energy Community[3] identify the procedures for issuing calls for proposals, for submission, evaluation, selection of proposals and award of grants.

18.2.4. The activities of the Joint Research Centre

The JRC is an autonomous Directorate General of the Commission and acts as **a science and technology and reference centre** for the Union. It has at its disposal a unique combination of facilities and skills which transcend national borders. Close to the policy formulation process while remaining independent of vested commercial or national interests, it serves the common interest of the Member States. The largest establishments of the JRC are situated at Ispra (Italy), while specialised institutes are located

---

[1] Decision 84/338, OJ L 177, 04.07.1984.

[2] Regulation 1906/2006, OJ L 391, 30.12.2006.

[3] Regulation 1908/2006, OJ L 400, 30.12.2006.

at Geel (Belgium), Petten (Netherlands), Karlsruhe (Germany) and Seville (Spain)[1].

The mission of JRC is to provide customer-driven scientific and technical support for the conception, development, implementation and monitoring of Community policies. In implementing its mission, the JRC endeavours to coordinate R & D activities carried out in the Member States. Its work depends on intensive networking with public and private institutions in the Member States through, for example, research networks, joint projects or staff exchanges[2]. This is important because the JRC's mission is complementary to the indirect action part of the framework programme. While the indirect actions are the main mechanism for developing and testing new ideas, the JRC's role is to help apply them in the service of the policy-maker. Thus, JRC operates in areas where its unique pan-European identity provides an added value to Community R & D. The JRC carries out two research programmes: one for the European Community and the other for the European Atomic Energy Community (Euratom).

18.2.5. Coordination of research in the European Union

Several scientific bodies assist the Commission in its tasks of conceiving and managing the Community policy of research and technological development. The **Scientific and Technical Research Committee (CREST)** is an advisory body which assists the Commission and the Council in the R & D field by identifying strategic priorities, establishing mutual consistency between national and Community policies, and helping to formulate Community strategy with regard to international cooperation[3]. The European Group on Ethics in Science and New Technologies (EGE) advises the Commission on ethical subjects related to research and new technologies[4].

In fact, in order to implement Article 165 of the EC Treaty, which requires the Community and the Member States to coordinate their research and technological development activities, the coordination of national and Community policies is based as far as possible on **European scientific networks**, notably CREST. These scientific networks help knit the scientific fabric of the European Union. In the framework of the Lisbon strategy and following the model of the Massachusetts Institute of Technology (MIT), the **European Institute of Innovation and Technology (EIT)** aims to contribute to the development of innovation capacity in the EU, by involving higher education, research and innovation activities at the highest standards[5] [see section 13.4.1].

---

[1] Decision 96/282, OJ L 107, 30.04.1996.
[2] COM/2001/215.
[3] Resolution, OJ C 264, 11.10.1995, p. 4-5.
[4] Directive 98/44, OJ L 213, 30.07.1998.
[5] Regulation 294/2008, OJ L 97, 09.04.2008.

18.2.6. Transnational R & D cooperation

Under the specific **programme "Cooperation"** for Community activities in the area of research and technological development support is provided to transnational cooperation in different forms across the Union and beyond[1]. This programme is open to the participation of countries having concluded agreements to this effect and of entities from third countries and of international organisations for scientific cooperation. It supports the whole range of research actions carried out in trans-national cooperation in the following thematic areas:
(a) Health;
(b) Food, Agriculture and Fisheries, Biotechnology;
(c) Information and communication technologies;
(d) Nano-sciences, Nano-technologies, Materials and new Production Technologies;
(e) Energy;
(f) Environment (including climate change);
(g) Transport (including aeronautics);
(h) Socio-economic Sciences and Humanities;
(i) Space;
(j) Security.

In particular, the specific research programmes of the Community are open to the participation of EFTA countries (Switzerland, Norway, Iceland, Liechtenstein) and of the countries of Central and Eastern Europe and the new independent States of the former Soviet Union [see sections 25.1, 25.2 and 25.4.]. **Scientific and technical cooperation (Cost)** covers the countries of the EFTA and of Central and Eastern Europe. It is managed by a Committee of Senior Officials and by specialised committees. It takes the form of memoranda of understanding by the Cost States on the execution of Cost activities in the most varied fields, such as medicine, transport or materials. The Council concludes coordination agreements between the Community and the Cost countries relating to concerted actions forming part of the Community research programme[2].

The Seventh Framework Programme provides for a Community contribution for the establishment of long term public-private partnerships in the form of Joint Technology Initiatives (JTIs) which could be implemented through **Joint Undertakings** within the meaning of Article 171 of the EC Treaty. Several Joint Undertakings were set up as public-private partnerships aimed at mobilising and pooling Community, national and private efforts, notably: the Joint Technology Initiative on Innovative Medicines[3]; the European Technology Platform on Nanoelectronics (**ENIAC** Technology Platform)[4]; and the **Clean Sky** Joint Undertaking[5].

[1]   Decision 2006/971, OJ L 400, 30.12.2006.
[2]   See e.g., Decision 88/615, OJ L 344, 13.12.1988 and Decision 92/181, OJ L 85, 31.03.1992.
[3]   Regulation 73/2008, OJ L 30, 04.02.2008.
[4]   Regulation 72/2008, OJ L 30, 04.02.2008.
[5]   Regulation 71/2007, OJ L 30.04.02.2008.

The Joint European Torus (JET) fusion research project, established in 1978 [see section 18.3.2.][1], has met its design objectives including demonstrating the release of significant amounts of fusion energy in a controlled manner. The Community has played a key role in the development of a **next step international fusion project (ITER)**, which, in 2001, produced a detailed engineering design for a research facility aimed at demonstrating the feasibility of fusion as an energy source. The seven parties to the ITER negotiations (Euratom, People's Republic of China, India, Japan, Republic of Korea, Russia and the United States) have concluded the Agreement on the Establishment of the **ITER International Fusion Energy Organisation**, with headquarters in St Paul-lez-Durance, Bouches-du-Rhône, France, which aims to demonstrate the scientific and technological feasibility of fusion energy for peaceful purposes[2].

18.3. Euratom and nuclear research

Nuclear energy has the potential to provide Europe with a secure and sustainable electricity supply at a competitive price. Efforts to develop the safety and security of nuclear energy systems can strengthen the Community's industrial competitiveness, through exploiting the European technological advance and enhance the public acceptance of nuclear energy. Minimising radiation exposure from all sources, including medical exposures and natural radiation, may improve the quality of life and may help in addressing health and environmental problems. The Commission has specific Treaty obligations in nuclear energy and it has always relied on the JRC to provide a technical support that can keep up with technological developments and face new challenges. However, both the focus of the Euratom Treaty and the missions of the JRC have undergone radical changes since the early days, the most important being that Euratom research is now mainly concerned with nuclear fission safety, on the one hand, and with thermonuclear fusion, on the other.

The Seventh Framework **Programme of the European Atomic Energy Community** (Euratom) for nuclear research and training activities (2007 to 2011) comprises Community research, technological development, international cooperation, dissemination of technical information and exploitation activities as well as training, set out in two specific programmes[3]:
(a) fusion energy research, with the objective of developing the technology for a safe, sustainable, environmentally responsible and economically viable energy source [see section 18.3.2];
(b) nuclear fission and radiation protection, with the objective of enhancing in particular the safety performance, resource efficiency and cost-

---

[1]   Decision 2002/837, OJ L 294, 29.10.2002.
[2]   Agreement, OJ L 358, 16.12.2006, p. 60.
[3]   Decision 2006/970, OJ L 460, 30.12.2006.

effectiveness of nuclear fission and other uses of radiation in industry and medicine [see section 18.3.1].

18.3.1. Nuclear fission

Nuclear fission energy supplies 35% of electricity in the Community. It constitutes an element in combating climate change and reducing Europe's dependence on imported energy. Some of the power plants of the current generation will continue to be operated for at least 20 years. For these reasons, the second thematic area of the specific programme implementing the Seventh Framework Programme of the European Atomic Energy Community (Euratom) for nuclear research and training activities (2007 to 2011) is **research on nuclear fission and radiation protection**[1]. This part of the programme aims to enhance in particular the safety performance, resource efficiency and cost-effectiveness of nuclear fission and uses of radiation in industry and medicine. The specific objectives of this part are:

(i) the management of radioactive waste aiming to establish a sound scientific and technical basis for demonstrating the technologies and safety of disposal of spent fuel and long-lived radioactive wastes in geological formations;

(ii) reactor systems research aiming to ensure the continued safe operation of all relevant types of existing installations and to explore the potential of more advanced technology;

(iii) radiation protection research aiming at the safe use of radiation in medicine and industry;

(iv) research infrastructures, ranging in size from very large and expensive plant and laboratory networks to much smaller facilities such as databases, numerical simulation tools and tissue banks

(v) Human resources, mobility and training aiming to guarantee the availability of suitably qualified researchers, engineers and technicians.

18.3.2. Controlled thermonuclear fusion

Euratom is also actively engaged in the development of controlled thermonuclear fusion, which is safe for the environment. **Thermonuclear fusion** is a process which occurs on the surface of the Sun, releasing prodigious energy. In the Sun's core at temperatures of 10 to 15 million degrees Celsius, hydrogen is converted to helium providing enough energy to sustain life on Earth. Man has conceived of reproducing on earth, in a controlled fashion, what happens on the Sun. In fact, by heating gases such as deuterium (abundant in all forms of water) and lithium (plentiful in the Earth's crust) or tritium (manufactured from lithium) to a temperature of 100 million degrees Celsius, their electrons are completely separated from the atomic nuclei, atoms fuse and a fantastic release of energy within that

---

[1] Decision 2006/976, OJ L 400, 30.12.2006.

"plasma" ensues. However, one must first obtain that extraordinary temperature, which is feasible, and the plasma must thereafter be confined within a magnetic space known as a "torus", which is more difficult. The objective of Community research is to produce and contain plasma, which has the properties required for the reactors of the future, in a magnetic field known as "tokamak". For reasons bound up with the complexity of fundamental knowledge in physics and the technological problems to be resolved, the developments needed for the possible application of fusion for energy production take the form of a process in several steps, each of which has an impact on the next one.

Thermonuclear fusion research is pursued since 1978 at Culham (United Kingdom) in an establishment which does not form part of the Joint Research Centre, but which is administered by a **joint undertaking**, the Joint European Torus (JET), within the meaning of Article 45 of the Euratom Treaty [see section 19.2.3.][1] and whose Board of Governors is made up of representatives of the participating States and of the Commission, with a budget 80% of which is financed by the Community[2]. The first thematic area of the specific programme implementing the Seventh Framework Programme of the European Atomic Energy Community (Euratom) for nuclear research and training activities (2007 to 2011) is **fusion energy research**[3]. The construction of ITER at Cadarache in France, and of "Broader Approach" projects to accelerate the development of fusion energy take place within the framework of international cooperation. An international ITER agreement established the ITER International Fusion Energy Organisation. The European Domestic Agency for ITER provides the means for Euratom to discharge its international obligations under the ITER Agreement [see section 18.2.6]. European industry, including SMEs, play a central role in the construction of ITER and participates fully in the development of fusion power technologies for DEMO (a "demonstration" fusion power station) and future fusion power plants.

18.4. Research activities of the European Community

The Seventh Framework Programme is carried out to pursue the general objectives described in Article 163 of the Treaty, to strengthen industrial competitiveness and to meet the research needs of other Community policies, thereby contributing to the creation of a knowledge-based society, building on a European Research Area and complementing activities at a national and regional level[4]. In line with the Lisbon strategy [see section

---

[1] Decisions 78/471 and 78/472, OJ L 151, 07.06.1978 and Decision 98/585, OJ L 282, 20.10.1998.
[2] Decision 96/305, OJ L 117, 14.05.1996.
[3] Decision 2006/976, OJ L 400, 30.12.2006.
[4] Decision 1982/2006, OJ L 412, 30.12.2006.

13.3.2], the overriding aim of the Seventh Framework Programme is to contribute to the Union becoming the world's leading research area. Therefore, the Framework Programme is strongly focused on promoting and investing in world-class state-of-the-art research, based primarily upon the principle of excellence in research. In order to realise these objectives, the Seventh Framework Programme promotes four types of activities: transnational cooperation on policy-defined themes (the "Cooperation" programme) [see section 18.2.6], investigator-driven research based on the initiative of the research community (the "Ideas" programme) [see section 18.4.1], support for individual researchers (the "People" programme) [see section 18.4.1], and support for research capacities (the "Capacities" programme) [see section 18.4.2].

In order to help the **development of SMEs in the knowledge society** and the use of the economic potential of SMEs in an enlarged and better integrated European Union, SMEs, including small and micro enterprises as well as craft enterprises, are encouraged to participate in all areas and all instruments of the seventh framework programme, ensuring complementarity with the Competitiveness and Innovation Framework Programme [see section 17.1.3]. The **"Regions of Knowledge"** initiative brings together regional actors involved in research, such as universities, research centres, industry, public authorities (regional councils or regional development agencies). This initiative comprises measures aiming at improving research networking and access to sources of research funding in close relationship with Community regional policy (structural funds) [see section 12.3], the Competitiveness and Innovation Framework Programme [see section 17.1.3] and the training programmes [see section 13.4.2].

18.4.1. People and ideas in European research

The **"People" programme** aims to increase the human R & D potential in Europe in terms of both quality and quantity, including by recognising the 'profession' of researcher with a view to maintaining the excellence in basic research and the organic development of technological research, and encouraging European researchers' mobility from, to and throughout Europe[1]. The mobility of researchers is the key not only to the career development of researchers but also to the sharing and transfer of knowledge between countries and sectors and to ensuring that innovative frontier research in various disciplines benefits from dedicated and competent researchers, as well as increased financial resources. The "People" programme aspires to stimulate individuals to enter into the profession of researcher, to encourage European researchers to stay in Europe, to attract to Europe researchers from the entire world and, in general, make Europe more attractive to the best researchers. Building on the positive experiences with the **"Marie Curie Actions"** under previous Framework Pro-

---

[1]   Decision 2006/973, OJ L 400, 30.12. 2006.

grammes, the "People" programme encourages individuals to enter the profession of researcher; structure the research training offer and options; encourage European researchers to stay in, or return to, Europe; encourage intersectoral mobility, and attract researchers from all over the world to Europe.

The **"Ideas" programme** aims to enhance the dynamism, creativity and excellence of European research at the frontier of knowledge[1]. This is done by supporting "investigator-driven" research projects carried out across all fields by individual teams in competition at the European level. Projects are funded on the basis of proposals presented by researchers both from the private and public sectors on subjects of their choice and evaluated on the sole criterion of excellence as judged by peer review. The Community activities in frontier research are implemented by a **European Research Council (ERC)**, consisting of an independent scientific council and a dedicated implementation structure. The Scientific Council establishes, inter alia, an overall scientific strategy, has full authority over decisions on the type of research to be funded and acts as guarantor of the quality of the activity from the scientific perspective.

18.4.2. Infrastructures in the European research area

The term **"research infrastructures"** in the context of the Community Framework Programme for research and technological development refers to facilities, resources or services that are needed by the research community to conduct research in all scientific and technological fields. Research infrastructures play an increasing role in the advancement of knowledge and technology and their exploitation. They are expensive, need a broad range of expertise to be developed, and should be used and exploited by a large community of scientist and customer industries on a European scale. The development of a European approach with regard to research infrastructures and the carrying out of activities in this area at Union level can make a significant contribution to boosting the potential of European research and its exploitation and contributing to the development of the European Research Area. In this respect, the **European Strategy Forum on Research Infrastructures (ESFRI)** plays a key role in identifying needs and a roadmap for European research infrastructures.

The **"Capacities" programme** of the Seventh Framework Programme aims at optimising the use and development of the best research infrastructures existing in Europe, and helping to create in all fields of science and technology new research infrastructures of pan-European interest needed by the European scientific community to remain at the forefront of the advancement of research, and able to help industry to strengthen its base of knowledge and its technological know-how[2]. To pursue this objective the

---

[1]   Decision 2006/972, OJ L 400, 30.12. 2006.
[2]   Decision 2006/974, OJ L 400, 30.12. 2006.

Capacities programme supports key aspects of European research and innovation capacities such as: research infrastructures; regional research driven clusters; the development of a full research potential in the Community's convergence and outermost regions; research for the benefit of small and medium-sized enterprises (SMEs); "Science in Society" issues; the coherent development of policies; and horizontal activities of international cooperation.

18.5. Appraisal and outlook

Competitiveness and sustainability are the keys to the long-term future of the Union's economy. They entail the capacity of citizens, enterprises, regions, nations and the Community to generate and use the knowledge, science and technology of tomorrow, in high-quality goods, processes and services, and in new and more efficient organisational forms. By strengthening the innovative capacity of the European industrial system and by fostering the creation of businesses and services built on emerging technologies and new market opportunities, European R & D helps EU countries face the major challenges of society, in particular employment. In parallel, research into sustainable mobility and environmentally and consumer friendly processes, products and services may contribute to improving quality of life and working conditions.

The promotion of sustainable development in Europe is not possible unless economic objectives relating to technological development, competitiveness and growth are reconciled with **societal goals** such as quality of life, employment, security, health and a high quality environment. Moreover, improving the quality of life of European citizens and disconnecting economic growth from environmental degradation contributes to European competitiveness and employment.

The individual and collective expertise of the Community's researchers is a considerable asset. However, scientific research takes place in **a strongly competitive worldwide environment** and compared with its main competitors, the Community has a relative shortage of researchers, a high fragmentation and duplication of research effort and a certain isolation of research teams, particularly in the peripheral and less-favoured regions of the Community.

Europe has established **a leading R & D role in many areas,** notably nuclear safety, thermonuclear fusion, telecommunications' technologies and biochemistry. In other areas improvements are needed for the future benefit of society, as well as the business and industrial sectors. It is essential to increase knowledge in order to achieve the Lisbon objective. Investing in knowledge is the best way for the European Union to foster economic growth and create more and better jobs, while at the same time ensuring social progress and environmental sustainability.

Bibliography on research policy

- AKRICH Madeleine, MILLER Riel (eds.). *The Future of Key Actors in the European Research Area: synthesis paper*. European Commission. Luxembourg: EUR-OP*, 2007.
- CARSA. *Remuneration of researchers in the public and private sector*. European Commission. Luxembourg: EUR-OP*, 2007.
- CIESLIKIEWICZ Witold (ed.). Proceedings of the EurOCEAN 2004: European conference on marine science & ocean technology. European Commission. Luxembourg: EUR-OP*, 2007.
- EUROPEAN COMMISSION. *Improving knowledge transfer between research institutions and industry across Europe*. Luxembourg: EUR-OP, 2007.

  - *People programme: Marie Curie Actions: 7th Framework programme for research and technological development*. Luxembourg: EUR-OP, 2007.
- HOUGHTON James (ed.). *Ethics, research & globalisation: Europe and its partners building capacity in research ethics*. European Commission. Luxembourg: EUR-OP*, 2007.
- MULDUR Ugur. *A new deal for an effective European research policy : the design and impacts of the 7th Framework Programme*. Dordrecht: Springer, 2006.
- ORGANISATION FOR ECONOMIC COOPERATION AND DEVELOPMENT. *Government R&D funding and company behaviour: measuring behavioural additionality*. Paris: OECD, 2006.
- RUBIN DE CERVIN Almoro, ZULEGER Volker. *Large R&D projects: Commission practice under the R&D framework from 1996 to 2006*. Berlin: Lexxion Verlag - NP NewLaw Publishers, 2006.
- TAPLIN Ruth (ed.). *Innovation and business partnering in Japan, Europe and the United States*. London: Routledge, 2006.

DISCUSSION TOPICS

1. Does the common research policy weaken or strengthen national research efforts?
2. What are the main types of Community RTD?
3. What is the role of the Common Research Centre?
4. Outline the activities of Euratom's nuclear research.
5. Outline the objectives of the specific research programmes of the European Community.

Chapter 19

ENERGY POLICY

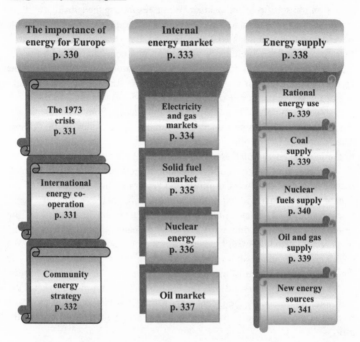
Successive oil shocks, their impact on the economic and monetary system at international and EEC level and Community efforts to reduce its dependence on imported oil are the closely interrelated problems which topped the economic agenda in the 1970s. The Community was ill prepared to cope with these problems, for when the founding Treaties were signed in the 1950s, it was almost self-sufficient in energy and hoped that a new source - atomic energy - would soon take over from coal, the traditional source. Time proved otherwise and it was oil which made a spectacular entry onto the Community market in the 1960s.

In that **two Community Treaties dealt** uniquely with the energy of the past (coal - ECSC) and the perceived one of the future (nuclear - Euratom), the Commission did not have the legal instruments at its disposal to assume responsibilities in the energy sector (oil - EEC) which had since become the dominant player. The Community perceived the risks of its dependence from imported oil during the October 1973 energy crisis. It was from this point that a common energy policy began to take shape at a snail's pace.

19.1. The importance of energy for Europe

Energy policy is important because **energy is at the core of economic and social activity** in industrialised countries. Energy costs affect not only industries with large energy consumption but also industry as a whole and even the cost of living of citizens, notably because of the impact of energy prices on transport cost and heating. While respecting the subsidiarity principle [see section 3.2.] and the environmental requirements for sustainable development [see sections 16.2. and 16.3.4.], European energy policy aims, therefore, at influencing energy production and consumption with the objective of securing economic growth and safeguarding the wellbeing of the citizens of the Union. It must, on the one hand, ensure the smooth functioning of the single market in energy products and services and, on the other, guarantee the supply of relatively cheap and secure (from the strategic and environmental viewpoints) energy resources to the States of the Union. The common energy policy thus revolves around two axes: the functioning of the internal energy market and the security of energy supplies.

The common energy policy was not forgotten by the "founding fathers", who **devoted two Community Treaties to this sector**: the ECSC Treaty, which deals with coal and Euratom, which covers nuclear energy [see section 2.1.]. They failed, however, to give the institutions of the European Economic Community any clear responsibility for the hydrocarbons sector. Although with hindsight this may be questioned, in the 1950s coal was in abundant supply, was relatively inexpensive and met 65% of the energy requirements of the six founding countries. It was therefore seen as the energy, which would fuel the creation of the common market. Furthermore, impressed by the recent demonstration at Hiroshima of the force of atomic energy, experts were predicting a bright future for its peaceful use.

No clear need for a common or even national oil policy was perceived in **the years when oil was cheap and supply certain**, which was the case throughout the post-war years up to the early 1970s. This golden era was anchored in major oil discoveries by Western oil companies in the Middle East and Africa and in the legal system governing the exploitation of oil reserves. The central principle of this system was the granting of a prospecting and working monopoly over a given area by the producer country to one or several foreign companies (licence). The activity spectrum of these companies covered all of the petroleum industry activities (prospecting, production, transport, refining, storage and distribution) and they enjoyed a strong position enabling them, in the vast majority of exporting countries and in relation to most of the importing countries, to regulate petroleum output and marketing terms.

19.1.1. The 1973 crisis

The first occasion for a showdown between producer countries on the one hand and consumer countries and their oil companies on the other came with **the Kippur war between Israel and the Arab countries** from October 6 to 16, 1973. During this war and in the following months, the Arab countries successfully wielded the weapon represented by their oil resources. They notably placed an embargo, for several months, on exports to countries which were branded "enemies of the Arab cause" - including practically all the countries of Western Europe - while reducing their overall oil output level. They decided to overturn the principle of price setting for crude oil through agreements with the oil companies and hiked up prices on a unilateral basis. Finally, they stepped up their claims to holdings in the companies producing crude oil. Under the combined impact of these measures, oil prices quadrupled in just a few months and uncertainty clouded the quantity and price situation which the world's biggest importer, the European Community, would have to face. A common trade policy for oil could have considerably boosted the negotiating leverage of the EEC Member States, if only it had existed; but even after the bitter lesson of their weakness in the face of a united front of producing countries, the European States were **not ready to shed a bit of their sovereignty** in the oil sector in order to collectively negotiate the terms of their supply.

19.1.2. International energy cooperation

The **European Energy Charter** attempts to put some order in energy supply and demand conditions in Europe. It lays down the principles, the objectives and ways of achieving pan-European cooperation in the field of energy. Signed in the Hague on December 17, 1991 by almost all European countries as well as by the Community, Canada, the United States, and Japan, the Charter is in fact a code of good practice. The implementation of the Charter is provided by the **European Energy Charter Treaty**, signed in Lisbon on 17 December 1994[1]. This Treaty is designed to develop new relations between the main European countries, most of the independent States of the former Soviet Union and Central and Eastern Europe, Canada, the United States and Japan concerning the transit of energy products between east and west, trade, investment and energy cooperation. The European Commission assists the Secretariat of the Conference, which is established in Brussels. The practical implication of the Energy Charter is the diversification of the supplies of European Union countries in oil and natural gas and, hence, their decreasing dependence from Middle Eastern sources.

---

[1] Final Act of the Conference, Annex 1, Annex 3 and Decision 94/998, OJ L 380, 31.12.1994, Amendment to the Treaty and Decision 98/537, OJ L 252, 12.09.1998 and Decision 2001/595, OJ L 209, 02.08.2001.

Russia has signed but not ratified the Energy Charter Treaty and the Partnership and Cooperation Agreement between **the EU and Russia** (signed in 1994 and in force since 1997) has not solved the energy problems between the two parties. Therefore an energy dialogue was deemed necessary to resolve energy questions. Since its launch in 2000, the energy dialogue between the European Union and Russia has resolved a number of difficulties between the two parties. It has contributed to the smooth operation of the internal market, sustainable development with the ratification by the Russian Federation of the Kyoto Protocol, and the security of energy supply. This exchange has also resolved important questions such as the preservation of long-term supply contracts and the abolition of measures which are contrary to Community competition rules. European and Russian companies investing in the energy sector have benefited from this dialogue, which thus helps the creation of a pan-European energy market[1].

On 25 October 2005, the EU and eight partners in south-east Europe (Albania, Bosnia and Herzegovina, Bulgaria, Croatia, Former Yugoslav Republic of Macedonia, Romania, Serbia and Montenegro and UNMIK, on behalf of Kosovo) signed the **Energy Community Treaty** in order to create the legal framework for an integrated energy market[2]. As a result of this treaty, the internal market for energy will be extended into the Balkan peninsula as a whole. This means that the relevant *acquis communautaire* on energy, environment and competition will be implemented there. Market opening, investment guarantees and firm regulatory control of the energy sectors will also be enhanced.

19.1.3. Community energy strategy

European **energy markets** face a number of problems: the growing threats of climate change, slow progress in energy efficiency and the use of renewables, the need for transparency, further integration and interconnection of national energy markets and the need for large investments in energy infrastructure. Moreover, Europe has to deal with major challenges in **energy supply**: the ongoing difficult situation on the oil and gas markets, the increasing import dependency and limited diversification achieved so far, high and volatile energy prices, growing global energy demand, security risks affecting producing and transit countries as well as transport routes.

In a 2006 Green Paper the Commission defines a European energy policy, which should aim at three major objectives: sustainable development, competitiveness and security of supply[3]. It calls for a debate in six major domains: the achievement of an internal energy market; the security of energy supply; a more sustainable, efficient and diverse energy mix; an ac-

---

[1]   COM (2004) 777, 13 December 2004.

[2]   Treaty, OJ L 198, 20.07.2006 and Decision 2005/905, OJ L 329, 16.12.2005.

[3]   COM/2006/105, 08.03.2006.

tion plan on energy efficiency and renewable energy sources; a plan for strategic energy technologies; and a common external energy policy.

19.2. Internal energy market

The **first wing of the common energy policy** aims to establish a genuine internal market for the products and services of the energy sector. Through the removal of barriers, whether of public or private origin, and the establishment of common rules, the opening up of energy markets should ensure the availability of energy on the most economic conditions for the end-users whether these are high energy consuming industries or just private individuals. The energy sector, a source of high value contracts, finds itself in the front-line of general public procurement policy and should benefit from the openness it provides [see section 6.3.]. Fiscal alignment by the convergence of the real rates of excise taxes, pursued by taxation policy, is crucially important for the completion of the internal market for oil products [see section 14.2.3.]. Last but not least, the introduction of competition in those sectors in which public monopolies persist could play a prime role in the integration of the markets and in the competitiveness of the EU economy [see section 15.5.4.].

The establishment of a real internal market for energy also depends on the development of **energy trans-European networks**, which should "irrigate" the whole territory of the European Union with cheap, diversified - from the supply point of view - and environment-friendly energy [see section 6.8.]. This development is particularly important for the less favoured regions, which previously had no access to the big interconnected networks for gas and electricity, this being a cause but also a consequence of their underdevelopment [see section 12.1.1.]. In the meantime, the Regulation on notifying the Commission of investment projects of interest to the Community in the petroleum, natural gas and electricity sectors aims at a certain coordination of trans-European energy investments[1].

In general, the full **application of Community internal market law** - and in particular of provisions relating to the free movement of goods and services, to monopolies, to undertakings (firms, businesses) and to State aids - is the main path to a better integrated energy market. The integration of this market is fundamental for the competitivity of the economy of the EU and for the wellbeing of its citizens. But the energy sector does not fully benefit from this integration because the Member States still use the security of supply and the diversity of their energy situation as excuse for the preservation of their national monopolies and of their different regulatory frameworks.

---

[1] Regulation 736/96, OJ L 102, 25.04.1996.

19.2.1. Electricity and gas markets

The prime objective in the field of the internal energy market is to **liberalise and integrate the electricity and natural gas markets**. The most important challenge here is to apply the competition rules of the Treaty to the monopolies for transmission and distribution of gas and electricity, even though these are entrusted with the operation of services of general economic interest [see sections 6.6.4. and 15.5.4.]. Another issue is the reconciliation of the objectives of the prevention of trade barriers and of energy efficiency by way of the adoption of European standards established by the European Standardisation Bodies (CEN/CENELEC) [see section 6.2.3.]. A final problem is in the monitoring of the markets and the co-operation on interconnected systems between national regulatory authorities in both the gas and electricity sectors.

In the early 1990s, some concrete steps were taken in the direction of the integration of the electricity and gas markets, notably the **transit of electricity** and **of natural gas** through major networks[1]. Contracts on the transit of electricity and natural gas between major networks are negotiated between the entities with responsibility for these networks and the relevant bodies in the Member States. Transit conditions must be non-discriminatory and impartial as regards all the parties involved, must not contain unfair clauses or unjustified restrictions and must not place in danger either supply security or the quality of the service provided. Should a disagreement arise, parties concerned by transit contracts have the right to take their case to a conciliation body set up and presided by the Commission. A Directive, on the **transparency of gas and electricity prices** charged to industrial end-users, makes it compulsory for gas and electricity distribution concerns to communicate price data twice a year covering all the main categories of gas and electricity consumers[2].

Serious steps towards the **liberalisation of the electricity and gas sectors** were taken in the late 1990s. Community Directives, revised in 2003, set up common rules for the internal market in electricity[3] and gas[4]. They are based on a balanced approach concerning access to the systems, public service obligations and competition rules and on the broad application of the subsidiarity principle [see section 3.2.], in order to take account of the different national electricity and gas systems, thus facilitating their incorporation into national law.

A Regulation set up fair rules for **cross-border exchanges in electricity**, thus enhancing competition within the internal electricity market, tak-

---

[1] Directive 2003/55, OJ L 176, 15.07.2003.
[2] Directive 90/377, OJ L 185, 17.07.1990 and Directive 93/87, OJ L 277, 10.11.1993.
[3] Directive 2003/54, OJ L 176, 15.07.2003 last amended by Decision 2006/859, OJ L 332, 30.11.2006.
[4] Directive 2003/55, OJ L 176, 15.07.2003.

ing into account the specificities of national and regional markets[1]. To this end, it established a compensation mechanism for cross border flows of electricity and set up harmonised principles on cross-border transmission charges and the allocation of available capacities of interconnections between national transmission systems.

Directive 2005/89 establishes measures aimed at safeguarding **security of electricity supply** so as to ensure the proper functioning of the internal market for electricity and to ensure: (a) an adequate level of generation capacity; (b) an adequate balance between supply and demand; and (c) an appropriate level of interconnection between Member States for the development of the internal market[2].

Regulation 1775/2005 aims at setting non-discriminatory rules for **access conditions to natural gas transmission systems** taking into account the specificities of national and regional markets with a view to ensuring the proper functioning of the internal gas market[3]. This objective includes the setting of harmonised principles for tariffs, or the methodologies underlying their calculation, for access to the network, the establishment of third party access services and harmonised principles for capacity allocation and congestion management, the determination of transparency requirements, balancing rules and imbalance charges and facilitating capacity trading.

19.2.2. Solid fuel market

The single market in the coal sector was **regulated, until July 2002, by the European Coal and Steel Community (ECSC) Treaty** [see section 2.1.]. Thanks to this Treaty, import and export taxes, taxes having equivalent effect, and quantitative restrictions on product movement were abolished. The Paris Treaty laid down rules for agreements, company concentrations and dominant positions, and prohibited unfair competitive practices and discriminatory practices, i.e. the application by a seller of dissimilar conditions to comparable transactions and especially on the grounds of the nationality of the buyer. It thus succeeded to ensure that users have equal access to sources of production and to promote the development of international trade. The "acquis communautaire" in the coal sector is now guaranteed by the EC Treaty.

The ECSC has enabled Europe to maintain a leading position in the field of mining technology and clean coal combustion. Considerable spin off effects have also been seen in other industries. Although the ECSC Treaty succeeded in creating a common coal market, it was **not able to prevent coal from being swept aside by oil,** which is a more flexible, easier to handle and a less expensive product. Preservation of coal's suprem-

---

[1] Regulation 1228/2003, OJ L 176, 15.07.2003 last amended by Decision 2006/770, OJ L 312, 11.11.2006.

[2] Directive 2005/89, OJ L 33, 04.02.2006.

[3] Regulation 1775/2005, OJ L 289, 03.11.2005.

acy would have required measures much more drastic and expensive, in the form of a coal policy modelled on the Common Agricultural Policy [see sections 21.1.1 and 21.4.]. Europe of the 1960's, awash with oil supply, was not prepared to pay the price of its energy independence. Thus, investment in the coal industry of the EU continued to fall during the 1990s in the face of international competition and as a result of the gradual shift in Member States' domestic policies.

19.2.3. Nuclear energy market

The economic factors pertaining to the nuclear energy market have also not evolved in the manner predicted at the time of signature of the Euratom Treaty [see section 2.1.]. In the1950's, it was thought that the arrival on the industrial scene of nuclear energy was just around the corner and the drop in energy prices, which caused this event to be postponed, could not have been foreseen. Nuclear energy in fact only attained economic competitiveness after the 1973 crisis and the momentous increase of oil prices. In the period prior to this, the **absence of a genuine nuclear energy market** forced each Member State to create an artificial one through vast government research programmes targeted more at the acquisition of basic knowledge than at the encouragement of industrial projects. This pushed the Member States off the straight and narrow path defined by the EAEC (Euratom) Treaty onto parallel technological roads, such as uranium enrichment systems, and sparked off a serious crisis in Euratom between 1965 and 1972.

Nevertheless, the Euratom Treaty provides for a well-functioning **common nuclear energy market**, characterised by: the abolition of customs duties, charges having equivalent effect and all quantitative restrictions on imports and exports of natural and enriched uranium and other nuclear materials (Art. 93 EAEC); the free movement and free establishment of individuals and companies in the common nuclear energy market (Art. 96 and 97 EAEC); the free movement of capital for the financing of nuclear activities (Art. 99 and 100 EAEC); the free determination of prices as a result of balancing supply and demand within the Supply Agency (Art. 67 EAEC) and the prohibition of discriminatory pricing practices designed to secure a privileged position for certain users (Art. 68 EAEC). Economic operators have to inform the Commission of major investment projects prior to their implementation (Art. 41 EAEC) and thus the Commission can inform governments and economic operators in the Member States of the aims and prospects for nuclear energy production in the Community (Art. 40 EAEC).

One interesting feature of the Euratom Treaty is that it offers special status and certain advantages to **joint undertakings**, which are of primordial importance to the development of the Community's nuclear industry (Art. 45 EAEC). The Council, acting unanimously on a Commission proposal, can grant each joint undertaking all or some of the advantages listed in Annex III to the Euratom Treaty, such as recognition that public interest status applies to the acquisition of immovable property required for the establishment of the joint undertakings or the exemption from all duties and charges when a venture is established (Art. 48 EAEC). In 1978, this status was granted to an undertaking of vital importance for the growth of the Community nuclear industry, namely the joint venture which, as seen in the previous chapter, builds the **Joint European Torus (JET)**, a thermonuclear fusion prototype [see section 18.3.2.][1].

Safety, a major feature of the common nuclear energy market, is perhaps the most important joint achievement in this field. This achievement is, however, of fundamental importance, because it determines the acceptance of the nuclear energy by the public. **Nuclear safety** is moreover approached from various different angles. Chapter VII of the Euratom Treaty provides for "safeguards". The Commission must be informed of the basic technical specifications of any nuclear plant. The Commission also has to approve procedures for the chemical processing of irradiated materials (Art. 78 EAEC). It must check that all ores, source materials and special fissile materials are not diverted from their intended uses as declared by the users (Art. 77 EAEC) and that the latter respect international safeguards and non-proliferation arrangements laid down by an Euratom Regulation[2]. The Commission can send inspectors to the Member States who must be given access at any time to all premises, all information and all individuals to the extent necessary to check the ores, source materials and special fissile materials used by the 750 or so nuclear installations, including some 130 reactors, in the Community (Art. 81 EAEC). The **Euratom Safeguards Office** has the task of ensuring that nuclear material is not diverted from its intended use within the European Union and that the Community's safeguards obligations under agreements with third countries or international organisations are complied with.

19.2.4. Oil market

Although it is less developed than the nuclear market, a **single market in petroleum products exists** in many respects. On the basis of the EEC (now the EC) Treaty governing the oil market, all quantitative restrictions to trade between Member States and all measures having equivalent effect have been abolished. Tariff obstacles to trade in petroleum products were phased out in July 1968. On the external market, the Common Customs Tariff set a zero rate for oil and very low rates for refined products. The latter were further reduced in the framework of the General Agreement on Tariffs and Trade [see section 23.4.]. All the freedoms written into the

---

[1] Decision 78/471 and 78/472, OJ L 151, 07.06.1978 and Decision 98/585, OJ L 282, 20.10.1998.

[2] Regulation 302/2005, OJ L 54, 28.02.2005.

Treaty of Rome, such as freedom of establishment and the freedom to provide services, are applicable in the oil sector [see chapter 6].

Even if the **common oil market is not yet perfect**, petroleum products can move freely from Member State to Member State. The big oil companies have been able to build refineries at certain nerve centres in the common market to supply refined products to networks covering neighbouring regions in two or more Member States. This means that refinery production and distribution activities can be rationalised to meet supply in surrounding regions without regard to national borders. Oil and gas pipelines consequently start their journey from the major ports of the Mediterranean and the North Sea, cut across one or several Member States and supply crude oil to the refineries of different oil companies situated in another Member State. Before the creation of the common market, it would have been unthinkable for a European state to entrust the supply of a product as vital as oil to the good will of one or several neighbouring countries. The European Community has rendered self-evident certain situations, which would have been inconceivable in the protectionist post-war period [see section 1.1.2.].

19.3. Energy supply

Security of energy supply, the second wing of the common energy policy, is defined as the ability to ensure the continued satisfaction of essential energy needs by means of, on the one hand, sufficient internal resources exploited under acceptable economic conditions and, on the other, of accessible, stable and diversified external sources. With this definition, most European countries had a more secure energy supply in the 1950s than they had in the 1970s or even in the 1990s, despite their efforts in those three decades. Indeed, at the beginning of the 1950s, the Community's energy economy revolved around indigenous resources, chiefly coal. In 1955, coal met 64% of gross internal energy consumption in the then Community of Six; but little by little, **demand switched from primary energy to processed energy**, chiefly electricity and petroleum products. Due to strong growth in demand for light petroleum products (chiefly petrol), heavy fuels became residual products, which refiners wanted to get rid of at any price, often below that of crude oil. Unfortunately for coal, its main competitors were these heavy, industrial use fuels. In that oil was almost exclusively imported from third countries, the consequences on the Community's energy independence were plain to see. Energy independence was sacrificed on the altar of rapid industrial growth, stimulated by low energy prices.

19.3.1. Energy objectives and rational energy use

Energy objectives converge with the environmental objectives pursued by the Directive on **energy end-use efficiency and energy services**[1] [see section 16.3.4], which seeks to enhance the cost-effective improvement of energy end-use efficiency in the Member States by: (a) providing the necessary indicative targets to remove market barriers and imperfections that impede the efficient end use of energy; and (b) creating the conditions for the development of a market for energy services and other energy efficiency improvement measures.

Thanks in part to various measures taken by the Member States at the prompting of Community institutions and in part to the reduction of energy demand and the increase of internal production, notably in the North Sea, the EU, in 2000, imported about half of its total energy needs compared with two-thirds twenty five years earlier. However, despite these improvements, the problems have not gone away. The **European Union still has to cope with a massive oil bill**, vast amounts of investment, and the implications for environmental pollution and energy dependence that cannot be reduced in any significant manner in the medium term. This is why, the Commission is proposing more drastic measures, notably a tax based on the consumption of carbon dioxide[2].

19.3.2. Coal supply

Coal is the most abundant non-renewable energy source available and will continue to play a very important role as a regulator of the Union's energy market, particularly in the generation of energy. In any case, **the European Union does not face a problem in coal supply**, both as far as indigenous resources are concerned, which are abundant, and imports from several third countries, which are more competitive. After the expiration of the ECSC Treaty in July 2002, the common commercial policy of the EC covers the coal products [see chapter 23]. Any imported coal released for free movement in a Member State circulates freely in all the Community. However, there is Community surveillance of imports of hard coal originating in third countries[3]. The monitoring system entails the provision by the Member States of information concerning their imports of hard coal, including the prices charged and the breakdown of hard coal imports between electricity production and use in the Community steel industry.

---

[1] Directive 2006/32, OJ L 114, 27.04.2006.
[2] COM (92)226, 27.05.1992.
[3] Regulation 405/2003, OJ L 62, 06.03.2003.

19.3.3. Supply of nuclear fuels

Nuclear energy makes a significant contribution to the policy of diversifying energy supply and reducing overall emissions of CO_2. Supply of nuclear fuels is **a matter dealt with in some depth in the Euratom Treaty** [see section 2.1.]. Article 52 of this Treaty stipulates that supply of ores, source materials and special fissile materials is accomplished with respect of the principle of equal access to resources and through a common supply policy. For this purpose, all practices that seek to provide certain users with a privileged position are forbidden. The Treaty set up a **Supply Agency,** the organisation of which is provided for in Articles 53 and 54 (EAEC). The Agency, which has legal status and is financially independent, is governed by Statutes adopted by the Council on the basis of a Commission proposal. The Euratom Supply Agency is under the control of the Commission, which issues it with policy guidelines, has a right of veto on its decisions and appoints its Director General[1]. In contrast with the coal and oil sectors, the nuclear sector is endowed with a strong common supply policy, exercised by the Agency, under the control of the Commission.

Article 52 (EAEC) grants the Agency two fundamental rights: (a) an option right on ores, source material and special fissile materials produced in the Member States and (b) the exclusive right to conclude contracts for the supply of ores, source materials and special fissile materials originating inside or outside the Community. The Agency's main role is to act as an **intermediary between producers and users.** Under Article 60 (EAEC), possible users periodically inform the Agency of their supply needs. Producers inform the Agency of the supplies that they can put on the market. The Agency informs all potential users of supplies and of the demand volume brought to its attention, and invites them to order. Once it has all the orders, it makes known the terms at which they can be satisfied. In fact, the option right of the Agency, described in Article 57 (EAEC), gives it a *"de jure"* **monopoly** on the trade of ores, raw materials and special fissile materials intended for peaceful nuclear use in the Community.

19.3.4. Oil and natural gas supply

Contrary to the EAEC Treaty's concern for the supply of nuclear fuels, the **EEC Treaty did not show any particular interest** for the supply of oil and natural gas. The general clauses under the title "trade policy" clearly could not form the basis of a supply policy for products as important as oil and natural gas. The EEC Treaty did not even give the Community institutions the possibility of collecting and publishing information of vital importance for the common oil market, such as those covering investments, production or imports, as is done by the ECSC and Euratom

---

[1]   Decision 2008/114, OJ L 41, 15.02.2008.

Treaties for their respective areas. In light of the growing importance of oil in the1960s, this vacuum was partly filled by the Council.

The most important measure is the **strategic storage of petroleum products**. A Council Directive obliges the Member States to maintain a minimum stock level of 90 days' consumption for crude oil and/or petroleum products, as a buffer against the effects of accidental or deliberate interruption in supplies and against the economic and political leverage enjoyed by suppliers[1]. Another measure is a Council Decision setting a Community target for the reduction of primary energy consumption in the event of supply difficulties of crude oil and petroleum products in order to ensure that these difficulties are spread fairly among all consumers[2].

A directive establishes measures to safeguard an adequate level of **security of gas supply**[3]. It clarifies the general roles and responsibilities of the different market players and implements specific non-discriminatory procedures to safeguard security of gas supply. While contributing to the smooth functioning of the internal gas market, it provides for a common framework within which Member States should define general, transparent and non-discriminatory security of supply policies compatible with the requirements of the competitive internal gas market.

In the context of the completion of the internal market, a Directive on the conditions for granting and using **authorisations for oil and gas prospecting, exploration and extraction** is designed to ensure non-discriminatory access to and pursuit of these activities by Community companies in non-member countries under conditions which encourage greater competition in this sector[4]. However, Member States have sovereign rights over oil and gas resources on their territories. They therefore retain the right to determine the areas within their territory to be made available for oil and gas prospecting, exploration and production.

19.3.5. New technologies and new energy sources

Fortunately for the Union, new energy technologies and new energy sources offer **an alternative route to supply security**. Moreover, **new and renewable energies** (solar, wind, hydroelectric, geothermal, biomass) can generate economic activity, thereby creating added value and employment in Europe. Furthermore, they both improve the quality of the environment and standards of living, and are particularly important for the less developed regions of the EU, which have considerable potential for the development of renewable energy resources. For these reasons, a directive commits the Member States to meeting national targets for their future consumption of **electricity from renewable energy sources** consistent

[1] Directive 2006/67, OJ L 217, 08.08.2006.
[2] Decision 77/706, OJ L 292, 16.11.1977.
[3] Directive 2004/67, OJ L 127, 29.04.2004.
[4] Directive 94/22, OJ L 164, 30.06.1994.

with the indicative overall target of 12% of gross inland energy consumption in 2010[1]. In this context, a directive establishes a framework for the promotion and development of cogeneration, that is, the simultaneous generation in one process of heat and electrical and/mechanical power, as a means of improving security of energy supply[2].

The **common research policy** tries to encourage the deployment of technologies and to help promote changes in energy demand patterns and consumption behaviour by improving energy efficiency and integrating renewable energy into the energy system[3]. The aim is to bring to the market improved renewable energy technologies and to integrate renewable energy into networks and supply chains [see sections 18.3 and 18.4]. The research effort is focused notably on: energy savings and energy efficiency, including those to be achieved through the use of renewable raw materials; the efficiency of combined production of electricity, heating and cooling services, by using new technologies; and alternative motor fuels, such biofuels, natural gas and hydrogen.

19.4. Appraisal and outlook

There is a general impression that a common energy policy is non-existent or, at best, ineffective. This impression arises chiefly from **confusion between energy policy and oil supply policy**. The latter is clearly of vital importance and is still lacking. But it is only a part of energy policy. It cannot be denied that the common coal, oil and nuclear energy markets have been largely achieved thanks to Community policy. But their existence tends to be taken for granted and similarly significant achievements are expected in the area of supply, notably oil supply. The fact that the EEC Treaty and now the EC Treaty did not provide for such a policy is often forgotten. The silence of the Treaty means, however, that the Member States do not want to commit themselves in a common policy for oil and gas supply.

Another fact often overlooked is that in the1960s, all the Member States chose to boost industrial growth through low energy prices rather than promoting indigenous energy production by high prices. This preference for the industrial rather than energy sector culminated, at Community level, in a system diametrically opposed to the one existing for agriculture [see section 21.2.]. It was a political decision, the advantages of which cannot be denied, even with hindsight of the post-1973 events. In any case, the Member States, due to their different energy situations and interests, have proven unable to conduct a common supply policy, which would have increased their negotiation power towards their main oil suppliers.

---

[1]   Directive 2001/77, OJ L 283, 27.10.2001.
[2]   Directive 2004/8, OJ L 52, 21.02.2004.
[3]   Decision 2002/834, OJ L 294, 29.10.2002.

Thanks to the increase of internal production - notably in the North Sea - and to the diversification of fuels and suppliers, the Union is now in a much more comfortable situation than the one the Community has experienced in the mid-1970s. However, despite these improvements, the problems have not gone away. Since international political and economic developments are liable at any time to cause considerable increases in the price of oil and of products indexed to it, **the EU is always at risk** as regards competitiveness, employment and growth. This is why, a policy framework is needed in which Member States would be working towards agreed common objectives, notably balance and diversification in relation to the different sources of supply (by products and by geographical zones), the development of renewable sources and clean technologies, assisted by Community financial and fiscal measures and closely coordinated with other common policies, particularly the environment, transport and enterprise policies. Concerning hydrocarbon supply, in particular, the EU should ideally develop a common policy similar, as far as possible, to the one for the supply of nuclear fuels [see section 19.3.3.]. At least, it should promote greater coherence between national policies and develop a common voice in support of energy policy objectives when addressing third countries, more open relations with the producer countries, notably the OPEC countries, and enhanced cooperation with Central European countries and Russia.

Energy is certainly an important factor determining the economic performance of a country or of a group of countries such as the EU. The absence of a common oil and gas supply policy handicaps the common energy market and renders energy prices higher than they could be if the Union could use its economic weight to negotiate its overall supplies with producing countries as it does concerning its supplies of nuclear fuels. High energy prices mean a serious **competitive disadvantage for the businesses of the European Union** as compared with those of its main trading partners. Furthermore, economic performance is not measured only by industrial competitiveness, but also by the welfare of citizens in terms of the employment situation and the state of the environment. The reduction of greenhouse gas emissions requires common policies, such as a sustained commitment to energy efficiency and energy saving, a commitment to make more systematic use of energy sources with low or no CO_2 emissions and a reduction in the impact of the use of energy sources with high CO_2 emissions.

Bibliography on energy policy

- ALARIO Juan. *An efficient, sustainable and secure supply of energy for Europe: global and European policy perspectives*. Luxembourg: European Investment Bank, 2007.
- COOP Graham, GAITIS James. "Energy dispute settlement", in *Journal of Energy & Natural Resources Law*, v. 25, n. 3, August 2007, p. 199-344.

- CRUCIANI Michel. "La sécurité d'approvisionnement de l'Europe en gaz naturel: séminaire du Centre de géopolitique de l'énergie et des matières premières (CGEMP)", in *Revue de l'énergie*, v. 58, n. 577, mai-juin 2007, p. 171-175.
- DEHOUSSE Franklin (ed.). "Towards a real European energy policy?" in *Studia diplomatica*, v. 60, n. 2, 2007, 1-227.
- EURELECTRIC. *European electricity: Flashback on a momentous era, spotlight on an exciting future*. Brussels: Eurelectric, 2007.
- EUROPEAN COMMISSION. *Towards a European Charter on the Rights of Energy Consumers*. Luxembourg: EUR-OP, 2007.
  - *2020 vision: saving our energy*. Luxembourg: EUR-OP, 2007.
- HAGHIGHI Sanam Salem. *Energy security: the external legal relations of the European Union with major oil and gas supplying countries*. London: Hart Publishing, 2007.
- ROGGENKAMP M. (et al. eds.). *Energy law in Europe: national, EU and international regulation*. Oxford: Oxford University Press, 2007.
- RÖLLER Lars-Hendrik, DELGADO Juan, FRIEDERISZICK Hans. *Energy: choices for Europe*. Brussels: Bruegel, 2007.

DISCUSSION TOPICS

1. Discuss the energy objectives of the ECSC, the EC and Euratom Treaties.
2. How has the completion of the single market influenced the energy sector?
3. What measures has the EC/EU taken to promote its energy supply security?
4. Discuss the issue of security of Europe's oil supplies.
5. How can the common energy policy contribute to the attainment of the sustainable development objective of the common environment policy?

Chapter 20

TRANSPORT POLICY

Diagram of the chapter

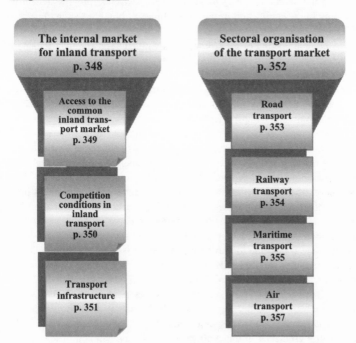

The internal market for inland transport p. 348

Access to the common inland transport market p. 349

Competition conditions in inland transport p. 350

Transport infrastructure p. 351

Sectoral organisation of the transport market p. 352

Road transport p. 353

Railway transport p. 354

Maritime transport p. 355

Air transport p. 357

The EEC Treaty sought **a common policy for inland transport**, namely roads, rail and inland waterways, but not for maritime and air transport (Art 84 EEC, Art. 80 TEC). The concept of a common transport market was consequently limited at the outset to inland transport and more specifically, in light of the highly specific situation of railway and inland waterway undertakings, to road transport. However road haulage services represent by far the bulk of goods carriage in the European Community. They, therefore, play a principal role in the good functioning of the single market by enabling the free movement of goods and persons. Thus, the common transport market had to be completed together with the single market for goods in 1992.

In addition to the integration of inland transport markets, Community policy in this sector seeks to **organise the various means of transport** in accordance with "Community rules", i.e. measures tending towards the approximation of the economic conditions and the structures of each mode of transport in the Member States. For many years, the Community institutions concentrated upon harmonising road haulage rates, but achievements are thin on the ground. The aim in the railway sector was to improve the financial situation of railway companies, but the many provisions adopted with this aim in mind have, thus far, had little impact. By way of contrast, sea and air transport which only made their entrance onto the Community stage in the middle of the 1970s, have seen spectacular progress recently, not only in the completion of the internal market in these sectors, but also of their Community organisation.

A communication of the Commission entitled "The common transport policy - Sustainable mobility: perspectives for the future" provides an updated **framework for the future development of the transport policy**[1]. The Commission identifies three priority areas for action, for which it lists the main measures designed to: improve the **efficiency and competitiveness** of Community transport by: liberalising market access, establishing integrated transport systems and developing the trans-European network; establishing **fair pricing** on the basis of the marginal social cost and improving working conditions; and improving **transport quality** through targeted action on safety, primarily on air, maritime and road transport, and protection of the environment. Concerning in particular environment protection, the Commission believes that the introduction of a rational policy for achieving a reduction in carbon dioxide emissions in the transport sector (accounting for 26% of total CO_2 emissions in the Union in 1995) would make it possible to halve them by 2010[2] [see also section 16.3.4.]. To this end, the "**Intelligent Energy – Europe**" programme, which is part of the competitiveness and innovation framework programme (CIP, 2007-2013)[3] [see section 17.1.3], supports initiatives relating to all energy aspects of transport, the diversification of fuels, such as through new developing and renewable energy sources, and the promotion of renewable fuels and energy efficiency in transport, including the preparation of legislative measures and their application.

20.1. The special interest for the transport sector

Article 51 TEC (ex-Art. 61 EEC) makes the provision of services in the transport sector dependent on the special clauses of the title relating to transport. Article 71 TEC (ex-Art. 75 EEC) stipulates that the common policy should take into account the **"distinctive features"** of (inland) transport sector. At the outset, these distinctive features were based on the facts: (a) that transport undertakings were dependent upon infrastructure decided and built by the States; (b) that in general, competition took place between large State controlled railway monopolies and a multitude of

---

[1]   COM (1998) 716, 1 December 1998.

[2]   COM (1998) 204, 31 March 1998.

[3]   Decision 1639/2006, OJ L 310, 09.11.2006.

small road haulage and inland waterway transport operators; (c) that the State required certain undertakings, notably the railways, to fulfil public service obligations, which distort competition conditions; and (d) that supply and demand were extremely rigid in this sector.

The Treaty of Rome and its successor, the Treaty establishing the European Community, show **special interest in the transport sector for several reasons**. First of all, economic integration was expected to lead to growth in trade and consequently in transport flows. The EEC Treaty therefore saw the transport sector as one of the major motors of economic integration. On its side, the healthy operation of the transport sector depended to a large extent on healthy trade and business in the Community.

Secondly, transport costs, which put a serious strain on the cost price of certain goods, **could act as a barrier to trade** or a source of discrimination between European businesses of various nationalities. At the outset, the situation was most complex in the road transport sector, which represents 80% of goods carriage between the Member States. Depending on the routes, international road traffic was either restriction free or subject to prior authorisation or to the granting of authorisations in the framework of a quota. Authorisation issuing provisions (length of validity, possibility of return trip loaded, etc.) varied from one route to the next. The conditions governing Community transit differed from one State to the next and provisions relating to combined rail/road transport were practically non-existent. It is obvious that all this had to be changed in order to create a common market for transport.

Infrastructure choices for means of communication, their construction and use have considerable impact on regional development, the environment, town and country planning, traffic safety and energy consumption. Coordination of investment decisions can eliminate the risk of works whose socio-economic profitability is not sufficient and can open the way to the economies of scale offered by the wider internal market. Nowadays, the priority in the transport sector is moving towards building modern infrastructures and, in particular, **trans-European networks**, which help complete the internal market by reinforcing the links between the Member States [see section 6.8.]. These networks also permit: better, safer travel at lower cost, thus improving both industrial competitiveness and quality of life; effective planning in Europe, thus avoiding a concentration of wealth and population; and bridge-building towards Central and Eastern European countries, which is essential in view of their integration into the Union. Building trans-European transport networks requires Community action to coordinate the various national activities and so complete the internal market and facilitate interconnection and interoperability in the transport sector.

The continuing integration of the economies of the Member States necessarily entails increased transport movements across frontiers and places new challenges for the European transport policy. Therefore, Article 71 of the EC Treaty declares that **transport safety** is one of the objectives to be attained by the transport policy. Safety requirements may fall within the area of the Community's exclusive powers, for example, because they affect the free circulation of vehicles or transport services. In other cases, in application of the subsidiarity principle [see section 3.2.], transport safety is a matter which should be addressed by the Community when it is in a position to act usefully.

20.2. The internal market for inland transport

Title V of the EC Treaty is devoted to transport policy. It states that common policy in the transport sector should be implemented via **common rules applicable to international transport**, through the admission of non-resident carriers to the national transport market and through all other appropriate provisions (Art 71 TEC). According to the Treaty, aids which respond to the need for the coordination of transport services or for the reimbursement for the discharge of certain obligations inherent in the concept of public service are compatible with the common market (Art. 73 TEC). Any discrimination, which takes the form of carriers charging different rates and imposing different conditions for the carriage of the same goods over the same transport links on grounds of the country of origin or destination of the country in question, must be abolished (Art. 75 TEC). The Member States may not impose rates and conditions involving any element of support or protection in the interest of one or more particular undertakings or industries, unless authorised by the Commission (Art. 76 TEC).

The first Community measures adopted in the inland transport sector sought **to integrate national transport markets** together with the creation of the general common market for goods and services. In this sector, it was necessary to create a genuine internal market in which transport operators from all the Member States would have access under the same conditions as those prevalent on their national markets. No special problems were encountered in the free movement of individuals and the right of establishment in the transport sector. The Regulation of 1968 on the **free movement of workers** within the Community was applied to the inland transport sector in the same way as to other economic sectors [see section 6.4.][1]. The **right of establishment** formed part of the general programme to remove restrictions to the freedom of establishment adopted by the Council in December 1961 [see section 6.5.1.], but was also the subject of a specific Directive on mutual recognition of diplomas and certificates of road carriers[2]. It was the **free movement of services**, meaning free access of all operators in the transport market, that was the source of complex problems,

---

[1]   Regulation 1612/68, OJ L 257, 19.10.1968 and Directive 2004/38, OJ L 158, 30.04.2004.
[2]   Directive 96/26, OJ L 124, 23.05.1996 and Directive 2004/66, OJ L 168, 01.05.2004.

due to restrictive national regulations in the Member States, particularly for road haulage services. This subject merits our particular attention.

20.2.1. Access to the common inland transport market

The **liberalisation of the internal goods carriage market** was at long last established by a Regulation on access to the market in the carriage of goods by road within the Community and departing from or en route to a Member State, or crossing the territory of one or several Member States[1]. This Regulation replaced the formerly existing quantitative restrictions and bilateral authorisations by qualitative conditions (fiscal, technical and safety) with which a carrier must conform in order to obtain the Community **road haulage operator licence** and which are specified in the directives on access to the transport profession, mentioned below. The licence is valid for six years, but the criteria for holding it have to be controlled every three years. Thanks to a uniform document, the **"driver attestation"**, the regularity of the employment status of a driver of a Community vehicle engaged in international carriage under cover of a Community authorisation can be effectively checked by inspecting officers of all Member States[2]. Should economic crisis hit the road haulage market, the Commission can take measures to prevent any further capacity increases on the market affected[3]. A Regulation laying down the conditions under which non-resident carriers may operate national **road haulage services within a Member State** (**cabotage**) is the culmination of many years of work towards the liberalisation of the road haulage sector[4]. These Regulations have completed the internal goods carriage market.

The **freedom to provide passenger transport services by road** for hire or reward or on one's own account is also guaranteed by a Council Regulation[5]. It notably provides for the liberalisation of shuttle services by coach and bus with sleeping accommodation, along with nearly all occasional services, and simplifies authorisation procedures by introducing a Community licence based on a harmonised model. The detailed rules with regard to documentation covering the international carriage of passengers are laid out in a Commission Regulation[6]. Another Council Regulation lays down the conditions under which non-resident carriers may operate **national road passenger transport services (cabotage)** within a Member State[7]. It authorises cabotage, under certain conditions, for regular services performed during a regular international service, excluding purely internal

---

[1] Regulation 881/92, OJ L 95, 09.04.1992 and Directive 2006/94, OJ L 374, 27.12.2006.
[2] Regulation 484/2002, OJ L 76, 19.03.2002.
[3] Regulation 3916/90, OJ L 375, 31.12.1990.
[4] Regulation 3118/93, OJ L 279, 12.11.1993 and Regulation 484/2002, OJ L 76, 19.03.2002.
[5] Regulation 684/92, OJ L 74, 20.03.1992 and Regulation 11/98, OJ L 4, 08.01.1998.
[6] Regulation 2121/98, OJ L 268, 03.10.1998 last amended by Regulation 1792/2006, OJ L 362, 20.12.2006.
[7] Regulation 12/98, OJ L 48, 04.01.1998.

urban and suburban services. Despite cabotage liberalisation, when a bus or coach company wants to gain a permanent foothold in another national market, the simplest way to do so remains to establish itself on that market and cabotage operations are carried out mainly in adjacent Member States.

The **admission to the occupation** of road haulage operator and road passenger transport operator and the mutual recognition of diplomas, certificates and other evidence of qualifications intended to facilitate for these operators the right to freedom of establishment in national and international transport operations are guaranteed by a Directive[1]. It stipulates that individuals or undertakings wishing to exercise the occupation of road haulier or road passenger transport operator must satisfy certain conditions relating to good repute (no insolvency), sufficient financial capacity for correct management of the undertaking and professional skills acquired through attendance of a training course or through practical experience.

20.2.2. Competition conditions in inland transport services

For there to be effective freedom to provide services, all transport operators in the Member States had to **be placed on an equal footing** from the viewpoint of competition conditions, a really difficult requirement. In effect, rail transport systems based on the exploitation of single networks constituted monopolies or oligopolies. Service obligations in the public interest tended to involve the granting of correlative special or exclusive rights. Rail transport operators frequently relied on public finance, including subsidies not compatible with the functioning of the common market.

After the achievement of customs union [see section 5.1.2.], a 1968 Regulation sanctioned the **application of competition rules** to the rail, road and inland waterway transport sectors[2]. This Regulation in principle forbids, for all three modes of transport, agreements between companies, decisions of association and concerted practices, along with abuse of a dominant position in the common market. Yet, an exemption is granted to agreements which contribute to productivity, along with certain types of agreements, decisions and concerted practices in the field of transport which have as sole object and impact the application of technical improvements or technical cooperation. A Commission Regulation facilitates the presentation of complaints, applications and notifications by natural or legal persons who claim a legitimate interest[3].

However, competition rules alone do not suffice to guarantee free competition in the transport sector. Competition conditions for different modes of transport and for the undertakings of different Member States

---

[1] Directive 96/26, OJ L 124, 23.05.1996 last amended by Directive 2004/66, OJ L 168, 01.05.2004.

[2] Regulation 1017/68, OJ L 175, 23.07.1968 and Regulation 1/2003, OJ L 1, 04.01.2003.

[3] Regulation 773/2004, OJ L 123, 27.04.2003 last amended by Regulation 1792/2006, OJ L 362, 20.12.2006.

running the same type of transport services must also be harmonised. The first step in this direction was taken by the Council Decision of May 13, 1965 on the harmonisation of **certain provisions affecting competition** in transport by rail, road and inland waterway[1]. Under this Decision, the Council agreed to take action in three fields: State intervention, taxation and social regimes in the transport sector. One of the most important measures was a Regulation providing for separate accounting of public service activities and commercial activities in transport undertakings, abolishing public service obligations and replacing them, when public interest justifies the preservation of transport services of no commercial viability for the operator, by **public service contracts** negotiated between governments and undertakings[2]. Many other measures harmonising the conditions of competition were taken in the fields of State aids, taxation and social legislation.

20.2.3. Transport infrastructure

Infrastructure plays a determinant role in the competition conditions enjoyed by the various modes of transport. Through its choice of means of communication, the State determines the expansion and link up possibilities of the various modes of transport. Transport undertakings are dependent upon the infrastructure, which they use, in as much as decisions on its construction and maintenance are taken by governments. However, transport users are usually **not obliged to pay the full cost of the infrastructures** that they use. This is particularly true of road infrastructures and has contributed to the phenomenal expansion of road transport. In other respects, transport networks having been designed largely from a national point of view, there were in post-war Europe many missing links, bottlenecks and obstacles to inter-operability between national networks. Moreover, whereas the central regions of the Community suffered from a growing congestion and had to bear a disproportionate burden of the costs of cross-frontier traffic, there was an under-investment in peripheral areas contributing to their economic underdevelopment.

The EEC Treaty did not give the Community institutions any powers in this field. However, at the instigation of the Commission, a **consultation procedure** and a Transport Infrastructure Committee were established in the late 1970s and improved over time[3]. This procedure enabled better planning at national level both as regards time scale and geographical aspects. In addition, the European Investment Bank and the Structural Funds have much helped the financing of infrastructures. But the overall infrastructure deficit of the Community has increased with the accession of peripheral States. This is why, the development of transport infrastructures

---

[1] Decision 65/271, OJ 88, 24.05.1965.
[2] Regulation 1191/69, OJ L 156, 28.06.1969 and Regulation 1893/91, OJ L 169, 29.06.1991.
[3] Decision 1692/96, OJ L 228, 09.09.1996, last amended by Decision 884/2004, OJ L 167, 30.04.2004.

was provided for in the EC Treaty under the heading of trans-European networks.

Indeed, the new Article 155 of the EC Treaty calls for a series of guidelines covering the objectives, priorities and broad lines of measures envisaged in the sphere of **trans-European networks** [see section 6.8.]. These networks are not only necessary in order to complete the internal market, improve the links between the European regions, avoid traffic congestions, reduce environment pollution and improve the competitiveness of European industries, but they can also enliven the European economy through the realisation of very big projects and thus contribute to its growth. Community financial assistance is granted under certain rules to projects of common interest[1]. Concerning trans-European transport networks (TEN-T) the goal is not so much the improvement of transport infrastructure in general but the integration of the Community's transport system through the completion and combination of its networks, taking particular account of its more geographically isolated regions.

A first measure in this sense is the creation of a European **electronic road toll service**, which aims to secure the interoperability of toll systems in the internal market and to contribute to the elaboration of infrastructure charging policies at European level, making it possible to fund, in part, new infrastructure and to ensure a better traffic flow on the main routes of the trans-European network[2].

20.3. Sectoral organisation of the transport market

In addition to the proper functioning of the internal market for transport, the common transport policy also tackles the sector-by-sector **organisation of the various modes of transport**. This requires the approximation of the economic conditions and the structures of each mode of transport in the Member States. The Treaty of Rome did not call for specific action in this field, but nevertheless stated that there should be common rules applicable to international transport to or from the territory of a Member State, or passing across the territory of one or more Member States (Article 75,1,a EEC). The European institutions slowly put in place common rules, first for road transport rates and for improving the financial situation of the railways and, then in reaction to the Court of Justice ruling of April 4, 1974 on the interpretation of Article 84 of the EEC Treaty[3], on the organisation of activities and the establishment of the internal market for the sea and air transport sectors. For concision's sake, all measures adopted in the last two sectors are examined in this part, since they often pursue simultaneously the two objectives of the common transport policy, namely the proper functioning of the internal market and the organisation of the sector.

---

[1]   Regulation 2236/95, OJ L 228, 23.09.1995 and Regulation 1159/2005, OJ L 191, 22.07.2005.

[2]   Directive 2004/52, OJ L 166, 30.04.2004.

[3]   Judgment of 4 April 1974, Case 167-73, Commission v French Republic, ECR 1974, p. 359.

20.3.1. Road transport

The part of road haulage in the total freight transport of the Community increased from around 50% in 1970 to almost 70% in 1990. This increase was partly due to the choice of the Member States **not to charge the prices of road transport with the cost of infrastructures**. In 1968, the Council, acting on a proposal by the Commission, had introduced bracket tariffs only for the carriage of goods by road between the Member States. This experimental system was replaced, since 1990, by a single system providing a **free price setting** applicable to all carriage of goods by road between the Member States[1]. This new tariff regime allows for the introduction of cost indexes, i.e. indicators of the various cost elements, which a haulier should take into account when drawing up a transport price to be negotiated with the client, but the real cost of infrastructures is not among those indicators. However, the Commission's approach to infrastructure charging based on the "user pays" principle [see section 20.2.3.] could have an important bearing on the harmonisation of road transport costs and prices in the Community[2].

The form and content of **registration certificates** for motor vehicles have been harmonised in order to facilitate road traffic within the Community, simplify procedures for the re-registration of vehicles in another Member State, and step up the fight against illegal vehicle trafficking[3]. Common rules command the recognition in intra-Community traffic of the distinguishing sign of the Member State in which motor vehicles and their trailers are registered[4].

The Community aims not only at the harmonisation of conditions of competition and the protection of the environment but also at **road safety**, which becomes an ever more important problem of the EU. The principal actions taken so far in the area of road safety have been concerned with the harmonisation of rules relating to vehicle construction and vehicle inspection, through the adoption of over 100 Directives, notably on: minimum tyre tread depth[5]; the periodic inspection of vehicles[6]; speed limiters for heavy vehicles[7]; the mandatory wearing of seat belts[8]; compulsory installation of digital equipment to monitor the activities, notably the working hours, of lorry drivers (tachographs)[9]; and the general standards for the

---

[1] Regulation 4058/89, OJ L 390, 30.12.1989 and EEA Agreement, OJ L 1, 03.01.1994.

[2] COM (1998) 466, 22 July 1998.

[3] Directive 1999/37, OJ L 138, 01.06.1999 last amended by Directive 2003/127, OJ L 10, 16.01.2004.

[4] Regulation 2411/98, OJ L 299, 10.11.1998.

[5] Directive 89/459, OJ L 226, 03.08.1989 and EEA Agreement, OJ L 1, 03.01.1994.

[6] Directive 96/96, OJ L 46, 17.02.1997 and Directive 2003/27, OJ L90, 08.04.2003.

[7] Directive 92/24, OJ L 129, 14.05.1992 last amended by Directive 2004/11, OJ L 44, 14.02.2004.

[8] Directive 91/671, OJ L 373, 31.12.1991 and Directive 2003/20, OJ L 115, 09.05.2003.

[9] Regulation 3821/85, OJ L 370, 31.12.1985 last amended by Regulation 561/2006, OJ L 102, 11.04.2006.

Community model driving licence in paper or "credit card" format, including harmonised codes for additional or restrictive information[1]. Minimum safety requirements for tunnels have become obligatory in the trans-European road network[2]. How many citizens realise that these life-saving measures are based on the - according to eurosceptic rhetoric - "niggling legislation of Brussels" [see section 10.1.]?

20.3.2. Railway transport

Railways, once the dominant means of transport, were **relegated by the car** in the 1960s. In the early 1990s, railway transport represented around 15% of freight transport in the Community, whereas twenty years before it represented practically the double. The bulky organisation of the railways has not given them sufficient flexibility to structure their service to new transport requirements, to the "European dimension" and to competition from other modes of transport. The Member States must shoulder part of the blame for the unfortunate situation in which their railways find themselves. They oblige the railways to bend to the requirements of public service and regional development, which is not required of their private competitors, the road hauliers, while not raising the capital endowment of railway undertakings in line with this obligation. This forces the railways into the red and hampers their modernisation.

Nowadays, however, there is some light at the end of the tunnel in the shape of the high speed trains, which have given a new lease of life to European railways. The new momentum has led to the **"railway package"** of measures designed to speed up market integration by removing major obstacles to cross-border services, ensure a high standard of operational safety on the railways and help to reduce costs and facilitate operations through greater harmonisation of technical standards in the railway industry.

Thus, a Directive on the **development of the Community's railways** purports to make relations between the railways and the public authorities more transparent and to ensure the financial, administrative, economic and accounting independence of the railway undertakings[3]. It entails the total opening of the rail freight markets. It also allows access to new railway operators into the combined transport market, in order to stimulate a higher quality of service from all concerned. Another Directive establishes the general framework for a uniform, non-discriminatory Community system regarding access to railway infrastructure, so that railway undertakings and their customers can reap the full benefits of the internal market in this sector, while ensuring high standards of safety[4]. However, undertakings ap-

---

[1] Directive 2006/126, OJ L 403, 30.12.2006.
[2] Directive 2004/54, OJ L 167, 30.04.2004.
[3] Directive 91/440, OJ L 237, 24.08.1991 and Directive 2004/51, OJ L 164, 30.04.2004.
[4] Directive 2001/14, OJ L 75, 15.03.2001 and Directive 2004/49, OJ L 164, 30.04.2004.

plying for a licence to the Community railway market must meet specified standards of financial fitness and professional competence[1]. The licences, granted by the Member State in which a railway undertaking is established, are valid throughout the territory of the Community. Harmonised technical specifications ensure the uninterrupted movement of high-speed trains throughout the European Union[2] as well the interoperability of the trans-European conventional rail system[3], while a uniform set of national safety rules purports to avoid distorting competition between modes for the transport of dangerous goods[4]. **Multimodal transport** is encouraged by granting Community financial assistance to improve the environmental performance of the freight transport system (Marco Polo programme)[5]. The **European Railway Agency** plays a key role in technically aligning the railway systems[6]. Working in close liaison with experts in the field, it provides technical support for the work on interoperability and safety.

20.3.3. Maritime transport

Established in the early 1990s, the **internal maritime transport market** is functioning quite well. In 1986, the Council applied the principle of freedom to provide services, (Art. 49 and 50 TEC) to shipping services between the Member States and third countries[7]. In 1992, the freedom to provide services was extended to maritime transport within Member States **(maritime cabotage)** for Community shipowners who have their ships registered in and flying the flag of a Member State, provided that these ships comply with all the conditions for cabotage in that Member State[8]. For vessels carrying out mainland cabotage and for cruise liners, all matters relating to manning are the responsibility of the State in which the vessel is registered. However, for ships smaller than 650 Gt. and for vessels carrying out island cabotage, all matters relating to manning are the responsibility of the host State. The ability to transfer ships from one register to another within the Community may improve the operating conditions and competitiveness of the Community merchant fleet[9]. A Directive concerning the Agreement on the organisation of working time of seafarers, concluded by the European Community Shipowners' Association and the Federation of Transport Workers' Union in the European Union, is important for levelling both working conditions of sailors and competition conditions in this area[10].

---

[1] Directive 95/18, OJ L 143, 27.06.1995 and Directive 2004/49, OJ L 164, 30.04.2004.
[2] Directive 96/48, OJ L 235, 17.09.1996 and Directive 2004/50, OJ L 164, 30.04.2004.
[3] Directive 2001/16, OJ L110, 20.04.2001 and Directive 2004/50, OJ L 164, 30.04.2004.
[4] Directive 96/49, OJ L 235, 17.09.1996 and Directive 2000/62, OJ L 279, 01.11.2000.
[5] Regulation 1692/2006, OJ L 328, 24.11.2006.
[6] Regulation 881/2004, OJ L 164, 30.04.2004.
[7] Regulation 4055/86, OJ L 378, 31.12.1986 and Regulation 3573/90, OJ L 353, 17.12.1990.
[8] Regulation 3577/92, OJ L 364, 12.12.1992.
[9] Regulation 789/2004, OJ L 138, 30.04.2004.
[10] Directive 1999/63, OJ L 167, 02.07.1999.

Detailed rules were laid down for the application of Articles 81 and 82 of the EC Treaty (ex-Articles 85 and 86) to maritime transport in order to ensure that competition is not unduly distorted within the common market. Community guidelines for **State aid in the maritime transport sector** are intended to make public assistance transparent and to define what kinds of aid scheme can be introduced to support the Community's maritime interests[1]. Block exemptions [see section 15.3.3.] exist for certain concerted practices between liner shipping companies (**maritime conferences and consortia**), which provide international liner shipping services from or to one or more Community ports[2]. Thanks to these exemptions from the general rules of Articles 81 and 82, shipowners may jointly organise services, thus rationalising their activities as maritime carriers and obtaining economies of scale and cost reductions, while at the same time providing users with a better-quality service. They allow notably the coordination and joint fixing of sailing timetables, the determination of ports of call, the exchange, sale or cross-chartering of space or "slots" on vessels, the pooling of vessels, port installations and operation offices.

International **safety standards for passenger vessels** are applied in the Community. Thus, the International Conventions for the Safety of Life at Sea (SOLAS) and for the prevention of pollution by ships (MARPOL) are applicable to the Member States - and therefore to ships flying their flags[3]. The Member States must subject cargo ships and passenger ships to initial and annual surveys to check in particular compliance with the SOLAS Convention[4]. Passenger ships operating on domestic voyages, which are not covered by the SOLAS international Convention, are covered by a Community Directive, which is intended to guarantee maximum safety for passengers and, at the same time, to provide a level playing field based on convergent standards in Community shipping[5]. In order to ensure that the maximum capacity of ships is not exceeded and to provide accurate information to the emergency services in the event of an accident, another Directive obliges shipping companies operating to or from Community ports to count and register the crew members and persons sailing on board passenger ships[6]. The Community implements the International Management Code for the Safe Operation of Ships and for Pollution Prevention adopted by the International Maritime Organisation (ISM Code)[7]. Ships using Community ports and sailing in the waters under the jurisdiction of the Member States must respect the international standards for ship safety, pollution prevention and shipboard living and working conditions (port State control)[8].

[1] OJ C 205, 05.07.1997.
[2] Regulation 823/2000, OJ L 100, 20.04.2000 and Regulation 611/2005, OJ L 101, 21.04.2005.
[3] Regulation 2158/93, OJ L 194, 03.08.1993.
[4] Directive 1999/35, OJ L 138, 01.06.1999 and Directive 2002/84, OJ L 324, 29.11.2002.
[5] Council Directive 98/18, OJ L 144, 15.05.1998 and Directive 2003/75, OJ L 190, 30.07.2003.
[6] Directive 98/41, OJ L 188, 02.07.1998 and Directive 2003/25, OJ L 123, 17.05.2003.
[7] Regulation 336/2006, OJ L 64, 04.03.2006.
[8] Directive 95/21, OJ L 157, 07.07.1995 and Directive 2002/84, OJ L 324, 29.11.2002.

The independent **European Maritime Safety Agency** assists the Commission with drafting maritime legislation, monitoring application by the Member States and coordinating inquiries after accidents at sea or after accidental or illicit pollution caused by ships[1]. A Directive sets up common rules and standards for ship inspection and survey organisations in order to ensure a high level of competence and independence of these organisations[2]. To prevent marine pollution (such as that caused by the "Erika" and "Prestige" accidents off the coasts of France in December 2000 and Spain in December 2002), a Regulation established an accelerated phasing-in scheme for the application of the double-hull or equivalent design requirements of the MARPOL 73/78 Convention to single hull oil tankers[3].

20.3.4. Air transport

The liberalisation of air transport in the Community was achieved progressively, between 1987 and 1992, with three packages of Regulations. The third air transport package, adopted by the Council on 22 June 1992, constituted the final stage in the liberalisation of Community air transport. It has achieved the freedom to provide services within the Community, technical and economic harmonisation and free price setting.

The Regulation on the **licensing of air carriers** defines the technical and economic requirements which airlines must meet in order to obtain national licences authorising them to operate on Community territory without restrictions on the grounds of nationality[4]. The licences in question are: the air operator's certificate (AOC), which affirms the technical quality and competence of the airline concerned; and the operating licence, granted to undertakings which comply with certain conditions regarding nationality and which meet certain economic criteria and are covered by a suitable insurance scheme. This Regulation guarantees, then, that only airlines under Community control, and with adequate technical and economic capacity, are able to take advantage of the opening up of the European market.

The Regulation on **access for air carriers** to intra-Community air routes opens up all airports on the territory of the Community to all those who are registered according to the above-mentioned Regulation[5]. It provides, in particular, for: the abolition of the previously existing sharing of passenger capacity between airlines; the unrestricted exercise of the **'fifth freedom'** (the right to pick up passengers in a Member State other than that in which the airline is registered and to disembark them in a third Member State); and the authorisation to undertake **cabotage operations**

---

[1] Regulation 1406/2002, OJ L 208, 05.08.2002 and Regulation 724/2004, OJ L 129, 29.04.2004.

[2] Directive 94/57, OJ L 319, 12.12.1994 and Directive 2002/84, OJ L 324, 29.11.2002.

[3] Regulation 417/2002, OJ L 64, 07.03.2002 and Regulation 1726/2003, OJ L 249, 01.10.2003.

[4] Regulation 2407/92, OJ L 240, 24.08.1992.

[5] Regulation 2408/92, OJ L 240, 24.08.1992 last amended by Regulation 1882/2003, OJ L 284, 31.10.2003.

(to pick up passengers in a Member State other than that in which the air-line is registered and to disembark them in that same Member State).

Finally, the Regulation on **fares and rates for air services** guarantees the unrestricted setting of new passenger fares and cargo rates for sched-uled air services and charter flights under certain conditions safeguarding the interests of both the industry and of consumers[1]. It defines, in particu-lar, the arrangements for the examination of new fares and rates by the Member States and the system of 'double disapproval' (whereby a new fare or rate may not be turned down unless both Member States concerned dis-approve of it). If this is not the case, Community air carriers may freely fix passenger fares. Charter fares and air cargo rates are freely fixed by the parties to the air transport contract.

The EU encourages better information for air passengers, greater pro-tection for passengers' rights, improved service and simplified handling of disputes[2]. A Regulation drawing up common rules for the **compensation of passengers refused the right to board** due to over-booking[3] is of par-ticular importance to the ordinary citizen. It stipulates that should a pas-senger be refused the right to board, he has the right to choose between full reimbursement of the price of the ticket for the part of the journey, which he was unable to carry out, or rescheduling on a later date of his choice. Regardless of the choice made by the passenger, the air carrier must pay, immediately after the boarding refusal, compensation that varies in line with the distance of the flight and the rescheduling delay. The carrier must moreover offer passengers refused the right to board meals, hotel accom-modation if necessary and the cost of a telephone call and/or telefax mes-sage to the place of destination.

As regards, more particularly, the operation of **air freight services,** a Council Regulation seeks to open up access to the market, liberalise fares and boost the operating flexibility of these services[4]. A Member State ap-proves airfreight carriers whose licence has been issued by another Mem-ber State and which has been authorised by the State of registration to ex-ercise third-, fourth- and fifth-freedom traffic rights. Fifth freedom traffic rights are exercised on a service, which is the extension of a service on de-parture from the State where the carrier is registered or a preliminary to a service whose end destination is this State. The prices applied by Commu-nity air carriers for freight transport are set freely by mutual agreement of the parties to the transport contract. Air carriers operating services within the Community must place all their standard freight rates at the disposal of the general public on request.

The establishment of **common rules in the field of civil aviation** aims at guaranteeing European citizens high safety and environmental protection

---

[1] Regulation 2409/92, OJ L 240, 24.08.1992.

[2] Council resolution, OJ C 293, 14.10.2000.

[3] Regulation 261/2004, OJ L 46, 17.02.2004.

[4] Regulation 2408/92, OJ L 240 of 24.08.1992 last amended by Regulation 1882/2003, OJ L 284, 31.10.2003.

standards and at facilitating activity in the aeronautics industry in Europe[1]. Aeronautical products are henceforth subject to certification to verify that they meet essential airworthiness and environmental protection requirements relating to civil aviation, notably to the design, production, maintenance and operation of aeronautical products, parts and appliances. Appropriate essential requirements cover operations of aircraft and flight crew licensing. They apply to third-country aircraft and other areas in the field of civil aviation safety. In addition, a Community blacklist contains airlines that are banned throughout the European Union and a series of measures aimed at better informing air passengers about the identity of the airline they are travelling with[2].

In order to respond to increasing concerns over the health and welfare of passengers during flights, the common rules aim, among other things, to develop aircraft designs which better protect the safety and health of passengers. An independent Community body, the **European Aviation Safety Agency** assists the Commission in the preparation of the necessary legislation and the Member States and the industry in its implementation[3]. It is able to issue certification specifications and certificates as required. It is allowed to develop its expertise in all aspects of civil aviation safety and environmental protection.

A package of common rules on the use of airspace throughout the Community, called the "**single European sky**" package, aims at improving and reinforcing safety, and at restructuring airspace on the basis of traffic flow rather than according to national boundaries, at encouraging cross-border air navigation service provision and at establishing a framework for the modernisation of systems[4]. The measures concern an integrated, harmonised management of Community airspace, which implies the supply of services by flexible and efficient providers guided by demand from airspace users and therefore they entail a less rigid interpretation by States of national sovereignty over their airspace. The project to modernise air traffic management in Europe and to enhance safety (**the SESAR project**) is the technological element of the single European sky[5]. Development of these measures requires, in addition to greater involvement of industry and the social partners, recourse to the technical expertise of the **European Organisation for the Safety of Air Navigation (Eurocontrol)** and the possible creation of a military cooperation framework.

As a matter of fact, the Regulation, which is designed to achieve the gradual harmonisation and integration of national air-traffic systems, makes mandatory the technical specifications drawn up by Eurocontrol, thus allowing the Commission to adopt Eurocontrol standards[6]. The acces-

---

[1] Regulation 216/2008, OJ L 79, 19.03.2008.
[2] Regulation 2111/2005, OJ L 344, 27.12.2005 and R. 715/2008, OJ L 197, 25.07.2008.
[3] Regulation 216/2008, OJ L 79, 19.03.2008.
[4] Regulations 549/2004 to 552/2004, OJ L 96, 31.03.2004.
[5] Regulation 219/2007, OJ L 64, 02.03.2007.
[6] Regulation 552/2004, OJ L 96, 31.03.2004.

sion by the European Community to Eurocontrol, aiming at ensuring consistency between the two institutions and improving the regulatory framework for air traffic management, forms part of the overall strategy to build up a single sky over the single market[1].

An Air Transport Agreement between the European Community and its Member States, on the one hand, and the United States of America, on the other hand, was signed on April 30, 2007[2]. The so-called **"Open Skies Agreement"** is applied since 30 March 2008. It removes all restrictions on routes, prices, or the number of weekly flights. All EU airlines are now able to operate direct flights to the US from anywhere in Europe and not just from their home country (and vice-versa for US airlines).

20.4. Appraisal and outlook

Until the end of the 1980s, the Community achievements in the transport sector did not measure up to the clear need for a policy expressly mentioned in the Treaty of Rome as **a crucial cornerstone of the common market**. In fact, during thirty years the Member States rejected measures of liberalisation proposed by the Commission which, they maintained, would upset competition conditions, both between the various modes of transport and within each one of them. Council deliberations revolved around the sophistic question of whether market liberalisation or harmonisation of competition conditions should come first. The Council's failure to act, forcefully pointed out by the European Parliament in its 1982 resolution, was chiefly due to an **absence of political commitment** to pushing economic integration in this field. As a consequence, national experts, who prepared the Council meetings, played a very important role in examining the Commission's proposals [see section 9.4.]. Since these proposals, by their very nature, were likely to perturb vested interests and the economic policy concepts of the Member States, very often there was exaggerated defence of national interest and sectoral perception of the problems, which did not make sufficient allowance for the requirements of European integration. These requirements finally prevailed, however. Whether under pressure from the European Parliament and public opinion or the need to integrate transport into the post-1992 single market, **transport policy stepped on the accelerator** in the middle of the 1980s, particularly in three fields: road haulage, maritime transport and air transport.

The greatest breakthrough for the common transport policy has undoubtedly been in the area of **liberalising international road haulage services**. All the quotas applicable to cross-border transport within the Community were replaced by a system of Community licences issued on the basis of qualitative criteria. The fact that the liberalisation introduced

---

[1]   Decision 2004/636, OJ L 304, 30.09.2004.
[2]   Decision 2007/339 and Agreement, OJ L 134, 25.05.2007.

gradually since the early 1990s has not upset the road haulage market, shows that the fears of some national administrations of the common transport market upsetting their national markets were exaggerated.

In the area of **maritime transport**, which is the carrier for 85% of the EEC's external trade, the Member States undertook to apply the rules of free competition and the principle of free provision of services to this sector. They also agreed to fight unfair tariff practices and unsafe seafaring methods, while guaranteeing free access to ocean trades and even to cabotage. All cabotage services in Europe have been liberalised between January 1999 and December 2002. The market has not been adversely affected. Cargo volumes and the number of passengers transported have remained relatively stable.

As regards **air transport**, the liberalisation measures completed in 1992 have had a major impact on competition between air carriers. Additional routes were opened, new services were introduced, monopolies were put under pressure, inefficient national companies were forced to modernise or close down and new companies were created. Nevertheless, basic fares are still too high if compared to those in other regions of the world, especially the United States. The costs of air transport remain high, largely because of heavy infrastructure charges and airport fees. Access to the market is still too difficult, mainly due to bilateral agreements between the Member States and third countries. The main concern for the future is the saturation of the Community's airports and air corridors, due to substantial increase in air traffic.

Bibliography on transport policy

* COMBES Michel (et al.). *Transport aérien: gagner ensemble = Air transport: winning together*. Paris: Publisud, 2006.
* DIDIER Michel, PRUD'HOMME Rémy. *Infrastructures de transport, mobilité et croissance*. Conseil d'analyse économique. Paris: Documentation française, 2007.
* EUROPEAN COMMISSION. *Flying together: EU air transport policy*. Luxembourg: EUR-OP, 2007.
    * Trans-European networks: towards an integrated approach. COM/2007/135. Luxembourg: EUR-OP, 2007.
    * Information society and transport: linking European policies. Luxembourg: EUR-OP, 2007.
* EUROPEAN CONFERENCE OF MINISTERS OF TRANSPORT. *Transport infrastructure Investment and economic productivity*. Paris: ECMT, 2007.
* EUROPEAN ENVIRONMENT AGENCY. *Transport and environment on the way to a new common transport policy: indicators tracking transport and environment in the European Union*. Luxembourg: EUR-OP*, 2007.
* GEENHUIZEN Marina van, REGGIANI Aura, RIETVELD Piet (eds.). *Policy analysis of transport networks*. Aldershot: Ashgate, 2007.
* KAEDING Michael. *Better regulation in the European Union: lost in translation or full steam ahead? The transposition of EU transport directives across member states*. Leiden: Leiden University Press, 2007.

- MOAVENZADEH F, MARKOW M.J. *Moving millions: transport strategies for sustainable development in megacities.* Dordrecht: Springer, 2007.

DISCUSSION TOPICS

1. Why was the common transport policy specifically provided for in the Treaty of Rome?
2. What are the relations between the single market for goods and the single market for transports?
3. Discuss the terms of competition between road and rail transport.
4. Can the common transport policy promote economic and social cohesion in the EU?
5. Has the upheaval of national policies and vested interests caused by the common transport policy been beneficial to EU citizens?

Chapter 21

AGRICULTURAL POLICY

Diagram of the chapter

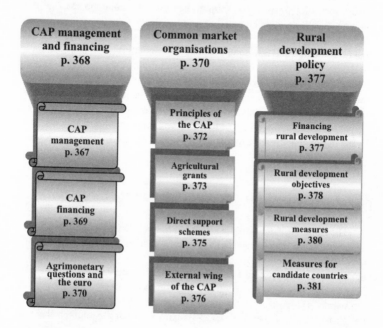

CAP management and financing p. 368	Common market organisations p. 370	Rural development policy p. 377
CAP management p. 367	Principles of the CAP p. 372	Financing rural development p. 377
CAP financing p. 369	Agricultural grants p. 373	Rural development objectives p. 378
	Direct support schemes p. 375	Rural development measures p. 380
Agrimonetary questions and the euro p. 370	External wing of the CAP p. 376	Measures for candidate countries p. 381

The share of agriculture in the Union's gross domestic product (GDP) is just under 3%; but the sector is the principal source of income in many rural communities, which would be devastated without its contribution. Moreover, food, beverages and tobacco account for about 20% of average European household consumer expenditure and form a substantial proportion of internal trade and exports of the Union. Finally and most importantly, the self-sufficiency of the EC/EU in basic agricultural products is vital, not only for the wellbeing of its citizens, but also for the political independence of its Member States. The economic, **social and political importance of agriculture** is, therefore, much greater than its share in the GDP of the Union.

Without a shadow of a doubt, agriculture is the economic sector where **the process of European integration is furthest advanced**. This achievement is all the more significant in that State interventionism and the conflicts of national interests complicated the task of creating a common policy in this sector. Indeed, prior to the common market, the Member

States were actively interventionist in agriculture [see section 21.1.]. National interventionism had to be corrected to enable free trade and free play of competition in the agricultural sector. The creation of the **Common Agricultural Policy (CAP)** is therefore an exemplary achievement of the multinational integration process.

Nonetheless, the common agricultural policy is **difficult to manage**, for it implies the use of common prices, common price management instruments, joint financing of support measures and common external protection. All these cumbersome but unavoidable mechanisms form part of the CAP's market organisation. The latter is one of **the CAP's two wings**, the other being rural development policy. Although the common market in agricultural products has ensured supply security of foodstuffs at reasonable prices for consumers, it would not have been sufficient in itself to attain the other objectives of the Treaty, namely increased agricultural productivity and a higher standard of living for farmers. The latter required an active socio-structural policy, interacting with other common policies, such as the regional and social, to guarantee the Community's rural areas a place in the single market.

21.1. Reasons for special treatment of agriculture

The founding fathers of the European Economic Community were well aware of the need to include the agricultural markets of the Member States in the future common market. But they were also aware that the **common agricultural market could not simply be achieved** by abolishing the barriers to free movement and introducing common competition rules, as in the sectors of industry and the services [see section 6.2.]. This is why Article 32 of the EC Treaty (ex Art. 38) states in its first paragraph that the common market includes agriculture and trade in agricultural products, while specifying in paragraph 4 that the operation and growth of the common market in agricultural products must be accompanied by the introduction of a common agricultural policy.

There are several reasons why agriculture was afforded "special treatment". The most important is that due to the **very nature of agriculture**, which is at the mercy of weather conditions, crop and livestock diseases and many other factors which often elude human control and make it very difficult to ensure a perfect balance between agricultural output and the demand for foodstuffs. In addition, demand has very pronounced social and political characteristics. Governments are obliged to ensure that demand for basic commodities is satisfied at all times and at reasonable prices. The original Community was far from self-sufficient in foodstuffs and conditions on the world market provided no justification for the unilateral opening up of markets. Consequently, if food security was to be guaranteed at stable prices, the Community had to organise its own agriculture. This was quite reasonable, since the agricultural output of the different

Member States was complementary. Northern Europe could supply cereals, dairy products and meat, whereas Southern Europe could specialise in fruit and vegetables, citrus fruit and wines.

However, the diversity of the agricultural sector of the six founding Member States, which increased with each enlargement of the Community, generated difficulties for the unification of their agricultural markets, providing further justification for an **interventionist agricultural policy**. Different natural, structural, social and trade conditions, the prominence of agriculture in the national economy and different farming traditions led to the use in each European State of agricultural policy instruments which diverged considerably as to their application scope and magnitude. The common policy therefore had to not only align structurally different agricultural systems, but also to iron out tenaciously held privileges resulting from the interplay of national political institutions: State monopolies or similar regulations, price guarantees, farm income aid, export subsidies, direct or indirect import restrictions, customs protection and so on. A new agricultural policy stepping in the shoes of the national ones had to be defined. The complexity of the latter created the need for the blending of national policies into one common agricultural policy.

One could ask **why organise agricultural markets at all?** The answer is that the agricultural markets of the Member States were already organised in various ways at national level. Indeed, almost all states in the world intervene in one way or another to ensure the income of their farmers and stable supply for their consumers. The only difference is that the system of intervention varies from one to the other. They can however be divided into two main categories: direct income aid systems for farmers, which existed in the United Kingdom before its entry to the Community and was called deficiency payments; and the system of price support on the internal market combined with external protection, the system chosen for the bulk of the original EEC's agricultural production[1].

The system of support for agricultural prices was thought, at the time, to be better adapted to the interests of the original Community. In effect, under the alternative **direct income aid** system, agricultural products are imported at world prices, generally low when they are in ample supply, and the income of national farmers topped up by a subsidy from the budget. Under the **system of price support**, on the other hand, in order to provide national farmers with sufficient income, internal prices which are higher than the world prices for agricultural products are practised and the difference is compensated by import levies or customs duties and by export refunds (subsidies)[2]. The higher prices stimulate agricultural output and productivity. They also tend to guarantee self-sufficiency in basic agricultural products and foodstuffs, which is another point in their favour. If they are set too high they can naturally lead to production surpluses, which is a

---

[1] OJ 11, 01.08.1958.

[2] Regulation 800/1999, OJ L 102, 17.04.1999 last amended by Regulation 1847/2006, OJ L 355, 15.12.2006.

negative point, but which results more from the manner in which the system is applied than from the system itself. Inasmuch, however, as agricultural prices determine farmer income, it is socio-politically very difficult for Agricultural Ministers within the Council to cut these prices, even if the Commission, in its pricing proposals, provides them with arguments in favour of reducing surplus production through prices [see section 4.3.]. These same Ministers are, however, conscious of their own failings, since they periodically accept to revise the system through a CAP reform [see section 21.2.2.].

As will be seen in the nest section, the CAP was reformed four times in forty years, blending gradually the systems of price and income support. Thus, after its major reforms, in 1999 and 2003, the **European model of agriculture** is based on competitive, multifunctional and sustainable farming. This means that European agriculture is broadening its horizons, since farmers also perform a range of additional tasks, notably in the fields of environment and countryside conservation. As a result of their high population density and geographical differentiation, European countries must produce these services in addition to actual farm produce itself. The EU cannot afford to confine nature and the environment to some reserves. Therefore, agriculture must also be maintained in less-favoured areas as well. Since it is not developed in a vacuum, however, the European model of agriculture has to prove its worth, both internally in addressing issues such as market development, rural development, satisfactory farm incomes and environmental protection, and externally, in facing the challenges of an enlarged Union and heightened competition inside the World Trade Organisation [see section 23.4.].

21.2. CAP foundations and reforms

The **objectives** of the common agricultural policy are specified in Article 33 of the EC Treaty (ex-Art. 39): higher agricultural productivity; guarantee of a fair standard of living to farmers; market stabilisation; supply security and reasonable prices for consumers. In order to attain these objectives, Article 40 of the EEC Treaty (actual Art. 34 TEC) called for the **common organisation of agricultural markets** which, depending on the product, could take one of three forms: common coordination rules, compulsory coordination of the various national market organisations or European market organisation. It is interesting to note that it is always this last and most stringent concept that has been applied to the common organisation of agricultural markets.

Established in July 1966, the CAP was reformed a first time in April 1972, a second time in February 1988, a third time in May 1992 and a fourth time in March 1999. Four major reforms of a common policy in 33 years may indicate that the Member States that conceived it and those that joined them later on have never considered it as perfect; but may also show that they were willing to learn from their experience and able to **adapt their common policy** to the changing internal and external circumstances.

Successive reforms have contributed to the competitiveness of European agriculture by reducing price support guarantees and encouraging structural adjustment. **The fifth CAP reform**, carried out in September 2003, provides for a single farm payment for European Union farmers, independent from production and subject to compliance with environmental, food safety, animal and plant health and animal welfare standards, and requirements to keep all farmland in good agricultural and environmental condition ("cross-compliance")[1]. The introduction of decoupled direct payments encourages farmers to respond to market signals generated by consumer demand rather than by quantity-related policy incentives. The reform is aimed at enabling the farmers of the twenty-seven Member States to be more competitive and be more market-oriented whilst stabilising their income, and at channelling more resources into programmes on the environment, quality and animal welfare by reducing direct payments to large farms. It is expected also to strengthen the European Union's hand in the trade negotiations in the World Trade Organisation.

After its fourth and fifth reforms, the CAP is targeted not just at agricultural producers but also at the wider rural population, consumers and society as a whole. Thus **the new CAP seeks to promote**:

- a clear connection between public support and the range of services which society as a whole receives from the farming community;
- a competitive agricultural sector which is capable of exploiting the opportunities existing on world markets without excessive subsidy, while at the same time ensuring a fair standard of living for the agricultural community;
- an agricultural sector that is sustainable in environmental terms, contributing to the preservation of natural resources and the natural and cultural heritage of the countryside;
- the maintenance of vibrant rural communities, capable of generating employment opportunities for the rural population [see section 21.5];
- production methods which are safe and capable of supplying quality products that meet consumer demand and reflect the diversified and rich tradition of European food production.

21.3. CAP management and financing

The unity of the European Union's agricultural market requires common prices, common support instruments for these prices, common external protection, joint financing and, in general, **joint management**, for which the European Commission has responsibility. The Commission, as

---

[1] Regulations 1782/2003 to 1788/2003, OJ L 270, 21.10.2003 and Regulation 674,/2008, OJ L 189, 17.07.2008.

for other areas of Community activity, is also invested with the power of initiative, i.e. the power to make proposals [see section 4.1.2.]. Hence, the genesis of any agricultural policy measure, adopted by politicians in the Parliament and the Council, is a Commission proposal, based on techno-cratic criteria.

Scientific committees, made up of experts from all Member States, give advice to the Commission on the very important matters of consumer health and food safety. Eight committees meet about ten times a year, and the Commission consults them whenever there is a legal requirement to do so, and whenever a matter of special relevance to one of them arises. A Scientific Steering Committee (SSC) has a multidisciplinary role. One of its tasks is to coordinate the work of the scientific committees to provide an overall view of consumer health matters, and to deliver scientific advice on matters not covered by the mandates of the other scientific committees, e.g. on transmissible spongiform encephalopathies. The operation of the scientific committees and, in particular, of the SSC, is based on the three principles of excellence, independence and transparency.

After all this preparatory work inside the services of the Commission, once a Commission proposal in the area of the common agricultural policy has been put before it, the Council entrusts the preparation of its proceed-ings to a committee of senior officials known as the **Special Committee on Agriculture** (SCA). In the area of agriculture, the SCA assumes the role normally fulfilled by the Committee of Permanent Representatives (Coreper) [see section 4.1.4.].

21.3.1. CAP Management

After adoption of the basic regulations by the Council comes manage-ment of the common organisations. Management is either the joint respon-sibility of the Commission and Council or that of the Commission alone. For general policy decisions such as the annual setting of farm prices, un-dertaken in application of the basic regulations, the **full procedure** is used: the Commission after consulting professional organisations submits a pro-posal to the Council, which takes a decision after consultation with the European Parliament and very often the Economic and Social Committee as well as the Committee of the Regions [see section 4.3.]. For long-application management provisions, such as adjustments of market mecha-nisms or of basic criteria, a **medium-length procedure** is used: the Com-mission proposes measures to the Council, which takes a decision without consulting either the European Parliament or the Economic and Social Committee.

The implementation provisions for basic regulations and management measures in the strict sense of the term, which are applicable on average for a few weeks or a few months, are adopted by the Commission using a procedure known as the **"Management Committee" procedure**, whereby the Commission acts after having received the opinion of the relevant management committee[1]. Management committees comprise representatives of the Member States dealing with a specific sector [see section 9.4.]. They give their opinion on the Commission's plans for the management of agricultural markets. There is a management committee for each category of product: cereals, milk products, beef and veal, wine, fruit and vegetables, etc. Very important management committees are notably: the Committee of the EAGF, which deals exclusively with matters relating to and the Committee on rural development, which assists the Commission with the management of the common agricultural and rural development policies. **Regulatory committees**, also made up of representatives of all the Member States, play a role similar to that of the management committees for decisions about the regulations that apply in general areas such as food safety legislation, common veterinary or plant health standards, etc.

21.3.2. CAP financing

Article 34 of the EC Treaty (Art. 40 EEC) - devoted to the gradual development of the common agricultural policy - declared that one or several agricultural guidance and guarantee funds should be created to enable the common organisation of agricultural markets to fulfil its goals. On January 14, 1962 during the first agricultural marathon, the Council opted for the creation of one single fund to finance all Community market and structural expenditure in the various agricultural sectors: the **European Agricultural Guidance and Guarantee Fund (EAGGF)**.

The reform of the common agricultural policy in June 2003 and April 2004 [see section 21.2.2] introduced major changes having a significant impact on the economy of rural territories of the Community in terms of agricultural production patterns, land management methods, employment and the wider social and economic conditions in the various rural areas. Consequently, the European Agricultural Guidance and Guarantee Fund (EAGGF) was abolished and two European agricultural funds were created in 2005, namely the **European Agricultural Guarantee Fund (EAGF)**, for the financing of market measures, and the **European Agricultural Fund for Rural Development (EAFRD)**, for the financing of rural development programmes[2].

As of January 2007, **the EAGF finances** in a context of shared management between the Member States and the Community the following expenditure, which is effected in accordance with Community law: (a) refunds for the exportation of agricultural products to third countries; (b) intervention measures to regulate agricultural markets; (c) direct payments to farmers under the common agricultural policy; and (d) the Community's financial contribution to information and promotion measures for agricultural products on the internal market of the Community and in third coun-

---

[1] Regulation 2602/69, OJ L 324, 27.12.1969.
[2] Regulation 1290/2005, OJ L 209, 11.08.2005 and R. 1437/2007, OJ L 322, 07.12.2007.

tries, undertaken by Member States on the basis of Community programmes and selected by the Commission. **The EAFRD finances** in a context of shared management between the Member States and the Community the Community's financial contribution to rural development programmes implemented in accordance with the Community legislation on support for rural development [see section 21.5]. Budget discipline takes account of the reform of the CAP as provided for by Regulation 1782/2003. The Commission and Member States share the costs of payments under the EAFRD and amounts to be recovered following the detection of irregularities and negligence.

21.3.3. Agrimonetary questions and the euro

The **introduction of the euro**, on 1 January 1999, ended the previously existing problems concerning the fixing of common prices and intervention measures[1]. It led to a major reform and simplification of the agrimonetary system. Agricultural conversion rates have been discontinued. Agricultural prices and aid in the participating Member States is paid in euros. Community aid too is paid and collected in euros[2]. In the case of the Member States outside the eurozone, the euro exchange rate is used for the necessary conversions into their national currencies, unless they decide to make payments in euro. For those Member States the value of a payment is determined by the exchange rate on the date of the operative event (a price or an aid) and not on the date of actual payment.

The use of **the euro benefits the CAP**, not only by simplifying its procedures and reducing its budget costs through the abolition of the green rates, but also through the simplification and transparency of aid schemes for farmers, price stability and increased competitiveness in Community agriculture. Thanks to the euro, Eurozone agricultural enterprises are able to invoice their products in the currency in which their costs are also denominated, thereby avoiding an exchange risk.

21.4. Common market organisations

The common agricultural market is underpinned by **common market organisations (CMOs)**, which remove obstacles to intra-Community trade and create common protection at the external borders. At present, almost all the Community's agricultural production is regulated by common organisations. Article 32 of the EC Treaty (ex-Art. 38) defines agricultural products as products of the soil, livestock products and fishery products, along with products of first-stage processing which are directly related to these products. Foodstuffs are considered as products of second-stage

---

[1] Regulation 2799/98, OJ L 349, 24.12.1998.
[2] Regulation 2800/98, OJ L 349, 24.12.1998 and Regulation 2813/98, OJ L 349, 24.12.1998.

processing and are therefore not included in agricultural products. To make matters as clear as possible, products covered by the provisions under the heading "agriculture" are listed in Annex I of the EC Treaty. This is why, in Community terminology, agricultural arrangements are often stated as being applicable to "Annex I products".

The market organisation regulations, which came into force in 2000 as a result of **the fourth reform of the CAP** [see section 21.2.2.], concern the arable crops, beef, milk and wine sectors, the new rural development framework, the horizontal rules for direct support schemes and the financing of the CAP[1]. These regulations introduced gradual cuts in institutional prices - compensated by income support - with the objective of bringing Europe's agricultural prices into closer touch with world market prices, thus helping improve the competitiveness of agricultural products on domestic and world markets with positive impacts on both internal demand and export levels [see sections 21.4.2. and 21.4.4.].

The **fifth CAP reform** (September 2003) established common rules for direct support schemes under the common agricultural policy and support schemes for producers of certain crops (durum wheat, protein crops, rice, nuts, energy crops, starch potatoes, milk, seeds, arable crops, sheep meat and goat meat, beef and veal and grain legumes)[2]. The reform takes account of increased consumer concerns over **food quality and safety and environmental protection**. Indeed, the full payment of direct aid is henceforth linked to compliance with rules relating to agricultural land, agricultural production and activity, which should serve to incorporate in the common market organisations basic standards for the environment, food safety, animal health and welfare and good agricultural and environmental condition. The reform includes a reduction in direct payments ("modulation") for bigger farms to finance the rural development policy and introduces a financial discipline mechanism to ensure that the farm budget fixed until 2013 is not exceeded. The reform of the support schemes for farmers concerns also the ten new Member States since May 2004[3].

The market organisation of each agricultural product uses different mechanisms defined by its basic regulation and adopted by the Council using the full-blown procedure [see section 21.3.2.], but all of them are underpinned by, on the one hand, internal market measures, more often than not relating to price setting and support, and, on the other, by a trade regime with third countries, which is in conformity with the Agreement on agriculture concluded in the context of the GATT Uruguay Round [see section 23.4.].

---

[1] Regulations 1251/1999 to 1259/1999, OJ L 160, 26.06.1999 and Regulation 1782/2003, OJ L 270, 21.10.2003.

[2] Regulations 1782/2003 to 1788/2003, OJ L 270, 21.10.2003 and Regulation 674,/2008, OJ L 189, 17.07.2008.

[3] Regulation 583/2004, OJ L 91, 30.03.2004 and Decision 2004/281, OJ L 93, 30.3.2004.

21.4.1. The principles of the CAP

Three basic principles defined in 1962 characterise the common agricultural market and consequently the common market organisations: market unity, Community preference and financial solidarity. Whereas, the introduction of the euro has consolidated market unity [see section 21.3.5.], the third and fourth reforms of the CAP [see section 21.2.2.] have had an important effect on Community preference and financial solidarity.

Market unity means that agricultural products move throughout the European Union under conditions similar to those in an internal market, thanks to the abolition of quantitative restrictions to trade (quotas, import monopolies...) and the removal of duties, taxes and measures having equivalent effect. Market unity supposes common agricultural prices throughout the EU. The Council, acting on a proposal from the Commission, thus, early in each marketing year, sets common agricultural prices expressed formerly in ecu and, since 1999, in euro[1] [see section 21.3.5.]. In principle, the common agricultural prices should be attained through the free play of supply and demand so that the only variations in the prices paid to farmers in all regions of the Union result from natural production conditions and distance from main centres of consumption.

Community preference, the second bulwark of the common agricultural market, signifies that products of Community origin are bought in preference to imported products, in order to protect the common market against low-price imports and fluctuations in world prices. This principle, spread throughout the world, is enacted through import and export measures. The European Union tries to bring the prices of imports into the EU at the prices practised on the common market. The price gap between the world market and the minimum guaranteed price in the EU was formerly covered by variable import levies, which after the GATT Uruguay Round have been progressively replaced by fixed customs duties [see section 21.4.4. and 23.5.]. To the extent that external prices taxed with import duties are at the same level as internal prices, it is not to the advantage of European traders to buy supplies from outside the EU and they therefore give preference to Community products. But whereas this was practically always the case with the import levies, it is much less certain with the customs duties.

The third basic principle of the common agricultural market is that of **financial solidarity**. It is implemented through the intermediary of the European Agricultural Guarantee Fund (EAGF) and signifies that the Member States are jointly liable as regards the financial consequences of the common agricultural markets policy. Since the European Union organises agricultural markets and defines and applies the intervention measures on them, it is logical that it is responsible for the financial consequences of

---

[1] See, e.g., Council Regulations 1400/1999 to 1405/1999, OJ L 164, 30.06.1999 and Council Regulations 1671/1999 to 1680/1999, OJ L 199, 30.07.1999.

these measures. The EAGF therefore covers all the expenditure rendered necessary by the common market organisations. The other side of the coin is that the customs duties, collected at the Union's frontiers on imports from third countries, do not go into the coffers of the Member States but are a source of revenue for the Community budget [see section 3.4.].

The 1992 CAP reform, which made possible the 1993 GATT Agreement [see sections 23.4 and 23.5.], has affected the fundamental principles of the CAP, since it has supplemented the original price support with a direct income aid system. It has, in fact, introduced a **mixed system**: price support was reduced, but the farmers' revenue was maintained at its previous level by subsidies. In other words, the reduction of price support was compensated by the support of the revenue of the farmers. This system was amplified by the 1999 reform. The new policy for rural development seeks to establish a coherent and sustainable framework for the future of Europe's rural areas. It seeks to complement the reforms introduced into the market sectors by promoting a competitive, multi-functional agricultural sector in the context of a comprehensive, integrated strategy for rural development [see section 21.5.3.]. The guiding principles of the new policy are those of decentralisation of responsibilities - thus strengthening subsidiarity and partnership - and flexibility of programming based on a "menu" of actions to be targeted and implemented according to Member States' specific needs.

21.4.2. Agricultural grants and product quality

The **2003 CAP reform** altered the basis of direct aid to producers, paid to farmers or producers' associations, progressively phasing it out and decoupling it from production [see section 21.4.3]. This decoupling, which began on 1 January 2005 for most Common Market Organisations (CMOs), separates grants received from production. The vast majority of subsidies is henceforth paid independently from the volume of production. To avoid abandonment of production, Member States may choose to maintain a limited link between subsidy and production under well defined conditions and within clear limits. These new "single farm payments" are linked to the respect of environmental, food safety and animal welfare standards. Severing the link between subsidies and production is intended to make EU farmers more competitive and market orientated, while providing the necessary income stability. More money will be available to farmers for environmental, quality or animal welfare programmes by reducing direct payments for bigger farms.

The key **elements of the reformed CAP are:**

- the "single farm payment" for EU farmers is independent from production and is linked to the respect of environmental, food safety, animal and plant health and animal welfare standards, as well as the requirement to keep all farmland in good agricultural and environmental condition ("cross-compliance"),

- limited coupled elements are intended to avoid abandonment of production,
- a strengthened rural development policy with new measures is intended to promote the environment, quality and animal welfare and to help farmers to meet EU production standards,
- a reduction in direct payments ("modulation") for bigger farms helps to finance the new rural development policy,
- a mechanism for financial discipline aims to ensure that the farm budget fixed until 2013 is not overshot,

Connected with the question of agricultural grants is the question of the **quality of agricultural products** and foodstuffs. The quality and characteristics of these products are often linked to their geographical origin. Two Council Regulations are designed to raise consumer awareness of the producers' efforts to improve the quality of their products. The first establishes a Community system for the protection of **geographical indications and designations of origin** for agricultural products and foodstuffs[1], supplemented by lists of some 480 names of agricultural and food products drawn up by the Commission[2]. It spells out with what requirements a product or foodstuff should comply in order to qualify for a protected designation of origin (PDO) or for a protected geographical indication (PGI). The other Regulation lays down the rules under which an agricultural product or foodstuff may be recognised and registered as **traditional speciality guaranteed**[3]. It introduces an instrument for registering the names of products, thus enabling producers who so wish to obtain certificates of the 'specific character' of a traditional product (or foodstuff), the specific character being defined as the feature which distinguishes the product or foodstuff clearly from other similar products or foodstuffs belonging to the same category.

Another Regulation concerns **organic production** of agricultural products and indications referring thereto (labelling) on agricultural products and foodstuffs[4]. A European Union symbol (logo), based on the 12 stars symbol of the EU, identifies agricultural products and foodstuffs whose names are registered under the rules on the protection of geographical indications and designations of origin[5]. The Community finances generic, collective information and promotion campaigns (public relations, publicity and dissemination of scientific information) for agricultural products on the internal market[6].

---

[1]   Regulation 510/2006, OJ L 93, 31.03.2006.
[2]   Regulation 1107/96, OJ L 148, 21.06.1996 last amended by Regulation 704/2005, OJ L 118, 05.05.2005.
[3]   Regulation 509/2006, OJ L 93, 31.03.2006.
[4]   Regulation 2092/91, OJ L 198, 22.07.1991 and Regulation 780/2006, OJ L 137, 25.05.2006.
[5]   Regulation 510/2006, OJ L 93, 31.03.2006.
[6]   Regulation 2826/2000, OJ L 328, 23.12.2000 and Regulation 2060/2004, OJ L 357, 02.12.2004.

21.4.3. Direct support schemes for farmers

In order to promote more market-oriented and sustainable agriculture, the 2003 reform of the CAP completed the shift from production support to producer support by introducing a system of **decoupled income support for each farm**[1]. Regulation 1782/2003 established common rules on direct payments under income support schemes in the framework of the common agricultural policy which are financed by the European Agricultural Guarantee Fund (EAGF)[2]. These schemes are: an income support for farmers (referred to as the "single payment scheme"); and- support schemes for farmers producing durum wheat, protein crops, rice, nuts, energy crops, starch potatoes, milk, seeds, arable crops, sheep meat and goat meat, beef and veal and grain legumes. In order to leave farmers free to choose what to produce on their land, including products which are still under coupled support, the single payment is not conditional on production of any specific product. However, in order to avoid distortions of competition some products are excluded from production on eligible land.

The new system combines a number of pre-existing direct payments received by a farmer from various schemes in a single payment, determined on the basis of previous entitlements, within a reference period, adjusted to take into account the full implementation of measures introduced by the reform of the CAP. While decoupling leaves the actual amounts paid to farmers unchanged, it is aimed to significantly increase the effectiveness of the income aid. The single farm payment is therefore made **conditional upon cross-compliance** with environmental, food safety, animal health and welfare, as well as the maintenance of the farm in good agricultural and environmental condition.

In order to establish the amount to which a farmer should be entitled under the new scheme, the single payment is based on the amounts granted to him during a reference period. This payment is established at farm level. The overall amount to which a farm is entitled is split into parts (**payment entitlements**) and linked to a certain number of eligible hectares. Specific provisions should be laid down for aid not directly linked to an area taking into account the peculiar situation of sheep and goat rearing. To take account of specific situations, a national reserve is established. That reserve may also be used to facilitate the participation of new farmers in the scheme.

All the amounts of direct payments to be granted in a given calendar year to a farmer in a given Member State are reduced progressively for each year until 2012 (**modulation**). The amounts resulting from application of these reductions are made available as additional Community support for measures under rural development programming financed by the

---

[1] Regulations 1782/2003, OJ L 270, 21.10.2003 and 674/2008, OJ L 189, 17.07.2008.
[2] Regulations 1290/2005, OJ L 209, 11.08.2005 and 1437/2007, OJ L 322, 07.12.2007.

European Agricultural Fund for Rural Development (EAFRD)[1] [see sections 21.3.3 and 21.5.1].

In order to improve the effectiveness and usefulness of the administration and control mechanisms, each Member State must establish an **integrated administration and control system (IACS)** for certain Community aid schemes with a view to including the single payment scheme, the various support schemes, specific regional aids as well as controls on the application of the rules on cross compliance, modulation and the farm advisory system[2] [see also section 21.3.4]. The integrated system must comprise: (a) a computerised data base, (b) an identification system for agricultural parcels, (c) a system for the identification and registration of payment entitlements, (d) aid applications, (e) an integrated control system, and (f) a single system to record the identity of each farmer who submits an aid application.

21.4.4. External wing of the CAP

The external wing of the common market organisations seeks to protect European agricultural prices against low price imports. In the same way as intervention on the internal market attempts to prevent the market prices falling too far below the intervention prices, intervention at the external borders tries to prevent low priced imports from upsetting the European market. The gap between the world price and the threshold price was originally bridged by import levies. Following the GATT agreements of December 1993, this gap is now partially closed by **customs duties**. However, for certain product groups such as cereals, rice, wine and fruit and vegetables, certain supplementary mechanisms that do not involve the collection of fixed customs duties are introduced in the basic regulations of the CAP by a Regulation, which lays down the adaptations and transitional measures required in order to implement the agreements concluded in the GATT framework [see sections 23.4. and 23.5.][3].

The across-the-board **tariff concessions** which result from multilateral trade negotiations, such as those of the GATT and now the WTO, are only part of the commitments weighing upon the EU's agricultural relationships. There are in addition preferential bilateral agreements with the ACP countries [see section 24.2.] and the majority of Mediterranean countries [see section 25.5.], in the form of association agreements or cooperation agreements, which provide for concessions in the agricultural sector [see also section 5.2.2.]. In addition, tariff reductions are granted by the Community under the Generalised System of Preferences (GSP) to almost all the developing countries [see section 24.5.], notably in the framework of the

---

[1]   Regulation 1698/2005, OJ L 277, 21.10.2005 last amended by Regulation 1944/2006, OJ L 367, 22.12.2006.

[2]   Regulation 1782/2003, OJ L 270, 21.10.2003 last amended by Regulation 674,/2008, OJ L 189, 17.07.2008.

[3]   Regulation 3290/94, OJ L 349, 31.12.1994 and Regulation 1340/98, OJ L 184, 27.06.1998.

United Nations Conference on Trade and Development (UNCTAD) and in the framework of the Europe Agreements with the countries of Central and Eastern Europe [see section 25.2.]. The Community supplies the Russian Federation agricultural products free of charge from intervention stocks or purchased on the EU market[1].

21.5. Rural development policy

According to the Treaty, in working out the common agricultural policy and the special methods for its application, account is to be taken of the particular nature of agricultural activity which results from the social structure of agriculture and from structural and natural disparities between the various rural areas. Main objectives of the common agricultural policy are: (a) to increase agricultural productivity by promoting technical progress and by ensuring the rational development of agricultural production and the optimum utilisation of the factors of production, in particular labour; and (b) thus to ensure a fair standard of living for the agricultural community, in particular by increasing the individual earnings of persons engaged in agriculture (Art. 33 TEC).

Rural areas face particular challenges as regards growth, jobs and sustainability in the enlarged Union. But they offer real opportunities in terms of their potential for growth in new sectors, the provision of rural amenities and tourism, their attractiveness as a place in which to live and work, and their role as a reservoir of natural resources and highly valued landscapes. Therefore, a **rural development policy** accompanies and complements the market and income support policies of the common agricultural policy and thus contributes to the achievement of that policy's objectives as laid down in the Treaty. The reformed rural development policy covers, since January 2007, all rural areas in the Community through a single instrument, the European Agricultural Fund for Rural Development (EAFRD) [see sections 21.3.3 and 21.5.1].

21.5.1. The financing of rural development

Rural development and accompanying measures during the period 2000-06 were financed by the EAGGF Guarantee Section or Guidance Section, depending on their regional context [see section 12.3.2.]. Thus, Community support for early retirement, less-favoured areas and areas with environmental restrictions, agri-environmental measures and afforestation were **financed by the EAGGF Guarantee Section** throughout the Community. Community support for other rural development measures was financed by the **EAGGF Guidance Section** in areas covered by Ob-

---

[1] Regulation 2802/98, OJ L 349, 24.12.1998.

jective 1 (integrated into the programmes) **and Guarantee Section** in areas outside Objective 1 [see sections 12.1.1. and 12.3.1.].

Through two Regulations adopted in 2005, the EAGGF was split in two different but complementary instruments: the European Agricultural Guarantee Fund (EAGF), for the financing of market measures, and the **European Agricultural Fund for Rural Development (EAFRD)** [see section 21.3.3]. Regulation 1698/2005 established **the European Agricultural Fund for Rural Development (EAFRD)**[1]. The EAFRD contributes to the promotion of sustainable rural development throughout the Community in a complementary manner to the market and income support policies of the common agricultural policy, to cohesion policy and to the common fisheries policy. Support for rural development should, in particular, contribute to achieving the following objectives: (a) improving the competitiveness of agriculture and forestry by supporting restructuring, development and innovation; (b) improving the environment and the countryside by supporting land management; and (c) improving the quality of life in rural areas and encouraging diversification of economic activity.

In the context of Regulation 1698/2005, the Council, on a proposal from the Commission, should adopt **strategic guidelines** aiming at reinforcing the content of rural development policy in line with the Community's priorities. On the basis of the strategic guidelines, each Member State should prepare its rural development national strategy plan constituting the reference framework for the preparation of the rural development programmes, whose duration should be of seven years. The programming of rural development should comply with Community and national priorities and complement the other Community policies, in particular the agricultural market policy, cohesion policy and common fisheries policy. In accordance with their respective responsibilities, the Commission and the Member States mustl ensure the coordination between the assistance from the different Funds, i.e. the ERDF, the ESF, the Cohesion Fund [see section 12.3], the European Fisheries Fund (EFF) [see section 22.4], and the interventions of the European Investment Bank (EIB), and of other Community financial instruments.

21.5.2. Rural development objectives and guidelines

According to **Article 33(2,a)** of the EC Treaty, in working out the common agricultural policy and the special methods for its application, account is to be taken of the particular nature of agricultural activity which results from the social structure of agriculture and from structural and natural disparities between the various agricultural regions. A common rural development policy should accompany and complement the other instruments of the common agricultural policy and thus contribute to the

---

[1] Regulation 1698/2005, OJ L 277, 21.10.2005 last amended by Regulation 1944/2006, OJ L 367, 22.12.2006.

achievement of the policy's objectives as laid down in Article 33(1) of the Treaty. This policy should take into account the objectives set out in Articles 158 and 160 (TEC) for the common policy of economic and social cohesion and contribute to their achievement [see section 12.1.2.]. Within the framework of the objectives established in Regulation 1698/2005, the strategic guidelines set out in Decision 2006/144 aim at the integration of **major policy priorities** as spelt out in the conclusions of the Lisbon and Göteborg European Councils[1] [see sections 13.3.2 and 16.2].

Enhancing the competitiveness of Community agriculture and promoting food quality and environment standards, under the fifth CAP reform, entail a drop in institutional prices for agricultural products and a shift from production support to producer support by a system of decoupled income support for each farm. While decoupling should leave the actual amounts paid to farmers unchanged, it should make the single farm payment conditional upon cross-compliance with environmental, food safety, animal health and welfare, as well as the maintenance of the farm in good agricultural and environmental condition. In order to help farmers to meet the standards of modern, high-quality agriculture the Member States should establish a comprehensive system offering advice to commercial farms. Therefore a national farm advisory system should help farmers to become more aware of material flows and on-farm processes relating to the environment, food safety, animal health and welfare.

The new generation of rural development strategies and programmes for the period 2007-2013 is built around four axes, namely:

- axis 1, on **improving the competitiveness** of the agricultural and forestry sector through a range of measures targeting human and physical capital in the agriculture, food and forestry sectors (promoting knowledge transfer and innovation) and quality production;
- axis 2, on **improving the environment and the countryside** by measures protecting and enhancing natural resources, as well as preserving highnature value farming and forestry systems and cultural landscapes in Europe's rural areas;
- axis 3, on **improving the quality of life** in rural areas and diversification of the rural economy by measures helping to develop local infrastructure and human capital in rural areas to improve the conditions for growth and job creation in all sectors and the diversification of economic activities; and
- axis 4, introducing possibilities for innovative governance through locally based, bottom-up **integrated approaches to rural development**, based on the Leader experience.

---

[1] Decision 2006/144, OJ L 55, 25.02.2006.

21.5.3. Rural development measures

In order to **improve the competitiveness** of the agricultural and forestry sector (axis 1 of the rural development strategy), Member States are encouraged to focus support on the following key actions:
* restructuring and modernisation of the agriculture sector;
* improving integration in the agrifood chain;
* facilitating innovation and access to research and development (R & D);
* encouraging the take-up and diffusion of information and communications technologies (ICT);
* fostering dynamic entrepreneurship and encouraging the entry of young farmers into the profession;
* developing new outlets for agricultural and forestry products;
* improving the environmental performance of farms and forestry.

So as to **improve the environment and the countryside** (axis 2 of the rural development strategy), Member States are encouraged to focus support on key actions such as:
* promoting environmental services and animal-friendly farming practices;
* preserving the farmed landscape and forests;
* combating climate change by appropriate agricultural and forestry practices;
* consolidating the contribution of organic farming;
* promoting territorial balance and the attractiveness of rural areas;

In order to **improve the quality of life** in rural areas and **encourage diversification** of the rural economy (axis 3 of the rural development strategy), Member States are encouraged to support the following key actions:
* raising economic activity and employment rates in the wider rural economy;
* encouraging the entry of women into the labour market;
* putting the heart back into villages by integrated initiatives combining diversification and business creation;
* developing micro-business and crafts, which can build on traditional skills or introduce new competencies;
* training young people in skills needed for the diversification of the local economy;
* encouraging the take-up and diffusion of information and communication technologies;
* developing the provision and innovative use of renewable energy sources;
* encouraging the development of tourism;
* upgrading local telecommunications, transport, energy and water infrastructures.

To build **local capacity for employment and diversification** (Leader or axis 4 of the rural development strategy), Member States are encouraged to focus support on key actions such as:

- building local partnership capacity and promoting skills acquisition;
- promoting private-public partnership by encouraging the Leader innovative approaches to rural development;
- promoting cooperation and innovation by local initiatives such as Leader and support for diversification;
- improving local governance by fostering Leader innovative approaches to linking agriculture, forestry and the local economy.

21.5.4. LEADER+

Since its launch in 1991, the LEADER Community initiative has encouraged the active involvement of local rural communities in the development of their local economy. This participative approach to rural development has produced positive results. In particular, the experience gained from LEADER I and II has demonstrated that the territorial development strategy was the appropriate one to restore vitality to the rural territories, to stimulate the creation and maintenance of activities and hence to increase their attractiveness. The Community initiative, **LEADER+** goes a step further. Its objective is to encourage the implementation of high quality, original strategies for integrated sustainable development of rural areas. Leader+ is at the same time an instrument of assistance in the new rural development policy, accompanying and complementing the CAP, and an instrument of assistance in the economic and social cohesion policy aiming to ensure the viability of rural Europe [see section 12.1.2.][1]. Its objective is to encourage, on the basis of local partnerships, the emergence and experimentation of rural territorial development strategies, integrated and in a pilot form.

LEADER+ is applicable in all rural areas of the Community, but the selected territories must have demonstrated their capacity to support the proposed development project in terms both of coherence and sufficient critical mass. The **development strategy** must demonstrate its foundation and coherence with the territory, its economic viability, its sustainable character (in environmental terms), its pilot character and more particularly its specificity and originality in relation to the operations of the mainstream programmes as well as the transferable character of the methods proposed.

21.5.5. Rural development measures for EU candidate countries

The **candidate countries for EU membership must adopt the massive body of EU legislation** - known as the "acquis communautaire" [see section 3.3.] - in order to take part fully in the internal market. In the field of agriculture, this means, for example, harmonising legislation in the areas

---

[1] Regulation 1083/2006, OJ L 210, 31.07.2006 and R. 1989/2006, OJ L 411, 30.12.2006.

of veterinary and phytosanitary health, and the free movement of animals and agricultural products. Therefore, EU pre-accession aid supports projects that help the candidates prepare for accession, while familiarising the authorities and other relevant organisations with the methods used to implement Community support measures.

The **Instrument for Pre-Accession Assistance (IPA)** [see section 12.3.4] stipulates that assistance for candidate countries should, inter alia, focus on the adoption and implementation of the full acquis communautaire, and in particular prepare candidate countries for the implementation of the Community's agricultural and cohesion policy[1]. The Rural Development Component of IPA provides support for countries listed in Annex I (Croatia, Turkey, the Former Yugoslav Republic of Macedonia) in policy development as well as preparation for the implementation and management of the Community's common agricultural policy. It contributes to the sustainable adaptation of the agricultural sector and rural areas and to the candidate countries' preparation for the implementation of the acquis communautaire concerning the Common Agricultural Policy and related policies. It may in particular contribute towards the financing of the type of actions provided for under Regulation 1698/2005 on support for rural development by the European Agricultural Fund for Rural Development (EAFRD).

21.6. Appraisal and outlook

The common agricultural policy intrigues those who take an interest in European integration, both because of its advance on other common policies and because of its complexity. The resources in its grasp represent nearly 50% of the Community budget [see section 3.4.]; the instruments that it applies are extremely varied and the terms that it uses to describe them would appear to be chosen precisely to prevent outsiders from understanding what they are. A close look, however, reveals that the complexity of the agricultural policy is due first and foremost to the variety of natural and economic situations which exist, the first relating to production and marketing conditions for different products, the second to the fact that the fifteen Member States have different structures and different climatic conditions.

Despite its complexity, the CAP has more than achieved its objectives. Customs duties, quantitative restrictions and measures having equivalent effect have been relegated to the dustbin of history and trade between the Member States has been fully liberalised. The **single agricultural market** signifies that a good originating in one Member State can be stored in another and marketed in a third. It can also be exported to third countries from any Member State. The merchandise of third countries gains entry to

---

[1]   Regulation 1085/2006, OJ L 210, 31.07.2006.

the common market by crossing just one of the Member States' borders. This liberalisation has led to considerable growth in the range of agricultural products and foodstuffs available to consumers.

In addition, the common market organisation has buffered the European agricultural market against major fluctuations on the world market. In normal times, it **has provided market stability** through a policy of staggering supply (storage, monthly increases), of surplus disposal (refunds, denaturing) or of diversifying supply (imports from third countries, export levies). In times of crisis, it has resorted to drastic measures ranging from import or export bans to the withdrawal from the market of part of production or even the reduction of production factors.

Market stabilisation is not an end in itself. It is a path to the other objectives of the common agricultural policy, notably that of food supply security. Thanks to the CAP, **the European Union has been spared any serious food shortages**, which would have jeopardised both the common agricultural policy and European integration itself. Comparison of the abundance of foodstuffs in Western Europe with the shortages in Eastern Europe, before and after the fall of communist regimes, is a sufficient gauge of the CAP's success. An additional and not less important one, is the independence of Western Europe in foodstuffs, which should be compared to its dependence on imported energy, namely oil [see section 19.1.1.]. The price of the Community's independence in foodstuffs has not been too high to pay. It goes without saying that the level of common prices corresponds to Europe's industrial and social development level. These prices are naturally enough not below those of the world market, but they are not much above them either.

The so-called **"European model of agriculture"** aims at a sustainable development of rural areas through a diversified and multifunctional agriculture. The new CAP is based on two elements: lowering institutional prices for key products and offsetting the impact of these cuts on producer incomes by means of direct payments. While improving competitiveness of European agricultural products at world level, the 1999 reform has consolidated the foundations for a diversified and multifunctional agriculture contributing to sustainable development. The production of renewable raw materials and high quality food products, the protection of the environment and the maintenance of the vitality of rural regions and the countryside are considered services to the society, which have to be rewarded to ensure that they continue to be available in future.

Bibliography on the common agricultural policy

- DAUGBJERG Carsten, SWINBANK Alan. "The politics of CAP reform: trade negotiations, institutional settings and blame avoidance", in *Journal of Common Market Studies*, v. 45, n. 1, March 2007, p. 1-22.
- EUROPEAN COMMISSION. *European policy for quality agricultural products*. Luxembourg: EUR-OP, 2007.

- GLEBE Thilo, LATACZ-LOHMANN Uwe. "Agricultural multifunctionality and trade liberalisation", in *Cahiers d'économie et sociologie rurales*, n. 82-83, 1er et 2e trimestres 2007, p. 57-73.
- LOMBANA Jahir. *Competitiveness and trade policy problems in agricultural exports: a perspective of producing/exporting countries in the case of banana trade to the European Union.* Saarbrücken: Verlag Dr. Müller, 2007.
- LYNGGAARD Kennet. "The institutional construction of a policy field: a discursive institutional perspective on change within the Common Agricultural Policy", in *Journal of European Public Policy*, v. 14, n. 2, 2007, p. 293-312.
- McMAHON Joseph. *EU agricultural law.* Oxford: Oxford University Press, 2007.
- MOEHLER Rolf. *EU bilateral and regional trade agreements: impacts on the CAP* The Hague: European Association of Agricultural Economists, in *Euro-Choices*, v. 6, n. 2, mars 2007, p. 28-34.
- ROBERTS Ivan, GUNNING-TRANT Caroline. *The European Unions's Common Agricultural Policy: a stocktake of reforms.* Canberra: Australian Bureau of Agricultural and Resource Economics, 2007.
- TNS Opinion & Social. "Europeans, Agriculture and the Common Agricultural Policy", in *Special Eurobarometer*, n. 276, 2007.
- WIJNANDS J.H.M. (et al.). *Competitiveness of the European Food Industry: an economic and legal assessment.* European Commission. Luxembourg: EUR-OP, 2007.

DISCUSSION TOPICS

1. Why had the Treaty of Rome called specifically for a common agricultural policy?
2. Could the EU rely on world markets for the supply of agricultural products and foodstuffs as it does for the supply of energy products?
3. Discuss the management of the CAP.
4. Why does the CAP need common financial instruments such as the EAGF and the EAFRD?
5. How does the CAP interact with regional, social and environment policies?

Chapter 22

COMMON FISHERIES POLICY

Diagram of the chapter

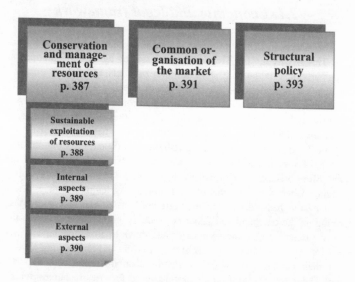

| Conservation and management of resources p. 387 | Common organisation of the market p. 391 | Structural policy p. 393 |

Sustainable exploitation of resources p. 388

Internal aspects p. 389

External aspects p. 390

Fisheries policy, which the Treaty of Rome initially made part of the Common Agricultural Policy by placing fishery products, products of the soil and stock-farming products in the same basket, became a fully-fledged common policy in 1983. It no longer has much in common with the CAP, apart from the fact that it makes use of instruments of market organisation comparable to those of the CAP. Although the fishery sector does not carry the same weight in the Gross Domestic Product and does not employ as many people as agriculture, the establishment of a common policy required just as much effort as the Common Agricultural Policy.

The fishery resources policy, which embraces both internal and external policy, was the most troublesome to put into practice. It is the forum for such thorny questions as total allowable catch (TAC), the sharing out of TAC between the Member States (quotas) and access of the vessels from one Member State to the territorial waters of the others. Resources policy also has to cope with difficult negotiations with third countries to settle questions of access for Community vessels to their waters and vice versa. Although this kingpin of the common fisheries policy (CFP) is analysed first, it was the last arrival on the fisheries scene.

The origins of the two other pillars of the CFP date back to 1970. The common organisation of markets has clearly covered a great deal of ground since then and its reform, in 1981, opened the door to the final compromise on fisheries. Structural policy, for its part, has been torn by national differences on the question of resource conservation. For many years it was restricted to interim measures and was only firmly established with the agreement on resources, reached in January 1983.

22.1. Economic and legal framework

The market in fishery products is similar to that in agricultural products. This is why the EC Treaty stipulates that by agricultural products is meant products of the soil, stock-farming products and fishery products and that the operation and establishment of a common market for all of these products must be accompanied by the introduction of a Common Agricultural Policy (Articles 32 and 33). This is therefore the fundamental reason for and legal basis of a common policy in the fisheries sector.

The Treaty consequently placed fisheries policy and the Common Agricultural Policy in the same basket and the two were initially one and the same. More precisely, the organisation of the market and structural policy covering fisheries formed part of the Common Agricultural Policy. There is however a basic difference between products of the soil and stock-farming on the one hand and fisheries products on the other. Whereas the first two remain within the boundaries laid down by man, fish have no respect for frontiers! Migratory fish, such as herring and tuna, do not have to show their passports when they enter the economic zone of a Member State! There are therefore problems relating to fisheries resources, which simply do not exist for products of the soil and stock farming. This is the first reason why a specific common policy was required for fisheries products. This specificity is now acknowledged by the EC Treaty in Article 3, which speaks of a common policy in the fields of agriculture and fisheries.

The second justification for a common fisheries policy is specific to this sector. Between 1956 and 1965, world fish production rose by 50%. Investments over this period of economic growth, vessel modernisation and higher productivity pushed up catches to such a high level that stock replenishment was threatened and the commoner species, such as herring, began to be exhausted. In times of surplus, storage aid, export subsidies and import restrictions were required. In times of shortage, on the other hand, it was necessary to regulate and monitor fishing to ensure that the seas fished by the Member States did not become empty of fish. All of this had to be achieved at Community level, if the aim was a common fisheries market.

The implementation of the rule of the United Nations of a **200 mile fishery conservation zone** provided a striking illustration of the need for a common conservation policy for these new Community resources. The principle of free access to the fishing zones of Member States was incorporated into the Regulation establishing the fisheries structural policy, adopted as far back as 1970, the year in which accession negotiations were opened with four countries - the United Kingdom, Ireland, Denmark and Norway - all major fishing nations, the total catch of which amounted to double that of the six founding Member States.

The principle of equal access to fishing zones therefore formed part of the "acquis communautaire" (existing Community legislation) which applicants had to accept. Although they attempted to abolish the rule of equal access during accession negotiations, they only succeeded in postponing its full application. Articles 100 to 103 of the **Act of Accession** granted a temporary derogation to the 1970 Community Regulation, authorising the Member States to maintain until December 31, 1982 exclusive fishing rights for their vessels in waters up to six nautical miles from their coasts (stretched to twelve miles for certain regions of the acceding States and of France), provided that the historic fishing rights of vessels from other Member States were respected in these waters. Despite this temporary derogation, the principle of equal access to economic zones was one of the main causes for the negative votes of the Norwegian people on Community membership, in 1973 as in 1994 [see section 1.2.].

The Commission felt that **the total allowable catch** should be shared out in accordance with the golden rule of the common market, namely freedom from all form of discrimination [see sections 5.1 and 6.1.]. This amounted to equality of access for the vessels of the Member States to Community waters. However, the very uneven spread of fishery resources between the waters of the Member States and the fact that fishermen consider it their exclusive right to fish in the strip of coastal water under the jurisdiction of their State and to continue to fish in areas where they have traditionally fished, even if these areas are no longer covered by open access but fall into the economic zone of another Member State, give a measure of the difficulties faced by a Community policy of fishery resources management and conservation.

22.2. Conservation and management of resources

The need for a policy to conserve fishery resources became evident towards the middle of the sixties, when, after long years of overfishing, production began to stagnate and the Community's levels of self-supply began to fall for certain popular species, notably herring and tuna. Since a similar situation prevailed in the rest of the world, the concept of a **total allowable catch (TAC)** was adopted by the United Nations Conference on the law of the sea, culminating in the extension of fishing zones to 200 miles[1]. Under the TAC rule, each coastal state uses scientific data to set a catch level which enables sufficient reproduction of fishery stocks, then it determines the amount which can be fished by its own vessels and that

---

[1] Decision 98/392, OJ C 155, 23.05.1997.

which can be granted to third countries in exchange for or through sale of catch rights. The central aim of the TAC is to conserve and enhance existing fishing zones in the interests of both the fishing industry and consumers.

In a Resolution of November 3, 1976 made public on May 7, 1981[1], the Council agreed that the Member States would extend, by concerted action, the limits of the fishing zones to 200 miles from January 1, 1977 for North Sea and North Atlantic coasts, without prejudice to action of a similar nature for other fishing zones under their jurisdiction, notably the Mediterranean. From January 1, 1977, the Community's exclusive economic zone therefore embraced numerous and potentially rich fishing grounds, the conservation and correct management of which was the responsibility of the Community.

While the extension of **the economic zones** to a distance of 200 miles off coasts - or to the median line when the distance between coasts did not permit a limit of 200 miles - extends the rights of coastal States in these zones, it also means greater obligations for them. The most significant of these obligations is that of conserving biological resources which, given the interdependence of fishery stocks, is a matter of some importance to fishermen and consumers both of the coastal state and of neighbouring states.

22.2.1. Sustainable exploitation of resources

The question of equal access conditions and that of the allocation of resources between Member States formed the crux of the design and implementation of the common fisheries policy. In this field as in many others, the diverging interests of the Member States proved to be a formidable obstacle. Many of them, pushed by the 200-mile rule out of the waters in which they had traditionally fished, had to fall back on the North Sea, where overfishing had already frittered away available resources. Since the three Member States, which had acceded to the Community in 1973 (United Kingdom, Ireland, Denmark), had much vaster and richer fishery zones than the founding members, the latter jealously coveted their resources. Founding members, to shore up their claims, called upon the Community principle of equal access to and working of fishing grounds in the sea waters under the sovereignty of the Member States by boats flying the flag of one of the Member States. This principle, embodied in the 1970 Regulation establishing the policy of fishery structures, was fiercely fought by applicant States, who succeeded in winning a temporary derogation running to December 31, 1982. Hence, the Community conservation and management of resources policy was first adopted in 1983 and was com-

---

[1]   OJ C 105, 07.05.1981.

pletely reviewed in 2002[1] [see section 22.2.2.]. This policy covered both internal and external aspects that we examine successively.

22.2.2. Internal aspects

The Council framework regulation on the **conservation and sustainable exploitation of fisheries resources** lays down the basis for ensuring the long-term viability of the fisheries sector[2]. The approach is founded on scientific advice and the precautionary principle on the one hand, and on good governance and consistency with the other Community policies on the other. Among the measures which the Council may adopt are multiannual recovery plans for the most threatened stocks, including measures to reduce fishing effort where necessary, and multiannual management plans for other stocks. Where there is a serious threat to the conservation of resources or the marine ecosystem, the Commission and the Member States may take the necessary emergency measures lasting for six and three months respectively. The Member States may also adopt conservation and management measures applicable to fishing vessels inside their 12 nautical mile zone, provided that they are non-discriminatory and prior consultation between the Commission and the Member States has taken place, and that the Community has not adopted measures specifically for that area. Concerning access to waters and resources, the regulation lays down rules on allocating fishing opportunities and reviewing the access rules, and extends until 31 December 2012 the existing rules restricting access to resources inside the 12 nautical mile zones of the Member States.

To ensure the **effective implementation of the common fisheries policy** a series of measures are provided for: the establishment of a Community system of fishing licences, administered by the Member States and applicable to all Community fishing vessels, both in its waters as in those of third countries[3]; the issuing and management by the Member States of special fishing permits (authorisation of exploitation of specific fisheries)[4]; the setting of the objectives and detailed rules for restructuring the Community fisheries sector with a view to achieving a balance on a sustainable basis between resources and their exploitation[5] and of multi-annual guidance programmes (MAGPs) designed to implement these objectives and rules[6]; and the establishment of systems for the management of fishing effort and for control of the CFP.

---

[1] Regulation 2371/2002, OJ L 358, 31.12.2002 and Regulation 1242/2004, OJ L 236, 07.07.2004.

[2] Regulation 2371/2002, OJ L 358, 31.12.2002 and Regulation 1242/2004, OJ L 236, 07.07.2004.

[3] Regulation 1281/2005, OJ L 203, 04.08.2005.

[4] Regulation 1627/94, OJ L 171, 06.07.1994.

[5] Decision 97/413, OJ L 175, 03.07.1997 and decision 2002/70, OJ L 31, 01.02.2002.

[6] Commission decisions 98/119 to 98/131, OJ L 39, 12.02.1998 and decision 2002/652, OJ L 215, 10.08.2002.

When, for a particular species or related species, restriction of catch volume is necessary, the total allowable catch (TAC) for certain fish stocks and groups of fish stocks, the share available to the Community, the allocation of this share between Member States, total catch allocated to third countries and the specific conditions under which all this must take place are drawn up every year[1]. The same is true of the setting of guidance prices for fishery products[2]. The **annual allocation of catch quotas** between the Member States is a process almost as difficult as the annual setting of agricultural prices. In both cases, a delicate balance must be struck between the aspirations of the different Member States.

The annual setting of TACs and their allocation between the Member States are, naturally enough, based on certain criteria. **TAC setting** takes into account scientific opinions on the need to protect fishing grounds and fish stocks, balancing them against the interests of Community consumers and fishermen. It was mentioned above that quite often the latter interests weigh more than the scientific opinions. However, TAC setting also takes into consideration the agreements which the Community has with third countries, such as Norway and Canada. The allocation of the TACs between Member States (catch quotas) is also carried out in light of traditional fishing activities, possible loss of fishing potential in the waters of third countries and the specific needs of regions which are particularly dependent on fishing and its related industries. In order to improve the conditions for exploiting resources, **special fishing permits** may be issued to Community fishing vessels and to vessels flying third-country flags operating in the Community fishing area[3], or, inversely, to Community vessels operating in the waters of a third country in the context of a fisheries agreement[4].

A Community framework covers specific measures to conserve and manage **fishery resources in the Mediterranean**[5]. Projects which can be financed by the Community notably include the restructuring of traditional fisheries, the adaptation of specialised fisheries (sponges, coral, sea urchin), the monitoring of fishing activities, the development of a statistical network and the coordination of research and the use of scientific data. A Regulation lays down certain technical measures for the conservation of fishery resources in the Mediterranean[6]. Technical measures exist also for the conservation of fishery resources in the waters of the Baltic Sea, the Belts and the Sound[7].

---

[1] See, for example, Regulation 40/2008, OJ L 19, 23.01.2008.
[2] Regulation 104/2000, OJ L 17, 21.01.2000 and Regulation 1759/2006, OJ L 335, 01.12.2006.
[3] Regulations 1626/94 and 1627/94, OJ L 171, 06.07.1994.
[4] Regulation 3317/94, OJ L 350, 31.12.1994.
[5] Regulation 3499/91, OJ L 331, 03.12.1991.
[6] Regulation 1626/94, OJ L 171, 06.07.1994 and Regulation 973/2001, OJ L 137, 19.05.2001.
[7] Regulation 2187/2005, OJ L 349, 31.12.2005.

22.2.3. External aspects

The external aspects of the resource policy are governed by the Council Resolution of November 3, 1976, known as **The Hague Agreements** and made public on May 7, 1981[1]. In this Resolution, the Council agreed that from January 1, 1977, fishing by third country vessels within the economic zone of the Community would be governed by agreements between the Community and the third countries in question. It also agreed that there was a need to ensure, through **Community agreements**, that the Community's fishing industry was granted or kept rights in the waters of third countries.

As a consequence, although the Community had not yet settled its internal fishery problems, by the end of 1976 it presented itself to the outside world as a single coastal State, obliging third countries which wished to fish in the fishing zones of the different Member States to conclude an agreement with the Community as such. The framework agreements negotiated by the Commission in the Community's name implied recognition of the Community's jurisdiction over the **Community 200 mile zone**, its right to set TACs within this zone and to give third countries access to the surplus part of TACs while obtaining access for the Member States to the surplus of co-signatory third countries.

Since this date, numerous fishery agreements have been concluded between the Community and countries with rich fishing grounds such as Madagascar, Angola, Mauritania, Morocco, Mozambique, the Seychelles and Senegal. These agreements and their renewal are negotiated by the Commission and concluded after a Council Decision, often in the form of an exchange of letters, defining the fishing rights of the Community and the financial compensation to be paid by it to the government of the country in question[2]. Fisheries agreements cover some 25% of supply of the Community market and are highly important to the sector, creating significant numbers of jobs in both the EU and partner countries[3].

22.3. Common organisation of the market

Contrasting sharply with the gestation of the policy for the management and conservation of fishery resources, the creation of a **common market for fishery products** did not come up against major difficulties. Such a market organisation was moreover expressly provided for by the Treaty, with Articles 32 and 34 (ex-Art. 38 and 40 TEC) stipulating that the operation and development of the common market for agricultural products (including fishery products) should be accompanied by the estab-

---

[1] OJ C 105, 07.05.1981.
[2] See, for example, Regulation 450/2007, OJ L 109, 26.04.2007 and Regulation 1446/2007, OJ L 331, 17.12.2007.
[3] COM (96) 488, 30 October 1996.

lishment of a common (agricultural) policy and that the latter should incorporate common organisation of the market. Common organisation of the market (CMO) in fishery and aquaculture products was born in October 1970 and amended several times at later stages. The most recent Regulation in this field aims at ensuring that the rules governing the organisation of the market in fishery products contribute positively to better management and utilisation of resources. It provides for consumers to be informed by means of labelling of fishery products when offered for retail sale, strengthens the role of producer organisations and overhauls the intervention mechanisms, the main purpose of which is to act as a safety net[1]. In fact, the current CMO laid down in Regulation 104/2000 has moved away from a mere intervention system and now lays more emphasis on sustainability-supportive fishing and marketing activities[2].

One of the measures necessary to implement the common organisation of markets is the application of **common standards for the marketing** of the products in question, to ensure that products which do not meet a sufficient quality level are not marketed and to stimulate trade on the basis of fair competition. A Regulation sets common marketing standards for certain fresh or chilled fish for human consumption[3]. In accordance with this Regulation, fish freshness plays a determinant role in assessment of its quality. The common marketing standards therefore take the form of a breaking down into freshness grading on the one hand and size grading on the other, the latter due to differences in consumers' buying habits. The application of these standards means that there must be inspection of the products subject to them. Member States must therefore submit products to a **conformity check**, which can take place at all the marketing stages and also during transport. The Member States must also take all appropriate steps to penalise infringements of marketing standards.

A **guide price** is set at the beginning of the fish marketing year for the main fresh or chilled products[4]. This price is based on the average of the prices recorded on wholesale markets or in representative ports during the three previous fish marketing years. It makes allowance for possible evolution in production and demand and for the need to ensure stable market prices and to contribute to supporting the income of producers, without forgetting consumers' interests. A **Community withdrawal price** is set in line with the freshness, size or weight and presentation of the product, which must be equal to at least 70% while not exceeding 90% of the guide price.

Within this range, producers' organisations can **set a withdrawal price** below which they no longer sell the products supplied by their members. Should this situation arise, the organisations must grant compensation to

---

[1]   Regulation 104/2000, OJ L 17, 21.02.2000 last amended by Regulation 1759/2006, OJ L 335, 01.12.2006.

[2]   COM (2006) 558, 29, September 2006.

[3]   Regulation 2406/96, OJ L 334, 23.12.1996 and Regulation 790/2005, OJ L 132, 26.05.2005.

[4]   See, for example, Regulations 1447/2007, OJ L 323, 08.12.2007.

member producers in line with the quantities of the main fresh or chilled products withdrawn from the market. The organisations set up intervention funds formed by contributions based on the quantities put on sale or run a compensation system to finance these withdrawal measures. A **producers' organisation** is taken as being any recognised organisation or association of such organisations, set up on the initiative of producers in order to take measures ensuring that fishing is carried out in a rational manner, to improve sales conditions for their production and to stabilise prices.

22.4. Structural policy

The fishery sector is at least as vulnerable as agriculture. Production depends on several factors that cannot be controlled by producers: weather, water pollution, delimitation of fishing zones. The sea-fishing sector, which makes up the bulk of the fishing industry, has a highly specific social structure and arduous living and working conditions. Fishing is moreover often economically vital in certain coastal regions without other economic resources and it is a major breadwinner for the people living in these regions. This is why the common organisation of the fishery market must be accompanied by a common structural policy. This fact was recognised in 1970, which saw the combined adoption of the Regulation establishing a common structural policy and that of the Regulation creating a common organisation of the market for the fishery products sector.

Despite the structural measures that were thus implemented during the seventies and the eighties, the fisheries sector was confronted in the early nineties by a very serious structural crisis, characterised notably by: the widespread chronic overcapacity of the fleets; the over-capitalisation and high debt levels of the companies; the restrictions brought to certain fishing techniques in respect of the conservation of resources; the setting of Community standards with regard to hygiene, health, product quality as well as safety on board. Moreover, many coastal regions suffered from a fragile socio-economic fabric, in particular the areas dependent on fishing, for many of which - if one took account of the induced activities - fishing was the principal or even the only activity.

On account of the aggravation of the structural problems of the fisheries sector in the enlarged EU, the former Financial Instrument for Fisheries Guidance (FIFG) was replaced in 2006 by the **European Fisheries Fund (EFF)**[1]. The assistance under the European Fisheries Fund (hereinafter EFF) aims in particular to: (a) support the common fisheries policy so as to ensure exploitation of living aquatic resources and support aquaculture to ensure durability; (b) promote a sustainable balance between resources and the fishing capacity of the Community fishing fleet; (c) promote a sustainable development of inland fishing; (d) strengthen the competitiveness of

---

[1] Regulation 1198/2006, OJ L 223, 15.08.2006.

the operating structures and the development of economically viable enterprises in the fisheries sector; (e) foster the protection and the enhancement of the environment and natural resources where related to the fisheries sector.

The objectives of the EFF are pursued within the framework of close cooperation (**"partnership"**) between the Commission and the Member State. This partnership concerns regional, local and other public authorities, as well as other appropriate bodies, including those responsible for the environment and for the promotion of equality between men and women, the economic and social partners and other competent bodies. The partners concerned should be involved in the preparation, implementation, monitoring and evaluation of assistance. The EFF provides assistance which complements national, regional and local actions, integrating into them the priorities of the Community. The programming system takes the form of one single operational programme per Member State, in accordance with its national structure. Programming should ensure coordination of the EFF with other funds geared to sustainable development and with the Structural Funds and other Community funds. The programming exercise covers the period from 1 January 2007 to 31 December 2013.

22.5. Appraisal and outlook

The Treaty of Rome did not provide for a fully-fledged fisheries policy, for it included fishery products in the products to be covered by the Common Agricultural Policy. Little by little, however, the specific characteristics of the fisheries sector pushed for a separate common policy. Towards the end of the sixties, therefore, the Community began to turn its attention to the need to protect its resources in the Atlantic and the North Sea, under serious threat from overfishing. Its concern was heightened by the creation of exclusive economic zones, decided upon within the United Nations Conference on the law of the sea. A Community policy to conserve fishery resources was necessary to protect the most threatened species in Community waters. Its main manifestations have been the setting of total allowable catches (TACs), the allocation of catch quotas between the Member States and technical management and surveillance measures. Through an external fisheries policy, the Community has sought to guarantee its own fleet access to the waters of countries with surplus resources and to restrict access to Community waters for foreign vessels, notably Soviet, Polish and Japanese factory ships.

Six years of negotiations were required before, on January 25, 1983, the Community reached one of its "historic compromises". On this date, a Community system of resource conservation, endeavouring to protect the biological resources of the sea under severe threat from modern fishing methods, was added to the common fisheries policy. This system introduced measures to restrict fishing and set conditions under which it could take place, along with measures governing access to the waters of the Member States. Measures to conserve and manage fishery resources thus came to join the "common organisation of the market", which sets common marketing standards for fisheries and aquaculture products, dividing them up into a freshness grading and seeking to ensure that products which do not reach a satisfactory quality level are not marketed. It obliges the Member States to carry out conformity control checks on these products and to apply sanctions to any infringements. This policy therefore helps protect consumer interests. Producers' interests are not neglected either in the common fisheries policy. Structural policy, inaugurated in 1970, makes use of common measures to restructure, modernise and develop the fishery sector, to develop aquaculture, encourage experimental fishing and adapt Community fishing capacities to disposal possibilities.

This does not mean that the Community fisheries sector is riding on the crest of a wave. The CFP currently faces multiple challenges: a number of stocks are in a critical state, the Community fleet is suffering from over-capacity, the fisheries sector is beset by economic fragility and employment is on the decline. The depletion of resources, due notably to the over-fishing of juveniles combined with fleet over-capacity, make the entire European fisheries sector extremely vulnerable from the economic and social viewpoint. The results achieved in the areas of surveillance systems, inspection and surveillance activities, fleet controls and the application of penalties are not satisfactory, because there are many differences in how the Member States are implementing controls at national level and the co-operation and coordination arrangements established by them are not adequate. Some Member States do not fulfil their obligation to notify catches to the Commission and the multi-annual guidance programmes (MAGPs) have not ensured effective control of the real capacity of the fleets. In order to redress this situation, there must be reduction in both fishing and fishing capacity through more stringent regulation of access to resources and closer monitoring of vessel movements in order to respect the general interest. At international level, the EU should coordinate its development co-operation policy and the external aspects of the common fisheries policy, stressing the importance of environmental and socioeconomic factors for promoting sustainable and responsible fisheries.

Bibliography on the common fisheries policy

- BJØRNDAL Trond (et al. eds.). *Advances in fisheries economics*: Festschrift in honour of Professor Gordon R. Munro. Oxford: Blackwell Publishing, 2007.
- EUROPEAN COMMISSION. *The European Fisheries Fund: 2007-2013*. Luxembourg: EUR-OP*, 2006.
  - *Report from the Commission to the Council and the European Parliament on the monitoring of the Member States' implementation of the Common Fisheries Policy 2003-2005*. Luxembourg: EUR-OP*, 2007.

- FOOD AND AGRICULTURE ORGANIZATION OF THE UNITED NATIONS. Model scheme on port state measures to combat illegal, unreported and unregulated fishing. Rome: FAO, 2007.
- LONG Ronán. *Marine resource law*. Dublin: Thompson Round Hall, 2007.
- MOLENAAR Erik. "Managing biodiversity in areas beyond national jurisdiction", in *The international journal of marine and coastal law*, v. 22, n. 1, April 2007, p. 89-124.
- NORDQUIST Myron (et al. eds.). *Law, science & ocean management*. Leiden: Martinus Nijhoff Publishers, 2007.
- ORGANISATION FOR ECONOMIC COOPERATION AND DEVELOPMENT. Structural change in fisheries: dealing with human development. Paris: OECD, 2007.
- SCHARE Teresa. *Europe and the "tragedy of the commons": a detailed analysis of the European common fisheries policy (CEP)*. Genève: Institut européen de l'Université de Genève, 2006.
- SERDY Andrew. "Law of the sea aspects of the negotiations in the WTO to harmonise rules of origin", in *The international journal of marine and coastal law*, v. 22, n. 2, June 2007, p. 235-256.

DISCUSSION TOPICS

1. What is the need of a common policy for the conservation of fishery resources?
2. How is the fisheries sector organised at Community level?
3. What is the structural policy of the Community for the fisheries sector?
4. Discuss the similarities and differences of the common agricultural and fisheries policies.
5. How does the common fisheries policy relate with the common regional and environment policies?

Part VI: External policies

The EU Treaty in its first pages (Article 2) declares that **the Union has the objective of asserting its identity on the international scene**, in particular through the implementation of a common foreign and security policy, including the progressive framing of a common defence policy, which might in time lead to a common defence. The **EC/EU is in fact present on the world stage in three roles**, played mainly under its European Community hat: common commercial policy, development aid policy and external relations. The first two are leading roles - as the EC/EU is the world's largest trading entity and the largest provider of funds for the developing countries - while the role of the external relations of the Community, which is for the time being secondary, is completed and often intermingled with the developing role of the Union in a common foreign and security policy (CFSP) [see chapter 8 and the European perspectives in the conclusions]. The three often overlap as development aid is tied in with commercial policy and commercial policy with the Community's external relations or the Union's CFSP. But, whereas the commercial and the development aid policies are managed with the successful Community method and have a global impact, the CFSP is run with the ineffective intergovernmental method and is common only in name. As the three policies should ideally support each other, the ineptness of the CFSP of the Union handicaps the performance of the policies of the Community.

The European Community/Union, through one or other of its international roles, has **diplomatic relations with 162 countries**, which for their part have representations in Brussels. The EC/EU has its own representations, set up by the Commission, in most of these countries and in **international organisations**. In organisations such as the World Trade Organisation (WTO) and in international fisheries organisations, the Community speaks in the name of and in place of the Member States, through the mouthpiece of the Commission [see section 4.1.2.]. It participates in the work of the Organisation for Economic Cooperation and Development (OECD) and has observer status in the United Nations and in some of its specialised organisations. It has relations with other international organisations, such as the Council of Europe. It is represented, by the President of the Commission, at the economic summits of the most industrialised countries, called "the G8", which bring together twice a year the Heads of State or Government of four of its Member States - France, Germany, the United

Kingdom and Italy - with those of the United States, Canada, Japan and Russia.

The European Community has signed and manages **association or co-operation agreements** with more than 120 countries and is also responsible for numerous multilateral agreements. When these agreements cover an area for which it has exclusive responsibility, such as international trade, agriculture or fisheries, the Community is the sole party to them on behalf of its Member States. In other cases (some agreements on the environment, transport and so on), the Community is a party in addition to its Member States.

If one adds the **international personalities** of the fifteen Member States - with their different and sometimes conflicting interests in the international arena - to the occasionally identical but at times distinct activities of the European Community and the European Union, one understands that the external relations of the former and the foreign policy of the later are bewildering subjects, not only for the partners of the Union, but also for the Member States themselves. Having examined the common foreign and security policy as a component of the future political integration of the Union, we now try to instil some systematic order in the study of the external relations of the Community.

Chapter 23

COMMERCIAL POLICY

Diagram of the chapter

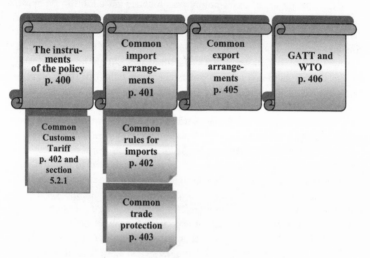

| The instruments of the policy p. 400 | Common import arrangements p. 401 | Common export arrangements p. 405 | GATT and WTO p. 406 |

| Common Customs Tariff p. 402 and section 5.2.1 | Common rules for imports p. 402 |

| Common trade protection p. 403 |

The creation of a **customs union** in the Community in 1968 was implemented internally through the abolition of customs duties, quantitative restrictions and measures having equivalent effect between Member States [see section 5.1.] and, on the external front, through the **introduction of a common customs tariff and a common commercial policy**. In fact, goods imported from third countries had to be treated in the same way by all Member States in order to circulate freely in the customs union [see section 5.2.]. But the customs union itself had to be integrated into the existing international economic order, regulated by the 1948 General Agreement on Tariffs and Trade (GATT).

This is why, in Article 110 of the EEC Treaty (Art. 131 TEC), the Member States declared that in creating a customs union, they intended to contribute, in accordance with the common interest, to the **harmonious development of world trade**, the gradual removal of restrictions to international trade and the lowering of customs barriers. They have kept their word. The creation of the customs union has led to strong growth in intra-Community trade, but the Community has not become introverted. Instead, it has developed into the world's biggest importer and exporter. In addition, the rules of the GATT [see section 23.4.], and the various international agreements drawn up under its aegis, formed the legal basis for the Community's own commercial policy instruments and action, notably in the field of tariffs, the application of safeguard measures, anti-dumping and anti-subsidies actions.

23.1. The instruments of the policy

The common commercial policy was founded on uniform principles, notably as regards tariff charges, the conclusion of tariff and commercial agreements and the harmonisation of liberalisation measures, export policies and trade defence measures, including those to be taken in cases of dumping and subsidies (Art. 133 TEC, ex-Art. 113 EEC). The implementation of the common commercial policy therefore falls **into the Community's sphere of competence**. The European institutions draw up and adapt the common customs tariff, conclude customs and trade agreements, harmonise measures to liberalise trade with third countries, specify export policy and take protective measures, notably to nip unfair trading practices in the bud. If agreements have to be negotiated with third countries, the Commission submits recommendations to the Council, which then authorises it to open negotiations. The Commission is the Community's negotiator and consults a special committee appointed by the Council to assist it in this task (known as "133 Committee"). It works within the framework of guidelines issued by the Council. In exercising the powers granted to it by Article 133 (TEC), including the conclusion of agreements, the Council acts by a qualified majority [see sections 4.1.4. and 4.3.].

In international agreements, **the Community as such, represented by the Commission** [see section 4.1.2.], is more often than not a party alongside the Member States, which means that it takes part in the negotiations, signs the agreements and if necessary participates in their management as a member of the organisation in question. In areas for which the Community has exclusive responsibility (agriculture, fisheries), the Member States are not at the forefront; the Commission negotiates and manages the agreements on the basis of a negotiating brief delivered by the Council (world commodity agreements, traditional trade agreements, preferential agreements, association agreements)[1]. According to Article 307 (TEC), rights and obligations arising from agreements concluded by the Member States before their accession to the Community [see section 1.2.] are not affected by the provisions of the EC Treaty [see sections 2.2. and 2.3.]; but to the extent that such agreements are not compatible with this Treaty, the Member States concerned must take all appropriate steps to eliminate the incompatibilities established[2].

Given the complexity of international relations and of external policy instruments in the broad sense of the term, the **Community powers occasionally spill out of the framework** defined in Article 133 (TEC). In such

---

[1] See: judgment of 31 March 1971, case 22/70, AETR, ECR 1971, p.263; and opinion of 26 April 1977, ECR 1977, p. 741.

[2] See judgment of 14 October 1980, case 812/79, Burgoa, ECR 1980, p.2787.

cases, the Community institutions cannot act alone [see section 4.3.]. They must draw in the Member States, a fact that considerably complicates the negotiating process and the conclusion of international agreements. However, the EC Treaty provides that the Council will be able, unanimously, to decide to extend the application of Article 133 (commercial policy) to international negotiations and agreements on services and intellectual property rights in addition to those already covered by this provision.

The **Common Customs Tariff (CCT)** is the key to the Community's commercial policy [see section 5.2.1.]. As seen in the Chapter on customs union and as will be seen later in this Chapter [see section 23.2.1.], the blueprinting and evolution of the CCT have taken place against the backdrop of the General Agreement on Tariffs and Trade (GATT). CCT tariffs were low at the outset, responding to the central objective of liberalisation of international trade. They have been cut even further in the framework of successive GATT negotiations [see section 23.4.]. It should be borne in mind that the Commission, acting on a negotiating brief issued by the Council, and not the Member States individually, is the Community's negotiator in the GATT/WTO arena.

Instead of becoming a **"Fortress Europe"** when the single market was completed in 1992 [see section 6.1.], as feared by some of its trade partners, the Community made important concessions in order to allow the conclusion of the GATT Uruguay Round in 1993. However, one of the central principles of GATT and WTO is that of balance of mutual advantages (global reciprocity). This means, for the European Union, that it can tie access for third country economic operators to the benefits of the single market with the existence of similar opportunities for European undertakings (businesses, companies) in the country in question, or at the least to the absence of any discrimination. This implies a case-by-case approach for third countries, but a common approach by the Member States. The single market obliges the latter to show a united face to third countries. At the same time, the globalisation of the economy is creating a state of interdependence and a growing realisation that trade problems need to be solved wherever possible in a multilateral framework.

23.2. Common import arrangements

The Customs Union is one of the linchpins of the common commercial policy. The other main elements are the **common import arrangements** and the **common protective measures**. Together they contribute to ensuring an even competition playing field for Community undertakings, giving them access to equal prices for imported raw materials and levelling the quantities and prices of competitor products.

23.2.1. Common rules for imports

The common rules for imports were established by Council Regulation of 22 December 1994[1]. **They apply to imports of products originating in third countries**, with the exception, on the one hand, of textiles subject to specific import arrangements, discussed under the heading of sectoral measures of the commercial policy, and, on the other, products originating from certain third countries, including Russia, North Korea and the People's Republic of China, mentioned below. Apart from those exceptions, imports into the Community are free and not subject to any quantitative restrictions. The Regulation strives to establish a balance between a Community market normally open to the world following the conclusion of the Uruguay Round and more rapid and simplified procedures in case of a risk of serious injury caused by imports of a product to Community producers.

The Regulation establishes a **Community information and consultation procedure**. The examination of the trend of imports, of the conditions under which they take place and of serious injury or threat of serious injury to Community producers resulting from such imports covers the following factors in practice: a) the volume of imports; b) the price of imports; and c) the consequent impact on the Community producers of similar or directly competitive products as indicated by trends in certain economic factors such as production, capacity utilisation, stocks, sales, market share, prices and so on.

Where the trend in imports of a product originating in a third country threatens to cause injury to Community producers, import of that product may be subject, as appropriate, to prior or retrospective **Community surveillance**. Products under prior Community surveillance may be put into free circulation only on production of an import document endorsed by the competent authority designated by Member States and valid throughout the EU, regardless of the Member State of issue. The surveillance may be confined to imports into one or more regions of the Community (regional surveillance).

Where a product is imported into the Community in such increased quantities and/or on such terms as to cause, or threaten to cause, serious injury to Community producers, the Commission may, acting at the request of a Member State or on its own initiative take **safeguard measures**, i.e.: limit the period of validity of import documents required in compliance with surveillance measures; alter the import rules for the product in question by making its release for free circulation conditional on production of an import authorisation granted under certain provisions and in certain limits laid down by the Commission. As regards Members of the World Trade Organisation (WTO), safeguard measures are taken only when the two conditions indicated above (quantities and terms of imports) are met. No safeguard measure may be applied to a product originating in a developing

---

[1] Regulation 3285/94, OJ L 349, 31.12.1994 and Regulation 2200/2004, OJ L 374, 22.12.2004.

country Member of the WTO as long as that country's share of Community imports of the product concerned does not exceed 3% and that the import share of all developing countries does not account for more than 9% of such imports.

23.2.2. Common trade defence

As seen above, the Community can introduce surveillance and safeguard measures in the framework of the common rules for imports when imports at prices viewed as normal are causing or risk causing serious injury to Community producers. In cases where the **export price is lower than the normal value of a like product (dumping)**, the Community can take trade protection measures, notably through the application of **anti-dumping duties**. Community rules being compatible with those of the World Trade Organisation, economic operators must comply with only one set of rules for imports into the EU [see sections 23.2.1. and 23.4.]. These rules apply automatically in the new States acceding to the EU, as of May 2004[1]. On the jurisdictional level, anti-dumping and anti-subsidy cases must be brought before the Court of First Instance[2].

According to the Regulation on **protection against dumped imports** from countries not members of the EC, anti-dumping duty may be applied to any dumped product whose release for free circulation in the Community causes injury[3]. A product is considered as having been dumped if its export price to the Community is less than a comparable price for the like product, in the ordinary course of trade, as established for the exporting country. The term like product means a product that is identical in all respects or has characteristics closely resembling those of the product under consideration. In order to determine the dumping, the normal price and the dumped price must be defined and these two values must then be compared. It should be noted that these definitions as well as the anti-dumping procedures are, after the Uruguay Round, similar in the EU and in other WTO countries.

Provisional measures may be taken by the Commission, after consultation with the Member States, no sooner than 60 days but not later than nine months from the initiation of the proceedings. The final conclusions of the investigation must be adopted within a further six months. The amount of the **provisional anti-dumping duty** must not exceed the margin of dumping as provisionally established. Investigation may be terminated without the imposition of provisional or definitive duties upon receipt of satisfactory voluntary undertakings from the exporter to revise his prices or to cease exports to the area in question at dumped prices.

---

[1] Commission notice, OJ C 91, 15.04.2004 and OJ 231, 16.09.2004.

[2] Decision 94/149, OJ L 66, 10.03.1994.

[3] Regulation 384/96, OJ L 56, 06.03.1996 and Regulation 2117/2005, OJ L 340, 23.12.2005.

Where a provisional duty has been applied and the facts established show that there is dumping and injury, the Council decides, irrespective of whether a definitive anti-dumping duty is to be imposed, what proportion of the provisional duty is to be definitively collected. If the **definitive anti-dumping** duty is higher than the provisional duty, the difference must not be collected. If the definitive duty is lower than the provisional duty, the duty must be recalculated. Provisional or definitive anti-dumping duties must be imposed by Regulation, and collected by Member States in the form, at the rate specified and according to the other criteria laid down in the Regulation imposing such duties.

The rules on **protection against subsidised imports** from countries not members of the European Community are also established by Regulation[1]. Here again the Community legislation is compatible with WTO rules and, therefore, business must comply with only one set of rules. A **countervailing duty** may be imposed for the purpose of offsetting any subsidy granted, directly or indirectly, for the manufacture, production, export or transport of any product whose release for free circulation in the Community causes injury. A subsidy is deemed to exist if: 1) there is a financial contribution by a government or by a private body entrusted by it (direct transfer of funds, loan guarantees, fiscal incentives, etc.); and 2) a benefit is thereby conferred.

Subsidies, which are not specific to an enterprise or industry or group of enterprises or industries, cannot be subjected to countervailing measures. Even when they are specific, subsidies cannot be subjected to countervailing duties, if they are given: for research activities; pursuant to a general framework of regional development; to promote adaptation of existing facilities to new environmental requirements. The amount of subsidies to be subjected to countervailing duties is calculated in terms of the benefit conferred to the recipient, which is found to exist during the investigation period. Where all conditions are met, a provisional or definitive **countervailing duty** is imposed following procedures similar to the ones described above concerning the imposition of anti-dumping duties.

In December 1994, the Council adopted a Regulation destined to improve Community **procedures on commercial defence** and to ensure the exercise of the Community's rights under international trade rules, in particular those established under the auspices of the World Trade Organisation (WTO)[2]. This Regulation allows the Community to respond to obstacles to trade, i.e. to any trade practice adopted or maintained by a third country in respect of which international trade rules establish a right of action. Thus, following the Community examination procedures and after consultation with the Member States, the Commission may take any commercial policy measures which are compatible with existing international obligations and procedures. The Commission has thus initiated procedures

---

[1] Regulation 2026/97, OJ L 288, 21.01.1997 and Regulation 461/2004, OJ L 77, 13.03.2004.
[2] Regulation 3286/94, OJ L 349, 31.12.1994 and Regulation 125/2008, OJ L 40, 14.02.2008.

concerning e.g.: the US Anti-dumping Act of 1916 and US practices with regard to cross-border music licensing[1]; trade practices maintained by South Korea affecting trade in commercial vessels[2] and practices followed by India affecting trade in wines and spirits[3].

An important trade defence instrument of the Community is related to customs action against goods suspected of **infringing certain intellectual property rights**, particularly counterfeit and pirated goods[4]. As these breaches have been escalating in recent years, notably as regards the methods used by fraud gangs and the internationalisation of traffic, and as other property rights such as geographical indications, designations of origin and new plant varieties are affected, the Community legislation has become more stringent [see sections 6.2.4 and 23.4.]. It gives customs administrations a legal arsenal enabling them, in collaboration with right holders, to better prevent and control intellectual property right infringements. The measures applicable to goods which have been found to be counterfeit, pirated or generally to infringe certain intellectual property rights aim to deprive those responsible for trading in such goods of the economic benefits of the transaction and penalise them so as to constitute an effective deterrent to further transactions of the same kind.

23.3. Common export arrangements

Article 132 of the EC Treaty stipulates that the **aid arrangements applied to exports** by the Member States should be harmonised to ensure that there is a level competition playing field for the Community's exporting undertakings. As regards **export credits**, the Community applies the arrangement concluded in the framework of the Organisation for Economic Cooperation and Development (OECD) and providing guidelines for officially supported export credits ("consensus")[5]. These guidelines confine official support to the interest rates for export credits to certain countries. Concerning **export credit insurance** for transactions with medium- and long-term cover, a Directive aims to harmonise the various public systems for such insurance in order to prevent distortion of competition among EU firms[6]. It lays down the common principles which must be observed by export credit insurers and which concern the constituents of cover (scope of cover, causes of loss and exclusions of liability and indemnification of claims), premiums, country cover policy and notification procedures.

The Commission contributes from the Community Budget [see section 3.4.] to **export promotion** and notably to closer cooperation at Community

---

[1]   Commission notices, OJ C 58, 25.02.1997 and OJ C 177, 11.06.1997.

[2]   Commission notice, OJ C345, 02.12.2000 and Decision 2002/818, OJ L 281, 19.10.2002.

[3]   Commission notice, OJ C 228, 17.09.2005.

[4]   Regulation 1383/2003, OJ L 196, 02.08.2003.

[5]   Decision 2001/76, OJ L 32, 02.02.2001 and Decision 2002/634, OJ L 206, 03.08.2002.

[6]   Directive 98/29, OJ L 148, 19.05.1998.

level and to research for joint action in favour of European exports (international exhibitions, trade forums, conferences, seminars) in coordination with Community programmes and with Member States' export promotion programmes. The cooperation with trade federations and with national export promotion organisations pursues two aims: first of all, to ensure that any activities on a particular market strengthen the Community dimension and secondly, to focus activities on a number of target countries, the list of which is topped by China, Japan and the countries of ASEAN (Association of South East Asian Nations) [see section 25.6.].

Community exports to third countries are free or, in other words, are not subject to quantitative restrictions, with the exception of a few products for certain Member States and of petroleum oil and gases for all the Member States[1]. However, when exceptional market trends, which cause scarcity of an essential product, justify protective measures in the opinion of a Member State, it can set in motion the **Community information and consultation procedure**. Consultations take place within an Advisory Committee and cover notably the conditions and terms of exports and, if necessary, the measures which should be adopted.

23.4. GATT and WTO

The **General Agreement on Tariffs and Trade (GATT)** came into being in 1947. Along with the International Monetary Fund and the World Bank it was one of the institutions set up in the post-war period to help regulate the international economy and prevent a recurrence of the disastrous protectionist policies undertaken between the two World Wars. GATT was charged with overseeing international trade in goods and, in particular, the liberalisation of this trade by means of a negotiated reduction in tariff barriers. The scope of the GATT was, therefore, somewhat limited initially, but the conclusion of the Uruguay Round negotiations enlarged its field of activities and placed them under the auspices of the **World Trade Organisation (WTO)**. The Member States of the EC were the contracting parties to the GATT, but, because of the common commercial policy, they participated as "the Community" in the work of GATT and now participate as such in the WTO, that superseded the GATT since 1995. The Commission is the single negotiator and spokesman of the European Community in WTO [see section 4.1.2.]. The Community as such is signatory to a number of international GATT agreements.

The EC Member States and other industrial countries made major tariff concessions - particularly in favour of the developing countries - during the successive GATT **negotiating rounds** between 1960 and 1979 under the aegis of the General Agreement on Tariffs and Trade [see section 5.2.2.]. Thanks to the Dillon (1960-1962) and Kennedy Rounds (1965-1967), the

---

[1]   Regulation 2603/69, OJ L 324, 27.12.1969 and Regulation 3918/91, OJ L 372, 31.12.1991.

customs tariffs of the States participating in the General Agreement were slashed by nearly 50%[1]. Following the Tokyo Round (1973-1979), a fresh one-third reduction in customs tariffs was agreed upon, to be implemented in eight stages the last of which was timed for January 1, 1987[2]. These tariff reductions made a considerable contribution to keeping the international trade system open, despite the fact that in the first years of the 1980s, the world economy went through the worst period in its post-war history causing protectionist pressures to flare up. Since 1985, the Community committed itself wholeheartedly to the process of launching a new cycle of multilateral trade negotiations under the GATT. The round got underway at the Punta del Este (Uruguay) Conference in September 1986.

The **Uruguay Round negotiations** encompassed the revision of GATT rules and disciplines, plus the adoption of disciplines for "new" areas: the trade-related aspects of intellectual property rights, trade-related investment measures and international trade in services. Also on the agenda were the sensitive issues of agriculture and textiles, areas in which trade was traditionally subject to special rules and for which the participants were to devise an agreement for their gradual incorporation into the GATT framework. The conclusion of the Uruguay Round, in December 1993, resulted in a strengthening of the rules and disciplines of international trade, thanks to the reform of the provisions on safeguards, subsidies, anti-dumping measures, the balance of payments, the "standards" and "public procurement" codes. All these GATT agreements have been incorporated into Community law [see sections 6.2.4 and 23.2.2.].

Market access for industrial products has been considerably improved by a reduction of one third or more in the customs duties imposed by the industrialised countries and many developing countries on the following sectors: building materials, agricultural machinery, medical equipment, steel, beer, spirits, pharmaceutical products, paper, toys and furniture [see section 5.2.]. The average level of tariffs for industrialised countries fell from 5% to about 3.5%, whereas it stood at 40% or more prior to the various rounds of GATT negotiations. In total, close to 40% of the EU's industrial imports are now duty free. On their part, developing countries apply substantial reductions of their customs duties on these products, whereas prior to the Uruguay Round they had taken very few such commitments. The EU played a major role in pushing through the conclusion, in March 1997, of the **Information Technology** Agreement under which tariffs on information technology products of countries accounting for 92% of world trade were phased out completely on 1 January 2000 [see also section 17.3.5.][3].

A first step was taken towards the liberalisation of world trade in services. It should be noted that trade is not limited to exchange of goods but also increasingly involves services, a sector which contributes nearly half

---

[1]   Agreement and Decision 68/411, OJ L 305, 19.12.1968.

[2]   Agreement and Decision 80/271, OJ L 71, 17.03.1980.

[3]   Decision 97/359, OJ L 155, 12.06.1997 and Regulation 2216/97, OJ L 305, 08.11.1997.

of the EU's GDP. The **General Agreement on Trade in Services (GATS)** includes general rules for trade in this area, specific provisions for certain service sectors and national schedules showing the services and activities which each country agrees to open up to competition, with possible limitations[1].

The Uruguay Round negotiations included also the protection of **trade-related intellectual property (TRIPs)**[2]. Intellectual property concerns an ever-increasing part of world trade, be it related to pharmaceuticals, computer software, books or records. As trade has increased so too have cheating, counterfeiting and copying. A further problem has been the appropriation of brand names and, in the case of wines and foodstuffs, certain geographical appellations. The conclusions of the Uruguay Round have reinforced existing international conventions, for example the Bern and Paris Conventions for the protection of literary and artistic works, by bringing them within the ambit of the GATT dispute settlement procedures.

The Uruguay Round resulted also on an Agreement on **trade-related investment measures (TRIMs)**[3]. An illustrative list of non-permissible measures is included in the agreement, covering such things as local content rules, trade balancing and local sales requirements. Such measures must be phased out over a two- to seven-year period, depending upon whether the country is developed or developing. The TRIMs Agreement is particularly important for the EU, which is responsible for 36% of direct foreign investment in the world and receives 19% of such investments on its territory.

The **World Trade Organisation (WTO)**, established in 1995, has replaced the GATT, taking all the agreements concluded under its auspices, and settling trade disputes on a multilateral basis[4]. In fact, the WTO brings together under a single decision-making and administrative body the three agreements resulting from the Uruguay Round: the General Agreement on Tariffs and Trade (GATT), the General Agreement on Trade in Services (GATS) and the Agreement on trade-related aspects of intellectual property rights (TRIPs). The WTO operates on the basis of a ministerial conference, which must meet at least once every two years, and of a General Council made up of representatives of all the member countries. The European Community as well as all its Member States are members of WTO, a code of conduct defining the participation of the Community and its Member States in areas of shared power.

Thus, **the GATT continues to exist**, while frozen in its pre-Uruguay Round situation, for those countries that are not in a position to accept the entire package of its conclusions. On the contrary, the WTO is open to those who agree to abide by the entire Uruguay Round package of rules. This increases the certainty of the world exchange system, since all the

---

[1]   Annex 1, OJ L 336, 23.12.1994, p 191-212 and Fifth Protocol, OJ L 20, 27.01.1999, p. 40-53.

[2]   Annex 1 – Annex 1C, OJ L 336, 23.12.1994, p. 214-233.

[3]   Annex 1 – Annex 1A, OJ L 336, 23.12.1994, p. 100-102.

[4]   Agreement and Decision 94/800, OJ L 336, 23.12.1994, p. 1-10.

members of the WTO are perfectly aware of their own rights and obligations and of those of their partners. The national law of each contracting party must be in conformity with the rules of the WTO, thus precluding unilateral action.

23.5. *Appraisal and outlook*

A little known fact in Europe is that **the Member States of the European Union no longer have an independent foreign trade policy**. More than 60% of their trade is intra-Community and as such depends on the rules of the single market which prohibit any trade protection or trade promotion measures [see section 6.1.]. For the remaining 40% of their trade, the main instruments of commercial policy, the Common Customs Tariff, the common import arrangements and the common protective measures are in the hands of the organs of the EU, the Commission and the Council. Together they contribute to ensuring an even competition playing field for Community businesses, giving them access to equal prices for imported raw materials and other products they need. At the same time, the common commercial policy facilitates the work of Community importers who can use a uniform import licence, valid throughout the EU.

Being the world's leading commercial power, the Community is certainly respected and heeded in the context of the GATT and of the World Trade Organisation. One of the central principles of the latter is that of **balancing mutual advantages (global reciprocity)**. This means, for the European Union, that it can tie access for third country economic operators to the benefits of its single market with the existence of similar opportunities for European businesses in the country in question, or at the least to the absence of any discrimination. This implies a case-by-case approach for third countries, but a common approach by the Member States. The single market obliges the latter to show a united face to third countries.

However, whereas the rules of the World Trade Organisation impose in principle the freedom of international exchanges, **European companies are still faced with obstacles to trade and investment** in a large number of countries. Thus, an environment conducive to international exchanges and investments is still lacking in many Asian and South American countries and even the United States resorts to protectionist measures under pressure from its industries in difficulties, such as steel [see section 25.7.]. The European Community has the necessary power to redress these situations through a bilateral approach (action vis-à-vis the countries concerned) and a multilateral approach (actions within the WTO); but the Member States must lend a supporting hand in combating trade barriers by joining forces with the Commission. To face the problems arising from the **globalisation of trade**, the EU should try to harness it by strict international rules and strong institutions [see European Perspectives in conclusions].

Bibliography on the common commercial policy

- BARTELS Lorand. "The trade and development policy of the European Union", in *European Journal of International Law*, v. 18, n. 4, September 2007, p. 715-756.

- BRADFORD Anu. "International antitrust negotiations and the false hope of the WTO", in *Harvard International Law Journal*, v. 48, n. 2, Summer 2007, p. 383-439.

- CARDWELL Michael, RODGERS Christopher. "Reforming the WTO legal order for agricultural trade: issues for European rural policy in the Doha Round" in *International and Comparative Law Quarterly*, v. 55, n. 4, October 2006, p. 805-838.

- CHAISSE Julien. "Adapting the European Community legal structure to the international trade" in *European Business Law Review*, v. 17, n. 6, 2006, p. 1615-1635.

- DÜR Andreas, ZIMMERMANN Hubert (eds.). "The EU in international trade negotiations", in *Special issue of: Journal of Common Market Studies*, v. 45, n. 4, November 2007.

- EUROPEAN COMMISSION. *Global Europe: Europe's trade defence instruments in a changing global economy: a Green Paper for public consultation.* Luxembourg: EUR-OP*, 2006.

- FLANAGAN Robert. *Globalization and labor conditions: working conditions and worker rights in a global economy.* Oxford: Oxford University Press, 2006.

- PETERSON John, YOUNG Alasdair (eds.). *The European Union and the new trade politics.* London: Routledge, 2007.

- SINGHAM Shanker. *A general theory of trade and competition: trade liberalisation and competitive markets.* London: Cameron May, 2007.

- WOOLCOCK Stephen (et al.). "Competing regionalism: patterns, economic impact and implications for the multilateral trading system", in *Intereconomics*, v. 42, n. 5, September/October 2007, p. 236-259.

DISCUSSION TOPICS

1. How does the customs union legislation interact with the common commercial policy?
2. Discuss the need and the scope of the common rules for imports.
3. Outline the common trade protection measures.
4. What are the functions of the World Trade Organisation?
5. Are the objectives of the common commercial policy compatible with the trade liberalisation objectives of the WTO?

Chapter 24

DEVELOPMENT AID POLICY

Diagram of the chapter

EC-ACP
Association
p. 413

Overseas
countries and
territories
p. 415

Aid for
sustainable
development
p. 416

Generalised
system of
preferences
p. 417

Cooperation
at world level
p. 418

Fight against
hunger in
the world
p. 419

Development aid reflects **both the search for solidarity** between the developed countries of the EU and the disadvantaged countries of the world **and the economic necessity for the Union** of guaranteeing its raw material supply and creating outlets for its products. Aware that advantages granted at world level, notably through the GATT negotiations mentioned in the previous chapter [see section 23.4.], diminished the attractiveness of regional preferences, the EC/EU has been caught up in a process of continually expanding its aid to developing countries. It now views every agreement with developing countries as an instrument in an all-embracing political, social and economic development strategy.

24.1. Objectives and instruments of the policy

Article 177 of the EC Treaty specifies that Community policy in the sphere of development cooperation is **complementary to the policies pursued by the Member States and must foster**: the sustainable economic and social development of the developing countries; the smooth and gradual integration of the developing countries in the world economy; and the campaign against poverty in the developing countries. Article 301 (TEC) allows the Community to apply politically motivated economic sanctions, thus making every cooperation agreement an instrument of a broad political, social and economic approach.

Indeed, within the framework of the Community cooperation policy, the Community provides financial aid for the implementation of both development cooperation operations[1] and other operations which contribute to the general **objective of developing and consolidating democracy** and the rule of law and to that of respecting human rights and fundamental freedoms in third countries[2]. In addition, the Community provides financial assistance and appropriate expertise aimed at promoting **gender equality** into all its development cooperation policies and interventions in developing countries[3]. Finally, the EU promotes the full integration of the **environmental dimension** in the development process and, in particular, the conservation and sustainable management of tropical forests and other forests in developing countries[4].

The EU has taken ambitious development commitments by deciding to raise its aid gradually to a level of 0.7% of gross national income by 2015 (€164 per European citizen a year). On 15 October 2007, the Council agreed a **strategy on aid for trade** that includes clear figures on the amount of aid potentially available, as well as clear dates for when the funds will be available[5]. The strategy is aimed at enabling all developing countries to better integrate into the world trade system and to use trade more effectively and in a sustainable way in the eradication of poverty.

The European Union currently has an impressive store of **development aid instruments**, spanning the Convention Africa, the Caribbean and the Pacific (ACP) countries, special relations with the Overseas Countries and Territories (OCTs), aid for non-associated countries, the Generalised System of Tariff Preferences, participation in world commodity agreements and aid provided through non-government organisations fighting global problems such as hunger. The **decentralised cooperation approach** places local actors at the focal point of implementation and hence pursues the dual aims of gearing operations to needs and making them viable[6]. The EU participates fully in the International Monetary Fund and World Bank initiative for heavily indebted ACP countries by helping them reduce the net value of their obligations[7].

The European Union also has a wide range of **development policy resources**, from industrial and technological cooperation to trade promotion, food aid and financial aid. Financial aid also takes the form of European

---

[1] Regulation 1905/2006, OJ L 378, 27.12.2006.
[2] Regulation 976/1999, OJ L 120, 08.05.1999 and Regulation 2112/2005, OJ L 344, 27.12.2005.
[3] Regulation 1905/2006, OJ L 378, 27.12.2006.
[4] Regulation 2494/2000, OJ L 288, 15.11.2000 repealed by Regulation 1905/2006, OJ L 378, 27.12.2006.
[5] COM/2007/158.
[6] Regulation 1659/98, OJ L 213, 30.07.1998 and Regulation 625/2004, OJ L 99, 03.04.2004.
[7] Decision 98/453, OJ L 198, 15.07.1998.

Investment Bank (EIB) loans and risk capital[1], EIB management of the Investment Facility of the Cotonou Agreement[2], European Development Fund (EDF) subsidies; or grants under other Articles of the Community Budget, concerning in particular food aid.

The **European Development Fund (EDF)** is the main instrument for providing Community aid for development cooperation in the ACP States and OCTs. The EDF does not yet come under the Community's general budget. It is funded by the Member States, is subject to its own financial rules and is managed by a specific committee. Each EDF is concluded for a period of around five years. The Council regulation on the implementation of the **10th EDF** under the ACP-EC partnership agreement is based on an EU internal agreement on the EDF for financing under the 2008-13 financial framework for Community aid and is aimed at improving programming and decision-making procedures[3].

24.2. EC-ACP Association

The Convention signed in Lomé (Togo) on February 28, 1975 between the then nine Member States of the EEC and 46 States of **Africa, the Caribbean and the Pacific (ACP)** signalled a fresh start for the common development aid policy. The fourth EEC-ACP Convention, also signed in Lomé on December 15, 1989, firmly cemented cooperation between the EC Member States and 70 ACP States, including the whole of sub-Saharan Africa and, in certain aspects, South Africa.

The fourth Lomé Convention expired on 29 February 2000. Its successor, **the partnership agreement signed at Cotonou** (Benin) on 23 June 2000, although it is still based on the acquis of the four Lomé Conventions, heralds a fundamental change in relations between the ACP States and the Community and its Member States[4]. The term of the new agreement is 20 years. The addition of six Pacific Island States has raised to 77 the list of members of the ACP group of countries.

The partnership agreement combines substantial **political dialogue between the partners** with innovative forms of economic and commercial cooperation and new development cooperation mechanisms and strategies. Thus the agreement is supported by five interdependent pillars, namely the overall political dimension, encouragement of a participatory approach, a stronger bias towards the aim of reducing poverty, a new framework for economic and trade cooperation and reform of financial cooperation. The objective of good governance has been added to those of respect for human rights, democratic principles and the rule of law as one of the essential

---

[1] Decision 97/256, OJ L 102, 19.04.1997 and Regulation 1085/2006, OJ L 210, 31.07.2006.

[2] Decision 2003/268, OJ L 99, 17.04.2003.

[3] Regulation 617/2007, OJ L 152, 13.06.2007 and Regulation 215/2008, OJ L 78, 19.03.2008.

[4] Agreement and Decision 2000/483, OJ L 317, 15.12.2000 and Decision 2008/373, OJ L 129, 17.05.2008.

elements of the partnership. Under Article 11 of the Cotonou Partnership Agreement "the parties shall pursue an active, comprehensive and integrated policy of peace-building and conflict prevention and resolution within the framework of the partnership".

The Cotonou Agreement also includes provisions on cooperation in trade-related areas leading each participating country to negotiate a trade agreement with the Community. The purpose of these agreements is to help developing countries **integrate into the world economy**, step up production and stimulate trade and investment in compliance with World Trade Organisation rules [see section 23.4.]. Where finances are concerned, the various instruments have been regrouped and rationalised so that all resources available under the European Development Fund (EDF) are disbursed via two instruments: a financial package from which subsidies are granted and another from which risk capital and loans are provided to the private sector. Operations must focus on a specific sector (health, transport, etc.) and combine many different aspects of cooperation (economic, environmental, social, etc.) in order to ensure that aid is better targeted. Geographic cooperation with the ACP countries and regions in the context of the 10th EDF are founded on the basic principles and values reflected in the general provisions of the ACP-EC Partnership Agreement and take into account the development objectives and cooperation strategies set out in Title XX of the EC Treaty[1].

The **joint institutions for cooperation** established by the former Lomé Conventions remain in force, namely:

- **the Council of Ministers**, consisting of members of the Council of the European Union, members of the European Commission and a member of the government of each ACP country, meets once a year to initiate political dialogue, adopt political guidelines and take decisions required for the implementation of the provisions of the Agreement[2];

- **the Committee of Ambassadors**, made up of the permanent representative of each Member State for the European Union, a Commission representative and a head of mission for each ACP state, assists the Council of Ministers[3];

- **the Joint Parliamentary Assembly**, made up of an equal number of representatives of Members of the European Parliament and representatives of the ACP States, may adopt resolutions and submit recommendations to the Council of Ministers.

The new system for programming the aid granted by the Community enhances the flexibility of the partnership and entrusts the ACP States with greater responsibility, particularly by establishing a system of **rolling programming** that eliminates the concept of non-programmable aid, i.e. aid programmed unilaterally by the Community. The ACP States now have greater responsibility for determining objectives, strategies and operations and for programme management and selection.

---

[1] Regulations 617/2007, OJ L 152, 13.06.2007 and 215/2008, OJ L 78, 19.03.2008.

[2] Decision 1/2005 ACP-EC, OJ L 95, 14.04.2005.

[3] Decision 3/2005 ACP-EC, OJ L 95, 14.04.2005.

The programming process is centred on results. Financial assistance of a set amount is no longer an automatic right. Grants are allocated on the basis of an assessment of requirements and performances in accordance with criteria negotiated between the ACP countries and the Community. These criteria reflect the partnership's main objectives, such as progress in institutional reform, poverty reduction, etc. The main instrument used for programming grants is the **country support strategy (CSS)**. A CSS is drawn up for each ACP country by the Commission and the country in question. The CSS sets out general guidelines for using the aid and is supplemented by an indicative operational programme containing specific operations and a timetable for their implementation.

In cases of fluctuation of export revenues, instead of the Stabex and Sysmin instruments of the previous Conventions, the new system of rolling and flexible programming (FLEX system) makes it possible to ensure additional support via the funds allocated within the framework of the CSS and the operational programmes (Annex II to the ACP-EC Partnership Agreement). Additional support in this area is needed because of the ACP States' vulnerability resulting from a high degree of dependence on export revenues in the agricultural or mining sectors in ACP States.

24.3. Overseas countries and territories

The regulations currently in force relating to the association of overseas countries and territories to the EC apply to twenty OCTs **dependent on France, the Netherlands, the United Kingdom and Denmark** (Greenland). While they come under the wing of Member States, and their nationals are recognised since 1996 as EU citizens, the OCTs do not form part of the Union, but they are associated with it and thus benefit from the EDF and the same types of development cooperation measures as ACP States. Community solidarity towards them is reflected chiefly by the near free access to the Community market for products originating in the OCTs, by the implementation of export stabilisation systems and by financial and technical cooperation drawing on the resources of the EDF and the European investment Bank[1].

The **fields covered by this financial and technical cooperation** are agricultural and rural development, fisheries, industrial development, the exploitation of mining and energy potential, transport and communications, the development of trade and services, regional cooperation and cultural and social cooperation. Depending on the development level and situation of the OCTs, an attempt is also made to establish firm cooperation between them and the ACP States. The partnership arrangements in favour of OCTs include many elements contained in the fourth Lomé Convention and establish a three-way Commission/Member State/OCT partnership. They

---

[1] Decision 2001/822, OJ L 314, 30.11.2001 and Decision 2007/249, OJ L 109, 26.04.2007.

also aim to improve the rights of individuals and the status of OCT nationals in the European Union.

24.4. Aid for sustainable development

The **European Consensus on Development**, adopted by the Council and the Representatives of the Governments of the Member States, the European Parliament and the Commission on 22 November 2005[1] states that the primary and overarching objective of EU development cooperation is the eradication of poverty in the context of sustainable development, including pursuit of the Millennium Development Goals (MDGs). The eight MDGs are to: eradicate extreme poverty and hunger; achieve universal primary education; promote gender equality and empower women; reduce the mortality rate of children; improve maternal health; combat HIV/AIDS, malaria and other diseases; ensure environmental sustainability and develop a global partnership for development. However, the Consensus states also that the EU acknowledges the essential oversight role of democratically elected citizens' representatives and encourages an increased involvement of national assemblies, parliaments and local authorities.

In this context the Community finances measures aimed at supporting cooperation with developing countries, territories and regions included in the list of aid recipients of the Development Assistance Committee of the Organization for Economic Cooperation and Development (OECD/DAC) - referred to as "partner countries and regions" in Annex I. The primary and overarching objective of cooperation under the Regulation establishing a **financing instrument for development cooperation** is the eradication of poverty in partner countries and regions in the context of sustainable development, including pursuit of the **Millennium Development Goals (MDGs)**, as well as the promotion of democracy, good governance and respect for human rights and for the rule of law[2]. Consistently with this objective, cooperation with partner countries and regions should:

- consolidate and support democracy, the rule of law, human rights and fundamental freedoms, good governance, gender equality and related instruments of international law;
- foster the sustainable development - including political, economic, social and environmental aspects - of partner countries and regions;
- encourage their smooth and gradual integration into the world economy;
- help develop international measures to preserve and improve the quality of the environment and the sustainable management of global natural resources; and
- strengthen the relationship between the Community and partner countries and regions.

---

[1] Joint Statement, OJ C 46, 24.02.2006.
[2] Regulation 1905/2006, OJ L 378, 27.12.2006.

A **financing instrument for the promotion of democracy and human rights** worldwide contributes also to the achievement of the objectives of the development policy statement on the "European Consensus on Development"[1]. It provides assistance, within the framework of the Community's policy on development cooperation, and economic, financial and technical cooperation with third countries, contributing to the development and consolidation of democracy and the rule of law, and of respect for all human rights and fundamental freedoms.

In addition to the Millennium Development Goals the EU **Programme for the Prevention of Violent Conflicts**, endorsed by the European Council, underlines the EU's "political commitment to pursue conflict prevention as one of the main objectives of the EU's external relations" and states that Community development cooperation instruments can contribute to this goal and to the development of the EU as a global player. In pursuit of this objective, Regulation 1717/2006, establishing an **Instrument for Stability** allows the Community to undertake development cooperation measures, as well as financial, economic and technical cooperation measures with third countries under the following conditions[2]: in a situation of crisis or emerging crisis, to contribute to stability by providing an effective response to help preserve, establish or re-establish the conditions essential to the proper implementation of the Community's development and cooperation policies; and (b) in the context of stable conditions for the implementation of Community cooperation policies in third countries, to help build capacity both to address specific global and transregional threats having a destabilising effect and to ensure preparedness to address pre- and post-crisis situations. Community assistance under the Instrument for Stability is complementary to that provided for under related Community instruments for external assistance [see also sections 25.6. and 25.8.]. It may be provided only to the extent that an adequate and effective response cannot be provided under those instruments.

24.5. Generalised System of Preferences

The Community provided the initiative behind the **Generalised System of Preferences (GSP)**, the principle of which was taken on board by the other industrialised countries at the 2nd Session of the United Nations Conference on Trade and Development (UNCTAD) in 1968. The objective of GSP is to assist developing countries' poverty reduction efforts by helping them to generate revenue through international trade and granting them tariff preferences. Although it has traditionally come under Article 133 of the EC Treaty (ex Art. 113) and, therefore, in theory, under the common commercial policy, the GSP is in practice a tool of development. It offers

---

[1]   Regulation 1889/2006, OJ L 396, 29/12/2006.
[2]   Regulation 1717/2006, OJ L 327, 24.11.2006.

some 130 developing countries tariff reductions or in some cases duty-free access for their manufactured exports and increasingly their agricultural exports as well. Being a tariff instrument, it operates purely at the level of tariffs which is already reduced thanks to GATT. Being an autonomous instrument, its preferences are granted (not negotiated) by the Community and are complementary to the multilateral liberalisation of trade within WTO [see section 23.4.].

The **reform of the GSP** involves simplification of the EU system of trade preferences through a reduction in the number of arrangements for the period 2006 to 2015[1]. It allows a range of 7.200 products duty-free access to the EU, representing an increase of 300 products, principally for the benefit of the agriculture and fisheries sectors. The "Everything but arms" arrangement grants duty- and quota-free access for all imports except arms from least developed countries. The new incentive system (GSP plus) is based on the concept of granting additional preferences to vulnerable developing countries that pursue good governance and sustainable development policies.

24.6. Cooperation at world level

Many developing countries are **heavily dependent on the export of just one or two commodities** and see their earnings rise and fall according to the fluctuations of the world prices of their products. As a consequence, international agreements concluded in the framework of the United Nations Conference on Trade and Development (UNCTAD) attempt to support or stabilise the production of certain commodities. These agreements generally cover three aspects: prices, quantities and mechanisms (production quotas, buffer stocks and so on). The producer countries see these agreements on commodities chiefly as a way of guaranteeing export earnings and ensuring a certain level of income for their producers, whereas importers view them as a way of guaranteeing supply of a given quantity of a product at a price set in advance. The agreements differ from one product to the next, some aiming at better marketing and heightened competitiveness, others involving attempts to intervene in the free play of market mechanisms at world level.

The United Nations **Common Fund for Commodities** supports the operation of agreements on certain commodities, which are regulated by organisations with specific responsibility for them. To this effect, the Fund has two "windows", one contributing to the financing of buffer stocks and national stocks coordinated at international level and managed by international organisations with specific responsibility for certain commodities; the other supporting measures other than storage (for example research and other measures seeking to improve productivity and marketing). The

---

[1]   Regulation 980/2005, OJ L 169, 30.06.2005.

Community is a member of the Fund on the same footing as its Member States[1].

24.7. *Fight against hunger and other afflictions*

The European Community considers food aid, first and foremost, as a structural instrument of long-term development. Community policy on **food security** has evolved towards supporting broad-based food security strategies at national, regional and global level, limiting the use of food aid to humanitarian situations and food crises and avoiding disruptive effects on local production and markets. It takes into account the specific situation of countries that are structurally fragile and highly dependent on support for food security, in order to avoid a steep reduction of Community assistance to these countries.

The objective of the **thematic programme on food security** of the Regulation establishing a financing instrument for development cooperation is to improve food security in favour of the poorest and most vulnerable people and contribute to achieving the Millennium Development Goals (MDGs) on poverty and hunger [see section 24.4], through a set of actions which ensure overall coherence, complementarity and continuity of Community interventions, including in the area of the transition from relief to development[2]. To achieve this objective the programme includes activities such as:

- contributing to the provision of international public goods, in particular pro-poor demand driven research and technological innovation;
- supporting global, continental and regional programmes which notably: support food security in specific fields such as agriculture, or promote national food security and poverty reduction strategies;
- addressing food insecurity in exceptional situations of transition and State fragility;
- developing innovative food security policies, strategies and approaches

Another Regulation lays down the objectives of **humanitarian aid** and the procedures governing aid and operations in this context[3]. The Community's humanitarian aid comprises assistance, relief and protection operations to help people in third countries, particularly the most vulnerable among them, and as a priority those in developing countries, victims of natural disasters, man-made crises, such as wars and outbreaks of fighting, or exceptional situations or circumstances comparable to natural or man-made disasters. The kinds of operation covered are specific projects or broader-based plans designed to bring in relief, prevent crises from worsening and help with the repatriation and resettlement of refugees back

---

[1] Agreement and Decision 1999/373, OJ L 182, 14.07.1990.
[2] Regulation 1905/2006, OJ L 378, 27.12.2006.
[3] Regulation 1257/96, OJ L 163, 02.07.1996.

home. Also included among the eligible operations are disaster-preparedness and activities to protect the victims of conflict.

The framework Regulation gives the **Commission overall control of all the aid mobilisation and delivery operations**. Commission control ends however when the aid is in the hands of the beneficiary country. Furthermore, the successful tenderer is responsible for the aid until its delivery to the location stipulated in the agreement concluded with the beneficiary countries. Finally, the Regulation stipulates that aid is to be monitored by professionals appointed by the Commission to ensure that the operation is correctly followed through. The Community focuses its attention on **food strategies** where food security tops the list of priorities. The European Community participates actively in the Food Aid Convention[1].

The **European Community Office for Humanitarian Aid (ECHO)**, run by the Commission, has the role of enhancing the Community's presence on the ground, of grouping together all its emergency humanitarian actions and improving coordination with the Member States, other donors, NGOs and specialised international agencies. ECHO is wholly responsible for administering humanitarian and emergency food aid, and disaster preparedness. At present, the humanitarian aid of the EU exceeds 1 billion euros a year and its scope has been broadened to cover the violent ethnic conflicts in Africa, the consequences of the collapse of the Soviet Union and the aftermath of the fratricidal wars in former Yugoslavia. In fact, more than 95% of ECHO's activities cover man-made disasters.

24.8. Appraisal and outlook

The European Union and its member countries are **by far the largest providers of development funds in the world**. Whereas, in the beginning, it was limited only to Associated Countries and Territories, the common development policy now covers almost all the underdeveloped countries of the world. Moreover, the contribution of the EU to the development of countries in Africa, Asia and Latin America is not limited to grants, through the Community budget, and loans through the European Investment Bank. An important part of its development aid takes the form of trade concessions both to ACP and OCT countries, through duty free imports of their products, and to Asian and Latin American countries, through the generalised system of trade preferences [see section 24.5.]. In addition, the Community development aid policy strives - without much success up to now - to support democratic regimes, human rights, women's position and environmental protection in the recipient countries [see section 24.1.].

While much clearly remains to be done, given an international backdrop of economic crisis in the developing countries and the fratricidal con-

---

[1]   Convention and Decision 96/88, OJ L 21, 27.01.1996 and Decision 2006/906, OJ L 346, 09.12.2006.

flicts and political instability in many of them, the association agreements of the EU with ACP and OCT countries and its cooperation agreements with Asian and Latin American countries are **a remarkable contribution to solidarity between the North and South** of the planet. Although aid cannot make up for a lack of sound domestic policies or trade outlets, it may be used as a lever for the implementation of economic and political reforms in the developing countries, on the basis of the four main themes expounded in the Treaty on European Union: consolidation and development of democracy, sustainable economic and social development, integration into the world economy and a battle against poverty. The adverse effects of climate change being particularly serious for the least advanced countries, the environmental dimension should be an integral part of the European Union's development policy, the principal objective being to create as many synergies as possible between action to combat poverty and that to tackle climate change.

By improving the arrangements for mobilising Community relief, the **European Community Office for Humanitarian Aid (ECHO)** is meant to provide both an efficient service to needy countries and a higher profile to European humanitarian interventions [see section 24.7.]. It should give, indeed, public opinion tangible evidence of the Community's role as an active contributor in the field of humanitarian aid. EU citizens are entitled to know that they, through the Community budget, make a small contribution to the alleviation of the sufferings of the people of developing countries that the media relate every day.

In the future, the EU should ensure consistency between development cooperation, the common commercial policy and the common foreign and security policy [see section 8.2.], while establishing close relations with the partner countries. Greater coordination of development aid is needed both at the European Union level and worldwide. Internal coordination between the Commission and Member States would enhance the Union's overall effort and increase the effectiveness of this effort. Food security policy should go hand in hand with poverty reduction in the most vulnerable countries and its objectives and instruments should be fully integrated into the Community's overall development policy.

On the global scene, the enlarged Union is the world's biggest economy. Its ability to influence **global economic governance** will accordingly be greater. As agreed at the Johannesburg World Summit on Sustainable Development in September 2002, the Union must defend a strategy for sustainable development based on the United Nations system and the international financial institutions and reject hegemony or unilateralism. To this end, it should promote the social dimension of globalisation, including bilateral and regional relations, development and external cooperation, trade policy, private initiatives and governance at global level. In view of the role they play in international development, the EU and its Member States should take the lead in revitalising the United Nations and its specialised organisations, the International Monetary Fund (IMF) and the World Bank in order to make them more effective.

Bibliography on development aid policy

- BORRMANN Axel, BUSSE Matthias. "The institutional challenge of the ACP/EU Economic Partnership Agreements", in *Development Policy Review*, v. 25, n. 4, July 2007, p. 403-416.
- BOURDET Yves, GULLSTRAND Joakin, OLOFSDOTTER Karin. *European Union and developing Countries: trade, aid and growth in an integrating world.* Cheltendam: Edward Elgar, 2007.
- COOK Paul, MOSEDALE Sarah (eds.). *Regulation, markets and poverty.* Cheltenham: Edward Elgar, 2007.
- EUROPEAN COMMISSION. *Towards a European consensus on humanitarian aid.* COM/2007/317. Luxembourg: EUR-OP*, 2007.
  - *Building a global climate change alliance between the European Union and poor developing countries most vulnerable to climate change* .Luxembourg: EUR-OP*, 2007.
- FABER Gerrit, ORBIE Jan (eds.). *European Union trade politics and development: 'everything but arms' unravelled* London: Routledge, 2007.
- GEBREWOLD Belachew (ed.). *Africa and fortress Europe: threats and opportunities.* Aldershot: Ashgate, 2007.
- HADFIELD Amelia. "Janus advances?: An analysis of the EC development policy and the 2005 amended Cotonou Partnership Agreement", in *European Foreign Affairs Review*, v. 12, n. 1, Spring 2007, p. 39-66.
- LIAPIS Peter. *Preferential trade agreements: how much do they benefit developing economies?* Paris: OECD, 2007.
- MOLD Andrew (ed.). *EU development policy in a changing world: challenges for the 21st century.* Amsterdam: Amsterdam University Press, 2007.

DISCUSSION TOPICS

1. Do the EU countries have common interests in helping the development of the less fortunate countries of the world?
2. Which are the main axes of the common development aid policy?
3. Outline the development mechanisms used by the EC-ACP association.
4. How does the EU help other than ACP countries?
5. Could the common development aid policy be better linked to the common commercial policy and to the common foreign and security policy?

Chapter 25

EXTERNAL RELATIONS

Diagram of the chapter

European Free Trade Association and EEA p. 424	**Candidates for accession** p. 425	**Balkan countries** p. 429	**European neighbour- hood policy** p. 430
Mediter- ranean countries p. 432	**Asian countries** p. 433	**North Ameri- can countries** p. 435	**Latin Ameri- can countries** p. 437

The **external relations of the European Community (EC)**, which date back to its first years of existence, should not be confused with the foreign policy of the European Union (EU), introduced by the Treaty of Maastricht, but which is governed by intergovernmental cooperation rather than by the Community procedure [see section 1.1.2]. As explained in chapter 8, the common foreign and security policy (CFSP) depends on a special decision-making process [see section 8.2.1.], whereas the external relations of the EC depend on the Community decision-making process [see section 4.3.]. However, the Community's external relations, tied in as they are with the common commercial policy and the Community's development aid policy, give a foretaste of a really common foreign policy and an indication of the scope which it will eventually assume.

The following pages will examine the relations which the European Community as a body has already established with many countries throughout the world. Although **these relations are of economic or commercial origin**, they have on more than one occasion stepped out of this setting into the purely political arena. This is notably the case of relations with other European countries. For the student of European integration it is interesting to distinguish the foreign affairs decisions taken under the common foreign and security policy procedure from those taken under the Community external relations procedure. In other words, it is interesting to see just where the European Community's external domain ends and that of the European Union begins. The answer to this question is not straightforward.

25.1. European Free Trade Association and European Economic Area

As stated in chapter 1, the **European Free Trade Association (EFTA)** was set up in 1959 on the initiative of the United Kingdom, which favoured trade liberalisation through intergovernmental cooperation rather than through the multinational integration process aimed at by ECSC and EEC [see sections 1.1.2. and 1.2.]. When the United Kingdom and Denmark switched allegiances from EFTA to the EEC in 1973, the scale of their commercial relations with the other EFTA countries made it necessary to abolish customs barriers between the two groups of countries. As a consequence, free trade agreements were signed in 1972 and 1973 between the Community and the EFTA countries. These agreements abolished customs duties and restrictions on trade in industrial products. Furthermore, the Community agreed to certain compromises on the Common Agricultural Policy, which were matched by reciprocal EFTA concessions in the agricultural field. EEC-EFTA free trade has operated in a satisfactory manner and has brought about sustained growth in trade between the two groups of countries. This trade, by the end of the 1980s, represented 25% of total Community trade and between 40% and 65% of that of the EFTA countries.

In 1989, Jacques Delors, then President of the European Commission, proposed and the European Council agreed to further strengthen the relations between the two European trade blocks. The negotiations were completed in October 1991 between the Community and EFTA as a body on the basic, legal and institutional aspects of such a global agreement. The **Agreement on the European Economic Area (EEA)** was signed in 1992 by the governments of twelve EU countries and six EFTA countries. However, as a result of the negative Swiss referendum on the EEA Treaty, on 6 December 1992, and the accession to the European Union since 1 January 1995 of the former EFTA members Austria, Sweden and Finland, the EEA Agreement associates to the EU **only Norway, Iceland and Liechtenstein**[1]. The new members of the EU have become contracting parties to the EEA Agreement.

The institutional framework of the EEA comprises: the EEA Council, which is made up of members of the Council of the EU and the Commission plus one member for each signatory EFTA government, and which

---

[1] Decisions 93/734 to 93/741, OJ L 346, 31.12.1993, Agreement on the EEA, OJ L 1, 03.01.1994, Decision of EEA Joint Committee 7/94, OJ L 160, 28.06.1994 , Decision 2004/368, OJ L 130, 29.04.2004 and Decision 2007/566, OJ L 221, 25.08.2007.

provides political impetus for the implementation of the Agreement and lays down general guidelines; the EEA Joint Committee, comprising representatives of the contracting parties and responsible for the implementation of the Agreement; the EEA Joint Parliamentary Committee; and the EEA Consultative Committee, which provides a forum for representatives of the social partners. The EFTA countries, members of the EEA, participate in the decision-shaping process of the EU in the ambit of the Commission.

The aim of the EEA Agreement is to establish a dynamic and homogeneous integrated economic entity based on common rules and equal conditions of competition. The EFTA States, minus Switzerland, undertook to take on board existing Community legislation concerning the free movement of goods, persons, services and capital, subject to a few exceptions and transitional periods in certain sectors. Apart from the **implementation of the "four freedoms" of the common market** [see chapter 6], the EEA Agreement also provides for close relations between the Community and the EFTA countries to be reinforced and extended in areas which have an impact on business activity[1], notably social policy, consumer protection, environment, statistics and company law, research and development, information, education, the audiovisual sector, SMEs and tourism. In fact, the EFTA countries (including Switzerland in some respects) participate practically in the common market without participating in the decision making process that governs it, adapting its legislation to their circumstances.

25.2. Candidates for accession

When, at the end of 1989, the pace of history suddenly accelerated with the rapid and successive collapse of the Communist regimes in Central and Eastern Europe, the Community rushed to help the people of these countries, working to promote political reform and develop a private sector in their economies. Less than fifteen years after the fall of the Berlin wall, in May 2004, eight of these countries have become **members of the European Community/Union**, but some mechanisms that helped them achieve this status are still in force, in order to prepare the accession of other candidates mentioned in this and the following section. It is interesting to review these mechanisms, which have proved their effectiveness.

This is notably the case concerning the **operation PHARE** (Poland and Hungary: Aid for Economic Restructuring)[2], which was extended in 2000 to Balkan countries[3] and in 2004 to Croatia[1] [see section 25.3.].

---

[1] Regulation 2894/94, OJ L 305, 30.11.1994.

[2] Regulation 3906/89, OJ L 375, 23.12.1989 and Regulations 1266/1999, 1267/1999, 1268/1999, OJ L 161, 26.06.1999 and Regulation 2257/2004, OJ L 389, 30.12.2004, all repealed by Regulation 1085/2006, OJ L 210, 31.07.2006.

[3] Regulation 2666/2000 repealed by Regulation 1085/2006, OJ L 210, 31.07.2006.

Aimed at gearing the programme to preparing the applicant countries for EU membership, the new guidelines are implemented by means of "accession partnerships" drawn up by the Commission. They provide the framework for the programming of PHARE funds focusing on two main priorities: institution building and financing investment. Institution building involves assistance to strengthen the applicant countries' democratic institutions and administrations with a view to facilitating adoption of the "*acquis communautaire*" (established Community law and practice) [see section 3.3.] and helping them meet the economic and political conditions for membership. Special attention under this priority is paid to justice and home affairs concerning notably fraud, illegal immigration and organised crime [see section 8.1.2.]. The second priority, the financing of investment, concerns areas where adoption of Community rules requires substantial resources (environment, transport, product quality, working conditions, etc.) and major infrastructure projects connected with the trans-European networks [see section 6.8.].

In parallel with PHARE and in relation with it three **specific but large-scale instruments** were designed for assistance to CEECs and are examined successively below: the European Bank for Reconstruction and Development, the European Training Foundation and the programme of trans-European mobility for university students.

On April 9, 1990 in Paris the text defining the operating provisions for the **European Bank for Reconstruction and Development (EBRD)** was signed[2]. It was inaugurated on April 14, 1991. Today the EBRD uses the tools of investment to help build market economies and democracies in 27 countries from central Europe to central Asia. The EBRD is the largest single investor in the region and mobilises significant foreign direct investment beyond its own financing. It is owned by 60 countries and two intergovernmental institutions, the European Commission and the European Investment Bank (EIB). It invests mainly in private enterprises, usually together with commercial partners. It provides project financing for banks, industries and businesses, both new ventures and investments in existing companies. It also works with publicly owned companies, to support privatisation, restructuring state-owned firms and improvement of municipal services. The Bank uses its close relationship with governments in the region to promote policies that will bolster the business environment. The mandate of the EBRD stipulates that it must only work in countries that are committed to democratic principles. Respect for the environment is part of the strong corporate governance attached to all EBRD investments.

The **European Training Foundation** is constituted in the form of an independent body which is cooperating closely with the European Centre for the Development of Vocational Training (**CEDEFOP**) [see section

---

[1]   Regulation 2257/2004, OJ L 389, 30.12.2004 and Decisions 2005/40 and 2005/41, OJ L 26, 28.01.2005.

[2]   Agreement and Decision 90/674, OJ L 372, 31.12.1990.

13.3.1.]. The Foundation is open to public or private sector participation by non-Community countries and focuses its action on vocational training, on-going training and training in certain specific sectors. Its role is to ensure efficient cooperation in the provision of aid to the countries in question, to help identify their training needs and to define a strategy which can help meet these needs. It acts as a kind of clearing house, matching up information on aid offers and requests and encouraging and helping multilateral assistance.

The **programme of trans-European mobility for university students (TEMPUS)** is cast in the same mould as existing Community exchange programmes, but is adapted to the specific needs of the countries in question [see section 13.4.2.][1]. In addition to various complementary activities, it makes provision for joint training projects between universities and companies in Eastern European countries and their counterparts in at least two EU States. It also seeks to encourage the mobility of teachers, students and administrative officials. Its priority action fields are management, business administration and language learning.

Although Central and Eastern European countries, finding themselves since the early 1990s in a very difficult transition from centrally planned to free trade and competition economies, could have chosen membership of the EFTA and through it of the EEA [see section 25.1.], they all **applied for membership to the EU**, thus clearly indicating their preference for the multinational integration process rather than for intergovernmental cooperation [see section 1.1.2.]. On their side, the EU Member States responded positively to this application, thus demonstrating that they did not view their successful enterprise as a club of rich countries.

The countries which request accession to the EU should, however, satisfy certain political and economic conditions. According to the **criteria established by the European Council in Copenhagen** in 1993, an applicant country should have: (a) stable institutions guaranteeing democracy, the rule of law, human rights and protection of minorities; (b) a functioning market economy and the capacity to cope with competitive pressure and market forces within the Union; and (c) the ability to take on the obligations of membership, including adherence to the aims of political, economic and monetary union. The EC/EU helps, however the candidate countries to comply with the criteria for their accession. In addition to their participation in various Community programmes and the assistance given through special programmes, notably PHARE, TEMPUS, ISPA and SAPARD [see sections 12.1.2 and 21.5.5.], pre-accession assistance is granted to the countries trying to meet the criteria set at Copenhagen[2]. A Technical Assistance Information Exchange Office (**TAIEX**) allows the associated countries as well as the European neighbourhood policy (ENP)

---

[1]   Decision 1999/311, OJ L 120, 08.05.1999 and Decision 2002/601, OJ L 195, 24.07.2002.

[2]   Regulation 622/98, OJ L 85, 20.03.1998 and Decisions 98/259 to 98/268, OJ L 121, 23.04.1998.

countries [see section 25.4] and Russia to call upon the experience of Commission and Member States officials in drafting, transposing and implementing legislation concerning the internal market and Community programmes[1].

Partnership agreements, containing the principles, priorities, intermediate objectives and conditions of accession, were signed, in 2003, with Bulgaria[2], Romania[3] and Turkey[4]. On 25 April 2005 the Council decided the admission of the Republics of Bulgaria and Romania to the European Union[5]. On 17 and 18 June 2004 the Brussels European Council recommended that accession negotiations should be opened with Croatia. The next Brussels European Council (16-17 December 2004) recommended that accession negotiations should be opened with Turkey.

In order to improve the efficiency of the Community's assistance to candidate countries, Regulation 1085/2006 established an **Instrument for Pre-Accession Assistance (IPA)**[6] [see section 12.3.4]. All the Western Balkan countries are considered as potential candidate countries; however, a distinction is made between candidate countries listed in Annex I of the Regulation (Croatia, Turkey and the former Yugoslav Republic of Macedonia) and potential candidate countries, listed in Annex II of the Regulation (Albania, Bosnia, Montenegro and Serbia, including Kosovo). The Community has agreed to assist all these countries in their progressive alignment with the standards and policies of the European Union, including where appropriate the acquis communautaire, with a view to membership.

The European Council of Brussels (16-17 December 2004) agreed that accession negotiations with individual candidate States should be based on **a framework for negotiations**. Each framework, which should be established by the Council on a proposal from the Commission, should address certain essential elements, while taking into consideration the own merits and specific situations and characteristics of each candidate State.

25.3. Balkan countries

Exceptional trade measures were introduced for **western Balkan countries** and territories (Albania, the Federal Republic of Yugoslavia, the Former Yugoslav Republic of Macedonia, Bosnia and Herzegovina, Croatia and the Kosovo) participating in or linked to the European Union's sta-

---

[1] Decision 2006/62, OJ L 32, 04.02.2006.
[2] Decision 2003/396, OJ L 145, 12.06.2003.
[3] Decision 2003/397, OJ L 145, 12.06.2003.
[4] Decision 2003/398, OJ L 145, 12.06.2003.
[5] Treaty and Council Decision, OJ L 157, 21.06.2005.
[6] Regulation 1085/2006, OJ L 210, 31.07.2006.

bilisation and association process (SAP)[1]. After the change of regime in Serbia, the Union has stepped up its assistance to the Balkans by bringing under a single legal basis and a single programme the initiatives covered by the Phare and Obnova[2] programmes, clarifying the objectives of Community action and promoting close regional cooperation between recipient countries[3]. The aim of the assistance is the reconstruction and stabilisation of the region, support for democracy and the rule of law, promotion of human and minority rights, and economic development and market economy reforms. Indeed, the European perspective provides a powerful incentive for political and economic reform in the region and has encouraged reconciliation among its peoples.

The Thessaloniki European Council (19-20 June 2003) enhanced the stabilisation and association process with elements from the enlargement process (twinning, allowing participation in selected Community programmes, European partnerships, strengthening of political dialogue and cooperation in the area of common foreign and security policy). In accordance, the Community pre-accession assistance programmes (Phare, ISPA and Sapard) were modified to allow the stabilisation and association process countries to participate in tenders, which were previously limited to the acceding or candidate countries, and therefore move towards EU integration[4].

The Thessaloniki European Council endorsed, in particular, the introduction of the Partnerships as a means of materialising the European perspective of the Western Balkan countries within the framework of the Stabilisation and Association Process. **European partnerships** now cover Albania, Bosnia and Herzegovina, Croatia, the Former Yugoslav Republic of Macedonia and Serbia and Montenegro, including Kosovo[5]. The partnerships provide a framework covering the priorities resulting from the analysis of the partners' different situations, the preparations for further integration into the European Union and the progress made in implementing the stabilisation and association process, including stabilisation agreements. The Council decides by qualified majority the principles, priorities and conditions to be contained in the European partnerships.

To **prepare for the European integration** of the countries concerned in the framework of the stabilisation and association process, the Council set out the principles, priorities and conditions to be contained in the respective partnerships with, respectively, Croatia[6], Turkey[7], Bosnia and

---

[1] Regulations 2007/2000, OJ L 240, 23.09.2000 and 530/2007, OJ L 125, 15.05.2007.
[2] Regulation 2454/1999, OJ L 299, 20.11.1999.
[3] Regulation 2666/2000, OJ L 306, 07.12.2000 and Regulation 769/2004, OJ L 123, 27.04.2004, all repealed by Regulation 1085/2006, OJ L 210, 31.07.2006.
[4] Regulation 769/2004, OJ L 123, 27.04.2004.
[5] Regulations 533/2004, OJ L 86, 24.03.2004 and 229/2008, OJ L 73, 15.03.2008.
[6] Decision 2008/119, OJ L 42, 16.02.2008.
[7] Decision 2008/157, OJ L 51, 26.02.2008.

Herzegovina[1], the Former Yugoslav Republic of Macedonia[2], Albania[3] and Serbia and Montenegro, including Kosovo[4]. In the light of the priorities set for each country, the Commission expects each partner to prepare an action plan and schedule listing the specific measures which it intends to take. The financial aid allocated under the Community assistance for reconstruction, development and stabilisation (CARDS) programme will be conditional upon progress achieved in the implementation of the Copenhagen political criteria [see section 25.2] and of the specific short- and medium-term priorities laid down in each of the European partnerships. While the EU is ready to provide all support possible, advancement in the process of European integration in the region depends primarily on each country's own commitment and capability to carry out political and economic reform and adhere to the core values and principles of the Union. In any case, all these countries may participate in Community programmes[5]. On 25 October 2005, the EU and eight Balkan countries signed the **Energy Community Treaty** in order to create the legal framework for an integrated energy market[6] [see section 19.1.2].

25.4. European neighbourhood policy

The Community plays a decisive role in the provision of technical assistance and food aid to the new republics of the Commonwealth of Independent States (CIS). In 1990, it introduced a technical assistance programme in favour of economic reform and recovery in the former Union of Soviet Socialist Republics. From 1996 to 1999, the Community provided assistance to economic reform and recovery in the New Independent States and Mongolia (TACIS programme)[7]. Such assistance generated significant impact on reform and led to partnership and cooperation agreements with 13 states in **Eastern Europe and Central Asia: Armenia, Azerbaijan, Belarus, Georgia, Kazakhstan, Kyrgyzstan, Moldova, Mongolia, Russian Federation, Tajikistan, Turkmenistan, Ukraine and Uzbekistan.**

Under the new **European Neighbourhood Policy**, a set of priorities are defined together by the European Union and the partner countries, to be incorporated in a series of jointly agreed Action Plans, covering a number of key areas for specific action, including political dialogue and reform, trade and economic reform, equitable social and economic development, justice and home affairs, energy, transport, information society, environ-

---

[1] Decision 2008/211, OJ L 80, 19.03.2008.
[2] Decision 2008/212, OJ L 80, 19.03.2008.
[3] Decision 2008/210, OJ L 80, 19.03.2008.
[4] Decision 2008/213, OJ L 80, 19.03.2008.
[5] Decisions 2005/524, 2005/525, 2005/526, 2005/527, 2005/528, OJ L 192, 22.07.2005.
[6] Decision 2005/905, OJ L 329, 16.12.2005.
[7] Regulation 1279/96, OJ L 165, 04.07.1996.

ment, research and innovation, the development of civil society and people-to-people contacts. These priorities are consistent with the objectives of the Partnership and Cooperation Agreements and of the Association Agreements. They are also coherent with the objectives and principles of the European Community Development Policy, as outlined in the Joint Statement entitled **"The European Consensus on Development"** [see section 24.4].

In Eastern Europe and the southern Caucasus, the Partnership and Cooperation Agreements provide the basis for contractual relations. Since the European Union and **Russia** have decided to develop their specific strategic partnership through the creation of four common spaces, Community assistance is used to support the development of this partnership and to promote cross-border cooperation at the border between Russia and its European Union neighbours. In the Mediterranean, the **Euro-Mediterranean Partnership** (the Barcelona Process) [see section 25.5] provides a regional framework for cooperation which is complemented by a network of Association Agreements. Hence, the neighbourhood policy for Mediterranean partners takes into account the agreement reached in that context on establishing a free-trade area for goods by 2010 and beginning a process of asymmetric liberalisation.

In order to support the partner countries' commitment to common values and principles and their efforts in the implementation of the action plans, the Community provides assistance to those countries and supports various forms of cooperation among them and between them and the Member States with the aim of developing a **zone of shared stability, security and prosperity** involving a significant degree of economic integration and political cooperation. To this end, the Community created a single policy-driven instrument, the **European Neighbourhood and Partnership Instrument (ENPI)**, which replaced, since 1 January 2007, a number of pre-existing instruments (such as MEDA and in part TACIS), ensuring coherence and simplifying assistance programming and management[1].

Community assistance by the European Neighbourhood and Partnership Instrument should promote enhanced cooperation and **progressive economic integration** between the European Union and the partner countries. Since the European Union is founded on the values of liberty, democracy, respect for human rights and fundamental freedoms and the rule of law, Community assistance seeks to promote commitment to these values in partner countries through dialogue and cooperation inside an area of prosperity and good neighbourhood. The ENPI assists the implementation of partnership and cooperation agreements, association agreements or other existing and future agreements with the following countries and territories (ENP countries): Algeria, Armenia, Azerbaijan, Belarus, Egypt, Georgia, Israel, Jordan, Lebanon, Libya, Moldova, Morocco, the Palestinian Author-

---

[1]   Regulation 1638/2006, OJ L 310, 09.11.2006.

ity, the Russian Federation, Syria, Tunisia and Ukraine. A total of over EUR 11.1 billion under the European Union's 2007-13 financial framework will be provided from the Community budget for implementation of the regulation, of which at least 95% will be allocated to country and multi-country programmes, and up to 5% will be devoted to cross-border cooperation programmes. ENP countries have access to the assistance of the Technical Assistance Information Exchange Office (**TAIEX**)[1] [see section 25.2].

25.5. Mediterranean, Middle East

The countries of the Mediterranean are of considerable economic significance for the European Union, constituting as a group one of its largest trading partners and having close historic and cultural ties with some of its Member States. A prosperous, democratic, stable and secure Mediterranean region, having close economic and political relations with Europe, is in the best interests of the EU. Relations between the Community/Union and the Mediterranean countries have become ever closer since the 1960s, with a new phase of close cooperation beginning in 1995.

An important Euro-Mediterranean ministerial conference took place on 27 and 28 November 1995 in Barcelona between the European Union and its twelve Mediterranean partners (Algeria, Cyprus, Egypt, Israel, Jordan, Lebanon, Malta, Morocco, Syria, Tunisia, Turkey and the Palestinian Authority). At the end of the proceedings, the ministers adopted a Declaration and a work programme instituting a regular political dialogue and enhanced cooperation fostering peace, security, stability and prosperity in the region. The three key components of the **Euro-Mediterranean partnership** based on the Barcelona Declaration are: to establish a common area of peace and stability through a political and security partnership; to create an area of shared prosperity through an economic and financial partnership; to establish a partnership in social, cultural and human affairs, thus developing human resources, promoting understanding between cultures and exchanges between civil societies.

The EU enlargement, on 1st May 2004, has brought two Mediterranean Partners (Cyprus and Malta) into the European Union. Nowadays, the Euro-Mediterranean partnership comprises 37 members, 27 EU Member States and 10 Mediterranean Partners. Libya has an observer status since 1999. The Euro-Mediterranean partners participate in the **European Neighbourhood policy** and benefit from the European Neighbourhood and Partnership Instrument (ENPI), which replaced, since 1 January 2007, the pre-existing financial instrument MEDA [see section 25.4]. A key objective over the next few years will be deeper integration between the partners

---

[1]   Decision 2006/62, OJ L 32, 04.02.2006.

through liberalisation of trade and services, increased investment and regulatory convergence[1].

The Euro-Mediterranean Partnership comprises a complementary **bilateral dimension**. Indeed, the European Union has bilateral agreements with each country. The most important are the Euro-Mediterranean Association Agreements that the Union negotiates and concludes with Mediterranean countries individually. They reflect the general principles governing the new Euro-Mediterranean relationship, although they each contain characteristics specific to the relations between the EU and each Mediterranean country.

25.6. Asian countries

The **Community Strategy for Asia** is founded on a development partnership and on political dialogue[2]. The priorities of this strategy include notably: backing cooperation schemes aimed at safeguarding peace and security; improving Europe's image in Asia and creating a climate conducive to the development of trade and investment; and improving coordination in the management of development aid so that the region's less prosperous countries experience economic growth and poverty is reduced. Many Asiatic countries benefit from the Community **financing instrument for development cooperation** [see section 24.4.].

The new agreement concluded with **India** is an advanced framework cooperation agreement emphasising economic cooperation and private sector investment, intellectual property rights, technology transfer and diversification of economic and trade relations[3]. Similar **non-preferential agreements, called "third generation"**, comprising three areas of cooperation, namely trade, economic and development cooperation, and making respect for human rights a key condition for the development of dialogue and partnership have been concluded with **Mongolia**[4], **Sri Lanka**[5], **Vietnam**[6] and **Nepal**[7].

Community aid has had a relatively positive impact in the countries belonging to the **Association of South-East Asian Nations (ASEAN)**, which comprises **Brunei, Indonesia, Malaysia, the Philippines, Singapore, Thailand and Vietnam**. The cooperation agreement between the Community and most of these countries dates back to 1980[8]. It is completed by

---

[1] COM (2005) 139, 12 April 2005.

[2] COM (94) 314.

[3] Agreement and Decision 94/578, OJ L 223, 27.08.1994.

[4] Agreement and Decision 92/101, OJ L 41, 18.02.1993.

[5] Agreement and Decision 95/129, OJ L 85, 19.04.1995.

[6] Agreement and Decision 96/351, OJ L 136, 07.06. 1996.

[7] Agreement and Decision 96/354, OJ L 137, 08.06.1996.

[8] Regulation 1440/80, OJ L 144, 10.06.1980 and Decision 1999/295, OJ L 117, 05.05.1999.

trade agreements on manioc from Thailand and Indonesia[1] granting better access for their products to the Community market. As a follow-up to its communication on "Europe and Asia: a strategic framework for enhanced partnerships"[2], the Commission proposes revitalising the relations between the EU, ASEAN and the countries of South-East Asia, and identifies the strategic priorities, creating a framework for future bilateral agreements[3].

Relations between the Community and **China**, after the retrogression that followed the events of Tiananmen Square on June 4, 1989, are marking a steady improvement. A 1978 framework trade agreement evolved into the 1985 trade and economic cooperation agreement covering industrial and technical fields[4] and trade in textiles[5]. A 1998 Commission communication on "a comprehensive **partnership with China**"[6] opened the way for a new EU-China relationship embracing four main areas: upgrading the political dialogue; supporting China's transition to an open society based on the rule of law and respect for human rights; integrating China further into the world economy; and raising the profile of the EU in China. On behalf of the Community and its Member States, the Commission negotiated with China a whole series of commitments on the opening up of markets which are of particular importance to the European Union. These commitments were listed in the bilateral agreement signed by the People's Republic of China and the European Community on 19 May 2000, and are set out in the protocol of accession by China to the WTO[7] [see section 23.4.]. The EU's cooperation programme with China has expanded steadily and now focuses on supporting sustainable development to assist the overall reform process in China and the implementation of its WTO commitments[8].

Japan poses problems of a completely different nature for the European Union. Japan has a huge trade surplus with the Community, with its exports to the EU running at three times its imports from it. Japan is at an advantage compared with the other industrialised countries due to such specificities as a limited social security budget, low military expenditure and low aid level to the developing countries. But the success of Japanese policy is chiefly due to certain basic economic factors: strong competitiveness and productivity, rigid organisation of the domestic market, integrated industrial and trade strategy working towards precise and planned objectives. As regards more specifically trade relations with the EU, the determinant factors in the disequilibrium are: the concentration of Japanese exports on a limited number of sectors, high quality, leading-edge products,

---

[1] Decisions 82/495 and 82/496, OJ L 219, 28.07.1982 and Decision 90/637, OJ L 347, 12.12.1990.
[2] COM (2001) 469.
[3] COM (2003) 399.
[4] Agreement and Regulation 2616/85, OJ L 250, 19.09.1985.
[5] Agreement and Decision 95/155, OJ L 104, 06.05.1995.
[6] COM (1998) 181.
[7] COM (2001) 517 and 518, 19 September 2001.
[8] COM (2000) 552, 8 September 2000.

marketed with highly effective marketing methods supported by a favourable financing system; and, on the other side of the equation, the closing of the Japanese market by various technical and administrative barriers as well as by prevalent Japanese national habits and attitudes. Nevertheless, the Community is becoming an increasingly important trading partner for Japan because of the size of the single European market and the efforts made to develop trade and cooperation.

Closer relations between the Community and Japan culminated in the adoption, on July 18, 1991, of a **joint declaration** similar to those defining the Community's relations with the United States and Canada. It sets out the general principles and objectives of cooperation between the two parties, notably stipulating that access to respective markets must be equitable and offer comparable opportunities through the removal of obstacles to trade and investments. It also stipulates the framework for dialogue, with annual summits and other meetings. As regards more especially trade in motor vehicles, the Community and Japan agreed on July 31, 1991 on a solution aiming at gradual liberalisation of the Community market as part of the completion of the single market, while avoiding market distortion caused by exports from Japan [see section 23.5.].

25.7. North American countries

The European Union is **the biggest trading partner of the United States** and is linked to this country by culture, tradition and cross-investments as well as by common economic and political interests embodied within international organisations such as the Organisation for Economic Cooperation and Development (OECD) and the North Atlantic Treaty Organisation (NATO). The United States were in 2000 the EU's leading investment partner: almost half of the extra-EU investments by Member States went to the United States (EUR 147 out of EUR 304 billion), and almost 80% of investments by non-member countries in the EU came from the United States (EUR 98 out of EUR 125 billion). From the political viewpoint, the United States has always supported European integration. This has not prevented strong economic antagonism between the two richest regions of the planet.

The fall of the Soviet Union and the emergence of the United States as the sole superpower led to the adoption on November 22, 1990 by the United States on the one hand and by the Community and its Member States on the other of a joint **transatlantic declaration**. Considering that their relationship is a vital factor for political stability in a changing world, the two parties confirmed their commitment to continuing and developing cooperation on an equal footing and, for this purpose, they agreed to consult one another on important subjects of common interest and to intensify their dialogue in a formal contact structure. The **transatlantic agenda**, signed in 1995, completed the Transatlantic Declaration and organised the cooperation between the two partners around four pillars: promoting peace, stability, democracy and development throughout the world, responding to global challenges, contributing to the expansion of world trade and closer economic relations, and establishing closer ties between the partners. In addition, an agreement between the Community and the United States established a cooperation programme in the field of higher education and vocational training[1].

After the **terrorist attacks** of 11 September 2001 against the United States, the European Council meeting in extraordinary session on 21 September 2001 declared its total support to the American people in the face of the deadly terrorist attacks and its willingness to cooperate with the United States in bringing to justice and punishing the perpetrators, sponsors and accomplices of such barbaric acts [see section 8.2.3.]. On 8 October 2001, the Council declared that the military action taken by the US in self-defence and in conformity with the UN Charter and the UNSCR 1368 was part of a wider multilateral strategy in which the European Union was committed to playing its part, including a comprehensive assault on the organisations and financing structures that underpin terrorism.

However, transatlantic relations are often a **controversial subject** for the EU, since the degree of solidarity with the United States differs considerably from one European country to another. It is, therefore, usually difficult to work out a common reaction to the initiatives of Washington. In general, the vision of the world and of international relations of the USA, which is largely based on national interest and the use of military force, is basically contrasting with the concept of international law that the European nations tend to place above national law. Even the best friends of the USA in Europe are sad to see the new American policy depart from the rules of international law, enacted with the active participation of the USA themselves, on issues such as: the ratification of the Kyoto protocol for the reduction of atmospheric pollution [see section 16.3.4.]; the exemption of American citizens from the jurisdiction of the International Criminal Court for war crimes [see section 8.1.2.]; the disrespect of the rules of the World Trade Organisation in general and particularly concerning the huge increase in American farm subsidies (70%) and the protection of American steel products; the invasion of Iraq without agreement of the UN Security Council; and, last but not least, the uneven interposition in the conflict between Israelis and Palestinians. On all these subjects the transatlantic declaration of 1990 has not served as a basis of dialogue and cooperation between equal partners. If this situation continues, the European Union will, sooner or later, adopt a foreign policy, which will increasingly diverge from that of the USA.

The Community's relations with **Canada** have originally been based on a cooperation agreement between Euratom and Canada on the peaceful use

---

of atomic energy[1], on a cooperation agreement between the EEC and Canada on commercial and economic cooperation[2] and on a fisheries agreement[3]. The two parties adopted on November 22, 1990 a **joint declaration** based on the preferential relations introduced by the framework cooperation agreement which reinforces the institutional framework for consultations in order to give them a long-term horizon.

25.8. Latin American countries

The Community has been **granting aid to Latin America** as a group of non-associated countries for many years [see section 24.4.]. The Community is aware of its responsibility for development in these countries, home to some of the poorest people in the world. This awareness has been further accentuated since the entry of Spain and Portugal to the Community, two countries which share the same cultural heritage with Latin America. Thus, the Community develops ever closer relations with **regional groupings** in Latin America, i.e. the **Rio Group** (Argentina, Bolivia, Brazil, Chile, Colombia, Costa Rica, Dominican Republic, El Salvador, Ecuador, Guatemala, Honduras, Mexico, Nicaragua, Panama, Paraguay, Peru, Uruguay, Venezuela), the **Central American Integration**, the **Andean Pact** and **Mercosur**.

In 1986 the Community concluded a framework agreement for commercial and economic cooperation and development with the countries of the Central American Economic Integration or **San José Group (Costa Rica, El Salvador, Guatemala, Honduras, Nicaragua) and with Panama**[4]. The cooperation agreement between the Community and the countries of the **Andean Pact or Cartagena Agreement (Bolivia, Colombia, Ecuador, Peru and Venezuela)**, places particular emphasis on the consolidation of the regional integration systems and on the respect of democratic principles and human rights[5]. The main aims of the agreement are: to stimulate, diversify and improve trade; to encourage cooperation between industrialists; and to stimulate scientific and technical cooperation.

The European Union is also providing technical assistance to the common market between the **Mercosur** countries **(Argentina, Brazil, Paraguay and Uruguay)**. In the wake of the Solemn Joint Declaration between the European Union and Mercosur[6], an interregional commercial and economic cooperation framework Agreement between the EU and Mercosur

---

[1] 1959 Agreement, OJ 60, 24.11.1959 and 1995 Agreement OJ L 211, 06.09.1995.
[2] Agreement and Decisions, OJ L 260, 24.09.1976 and new Agreement, OJ L 346, 22.12.1998.
[3] Decisions 81/1053 and 81/1054, OJ L 379, 31.12.1981 and Agreement and Regulation 3675/93, OJ L 340, 31.12.1993.
[4] Agreement and Regulation 2009/86, OJ L 172, 30.06.1986.
[5] Agreement and Decision 98/278, OJ L 127, 29.04.1998.
[6] Framework Agreement and Decision 96/205, OJ L 69, 19.03.1996.

was signed in Madrid on 15 December 1995[1]. Aimed at strengthening existing ties and preparing for eventual association, this Agreement provides: regular, institutionalised political dialogue; trade cooperation leading to trade liberalisation; economic cooperation geared to promoting reciprocal investment; cooperation on regional integration, intended to allow Mercosur to draw upon the experience of the European Union; and wider cooperation in fields of mutual interest, such as culture, information and communication, training on the multinational integration process and on the prevention of drug abuse.

The new opening provided by the Uruguay Round Agreements [see section 23.4.] and the developments in the various integration processes in Latin America are the two vital elements for **intensifying cooperation** between the EU and Latin American countries. In giving its support to the development efforts of the latter (at bilateral level) and to their integration efforts (at multilateral level) the European Union hopes to contribute to the political stability and economic and social development of a region of the world which, despite its current economic and social difficulties, is rich in raw materials and is a vast potential market.

25.9. Appraisal and outlook

Whereas at the outset the Community was viewed with indifference, scepticism or even hostility by the rest of the world, it is now **recognised as being a major economic, commercial and, potentially, political power**. In this and in the two preceding chapters we saw that the Community is dealing, negotiating and conversing with many countries large and small throughout the world, which see it as an important group of prosperous, democratic and peaceful countries. Curiously enough, those outside better perceive the common policies of EC/EU countries than those inside it [see sections 10.1. and 10.4.]. In fact, the Union's external policy is made up of a number of common policies, which support one another. It goes beyond the traditional diplomatic and military aspects, which are ostensibly in the ambit of the Union, and stretches to Community areas such as trade and customs affairs, development aid, justice and police matters, environment protection, external relations of agricultural and fisheries policies and external representation of the euro zone. Through its development aid policy, its common commercial policy and its external relations, the European Community has a **strong presence on the world stage**. It notably exerts a strong pressure, through its statements, representations and economic sanctions, on many countries practising serious violations of democratic principles and human rights [see section 24.1.]. It also advo-

---

[1]   Agreement and Decision 96/205, OJ L 69, 19.03.1996 and Council Decision 1999/279, OJ L 112, 29.04.1999.

cates an effective multiterism in the framework of an international society based on the rule of law.

However, the fragmentation of initiative, decision and action causes the **inadequacy of the Union's foreign policy**. The European Union cannot exert a political influence commensurate to its economic weight in the world affairs, as long as the external policies of the Community, examined in this part, are not well coordinated or better integrated in the common foreign and security policy of the Union [see section 8.2.]. As we will see in the "European outlook", it is up to its Member States to let the European Union become a world power by accepting to share their political sovereignty in the same way they share their economic and monetary sovereignty [see chapter 7].

The Union has the potential to **play a role as a world power**. To this end, it must propound its democratic values and its integration paradigm, stand up and be counted as the bearer of a shared and sustainable model of development. It must pursue an external policy open to dialogue between civilisations, cultures and religions, and based on cooperation with the countries at its borders and on the resolve to help the economic, political and social development of all the countries in the world [see the European perspectives in the conclusions]. It is significant that after the fall of their communist regimes Central and Eastern European countries ignored the possibility of acceding to the European Economic Area and applied for membership to the EU in order to strengthen their feeble economies and stabilise their fragile democratic systems. By enhancing its power and image in the world arena, the EU could better help other countries in the world, torn by their economic and political differences, imitate its successful formula of multinational integration. In fact, Europe's experience with economic and political unification is being watched with close attention throughout the world and countries in other regions of the globe, notably in Latin America, are trying to imitate it. This could be a valuable contribution of the European Union to world peace and prosperity.

Bibliography on external relations

- BLOCKMANS Steven. *Tough love: the European Union's relations with the Western Balkans*. The Hague: T.M.C. Asser Press, 2007.
- BRIMMER Esther. *Seeing blue: American visions of the European Union*. Paris: Institute for Security Studies (ISS), 2007.
- CASARINI Nicola, MUSU Costanza (eds.). *European foreign policy in an evolving international system: the road towards convergence*. Basingstoke: Palgrave Macmillan, 2007.
- DELEVIC Milica. *Regional cooperation in the Western Balkans. Paris:* Institute for Security Studies, 2007.
- EUROPEAN COMMISSION. *The EU in the world: the foreign policy of the European Union*. Luxembourg: EUR-OP*, 2007.

- • *European Neighbourhood Policy: Economic Review of EU Neighbour Countries.* Luxembourg: EUR-OP*, 2007.
- • GREVI Giovanni. *Pioneering foreign policy: the EU special representatives.* Paris: Institute for Security Studies (ISS), 2007.
- • LERAIS Frederic (et al.). *China, the EU and the world: Growing in harmony?* European Commission, Bureau of European Policy Advisers. Luxembourg: EUR-OP, 2007.
- • LIPPERT Barbara (et al.). "The Neighbourhood Policy of the European Union", in *Intereconomics*, v. 42, n. 4, July-August 2007, p. 180-204.
- • NIBLETT Robin. "Choosing between America and Europe: a new context for British foreign policy", in *International Affairs*, v. 83, n. 4, July 2007, p. 627-641.

DISCUSSION TOPICS

1. What distinguishes the external relations of the EC from the common foreign and security policy of the EU?
2. Why have Central and Eastern European countries applied for membership to the EU rather than to the European Economic Area?
3. Could Russia and other Eastern European countries become one day members of the EU or else of the EEA?
4. Does competition in the world arena encourage or hamper the partnership between the EU and the USA?
5. How do the relations of the Community with Asian and Latin American countries interact with the common commercial policy and with the common aid to development policy?

Conclusions

EUROPEAN INTEGRATION
AND ITS PERSPECTIVES

Europe's history relates in the main the wars for the domination of some nations over the others and the battles of those others for their liberation from their oppressor or oppressors. After centuries of incessant wars, recurring aggressions, revolutions, massacres, human sacrifices, genocides, material destructions, economic disasters, Europe has arrived in the middle of the last century at the most devastating war of world history, the economic downfall of all European nations and the world supremacy of a non-European power. Fortunately, however, right after the Second World War, some inspired politicians, like Schuman, Adenauer, De Gasperi and Spaak, realised that the European nations, which had just ruined each other in a nonsensical war for the enlargement of their economic space, were in fact parts of **a single geographic, economic and political entity**, that could guarantee the prosperity of all in a single market.

Realists rather than idealists, those wise political leaders were fully aware of the difficulties of uniting Europe. The famous declaration of Robert Schuman of the 9th May 1950, inspired by Jean Monnet, was clear as to the step by step approach to be followed for European integration. The realisation of a customs union would fulfil the requirements for building a large common market and this would in turn establish the conditions and exert the pressures needed for the attainment of an economic and monetary union. This close economic integration would eventually necessitate a common foreign policy. Thus, political integration would follow the economic one.

Fifty years after the "invitation to union" of Robert Schuman we may say with confidence that the expectations of the fathers of European unification have been largely fulfilled. The European Community/Union has built the three first floors of its edifice – the customs union, the common market and economic and monetary union – and although work is still needed and done daily on them, it has started building the last floor, that of political union. Work at the one wing of this floor, that of home and judicial policy, is advancing satisfactorily. The big question is if and when will work get started on the wing of foreign and security policy.

The work already accomplished qualifies the European model as a **success story**. Multinational integration has established peace in Western Europe, has turned the former enemies into good partners, has secured the equality of all participating nations under common laws, has ensured development opportunities and thus the relative prosperity of all. In short, the European Community/Union has become an island of peace and prosperity in a world that is, unfortunately, still suffering from skilfully cultivated ethnic, racial, religious and other differences, battles for the glory of war-mongers, the slaughter and displacement of populations for ethnic and/or economic reasons and, finally, the exploitation of the vast majority of mankind by an unscrupulous minority, equally distributed among various nations.

Unfortunately, despite the fantastic progress of science and technology during the previous century, civilisation has not much advanced in the world. Indeed, if "Civilisation" is taken to mean an advanced system of human values and social development guaranteeing peace, freedom of opinion and welfare for all persons, civilisation is not yet enjoyed by a huge part of mankind. In this sense of civilisation, multinational integration may be considered the **most important socio-political invention since the invention of democracy**, because it spreads and consolidates the values of the latter: the rule of law, the separation of the state from religion, freedom of initiative, equality of nations and individuals, well distributed welfare for all regions and social categories. These capital socio-political discoveries, which go hand in hand (since the concept of integration is inseparable from that of democracy) [see section 1.1.2.], were made on European soil. It is true that Europe also invented colonialism, fascism, anti-semitism and bolshevism and other "isms", but these bad inventions ended in failures and are currently disavowed by the immense majority of Europeans. On the other hand, Europeans have a vital reason to promote the models of democracy, humanism and integration, that they have developed and are still improving, to the nations that are torn apart and starving, exploited by demagogues and plutocrats without scruples carrying all kinds of fanciful banners and propagating myths stirring the hatred of others. The reason is the protection of their own safety and wellbeing against all these false prophets.

In this book we have tried to throw light on all aspects of the phenomenon called multinational integration, which is complicated and difficult to understand even for those who are involved in it. The sad fact is that, because of the complex nature of the integration process and the lack of adequate edification, the citizens of the Member States do not realise that they take part in an experiment that may change for the better not only their own lives but also the course of history. If they did realise the potential of the multinational integration process, they would better accept the hurdles that it has to overcome and they would better appreciate its accomplishments. By presenting all the achievements of the integration process to date, our objective was not advertising **the success story of European integration** in order to embellish its institutions, which are far from perfect, but scrutinising the phenomenon in order to infer certain conclusions concerning its possible evolution and dissemination to other parts of the world. In what follows, we will try to assess the main findings of the study and propose some estimates concerning the advancement of the evolutionary process of multinational integration.

1. Main facts regarding European integration

The course of the multinational integration process in the European Community/Union is determined by **three currents that converge at certain points** and strengthen the main flow: (a) the increasing number of the participants; (b) the continuous raising of their goals through the passage from one integration stage to another; and (c) the constant increase of their activities by the development of common policies. It is worth recapitulating the main findings of our study on these major trends of European integration.

The membership has kept growing together with the tasks assumed by the team. The multinational integration process began in 1951 as a customs union concerning only the coal and steel sectors of six countries on the basis of the ECSC Treaty. In 1958, these same countries extended the operation of the customs union and of the common market to all the sectors of their economies, thanks to the EEC Treaty. In 1973, they were joined by three countries, which had originally preferred intergovernmental cooperation inside a free trade area. In 1992, the builders of the common market had become twelve, had completed the work on that stage of their integration on the basis of the Single European Act and had signed the Treaty of Maastricht leading them to the next stage of their integration [see sections 2.2 and 6.1]. In 1995, the builders of the union were joined by three more states, which had originally believed in the benefits of the free trade area. In 2007, the fifteen had opened the door of their enterprise to twelve more states, most of which had been their antagonists less than twenty years before. The twenty-seven were endeavouring to improve the functioning of the institutions of the enlarged Union thanks to the reform treaty that they had signed in Lisbon [see section 2.5].

Despite the successive enlargements, the multinational integration process in Europe has followed **a steady evolution in stages of ever closer economic convergence** - customs union, common market, economic and monetary union - and is proceeding towards the final stage of political union. The **customs union**, nowadays taken for granted and almost forgotten, formed the solid foundation of the entire European edifice. The problem-free removal of customs barriers to trade filled the apprentices of European construction with the enthusiasm necessary for climbing up the steep and unfamiliar road of integration [see section 5.1.1.]. The stage of the **common market**, completed in 1992, meant the freedom of movement within the single market of goods, persons, services and capital [see chapter 6]. These freedoms revolutionised trade and competition, the working methods and the economic conditions in the Member States of the Community. The reduction of administrative and financial costs of intra-Community trade and the realisation of economies of scale liberated the dynamism and the creativity of European businessmen and gave them a solid foothold from which to sustain international competitiveness [see section 6.2.].

In December 1991 in Maastricht, the Member States decided to initiate the next stage of their integration, viz. **economic and monetary union (EMU),** implying a single monetary policy, necessary for the management of a single currency, and the convergence of national economic policies, with a view to achieving economic and social cohesion. EMU was based on the common market in goods and services, but itself served the proper functioning of the common market, by eliminating exchange rate variations between Member States' currencies, which hindered the interpenetration of capital markets, disturbed the common agricultural market and prevented the common industrial market from wholly resembling an internal market. This stage of the integration process was completed with the successful circulation of the euro, on 1st January 2002, just ten years after its conception.

At the same time that they designed their monetary integration, in Maastricht, the Member States decided to coordinate their non-economic policies as well, i.e.: justice and home affairs policies, in order to achieve a common area of freedom, security and justice; and their foreign and security policies, so that the economic giant that they were creating through economic integration would have a voice commensurate with its size in the international arena [see section 2.3.and chapter 8]. They have, thus, reached the threshold of **political integration;** but although the new common policies in the political field were given a boost with the Treaty of Amsterdam, foreign and security policy is still detached from the prime objective of the EC/EU, that of an **"ever closer union among the peoples of Europe".**

The preceding summary of events and trends demonstrates the **extraordinary success of the multinational integration process** as practised in Europe since the early 1950s. This success was due to the construction method taught by Monnet and Schuman, which is that of a step by step advance after careful evaluation of the previous experience. Brick upon brick, act after act, as taught by the old masters, the European edifice has been built up and is still expanding. Every new measure fits so well into the adjoining provisions that it fills a gap while consolidating the whole structure [see section 3.1.]. In fact, the successful formula of European integration is based on **common policies** built by **common institutions** following the **Community method** [see section 1.1.2.]. These three ingredients of the integration formula, amply brought out in the various chapters of this book, merit some concluding observations.

In the introduction of this book, we made the hypothesis that the fundamental elements of the multinational integration process are **common policies** pursuing common goals and **serving common interests** [see section 1.1.2.]. We supposed that the supreme interests of the citizens of the participating states are the assurance of peace with their neighbours and the increase of their wellbeing. On the basis of the findings brought out in the book, we may assert that the common policies of the European Community/Union serve those interests well. They have transformed the former enemies into partners. War between the members of the Union has become unthinkable and the wellbeing of their citizens has greatly increased through the constant development of their economies and through the abundance of good quality products and services inside the single market. In addition, the common policies attain a great number of secondary common goals. They monitor the free exchange of industrial and agricultural goods between the Member States. They stimulate and support the development of the poorer regions of the Union. They guarantee the rights of the citizens of the Member States to travel, to live and to work wherever they choose within its territory. They facilitate the access of all citizens to the universal banking, insurance, telecommunication and audiovisual services offered in the large European market. They bolster the competitiveness of European industries by imposing uniform rules of competition and by supporting their efforts in research and development. They prepare the future by laying the foundations of the information society and of transport, energy and telecommunications trans-European networks spanning the whole Continent. They try to protect in a uniform way the environment and the consumers of the member countries. Certainly, none of these policies is perfect, but all of them are under the constant scrutiny of the common institutions and they are amended very often, in order to be adapted to the new needs that emerge from internal or external causes.

The **common policies are closely knit together** and support each other. Two horizontal policies - regional and social - pursue the objective of economic and social cohesion [see section 12.1.2.], which is linked to the objective of economic and monetary union. Such a union, implying abandonment of the use of exchange rate adjustment as a means of balance of national economies, would be to the detriment of the poorer Member States, if there was not an efficient **common regional policy** operating capital transfers from the richer to the poorer regions of the EU [see section 12.1.]. In fact, thanks to the common regional policy the standard of living in the Union's poor regions increased considerably and they recovered a great part of their disadvantages. Likewise, inside an economic and monetary union, where governments gradually lose the ability to confront separately the social problems of their peoples, since monetary and many economic decisions are taken in common [see section 13.1.], the process of social integration is pursued through common employment, vocational training and social protection policies. The **common social policy** has already built a "European social model" which guarantees, not only fundamental human rights and the democratic and pluralistic principles, but also the fundamental rights of workers: training adapted to the technical progress, fair pay allowing decent living conditions and social protection covering the hazards of life, illness, unemployment and old age [see chapter 13]. This model is the social bedrock of the European integration process.

Three other **horizontal common policies** - on taxation, competition and environment protection - ensure a level playing field for European businesses. The harmonisation of indirect taxes brought about by the common taxation policy is instrumental for levelling the competition conditions inside the single market of products and services. The common competition policy is not only a necessary instrument for the smooth functioning of the internal market, preventing new compartmentalisation by the agreements of large companies and protectionism by national administrations through national aids, but is also a complement to common sectoral policies - industrial, agricultural, energy, transport - aimed at improving production structures and achieving international competitiveness. The common environment policy is essential, both for even-handed competition between nations respecting both market laws and citizens' welfare and for the sustainable development of the European and world economy.

The large sectors of the European economy - industry, energy, transports and agriculture - are organised gradually at European level by the legislation of the single market and by specific legislation adopted in the context of **sectoral common policies** [see Part V]. In fact, the freedoms of the common market apply to the businesses of those sectors, either directly or through sector-specific adaptations. The sectoral common policies are therefore necessary for the smooth functioning of the customs union, the common market and the economic and monetary union. Both horizontal and sectoral policies, including research and development, strive to boost the international competitiveness of European businesses, while cementing the economic integration of the States of the Union.

The economies of the member states are greatly influenced by common policies. As these economies are gradually opened up to multinational trade and competition, **all economic parameters change**: trade increases enormously within the large internal market, both supply and demand conditions are modified dramatically, state intervention is curbed and new dynamics are set in motion, notably concerning trade and investment opportunities, mergers and joint ventures. The creation and/or extension of multinational companies and the cross investments between them tend to connect the national economies to one another. The common policies build, in fact, a new concept and context of political economy, which has to be reckoned with by politicians, economists and businessmen.

2. European perspectives

Common policies, as all other public policies, are there to meet the societal needs which arise in a defined community of nations at a given time. Therefore, not only the objectives which the member states set for each common policy, but the means which they give to the common institutions to attain them and the measures which the latter adopt to implement them change in accordance with the economic, political and social needs which the participating states experience at a certain time. In the case of the EC/EU, the common policies are **in permanent evolution**, demonstrated, for all of them, by the constant amendment of the Community laws (regulations, directives, etc.) that form them, and, for some of them (e.g., agricultural, regional, social and research policies), by the amendment of the Treaty provisions that concern them. Moreover, a common policy tends to spill over into other common policies, to produce needs, to cause reactions and to nourish their development.

The constant evolution of all common policies, requiring the regular updating of this book, causes the endless evolution of the multinational integration process. In fact, the development of common policies creates ever-stronger economic and political links between the peoples of Europe. Paradoxically, the constant progress of integration in all fields demonstrates both the soundness and the imperfection of the Community model. A process and an organisation that are in a state of permanent evolution can never be perfect. They can only be improved constantly. The "**constant progress syndrome**" is the strong point and the permanent challenge of the European model of integration. It means that the European Union will normally keep developing all the time, trying to reach an integration ideal that it will never attain, since ideals, by definition, cannot be completely achieved.

Although, due to the constant progress syndrome, the common policies examined in this book are expected to develop in scope and improve in efficiency over time, two are exceptionally sluggish: a common information policy and a common foreign and security policy. Both these failures are due to the reluctance of the Member States to entrust the common institutions with large scale tasks in these fields. They both cause the frustration of the citizens of the Union and endanger the very existence of the European integration model.

The absence of a common information policy results in the **information deficit** of the European Union, i.e. a deficiency of reliable information, readily available to the citizens, concerning European affairs and the integration process. Due to the information deficit, most citizens ignore or take for granted the positive and palpable effects of European integration, such as the customs free availability of goods from all over Europe, border free travel and, above all, peace and friendship among their erstwhile bellicose nations. They are unaware of the extent to which they are surrounded by the workings of the Union in their daily and professional lives [see sections 10.1. and 10.4.].

The information deficit endangers the integration process. If the majority of the media adopt attitudes different from the majority of the political elite of a nation, concerning the issue of integration or particular aspects of it, this may lead to a different stance of the majority of the public from that of the majority of the political elite of the nation. We may thus have the following antidemocratic phenomenon: the popular media transforming the political consensus existing among the democratically elected leaders of a nation, concerning the major political issues discussed at European level [see section 9.5], into a public opinion dissent on those issues, orchestrated by non-elected opinion leaders (media tycoons, trendy journalists, popular television speakers, etc.) and/or a vociferous minority (party, movement or union).

In a community of people, where a silent majority has no interest in the common affairs and goals, while a determined minority is strongly opposed to its objectives and institutions, there is a high probability that the minority group would tend to grow over time and to become stronger and ever more convinced of its ideas and ideals. Unopposed by the silent majority, it might thus eventually succeed in reversing the working system that holds the community together. If European citizens were led to believe that the disadvantages of European integration were greater than its benefits, they might be led to press their political leaders to disengage their country or countries from the integration process or, worse, to halt this process altogether and return to the ante-integration status; i.e. the situation where each European state would be fighting for its interests against all others in the adverse environment of globalisation and each, in turn, would be falling easy prey to the "divide and rule" techniques of non-European superpowers naturally promoting their own interests. If we consider the effects of the information deficit on some referenda, in the past (the Danish concerning the Treaty of Maastricht, the Irish concerning the Treaty of Nice, the French and Dutch concerning the Constitutional Treaty and the Irish again concerning the treaty of Lisbon), this scenario is not as absurd as it seems at first sight.

Not only all governments but also all major political parties, which are generally pro-integration, should recognize that the information deficit combined with a systematic disinformation on the part of some europhobic media is undermining the common policies that they want to carry through, is debasing the democratic institutions set up and empowered by them to implement those common policies and is halting the progress of European integration. In other words, the political elite should acknowledge that a common information policy, which might have been a luxury as long as the integration process was confined to customs and technical matters, is a necessity now that the process is spreading ever more from the purely economic to the political field. It is high time for the European institutions to forsake the old habits of discretion and neglect of the citizens' opinion. In chapter 10 we called for the inauguration of **a common information and communication policy**, covering all the activities of the European institutions and implemented by a European Press Agency in close cooperation with the governments of the Member States [see section 10.1.3.]. Such a common communication policy, combined with the civic education of young Europeans at school, would bring the citizens closer to the Union and would secure the achievements of all the other common policies.

A paradoxical effect of the information deficit and the absence of civic education on European integration is that, while citizens seem to be indifferent to the European Union, they simultaneously expect ever more important results from it. This is notably the case concerning the **European presence on the world stage**, the second serious flaw of the European edifice. Eurobarometer surveys indicate constantly over a long period of years that two out of three Europeans believe that the European Union should have an effective common foreign policy [see introduction to chapter 10]. Three out of four citizens of the Union back a really common security and defence policy. These and many more specific findings of the opinion polls indicate that Europeans fail to understand how the economic giant that they have created, the most important power in international trade, now endowed with the strongest currency in the world, cannot make its voice heard in the world arena. They expect the Union to take the lead in monitoring regional conflicts, globalisation, environmental challenges and famines in the world. The tragic inability of the Union to prevent the Balkan wars at its doorstep or to enforce the rules of international law in the resolution of conflicts in the Middle East has greatly reduced the respect of Europeans for their common institutions. Public reasoning is quite simple: as long as the Union cannot act as a mature political giant, it cannot be respected. It is time for the infant giant to grow up.

The citizens' expectations for a powerful Union in the world include the dissemination and defence of the European ideals of peace, welfare, democracy, the rule of law and social justice on the world stage. Europe is open to the world and its citizens understand that they cannot live merrily in a prosperous island surrounded by the misery and envy of other nations. They understand that, for their own peace and security, the Union should contribute more to peace and sustainable development in the world. Europeans know as well that they cannot prevent the new technologies and free enterprise from shrinking the world to the virtual dimensions of a village; but they feel that this, as any village, should have a town hall and that they should have their representatives inside it. In other words, they expect the Union to play **an active role in the globalisation phenomenon** by enhancing the legitimacy and effectiveness of international institutions, notably the United Nations Organisation and its specialised agencies, so that these may impose the law in the fields of peace, durable development, social protection, commerce and competition.

There is no doubt that the vast majority of European citizens want their integration to step up to the **stage of political union**, including a strong and independent foreign policy and an even stronger and more independent security and defence policy. Why do citizens understand that in an era of integration, globalisation and world predominance of a superpower, national sovereignty in matters of foreign policy and security has no real meaning, while their political leaders do not understand it? Because, for the later, national sovereignty is closely related to their own power, which they do not want to share with their partners, even though this power, in the present geopolitical environment, is waning all the time and only unity can bolster it.

One might suppose that the common foreign and security policy could develop as other common policies have developed in the past. There is, however, a fundamental difference between the common foreign and security policy and the common policies of the Community. Whereas the latter are governed by the Community method of decision-making [see section 4.3.], **the CFSP depends on intergovernmental cooperation**. This means that unanimity is required to make decisions in these fields, that the European Parliament does not participate in the decision-making process, that the Commission is not required to execute the decisions taken by the Council and that the Court of Justice is not competent to settle disputes and enforce the implementation of the decisions taken. Thanks to the intergovernmental method of the CFSP, any Member State may block a common position or common action on an important matter, thus frustrating the will of all the others. Moreover, any Member State may eventually disengage itself from a decision taken, thus thwarting a common action agreed upon. Obviously, the foreign and security policy cannot become "common" as long as it depends on intergovernmental cooperation.

The **Treaty of Lisbon** (like the stillborn Constitutional Treaty) would increase the European Union's visibility and efficiency in the world scene [see section 2.5]. The **permanent president** of the European Council would represent the Union in discussions among world leaders, such as the G8, "putting a face" on the Union [see section 4.1.1]. The fact that the new **High Representative for Foreign Affairs and Security Policy** would be Vice-President of the Commission and would chair the "foreign affairs Council" would help the EU work more effectively and consistently on the world scene [see section 4.1.2]. The High Representative - assisted by a new European external action service, composed of officials from the Council, Commission and national diplomatic services - should connect different strands of EU external policy, such as diplomacy, security, trade, aid to development, humanitarian aid and international negotiations. Also, the fact that the new Treaty, does away with the European Community and introduces a single legal personality for the European Union would enabble it to conclude international agreements and join international organisations as such, raising its profile worldwide [see section 3.1]. The common security and defence policy would be an integral part of the common foreign and security policy and would provide the Union with an operational capacity drawing on civilian and military assets, which could be used on missions outside the Union for peace-keeping, conflict prevention and strengthening international security. Inside the Union, Member States should act jointly if a Member State is the target of a terrorist attack. Moreover, a European Defence Agency should identify operational requirements, should promote measures to satisfy those requirements, should contribute to identifying and, where appropriate, implementing any measure needed to strengthen the industrial and technological base of the defence sector and shall assist the Council in evaluating the improvement of military capabilities (Article 28 A TEU, Lisbon).

These provisions mean a certain progress; but, **the unanimity rule still prevails** in the Treaty of Lisbon (as in the draft Constitution) concerning the CFSP. This policy would still be defined and implemented by the

European Council and the Council acting unanimously, except where the Treaties provide otherwise. The adoption of legislative acts would be excluded (Article 10 c, Lisbon). In fact, European decisions relating to CFSP would be adopted by the European Council and the Council of Ministers unanimously, except when they would be implementing decisions of the European Council taken unanimously or if the European Council would unanimously decide that the Council of Ministers should act by qualified majority (Article 15b, Lisbon). Moreover, the unanimity rule prevents not only a genuine common foreign and security policy but also the ratification and putting into force of the treaty of Lisbon itself. At the moment of writing, the ratification of the Lisbon treaty is suspended, because it was rejected, in a referendum on 12 June 2008, by the Irish people, representing 1.7% of the total EU population. Whatever eurosceptic circles may say to the contrary, this is **democratic deficit par excellence**, i.e. disregard of the will of the people concerning the progress of the integration process and the political maturity of their union [see section 9.5].

However, it is practically certain that not all the Member States of the actual EU would be willing to confer on the Union the competences necessary for building a genuine common foreign and security policy. Experience to date shows that if the public opinion in some countries is negative on an issue, e.g. the common currency, then, even if they want to, the politicians of those countries cannot follow the common march [see section 7.2.3]. Hence, in a Community/Union of twenty-seven states, it is quite probable that one government, one parliament or a referendum in one country may stop the march of all the others by vetoing the amendment of a treaty (be it named constitutional or otherwise).

The question arises consequently: the Member States whose citizens aspire for a really common foreign and security policy should be **eternally blocked by their partners** who prefer to guard their national prerogatives rather than unite their forces in order to build a superpower able to better serve their common interests? The probable answer is that sooner or later a number of states, under the pressure of their citizens, would like to gain their freedom to proceed at the stage of integration of the political union and to thus establish a truly common foreign and security policy. It is probable that this would be the group of states, which would have a single currency on top of the single market. In fact, the interests of those states would become ever more common and it is natural that sooner rather than later they would feel the need to defend them in common by a genuine common foreign and security policy.

The subsidiary question to the one above is: given the unanimity rule required for the amendment of the Treaty on the European Union, how the Member States of the EU, which would want to advance towards the stage of the political union, could do it, if some of the signatories of this Treaty would oppose the concessions of national sovereignties necessary for taking this step? There are two possible answers to this question. The relatively easier but limited way for building a common foreign and security policy would be by the enhanced cooperation of some Member States, provided for by the actual Treaty of Nice and reinforced by the Treaty of Lisbon. The more difficult but sturdier way of proceeding towards the political union of Europe would be by **a treaty democratically drafted and adopted**, which would engage only the Member States which would have signed and ratified it. Let us consider these two possibilities.

Enhanced cooperation in the field of the common foreign and security policy is facilitated by the Treaty of Nice [see sections 4.3 and 8.1.2.] and even more so by the Treaty of Lisbon. The latter provides that authorisation to proceed with enhanced cooperation should be granted by the Council (of Ministers) as a last resort, when it has been established that the objectives of such cooperation could not be attained within a reasonable period by the Union as a whole, and provided that at least nine Member States would participate in it (Article 10, Lisbon). But, with the method of enhanced cooperation, progress in the fields of foreign and security policies would proceed in bits and pieces and might involve a number of Member States in certain cases and another number in other cases.

It would be much better, if Member States willing to build a real common foreign and security policy set down in a "Treaty on European Political Union" all the rules that should govern this common policy. Of course, the great hurdle to the conception, the signing and the ratification of such a treaty would be the **unanimity requirement**. On top of this problem would come the supplementary one of the possibility left for some countries to hold referendums for the ratification of European treaties, despite all evidence proving that such solitary referendums (i.e. in some countries of the Union and not in all simultaneously) are usually destined to turn negative results, because of the information deficit and the undermining work of eurosceptic media and europhobic parties [see sections 2.5 and 9.5]. Therefore, the search for a way out of the imbroglio caused by the Irish rejection of the treaty of Lisbon should, at the same time, point on a way for preventing its recurrence in a future amendment of the European treaties.

The solution to the unanimity problem of European treaties is conceptually easy. Article 6, paragraph 1, of the **Final Provisions of the Treaty of Lisbon** says: "This Treaty shall be ratified by the High Contracting Parties in accordance with their respective constitutional requirements. The instruments of ratification shall be deposited with the Government of the Italian Republic". This paragraph could be left as it is, but the second paragraph of this Article should be amended to stipulate (instead of "This Treaty shall enter into force on 1 January 2009, provided that all the instruments of ratification have been deposited"...): " This Treaty shall enter into force after **three fourths of the High Contracting Parties** have deposited their instruments of ratification". A third paragraph should be added saying: "Immediately after the coming into force of this Treaty, the High Contracting Parties shall convene an Intergovernmental Conference with the task of drafting **a connecting treaty** determining the transitional provisions governing the relations between the High Contracting Parties having ratified this treaty and the other signatories of the treaty of Nice. It would be implied by this drafting that any Member State(s) that had not ratified on time the new treaty could do so at a later day and in the mean-time provisional solutions would be applied to the common institutions and policies. These solutions could imitate the existing provisions applying to the "opt out" provisions for Member States not participating in the final stage of the economic and monetary union and/or in the Schengen coopera-tion agreement.

It should be noted that the proposed method for the ratification of the amendments to European treaties is very **similar to the American consti-tutional law**. Under Article Five of the United States Constitution, Con-gress can propose an amendment to this Constitution by a two-thirds vote (of a quorum, not necessarily of the entire body) of the Senate and of the House of Representatives. Amendments must then be ratified by three-fourths of the states to take effect. Article Five gives Congress the option of requiring ratification by state legislatures or by special conventions as-sembled in the states. The convention method of ratification has been used only once (to approve the 21st Amendment repealing Prohibition). The USA could not have become the superpower that we know today, if any state of the federation - say Texas or Alaska - could veto a foreign policy decision of the Congress.

This way out of the Irish imbroglio seems simple, but of course it will not be too easy to find the necessary unanimity in the present political situation, notably because of the bad habit acquired with past ratifications of the treaties. If, however, some pioneers, notably France and Germany, showed the way, others would follow on their steps. This has happened in all the history of the European unification. The common market for coal and steel products and then for all products and services was initiated by six countries. The others followed, when the experiment proved to be a success. The economic and monetary union started with twelve countries and now others are hastening to join the Eurozone. The same happened with the Schengen arrangements for the abolition of border controls, which were adopted even by countries outside the EU, like Norway and Iceland. Some pioneers have again to show the way for the reform of the European Union, by adopting the treaty of Lisbon at a majority of three fourths.

Once adopted for the ratification of the treaty of Lisbon, the new for-mulation of the Final provisions could and should be **applied to future amendments of the treaties**, thus allowing the European integration proc-ess to step into the stage of the political union, comporting a really com-mon foreign and security policy. A real CFSP should, it too, as the treaty, be based on qualified majority voting, but the vital interests of each one of the participating Member States should be taken into consideration and guaranteed. A provision, similar to the Luxembourg compromise, should block any decision of the Council, if a Member State felt that it countered its vital national interests. Moreover the **mutual defence clause** already in-serted in the Treaty of Lisbon would assert that, if a Member State was the victim of armed aggression on its territory, the other Member States would have towards it an obligation of aid and assistance by all the means in their power [see section 8.2.3]. These clauses would incite many Member States, which feel insecure in the present geopolitical situation, to participate in the making of a European Political Union.

The possibilities of an improved political union were amply demonstrated during the Caucasus crisis, which began on 8 August 2008, when Georgia launched a large-scale attack against the South Ossetian capital of Tskhinvali and Russia riposted by invading a large part of Georgia. In this crisis, **the European Union emerged as the mediator** in conflict management and conflict resolution. The French Presidency of the Union was able to make Russia and Georgia accept the EU's plan aimed at defusing the conflict between the warring states. The European Council, held on 1 September, was able to **achieve rare unity** and issue a muscular response to Russia's military intervention in Georgia. But, in view of the unanimity requirement for all decisions of the common foreign and security policy, it is doubtful that the EU could permanently play this useful role of international mediator and pacificator. To become a credible mediator and peacekeeper in the world, the EU should have a really common and effective foreign and security policy. Such a policy could be obtained if the three-fourths majority vote - proposed above for the ratification of European treaties - was also applied to the CFSP, either by enhanced cooperation or, better, by a treaty on Political Union agreed by at least three-fourths of the actual Member States.

The Treaty on Political Union would engage the States which would have ratified it and them only to establish a foreign and security policy managed by qualified (three-fourths) majority voting. There would thus come into being in Europe **a core of States** pursuing their economic, monetary and political integration with the method of integration provided in the Treaties on the European Union and on the European Political Union. This would be the first of three concentric circles grouping the European countries - the circle of the European Political Union. A truly common foreign and security policy, which would be an attribute of the political union of Europe, would certainly entail new transfers of national sovereignties to the Union [see section 3.2], but would not mean the loss of the political independence of the participating states. These states **would not necessarily form a federation**. In fact, the very concept of the common policy [see section 1.1.2] excludes the concept of the single policy, which is an attribute of a federation of states. It means that a policy is built up and implemented in common by the common institutions and the governments of the Member States [see section 3.2].

Each member of the group participating in a real CFSP, whether by enhanced cooperation or by a Treaty on political union, **would keep intact its legal personality and sovereignty** in all areas not placed under the common competence of the group. It could sign international agreements not conflicting with Community competence. It could keep its diplomatic representations in third countries and in international institutions. The representations of the members of the group would simply have instructions to follow the positions agreed in common, a fact that would enhance the position of the participating states in world affairs [see section 25.9]. In the field of defence as well, each member of the inner group would keep its own army, its armaments and its defence budget. The willing states would only place them under an integrated command, which would be responsible for their coordinated actions. This would not prevent separate actions, compatible with the CFSP, in case of non-agreement by the partners on a common action.

If and when some Member States of the actual European Union decided to proceed to enhanced cooperation in the field of common foreign and security policy or adopted a specific treaty to this end, **Europe would be divided into three concentric circles**. The first circle would comprise the countries having decided to proceed to their political integration by enhanced cooperation or on the basis of a Treaty on European Political Union. The second circle would encompass all the countries of the first circle and the other countries of the actual European Union, which would like to continue their economic integration in the framework of the EU Treaty, but would not want to proceed to their political integration. The third circle would include both the countries of the first two circles and the European countries which would like to remain apart from the political as well as the economic integration process and have only an intergovernmental cooperation with the EU countries.

The separation in three groups of States having more or less close relations between them would mean **a European integration at several speeds**, a situation that has been shunned until now with the result of obliging the whole group of the former European Community and now the European Union countries to march to the step of the slowest of its members. A "multi-speed Europe" would solve the problem of the conduct of the integration process in a democratic way, since each country would have the possibility of choosing the rhythm of integration which would suit better its traditions, its interests and its goals. The European States which want to advance in their union could finally do it without being slowed down by the laggards. The latter would voluntarily remain behind the leading group, but could later, if they changed opinion, run to catch up with it. They have done it in the past. They could do it again in the future.

For the countries which would choose to leave the process of integration altogether, a case envisaged by the Treaty of Lisbon [see section 2.5], there exists an all set solution concerning the organisation of their relations with the countries of the European Political Union (first circle) and those of the European Union (second circle). It is offered by the **European Economic Area (EEA)**, whose Treaty signed in 1992 currently binds Norway, Iceland and the Liechtenstein with the twenty-seven States of the EU [see section 25.1]. This Treaty aims to establish a large market based on common rules and equal conditions of competition concerning the freedom of movement of goods, people, services and capital and a reinforcement of the relations between the two groups of countries in fields having an impact on the activity of the companies, like consumer protection, the environment, research and technological development, education and tourism. The Treaty on the EEA could thus become the charter of the third circle of the European countries.

EEA membership could serve the objectives of the **countries which prefer a free trade area** governed by an intergovernmental cooperation rather than the process of European integration, which entails important transfers of national sovereignty. Indeed, certain countries wished, after the Second World War and even after their accession to the EC/EU, to participate in a simple free trade area open to the two coasts of the Atlantic. They reluctantly reached the stage of the European single market, while regretting the transfers of sovereignty and the constraints necessitated by it [see section 1.2]. Their press abounds with misrepresentations of the "meddling and malevolent" bureaucracy of Brussels, which manages this market and which, according to this press, assaults their sacrosanct national sovereignty just for the pleasure of overwhelming it. On the other hand, the majority of the other countries of EC/EU wanted and succeeded to reach the stage of the economic and monetary union and, by adopting the Treaty on European Political Union, they would demonstrate their will to advance towards their political union. The membership of all in the European Economic Area could satisfy the wishes of the ones and the others. The members of the EEA would have excellent trade relations with countries of the first two circles, but they would not be held by the rigours of the process of integration that the latter would wish to perfect. The relations of the countries participating in this third European concentric circle would indeed be governed by intergovernmental cooperation [see section 1.1.2].

The circle of the EEA, thus reinforced by the countries which would like to leave the process of integration, could be widened one day to include all other countries, which would belong to the **large family of nations established many centuries ago on the European continent** and which would have efficient market economies and political and societal institutions and cultural values similar to those of the current members of the EEA. All these countries would develop an effective intergovernmental cooperation from the economic and commercial points of view, a cooperation which would not link to the European construction those nations that would not like it. However, the door of the EU would remain open for the European countries of the third circle which would like to sign and ratify its Treaty. By their membership in the European Economic Area these countries could, indeed, obtain a good preparation of their economies before plunging into the deep water of the integration process.

With non-European countries in its periphery - i.e. Mediterranean countries in Asia and Africa, which have different cultures, traditions and regimes - the European Union should build strong economic and political links through **partnership and/or new neighbourhood agreements** [see section 25.4]. Already under the Treaty of Lisbon, a task of the common foreign and security policy of the Union would be to coordinate the commercial, aid to development and foreign policies of the Member States of the Union so as to create a friendly and therefore secure area around Europe, notably in the Mediterranean and the Middle East [see section 25.5].

The European countries which would succeed their political as well as their economic integration would greatly enhance their position in the world. The links which these countries would have with the other European countries in the two external circles and with other friendly countries in the world would make them **a world actor of primary importance**, basing the prestige and security of its members less on the force of weapons and more on the assistance for a sustainable development of friendly countries. Hence, the European Political Union would not need to match the military power of the United States. Actually, the EU countries are not threatened by any organised state and do not have any hegemonic or policing ambitions in the world. In order to take their place in the global chessboard, they do not need large armed forces, bases and armaments deployed around the globe. They only need the goodwill of governments and peoples of the rest of the world by fostering sustainable development, democracy, multinational integration (resembling the European model) and the overall respect of international law (mistreated by other actual or emerging superpowers). These could be the common goals of the unified European foreign, commercial, development and defence policies, based on an amended treaty of Lisbon.

In a world which aspires to peace, security, social and economic progress and the rule of law, it is very important that a democratic and pluralistic Europe, without hegemonic ambitions, assumes the international role which its history, its culture and its economic power reserve for it. Its successful experiment of peaceful and voluntary integration of nations, which only yesterday were fighting each other, is observed with attention by several nations in the world which suffer from their ethnic, religious and other discords and which are the victims of their dissensions. Carried out at its final stage, which is the political union [see the introduction to part II], the process of integration could place the old continent **at the vanguard of the march of civilization**, defined as an advanced system of human values, of political freedom, of economic development and of social progress, guaranteeing peace, freedom of thought and the wellbeing of all human beings.

Bibliography on European perspectives

- BEITTER Ursula (ed.). *Reflections on Europe in transition*. New York, NY ; Frankfurt am Main: P. Lang, 2007.
- BISCOP Sven (ed.). *Global Europe*. Brussels: Egmont - The Royal Institute for International Relations, 2007.

- BROWN David, SHEPHERD Alistair. *The security dimensions of EU enlargement: Wider Europe, weaker Europe?* Manchester: Manchester University Press, 2007.

- EUROPEAN COMMISSION. *Europe's challenges in a globalised world = Les défis de l'Europe dans un monde globalisé.* Luxembourg: EUR-OP*, 2007.

- FABBRINI Sergio *Compound democracies: why the United States and Europe are becoming similar.* Oxford: Oxford University Press, 2007.

- McCORMICK John. Weber, *Habermas and transformations of the European state: constitutional, social and supranational democracy.* Cambridge: Cambridge University Press, 2007.

- MEUNIER Sophie, McNAMARA Kathleen (eds.). *The state of the European Union. V. 8, Making history: European integration and institutional change at fifty.* Oxford: Oxford University Press, 2007.

- SAPIR André (ed.). *Fragmented power: Europe and the global economy.* Brussels: Bruegel, 2007.

- SNYDER Francis (ed.). *Designing the European Union = L'Union européenne: projets de société en devenir.* Bruxelles: Bruylant, 2007.

- VERHOFSTADT Guy. *The United States of Europe: manifesto for a new Europe.* London: Federal Trust for Education and Research, 2006.

DISCUSSION TOPICS

1. On the basis of the data provided in this book, assess the role played by common policies in the European integration process.
2. What are the effects of common policies on the legal and political systems of the member states of a multinational integration process?
3. Is multinational integration a process with a definite or an open end?
4. Discuss the need of a Constitution (the one already signed or another one) for the advancement of the European integration process.
5. What is your opinion about the possible division of European States into three concentric circles?

INDEX AND GLOSSARY